The Ornament Collector's

Official Price Guide For Past Years'

Hallmark Ornaments

1996

10th Edition
Rosie Wells
Editor & Collector

*Check in with "Elvin the Elf"
in the next issue of
The Ornament Collector™
magazine for news, views,
collector ads, and
collecting information on
Hallmark's ornaments and
collectibles plus other
companies' ornament offerings.*

*If you're looking for an older ornament...
Look to **The Ornament Collector™**
magazine's Classified ads!
1- 800-445-8745*

Published by
Rosie Wells Enterprises, Inc.
22341 E. Wells Rd., Canton, IL 61520
Ph. 1-800-445-8745

©1996, Rosie Wells Enterprises, Inc.
All rights reserved. No part of this book may be reproduced
in any form by any means without written permission
from Rosie Wells Enterprises, Inc.
(Not affiliated with Hallmark Cards, Inc.)

Photos of ornaments used from Hallmark's literature with permission. ©1996 Hallmark Cards, Inc.

Table of Contents

Lois Winter colors her holiday season happy with Hallmark Ornaments!

Rosalie "Rosie" Wells

Author, Editor, Collector,
Wife, Mother, Grandma
Bringing Collectors Together Since 1983.

Rosie Wells lives in Central Illinois, "down on the farm" and has been a collector ever since she can remember. Even as a child, she cherished her comic books, pins, little steel cars (instead of dolls) and WWII bubble gum. She ordered by radio all the *Straight Arrow* drums she could get with Shredded Wheat box tops!

Rosie is married to Dave. They have two children, Tim and Beth, and one precious, outstanding, super-smart, cute, little grandson named Hunter who will be three this year in June! Hunter and his mommy live down on the farm with Grandma and Grandpa. Rosie loves animals and enjoys her chickens, peacocks, swans, turkeys, rheas and ostriches as well as Dave's White Park cattle. Three loyal dogs and a parrot also make their home with Rosie and Dave. Rosie also has a hobby floral shop "down on the farm." Many types of woodland animals are seen on the farm and part of the fields are planted to provide winter food for wildlife. Canadian Geese inhabit the land year round; white tail deer are frequently spotted from the view at the office which is across the gravel road from the farm house. Rosie says she walks to work every day! Her career in publishing began at her kitchen table and she now has a staff of twenty five! Her Secondary Market guides for Hallmark, Precious Moments® collectibles, Enescos' Cherished Teddies™ as well as *Collectors' Bulletin*™, *The Ornament Collector*™ and *Precious Collectibles*™, the three collector magazines, are published to inform collectors of what is happening in the world of collecting. Rosie also publishes a *Weekly Collectors' Gazette* filled with news on Hallmark collectibles and other Limited Edition collectibles. She and Dave also host the Midwest Collectibles Shows in Illinois (the largest in the nation with over 180 dealer tables each time!).

Rosie is known as an authority on collecting and can spot a "hot" collectible in the making almost from day one! She has helped guide retailers as to what ornament "picks" would be best to order for the current year, also! She has helped many collectibles gain recognition through her three international collectors' magazines and through shows and seminars throughout the United States. Her sense of humor is enjoyed by others through the many articles she has written for collectors and her "down home talk" brings collectors together. Hallmark ornaments have been a fascination to Rosie from the beginning; she has a collection of several hundred ornaments. Rosie has also collected Hallmark Merry Miniatures, lapel pins, cookie cutters and magnets and published guides for Hallmark Merry Miniatures, lapel pins and cookie cutters.

Rosie says if she has only one life to live, then she hopes to collect as much as her basement, shelves, drawers and walls can hold, then everyone will know she was a fun lovin', crazy collector! Collectors are fun folks, you know!

Rosie invites calls and letters to her office down on the farm ... Enjoy collecting!

Hallmark Ball Ornaments

In general, ball ornaments have not proven to be as collectible as the other Hallmark ornaments although some are very difficult to locate, especially mint in box condition. Many older ball ornaments are found with discoloration, spotting and with no boxes.

According to an article written by Shirley Trexler which appeared in the June 1994 issue of ***The Ornament Collector***™ magazine: "*Difficulty faces ball ornament collectors who try, in vain, to find ball ornaments that had low production and a high breakage and spotting potential. Few secondary market dealers have any ball or yarn ornaments listed on price lists or show tables. Many times collectors are unable to replace a broken, cherished ball ornament because these ornaments are so few in number anymore. A few examples of such rare older ball ornaments include: 1973* ***Manger Scene*** *and* ***Christmas Is Love;*** *1974* ***Angel*** *ball and* ***Snow Goose*** *ball; 1975* ***Buttons and Bo*** *collection and* ***Little Miracles*** *group of balls; 1976* ***Rudolph and Santa****; and the* ***Baby's First Christmas*** *and* ***Drummer Boy*** *balls; 1979* ***Light of Christmas*** *ball; 1980* ***Christmas Choir*** *ball and the 1983* ***Christmas Wonderland*** *ball. These are just a few of many which are fading from existence.*"

Some ball ornaments are scarce, not because of tremendous popularity but because of the reasons listed above; low production, breakage and spotting. Some of the older ball ornaments are sought after but not many. If you're thinking of the future secondary market for ball ornaments, don't "go overboard." Three or four of each of the new ones per secondary market dealer would overload the supply, in my opinion. Ball ornaments are lovely and enjoyable, but not an investment, in my opinion, unless they are rare or unusual.

Insure Your Collection

This guide will be especially helpful for insuring your collection; many insurance companies use it as proof of value in settling claims. Your agent may need additional documentation, such as photos of your collection and inventory records. Before appraising your collection for insuring, you may wish to contact your insurance agent and ask about the actual details which he/she requires. Be sure your agent insures your collection at today's replacement prices, not the original retail price. In this guide, you will find space to record your ornament purchases as well as the condition of each ornament (mint in box, damaged box, etc.). It is very important to have a current inventory of your collection in the event you need to file a claim.

One should also be aware of the value of these ornaments in "planning estates." Sadly, many valuable Hallmark ornaments have been sold as a group for a very few dollars because of a lack of knowledge. Although you might never sell your collection, it's always best to keep a record of its monetary value.

New Collector? Then Read On!

Buying just "one more" Hallmark ornament is what thousands do to ease their Hallmark fever. It seems that everyone buys Hallmark ornaments! They buy their favorites! They buy them for gifts! They buy them for sentimental reasons and they buy the ones which remind them of a special person, a special event or just "because."

Yes, some people even buy Hallmark ornaments as an investment in hopes of making a little extra cash later on. There's a good chance if you're involved in the buyers circle you may double your money or more on the scarce ornaments and the "popular" first in series ornaments. For example, the 1993 *Holiday Barbie*, with a retail price of $14.75, went to $50 within two months and now on the secondary market it has gone up to $125! (Not all first in series ornaments are a sure thing; some, like *Winter Surprise*, didn't do well on the secondary market.)

Of course, collectors and dealers were caught unaware of how popular the 1991 *Starship Enterprise* would become; the scarcity of this ornament caused the price to climb to the $300 mark, with seekers still out there looking. After a "hot" ornament is produced, don't get overly excited thinking that the second edition will be as scarce. Retailers remember the response to the "firsts" and usually order extra of "number two." Study the market carefully.

Fads come and go and "pop culture" ornaments are good sellers, such as the 1994 *Beatles* set. Retailers may not have ordered many of these because of the $48 retail price, but one must study the market! Someone, somewhere had over 1000 of these to release on the secondary market thus the secondary market has been hindered. I hope you purchased the first edition 1995 mini *Blue Murray Kiddie Car*. It's a must for your collection!

In my opinion, the only way the personalized ornaments will rise in value on the secondary market will be if you had a clever saying put on, maybe a famous name. For example, on the 1995 *Reindeer Rooters* (QP 605-6) I would put, "Hey Santa, may we ride too?" on the sign to be displayed with the 1993 *Cheery Cyclists* (QX 578-6) or Vote for Clinton - or Vote for Perot - or Vote for Rosie! Ha!

Most light, motion and talking ornaments have not been favorites for secondary market folks to invest in. Many collectors are cautious about the life expectancy of the motors. Of course, if one has these ornaments, one could easily make a few folks happy.

If you're lucky to find ornaments from the '70s and early '80s at a bargain price, these would be great to resell on the secondary market. (Only a few of the ball ornaments are money makers.)

Before you decide to invest in ornaments, my advice is to attend several swap meets and watch what sells. ***Although 99% of the listed ornaments in this guide have a higher value than their original retail, it's still not a guarantee they will "sell" immediately at these prices.*** These prices are averages of selling prices across the country and are prices for a guide to insure your collection.

Write to me if you have any questions. We also may be able to help you locate a much sought after ornament. Thank you for purchasing our guide; we hope you enjoy reading and learning the values for your ornaments. Our goal is "Bringing CollectorsTogether." We know the family who prays together stays together and we've also found that when families collect together they enjoy being together. I hope to see you sometime at a Collectibles Show! (Ask about our three Collectibles Shows in Illinois, for March, Sept. and Oct. 1996)

Rosie

What About The Boxes?

This guide was the first to research "no box" prices on the majority of the ornaments. No **NB** prices have been established on '95 ornaments.

We have found that the older the ornament is, the less having the box means to collectors who are really wanting a hard-to-find ornament. They will pay a good price to get what they want with or without the box. Even though many collectors want the box with the ornament, no box older ornaments are the only choice for many since ornaments without the box are more readily available. Why? Because 20 years ago, many of those who bought Hallmark ornaments didn't keep the boxes and didn't know what boxes would mean to us in the future. It wasn't even in the minds of many that in 15 to 20 years a Hallmark ornament might be looked upon as a collectible valued at many times its original retail price!

You may feel that if you have the original box with a valuable ornament such as the first in series *Here Comes Santa* then you should be able to sell it for a considerable amount more than the same ornament without a box. A buyer probably will be found who will pay Mint in Box price, but this ornament is so sought after that even without the box the price is still high. Boxes are a plus with older ornaments, but we've found that, with or without the box, these sought-after ornaments will still bring a good price and should be insured accordingly.

When ornaments are easy to find, especially due to shows and secondary market dealers offering many recent years' ornaments, we feel that collectors should be aware of keeping the boxes in case there is a decision to sell in the future. These ornaments will be offered to a new generation of well informed collectors who may still want the boxes. This guide reflects less value on ornaments without a box if they have debuted in recent (five to six) years. Since it is very unlikely that the most recent years' ornaments will be sold without boxes, the no box prices have been excluded from those entries. When insuring your collection, take off 15% of the original price for ornaments from recent years that do not have boxes. Once an ornament becomes older, then you may find the no box price will escalate, as with the present 15-20 year old ornaments. There are differences of opinion on this subject, each with valid points to be made.

To locate an ornament/collectibles show in your area, search the ads in *The Ornament Collector*™ magazine! Shows are a lot of fun and you can find some of your favorite ornaments since secondary market dealers offer hundreds of ornaments for sale. In *The Ornament Collector*™ magazine *"We Bring Ornament Collectors Together"* to enjoy their collections. Give us a call at 1-800-445-8745. We'll be glad help you get started and put you in touch with collectors across the U.S.A.!

For Hot Tips on:

Hallmark Ornaments & Merry Miniatures

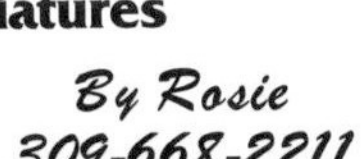

Call **1-900-740-7575** *By Rosie* 309-668-2211

Touch-tone phone required. $2.00 per minute. Must be 18 years of age.
Changes every Thursday at Noon CST.

★ All 1995 Showcase Ornaments were sold out at the Hallmark warehouse by mid October.

★ Errors, such as missing decals, upside down labels on ball ornaments and missing painted parts, are sometimes found on ornaments. Errors are few; secondary market prices rise on these pieces.

★ Production quantities of ornaments most often depends on the early orders of retailers.

★ The ornament *Joyous Song*, depicting a young choir girl, was modeled after a niece of Lynetta White of the Hallmark Collectors' Club.

★ More than several collectors found the words "Display Only/Not for Resale" on their '95 Club pieces. An error.

★ Usually attractive first editions increase in value immediately after Christmas. Always buy the first editions of the ornaments that you like as soon as they debut...next year you'll pay more!

★ There are local clubs in many states. Ask your favorite dealer, subscribe to *The Ornament Collector*™ magazine for locations or call the Keepsake Ornament Club at Hallmark in Kansas City at 816/274-4000 or 816/274-7463.

★ Many children, when they marry and leave home, leave the family dog and take their ornaments with them.

★ Remember, not all ornaments produced by Hallmark are "Keepsake Ornaments." Some are "Tree Trimmers." These are not in this guide and are not as sought after as the Keepsake Collection.

★ There may be a local Hallmark Club in your area! Call Hallmark, Inc., ph. 816/274-5387 for the location!

★ Many collectors display their ornaments all year 'round. *Many*, I say *many*, collectors put up three, four, five or even more trees at Christmas time! Each year we give a Collector of the Year award! You'd be amazed at the photo entries we receive.

★ Back yard sales and auctions bring great finds to collectors. Advertise in your local paper for these collectibles!

★ Quality Looney Tunes ornaments (not Hallmark) were available at discount stores at affordable prices in '95.

★ Baby's First through Third Birthday ornaments are more sought after than the other numerated ones.

★ "Personalized" ornaments on which you have your own name or message placed usually do not escalate in value; only heirloom value.

★ The 1987 Hallmark Crayola® ornament *Bright Christmas Dreams* was not actually a part of the Hallmark Crayola® Crayon series which officially started in 1989 with *Bright Journey*, although many collectors consider it a "must have" to complete this series.

★ Showcase Ornaments were new from Hallmark in 1993. Many collectors had trouble locating these ornaments because this was an optional line and many dealers chose not to carry them. The most popular one on the secondary market to date is the 1993 *Santa Claus* from the Folk Art Americana Collection.

★ Be careful with packing and unpacking of ornaments. The 1994 *Beatles* have been found with Ringo having broken drum sticks.

★ It's best to put your favorite ornaments on layaway when they debut in July and August. Many people were accustomed to waiting for after Christmas sales to purchase some of their Hallmark ornaments but in the past three years some collectors have been sorely disappointed, finding that many ornaments were sold out by this time.

★ Hallmark hosted one-day Ornament Expos across the country in 1994 and 1995 in lieu of one large convention as in 1991 and 1993. A special piece, *Mrs. Claus' Cupboard*, was available for purchase at the 1994 Expo and *Christmas Eve Bake-Off* was available at the 1995 Expo. Hallmark also produced variations of popular ornaments to be given away at the Expos as door prizes and other special Expo offerings which collectors may purchase. (The 1995 miniature Pewter Rocking Horse is Hot!) Also, Artist Signing Events are held throughout the country each year, giving collectors a chance to meet Hallmark artists and have their favorite ornaments signed.

★ The 1980 *Cool Yule* is a very coveted ornament in the Hallmark line. *Here Comes Santa* and *Rocking Horse* are also two very popular Hallmark series.

★ Sleepers are ornaments which sell out at dealers more quickly than those predicted to do so. This is because there are usually less of them available.

★ Generally, any train or Classic Car ornament is good for secondary market holdings. The '95 Mini *Murray Champion* was Hot!

★ Did you know there are many channels through which you may find the older ornaments? These include ornament swap meets and secondary market dealers' ads and some Hallmark stores have added rooms for older ornaments. Advertise; you'll probably find what you want!

★ *Baby-Sitter* and *Teacher* ornaments usually have not been sought after to date on the secondary market.

★ Know who you are dealing with when buying, selling and trading through the mail. Generally, most collectors are trustworthy folks but there's always that one bad onion! There's a very good method to use to mark your ornaments when selling. Use a black light marking pen to put a dot or two on each ornament in case a broken or scratched ornament is returned. These marks will show up under a black light, proving whether or not the ornament returned is the one you sent. When shipping UPS, we advise shipping with the label AOD (Acknowledgment of Delivery). The recipient must "sign" for the package.

★ In the future we may see new series of different dog breeds, cat breeds, actual nursery rhyme characters, more licensee product ornaments, bicycles, football stars, mermaids and computers, plus Victorian dolls, Nativity pieces, a special line of Santas, trains and definitely a new series of angels. The farmers have hoped for antique tractors; replicas of old toys and mechanical banks have been thought about as well as whimsical little vegetables! Mice will be around for years to come and surely, before the fad is over, a few black and white cows will debut. Hallmark artists plan designs several years ahead; as you read this the '96 and some '97 ornaments are well ahead on the production line in the Far East.

★ An unpainted 1989 Hallmark *Backstage Bear* ornament was found at a garage sale – a sample before final approval. Great find!

★ The *Classic American Cars* series is very popular as many men receive them as gifts. In the future we may see a similar line of foreign cars. Car enthusiasts are offering these at their Swap 'n Sells also.

★ For Hallmark Artist interviews - read *The Ornament Collector*™ magazine.

★ The 1994 *Here Comes Santa* ornament proved to be very popular among farm toy collectors. One collector in particular reported he customized his with the John Deere colors and decal.

★ Read **"ROSIE'S PICKS"** in *The Ornament Collector™* for **FUTURE** ornaments' popularity. She has a Retailer Guide each year, also! Tell your dealer!

★ Sometimes the value of an ornament may fall after a peak, later to rise or level off. It pays to study the market.

★ Most of the 1994 *Holiday Barbie* ornament boxes sold in Canada had French writing on the box.

★ Many collectors feel that ornaments shouldn't be stored in the original bubble wrap packing as this bubble wrap may emit a gas which discolors the ornament. As of 1994, Hallmark replaced bubble wrap with tissue paper as packing material. One reason for this change is that tissue paper is more environmentally friendly. However, we saw bubble wrap used as packing again in 1995. Many collectors also store their ornaments in sectioned storage boxes, thus eliminating the wear and tear on individual ornament boxes, if they decide to keep them. This also makes it simpler when decorating or putting away ornaments for the year. Ornament boxes may be carefully flattened and stored.

★ Many collectors want to know the relationship between Ambassador and Hallmark. Ambassador was a subsidiary of Hallmark and produced ornaments in the early '80s. Packaging for the Ambassador line consisted of white boxes with green inner boxes and a clear, see-through front. Printed on the outside of each box is *The Holiday House Collection*. It is difficult to find Ambassador ornaments in the original boxes.

★ You have joined the National Hallmark Club, haven't you?

★ The 1986 *Cinnamon Teddy* has two different stock numbers. It was done due to the computer's capacity being too small. Hallmark was obtaining the ornament from more than one manufacturer and they identified them with different numerals to regulate inventory.

★ Upside down decals sometimes are found on ornaments. Such was the case on the '94 third in series *Betsey's Country Christmas.*

★ The large Keepsake ornament book which retailers offer for sale every two years will not be published again until 1998 when a 25th Anniversary book will be issued.

★ Did you know Hallmark aired a very catchy television commercial featuring the *Solo in the Spotlight Barbie* ornament in the Fall of 1995?

★ There were three souvenir ornaments available only at Hallmark Expos in 1995. These included a Hallmark Artists' Caricature ball ornament, a miniature pewter Rocking Horse and a Cookie tree ornament. See page 228. The three ornaments were limited to one each per registered membership. The pewter rocking horse was the most popular!

★ Did you know Hallmark is on America On Line? You can access them if you're registered with that service by clicking or double clicking through these steps: Clubs and Interests, Hobbies and Interests, The Exchange, Other Collectors Board, Find, Other Collector's B/Hallmark Ornaments.

★ There will be three new series available in the '96 Easter ornaments. These include *Peter Rabbit* from the Beatrix Potter books, the *Cotton Tail Express* and the *Joyful Angel.*

★ *Holiday Carousel,* designed by Tobin Fraley, has a manufacturing defect. The designed side of the horse is on the inside and the plain side of the horse is facing outside. Mr. Fraley is no longer with Hallmark.

★ The Hallmark at Home catalog features several of the ornaments found in the Dream Book.

★ There were only three lighted ornaments that were not sold out by the middle part of October, 1995. These were *Superman,* the *Victorian Toybox* and the *Space Shuttle.*

★ There will be six Keepsake Ornaments in the 1996 Olympic Spirit Collection. They are: *Invitation to the Games,* two dated, trading-card size ceramic plaque ornaments; *Lighting the Flame,* a Magic Ornament which features flickering light and plays *Bugler's Dream; Olympic Triumph, Cloisonné Medallion, Parade of Nations* and *Izzy*, the 1996 Olympic mascot. See page 230.

★ *The Fireman,* a Showcase ornament, is a first in series. However, it was not advertised as a first in series, only as a Showcase ornament.

★ The *Collector's Rocking Horse* from the Hallmark at Home catalog nearly sold out at $199 in 1995. We are of the opinion that you may see another rocking horse in 1996. If that is the case, this first Collector's Rocking Horse of 1,000 could become collectible. It is a replica of the *Rocking Horse* ornament series #1. If one is produced next year, it may be a replica of the #2 and possibly the Gold Crown stores will offer this #2 piece. Time will tell.

The Ornament Collector's
Collector of the Year
Marty Tonomura
Spring, Texas

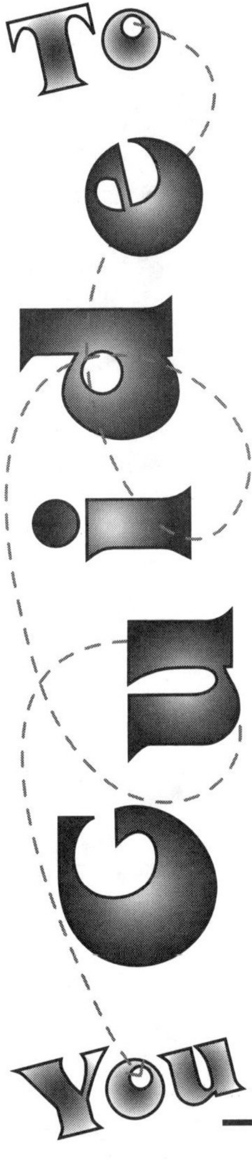

We have conducted extensive research in recording values for ornaments found in this guide. Use these values as a "guide" in insuring, as well as buying and selling. Expect prices on recent years' ornaments to increase proportionally more in the next few years than ornaments from early years.

MIB Sec. Mkt. prices quoted are for ornaments which are in mint condition and in their original boxes with price tab still attached to the box. The price tab is the removable perforated price tag found on each Hallmark ornament box. There were also "strips" running across the box or "gift tags" on some earlier boxes (i.e. 1977-1978 Trimmer Collection). When purchasing new ornaments be sure the perforated price tab remains on the box if you plan to resell later. If you give Hallmark ornaments as gifts to friends or loved ones who are collectors, they may want you to leave the tabs on. (Normally, this would be considered a breach in good manners, but collectors are a rare breed!)

Photos of each ornament have been included next to each listing in this guide. Care has been taken to ensure the clarity of each photo, however some detail has been lost as the photos in this guide have been reduced from larger color photos. **A secondary market price has been given for each ornament with a high-low range to guide you throughout 1995. In our opinion, by mid '96 the ornaments should be at the high price.**

*Read **The Ornament Collector**™ for price updates and current news on Hallmark ornaments! Each issue is packed with hot news on Hallmark ornaments and other Christmas theme collectibles, Collectors' Comments, classified ads, show listings, club information and much more!*

$23.95 Yr/4 issues, 22341 E. Wells Rd., Dept. G, Canton, IL 61520

Phone: 1-800-445-8745; Fax: 309/668-2795

May be found on most newsstands!

This guide is arranged first by year of production, then each ornament is alphabetized and listed by name.

Ornaments in a series or collection are listed by the name of the series or collection.

①

② **QLX 719-9 STARSHIP ENTERPRISE**③

④ *Comments:* Blinking Lights, Handcrafted, 1-5/8" tall Dated 1991. Commemorating the 25th anniversary of the television series *Star Trek*. Many *Star Trek* collectors were unaware of its debut. Production was much less than '92's Shuttlecraft Galileo, which was abundant. ('93 is now somewhat hard to find.) **Artist:** Lynn Norton

⑤ ☐ Purchased 19___ Pd $_______ MIB NB DB BNT

☐ Want ⑥ Orig. Ret. $20.00 **Lights Not Working** $100

⑦**NB** $280 ⑧**MIB** Sec. Mkt. $300-$325

1 .... **PHOTOGRAPH** of the Ornament. "Not Shown" means no photo of the piece was available. Photos welcomed!

2 .... **NUMBER:** Ornament's style number.

3 .... **NAME** of the Ornament. If the ornament is part of a series, the name of the series will appear first.

4 .... **COMMENTS:** Descriptions of each ornament include: Whether or not the ornament is part of a series and its standing in that series; if it is a ball ornament, acrylic, handcrafted, etc.; the size of the ornament (if available); whether or not it is dated; a short descriptive phrase; anything unusual or out of the ordinary.

5 .... This guide can also be used as a personal inventory book, keeping a record of ornaments you want or already own and the condition of your ornaments. MIB = mint in box, NB = no box, DB = damaged box and BNT = box with original price tab removed, NE = not established.

6 .... **ORIG. RET.:** Retail price of the ornament when it debuted.

7 .... **NB:** The value of the ornament without its original box. (NB-P signifies the fact that there is a plentiful supply of the ornament with No Box.)

8 .... **MIB** Sec. Mkt.: Today's secondary market price (collectors' and dealers' selling/buying prices). A high-low price range has been given for most of the ornaments. Ninety-nine percent of the time you'll be able to find that special ornament at these prices. To sell a large collection quickly, expect to reduce your prices by 20%-30%. When selling to dealers, it may be necessary to take 50%-60% off as they buy to resell. Remember, use these prices as a guide; use them to insure as this would be the replacement cost.

1973 Collection

(Deduct $15-$20 on "old age" spots, depending on the amount.)

XHD 100-2 BETSEY CLARK
Comments: White Glass Ball, 3-1/4" dia.
Five pretty girls are joyfully singing around a Christmas tree.
☐ Purchased 19___ Pd $_______ MIB NB DB BNT
☐ Want Orig. Ret. $2.50 **NB** $65 **MIB** Sec. Mkt. **$85-$90**

XHD 110-2 BETSEY CLARK SERIES
Comments: ***FIRST IN SERIES***, Dated 1973
White Glass Ball, 3-1/4" dia.
One little girl is feeding a deer; the other is cuddling a lamb.
☐ Purchased 19___ Pd $_______ MIB NB DB BNT
☐ Want Orig. Ret. $2.50 **NB** $85 **MIB** Sec. Mkt. **$125-$130**

XHD 106-2 CHRISTMAS IS LOVE
Comments: White Glass Ball, 3-1/4" dia.
Two angels play mandolins; in shades of green and lavender. Caption: "Christmas Is Love - Christmas Is You."
☐ Purchased 19___ Pd $_______ MIB NB DB BNT
☐ Want Orig. Ret. $2.50 **NB** $60 **MIB** Sec. Mkt. **$65-$70**

XHD 103-5 ELVES
Comments: White Glass Ball, 3-1/4" dia. Ice skating elves.
☐ Purchased 19___ Pd $_______ MIB NB DB BNT
☐ Want Orig. Ret. $2.50 **NB** $55 **MIB** Sec. Mkt. **$65-$70**

XHD 102-2 MANGER SCENE
Comments: White Glass Ball, 3-1/4" dia.
Designed scene on dark red background.
☐ Purchased 19___ Pd $_______ MIB NB DB BNT
☐ Want Orig. Ret. $2.50 **NB** $65 **MIB** Sec. Mkt. **$70-$75**

XHD 101-5 SANTA WITH ELVES
Comments: White Glass Ball, 3-1/4" dia.
☐ Purchased 19___ Pd $_______ MIB NB DB BNT
☐ Want Orig. Ret. $2.50 **NB** $65 **MIB** Sec. Mkt. **$75-$80**

No secondary market value has been established for yarn and fabric ornaments found in original cellophane package.

XHD 78-5 YARN ORNAMENT - ANGEL
Comments: 4-1/2" tall
☐ Purchased 19___ Pd $_______ MIB NB DB BNT
☐ Want Orig. Ret. $1.25
White Wings: $28-$30
Gold Wings: $28-$30

XHD 85-2 YARN ORNAMENT - BLUE GIRL
Comments: 4-1/2" tall
☐ Purchased 19___ Pd $_______ MIB NB DB BNT
☐ Want Orig. Ret. $1.25 Sec. Mkt. **$24-$26**

XHD 83-2 YARN ORNAMENT - BOY CAROLER
Comments: 4-1/2" tall. Blue hat and coat.
☐ Purchased 19___ Pd $_______ MIB NB DB BNT
☐ Want Orig. Ret. $1.25 Sec. Mkt. **$25-$28**

XHD 80-5 YARN ORNAMENT - CHOIR BOY
Comments: 4-1/2" tall
☐ Purchased 19___ Pd $_______ MIB NB DB BNT
☐ Want Orig. Ret. $1.25 Sec. Mkt. **$25-$30**

XHD 79-2 YARN ORNAMENT - ELF
Comments: 4-1/2" tall
☐ Purchased 19___ Pd $_______ MIB NB DB BNT
☐ Want Orig. Ret. $1.25 Sec. Mkt. **$25-$27**

XHD 84-5 YARN ORNAMENT - GREEN GIRL
Comments: 4-1/2" tall. Green with red hat and song book.
☐ Purchased 19___ Pd $_______ MIB NB DB BNT
☐ Want Orig. Ret. $1.25 Sec. Mkt. **$25-$27**

XHD 82-5 YARN ORNAMENT - LITTLE GIRL
Comments: 4-1/2" tall. Pink dress, blonde hair.
☐ Purchased 19___ Pd $_______ MIB NB DB BNT
☐ Want Orig. Ret. $1.25 Sec. Mkt. **$22-$25**

XHD 74-5 YARN ORNAMENT - MR. SANTA
Comments: 4-1/2" tall
☐ Purchased 19___ Pd $_______ MIB NB DB BNT
☐ Want Orig. Ret. $1.25 Sec. Mkt. **$25-$30**

XHD 75-2 YARN ORNAMENT - MRS. SANTA
Comments: 4-1/2" tall
☐ Purchased 19___ Pd $_______ MIB NB DB BNT
☐ Want Orig. Ret. $1.25 Sec. Mkt. **$22-$28**

XHD 76-5 YARN ORNAMENT - MR. SNOWMAN
Comments: 4-1/2" tall. Blue scarf, black top hat.
☐ Purchased 19___ Pd $_______ MIB NB DB BNT
☐ Want Orig. Ret. $1.25 Sec. Mkt. **$22-$25**

XHD 77-2 YARN ORNAMENT - MRS. SNOWMAN
Comments: 4-1/2" tall. Pink hat and scarf.
☐ Purchased 19___ Pd $_______ MIB NB DB BNT
☐ Want Orig. Ret. $1.25 Sec. Mkt. **$22-$25**

XHD 81-2 YARN ORNAMENT - SOLDIER
Comments: 4-1/2" tall. Blue with red hat, boots and bands.
☐ Purchased 19___ Pd $_______ MIB NB DB BNT
☐ Want Orig. Ret. $1.00 Sec. Mkt. **$22-$25**

1974 Collection

QX 110-1 ANGEL
Comments: White Glass Ball, 3-1/4" dia.
☐ Purchased 19___ Pd $_______ MIB NB DB BNT
☐ Want Orig. Ret. $2.50 **NB** $55 **MIB** Sec. Mkt. **$70-$75**

QX 108-1 BETSEY CLARK SERIES
Comments: **Second in Series**, Dated 1974
White Glass Ball, 3-1/4" dia.
Features an orchestra and choir of youngsters.
☐ Purchased 19___ Pd $_______ MIB NB DB BNT
☐ Want Orig. Ret. $2.50 **NB** $60 **MIB** Sec. Mkt. **$75-$80**

ERROR - Sleeve Upside Down
Other ornaments have also been reported with the sleeves upside down. Add $25-$30 over the secondary market to these.

QX 113-1 BUTTONS & BO
Comments: White Glass Ball, 2-1/4" dia., Set of 2
☐ Purchased 19___ Pd $_______ MIB NB DB BNT
☐ Want Orig. Ret. $3.50 **NB** $40 **MIB** Sec. Mkt. **$50-$55**

QX 109-1 CHARMERS
Comments: White Glass Ball, 3-1/4" dia., Dated 1974
☐ Purchased 19___ Pd $_______ MIB NB DB BNT
☐ Want Orig. Ret. $2.50 **NB** $30 **MIB** Sec. Mkt. **$42-$45**

QX 112-1 CURRIER & IVES
Comments: White Glass Ball, 2-1/4" dia., Set of 2
Winter farmstead and horse-drawn sleigh.
☐ Purchased 19___ Pd $_______ MIB NB DB BNT
☐ Want Orig. Ret. $3.50 **NB** $40 **MIB** Sec. Mkt. **$55-$60**

QX 115-1 LITTLE MIRACLES
Comments: White Glass Ball, 1-3/4" dia., Set of 4
Little boy and his rabbit companion in play.
☐ Purchased 19___ Pd $_______ MIB NB DB BNT
☐ Want Orig. Ret. $4.50 **NB** $50 **MIB** Sec. Mkt. **$55-$60**

QX 111-1 NORMAN ROCKWELL
Comments: White Glass Ball, 3-1/4" dia.
Santa wears an apron with tools in his pockets. He naps in a chair while the elves work. On the opposite side is Santa with two boys.
☐ Purchased 19___ Pd $_______ MIB NB DB BNT
☐ Want Orig. Ret. $2.50 **NB** $65 **MIB** Sec. Mkt. **$75-$80**

QX 106-1 NORMAN ROCKWELL SERIES
Comments: White Glass Ball, 3-1/4" dia., Dated 1974
Two of Rockwell's famous illustrations on this ball include the "Jolly Postman" and on the back, a father and son bringing home the perfect Christmas tree.
☐ Purchased 19___ Pd $_______ MIB NB DB BNT
☐ Want Orig. Ret. $2.50 **NB** $65 **MIB** Sec. Mkt. **$85-$90**

QX 114-1 RAGGEDY ANN™ AND RAGGEDY ANDY™
Comments: White Glass Ball, 1-3/4" dia.
A pretty set of 4.
☐ Purchased 19___ Pd $_______ MIB NB DB BNT
☐ Want Orig. Ret. $4.50 **NB** $75 **MIB** Sec. Mkt. **$80-$85**

QX 107-1 SNOWGOOSE
Comments: White Glass Ball, 3-1/4" dia.
☐ Purchased 19___ Pd $_______ MIB NB DB BNT
☐ Want Orig. Ret. $2.50 **NB** $70 **MIB** Sec. Mkt. **$75-$80**

QX 103-1 YARN ORNAMENT - ANGEL
Comments: 4-3/4" tall
☐ Purchased 19___ Pd $_______ MIB NB DB BNT
☐ Want Orig. Ret. $1.50 Sec. Mkt. **$25-$30**

QX 101-1 YARN ORNAMENT - ELF
Comments: 4-3/4" tall
☐ Purchased 19___ Pd $_______ MIB NB DB BNT
☐ Want Orig. Ret. $1.50 Sec. Mkt. **$22-$25**

QX 100-1 YARN ORNAMENT - MRS. SANTA
Comments: 4-3/4" tall. Red dress with white pinafore.
☐ Purchased 19___ Pd $_______ MIB NB DB BNT
☐ Want Orig. Ret. $1.50 Sec. Mkt. **$25-$30**

QX 105-1 YARN ORNAMENT - SANTA
Comments: 4-3/4" tall. Traditional Santa in red.
☐ Purchased 19___ Pd $_______ MIB NB DB BNT
☐ Want Orig. Ret. $1.50 Sec. Mkt. **$25-$30**

XHD 104-1 YARN ORNAMENT - SNOWMAN
Comments: 4-3/4" tall. Plaid scarf, black top hat.
☐ Purchased 19___ Pd $_______ MIB NB DB BNT
☐ Want Orig. Ret. $1.50 Sec. Mkt. **$22-$25**

XHD 102-1 YARN ORNAMENT - SOLDIER
Comments: 4-3/4" tall. Blue with red hat and boots, white bands.
☐ Purchased 19___ Pd $_______ MIB NB DB BNT
☐ Want Orig. Ret. $1.50 Sec. Mkt. **$22-$25**

No secondary market value has been established for yarn and fabric ornaments found in original cellophane package.

1975 Collection

QX 157-1 ADORABLE ADORNMENTS: BETSEY CLARK
Comments: 3-1/2" tall. **Artist:** Donna Lee
☐ Purchased 19___ Pd $_______ MIB NB DB BNT
☐ Want Orig. Ret. $2.50 **NB** $215 **MIB** Sec. Mkt. **$230-$250**

QX 161-1 ADORABLE ADORNMENTS: DRUMMER BOY
Comments: Handcrafted, 3-1/2" tall. **Artist:** Donna Lee
☐ Purchased 19___ Pd $_______ MIB NB DB BNT
☐ Want Orig. Ret. $2.50 **NB** $150 **MIB** Sec. Mkt **$230-$250**

QX 156-1 ADORABLE ADORNMENTS: MRS. SANTA
Comments: Handcrafted, 3-1/2" tall. This ornament came in an individual package. Reissued with Mr. Santa in 1981 in a box as "Mr. and Mrs. Claus." Only the original packaging proves whether or not this ornament is the 1975 version or the reissued 1981 ornament. This is why the no box price is considerably lower than MIB price.
Artist: Donna Lee
☐ Purchased 19___ Pd $_______ MIB NB DB BNT
☐ Want Orig. Ret. $2.50 **NB** $65 **MIB** Sec. Mkt. **$250-$275**

QX 159-1 ADORABLE ADORNMENTS: RAGGEDY ANN™
Comments: Handcrafted, 3-1/2" tall. RARE!
Collectors are willing to pay nearly the same with or without the box.
Artist: Donna Lee
☐ Purchased 19___ Pd $_______ MIB NB DB BNT
☐ Want Orig. Ret. $2.50 **NB** $275 **MIB** Sec. Mkt. **$295-$325**

QX 160-1 ADORABLE ADORNMENTS: RAGGEDY ANDY™
Comments: Handcrafted, 3-1/2" tall. RARE!
Artist: Donna Lee
☐ Purchased 19___ Pd $_______ MIB NB DB BNT
☐ Want Orig. Ret. $2.50 **NB** $280 **MIB** Sec. Mkt. **$350-$375**

QX 155-1 ADORABLE ADORNMENTS: SANTA
Comments: Handcrafted, 3-1/2" tall. This ornament came in an individual package. Reissued with Mrs. Santa in 1981 in box as "Mr. and Mrs. Claus." No real difference between these two years' ornaments.
Artist: Donna Lee
☐ Purchased 19___ Pd $_______ MIB NB DB BNT
☐ Want Orig. Ret. $2.50 **NB** $70 **MIB** Sec. Mkt. **$260-$285**

QX 168-1 BETSEY CLARK
Comments: White Satin Ball, Dated 1975, 2" dia., Set of 4
Caption: "Christmas 1975." Four different scenes of children with the animals and birds.
☐ Purchased 19___ Pd $_______ MIB NB DB BNT
☐ Want Orig. Ret. $4.50 **NB** $35-$45 **MIB** Sec. Mkt. **$50-$55**

QX 167-1 BETSEY CLARK
Comments: White Satin Ball, 2-1/2" dia., Set of 2
Caption: "Christmas 1975." Two skaters on one ornament and girl in stocking cap on other.
☐ Purchased 19___ Pd $_______ MIB NB DB BNT
☐ Want Orig. Ret. $3.50 **NB** $20-$30 **MIB** Sec. Mkt. **$45-$50**

QX 163-1 BETSEY CLARK
Comments: White Satin Ball, Dated 1975, 3" dia.
Youngster in pajamas, saying bedtime prayers.
Artist: Linda Sickman
☐ Purchased 19___ Pd $_______ MIB NB DB BNT
☐ Want Orig. Ret. $2.50 **NB** $22 **MIB** Sec. Mkt. **$35-$42**

QX 133-1 BETSEY CLARK SERIES
Comments: **Third in Series,** Caption: "Christmas 1975"
White Glass Ball, 3-1/4" dia. Three girls dressed in pink, blue and yellow calico with song book.
☐ Purchased 19___ Pd $_______ MIB NB DB BNT
☐ Want Orig. Ret. $3.00` **NB** $35 **MIB** Sec. Mkt. **$55-$60**

QX 139-1 BUTTONS & BO
Comments: White Glass Ball, 1-3/4" dia., Set of 4
Dated 1975 on back.
☐ Purchased 19___ Pd $_______ MIB NB DB BNT
☐ Want Orig. Ret. $5.00 **NB** $35 **MIB** Sec. Mkt. **$45-$50**

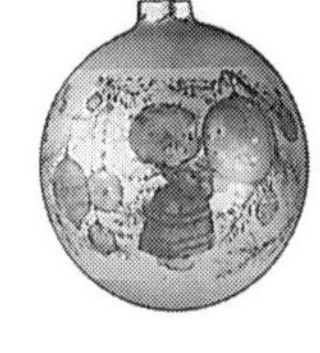

QX 135-1 CHARMERS
Comments: White Glass Ball, 3-1/2" dia.
Dated 1975 on back.
☐ Purchased 19___ Pd $_______ MIB NB DB BNT
☐ Want Orig. Ret. $3.00 **NB** $30 **MIB** Sec. Mkt. **$40-$45**

QX 164-1 CURRIER & IVES
Comments: White Satin Ball, 3" dia.
Winter scene of farmhouse and farm buildings.
Artist: Linda Sickman
☐ Purchased 19___ Pd $_______ MIB NB DB BNT
☐ Want Orig. Ret. $2.50 **NB** $25 **MIB** Sec. Mkt. **$35-$40**

QX 137-1 CURRIER & IVES
Comments: White Glass Ball, 2-1/4" dia., Set of 2
Snow scenes of Victorian ice skaters and old mill.
Artist: Linda Sickman
☐ Purchased 19___ Pd $_______ MIB NB DB BNT
☐ Want Orig. Ret. $4.00 **NB** $28 **MIB** Sec. Mkt. **$40-$45**

QX 140-1 LITTLE MIRACLES
Comments: White Glass Ball, 1-3/4" dia., Set of 4
A cherub and his forest friends.
Caption on back: "Christmas 1975."
☐ Purchased 19___ Pd $_______ MIB NB DB BNT
☐ Want Orig. Ret. $5.00 **NB** $35 **MIB** Sec. Mkt. **$42-$45**

QX 136-1 MARTY LINKS™
Comments: White Glass Ball, 3-1/4" dia.
On back: "Merry Christmas 1975."
☐ Purchased 19___ Pd $_______ MIB NB DB BNT
☐ Want Orig. Ret. $3.00 **NB** $28 **MIB** Sec. Mkt. **$34-$38**

QX 166-1 NORMAN ROCKWELL
Comments: White Satin Ball, 3" dia.
Front: Santa writes in book while checking on boys through his telescope. Back: Santa with bag of toys.
☐ Purchased 19___ Pd $_______ MIB NB DB BNT
☐ Want Orig. Ret. $2.50 **NB** $45 **MIB** Sec. Mkt. **$55-$60**

QX 134-1 NORMAN ROCKWELL
Comments: White Glass Ball, 3-1/4" dia., Dated 1975
Santa peeks at two small boys asleep in a chair. Back: A young child is kneeling at the bed, saying prayers.
☐ Purchased 19___ Pd $_______ MIB NB DB BNT
☐ Want Orig. Ret. $3.00 **NB** $40 **MIB** Sec. Mkt. **$50-$60**

QX 130-1 NOSTALGIA ORNAMENTS: DRUMMER BOY
Comments: 3-1/4" dia., Reissued in 1976.
A little boy marches to the beat of his drum. **Artist:** Linda Sickman
☐ Purchased 19___ Pd $_______ MIB NB DB BNT
☐ Want Orig. Ret. $3.50 **NB** $125 **MIB** Sec. Mkt. **$165-$175**

QX 132-1 NOSTALGIA ORNAMENTS: JOY
Comments: 3-1/4" dia., RARE!
Baby Jesus lies peacefully in the center of the word "Joy."
Artist: Linda Sickman
☐ Purchased 19___ Pd $_______ MIB NB DB BNT
☐ Want Orig. Ret. $3.50 **NB** $180 **MIB** Sec. Mkt. **$230-$235**

QX 127-1 NOSTALGIA ORNAMENTS: LOCOMOTIVE
Comments: 3-1/4" dia., Dated 1975
Artist: Linda Sickman
☐ Purchased 19___ Pd $_______ MIB NB DB BNT
☐ Want Orig. Ret. $3.50 **NB** $120 **MIB** Sec. Mkt. **$165-$170**

QX 131-1 NOSTALGIA ORNAMENTS: PEACE ON EARTH
Comments: 3-1/4" dia., Dated 1975
"Peace On Earth" is the perfect caption for this snowy village scene.
Artist: Linda Sickman
☐ Purchased 19___ Pd $_______ MIB NB DB BNT
☐ Want Orig. Ret. $3.50 **NB** $115 **MIB** Sec. Mkt. **$165-$170**

QX 128-1 NOSTALGIA ORNAMENTS: ROCKING HORSE
Comments: 3-1/4" dia., Reissued in 1976.
Artist: Linda Sickman
☐ Purchased 19___ Pd $_______ MIB NB DB BNT
☐ Want Orig. Ret. $3.50 **NB** $125 **MIB** Sec. Mkt. **$160-$165**

QX 129-1 NOSTALGIA ORNAMENTS: SANTA AND SLEIGH
Comments: 3-1/4" dia., RARE!
Artist: Linda Sickman
☐ Purchased 19___ Pd $_______ MIB NB DB BNT
☐ Want Orig. Ret. $3.50 **NB** $185 **MIB** Sec. Mkt. **$250-$255**

QX 165-1 RAGGEDY ANN™
Comments: White Satin Ball, 3" dia., Dated 1975
Poinsettias and holly make a lovely frame for Raggedy Ann.
Artist: Linda Sickman
☐ Purchased 19___ Pd $_______ MIB NB DB BNT
☐ Want Orig. Ret. $2.50 **NB** $30 **MIB** Sec. Mkt. **$45-$50**

QX 138-1 RAGGEDY ANN™ AND RAGGEDY ANDY™
Comments: White Glass Ball, 2-1/4" dia., Set of 2
Front: Ann and Andy are seated beside each other with a green wreath encircling them. Back: They hold a "Merry Christmas" banner. Front of second ornament: Decorating the tree; Back: "Christmas 1975." **Artist:** Linda Sickman
☐ Purchased 19___ Pd $_______ MIB NB DB BNT
☐ Want Orig. Ret. $4.00 **NB** $50 **MIB** Sec. Mkt. **$65-$70**

No secondary market value has been established for yarn and fabric ornaments found in original cellophane package.

QX 123-1 YARN ORNAMENTS: DRUMMER BOY
Comments: 4-1/2" tall. Reissued in 1976.
Green with red hat.
☐ Purchased 19___ Pd $_______ MIB NB DB BNT
☐ Want Orig. Ret. $1.75 Sec. Mkt. **$25-$28**

QX 126-1 YARN ORNAMENTS: CAROLER (Little Girl)
Comments: 4-1/2" tall. Reissued in 1976.
Green dress, with green hat and white muff.
☐ Purchased 19___ Pd $_______ MIB NB DB BNT
☐ Want Orig. Ret. $1.75 Sec. Mkt. **$20-$24**

QX 125-1 YARN ORNAMENTS: MRS. SANTA
Comments: 4-1/2" tall
White apron with red checked pockets.
☐ Purchased 19___ Pd $_______ MIB NB DB BNT
☐ Want Orig. Ret. $1.75 Sec. Mkt. **$22-$25**

QX 121-1 YARN ORNAMENTS: RAGGEDY ANN™
Comments: 4-1/2" tall, RARE! Reissued in 1976.
Blue dress with white pinafore.
☐ Purchased 19___ Pd $_______ MIB NB DB BNT
☐ Want Orig. Ret. $1.75 Sec. Mkt. **$35-$40**

QX 122-1 YARN ORNAMENTS: RAGGEDY ANDY™
Comments: 4-1/2" tall, RARE! Reissued in 1976.
Blue with red-white checked shirt.
☐ Purchased 19___ Pd $_______ MIB NB DB BNT
☐ Want Orig. Ret. $1.75 Sec. Mkt. **$40-$45**

QX 124-1 YARN ORNAMENTS: SANTA
Comments: 4-1/2" tall. Reissued in 1976.
☐ Purchased 19___ Pd $_______ MIB NB DB BNT
☐ Want Orig. Ret. $1.75 Sec. Mkt. **$22-$24**

1976 Collection

QX 211-1 BABY'S FIRST CHRISTMAS
Comments: White Satin Ball, 3" dia., Dated 1976
Caption: "Baby's First Christmas." Price up from '95.
☐ Purchased 19___ Pd $_______ MIB NB DB BNT
☐ Want Orig. Ret. $2.50 **NB** $80 **MIB** Sec. Mkt. **$110-$115**

QX 218-1 BETSEY CLARK
Comments: White Satin Ball, 2" dia., Set of 3
All Dated 1976 on back.
☐ Purchased 19___ Pd $_______ MIB NB DB BNT
☐ Want Orig. Ret. $4.50 **NB** $35 **MIB** Sec. Mkt. **$50-$55**

QX 210-1 BETSEY CLARK
Comments: White Satin Ball, 3" dia.
Caption: "Christmas 1976"
☐ Purchased 19___ Pd $_______ MIB NB DB BNT
☐ Want Orig. Ret. $2.50 **NB** $28 **MIB** Sec. Mkt. **$42-$45**

QX 195-1 BETSEY CLARK SERIES
Comments: **Fourth in Series**
White Glass Ball, 3-1/4" dia. Caption: "Christmas 1976"
☐ Purchased 19___ Pd $_______ MIB NB DB BNT
☐ Want Orig. Ret. $3.00 **NB** $70 **MIB** Sec. Mkt. **$95-$100**

QX 203-1 BICENTENNIAL '76 COMMEMORATIVE
Comments: White Satin Ball, 3" dia.
Charmers dressed in 1776 fashions.
Caption: "1976 Commemorative"
☐ Purchased 19___ Pd $_______ MIB NB DB BNT
☐ Want Orig. Ret. $2.50 **NB** $42-$47 **MIB** Sec. Mkt. **$60-$62**

QX 198-1 BICENTENNIAL CHARMERS
Comments: White Glass Ball, 3-1/4" dia.
Caption: "Merry Christmas 1976." Very little trading found since 1992.
☐ Purchased 19___ Pd $_______ MIB NB DB BNT
☐ Want Orig. Ret. $3.00 **NB** $29 **MIB** Sec. Mkt. **$42-$45**

QX 205-1 CARDINALS
Comments: White Glass Ball, 2-5/8" dia.
Caption: "Christmas 1976."
☐ Purchased 19___ Pd $_______ MIB NB DB BNT
☐ Want Orig. Ret. $2.25 **NB** $30 **MIB** Sec. Mkt. **$45-$50**

QX 215-1 CHARMERS
Comments: White Satin Ball, 2-1/2" dia., Set of 2
Caption on Both: "Christmas 1976."
☐ Purchased 19___ Pd $_______ MIB NB DB BNT
☐ Want Orig. Ret. $3.50 **NB** $40 **MIB** Sec. Mkt. **$50-$55**

QX 204-1 CHICKADEES
Comments: White Glass Ball, 2-5/8" dia.
Caption: "Christmas 1976."
☐ Purchased 19___ Pd $_______ MIB NB DB BNT
☐ Want Orig. Ret. $2.25 **NB** $27 **MIB** Sec. Mkt. **$42-$45**

QX 208-1 COLONIAL CHILDREN
Comments: White Glass Ball, 2-1/4" dia., Set of 2, Dated 1976
Front: Children in colonial clothing, build and dress a snowman. Back: "Christmas 1976." Front of second design: Colonial youngsters bring home the Christmas tree. Back: "Merry Christmas 1976."
☐ Purchased 19___ Pd $_______ MIB NB DB BNT
☐ Want Orig. Ret. $4.00 **NB** $30 **MIB** Sec. Mkt. **$40-$45**

QX 209-1 CURRIER & IVES
Comments: White Satin Ball, 3" dia.
Caption: "To Commemorate Christmas 1976." A farmyard in winter with sleigh and skaters.
☐ Purchased 19___ Pd $_______ MIB NB DB BNT
☐ Want Orig. Ret. $2.50 **NB** $37 **MIB** Sec. Mkt. **$45-$50**

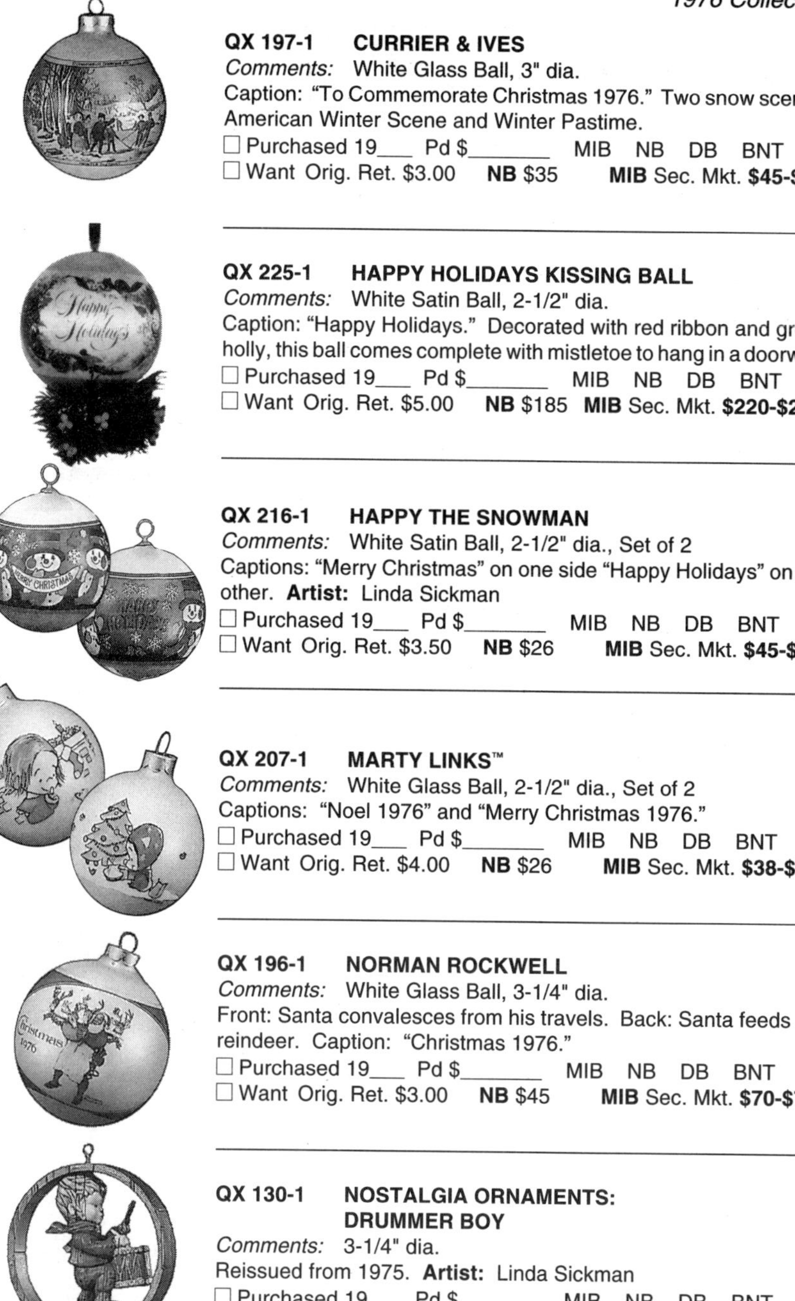

QX 197-1 CURRIER & IVES
Comments: White Glass Ball, 3" dia.
Caption: "To Commemorate Christmas 1976." Two snow scenes, American Winter Scene and Winter Pastime.
☐ Purchased 19___ Pd $_______ MIB NB DB BNT
☐ Want Orig. Ret. $3.00 **NB** $35 **MIB** Sec. Mkt. **$45-$50**

QX 225-1 HAPPY HOLIDAYS KISSING BALL
Comments: White Satin Ball, 2-1/2" dia.
Caption: "Happy Holidays." Decorated with red ribbon and green holly, this ball comes complete with mistletoe to hang in a doorway.
☐ Purchased 19___ Pd $_______ MIB NB DB BNT
☐ Want Orig. Ret. $5.00 **NB** $185 **MIB** Sec. Mkt. **$220-$230**

QX 216-1 HAPPY THE SNOWMAN
Comments: White Satin Ball, 2-1/2" dia., Set of 2
Captions: "Merry Christmas" on one side "Happy Holidays" on the other. **Artist:** Linda Sickman
☐ Purchased 19___ Pd $_______ MIB NB DB BNT
☐ Want Orig. Ret. $3.50 **NB** $26 **MIB** Sec. Mkt. **$45-$50**

QX 207-1 MARTY LINKS™
Comments: White Glass Ball, 2-1/2" dia., Set of 2
Captions: "Noel 1976" and "Merry Christmas 1976."
☐ Purchased 19___ Pd $_______ MIB NB DB BNT
☐ Want Orig. Ret. $4.00 **NB** $26 **MIB** Sec. Mkt. **$38-$42**

QX 196-1 NORMAN ROCKWELL
Comments: White Glass Ball, 3-1/4" dia.
Front: Santa convalesces from his travels. Back: Santa feeds his reindeer. Caption: "Christmas 1976."
☐ Purchased 19___ Pd $_______ MIB NB DB BNT
☐ Want Orig. Ret. $3.00 **NB** $45 **MIB** Sec. Mkt. **$70-$75**

QX 130-1 NOSTALGIA ORNAMENTS: DRUMMER BOY
Comments: 3-1/4" dia.
Reissued from 1975. **Artist:** Linda Sickman
☐ Purchased 19___ Pd $_______ MIB NB DB BNT
☐ Want 1976 Ret. $4.00 **NB** $125 **MIB** Sec. Mkt. **$165-$175**

QX 222-1 NOSTALGIA ORNAMENTS: LOCOMOTIVE
Comments: 3-1/4" dia., Dated 1976
Same design as 1975, but fewer available. **Artist:** Linda Sickman
☐ Purchased 19___ Pd $_______ MIB NB DB BNT
☐ Want Orig. Ret. $4.00 **NB** $155 **MIB** Sec. Mkt. **$170-$175**

QX 223-1 NOSTALGIA ORNAMENTS: PEACE ON EARTH
Comments: 3-1/4" dia., Dated 1976
Same design as 1975. **Artist:** Linda Sickman
☐ Purchased 19___ Pd $_______ MIB NB DB BNT
☐ Want Orig. Ret. $4.00 **NB** $90 **MIB** Sec. Mkt. **$140-$145**

QX 128-1 NOSTALGIA ORNAMENTS: ROCKING HORSE
Comments: 3-1/4" dia.
Reissued from 1975. **Artist:** Linda Sickman
☐ Purchased 19___ Pd $_______ MIB NB DB BNT
☐ Want 1976 Retail $4.00 **NB** $120 **MIB** Sec. Mkt. **$162-$165**

QX 212-1 RAGGEDY ANN™
Comments: White Satin Ball, 2-1/2" dia., Dated 1976
Ann is hanging stockings at fireplace. Caption on back: "Merry Christmas 1976." Very cute!
☐ Purchased 19___ Pd $_______ MIB NB DB BNT
☐ Want Orig. Ret. $2.50 **NB** $40 **MIB** Sec. Mkt. **$60-$65**

QX 213-1 RUDOLPH AND SANTA
Comments: White Satin Ball, 2-1/2" dia., Dated 1976
Front: "Rudolph the Red-Nosed Reindeer." Back: "Merry Christmas 1976."
☐ Purchased 19___ Pd $_______ MIB NB DB BNT
☐ Want Orig. Ret. $2.50 **NB** $65 **MIB** Sec. Mkt. **$75-$80**

QX 176-1 TREE TREATS: ANGEL
Comments: Vary in size from 2-3/4" to 3-5/8" tall
Resembles baker's dough. Caption: "Merry Christmas 1976."
☐ Purchased 19___ Pd $_______ MIB NB DB BNT
☐ Want Orig. Ret. $3.00 **NB** $130 **MIB** Sec. Mkt. **$195-$200**

QX 178-1 TREE TREATS: REINDEER
Comments: Vary in size from 2-3/4" to 3-5/8" tall, Dated 1976
Made from material resembling baker's dough.
Caption: "Merry Christmas 1976."
☐ Purchased 19___ Pd $_______ MIB NB DB BNT
☐ Want Orig. Ret. $3.00 **NB** $105 **MIB** Sec. Mkt. **$115-$120**

QX 177-1 TREE TREATS: SANTA
Comments: Vary in size from 2-3/4" to 3-5/8" tall, Dated 1976
Made from material resembling baker's dough.
Caption: "Season's Greetings 1976."
☐ Purchased 19___ Pd $_______ MIB NB DB BNT
☐ Want Orig. Ret. $3.00 **NB** $180 **MIB** Sec. Mkt. **$195-$200**

QX 175-1 TREE TREATS: SHEPHERD
Comments: Vary in size from 2-3/4" to 3-5/8" tall
Made from material resembling baker's dough. Caption: "Season's Greetings 1976."
☐ Purchased 19___ Pd $_______ MIB NB DB BNT
☐ Want Orig. Ret. $3.00 **NB** $95 **MIB** Sec. Mkt. **$115-$120**

QX 171-1 TWIRL-ABOUTS: ANGEL
Comments: Vary in size from 3-1/2" to 4" tall, Dated 1976
Center figures rotate on a brass pin. Angel in Christmas Tree.
Caption: "Merry Christmas 1976." **Artist:** Linda Sickman
☐ Purchased 19___ Pd $_______ MIB NB DB BNT
☐ Want Orig. Ret. $4.50 **NB** $115 **MIB** Sec. Mkt. **$165-$170**

QX 174-1 TWIRL-ABOUTS: PARTRIDGE
Comments: Vary in size from 3-1/2" to 4" tall, Dated 1976
Partridge rotates on a brass pin in the center of a pear wreath.
Artist: Linda Sickman
☐ Purchased 19___ Pd $_______ MIB NB DB BNT
☐ Want Orig. Ret. $4.50 **NB** $155 **MIB** Sec. Mkt. **$195-$200**

QX 172-1 TWIRL-ABOUTS: SANTA
Comments: Vary in size from 3-1/2" to 4" tall.
Santa rotates on a brass pin in the center of a wreath.
Artist: Linda Sickman
☐ Purchased 19___ Pd $_______ MIB NB DB BNT
☐ Want Orig. Ret. $4.50 **NB** $95 **MIB** Sec. Mkt. **$115-$125**

QX 173-1 TWIRL-ABOUTS: SOLDIER
Comments: Vary in size from 3-1/2" to 4" tall, Dated 1976
Soldier rotates on a brass pin at the center of Guard House.
Artist: Linda Sickman
☐ Purchased 19___ Pd $_______ MIB NB DB BNT
☐ Want Orig. Ret. $4.50 **NB** $75 **MIB** Sec. Mkt. **$100-$105**

QX 126-1 YARN ORNAMENTS: CAROLER (Little Girl)
Comments: 4-1/2" tall. Reissued from 1975.
Green, with white muff and green hat.
☐ Purchased 19___ Pd $_______ MIB NB DB BNT
☐ Want Orig. Ret. $1.75 Sec. Mkt. **$20-$24**

QX 123-1 YARN ORNAMENTS: DRUMMER BOY
Comments: 4-1/2" tall. Reissued from 1975.
Green with red hat.
☐ Purchased 19___ Pd $_______ MIB NB DB BNT
☐ Want Orig. Ret. $1.75 Sec. Mkt. **$25-$28**

QX 125-1 YARN ORNAMENTS: MRS. SANTA
Comments: 4-1/2" tall. Reissued from 1975.
White apron with red checked pockets.
☐ Purchased 19___ Pd $_______ MIB NB DB BNT
☐ Want Orig. Ret. $1.75 Sec. Mkt. **$22-$25**

QX 121-1 YARN ORNAMENTS: RAGGEDY ANN™
Comments: 4-1/2" tall, RARE!
Reissued from 1975. Blue dress with white pinafore.
☐ Purchased 19___ Pd $_______ MIB NB DB BNT
☐ Want Orig. Ret. $1.75 Sec. Mkt. **$35-$40**

QX 122-1 YARN ORNAMENTS: RAGGEDY ANDY™
Comments: 4-1/2" tall, RARE!
Reissued from 1975. Blue with red-white checked shirt.
☐ Purchased 19___ Pd $_______ MIB NB DB BNT
☐ Want Orig. Ret. $1.75 Sec. Mkt. **$40-$45**

Swap 'n Sell Meets are a great place to find that hard-to-find ornament. Subscribe to

THE ORNAMENT COLLECTOR™
and ***Weekly Collectors' Gazette***™

for Show locations!
CALL FOR DETAILS – 309/668-2565

No secondary market value has been established for yarn and fabric ornaments found in original cellophane package.

QX 124-1 YARN ORNAMENTS: SANTA
Comments: 4-1/2" tall. Reissued from 1975.
☐ Purchased 19___ Pd $_______ MIB NB DB BNT
☐ Want Orig. Ret. $1.75 Sec. Mkt. **$22-$24**

QX 184-1 YESTERYEARS: DRUMMER BOY
Comments: Vary in size from 2-3/4" to 4" tall, Dated 1976
The look of "wood" designed in "old world" tradition.
☐ Purchased 19___ Pd $_______ MIB NB DB BNT
☐ Want Orig. Ret. $5.00 **NB** $90 **MIB** Sec. Mkt. **$155-$160**

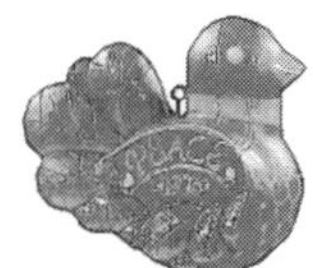

QX 183-1 YESTERYEARS: PARTRIDGE
Comments: Vary in size from 2-3/4" to 4" tall, Dated 1976
"Wood look" designs in "old world" character.
☐ Purchased 19___ Pd $_______ MIB NB DB BNT
☐ Want Orig. Ret. $5.00 **NB** $80 **MIB** Sec. Mkt. **$115-$120**

QX 182-1 YESTERYEARS: SANTA
Comments: Vary in size from 2-3/4" to 4" tall, Dated 1976
Simulated wood design in "old world" character.
☐ Purchased 19___ Pd $_______ MIB NB DB BNT
☐ Want Orig. Ret. $5.00 **NB** $132 **MIB** Sec. Mkt. **$170-$175**

QX 181-1 YESTERYEARS: TRAIN
Comments: Vary in size from 2-3/4" to 4" tall, Dated 1976
"Wood look" designs in "old world" character.
☐ Purchased 19___ Pd $_______ MIB NB DB BNT
☐ Want Orig. Ret. $5.00 **NB** $115 **MIB** Sec. Mkt. **$170-$175**

1977 Collection

QX 220-2 ANGEL
Comments: 4" tall.
Quilted and stuffed doll made from silk-screened fabric.
☐ Purchased 19___ Pd $_______ MIB NB DB BNT
☐ Want Orig. Ret. $1.75 Sec. Mkt. **$50-$55**

QSD 230-2 ANGEL TREE TOPPER
Comments: Country style simulated wood angel.
Dress is in cream, pink, turquoise and gold.
☐ Purchased 19___ Pd $_______ MIB NB DB BNT
☐ Want Orig. Ret. $9.00 **NB** $250 **MIB** Sec. Mkt. **$370-$385**

QX 131-5 BABY'S FIRST CHRISTMAS
Comments: White Satin Ball, 3-1/4" dia., Dated 1977
Caption: "Baby's First Christmas"
☐ Purchased 19___ Pd $_______ MIB NB DB BNT
☐ Want Orig. Ret. $3.50 **NB** $40-$45 **MIB** Sec. Mkt. **$70-$75**

QX 159-5 BEAUTY OF AMERICA COLLECTION: DESERT
Comments: White Glass Ball, 2-5/8" dia.
A desert mission at sunset. Caption: "Ring Out Christmas Bells And Let All The World Hear Your Joyful Song."
☐ Purchased 19___ Pd $_______ MIB NB DB BNT
☐ Want Orig. Ret. $2.50 **NB** $15 **MIB** Sec. Mkt. **$28-$32**

QX 158-2 BEAUTY OF AMERICA COLLECTION: MOUNTAINS
Comments: White Glass Ball, 2-5/8" dia.
Caption: "The Spirit Of Christmas Is Peace... The Message Of Christmas Is Love."
☐ Purchased 19___ Pd $_______ MIB NB DB BNT
☐ Want Orig. Ret. $2.50 **B** $15 **MIB** Sec. Mkt. **$25-$30**

QX 160-2 BEAUTY OF AMERICA COLLECTION: SEASHORE
Comments: White Glass Ball, 2-5/8" dia.
Caption: "Christmas Is--The Company Of Good Friends, The Warmth Of Goodwill And The Memory Of Good Times."
☐ Purchased 19___ Pd $_______ MIB NB DB BNT
☐ Want Orig. Ret. $2.50 **NB** $20 **MIB** Sec. Mkt. **$45-$50**

QX 161-5 BEAUTY OF AMERICA COLLECTION: WHARF
Comments: White Glass Ball, 2-5/8" dia.
Caption: "Christmas... When The World Stands Silent And The Spirit Of Hope Touches Every Heart."
☐ Purchased 19___ Pd $_______ MIB NB DB BNT
☐ Want Orig. Ret. $2.50 **NB** $18 **MIB** Sec. Mkt. **$35-$38**

QX 264-2 BETSEY CLARK SERIES
Comments: **Fifth in Series**, White Glass Ball, 3-1/4" dia. Captions: "Christmas 1977" and "The Truest Joys Of Christmas Come From Deep Inside." Most scarce of Bestey Clark Series. Very little trading for several years. Insure at price listed.
☐ Purchased 19___ Pd $_______ MIB NB DB BNT
☐ Want Orig. Ret. $3.50 **NB** $375 **MIB** Sec. Mkt. **$400-$425**

QX 153-5 CHARMERS
Comments: Gold Glass Ball, 3-1/4" dia. Dated 1977
Caption: "We Wish You A Merry Christmas."
☐ Purchased 19___ Pd $_______ MIB NB DB BNT
☐ Want Orig. Ret. $3.50 **NB** $40 **MIB** Sec. Mkt. **$50-$52**

QX 154-2 CHRISTMAS EXPRESSIONS: BELL
Comments: White Glass Ball, 3-1/4" dia.
Caption: "I Heard The Bells On Christmas Day, Their Old Familiar Carols Play, And Wild and Sweet, The Words Repeat, Of Peace On Earth, Good Will To Men." Henry Wadsworth Longfellow.
☐ Purchased 19___ Pd $_______ MIB NB DB BNT
☐ Want Orig. Ret. $3.50 **NB** $30 **MIB** Sec. Mkt. **$38-$42**

QX 157-5 CHRISTMAS EXPRESSIONS: MANDOLIN
Comments: White Glass Ball, 3-1/4" dia.
Caption: "Sing A Song Of Seasons; Something Bright In All..." Robert Louis Stevenson.
☐ Purchased 19___ Pd $_______ MIB NB DB BNT
☐ Want Orig. Ret. $3.50 **NB** $35 **MIB** Sec. Mkt. **$40-$45**

QX 155-5 CHRISTMAS EXPRESSIONS: ORNAMENTS
Comments: White Glass Ball, 3-1/4" dia.
Caption: "The Spirit Of Christmas Is Peace...The Message Of Christmas Is Love." Marjorie Frances Ames.
☐ Purchased 19___ Pd $_______ MIB NB DB BNT
☐ Want Orig. Ret. $3.50 **NB** $35 **MIB** Sec. Mkt. **$40-$45**

QX 156-2 CHRISTMAS EXPRESSIONS: WREATH
Comments: White Glass Ball, 3-1/4" dia.
Caption: "Christmas Is A Special Time. A Season Set Apart -- A Warm And Glad Remembering Time. A Season Of The Heart." Thomas Malloy.
☐ Purchased 19___ Pd $_______ MIB NB DB BNT
☐ Want Orig. Ret. $3.50 **NB** $20 **MIB** Sec. Mkt. **$35-$40**

QX 134-2 CHRISTMAS MOUSE
Comments: White Satin Ball, 3-1/4" dia.
Mice decorate their tree. Caption: "Tinsel And Lights Make The Season So Bright."
☐ Purchased 19___ Pd $_______ MIB NB DB BNT
☐ Want Orig. Ret. $3.50 **NB** $45 **MIB** Sec. Mkt. **$65-$70**

QX 200-2 COLORS OF CHRISTMAS: BELL
Comments: Acrylic, 3-1/4" dia.
Stained glass look. Bell with green ribbon. **Artist:** Linda Sickman
☐ Purchased 19___ Pd $_______ MIB NB DB BNT
☐ Want Orig. Ret. $3.50 **NB** $40 **MIB** Sec. Mkt. **$50-$55**

QX 203-5 COLORS OF CHRISTMAS: CANDLE
Comments: Acrylic, 3-1/4" dia., Dated 1977
The look of stained glass. Three lit candles.
☐ Purchased 19___ Pd $_______ MIB NB DB BNT
☐ Want Orig. Ret. $3.50 **NB** $42 **MIB** Sec. Mkt. **$58-$60**

QX 201-5 COLORS OF CHRISTMAS: JOY
Comments: Acrylic, 3-1/4" dia., Dated 1977
Stained glass look. The word "JOY."
☐ Purchased 19___ Pd $_______ MIB NB DB BNT
☐ Want Orig. Ret. $3.50 **NB** $45 **MIB** Sec. Mkt. **$58-$60**

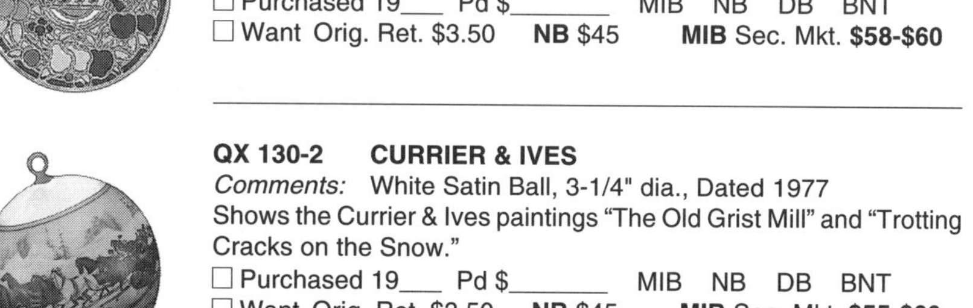

QX 202-2 COLORS OF CHRISTMAS: WREATH
Comments: Acrylic, 3-1/4" dia., Dated 1977
Stained glass look. Wreath with fruit.
☐ Purchased 19___ Pd $_______ MIB NB DB BNT
☐ Want Orig. Ret. $3.50 **NB** $45 **MIB** Sec. Mkt. **$58-$60**

QX 130-2 CURRIER & IVES
Comments: White Satin Ball, 3-1/4" dia., Dated 1977
Shows the Currier & Ives paintings "The Old Grist Mill" and "Trotting Cracks on the Snow."
☐ Purchased 19___ Pd $_______ MIB NB DB BNT
☐ Want Orig. Ret. $3.50 **NB** $45 **MIB** Sec. Mkt. **$55-$60**

QX 133-5 DISNEY
Comments: White Satin Ball, 3-1/4" dia. Dated 1977
Mickey's face is captured in a wreath with Donald Duck and Goofy on either side. Caption: "Merry Christmas 1977."
☐ Purchased 19___ Pd $_______ MIB NB DB BNT
☐ Want Orig. Ret. $3.50 **NB** $35 **MIB** Sec. Mkt. **$45-$50**

QX 137-5 DISNEY
Comments: White Satin Ball, 3-1/4" dia., Set of 2
Two Designs: One is Donald, Huey, Duey, & Luey with Caption: "Happy Holidays." The second is Mickey and Minnie with Caption: "Merry Christmas." Popular Disney ornaments.
☐ Purchased 19___ Pd $_______ MIB NB DB BNT
☐ Want Orig. Ret. $4.00 **NB** $30 **MIB** Sec. Mkt. **$40-$45**

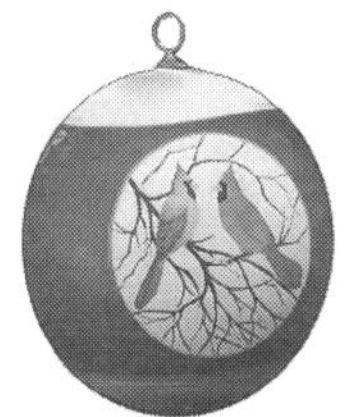

QX 132-2 FIRST CHRISTMAS TOGETHER
Comments: White Satin Ball, 3-1/4" dia., Dated 1977
Caption: "Our First Christmas Together." Date and caption printed in gold.
☐ Purchased 19___ Pd $_______ MIB NB DB BNT
☐ Want Orig. Ret. $3.50 **NB** $35 **MIB** Sec. Mkt. **$62-$65**

QX 263-5 FOR YOUR NEW HOME
Comments: Gold Glass Ball, 3-1/4" dia.
Dated 1977 on doormat. Very little trading in past four years.
☐ Purchased 19___ Pd $_______ MIB NB DB BNT
☐ Want Orig. Ret. $3.50 **NB** $20 **MIB** Sec. Mkt. **$35-$40**

QX 208-2 GRANDDAUGHTER
Comments: White Satin Ball, 3-1/4" dia.
Caption: "A Granddaughter Is A Gift Whose Worth Cannot Be Measured Except By The Heart." Very little trading in past six years.
☐ Purchased 19___ Pd $_______ MIB NB DB BNT
☐ Want Orig. Ret. $3.50 **NB** $20 **MIB** Sec. Mkt. **$25-$30**

QX 150-2 GRANDMA MOSES
Comments: White Glass Ball, 3-1/4" dia.
RARE! Two snow scenes from the paintings "Green Sleigh" and "Sugartime." A pamphlet giving the history of Grandma Moses and her paintings was included with each ornament.
☐ Purchased 19___ Pd $_______ MIB NB DB BNT
☐ Want Orig. Ret. $3.50 **NB** $45 (without pamphlet)
MIB Sec. Mkt. **$55-$60**

QX 260-2 GRANDMOTHER
Comments: Gold Glass Ball, 3-1/4" dia.
Caption: "Grandmother Is Another Word For Love."
☐ Purchased 19___ Pd $_______ MIB NB DB BNT
☐ Want Orig. Ret. $3.50 **NB** $25 **MIB** Sec. Mkt. **$40-$45**

QX 209-5 GRANDSON
Comments: White Satin Ball, 3-1/2" dia.
Caption: "A Grandson Is... A Joy Bringer... A Memory Maker... A Grandson Is Love."
☐ Purchased 19___ Pd $_______ MIB NB DB BNT
☐ Want Orig. Ret. $3.50 **NB** $15 **MIB** Sec. Mkt. **$25-$30**

QX 312-2 HOLIDAY HIGHLIGHTS: DRUMMER BOY
Comments: Acrylic, 3-1/4" dia.
Drummer boy marches to beat of his drum. Caption repeated around border: "Rum-Pa-Pum-Pum."
☐ Purchased 19___ Pd $_______ MIB NB DB BNT
☐ Want Orig. Ret. $3.50 **NB** $52 **MIB** Sec. Mkt. **$68-$70**

QX 310-2 HOLIDAY HIGHLIGHTS: JOY
Comments: Acrylic, 3-1/4" dia.
Caption: "JOY 1977"
☐ Purchased 19___ Pd $_______ MIB NB DB BNT
☐ Want Orig. Ret. $3.50 **NB** $20 **MIB** Sec. Mkt. **$45-$48**

QX 311-5 HOLIDAY HIGHLIGHTS: PEACE ON EARTH
Comments: Acrylic, 3-1/4" dia.
A picturesque village scene with snow-covered houses, pine trees, and a church in the center. Caption: "Peace On Earth, Good Will Toward Men. 1977"
☐ Purchased 19___ Pd $_______ MIB NB DB BNT
☐ Want Orig. Ret. $3.50 **NB** $55 **MIB** Sec. Mkt. **$68-$70**

QX 313-5 HOLIDAY HIGHLIGHTS: STAR
Comments: Acrylic, 3-1/4" dia.
Star at top of ornament with radiating beams over the ornament's surface. Caption: "Once For A Shining Hour Heaven Touched Earth."
☐ Purchased 19___ Pd $_______ MIB NB DB BNT
☐ Want Orig. Ret. $3.50 **NB** $45 **MIB** Sec. Mkt. **$50-$55**

OHD 320-2 HOLLY & POINSETTIA TABLE DECORATION
Comments: With special base.
☐ Purchased 19___ Pd $_______ MIB NB DB BNT
☐ Want Orig. Ret. $8.00 **NB** $125 **MIB** Sec. Mkt. **$130-$135**

QX 262-2 LOVE
Comments: Gold Glass Ball, 3-1/4" dia.
Caption: "Christmas 1977."
☐ Purchased 19___ Pd $_______ MIB NB DB BNT
☐ Want Orig. Ret. $3.50 **NB** $10 **MIB** Sec. Mkt. **$25-$30**

QX 210-2 METAL ORNAMENTS: SNOWFLAKES
Comments: Chrome Plated Zinc, 2-1/8" dia., Set of 4 die-cast in lightweight, chrome plated zinc. Packaged in peek-through gift box. This is the only year the snowflake set was offered. This set is hard to find. **Artist:** Linda Sickman
☐ Purchased 19___ Pd $_______ MIB NB DB BNT
☐ Want Orig. Ret. $5.00 **NB** $65 **MIB** Sec. Mkt. **$90-$95**

QX 261-5 MOTHER
Comments: White Glass Ball, 3-1/4" dia.
Pink roses and green holly. Caption: "In A Mother's Heart, There Is Love... The Very Heart Of Christmas."
☐ Purchased 19___ Pd $_______ MIB NB DB BNT
☐ Want Orig. Ret. $3.50 **NB** $15 **MIB** Sec. Mkt. **$20-$25**

QX 225-2 MR. AND MRS. SNOWMAN KISSING BALL
Not Shown. Photo welcomed.
☐ Purchased 19___ Pd $_______ MIB NB DB BNT
☐ Want Orig. Ret. $5.00 **NB** $85 **MIB** Sec. Mkt. **$100-$115**

QX 151-5 NORMAN ROCKWELL
Comments: White Glass Ball, 3-1/4" dia., Dated 1977
Four favorite Rockwell designs reproduced in separate panels. Caption: "Christmas 1977"
☐ Purchased 19___ Pd $_______ MIB NB DB BNT
☐ Want Orig. Ret. $3.50 **NB** $50 **MIB** Sec. Mkt. **$65-$70**

QX 182-2 NOSTALGIA COLLECTION: ANGEL
Comments: Handcrafted, 3-1/4" dia.
An angel flying in the center of a wide outer ring. Caption: "Peace On Earth" and "Good Will Toward Men." Gift tag was included.
Artist: Donna Lee
☐ Purchased 19___ Pd $_______ MIB NB DB BNT
☐ Want Orig. Ret. $5.00 **NB** $70 **MIB** Sec. Mkt. **$125-$130**

QX 180-2 NOSTALGIA COLLECTION: ANTIQUE CAR
Comments: Handcrafted, 3-1/4" dia.
Green car trimmed in red. Caption: "Season's Greetings 1977." Gift tag was included. **Artist:** Linda Sickman
☐ Purchased 19___ Pd $_______ MIB NB DB BNT
☐ Want Orig. Ret. $5.00 **NB** $50 **MIB** Sec. Mkt. **$65-$70**

QX 181-5 NOSTALGIA COLLECTION: NATIVITY
Comments: Handcrafted, 3-1/4" dia.
The Holy Family and animals in a stable with pine trees on either side. Caption: "O Come, Let Us Adore Him." Gift tag was included.
☐ Purchased 19___ Pd $_______ MIB NB DB BNT
☐ Want Orig. Ret. $5.00 **NB** $100 **MIB** Sec. Mkt. **$170-$175**

QX 183-5 NOSTALGIA COLLECTION: TOYS
Comments: Handcrafted, 3-1/4" dia., Dated 1977
Toys in the center of a red and yellow ring. Gift tag was included.
Artist: Linda Sickman
☐ Purchased 19___ Pd $_______ MIB NB DB BNT
☐ Want Orig. Ret. $5.00 **NB** $90 **MIB** Sec. Mkt. **$150-$155**

QX 225-5 OLD FASHIONED CUSTOMS KISSING BALL
Comments: White Satin Ball
☐ Purchased 19___ Pd $_______ MIB NB DB BNT
☐ Want Orig. Ret. $5.00 **NB** $125 **MIB** Sec. Mkt. **$145-$150**

QX 162-2 PEANUTS®
Comments: White Glass Ball, 2-5/8" dia.
Front: Charlie Brown and his sister Sally watch the stockings on the fireplace. Caption: "A Watched Stocking Never Fills." Back: Schroeder plays the piano as Lucy gives him a gift. Caption: "Merry Christmas." Packaged in Snoopy's Christmas-decorated dog-house.
☐ Purchased 19___ Pd $_______ MIB NB DB BNT
☐ Want Orig. Ret. $2.50 **NB** $45 **MIB** Sec. Mkt. **$55-$60**

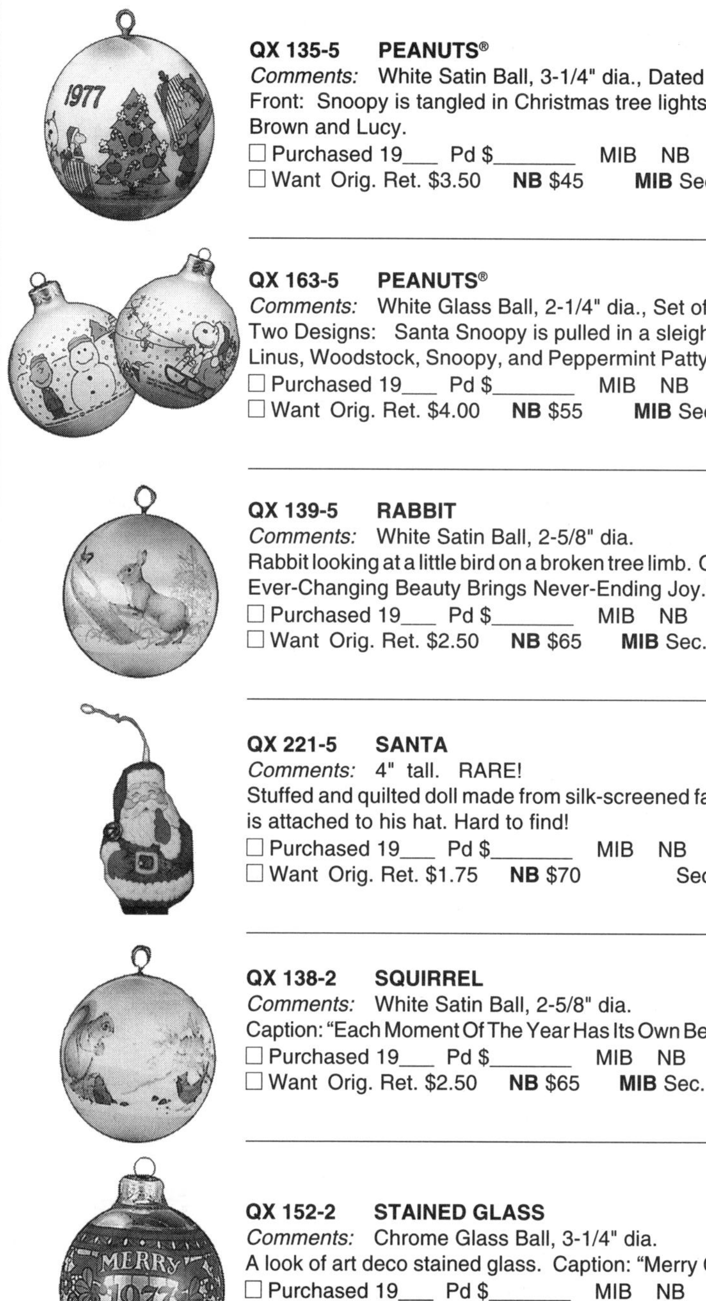

QX 135-5 PEANUTS®
Comments: White Satin Ball, 3-1/4" dia., Dated 1977
Front: Snoopy is tangled in Christmas tree lights. Back: Charlie Brown and Lucy.
☐ Purchased 19___ Pd $_______ MIB NB DB BNT
☐ Want Orig. Ret. $3.50 **NB** $45 **MIB** Sec. Mkt. **$60-$62**

QX 163-5 PEANUTS®
Comments: White Glass Ball, 2-1/4" dia., Set of 2, Dated 1977
Two Designs: Santa Snoopy is pulled in a sleigh. Charlie Brown, Linus, Woodstock, Snoopy, and Peppermint Patty play in the snow.
☐ Purchased 19___ Pd $_______ MIB NB DB BNT
☐ Want Orig. Ret. $4.00 **NB** $55 **MIB** Sec. Mkt. **$70-$75**

QX 139-5 RABBIT
Comments: White Satin Ball, 2-5/8" dia.
Rabbit looking at a little bird on a broken tree limb. Caption: "Nature's Ever-Changing Beauty Brings Never-Ending Joy." Karl Lawrence.
☐ Purchased 19___ Pd $_______ MIB NB DB BNT
☐ Want Orig. Ret. $2.50 **NB** $65 **MIB** Sec. Mkt. **$98-$100**

QX 221-5 SANTA
Comments: 4" tall. RARE!
Stuffed and quilted doll made from silk-screened fabric. A jingle bell is attached to his hat. Hard to find!
☐ Purchased 19___ Pd $_______ MIB NB DB BNT
☐ Want Orig. Ret. $1.75 **NB** $70 Sec. Mkt. **$80-$85**

QX 138-2 SQUIRREL
Comments: White Satin Ball, 2-5/8" dia.
Caption: "Each Moment Of The Year Has Its Own Beauty..." Emerson.
☐ Purchased 19___ Pd $_______ MIB NB DB BNT
☐ Want Orig. Ret. $2.50 **NB** $65 **MIB** Sec. Mkt. **$90-$100**

QX 152-2 STAINED GLASS
Comments: Chrome Glass Ball, 3-1/4" dia.
A look of art deco stained glass. Caption: "Merry Christmas 1977."
☐ Purchased 19___ Pd $_______ MIB NB DB BNT
☐ Want Orig. Ret. $3.50 **NB** $35 **MIB** Sec. Mkt. **$40-$45**

QX 192-2 TWIRL-ABOUT COLLECTION: BELLRINGER
Comments: Handcrafted, 3-11/16" tall, Dated 1977
A little boy strikes a bell as he rotates inside an arched gate decorated with red bows.
☐ Purchased 19___ Pd $_______ MIB NB DB BNT
☐ Want Orig. Ret. $6.00 **NB-P** $35 **MIB** Sec. Mkt. **$60-$65**

QX 193-5 TWIRL-ABOUT COLLECTION: DELLA ROBIA WREATH
Comments: Handcrafted, 3-9/16" tall, Dated 1977
A little girl, kneeling in prayer, twirls in the center of the traditional Della Robia wreath. **Artist:** Donna Lee
☐ Purchased 19___ Pd $_______ MIB NB DB BNT
☐ Want Orig. Ret. $4.50 **NB** $70 **MIB** Sec. Mkt. **$115-$120**

QX 190-2 TWIRL-ABOUT COLLECTION: SNOWMAN
Comments: Handcrafted, 3-3/4" tall, Dated 1977
A snowman rotates in the center of a three-dimensional snowflake.
Artist: Linda Sickman
☐ Purchased 19___ Pd $_______ MIB NB DB BNT
☐ Want Orig. Ret. $4.50 **NB** $45 **MIB** Sec. Mkt. **$70-$78**

QX 191-5 TWIRL-ABOUT COLLECTION: WEATHER HOUSE
Comments: Handcrafted, 3-15/16" tall, Dated 1977
Swiss dressed boy and girl rotate in and out of double doorways.
☐ Purchased 19___ Pd $_______ MIB NB DB BNT
☐ Want Orig. Ret. $6.00 **NB-P** $75 **MIB** Sec. Mkt. **$98-$105**

QX 172-2 YESTERYEARS COLLECTION: ANGEL
Comments: Handcrafted, 3-1/2" tall
Smiling folk-art angel wears a blue gown. Caption: "Joy To The World 1977." Price down from '95.
☐ Purchased 19___ Pd $_______ MIB NB DB BNT
☐ Want Orig. Ret. $6.00 **NB-P** $60 **MIB** Sec. Mkt. **$85-$95**

QX 170-2 YESTERYEARS COLLECTION: HOUSE
Comments: Handcrafted, 3-11/16" tall
This quaint cottage has a red roof and green shutters with painted designs. Caption: "Happy Holidays 1977."
☐ Purchased 19___ Pd $_______ MIB NB DB BNT
☐ Want Orig. Ret. $6.00 **NB** $85 **MIB** Sec. Mkt. **$120-$125**

QX 171-5 YESTERYEARS COLLECTION: JACK-IN-THE-BOX
Comments: Handcrafted, 3-13/16" tall
Green, blue and red Jack in a red and pink box. Caption: "Merry Christmas 1977." More readily available than most of 1970's ornaments.
☐ Purchased 19___ Pd $_______ MIB NB DB BNT
☐ Want Orig. Ret. $6.00 **NB-P** $80 **MIB** Sec. Mkt. **$120-$125**

QX 173-5 YESTERYEARS COLLECTION: REINDEER
Comments: Handcrafted, 4-1/4" tall, Dated 1977
Ivory painted reindeer on wheels has the look of a nostalgic child's toy. Hard to find!
☐ Purchased 19___ Pd $_______ MIB NB DB BNT
☐ Want Orig. Ret. $6.00 **NB** $100 **MIB** Sec. Mkt. **$125-$130**

QX 139-6 ANGEL
Comments: Handcrafted, 2-15/16" tall, Reissued in 1981.
Made with the bread-dough look, a barefoot angel dressed in blue and white holds a star. **Artist:** Donna Lee
☐ Purchased 19___ Pd $_______ MIB NB DB BNT
☐ Want Orig. Ret. $4.50 **NB** $70 **MIB** Sec. Mkt. **$90-$95**

QX 150-3 ANGELS
Comments: Handcrafted, 3-7/8" tall, Dated 1978
Angels fly around decorating a Christmas tree.
☐ Purchased 19___ Pd $_______ MIB NB DB BNT
☐ Want Orig. Ret. $8.00 **NB** $275 **MIB** Sec. Mkt. **$345-$350**

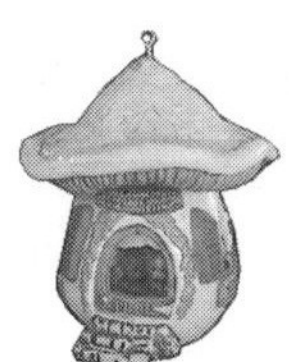

QX 149-6 ANIMAL HOME
Comments: Handcrafted, 2-9/16" tall
A darling little mushroom has become the home of a family of mice.
Artist: Donna Lee
☐ Purchased 19___ Pd $_______ MIB NB DB BNT
☐ Want Orig. Ret. $6.00 **NB** $150 **MIB** Sec. Mkt. **$180-$185**

QX 200-3 BABY'S FIRST CHRISTMAS
Comments: White Satin Ball, 3-1/4" dia.
A baby dressed in yellow plays with a stuffed teddy bear and a kitten. Caption: "Baby's First Christmas 1978."
☐ Purchased 19___ Pd $_______ MIB NB DB BNT
☐ Want Orig. Ret. $3.50 **NB** $45 **MIB** Sec. Mkt. **$65-$70**

QX 201-6 BETSEY CLARK SERIES
Comments: **Sixth in series**, Ecru Soft-Sheen Satin Ball 3-1/4" dia., Dated 1978. A little girl wraps a gift and delivers it to a friend. Caption: "The Christmas Spirit Seems To Bring A Cheerful Glow To Everything."
☐ Purchased 19___ Pd $_______ MIB NB DB BNT
☐ Want Orig. Ret. $3.50 **NB** $50 **MIB** Sec. Mkt. **$60-$65**

QX 137-6 CALICO MOUSE
Comments: Handcrafted, 3-7/16" tall
Smiling red calico mouse with green ears and nose, holds a sprig of holly. Similar to the Merry Miniature.
☐ Purchased 19___ Pd $_______ MIB NB DB BNT
☐ Want Orig. Ret. $4.50 **NB** $150 **MIB** Sec. Mkt. **$195-$198**

QX 146-3 CARROUSEL SERIES
Comments: ***FIRST IN SERIES,*** Handcrafted, 3" tall
Caption: "Christmas 1978." This carrousel has toys that spin around, hand painted in red, yellow, blue and green.
☐ Purchased 19___ Pd $_______ MIB NB DB BNT
☐ Want Orig. Ret. $6.00 **NB** $300 **MIB** Sec. Mkt. **$390-$405**

QX 702-3 CHRISTMAS STAR TREE TOPPER
Comments: Acrylic, 9-3/4" tall
A nine-point acrylic star with an etched snowflake in the center makes a lovely addition to any Christmas tree.
☐ Purchased 19___ Pd $_______ MIB NB DB BNT
☐ Want Orig. Ret. $7.50 **NB** $35 **MIB** Sec. Mkt. **$40-$45**

QX 354-3 COLORS OF CHRISTMAS: ANGEL
Comments: Acrylic, stained glass look, 3-5/8" tall
An angel wearing a red dress and halo with golden hair and wings. More no box trading than boxed trading.
☐ Purchased 19___ Pd $_______ MIB NB DB BNT
☐ Want Orig. Ret. $3.50 **NB** $35 **MIB** Sec. Mkt. **$55-$58**

QX 357-6 COLORS OF CHRISTMAS: CANDLE
Comments: Acrylic, stained glass look, 3-5/8" tall
Classic Christmas candle, with holly and berries at the base.
☐ Purchased 19___ Pd $_______ MIB NB DB BNT
☐ Want Orig. Ret. $3.50 **NB** $80 **MIB** Sec. Mkt. **$90-$95**

QX 356-3 COLORS OF CHRISTMAS: LOCOMOTIVE
Comments: Acrylic, stained glass look, 3-1/4" tall
Dated 1978. Red locomotive framed in blue and green.
☐ Purchased 19___ Pd $_______ MIB NB DB BNT
☐ Want Orig. Ret. $3.50 **NB** $40 **MIB** Sec. Mkt. **$50-$55**

QX 355-6 COLORS OF CHRISTMAS: MERRY CHRISTMAS
Comments: Acrylic, stained glass look, 4-1/8" tall
"Merry Christmas" in gold on red and green oval ornament.
Artist: Don Palmiter
☐ Purchased 19___ Pd $_______ MIB NB DB BNT
☐ Want Orig. Ret. $3.50 **NB** $40 **MIB** Sec. Mkt. **$50-$55**

QX 207-6 DISNEY
Comments: White Satin Ball, 3-1/4" dia., Dated 1978
Disney characters ride a wooden train. Mickey, as Santa, rings a bell.
☐ Purchased 19___ Pd $_______ MIB NB DB BNT
☐ Want Orig. Ret. $3.50 **NB** $65 **MIB** Sec. Mkt. **$78-$82**

QX 190-3 DOVE
Comments: Handcrafted, 3-9/16" tall, Dated 1978
A white dove twirls in the center of a white lacy snowflake.
Artist: Linda Sickman
☐ Purchased 19___ Pd $_______ MIB NB DB BNT
☐ Want Orig. Ret. $4.50 **NB** $70 **MIB** Sec. Mkt. **$85-$90**

QX 252-3 DRUMMER BOY
Comments: Gold Glass Ball, 3-1/4" dia., Dated 1978
Followed by sheep and geese, a little drummer boy marches to the Christ Child in the manger.
☐ Purchased 19___ Pd $_______ MIB NB DB BNT
☐ Want Orig. Ret. $3.50 **NB** $20 **MIB** Sec. Mkt. **$27-$30**

QX 218-3 FIRST CHRISTMAS TOGETHER
Comments: White Satin Ball, 3-1/4" dia.
Red hearts, fruits, flowers, greenery and pair of red birds. Caption: "Sharing Is The Heart Of Loving" and "First Christmas Together 1978."
☐ Purchased 19___ Pd $_______ MIB NB DB BNT
☐ Want Orig. Ret. $3.50 **NB** $32 **MIB** Sec. Mkt. **$40-$45**

QX 217-6 FOR YOUR NEW HOME
Comments: White Satin Ball, 3-1/4" dia.; Christmas 1978
A wreath with a glowing candle hangs from a brightly lighted window. Caption: "Home... Where The Light Of Love Shines Brightest."
☐ Purchased 19___ Pd $_______ MIB NB DB BNT
☐ Want Orig. Ret. $3.50 **NB** $20 **MIB** Sec. Mkt. **$25-$35**

QX 216-3 GRANDDAUGHTER
Comments: White Satin Ball, 3-1/4" dia.
A little girl decorates her Christmas tree. Caption: "A Granddaughter...Never Far From Thought, Ever Near In Love."
☐ Purchased 19___ Pd $_______ MIB NB DB BNT
☐ Want Orig. Ret. $3.50 **NB** $25 **MIB** Sec. Mkt. **$40-$45**

QX 267-6 GRANDMOTHER
Comments: White Satin Ball, 3-1/4" dia.
Red American Beauty roses and holly. Caption: "A Grandmother Has A Special Way Of Bringing Joy To Every Day."
☐ Purchased 19___ Pd $_______ MIB NB DB BNT
☐ Want Orig. Ret. $3.50 **NB** $30 **MIB** Sec. Mkt. **$40-$48**

QX 215-6 GRANDSON
Comments: White Satin Ball, 3-1/4" dia.
Raccoons ice skating, building a snowman, and sledding. Caption: "A Grandson Is Loved In A Special Way For The Special Joy He Brings."
☐ Purchased 19___ Pd $_______ MIB NB DB BNT
☐ Want Orig. Ret. $3.50 **NB** $30 **MIB** Sec. Mkt. **$40-$45**

QX 220-3 HALLMARK'S ANTIQUE CARD COLLECTION DESIGN
Comments: Ecru Soft-Sheen Satin Ball, 3-1/4" dia.
Reproduced from an antique Hallmark card. Caption: "Christmas Is A Special Time, A Season Set Apart-- A Warm And Glad Remembering Time, A Season Of The Heart." Very little trading.
☐ Purchased 19___ Pd $_______ MIB NB DB BNT
☐ Want Orig. Ret. $3.50 **NB** $35 **MIB** Sec. Mkt. **$40-$45**

QHD 921-9 HEAVENLY MINSTREL TABLETOP
Comments: Very similar to the Heavenly Minstrel ornament. Comes with walnut base with stained-glass look and brass background.

☐ Purchased 19___ Pd $_______ MIB NB DB BNT
☐ Want Orig. Ret. $35.00 **NB** $325 **MIB** Sec. Mkt. **$400-$425**

QX 320-3 HOLIDAY CHIMES: REINDEER CHIMES
Comments: Reissued in 1979, Chrome plated brass, 5-1/2" tall
Three prancing reindeer are suspended from a large snowflake.
Artist: Linda Sickman
☐ Purchased 19___ Pd $_______ MIB NB DB BNT
☐ Want Orig. Ret. $4.50 **NB** $30 **MIB** Sec. Mkt. **$42-$48**

QX 310-3 HOLIDAY HIGHLIGHTS: DOVE
Comments: Acrylic with the look of hand-cut crystal
Ranged from 2-11/16" to 3-5/8" tall. RARE! This dove in flight is of frosted acrylic with clear acrylic wing tips.
☐ Purchased 19___ Pd $_______ MIB NB DB BNT
☐ Want Orig. Ret. $3.50 **NB** $90 **MIB** Sec. Mkt. **$125-$130**

QX 309-6 HOLIDAY HIGHLIGHTS: NATIVITY
Comments: Acrylic with the look of hand-cut crystal
Ranged from 2-11/16" to 3-5/8" tall. **Artist:** Don Palmiter
☐ Purchased 19___ Pd $_______ MIB NB DB BNT
☐ Want Orig. Ret. $3.50 **NB** $60 **MIB** Sec. Mkt. **$80-$85**

QX 307-6 HOLIDAY HIGHLIGHTS: SANTA
Comments: Acrylic with the look of hand-cut crystal
Ranged from 2-11/16" to 3-5/8" tall.
Santa's face is etched into a round disc.
☐ Purchased 19___ Pd $_______ MIB NB DB BNT
☐ Want Orig. Ret. $3.50 **NB** $65 **MIB** Sec. Mkt. **$75-$80**

QX 308-3 HOLIDAY HIGHLIGHTS: SNOWFLAKE
Comments: Acrylic with the look of hand-cut crystal.
Ranged from 2-11/16" to 3-5/8" tall. Dated 1978.
Snowflake design etched into round acrylic disc.
☐ Purchased 19___ Pd $_______ MIB NB DB BNT
☐ Want Orig. Ret. $3.50 **NB** $40 **MIB** Sec. Mkt. **$60-$65**

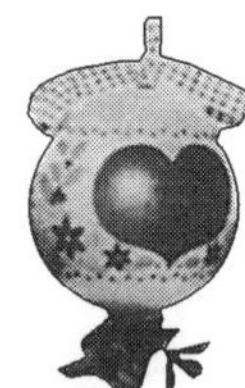

QHD 900-3 HOLIDAY MEMORIES KISSING BALL
Comments: Mistletoe Ball Ornament
"Holiday Memories Are Treasures Of The Heart."
☐ Purchased 19___ Pd $_______ MIB NB DB BNT
☐ Want Orig. Ret. $5.00 **NB** $100 **MIB** Sec. Mkt. **$130-$140**

QX 147-6 HOLLY AND POINSETTIA BALL
Comments: Handcrafted Ball, 3-1/2" dia.
With the look of intricate hand carving, this ball is circled with poinsettias and greenery. **Artist:** Linda Sickman
☐ Purchased 19___ Pd $_______ MIB NB DB BNT
☐ Want Orig. Ret. $6.00 **NB** $70 **MIB** Sec. Mkt. **$88-$90**

QX 221-6 JOAN WALSH ANGLUND©
Comments: White Satin Ball, 3-1/4" dia.
Front: Children caroling in the snow. Back: children decorating a snow-covered tree. Caption: "As Long As We Have Love And Friends, Christmas Never Really Ends. 1978"
☐ Purchased 19___ Pd $_______ MIB NB DB BNT
☐ Want Orig. Ret. $3.50 **NB** $55 **MIB** Sec. Mkt. **$65-$70**

QX 254-3 JOY
Comments: Gold Glass Ball, 3-1/4" dia.
Front: A stained glass look complements the word "JOY." Back: Christmas message in a matching oval. Caption on back: "The Beauty Of Christmas Shines All Around Us."
☐ Purchased 19___ Pd $_______ MIB NB DB BNT
☐ Want Orig. Ret. $3.50 **NB** $20 **MIB** Sec. Mkt. **$35-$38**

QX 138-3 JOY
Comments: Handcrafted, 4-3/16" tall
Red "bread dough" letters spell the word "JOY" as a little blue-dressed elf pops through the "O".
☐ Purchased 19___ Pd $_______ MIB NB DB BNT
☐ Want Orig. Ret. $4.50 **NB** $55-$60 **MIB** Sec. Mkt. **$88-$90**

QX 136-3 LITTLE TRIMMERS: DRUMMER BOY
Comments: Handcrafted, 2-1/16" tall
Drummer boy dressed in red, green and blue, beating his drum. Beware of missing or broken drumsticks.
☐ Purchased 19___ Pd $_______ MIB NB DB BNT
☐ Want Orig. Ret. $2.50 **NB** $45 **MIB** Sec. Mkt. **$65-$70**

QX 134-3 LITTLE TRIMMERS: PRAYING ANGEL
Comments: Handcrafted, 2" tall
Pink-clad angel kneeling in prayer. **Artist:** Donna Lee
☐ Purchased 19___ Pd $_______ MIB NB DB BNT
☐ Want Orig. Ret. $2.50 **NB** $60 **MIB** Sec. Mkt. **$90-$95**

QX 135-6 LITTLE TRIMMERS: SANTA
Comments: Handcrafted, 2-1/4" tall
Reissued in 1979. Waving Santa, holding a gift.
☐ Purchased 19___ Pd $_______ MIB NB DB BNT
☐ Want Orig. Ret. $2.50 **NB** $45 **MIB** Sec. Mkt. **$65-$70**

QX 133-6 LITTLE TRIMMERS: THIMBLE SERIES (MOUSE)
Comments: ***FIRST IN SERIES***, Handcrafted, 1-3/4" tall
A white mouse with red cap peeks out of a silver thimble.
Later known as Thimble Series.
☐ Purchased 19___ Pd $_______ MIB NB DB BNT
☐ Want Orig. Ret. $2.50 **NB** $220 **MIB** Sec. Mkt. **$300-$310**

QX 132-3 LITTLE TRIMMER COLLECTION
Comments: Handcrafted, Set of 4
Miniature versions of Thimble Mouse, Praying Angel, Drummer Boy, and Santa. RARE!
☐ Purchased 19___ Pd $_______ MIB NB DB BNT
☐ Want Orig. Ret. $9.00 **NB** $240 **MIB** Sec. Mkt. **$315-$325**

QX 268-3 LOVE
Comments: Gold Glass Ball, 3-1/4" dia., Dated 1978
A heart which contains the year 1978 is surrounded by poinsettias and birds. Caption: "Of Life's Many Treasures, The Most Beautiful Is Love."
☐ Purchased 19___ Pd $_______ MIB NB DB BNT
☐ Want Orig. Ret. $3.50 **NB** $25 **MIB** Sec. Mkt. **$40-$45**

QX 202-3 MERRY CHRISTMAS (SANTA)
Comments: White Satin Ball, 3-1/4" dia., Dated 1978
Santa with his pack of gifts is later seen flying over rooftops on Christmas eve. Caption: "Merry Christmas."
☐ Purchased 19___ Pd $_______ MIB NB DB BNT
☐ Want Orig. Ret. $3.50 **NB** $40 **MIB** Sec. Mkt. **$50-$55**

QX 266-3 MOTHER
Comments: White Glass Ball, 3-1/4" dia.
Caption: "The Wonderful Meaning Of Christmas Is Found In A Mother's Love" and "Christmas 1978."
☐ Purchased 19___ Pd $_______ MIB NB DB BNT
☐ Want Orig. Ret. $3.50 **NB** $25 **MIB** Sec. Mkt. **$35-$45**

QX 253-6 NATIVITY
Comments: White Glass Ball, 3-1/4" dia.
An Old World Nativity scene. Caption: "The Joy Of Heaven Is Come To Earth."
☐ Purchased 19___ Pd $_______ MIB NB DB BNT
☐ Want Orig. Ret. $3.50 **NB** $30 **MIB** Sec. Mkt. **$55-$57**

QX 145-6 PANORAMA BALL
Comments: Handcrafted Panorama Ball, 3-5/8" dia.
A little boy has fallen on the ice, viewed through a peek-through window in the ornament. Caption: "Merry Christmas 1978."
☐ Purchased 19___ Pd $_______ MIB NB DB BNT
☐ Want Orig. Ret. $6.00 **NB** $120 **MIB** Sec. Mkt. **$135-$140**

QX 204-3 PEANUTS®
Comments: White Satin Ball, 2-5/8" dia., Dated 1978
Snoopy and Woodstock decorate their freshly cut Christmas tree.
☐ Purchased 19___ Pd $_______ MIB NB DB BNT
☐ Want Orig. Ret. $2.50 **NB** $45 **MIB** Sec. Mkt. **$55-$60**

QX 205-6 PEANUTS®
Comments: White Satin Ball, 3-1/4" dia.
The gang sings while Linus holds a dated wreath. Caption: "Joy To The World 1978."
☐ Purchased 19___ Pd $_______ MIB NB DB BNT
☐ Want Orig. Ret. $3.50 **NB** $50 **MIB** Sec. Mkt. **$55-$60**

QX 206-3 PEANUTS®
Comments: White Satin Ball, 3-1/4" dia., Dated 1978
Front: Snoopy, Woodstock and his flock are playing in a toy store. Back: Snoopy plays Santa.
☐ Purchased 19___ Pd $_______ MIB NB DB BNT
☐ Want Orig. Ret. $3.50 **NB** $45 **MIB** Sec. Mkt. **$50-$55**

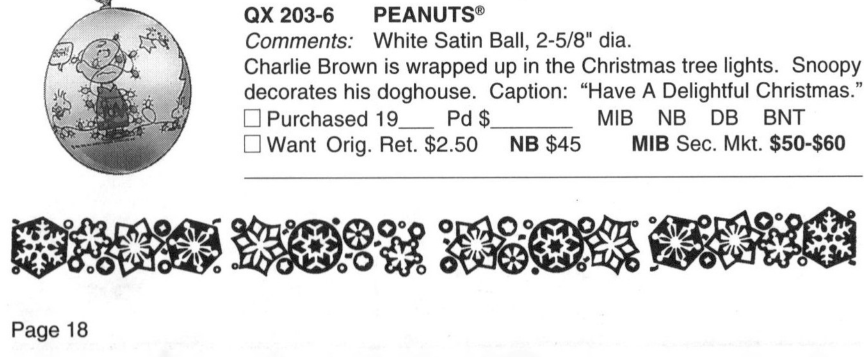

QX 203-6 PEANUTS®
Comments: White Satin Ball, 2-5/8" dia.
Charlie Brown is wrapped up in the Christmas tree lights. Snoopy decorates his doghouse. Caption: "Have A Delightful Christmas."
☐ Purchased 19___ Pd $_______ MIB NB DB BNT
☐ Want Orig. Ret. $2.50 **NB** $45 **MIB** Sec. Mkt. **$50-$60**

QX 251-6 QUAIL, THE
Comments: Gold Glass Ball, 3-1/4" dia., Dated 1978
Caption: "Nature Has A Wonderful Way Of Making A Wonder-Filled World."
☐ Purchased 19___ Pd $_______ MIB NB DB BNT
☐ Want Orig. Ret. $3.50 **NB** $25 **MIB** Sec. Mkt. **$35-$40**

QX 144-3 RED CARDINAL
Comments: Handcrafted, 4" tall
This cardinal clips on the branch of the tree.
☐ Purchased 19___ Pd $_______ MIB NB DB BNT
☐ Want Orig. Ret. $4.50 **NB-P** $135 **MIB** Sec. Mkt. **$175-$180**

QX 148-3 ROCKING HORSE
Comments: Handcrafted, 3-9/16" tall, Dated 1978
Hand-painted polka-dot horse with white yarn mane and red rockers.
☐ Purchased 19___ Pd $_______ MIB NB DB BNT
☐ Want Orig. Ret. $6.00 **NB** $80 **MIB** Sec. Mkt. **$85-$95**

QX 152-3 SCHNEEBERG BELL
Comments: Handcrafted, 4" tall
Reproduction of an intricate Schneeberg wood carving collage (82 decorating steps were required to achieve the natural wood look). Caption: "Christmas 1978."
☐ Purchased 19___ Pd $_______ MIB NB DB BNT
☐ Want Orig. Ret. $8.00 **NB** $160 **MIB** Sec. Mkt. **$195-$205**

QX 142-3 SKATING RACCOON
Comments: Handcrafted, 2-3/4" tall. Reissued in 1979.
Raccoon with red mittens and scarf wears real metal skates.
Artist: Donna Lee
☐ Purchased 19___ Pd $_______ MIB NB DB BNT
☐ Want Orig. Ret. $6.00 **NB** $60 **MIB** Sec. Mkt. **$90-$95**

QX 219-6 SPENCER ™ SPARROW, ESQ.
Comments: Ecru Soft-Sheen Satin Ball, 3-1/4" dia.
A little sparrow named Spencer sits in a wreath and on the reverse, pulls a sled loaded with gifts. Caption: "Holly Days Are Jolly Days" and "Christmas 1978."
☐ Purchased 19___ Pd $_______ MIB NB DB BNT
☐ Want Orig. Ret. $3.50 **NB** $45 **MIB** Sec. Mkt. **$50-$55**

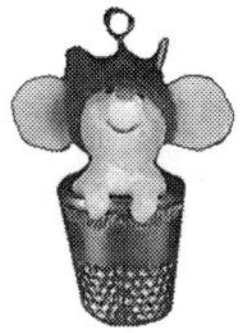

QX 133-6 THIMBLE SERIES: MOUSE
Comments: ***FIRST IN SERIES***, Handcrafted, 1-3/4" tall
Reissued from Little Trimmers Series - Thimble Mouse.
☐ Purchased 19___ Pd $_______ MIB NB DB BNT
☐ Want Orig. Ret. $2.50 **NB** $220 **MIB** Sec. Mkt. **$300-$310**

QX 269-6 TWENTY-FIFTH CHRISTMAS TOGETHER
Comments: White Glass Ball, 3-1/4" dia., Dated 1978
Front: Caption "25th Christmas Together." Caption: "Time Endears But Cannot Fade The Memories That Love Has Made."
☐ Purchased 19___ Pd $_______ MIB NB DB BNT
☐ Want Orig. Ret. $3.50 **NB** $20 **MIB** Sec. Mkt. **$25-$30**

QX 123-1 YARN ORNAMENTS: GREEN BOY
Comments: 4-1/2" tall. Green with red hat.
Slight changes from 1975. Reissued in 1979.
☐ Purchased 19___ Pd $_______ MIB NB DB BNT
☐ Want Orig. Ret. $2.00 Sec. Mkt. **$22-$25**

QX 126-1 YARN ORNAMENTS: GREEN GIRL
Comments: 4-1/2" tall. Green with white muff.
Slight changes from 1975. Reissued in 1979.
☐ Purchased 19___ Pd $_______ MIB NB DB BNT
☐ Want Orig. Ret. $2.00 Sec. Mkt. **$18-$20**

QX 340-3 YARN ORNAMENTS: MR. CLAUS
Comments: 4-1/2" tall.
Identical to 1975. Reissued in 1979.
☐ Purchased 19___ Pd $_______ MIB NB DB BNT
☐ Want Orig. Ret. $2.00 Sec. Mkt. **$22-$24**

QX 125-1 YARN ORNAMENTS: MRS. CLAUS
Comments: 4-1/2" tall
Identical to 1975. Reissued in 1979.
White apron with red checked pockets.
☐ Purchased 19___ Pd $_______ MIB NB DB BNT
☐ Want Orig. Ret. $2.00 Sec. Mkt. **$22-$25**

QX 250-3 YESTERDAY'S TOYS
Comments: Gold Glass Ball, 3-1/4" dia., Dated 1978
Caption: "Every Joy Of Yesterday Is A Memory For Tomorrow. 1978"
☐ Purchased 19___ Pd $_______ MIB NB DB BNT
☐ Want Orig. Ret. $3.50 **NB** $15 **MIB** Sec. Mkt. **$25-$35**

1979 Collection

QX 134-7 A CHRISTMAS TREAT
Comments: Handcrafted, 4-3/4" tall. Reissued in 1980.
A teddy bear with a red cap and coat holds a giant candy cane. The 1979 ornament has "grooves"around the candy cane; the 1980 ornament does not.
☐ Purchased 19___ Pd $_______ MIB NB DB BNT
☐ Want Orig. Ret. $5.00 **NB** $55 **MIB** Sec. Mkt. **$70-$75**

QX 343-9 ANGEL MUSIC
Comments: Sewn Fabric, 4-5" tall. Reissued in 1980.
Flying angel in blue flowered gown with pink and white wings, carrying a harp.
☐ Purchased 19___ Pd $_______ MIB NB DB BNT
☐ Want Orig. Ret. $2.00 Sec. Mkt. **$20-$22**

QX 208-7 BABY'S FIRST CHRISTMAS
Comments: White Satin Ball, 3-1/4" dia., Dated 1979
Toys and gifts are pulled on a sleigh. Back: A Christmas tree is decorated by birds. Caption: "Baby's First Christmas 1979."
☐ Purchased 19___ Pd $_______ MIB NB DB BNT
☐ Want Orig. Ret. $3.50 **NB** $20 **MIB** Sec. Mkt. **$25-$30**

QX 154-7 BABY'S FIRST CHRISTMAS
Comments: Handcrafted, 4" tall, Dated 1979
RARE!! Knitted stocking filled with toys. The first handcrafted ornament for Baby's First Christmas. Caption: "Baby's First Christmas 1979."
☐ Purchased 19___ Pd $_______ MIB NB DB BNT
☐ Want Orig. Ret. $8.00 **NB** $90 **MIB** Sec. Mkt. **$125-$130**

QX 255-9 BEHOLD THE STAR
Comments: White Satin Ball, 3-1/4" dia.
Caption: "And The Light Was For All Time; And The Love Was For All Men."
☐ Purchased 19___ Pd $_______ MIB NB DB BNT
☐ Want Orig. Ret. $3.50 **NB** $20 **MIB** Sec. Mkt. **$35-$40**

QX 147-9 BELLRINGER - "BELLSWINGER"
Comments: ***FIRST IN SERIES***, Dated 1979
Porcelain and Handcrafted, 4" tall. A happy elf swings on the clapper of a white porcelain bell decorated with a wreath.
☐ Purchased 19___ Pd $_______ MIB NB DB BNT
☐ Want Orig. Ret. $10.00 **NB** $300 **MIB** Sec. Mkt. **$385-$400**

QX 201-9 BETSEY CLARK SERIES
Comments: **Seventh in Series**, White Satin Ball, 3-1/4" dia.
Children sit at home reading and then they pull a sled with a tree and gifts. Caption: "Holiday Fun Times Make Memories To Treasure. 1979"
☐ Purchased 19___ Pd $_______ MIB NB DB BNT
☐ Want Orig. Ret. $3.50 **NB** $20 **MIB** Sec. Mkt. **$35-$42**

QX 207-9 BLACK ANGEL
Comments: Gold Glass Ball, 3-1/4" dia., Dated 1979
Young adult angel dressed in a red and white robe. Caption: "Merry Christmas 1979." **Artist:** Thomas Blackshear
☐ Purchased 19___ Pd $_______ MIB NB DB BNT
☐ Want Orig. Ret. $3.50 **NB** $10 **MIB** Sec. Mkt. **$22-$28**

QX 146-7 CARROUSEL SERIES: CHRISTMAS CARROUSEL
Comments: **Second in Series**, Handcrafted, 3-1/2" tall
Four angel musicians revolve on a carrousel.
Caption: "Christmas 1979."
☐ Purchased 19___ Pd $_______ MIB NB DB BNT
☐ Want Orig. Ret. $6.50 **NB** $145 **MIB** Sec. Mkt. **$188-$190**

QX 204-7 CHRISTMAS CHICKADEES
Comments: Gold Glass Ball, 3-1/4" dia.
A pair of chickadees enjoy holly berries. Caption: "Beauty Is A Gift Nature Gives Every Day" and "Christmas 1979."
☐ Purchased 19___ Pd $_______ MIB NB DB BNT
☐ Want Orig. Ret. $3.50 **NB** $15 **MIB** Sec. Mkt. **$25-$35**

QX 257-9 CHRISTMAS COLLAGE
Comments: Gold Glass Ball, 3-1/4" dia., Dated 1979
Old fashioned toys reproduced from a photograph of a Schneeberg collage. Caption: "Season's Greetings."
☐ Purchased 19___ Pd $_______ MIB NB DB BNT
☐ Want Orig. Ret. $3.50 **NB** $12 **MIB** Sec. Mkt. **$28-$30**

QX 157-9 CHRISTMAS EVE SURPRISE
Comments: Handcrafted, 4-1/4" tall, Dated 1979
A wood-look shadow box shows Santa going down the chimney.
☐ Purchased 19___ Pd $_______ MIB NB DB BNT
☐ Want Orig. Ret. $6.50 **NB** $45 **MIB** Sec. Mkt. **$60-$65**

QX 140-7 CHRISTMAS HEART
Comments: Handcrafted, 3-1/2" tall, Dated 1979
Two doves rotate through the center of this heart-shaped ornament.
Artist: Linda Sickman
☐ Purchased 19___ Pd $_______ MIB NB DB BNT
☐ Want Orig. Ret. $6.50 **NB** $80 **MIB** Sec. Mkt. **$115-$125**

QX 135-9 CHRISTMAS IS FOR CHILDREN
Comments: Handcrafted, 4-1/4" tall. Reissued in 1980.
A young girl dressed in a green bonnet and red dress holds a white kitten as she swings.
☐ Purchased 19___ Pd $_______ MIB NB DB BNT
☐ Want Orig. Ret. $5.00 **NB** $60 **MIB** Sec. Mkt. **$95-$100**

QX 253-9 CHRISTMAS TRADITIONS
Comments: Gold Glass Ball, 3-1/4" dia., Dated 1979
Homey Christmas traditions are portrayed. Caption: "The Old May Be Replaced With New, Traditions Rearranged, But The Wonder That Is Christmas Will Never Ever Change."
Artist: Linda Sickman
☐ Purchased 19___ Pd $_______ MIB NB DB BNT
☐ Want Orig. Ret. $3.50 **NB** $20 **MIB** Sec. Mkt. **$35-$38**

QX 353-9 COLORS OF CHRISTMAS: HOLIDAY WREATH
Comments: Acrylic, 3-1/2" tall, Dated 1979
Stained-Glass Look. Wreath decorated with colorful ornaments and a red bow.
☐ Purchased 19___ Pd $_______ MIB NB DB BNT
☐ Want Orig. Ret. $3.50 **NB** $30 **MIB** Sec. Mkt. **$42-$48**

QX 351-9 COLORS OF CHRISTMAS: PARTRIDGE IN A PEAR TREE
Comments: Acrylic, 3-1/4" dia., Dated 1979
Stained-Glass Look. A richly colored partridge surrounded by golden pears and green leaves.
☐ Purchased 19___ Pd $_______ MIB NB DB BNT
☐ Want Orig. Ret. $3.50 **NB** $30 **MIB** Sec. Mkt. **$40-$45**

QX 352-7 COLORS OF CHRISTMAS: STAR OVER BETHLEHEM
Comments: Acrylic, 3-1/2" dia.
Stained-Glass Look. The Star shines brightly over Bethlehem as the shepherds watch. **Artist:** Linda Sickman
☐ Purchased 19___ Pd $_______ MIB NB DB BNT
☐ Want Orig. Ret. $3.50 **NB** $50 **MIB** Sec. Mkt. **$70-$75**

QX 350-7 COLORS OF CHRISTMAS: WORDS OF CHRISTMAS
Comments: Acrylic, 3-3/4" tall, Stained-Glass Look.
Caption: "The Message Of Christmas Is Love."
☐ Purchased 19___ Pd $_______ MIB NB DB BNT
☐ Want Orig. Ret. $3.50 **NB** $65 **MIB** Sec. Mkt. **$80-$85**

QHD 950-7 CRECHE TABLETOP DECORATION
Comments: Frosted acrylic Creche on clear acrylic base.
Caption: "O Come Let Us Adore Him."
☐ Purchased 19___ Pd $_______ MIB NB DB BNT
☐ Want Orig. Ret. $25.00 **NB** $120 **MIB** Sec. Mkt. **$175-$180**

QX 145-9 DOWNHILL RUN, THE
Comments: Handcrafted, 3" tall
A rabbit in a blue scarf and a squirrel with a red cap are making a downhill run on a red toboggan. **Artist:** Donna Lee
☐ Purchased 19___ Pd $_______ MIB NB DB BNT
☐ Want Orig. Ret. $6.50 **NB** $120 **MIB** Sec. Mkt. **$150-$160**

QX 143-9 DRUMMER BOY, THE
Comments: Handcrafted Panorama Ball, 3-1/4" dia.
A red-capped drummer boy stands in the snow and plays for a lamb and a duck.
☐ Purchased 19___ Pd $_______ MIB NB DB BNT
☐ Want Orig. Ret. $8.00 **NB** $90 **MIB** Sec. Mkt. **$130-$135**

QX 209-9 FIRST CHRISTMAS TOGETHER, OUR
Comments: Gold Glass Ball, 3-1/4" dia.
Caption: "Our First Christmas Together 1979" and "Christmas And Love Are For Sharing."
☐ Purchased 19___ Pd $_______ MIB NB DB BNT
☐ Want Orig. Ret. $3.50 **NB** $35 **MIB** Sec. Mkt. **$50-$60**

QX 203-9 FRIENDSHIP
Comments: White Glass Ball, 3-1/4" dia.
Ice skating and a sleigh ride. Caption: "There Is No Time Quite Like Christmas For Remembering Friendships We Cherish" and "Christmas 1979."
☐ Purchased 19___ Pd $_______ MIB NB DB BNT
☐ Want Orig. Ret. $3.50 **NB** $15 **MIB** Sec. Mkt. **$32-$35**

QX 211-9 GRANDDAUGHTER
Comments: White Satin Ball, 3-1/4" dia., Dated 1979
A little girl in a white cap and a red coat feeds the animals. Caption: "A Granddaughter Fills Each Day With Joy By Filling Hearts With Love."
☐ Purchased 19___ Pd $_______ MIB NB DB BNT
☐ Want Orig. Ret. $3.50 **NB** $20 **MIB** Sec. Mkt. **$30-$35**

QX 252-7 GRANDMOTHER
Comments: White Glass Ball, 3-1/4" dia., Dated 1979
Birds fly about a basket of Christmas flowers. Caption: "Grandmothers Bring Happy Times--Time And Time Again."
☐ Purchased 19___ Pd $_______ MIB NB DB BNT
☐ Want Orig. Ret. $3.50 **NB** $10 **MIB** Sec. Mkt. **$20-$25**

QX 210-7 GRANDSON
Comments: White Satin Ball, 3-1/4" dia.
Snoopy and Woodstock sledding in the snow. Caption: "A Grandson... A Special Someone Whose Merry Ways Bring Extra Joy To The Holidays. Christmas 1979."
☐ Purchased 19___ Pd $_______ MIB NB DB BNT
☐ Want Orig. Ret. $3.50 **NB** $20 **MIB** Sec. Mkt. **$30-$35**

QX 155-9 HERE COMES SANTA SERIES: SANTA'S MOTORCAR
Comments: ***FIRST IN SERIES,*** Handcrafted, 3-1/2" tall
Dated 1979. Turning wheels on the antique car that Santa drives makes this a special ornament.
☐ Purchased 19___ Pd $_______ MIB NB DB BNT
☐ Want Orig. Ret. $9.00 **NB** $525 **MIB** Sec. Mkt. **$625**

QX 320-3 HOLIDAY CHIMES: REINDEER CHIMES
Comments: Chrome plated brass, 5-1/2" tall
Issued in 1978, 1979 and 1980
Artist: Linda Sickman
☐ Purchased 19___ Pd $_______ MIB NB DB BNT
☐ Want Orig. Ret. $4.50 **NB** $30 **MIB** Sec. Mkt. **$42-$48**

QX 137-9 HOLIDAY CHIMES: STAR CHIMES
Comments: Chrome Plate, 4" tall, Dated 1979
Stars circle within stars. Year date is in the center star.
Artist: Linda Sickman
☐ Purchased 19___ Pd $_______ MIB NB DB BNT
☐ Want Orig. Ret. $4.50 **NB** $50 **MIB** Sec. Mkt. **$65-$70**

QX 300-7 HOLIDAY HIGHLIGHTS: CHRISTMAS ANGEL
Comments: Acrylic, 4-1/4" wide, Hard to Find
Flying angel with long floral dress, feathery wings and halo, holding a nosegay of flowers. Caption: "Christmas 1979."
☐ Purchased 19___ Pd $_______ MIB NB DB BNT
☐ Want Orig. Ret. $3.50 **NB** $60 **MIB** Sec. Mkt. **$90-$95**

QX 303-9 HOLIDAY HIGHLIGHTS: CHRISTMAS CHEER
Comments: Acrylic, 3-1/2" dia., Dated 1979
A little bird with berries in its beak is perched on a holly bough.
☐ Purchased 19___ Pd $_______ MIB NB DB BNT
☐ Want Orig. Ret. $3.50 **NB** $45 **MIB** Sec. Mkt. **$70-$80**

QX 302-7 HOLIDAY HIGHLIGHTS: CHRISTMAS TREE
Comments: Acrylic, 4-1/2" tall, Dated 1979
A tree of leaves and flowers with a dove near the top. The date is stamped in silver foil.
☐ Purchased 19___ Pd $_______ MIB NB DB BNT
☐ Want Orig. Ret. $3.50 **NB** $45 **MIB** Sec. Mkt. **$75-$80**

QX 304-7 HOLIDAY HIGHLIGHTS: LOVE
Comments: Acrylic, 3-1/2" tall
The caption is stamped in silver foil on this heart: "Time Of Memories And Dreams... Time Of Love. Christmas 1979."
☐ Purchased 19___ Pd $_______ MIB NB DB BNT
☐ Want Orig. Ret. $3.50 **NB** $85 **MIB** Sec. Mkt. **$90-$95**

QX 301-9 HOLIDAY HIGHLIGHTS SNOWFLAKE
Comments: Acrylic, 3-1/2" dia., Dated 1979
This lovely snowflake has the date "etched" in the center hexagon.
☐ Purchased 19___ Pd $_______ MIB NB DB BNT
☐ Want Orig. Ret. $3.50 **NB** $30 **MIB** Sec. Mkt. **$40-$45**

QX 152-7 HOLIDAY SCRIMSHAW
Comments: Handcrafted, 3-1/2" tall
Ivory angel with widespread wings resembles scrimshaw carving. Caption: "Peace - Love - Joy 1979."
☐ Purchased 19___ Pd $_______ MIB NB DB BNT
☐ Want Orig. Ret. $4.00
NB $195 **MIB** Sec. Mkt. **$225-$230**

QX 205-9 JOAN WALSH ANGLUND©
Comments: White Satin Ball, 3-1/4" dia., Dated 1979
Children hang their stockings by the fireplace. Children with their gifts. Caption: "The Smallest Pleasure Is Big Enough To Share."
☐ Purchased 19___ Pd $_______ MIB NB DB BNT
☐ Want Orig. Ret. $3.50 **NB** $25 **MIB** Sec. Mkt. **$38-$40**

QX 256-7 LIGHT OF CHRISTMAS, THE
Comments: Chrome Glass Ball, 3-1/4" dia., Dated 1979
Stained Glass Art Deco design. Caption: "There's No Light As Bright As Christmas To Adorn And Warm The Night."
☐ Purchased 19___ Pd $_______ MIB NB DB BNT
☐ Want Orig. Ret. $3.50 **NB** $12 **MIB** Sec. Mkt. **$25-$30**

QX 132-7 LITTLE TRIMMER COLLECTION: A MATCHLESS CHRISTMAS
Comments: Handcrafted, 2-1/2" long
A little white mouse wearing a red nightcap makes a cozy bed from a red match box.
☐ Purchased 19___ Pd $_______ MIB NB DB BNT
☐ Want Orig. Ret. $4.00 **NB** $35-$40 **MIB** Sec. Mkt. **$65-$75**

QX 130-7 LITTLE TRIMMER COLLECTION: ANGEL DELIGHT
Comments: Handcrafted, 1-3/4" tall
A little angel in a blue gown rides in her walnut shell.
☐ Purchased 19___ Pd $_______ MIB NB DB BNT
☐ Want Orig. Ret. $3.00 **NB** $80 **MIB** Sec. Mkt. **$95-$100**

QX 135-6 LITTLE TRIMMERS: SANTA
Comments: Handcrafted, 2-1/4" tall
Reissued from 1978.
☐ Purchased 19___ Pd $_______ MIB NB DB BNT
☐ Want 1979 Retail $3.00 **NB** $45 **MIB** Sec. Mkt. **$65-$70**

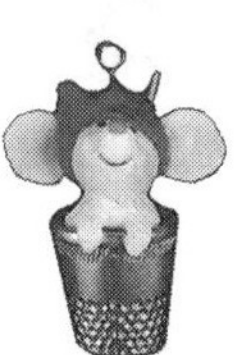

QX 133-6 LITTLE TRIMMERS: THIMBLE SERIES
Comments: ***FIRST IN SERIES***, Handcrafted, 1-3/4" tall
Reissued from 1978.
☐ Purchased 19___ Pd $_______ MIB NB DB BNT
☐ Want 1979 Retail $3.00 **NB** $220 **MIB** Sec. Mkt. **$300-$310**

QX 159-9 LITTLE TRIMMER SET
Comments: Handcrafted.
The Angel, Matchless Christmas and Soldier were packaged together as a trio of Trimmers.
☐ Purchased 19___ Pd $_______ MIB NB DB BNT
☐ Want Orig. Ret. $9.00 **NB** $255 **MIB** Sec. Mkt. **$330-$350**

QX 258-7 LOVE
Comments: White Glass Ball, 3-1/4" dia.
Caption: "Love... Warm As Candleglow, Wondrous As Snowfall, Welcome As Christmas" and "Christmas 1979."
☐ Purchased 19___ Pd $_______ MIB NB DB BNT
☐ Want Orig. Ret. $3.50 **NB** $18 **MIB** Sec. Mkt. **$30-$35**

QX 254-7 MARY HAMILTON
Comments: Ecru Soft-Sheen Satin Ball, 3-1/4" dia.
Dated 1979. A choir of angels sings to forest creatures.
Caption: "... And Heaven And Nature Sing."
☐ Purchased 19___ Pd $_______ MIB NB DB BNT
☐ Want Orig. Ret. $3.50 **NB** $15 **MIB** Sec. Mkt. **$22-$27**

QX 342-7 MERRY SANTA
Comments: Fabric, 4"-5" tall
Whimsical Santa with a pack of toys on his back.
☐ Purchased 19___ Pd $_______ MIB NB DB BNT
☐ Want Orig. Ret. $2.00 Sec. Mkt. **$20-$22**

QX 251-9 MOTHER
Comments: White Glass Ball, 3-1/4" dia.
Caption: "It's Love That Makes Christmas So Special - And Mother Who Makes Us Feel Loved."
☐ Purchased 19___ Pd $_______ MIB NB DB BNT
☐ Want Orig. Ret. $3.50 **NB** $15 **MIB** Sec. Mkt. **$22-$25**

QX 212-7 NEW HOME
Comments: Ecru Soft-Sheen Satin Ball, 3-1/4" dia.
Dated 1979. A colorful snow-covered village and pond. Caption: "Christmas... When Love Fills The Heart, When Hearts Look To Home."
☐ Purchased 19___ Pd $_______ MIB NB DB BNT
☐ Want Orig. Ret. $3.50 **NB** $15 **MIB** Sec. Mkt. **$35-$40**

QX 214-7 NIGHT BEFORE CHRISTMAS
Comments: White Satin Ball, 3-1/4" dia., Dated 1979
Santa fills the stockings and continues on his journey. Caption: "... I Heard Him Exclaim, Ere He Drove Out Of Sight, Happy Christmas To All, And To All A Good Night." C. C. Moore
☐ Purchased 19___ Pd $_______ MIB NB DB BNT
☐ Want Orig. Ret. $3.50 **NB** $30 **MIB** Sec. Mkt. **$40-$45**

QX 150-7 OUTDOOR FUN
Comments: Handcrafted, 3" tall
A little girl swings between two fir trees. **Artist:** Linda Sickman
☐ Purchased 19___ Pd $_______ MIB NB DB BNT
☐ Want Orig. Ret. $8.00 **NB** $90 **MIB** Sec. Mkt. **$120-$125**

QX 202-7 PEANUTS® (TIME TO TRIM)
Comments: White Satin Ball, 3-1/4" dia., Dated 1979
Woodstock and his green-capped flock decorate the tree with candy canes Snoopy is giving them.
Caption: "Merry Christmas 1979."
☐ Purchased 19___ Pd $_______ MIB NB DB BNT
☐ Want Orig. Ret. $3.50 **NB** $25 **MIB** Sec. Mkt. **$38-$42**

QX 133-9 READY FOR CHRISTMAS
Comments: Handcrafted, 3" tall, Dated 1979
White birdhouse with snow-capped roof and green garland over the door. **Artist:** Donna Lee
☐ Purchased 19___ Pd $_______ MIB NB DB BNT
☐ Want Orig. Ret. $6.50 **NB** $90 **MIB** Sec. Mkt. **$145-$150**

QX 340-7 THE ROCKING HORSE
Comments: Quilted Fabric, 4" - 5" tall. Reissued in 1980.
A brown spotted rocking horse on blue rockers. The ornament is trimmed in red.
☐ Purchased 19___ Pd $_______ MIB NB DB BNT
☐ Want Orig. Ret. $2.00 Sec. Mkt. **$22-$25**

QX 138-7 SANTA'S HERE
Comments: Handcrafted, 4" dia., Dated 1979
Santa, with his pack, waves as he rotates inside a white snowflake.
Artist: Linda Sickman
☐ Purchased 19___ Pd $_______ MIB NB DB BNT
☐ Want Orig. Ret. $5.00 **NB** $50 **MIB** Sec. Mkt. **$70-$75**

QX 142-3 SKATING RACCOON
Comments: Handcrafted, 2" tall.
Reissued from 1978.
Artist: Donna Lee
☐ Purchased 19___ Pd $_______ MIB NB DB BNT
☐ Want 1979 Retail $6.50 **NB** $60 **MIB** Sec. Mkt. **$90-$95**

QX 139-9 SKATING SNOWMAN, THE
Comments: Handcrafted, 4-1/4" tall, Reissued in 1980.
This happy snowman wears metal ice skates, a black top hat and a green and white scarf.
☐ Purchased 19___ Pd $_______ MIB NB DB BNT
☐ Want Orig. Ret. $5.00 **NB** $60 **MIB** Sec. Mkt. **$80-$85**

QX 141-9 SNOOPY & FRIENDS SERIES: ICE HOCKEY HOLIDAY
Comments: ***FIRST IN SERIES***, Dated 1979
Handcrafted Panorama Ball, 3-1/4" dia.
Snoopy and Woodstock play ice hockey on a frozen pond.
☐ Purchased 19___ Pd $_______ MIB NB DB BNT
☐ Want Orig. Ret. $8.00 **NB** $90 **MIB** Sec. Mkt. **$120-$125**

QX 200-7 SPENCER ™ SPARROW, ESQ.
Comments: Ecru Soft-Sheen Satin Ball, 3-1/4" dia.
Dated 1979. Spencer swings on a garland of popcorn and cranberries. Caption: "Christmas Time Means Decorating, Spreading Cheer And Celebrating."
☐ Purchased 19___ Pd $_______ MIB NB DB BNT
☐ Want Orig. Ret. $3.50 **NB** $16 **MIB** Sec. Mkt. **$30-$35**

QX 341-9 STUFFED FULL STOCKING
Comments: Quilted Fabric, 4" - 5" tall, Reissued in 1980.
Blue patchwork stocking holds a doll and other gifts to delight a child.
☐ Purchased 19___ Pd $_______ MIB NB DB BNT
☐ Want Orig. Ret. $2.00 Sec. Mkt. **$22-$27**

QX 213-9 TEACHER
Comments: White Satin Ball, 3-1/4" dia., Dated 1979
Front: A raccoon writes a message to the teacher. Back: A sleigh with a gift. Caption: "To A Special Teacher" and "Merry Christmas 1979."
☐ Purchased 19___ Pd $_______ MIB NB DB BNT
☐ Want Orig. Ret. $3.50 **NB** $8 **MIB** Sec. Mkt. **$15-$18**

QX 131-9 THIMBLE SERIES: A CHRISTMAS SALUTE
Comments: **Second in Series**, Handcrafted, 2-1/4" tall
Reissued in 1980. A cute soldier dressed in red and blue wears a thimble hat.
☐ Purchased 19___ Pd $_______ MIB NB DB BNT
☐ Want Orig. Ret. $3.00 **NB** $135 **MIB** Sec. Mkt. **$170-$175**

QX 703-7 TIFFANY ANGEL TREE TOPPER
Comments: This stained-glass look angel plays her lute.
Multicolored with silver "leading," she complements other stained-glass look ornaments.
☐ Purchased 19___ Pd $_______ MIB NB DB BNT
☐ Want Orig. Ret. $10.00 **NB** $25 **MIB** Sec. Mkt. **$32-$37**

QX 250-7 TWENTY-FIFTH ANNIVERSARY, OUR
Comments: White Glass Ball, 3-1/4" dia., Dated 1979
Greenery and holly berries make a lovely background for white ribbon and wedding bells. Caption: "Year Of Our 25th Anniversary" and "Those Warm Times Shared In Past Decembers. The Mind Still Sees, The Heart Remembers."
☐ Purchased 19___ Pd $_______ MIB NB DB BNT
☐ Want Orig. Ret. $3.50 **NB** $15 **MIB** Sec. Mkt. **$25-$30**

QX 206-7 WINNIE-THE-POOH
Comments: White Satin Ball, 3-1/4" dia.
This Walt Disney design shows Winnie with his all-time favorite "hunny." Caption: "Merry Christmas 1979." Winnie is popular!
☐ Purchased 19___ Pd $_______ MIB NB DB BNT
☐ Want Orig. Ret. $3.50 **NB** $20 **MIB** Sec. Mkt. **$35-$38**

QX 123-1 YARN ORNAMENTS: GREEN BOY
Comments: 4-1/2" tall, Slight changes from 1975.
Reissued from 1978. Green with red hat.
☐ Purchased 19___ Pd $_______ MIB NB DB BNT
☐ Want Orig. Ret. $2.00 Sec. Mkt. **$22-$25**

QX 126-1 YARN ORNAMENTS: GREEN GIRL
Comments: 4-1/2" tall, Slight changes from 1975.
Reissued from 1978. Green with white muff.
☐ Purchased 19___ Pd $_______ MIB NB DB BNT
☐ Want Orig. Ret. $2.00 Sec. Mkt. **$18-$20**

QX 340-3 YARN ORNAMENTS: MR. CLAUS
Comments: 4-1/2" tall. Identical to 1975.
Reissued from 1978.
☐ Purchased 19___ Pd $_______ MIB NB DB BNT
☐ Want Orig. Ret. $2.00 Sec. Mkt. **$22-$24**

QX 125-1 YARN ORNAMENTS: MRS. CLAUS
Comments: 4-1/2" tall. Identical to 1975.
Reissued from 1978.
☐ Purchased 19___ Pd $_______ MIB NB DB BNT
☐ Want Orig. Ret. $2.00 Sec. Mkt. **$22-$25**

1980 Collection

QX 134-7 A CHRISTMAS TREAT
Comments: Handcrafted, 4-3/4" tall
Reissued from 1979. The 1979 ornament has "grooves" around the candy cane; the 1980 ornament does not.
☐ Purchased 19___ Pd $_______ MIB NB DB BNT
☐ Want Orig. Retail $5.50 **NB** $55 **MIB** Sec. Mkt. **$70-$75**

QX 144-1 A CHRISTMAS VIGIL
Comments: Handcrafted Panorama Ball, 3-13/16" tall
A little boy and his dog look through a window in time to see Santa and his reindeer. Panorama Balls are usually not MIB. **Artist:** Donna Lee
☐ Purchased 19___ Pd $_______ MIB NB DB BNT
☐ Want Orig. Ret. $9.00 **NB** $85 **MIB** Sec. Mkt. **$110-$115**

QX 139-4 A HEAVENLY NAP
Comments: Handcrafted, 3-1/2" tall. Reissued in 1981.
A frosted acrylic moon, sound asleep, holds a sleeping angel dressed in blue. **Artist:** Donna Lee
☐ Purchased 19___ Pd $_______ MIB NB DB BNT
☐ Want Orig. Ret. $6.50 **NB-P** $25 **MIB** Sec. Mkt. **$55-$60**

QX 153-4 A SPOT OF CHRISTMAS CHEER
Comments: Handcrafted, 2-47/64" tall, Dated 1980
A chipmunk trims a Christmas tree inside a teapot decorated with green garland. **Artist:** Donna Lee
☐ Purchased 19___ Pd $_______ MIB NB DB BNT
☐ Want Orig. Ret. $8.00 **NB** $95 **MIB** Sec. Mkt. **$145-$150**

QX 343-9 ANGEL MUSIC
Comments: Quilted Fabric. Reissued from 1979.
☐ Purchased 19___ Pd $_______ MIB NB DB BNT
☐ Want Orig. Ret. $2.00 Sec. Mkt. **$20-$22**

QX 150-1 ANIMALS' CHRISTMAS, THE
Comments: Handcrafted, 2-37/64" tall
A brown rabbit and a brown bird decorate a tree with red ribbon and a gold star. **Artist:** Donna Lee
☐ Purchased 19___ Pd $_______ MIB NB DB BNT
☐ Want Orig. Ret. $8.00 **NB** $45 **MIB** Sec. Mkt. **$55-$65**

QX 200-1 BABY'S FIRST CHRISTMAS
Comments: White Satin Ball, 3-1/4" dia.
Santa with his pack on his back talks to a baby. Caption: "Baby's First Christmas, 1980."
☐ Purchased 19___ Pd $_______ MIB NB DB BNT
☐ Want Orig. Ret. $4.00 **NB** $15 **MIB** Sec. Mkt. **$30-$32**

QX 156-1 BABY'S FIRST CHRISTMAS
Comments: Handcrafted, 3-57/64" tall, Dated 1980
A shadow box in the shape of a Christmas tree. Caption: "Baby's First Christmas." **Artist:** Linda Sickman
☐ Purchased 19___ Pd $_______ MIB NB DB BNT
☐ Want Orig. Ret. $12.00 **NB** $38 **MIB** Sec. Mkt. **$48-$52**

QX 303-4 BEAUTY OF FRIENDSHIP
Comments: Acrylic, 3-1/4" dia., Dated 1980
Caption: "Friendship Brings Beauty To Our Days, Joy To Our World. Christmas 1980."
☐ Purchased 19___ Pd $_______ MIB NB DB BNT
☐ Want Orig. Ret. $4.00 **NB** $40 **MIB** Sec. Mkt. **$45-$55**

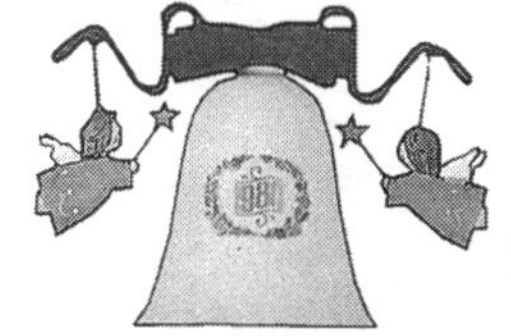

QX 157-4 BELLRINGERS SERIES
Comments: **Second in Series**, Handcrafted, 2-7/64" tall
Dated 1980. Two angels in blue gowns circle and ring a white porcelain bell with the star "clappers" they are holding.
☐ Purchased 19___ Pd $_______ MIB NB DB BNT
☐ Want Orig. Ret. $15.00 **NB** $65 **MIB** Sec. Mkt. **$85-$88**

QX 215-4 BETSEY CLARK SERIES
Comments: **Eighth in Series,** White Glass Ball, 3-1/4" dia.
Two children sled past a sign that says "Christmas 1980."
Caption: "It's Joy-In-The-Air Time, Love Everywhere Time, Good-Fun-To-Share Time, It's Christmas."
☐ Purchased 19___ Pd $_______ MIB NB DB BNT
☐ Want Orig. Ret. $4.00 **NB** $21 **MIB** Sec. Mkt. **$30-$35**

QX 307-4 BETSEY CLARK
Comments: Lt. Blue Cameo, 3-3/8" dia., Dated 1980
Angel is kneeling in prayer. Caption: "Love Came Down At Christmas, Love All Lovely, Love Divine: Love Was Born At Christmas, Star And Angels Gave The Sign" and "Christmas 1980."
☐ Purchased 19___ Pd $_______ MIB NB DB BNT
☐ Want Orig. Ret. $6.50 **NB** $38 **MIB** Sec. Mkt. **$60-$65**

QX 149-4 BETSEY CLARK'S CHRISTMAS
Comments: Handcrafted, 4" tall, Dated 1980
A shadow box trimmed in white and red shows a girl in a three-dimensional snow scene.
☐ Purchased 19___ Pd $_______ MIB NB DB BNT
☐ Want Orig. Ret. $7.50 **NB** $25 **MIB** Sec. Mkt. **$35-$40**

QX 229-4 BLACK BABY'S FIRST CHRISTMAS
Comments: White Satin Ball, 3-1/4" dia., Dated 1980
A black baby sits by a decorated tree that holds nested birds. Toys surround the tree. Caption: "Baby's First Christmas, 1980."
☐ Purchased 19___ Pd $_______ MIB NB DB BNT
☐ Want Orig. Ret. $4.00 **NB** $15 **MIB** Sec. Mkt. **$22-$25**

OX 705-4 BRASS STAR TREE TOPPER
Comments: A lacy design was used for this interlocking brass star.
☐ Purchased 19___ Pd $_______ MIB NB DB BNT
☐ Want Orig. Ret. $25.00 **NB** $45 **MIB** Sec. Mkt. **$60**

QX 140-1 CAROLING BEAR
Comments: Handcrafted, 3-7/33" tall, Dated 1980
A brown bear wearing a red and green striped scarf sings a duet with a red bird on his arm. Caption: "Carols 1980."
Artist: Donna Lee
☐ Purchased 19___ Pd $_______ MIB NB DB BNT
☐ Want Orig. Ret. $7.50 **NB** $95 **MIB** Sec. Mkt. **$150-$155**

QX 141-4 CARROUSEL SERIES: MERRY CARROUSEL
Comments: **Third in Series,** Handcrafted, 3-1/8" tall, Dated 1980
Santa and his reindeer make their "rounds." Caption on top: "Christmas 1980."
☐ Purchased 19___ Pd $_______ MIB NB DB BNT
☐ Want Orig. Ret. $7.50 **NB** $110 **MIB** Sec. Mkt. **$165-$170**

QX 158-4 CHECKING IT TWICE
Comments: Handcrafted, 5-15/16" tall, Special Edition
Reissued in 1981. Santa checks his list. He wears spectacles of real metal. **Artist:** Thomas Blackshear
☐ Purchased 19___ Pd $_______ MIB NB DB BNT
☐ Want Orig. Ret. $20.00 **NB** $155 **MIB** Sec. Mkt. **$195-$200**

QX 210-1 CHRISTMAS AT HOME
Comments: Gold Glass Ball, 3-1/4" dia., Dated 1980
Caption: "A Home That's Filled With Christmas Glows With The Joyful Light Of The Special Warmth And Happiness That Makes The Season Bright. Christmas 1980."
☐ Purchased 19___ Pd $_______ MIB NB DB BNT
☐ Want Orig. Ret. $4.00 **NB** $8 **MIB** Sec. Mkt. **$15-$20**

QX 224-1 CHRISTMAS CARDINALS
Comments: White Glass Ball, 3-1/4" dia., Dated 1980
Two cardinals sit on berry-laden branches of holly. Caption: "Nature At Christmas... A Wonderland Of Wintry Art. Christmas 1980."
☐ Purchased 19___ Pd $_______ MIB NB DB BNT
☐ Want Orig. Ret. $4.00 **NB** $15 **MIB** Sec. Mkt. **$30-$32**

QX 228-1 CHRISTMAS CHOIR
Comments: Gold Glass Ball, 3-1/4" dia., Dated 1980
Three children dressed in choir robes sing the message of Christmas. Caption: "Go Tell It On The Mountain... Jesus Christ Is Born!" and "Christmas 1980."
☐ Purchased 19___ Pd $_______ MIB NB DB BNT
☐ Want Orig. Ret. $4.00 **NB** $45 **MIB** Sec. Mkt. **$65-$72**

QX 135-9 CHRISTMAS IS FOR CHILDREN
Comments: Handcrafted, 4-1/4" tall
Reissued from 1979.
☐ Purchased 19___ Pd $_______ MIB NB DB BNT
☐ Want 1980 Retail $5.50 **NB** $60 **MIB** Sec. Mkt. **$95-$100**

QX 353-4 CHRISTMAS KITTEN TEST ORNAMENT
Comments: *VERY RARE! ONLY 200 MADE.*
Very limited "known" sold prices in past years. Until recently we had not seen this ornament in a box. No sales found for two years.
☐ Purchased 19___ Pd $_______ MIB NB DB BNT
☐ Want Orig. Ret. $4.00 **NB** $200-$220
MIB Sec. Mkt. **$300-$325**

QX 207-4 CHRISTMAS LOVE
Comments: White Glass Ball, 3-1/4" dia., Dated 1980
Reproduction of a Schneeberg collage in pastels. Caption: "Love At Christmas... Happy Moments Spent Together, Memories To Be Shared Forever. Christmas 1980"
☐ Purchased 19___ Pd $_______ MIB NB DB BNT
☐ Want Orig. Ret. $4.00 **NB** $20 **MIB** Sec. Mkt. **$32-$38**

QX 226-1 CHRISTMAS TIME
Comments: Ecru Soft-Sheen Satin Ball, 3-1/4" dia., Dated 1980
A stagecoach and a steaming mug of coffee. Caption: "These Are The Days Of Merrymaking Get-Togethers, Journey-Taking, Moments Of Delight And Love That Last In Memory. Christmas 1980."
☐ Purchased 19___ Pd $_______ MIB NB DB BNT
☐ Want Orig. Ret. $4.00 **NB** $18 **MIB** Sec. Mkt. **$25-$28**

QX 350-1 COLORS OF CHRISTMAS: JOY
Comments: Acrylic, 4" tall, Dated 1980
With a look of leaded stained glass, the ornament is molded to spell "JOY" with the year on a gold ribbon scroll over the "O."
☐ Purchased 19___ Pd $_______ MIB NB DB BNT
☐ Want Orig. Ret. $4.00 **NB** $15 **MIB** Sec. Mkt. **$22-$25**

QX 214-1 DAD
Comments: Gold Glass Ball, 3-1/4" dia., Dated 1980
"DAD" is printed on a red and green plaid background. Caption: "A Dad Is Always Caring, Always Sharing, Always Giving Of His Love. Christmas 1980."
☐ Purchased 19___ Pd $_______ MIB NB DB BNT
☐ Want Orig. Ret. $4.00 **NB** $10 **MIB** Sec. Mkt. **$18-$20**

QX 212-1 DAUGHTER
Comments: White Glass Ball, 3-1/4" dia., Dated 1980
A white kitten naps near a potted plant while another plays with an ornament. Caption: "A Daughter Is The Sweetest Gift A Lifetime Can Provide. Christmas 1980."
☐ Purchased 19___ Pd $_______ MIB NB DB BNT
☐ Want Orig. Ret. $4.00 **NB** $20 **MIB** Sec. Mkt. **$32-$35**

Family happiness is homemade.

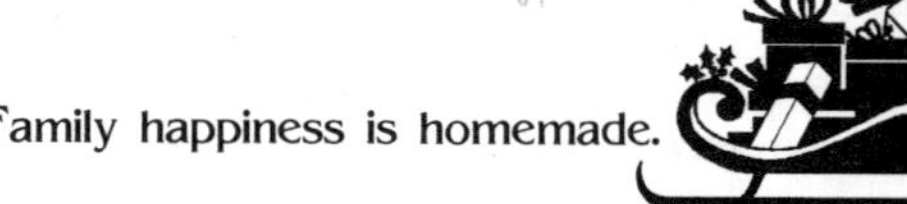

QX 218-1 DISNEY
Comments: White Satin Ball, 3-1/4" dia., Dated 1980
On one side, Mickey and Minnie Mouse ice skate. On the other, Mickey plays Santa. Caption: "Merry Christmas 1980."
☐ Purchased 19___ Pd $_______ MIB NB DB BNT
☐ Want Orig. Ret. $4.00 **NB** $20 **MIB** Sec. Mkt. **$28-$32**

QX 352-1 DOVE TEST ORNAMENT
Comments: *VERY RARE! ONLY 200 MADE.* More of these in collectors' hands than Christmas Kitten, p. 26. This ornament should have a flat white back; some have been found without back glued on. Not really sought after as in earlier years.
☐ Purchased 19___ Pd $_______ MIB NB DB BNT
☐ Want Orig. Ret. $4.00 **NB** $100 **MIB** Sec. Mkt. **$195-$200**

QX 147-4 DRUMMER BOY
Comments: Handcrafted, 3-3/64" tall, Dated 1980
In bread-dough design, this drummer boy is dressed in green with brown sandals and stocking cap. He plays a red and gold drum.
Artist: Donna Lee
☐ Purchased 19___ Pd $_______ MIB NB DB BNT
☐ Want Orig. Ret. $5.50 **NB** $80 **MIB** Sec. Mkt. **$90-$95**

QX 142-1 ELFIN ANTICS
Comments: *HARD TO FIND/POPULAR!* Handcrafted 4-9/16" tall. Three elves tumble down from your Christmas tree branch. The bottom elf rings a gold bell. Very popular!
☐ Purchased 19___ Pd $_______ MIB NB DB BNT
☐ Want Orig. Ret. $9.00 **NB** $190 **MIB** Sec. Mkt. **$220-$225**

QX 205-4 FIRST CHRISTMAS TOGETHER
Comments: White Glass Ball, 3-1/4" dia., Dated 1980
A man and wife take a moonlight sleigh ride. Caption: "First Christmas Together. Christmas Is A Love Story Written In Our Hearts."
☐ Purchased 19___ Pd $_______ MIB NB DB BNT
☐ Want Orig. Ret. $4.00 **NB** $18 **MIB** Sec. Mkt. **$25-$30**

QX 305-4 FIRST CHRISTMAS TOGETHER
Comments: Acrylic, 3-1/2" tall, Dated 1980
An acrylic heart has a floral and ribbon border surrounding the caption stamped in silver foil. Caption: "First Christmas Together 1980."
☐ Purchased 19___ Pd $_______ MIB NB DB BNT
☐ Want Orig. Ret. $4.00 **NB** $40 **MIB** Sec. Mkt. **$50-$55**

QX 208-1 FRIENDSHIP
Comments: White Glass Ball, 3-1/4" dia., Dated 1980
White lace and red ribbon border. Caption: "Hold Christmas Ever In Your Heart -- For Its Meaning Never Ends; Its Spirit Is The Warmth And Joy Of Remembering Friends."
☐ Purchased 19___ Pd $_______ MIB NB DB BNT
☐ Want Orig. Ret. $4.00 **NB** $10 **MIB** Sec. Mkt. **$18-$20**

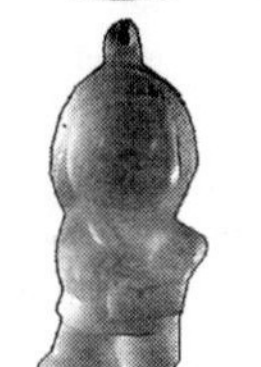

QX 309-4 FROSTED IMAGES: DRUMMER BOY
Comments: Acrylic, 1-7/8" to 2-1/4" tall
Look of etched crystal. Three dimensional frosted acrylic ornament depicts a boy playing his drum.
☐ Purchased 19___ Pd $_______ MIB NB DB BNT
☐ Want Orig. Ret. $4.00 **NB** $18 **MIB** Sec. Mkt. **$22-$24**

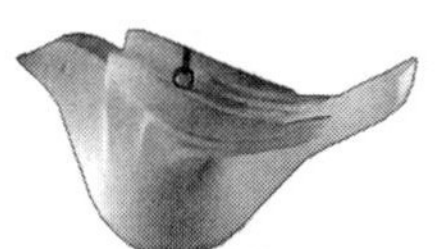

QX 308-1 FROSTED IMAGES: DOVE
Comments: Acrylic, 1-7/8" to 2-1/4" tall
Look of etched crystal. Three dimensional frosted acrylic ornament depicts a dove in flight.
☐ Purchased 19___ Pd $_______ MIB NB DB BNT
☐ Want Orig. Ret. $4.00 **NB** $30 **MIB** Sec. Mkt. **$35-$40**

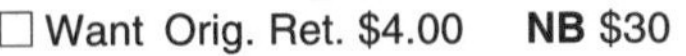

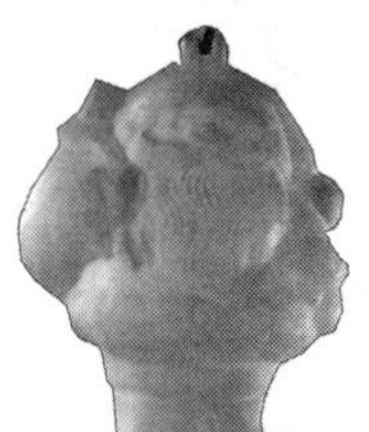

QX 310-1 FROSTED IMAGES: SANTA
Comments: Acrylic, 1-7/8" to 2-1/4" tall
Look of etched crystal. Three dimensional frosted acrylic ornament depicts Santa with his pack on his back.
☐ Purchased 19___ Pd $_______ MIB NB DB BNT
☐ Want Orig. Ret. $4.00 **NB** $15 **MIB** Sec. Mkt. **$20-$25**

QX 137-4 FROSTY FRIENDS SERIES: A COOL YULE
Comments: ***FIRST IN SERIES***, Handcrafted, 2-63/64" tall
This cute little Eskimo boy and his polar bear pal sit atop an ice cube reading their books. Caption: "Merry Christmas 1980." Most talked about ornament! Music books have been falling off.
Sec. mkt. value without book $400 in box.
☐ Purchased 19___ Pd $_______ MIB NB DB BNT
☐ Want Orig. Ret. $6.50 **NB** $450 **MIB** Sec. Mkt. **$550-$600**

QX 202-1 GRANDDAUGHTER
Comments: Ecru Soft-Sheen Satin Ball, 3-1/4" dia.
Caption: "A Granddaughter Is A Dream Fulfilled, A Treasure To Hold Dear, A Joy To Warmly Cherish, A Comfort Through The Year. Christmas 1980."
☐ Purchased 19___ Pd $_______ MIB NB DB BNT
☐ Want Orig. Ret. $4.00 **NB** $15 **MIB** Sec. Mkt. **$32-$35**

QX 231-4 GRANDFATHER
Comments: White Glass Ball, 3-1/4" dia., Dated 1980
Two snow scenes, one of a covered bridge and the other of an old wagon in a barn yard. Caption: "A Grandfather Is... Strong In His Wisdom, Gentle In His Love. Christmas 1980."
☐ Purchased 19___ Pd $_______ MIB NB DB BNT
☐ Want Orig. Ret. $4.00 **NB** $14 **MIB** Sec. Mkt. **$18-$20**

QX 204-1 GRANDMOTHER
Comments: White Glass Ball, 3-1/4" dia., Dated 1980
The caption and date are framed by flowers, birds and animals. Caption: "Love And Joy And Comfort And Cheer Are Gifts A Grandmother Gives All Year. Christmas 1980."
☐ Purchased 19___ Pd $_______ MIB NB DB BNT
☐ Want Orig. Ret. $4.00 **NB** $10 **MIB** Sec. Mkt. **$15-$18**

QX 213-4 GRANDPARENTS
Comments: Gold Glass Ball, 3-1/4" dia., Dated 1980
Reproduced from the Currier & Ives print, "Early Winter," the design is of a large home by a pond. Caption: "Grandparents Have Beautiful Ways Of Giving, Of Helping, Of Teaching... Especially Of Loving."
☐ Purchased 19___ Pd $_______ MIB NB DB BNT
☐ Want Orig. Ret. $4.00 **NB** $15 **MIB** Sec. Mkt. **$25-$30**

QX 201-4 GRANDSON
Comments: White Satin Ball, 3-1/4" dia.
Front: raccoons pull a snowman on a sled. Back: a snowman adds a candy cane to a tree. Caption: "Grandsons And Christmas Are Joys That Go Together. Christmas 1980."
☐ Purchased 19___ Pd $_______ MIB NB DB BNT
☐ Want Orig. Ret. $4.00 **NB** $15 **MIB** Sec. Mkt. **$25-$30**

QX 222-1 HAPPY CHRISTMAS
Comments: Ecru Soft-Sheen Satin Ball, 3-1/4" dia.
A Koala bear waters a potted tree which grows into a "pear tree" with a small bird at the top. Caption: "Tis The Season When Hearts Are Glowing, Love Is Growing, And Happiness Rounds Out The Year!" and "Christmas 1980."
☐ Purchased 19___ Pd $_______ MIB NB DB BNT
☐ Want Orig. Ret. $4.00 **NB** $20 **MIB** Sec. Mkt. **$25-$30**

Your greatest Christmas cheer comes when you give.

QX 156-7 HEAVENLY MINSTREL
Comments: **Special Edition,** Handcrafted, 6-1/4" tall
A beautiful old world angel with widespread wings plays a lute. Price down from '95.
Artist: Donna Lee
☐ Purchased 19___ Pd $_______ MIB NB DB BNT
☐ Want Orig. Ret. $15.00 **NB** $290 **MIB** Sec. Mkt. **$340-$350**

QX 152-1 HEAVENLY SOUNDS
Comments: Handcrafted, 3-30/64" tall, Dated 1980
Angels dressed in pink and blue ring a gold metal bell as they twirl around in the center of a wood-look pink ring.
☐ Purchased 19___ Pd $_______ MIB NB DB BNT
☐ Want Orig. Ret. $7.50 **NB** $60 **MIB** Sec. Mkt. **$90-$95**

QX 143-4 HERE COMES SANTA SERIES: SANTA'S EXPRESS
Comments: **Second in Series,** Handcrafted, 3" tall
Dated 1980. Santa waves from an old-fashioned locomotive in red and green; the wheels turn.
☐ Purchased 19___ Pd $_______ MIB NB DB BNT
☐ Want Orig. Ret. $12.00 **NB** $90 **MIB** Sec. Mkt. **$180-$185**

QX 320-3 HOLIDAY CHIMES: REINDEER CHIMES
Comments: Chrome plated brass, 5-1/2" tall.
Issued in 1978, 1979, and 1980. **Artist:** Linda Sickman
☐ Purchased 19___ Pd $_______ MIB NB DB BNT
☐ Want 1980 Retail $5.50 **NB** $30 **MIB** Sec. Mkt. **$42-$48**

QX 136-1 HOLIDAY CHIMES: SANTA MOBILE
Comments: Chrome Plate, 3-57/64" tall Reissued in 1981.
His sleigh pulled by three reindeer, Santa flies over three homes with smoking chimneys.
☐ Purchased 19___ Pd $_______ MIB NB DB BNT
☐ Want Orig. Ret. $5.50 **NB-P** $35 **MIB** Sec. Mkt. **$42-$48**

QX 165-4 HOLIDAY CHIMES: SNOWFLAKE CHIMES
Comments: Chrome Plate, 1-59/64" dia. Reissued in 1981.
Three lacy snowflakes are suspended from a fourth snowflake.
Artist: Linda Sickman
☐ Purchased 19___ Pd $_______ MIB NB DB BNT
☐ Want Orig. Ret. $5.50 **NB-P** $15 **MIB** Sec. Mkt. **$22-$28**

QX 300-1 HOLIDAY HIGHLIGHTS: THREE WISE MEN
Comments: Acrylic, 4" tall, Dated 1980
Three wise men follow the star to Bethlehem. Caption: "Christmas 1980."
☐ Purchased 19___ Pd $_______ MIB NB DB BNT
☐ Want Orig. Ret. $4.00 **NB** $15 **MIB** Sec. Mkt. **$25-$28**

QX 301-4 HOLIDAY HIGHLIGHTS: WREATH
Comments: Acrylic, 3-1/4" dia., Dated 1980
Leaves and holly in frosted acrylic are set off by clear fruit and berries. Date is stamped in silver foil on a clear center.
☐ Purchased 19___ Pd $_______ MIB NB DB BNT
☐ Want Orig. Ret. $4.00 **NB** $60 **MIB** Sec. Mkt. **$80-$85**

QX 217-4 JOAN WALSH ANGLUND©
Comments: White Satin Ball, 3-1/4" dia., Dated 1980
Three children ice skate on a frozen lake. Caption: "Each And Every Bright December Brings The Best Times To Remember. Christmas 1980."
☐ Purchased 19___ Pd $_______ MIB NB DB BNT
☐ Want Orig. Ret. $4.00 **NB** $20 **MIB** Sec. Mkt. **$25-$28**

QX 227-4 JOLLY SANTA
Comments: White Glass Ball, 3-1/4" dia., Dated 1980
Santa and his reindeer spell out Christmas messages with ice skates. Caption: "Merry Christmas" and "Christmas 1980."
☐ Purchased 19___ Pd $_______ MIB NB DB BNT
☐ Want Orig. Ret. $4.00 **NB** $15 **MIB** Sec. Mkt. **$25-$30**

QX 131-4 LITTLE TRIMMERS: CHRISTMAS OWL
Comments: Handcrafted, 1-27/32" tall.
Reissued in 1982. This cute little owl wearing a Santa cap holds a sprig of holly in its beak.
☐ Purchased 19___ Pd $_______ MIB NB DB BNT
☐ Want Orig. Ret. $4.00 **NB-P** $30 **MIB** Sec. Mkt. **$45-$50**

QX 135-4 LITTLE TRIMMERS: CHRISTMAS TEDDY
Comments: Handcrafted, 1 1/4". A small brown teddy bear with a big smile painted on his face has a bread dough look.
☐ Purchased 19___ Pd $_______ MIB NB DB BNT
☐ Want Orig. Ret. $2.50 **NB** $85 **MIB** Sec. Mkt. **$130-$135**

QX 134-1 LITTLE TRIMMERS: CLOTHESPIN SOLDIER
Comments: Handcrafted, 2-15/16" tall
Blue and red soldier in the style of a clothespin stands at attention.
☐ Purchased 19___ Pd $_______ MIB NB DB BNT
☐ Want Orig. Ret. $3.50 **NB** $25 **MIB** Sec. Mkt. **$40-$45**

QX 160-1 LITTLE TRIMMERS: MERRY REDBIRD
Comments: Handcrafted-Flocked, 1-27/32" long
This little redbird wears flocked "feathers" and holds a sprig of holly in his bill.
☐ Purchased 19___ Pd $_______ MIB NB DB BNT
☐ Want Orig. Ret. $3.50 **NB** $45 **MIB** Sec. Mkt. **$65-$70**

QX 130-1 LITTLE TRIMMERS: SWINGIN' ON A STAR
Comments: Handcrafted, 2-5/32" tall
A tiny white mouse with a red and green striped cap swings on a brass star.
☐ Purchased 19___ Pd $_______ MIB NB DB BNT
☐ Want Orig. Ret. $4.00 **NB** $60 **MIB** Sec. Mkt. **$85-$90**

QX 302-1 LOVE
Comments: Acrylic, 4" tall, Dated 1980
The word LOVE is enhanced by silver foil stamping. Caption: "Where There Is Love, There Is The Spirit Of Christmas."
☐ Purchased 19___ Pd $_______ MIB NB DB BNT
☐ Want Orig. Ret. $4.00 **NB** $50 **MIB** Sec. Mkt. **$60-$65**

QX 221-4 MARTY LINKS™
Comments: White Satin Ball, 3-1/4" dia.
A little boy and animals carol in the snow under the direction of a little girl. Caption: "We Wish You A Merry Christmas And A Happy New Year" and "Christmas 1980."
☐ Purchased 19___ Pd $_______ MIB NB DB BNT
☐ Want Orig. Ret. $4.00 **NB** $6 **MIB** Sec. Mkt. **$20-$22**

QX 219-4 MARY HAMILTON
Comments: Gold Glass Ball, 3-1/4" dia.
Caption: "Christmas – The Warmest, Brightest Season Of All" and "Christmas 1980."
☐ Purchased 19___ Pd $_______ MIB NB DB BNT
☐ Want Orig. Ret. $4.00 **NB** $12 **MIB** Sec. Mkt. **$20-$22**

QX 342-7 MERRY SANTA
Comments: Quilted Fabric
Reissued from 1979.
☐ Purchased 19___ Pd $_______ MIB NB DB BNT
☐ Want Orig. Ret. $2.00 Sec. Mkt. **$20-$22**

QX 203-4 MOTHER
Comments: White Satin Ball, 3-1/4" dia., Dated 1980
Large poinsettias and other Christmas flowers. Caption: "A Mother Has The Special Gift Of Giving Of Herself. Christmas 1980."
☐ Purchased 19___ Pd $_______ MIB NB DB BNT
☐ Want Orig. Ret. $4.00 **NB** $10 **MIB** Sec. Mkt. **$18-$20**

QX 304-1 MOTHER
Comments: Acrylic, 3-1/2" tall, Dated 1980
Heart-shaped with a ribbon tied floral border. Caption and date are stamped in silver foil: "Mother Is Another Word For Love. Christmas 1980."
☐ Purchased 19___ Pd $_______ MIB NB DB BNT
☐ Want Orig. Ret. $4.00 **NB** $25 **MIB** Sec. Mkt. **$35-$37**

QX 230-1 MOTHER & DAD
Comments: White Glass Ball, 3-1/4" dia.
Sprigs of holly and berries. Caption: "When Homes Are Decked With Holly And Hearts Are Feeling Glad, It's A Wonderful Time To Remember A Wonderful Mother And Dad. Christmas 1980."
☐ Purchased 19___ Pd $_______ MIB NB DB BNT
☐ Want Orig. Ret. $4.00 **NB** $12 **MIB** Sec. Mkt. **$15-$20**

QX 220-1 MUPPETS™
Comments: White Satin Ball, 3-1/4" dia.
Kermit waves a greeting on the front. The Muppets sing carols. Caption: "Merry Christmas 1980."
☐ Purchased 19___ Pd $_______ MIB NB DB BNT
☐ Want Orig. Ret. $4.00 **NB** $22 **MIB** Sec. Mkt. **$35-$40**

QX 225-4 NATIVITY
Comments: Gold Glass Ball, 3-1/4" dia.
Animals and birds draw near children in prayer at the manger. Caption: "Silent Night.. Holy Night..." and "Christmas 1980."
☐ Purchased 19___ Pd $_______ MIB NB DB BNT
☐ Want Orig. Ret. $4.00 **NB** $20 **MIB** Sec. Mkt. **$30-$32**

Husband of one collector: "I told her something had to be done; I simply could not afford any more Hallmark ornaments. So she got me a second job!"

QX 306-1 NORMAN ROCKWELL SERIES: SANTA'S VISITORS

Comments: ***FIRST IN SERIES***, Cameo, 3-3/8" dia.
Rockwell's famous drawing is reproduced in white relief on a soft green background. Caption: "Santa's Visitors. The Norman Rockwell Collection, Christmas 1980."

☐ Purchased 19___ Pd $_______ MIB NB DB BNT
☐ Want Orig. Ret. $6.50 **NB** $170 **MIB** Sec. Mkt. **$200-$220**

QX 216-1 PEANUTS®

Comments: White Satin Ball, 3-1/4" dia.; Christmas 1980
Snoopy sings as Woodstock and his friends portray verses from a Christmas carol. Caption: "Four Colly Birds... Three French Hens... And A Partridge In A Pear Tree."

☐ Purchased 19___ Pd $_______ MIB NB DB BNT
☐ Want Orig. Ret. $4.00 **NB** $20 **MIB** Sec. Mkt. **$25-$30**

QX 340-7 ROCKING HORSE, THE

Comments: Quilted Fabric
Reissued from 1979.

☐ Purchased 19___ Pd $_______ MIB NB DB BNT
☐ Want Orig. Ret. $2.00 Sec. Mkt. **$22-$25**

QX 146-1 SANTA 1980

Comments: Handcrafted, 4-5/32" tall, Dated 1980
Dough-look material. Santa is seen popping into the chimney of a mouse's home. The date is incorporated into the design.

☐ Purchased 19___ Pd $_______ MIB NB DB BNT
☐ Want Orig. Ret. $5.50 **NB** $75 **MIB** Sec. Mkt. **$95-$100**

QX 138-1 SANTA'S FLIGHT

Comments: Pressed Tin, 4" tall
Santa makes his deliveries in a blue and gold dirigible decorated with a green garland and red ribbon. The propeller twirls around. Caption: "Merry Christmas 1980." **Artist:** Linda Sickman

☐ Purchased 19___ Pd $_______ MIB NB DB BNT
☐ Want Orig. Ret. $5.50 **NB** $95 **MIB** Sec. Mkt. **$115-$125**

QX 223-4 SANTA'S WORKSHOP

Comments: White Satin Ball, 3-1/4" dia.
Santa adds a scarf to his usual costume and checks his list. Caption: "What Merriment Is All Around When Dear Old Santa Comes To Town" and "Christmas 1980."

☐ Purchased 19___ Pd $_______ MIB NB DB BNT
☐ Want Orig. Ret. $4.00 **NB** $15 **MIB** Sec. Mkt. **$22-$25**

QHD 925-4 SANTA'S WORKSHOP TABLETOP DECORATIONS

Comments: Handcrafted, 8" tall

☐ Purchased 19___ Pd $_______ MIB NB DB BNT
☐ Want Orig. Ret. $40.00 **NB** $125 **MIB** Sec. Mkt. **$180-$185**

QX 139-9 SKATING SNOWMAN, THE

Comments: Handcrafted, 4-1/4" tall
Reissued from 1979.
Artist: Donna Lee

☐ Purchased 19___ Pd $_______ MIB NB DB BNT
☐ Want 1980 Retail $5.50 **NB** $60 **MIB** Sec. Mkt. **$80-$85**

QX 154-1 SNOOPY AND FRIENDS SERIES: SNOOPY SKI HOLIDAY

Comments: **Second in Series,** Dated 1980
Handcrafted Panorama Ball, 3-1/4" dia. Snoopy, on skis, wears a red and green stocking cap and Woodstock rides in Snoopy' personalized feeding bowl. Several of this style ornament have been found with scratched surfaces. **Artist:** John Francis (Collin)

☐ Purchased 19___ Pd $_______ MIB NB DB BNT
☐ Want Orig. Ret. $9.00 **NB** $90 **MIB** Sec. Mkt. **$100-$105**

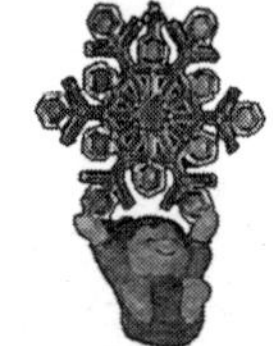

QX 133-4 SNOWFLAKE SWING, THE

Comments: Handcrafted, 3" tall
An angel swings from an acrylic snowflake.

☐ Purchased 19___ Pd $_______ MIB NB DB BNT
☐ Want Orig. Ret. $4.00 **NB** $35 **MIB** Sec. Mkt. **$45-$50**

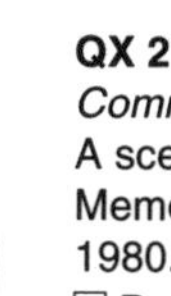

QX 211-4 SON

Comments: Gold Glass Ball, 3-1/4" dia.
A scene of a boy's favorite toys. Caption: "A Son Is... A Maker Of Memories, A Source Of Pride... A Son Is Love" and "Christmas 1980."

☐ Purchased 19___ Pd $_______ MIB NB DB BNT
☐ Want Orig. Ret. $4.00 **NB** $20 **MIB** Sec. Mkt. **$35-$38**

QX 341-9 STUFFED FULL STOCKING
Comments: Quilted Fabric
Reissued from 1979.
☐ Purchased 19___ Pd $_______ MIB NB DB BNT
☐ Want Orig. Ret. $2.00 Sec. Mkt. **$22-$27**

QX 209-4 TEACHER
Comments: White Satin Ball, 3-1/4" dia.
Kitten dressed in warm clothing is walking to school with a gift.
Back: He's placing the gift on the teacher's desk.
Caption: "Merry Christmas, Teacher" and "Christmas 1980."
☐ Purchased 19___ Pd $_______ MIB NB DB BNT
☐ Want Orig. Ret. $4.00 **NB** $10 **MIB** Sec. Mkt. **$16-$18**

QX 131-9 THIMBLE SERIES: A CHRISTMAS SALUTE
Comments: **Second in Series,** Handcrafted, 2-1/4" tall
Reissued from 1979.
☐ Purchased 19___ Pd $_______ MIB NB DB BNT
☐ Want 1980 Retail $4.00 **NB** $135 **MIB** Sec. Mkt. **$170-$175**

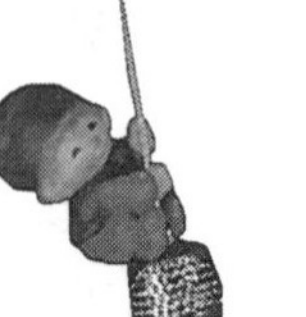

QX 132-1 THIMBLE SERIES: THIMBLE ELF
Comments: **Third in Series**, Handcrafted, 2-31/32" tall
Cute little elf dressed in red and green is swinging on a thimble "bell" which hangs from a golden rope.
☐ Purchased 19___ Pd $_______ MIB NB DB BNT
☐ Want Orig. Ret. $4.00 **NB** $125 **MIB** Sec. Mkt. **$178-$180**

QX 206-1 TWENTY-FIFTH CHRISTMAS TOGETHER
Comments: White Glass Ball, 3-1/4" dia., Dated 1980
Garlands, bells and ribbons frame the captions. "The Good Times Of The Present Blend With Memories Of The Past To Make Each Christmas Season Even Dearer Than The Last" and "25th Christmas Together 1980." A collector has reported this ball ornament being found without the date.
☐ Purchased 19___ Pd $_______ MIB NB DB BNT
☐ Want Orig. Ret. $4.00 **NB** $10 **MIB** Sec. Mkt. **$18-$20**

QX 162-1 YARN & FABRIC: ANGEL
Comments: Yarn with lace and felt accents, 5" tall
Reissued in 1981. This lovely blue angel with white wings, white pinafore and golden hair, holds a green wreath.
☐ Purchased 19___ Pd $_______ MIB NB DB BNT
☐ Want Orig. Ret. $3.00 Sec. Mkt. **$10-$12**

QX 161-4 YARN & FABRIC: SANTA
Comments: Yarn with lace and felt accents, 5" tall
Reissued in 1981. Santa with felt hat and boots.
☐ Purchased 19___ Pd $_______ MIB NB DB BNT
☐ Want Orig. Ret. $3.00 Sec. Mkt. **$10-$12**

QX 163-4 YARN & FABRIC: SNOWMAN
Comments: Yarn with lace and felt accents, 5" tall
Reissued in 1981. A happy, smiling snowman wears a holly-decorated black top hat and red and green plaid scarf.
☐ Purchased 19___ Pd $_______ MIB NB DB BNT
☐ Want Orig. Ret. $3.00 Sec. Mkt. **$10-$12**

QX 164-1 YARN & FABRIC: SOLDIER
Comments: Yarn with lace and felt accents, 5" tall
Reissued in 1981. This blue soldier is dressed with accents of red and green.
☐ Purchased 19___ Pd $_______ MIB NB DB BNT
☐ Want Orig. Ret. $3.00 Sec. Mkt. **$10-$12**

1981 Collection

QX 139-4 A HEAVENLY NAP
Comments: Handcrafted, 3-1/2" tall
Reissued from 1980.
Artist: Donna Lee
☐ Purchased 19___ Pd $_______ MIB NB DB BNT
☐ Want Orig. Ret. $6.50 **NB** $25 **MIB** Sec. Mkt. **$55-$60**

QX 154-7 A WELL-STOCKED STOCKING
Comments: Handcrafted, 4-1/2" tall
A red and white stocking is filled with toys including a doll, jack-in-the-box and others.
☐ Purchased 19___ Pd $_______ MIB NB DB BNT
☐ Want Orig. Ret. $9.00 **NB** $40 **MIB** Sec. Mkt. **$75-$80**

QX 139-6 ANGEL
Comments: Handcrafted, 2-15/16" tall
Reissued from 1978. Bread Dough Look.
Artist: Donna Lee
☐ Purchased 19___ Pd $_______ MIB NB DB BNT
☐ Want 1981 Retail $5.50 **NB** $70 **MIB** Sec. Mkt. **$90-$95**

QX 513-5 BABY'S FIRST CHRISTMAS
Comments: Lt. Green Cameo, 3-3/8" dia.
A large, gift-wrapped box, rocking horse on wheels and toys. Caption: "Baby's First Christmas 1981" and "A Baby Adds A Special Joy To All The Joys Of Christmas."
☐ Purchased 19___ Pd $_______ MIB NB DB BNT
☐ Want Orig. Ret. $8.50 **NB** $9 **MIB** Sec. Mkt. **$16-$18**

QX 440-2 BABY'S FIRST CHRISTMAS
Comments: Handcrafted, 3-3/4" long
Baby is in a "wicker" carriage. The wheels roll and the caption is on the fabric blanket: "Baby's First Christmas, 1981."
☐ Purchased 19___ Pd $_______ MIB NB DB BNT
☐ Want Orig. Ret. $13.00 **NB** $40 **MIB** Sec. Mkt. **$50-$55**

QX 516-2 BABY'S FIRST CHRISTMAS
Comments: Acrylic, 4" dia., Dated 1981
The wreath frames a photograph opening. Caption: "Baby's First Christmas."
☐ Purchased 19___ Pd $_______ MIB NB DB BNT
☐ Want Orig. Ret. $5.50 **NB** $20 **MIB** Sec. Mkt. **$30-$32**

QX 602-2 BABY'S FIRST CHRISTMAS - BLACK
Comments: Ecru Soft-Sheen Satin Ball, 3-1/4" dia.
A baby with his toys is playing peekaboo. Caption: "Baby's First Christmas 1981" and "A Baby Is A Gift Of Joy, A Gift Of Love At Christmas.
☐ Purchased 19___ Pd $_______ MIB NB DB BNT
☐ Want Orig. Ret. $4.50 **NB** $10 **MIB** Sec. Mkt. **$22-$25**

QX 601-5 BABY'S FIRST CHRISTMAS - BOY
Comments: White Satin Ball, 3-1/4" dia.
Caption: "Baby's First Christmas 1981" and "There's Nothing Like A Baby Boy To Bring A World Of Special Joy At Christmas."
☐ Purchased 19___ Pd $_______ MIB NB DB BNT
☐ Want Orig. Ret. $4.50 **NB** $10 **MIB** Sec. Mkt. **$18-$25**

QX 600-2 BABY'S FIRST CHRISTMAS - GIRL
Comments: White Satin Ball, 3-1/4" dia.
Caption: "Baby's First Christmas 1981" and "There's Nothing Like A Baby Girl To Cheer And Brighten All The World At Christmas."
☐ Purchased 19___ Pd $_______ MIB NB DB BNT
☐ Want Orig. Ret. $4.50 **NB** $12 **MIB** Sec. Mkt. **$22-$25**

QX 441-5 BELLRINGER SERIIIES: SWINGIN' BELLRINGER
Comments: **Third in Series,** Handcrafted, 4" tall
Dated 1981. A mouse swings on the candy cane clapper of this gold-rimmed bell.
☐ Purchased 19___ Pd $_______ MIB NB DB BNT
☐ Want Orig. Ret. $15.00 **NB** $65 **MIB** Sec. Mkt. **$95-$100**

QX 802-2 BETSEY CLARK SERIES
Comments: **Ninth in Series,** White Glass Ball, 3-1/4" dia.
A little girl leaves a gift for her friend. Back: She pulls a gift-filled sleigh. Caption: "Christmas 1981" and "The Greatest Joy Of Christmas Day Comes From The Joy We Give Away."
☐ Purchased 19___ Pd $_______ MIB NB DB BNT
☐ Want Orig. Ret. $4.50 **NB** $18 **MIB** Sec. Mkt. **$30-$35**

QX 423-5 BETSEY CLARK
Comments: Handcrafted, 3-9/32" tall
Betsey and a fawn look at a tree topped with a brilliant star.
Artist: John Francis (Collin)
☐ Purchased 19___ Pd $_______ MIB NB DB BNT
☐ Want Orig. Ret. $9.00 **NB** $45 **MIB** Sec. Mkt. **$75-$78**

QX 512-2 BETSEY CLARK BLUE CAMEO
Comments: Cameo, 3-3/8" dia.
A little girl pets a fawn. Caption: "Christmas, When Hearts Reach Out To Give And Receive The Gentle Gifts Of Love" and "Christmas 1981."
☐ Purchased 19___ Pd $_______ MIB NB DB BNT
☐ Want Orig. Ret. $8.50 **NB** $20 **MIB** Sec. Mkt. **$28-$30**

QX 403-5 CALICO KITTY
Comments: Sewn Fabric, 3" tall
Yellow Christmas fabric kitty has red bow.
☐ Purchased 19___ Pd $_______ MIB NB DB BNT
☐ Want Orig. Ret. $3.00 Sec. Mkt. **$18-$22**

QX 418-2 CANDYVILLE EXPRESS
Comments: Handcrafted, 3" long
Locomotive appears as if it has been crafted from gumdrops, cookies and licorice. Easily found Mint in Box.
☐ Purchased 19___ Pd $_______ MIB NB DB BNT
☐ Want Orig. Ret. $7.50 **NB** $75 **MIB** Sec. Mkt. **$90-$100**

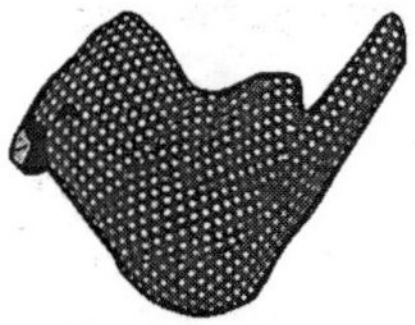

QX 400-2 CARDINAL CUTIE
Comments: Sewn Fabric, 3" tall
Red fabric with white dots.
☐ Purchased 19___ Pd $_______ MIB NB DB BNT
☐ Want Orig. Ret. $3.00 Sec. Mkt. **$22-$25**

QX 427-5 CARROUSEL SERIES: SKATERS CARROUSEL
Comments: **Fourth in Series**, Handcrafted, 2-15/32" tall
A family of four ice skates around a green pole. Date "1981" stamped on the top of roof.
☐ Purchased 19___ Pd $_______ MIB NB DB BNT
☐ Want Orig. Ret. $9.00 **NB** $75 **MIB** Sec. Mkt. **$90-$95**

QX 158-4 CHECKING IT TWICE
Comments: Special Edition, Handcrafted, 5-15/16" tall
Reissued from 1980.
Artist: Thomas Blackshear
☐ Purchased 19___ Pd $_______ MIB NB DB BNT
☐ Want 1981 Ret. $22.50 **NB** $155 **MIB** Sec. Mkt. **$195-$200**

QX 809-5 CHRISTMAS 1981 - SCHNEEBERG
Comments: White Satin Ball, 3-1/4" dia., Dated 1981
Schneeberg collage of a Christmas tree and sunburst of beads and colored glass.
☐ Purchased 19___ Pd $_______ MIB NB DB BNT
☐ Want Orig. Ret. $4.50 **NB** $10 **MIB** Sec. Mkt. **$22-$24**

Front

Back

QX 437-5 CHRISTMAS DREAMS
Comments: Handcrafted Panorama Ball, 3-1/4" dia.
Little boy looks through a toy shop window. Caption: "Toy Shop 1981." **Artist:** Donna Lee
☐ Purchased 19___ Pd $_______ MIB NB DB BNT
☐ Want Orig. Ret. $12.00 **NB** $195 **MIB** Sec. Mkt. **$225-$230**

QX 155-4 CHRISTMAS FANTASY
Comments: Handcrafted, 3-3/4" long, Reissued in 1982
An elf rides a white goose with a real brass ribbon in its bill.
☐ Purchased 19___ Pd $_______ MIB NB DB BNT
☐ Want Orig. Ret. $13.00 **NB** $60 **MIB** Sec. Mkt. **$85-$88**

QX 813-5 CHRISTMAS IN THE FOREST
Comments: White Glass Ball, 3-1/4" dia., Dated 1981. RARE!
Caption: "Softly... Gently... Joyfully... Christmas Arrives In The Heart" and "Christmas 1981." Big price increase in '95.
☐ Purchased 19___ Pd $_______ MIB NB DB BNT
☐ Want Orig. Ret. $4.50 **NB** $80 **MIB** Sec. Mkt. **$145-$150**

QX 810-2 CHRISTMAS MAGIC
Comments: White Satin Ball, 3-1/4" dia., Dated 1981
A gnome-like Santa ice skates with the animals. Caption: "Christmas 1981" and "It's Here, There, Everywhere... Christmas Magic's In The Air."
☐ Purchased 19___ Pd $_______ MIB NB DB BNT
☐ Want Orig. Ret. $4.50 **NB** $12 **MIB** Sec. Mkt. **$22-$25**

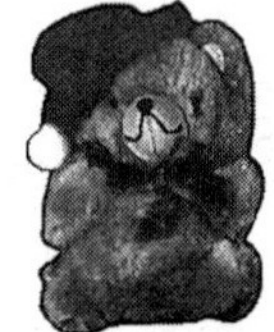

QX 404-2 CHRISTMAS TEDDY
Comments: Plush, 4" tall, packed in gift box
Cute little teddy with a green/red plaid bow and red stocking cap.
☐ Purchased 19___ Pd $_______ MIB NB DB BNT
☐ Want Orig. Ret. $5.50 **NB** $15 **MIB** Sec. Mkt. **$18-$20**

QX 507-5 CROWN CLASSICS COLLECTION: ANGEL
Comments: Acrylic, 3-3/4" tall, stained glass look
Golden-haired angel with white wings.
☐ Purchased 19___ Pd $_______ MIB NB DB BNT
☐ Want Orig. Ret. $4.50 **NB** $20 **MIB** Sec. Mkt. **$25-$28**

QX 515-5 CROWN CLASSICS COLLECTION: TREE PHOTOHOLDER
Comments: Acrylic, 3-27/32" tall, Dated 1981
Decorated tree has opening for photo. Caption: "Christmas 1981."
☐ Purchased 19___ Pd $_______ MIB NB DB BNT
☐ Want Orig. Ret. $5.50 **NB** $16 **MIB** Sec. Mkt. **$22-$25**

QX 516-5 CROWN CLASSICS COLLECTION: UNICORN
Comments: Cameo, 3-3/8" dia., Dated 1981
White unicorn on light green background. Caption: "A Time Of Magical Moments, Dreams Come True... Christmas 1981."
☐ Purchased 19___ Pd $_______ MIB NB DB BNT
☐ Want Orig. Ret. $8.50 **NB** $15 **MIB** Sec. Mkt. **$22-$25**

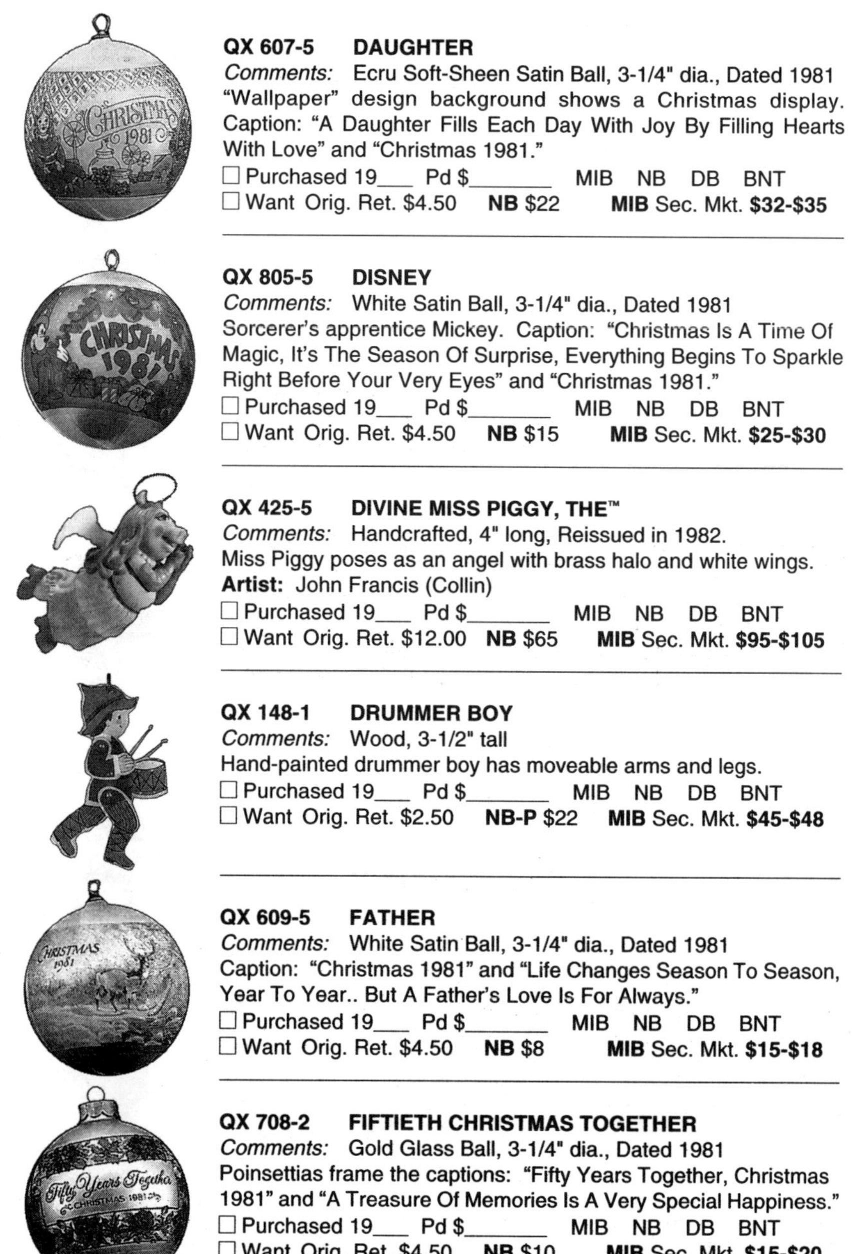

QX 607-5 DAUGHTER
Comments: Ecru Soft-Sheen Satin Ball, 3-1/4" dia., Dated 1981
"Wallpaper" design background shows a Christmas display. Caption: "A Daughter Fills Each Day With Joy By Filling Hearts With Love" and "Christmas 1981."
☐ Purchased 19___ Pd $_______ MIB NB DB BNT
☐ Want Orig. Ret. $4.50 **NB** $22 **MIB** Sec. Mkt. **$32-$35**

QX 805-5 DISNEY
Comments: White Satin Ball, 3-1/4" dia., Dated 1981
Sorcerer's apprentice Mickey. Caption: "Christmas Is A Time Of Magic, It's The Season Of Surprise, Everything Begins To Sparkle Right Before Your Very Eyes" and "Christmas 1981."
☐ Purchased 19___ Pd $_______ MIB NB DB BNT
☐ Want Orig. Ret. $4.50 **NB** $15 **MIB** Sec. Mkt. **$25-$30**

QX 425-5 DIVINE MISS PIGGY, THE™
Comments: Handcrafted, 4" long, Reissued in 1982.
Miss Piggy poses as an angel with brass halo and white wings.
Artist: John Francis (Collin)
☐ Purchased 19___ Pd $_______ MIB NB DB BNT
☐ Want Orig. Ret. $12.00 **NB** $65 **MIB** Sec. Mkt. **$95-$105**

QX 148-1 DRUMMER BOY
Comments: Wood, 3-1/2" tall
Hand-painted drummer boy has moveable arms and legs.
☐ Purchased 19___ Pd $_______ MIB NB DB BNT
☐ Want Orig. Ret. $2.50 **NB-P** $22 **MIB** Sec. Mkt. **$45-$48**

QX 609-5 FATHER
Comments: White Satin Ball, 3-1/4" dia., Dated 1981
Caption: "Christmas 1981" and "Life Changes Season To Season, Year To Year.. But A Father's Love Is For Always."
☐ Purchased 19___ Pd $_______ MIB NB DB BNT
☐ Want Orig. Ret. $4.50 **NB** $8 **MIB** Sec. Mkt. **$15-$18**

QX 708-2 FIFTIETH CHRISTMAS TOGETHER
Comments: Gold Glass Ball, 3-1/4" dia., Dated 1981
Poinsettias frame the captions: "Fifty Years Together, Christmas 1981" and "A Treasure Of Memories Is A Very Special Happiness."
☐ Purchased 19___ Pd $_______ MIB NB DB BNT
☐ Want Orig. Ret. $4.50 **NB** $10 **MIB** Sec. Mkt. **$15-$20**

Let your Hallmark dealer know of your wish list for new ornaments.
Most keep a customer wish list and will call you when the ornaments arrive.

QX 706-2 FIRST CHRISTMAS TOGETHER
Comments: Chrome Glass Ball, 3-1/4" dia., Dated 1981
An 1800s couple ice skates against a red background. Caption: "First Christmas Together 1981" and "Christmas... The Season For Sharing The Spirit Of Love."
☐ Purchased 19___ Pd $_______ MIB NB DB BNT
☐ Want Orig. Ret. $4.50 **NB** $12 **MIB** Sec. Mkt. **$24-$28**

QX 505-5 FIRST CHRISTMAS TOGETHER
Comments: Acrylic, 3" tall, Dated 1981
Caption stamped in gold foil: "First Christmas Together 1981."
☐ Purchased 19___ Pd $_______ MIB NB DB BNT
☐ Want Orig. Ret. $5.50 **NB** $10 **MIB** Sec. Mkt. **$20-$21**

QX 434-2 FRIENDLY FIDDLER, THE
Comments: Handcrafted, 3-5/32" tall
A rabbit wearing a red and green scarf fiddles a Christmas tune.
Artist: Donna Lee
☐ Purchased 19___ Pd $_______ MIB NB DB BNT
☐ Want Orig. Ret. $8.00 **NB** $55 **MIB** Sec. Mkt. **$75-$80**

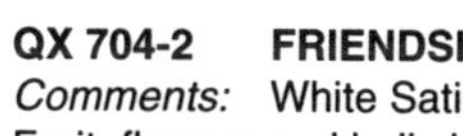

QX 704-2 FRIENDSHIP
Comments: White Satin Ball, 3-1/4" dia., Dated 1981
Fruit, flowers and holly border the caption: "The Beauty Of Friendship Never Ends" and "Christmas 1981."
☐ Purchased 19___ Pd $_______ MIB NB DB BNT
☐ Want Orig. Ret. $4.50 **NB** $10 **MIB** Sec. Mkt. **$15-$18**

QX 503-5 FRIENDSHIP
Comments: Acrylic, 3-1/4" dia., Dated 1981
A squirrel and bird sing a duet. Caption: "Friends Put The "Merry" In Christmas."
☐ Purchased 19___ Pd $_______ MIB NB DB BNT
☐ Want Orig. Ret. $5.50 **NB** $17 **MIB** Sec. Mkt. **$30-$35**

QX 509-5 FROSTED IMAGES: ANGEL
Comments: Look of Etched Crystal, 1-15/32" – 1-19/32" tall
Three-dimensional Angel has its hands folded.
☐ Purchased 19___ Pd $_______ MIB NB DB BNT
☐ Want Orig. Ret. $4.00 **NB** $40 **MIB** Sec. Mkt. **$50-$55**

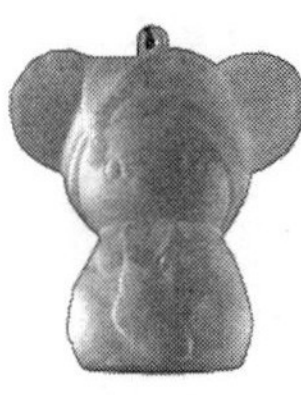

QX 508-2 FROSTED IMAGES: MOUSE
Comments: Look of Etched Crystal, 1-15/32" – 1-19/32" tall
Three-dimensional Mouse holds a stocking.
☐ Purchased 19___ Pd $_______ MIB NB DB BNT
☐ Want Orig. Ret. $4.00 **NB** $15 **MIB** Sec. Mkt. **$22-$24**

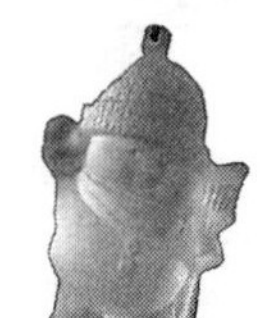

QX 510-2 FROSTED IMAGES: SNOWMAN
Comments: Look of Etched Crystal, 1-15/32" – 1-19/32" tall
Three-dimensional Snowman is waving.
☐ Purchased 19___ Pd $_______ MIB NB DB BNT
☐ Want Orig. Ret. $4.00 **NB** $16 **MIB** Sec. Mkt. **$22-$24**

QX 433-5 FROSTY FRIENDS
Comments: **Second in Series**, Handcrafted, 2" tall
Dated 1981. An Eskimo and Husky puppy sit snugly in an igloo.
☐ Purchased 19___ Pd $_______ MIB NB DB BNT
☐ Want Orig. Ret. $8.00 **NB** $295 **MIB** Sec. Mkt. **$400-$410**

QX 705-5 GIFT OF LOVE, THE
Comments: Gold Glass Ball, 3-1/4" dia., Dated 1981
Red roses and holly frame the date and caption: "Christmas 1981" and "Love Is A Precious Gift, Priceless And Perfect, Cherished Above All Life's Treasures."
☐ Purchased 19___ Pd $_______ MIB NB DB BNT
☐ Want Orig. Ret. $4.50 **NB** $10 **MIB** Sec. Mkt. **$22-$24**

QX 402-2 GINGHAM DOG
Comments: Sewn Fabric, 3" tall
Cute blue/white gingham dog has a red bow.
☐ Purchased 19___ Pd $_______ MIB NB DB BNT
☐ Want Orig. Ret. $3.00 Sec. Mkt. **$18-$20**

QX 603-5 GODCHILD
Comments: White Satin Ball, 3-1/4" dia.
An angel and puppy on a cloud are placing stars in a bag.
Caption: "Christmas 1981" and "For A Special Godchild."
☐ Purchased 19___ Pd $_______ MIB NB DB BNT
☐ Want Orig. Ret. $4.50 **NB** $8 **MIB** Sec. Mkt. **$14-$18**

QX 605-5 GRANDDAUGHTER
Comments: White Satin Ball, 3-1/4" dia., Dated 1981
A white rocking horse and toys are featured. Caption: "A Granddaughter Adds A Magical Touch To The Beauty And Joy Of Christmas."
☐ Purchased 19___ Pd $_______ MIB NB DB BNT
☐ Want Orig. Ret. $4.50 **NB** $14 **MIB** Sec. Mkt. **$24-$28**

QX 701-5 GRANDFATHER
Comments: Gold Glass Ball, 3-1/4" dia.
The caption in red and gold is bordered by sprigs of holly: "Grandfather Holds A Special Place In The Heart" and "Christmas 1981."
☐ Purchased 19___ Pd $_______ MIB NB DB BNT
☐ Want Orig. Ret. $4.50 **NB** $10 **MIB** Sec. Mkt. **$15-$18**

QX 702-2 GRANDMOTHER
Comments: Ecru Soft-Sheen Satin Ball, 3-1/4" dia.
Caption: "Christmas 1981" and "A Grandmother Is So Loving And Dear At Christmas And Throughout The Year."
☐ Purchased 19___ Pd $_______ MIB NB DB BNT
☐ Want Orig. Ret. $4.50 **NB** $12 **MIB** Sec. Mkt. **$15-$18**

QX 703-5 GRANDPARENTS
Comments: White Glass Ball, 3-1/4" dia., Dated 1981
Caption: "Grandparents Give The Gift Of Love At Christmas And All Year 'Round."
☐ Purchased 19___ Pd $_______ MIB NB DB BNT
☐ Want Orig. Ret. $4.50 **NB** $10 **MIB** Sec. Mkt. **$15-$18**

QX 604-2 GRANDSON
Comments: White Satin Ball, 3-1/4" dia.
Santa and reindeer are making toys. Caption: "A Grandson Makes The 'Holly Days' Extra Bright And Jolly Days" and "Christmas 1981."
☐ Purchased 19___ Pd $_______ MIB NB DB BNT
☐ Want Orig. Ret. $4.50 **NB** $12 **MIB** Sec. Mkt. **$24-$28**

QX 438-2 HERE COMES SANTA SERIES: ROOFTOP DELIVERIES
Comments: **Third in Series,** Handcrafted, 4-1/16" tall
Resembles an old milk truck. Caption: "1981 S. Claus & Co. Rooftop Deliveries."
☐ Purchased 19___ Pd $_______ MIB NB DB BNT
☐ Want Orig. Ret. $13.00 **NB** $230 **MIB** Sec. Mkt. **$295-$300**

QX 136-1 HOLIDAY CHIMES: SANTA MOBILE
Comments: Chrome Plated
Reissued from 1980.
☐ Purchased 19___ Pd $_______ MIB NB DB BNT
☐ Want Orig. Ret. $5.50 **NB-P** $35 **MIB** Sec. Mkt. **$42-$48**

QX 445-5 HOLIDAY CHIMES: SNOWMAN CHIMES
Comments: Chrome Plate, 4" tall
Mr. and Mrs. Snowman and Snowchild are suspended from a large snowflake.
☐ Purchased 19___ Pd $_______ MIB NB DB BNT
☐ Want Orig. Ret. $5.50 **MIB** Sec. Mkt. **$25-$28**

QX 165-4 HOLIDAY CHIMES: SNOWFLAKE CHIMES
Comments: Chrome Plate
Reissued from 1980.
Artist: Linda Sickman
☐ Purchased 19___ Pd $_______ MIB NB DB BNT
☐ Want Orig. Ret. $5.50 **NB** $15 **MIB** Sec. Mkt. **$22-$28**

QX 501-5 HOLIDAY HIGHLIGHTS: CHRISTMAS STAR
Comments: Clear Acrylic, 3-1/2" tall, Dated 1981
Star with raised, faceted border has emerald shapes between the points. Caption stamped in silver foil: "Christmas 1981."
☐ Purchased 19___ Pd $_______ MIB NB DB BNT
☐ Want Orig. Ret. $5.50 **NB** $15 **MIB** Sec. Mkt. **$22-$25**

QX 500-2 HOLIDAY HIGHLIGHTS: SHEPHERD SCENE
Comments: Clear Acrylic, 4" tall
A shepherd and his sheep watch the star over Bethlehem.
☐ Purchased 19___ Pd $_______ MIB NB DB BNT
☐ Want Orig. Ret. $5.50 **NB** $15 **MIB** Sec. Mkt. **$24-$28**

QX 709-5 HOME
Comments: White Satin Ball, 3-1/4" dia., Dated 1981
Victorian winter village scene. Caption: "Christmas 1981" and "Love In The Home Puts Joy In The Heart."
☐ Purchased 19___ Pd $_______ MIB NB DB BNT
☐ Want Orig. Ret. $4.50 **NB** $14 **MIB** Sec. Mkt. **$18-$20**

QX 431-5 ICE FAIRY
Comments: Acrylic & Handcrafted, 4-1/8" tall
A white frosted ice fairy with acrylic wings holds a clear acrylic snowflake. **Artist:** Donna Lee
☐ Purchased 19___ Pd $_______ MIB NB DB BNT
☐ Want Orig. Ret. $6.50 **NB** $45 **MIB** Sec. Mkt. **$85-$95**

QX 432-2 ICE SCULPTOR, THE
Comments: Handcrafted, 3-1/32" tall
A bear artist sculpts his self portrait in ice (clear acrylic).
Artist: Donna Lee
☐ Purchased 19___ Pd $_______ MIB NB DB BNT
☐ Want Orig. Ret. $8.00 **NB** $80 **MIB** Sec. Mkt. **$90-$98**

QX 804-2 JOAN WALSH ANGLUND©
Comments: White Satin Ball, 3-1/4" dia.
Three children read a book together then decorate the stair rail. Caption: " 'Tis The Time Of Dreams Come True. 'Tis The Time For Merrymaking" and "Christmas 1981."
☐ Purchased 19___ Pd $_______ MIB NB DB BNT
☐ Want Orig. Ret. $4.50 **NB** $15 **MIB** Sec. Mkt. **$20-$25**

QX 424-2 KERMIT the FROG™
Comments: Handcrafted, 3-11/32" long
Kermit, in a red stocking cap, rides his sled.
Artist: John Francis (Collin)
☐ Purchased 19___ Pd $_______ MIB NB DB BNT
☐ Want Orig. Ret. $9.00 **NB** $85 **MIB** Sec. Mkt. **$95-$110**

QX 811-5 LET US ADORE HIM
Comments: Gold Glass Ball, 3-1/4" dia.
Cherubs adore the Christ child in this lovely ball. Caption: "Christmas 1981" and "O Come Let Us Adore Him."
☐ Purchased 19___ Pd $_______ MIB NB DB BNT
☐ Want Orig. Ret. $4.50 **NB** $35 **MIB** Sec. Mkt. **$55-$60**

QX 408-2 LITTLE TRIMMERS: CLOTHESPIN DRUMMER BOY
Comments: Handcrafted, 2-13/16" tall
Drummer boy in black and brown beats a red drum.
☐ Purchased 19___ Pd $_______ MIB NB DB BNT
☐ Want Orig. Ret. $4.50 **NB** $35 **MIB** Sec. Mkt. **$45-$50**

QX 407-5 LITTLE TRIMMERS: JOLLY SNOWMAN
Comments: Handcrafted, 2-7/32" tall
Smiling snowman wears a black top hat and a fabric scarf.
☐ Purchased 19___ Pd $_______ MIB NB DB BNT
☐ Want Orig. Ret. $3.50 **NB** $30 **MIB** Sec. Mkt. **$52-$58**

QX 409-5 LITTLE TRIMMERS: PERKY PENGUIN
Comments: Handcrafted, 1-5/16" tall, Reissued in 1982.
Cute little penguin wears a red stocking cap and green and red striped scarf.
☐ Purchased 19___ Pd $_______ MIB NB DB BNT
☐ Want Orig. Ret. $3.50 **NB** $50 **MIB** Sec. Mkt. **$55-$62**

QX 406-2 LITTLE TRIMMERS: PUPPY LOVE
Comments: Handcrafted, 1-5/32" tall, bread dough look
This tan puppy has a red cord around his neck and a red heart on his chest.
☐ Purchased 19___ Pd $_______ MIB NB DB BNT
☐ Want Orig. Ret. $3.50 **NB** $26 **MIB** Sec. Mkt. **$38-$42**

QX 412-2 LITTLE TRIMMERS: STOCKING MOUSE, THE
Comments: Handcrafted, 2-1/4" tall
A little white mouse with a white and blue night cap peeks out of a red and green striped stocking.
☐ Purchased 19___ Pd $_______ MIB NB DB BNT
☐ Want Orig. Ret. $4.50 **NB** $85 **MIB** Sec. Mkt. **$98-$110**

QX 502-2 LOVE
Comments: Acrylic, 3-1/2" tall
Heart has silver foil caption in center. "Love... The Nicest Gift Of All. Christmas 1981."
☐ Purchased 19___ Pd $_______ MIB NB DB BNT
☐ Want Orig. Ret. $5.50 **NB** $40 **MIB** Sec. Mkt. **$45-$50**

QX 425-2 LOVE AND JOY (PORCELAIN CHIMES)
Comments: Porcelain, 3-3/4" tall, Dated 1981
Three white doves are suspended from a while porcelain heart tied in red fabric ribbon. Caption: "Love and Joy."
☐ Purchased 19___ Pd $_______ MIB NB DB BNT
☐ Want Orig. Ret. $9.00 **NB** $80 **MIB** Sec. Mkt. **$90-$95**

QX 808-2 MARTY LINKS
Comments: White Satin Ball, 3-1/4" dia.
Two children carry a large candy cane while another little girl holds mistletoe over her head. Caption: "Christmas 1981" and "Happy Hearts And Good Times Go Hand In Hand At Christmas."
☐ Purchased 19___ Pd $_______ MIB NB DB BNT
☐ Want Orig. Ret. $4.50 **NB** $12 **MIB** Sec. Mkt. **$18-$20**

QX 806-2 MARY HAMILTON
Comments: White Glass Ball, 3-1/4" dia.
Little angels take part in various activities. Caption: "Christmas 1981" and "Christmas Decorates The World With Wonder."
☐ Purchased 19___ Pd $_______ MIB NB DB BNT
☐ Want Orig. Ret. $4.50 **NB** $12 **MIB** Sec. Mkt. **$18-$22**

QX 814-2 MERRY CHRISTMAS
Comments: Gold Glass Ball, 3-1/4" dia., Dated 1981
A burgundy diamond design on a green background frames the date. Caption: "Merry Christmas" is framed in same design, colors reversed.
☐ Purchased 19___ Pd $_______ MIB NB DB BNT
☐ Want Orig. Ret. $4.50 **NB** $10 **MIB** Sec. Mkt. **$15-$20**

QX 608-2 MOTHER
Comments: White Satin Ball, 3-1/4" dia., Dated 1981
Red roses and Christmas greenery. Caption: "Christmas 1981" and "In A Mother's Heart There Is Love...The Very Heart Of Christmas."
☐ Purchased 19___ Pd $_______ MIB NB DB BNT
☐ Want Orig. Ret. $4.50 **NB** $12 **MIB** Sec. Mkt. **$15-$18**

QX 700-2 MOTHER AND DAD
Comments: Ecru Soft-Sheen Satin Ball, 3-1/4" dia., Dated 1981
Caption: "For Mother And Dad, Christmas 1981." and "The Wonderful Meaning Of Christmas Is Found In The Circle Of Family Love."
☐ Purchased 19___ Pd $_______ MIB NB DB BNT
☐ Want Orig. Ret. $4.50 **NB** $8 **MIB** Sec. Mkt. **$12-$14**

QX 448-5 MR. & MRS. CLAUS
Comments: 3-1/2" tall, Handcrafted
Boxed set of two ornaments. Originally issued in individual boxes in 1975 as Adorable Adornments: "Mrs. Santa" and "Santa." The only way to tell the difference is if you have the original packaging.
☐ Purchased 19___ Pd $_______ MIB NB DB BNT
☐ Want Orig. Ret. $12.00 **NB** $135 pr.
MIB Sec. Mkt. **$510 - $560 pr.**

QX 807-5 MUPPETS™
Comments: White Satin Ball, 3-1/4" dia., Dated 1981
Kermit "Santa" starts down the chimney; Miss Piggy awaits his visit. Caption: "Let's Hear It For Christmas" and "Let's Hear It For Santa."
☐ Purchased 19___ Pd $_______ MIB NB DB BNT
☐ Want Orig. Ret. $4.50 **NB** $25 **MIB** Sec. Mkt. **$30-$38**

QX 511-5 NORMAN ROCKWELL SERIES: CAROLERS
Comments: **Second in Series**, Cameo, 3-3/8" dia.
Rockwell's "Carolers" are depicted on dark blue background. Caption: "Carolers, Second In A Series, The Norman Rockwell Collection Christmas 1981."
☐ Purchased 19___ Pd $_______ MIB NB DB BNT
☐ Want Orig. Ret. $8.50 **NB** $25 **MIB** Sec. Mkt. **$45-$50**

QX 803-5 PEANUTS™
Comments: White Satin Ball, 3-1/4" dia.
Snoopy, Woodstock and friends sing. Caption: "Deck The Halls With Boughs Of Holly... Christmas 1981."
☐ Purchased 19___ Pd $_______ MIB NB DB BNT
☐ Want Orig. Ret. $4.50 **NB** $20 **MIB** Sec. Mkt. **$25-$30**

QX 401-5 PEPPERMINT MOUSE
Comments: Sewn Fabric, 3" tall
White mouse with red/white striped clothes.
☐ Purchased 19___ Pd $_______ MIB NB DB BNT
☐ Want Orig. Ret. $3.00 **NB** $20 **MIB** Sec. Mkt. **$25-$30**

QX 405-5 RACCOON TUNES
Comments: Plush, 4" tall
Raccoon caroler wears a felt vest and holds a felt song book.
☐ Purchased 19___ Pd $_______ MIB NB DB BNT
☐ Want Orig. Ret. $5.50 **NB** $15 **MIB** Sec. Mkt. **$18-$22**

QX 422-2 ROCKING HORSE
Comments: ***FIRST IN SERIES***, Handcrafted 2" tall, Dated 1981
Brown/white palomino horse on red rockers. Very much sought after.
Artist: Linda Sickman
☐ Purchased 19___ Pd $_______ MIB NB DB BNT
☐ Want Orig. Ret. $9.00 **NB** $550 **MIB** Sec. Mkt. **$625-$650**

QX 439-5 SAILING SANTA
Comments: Handcrafted, 5" tall, Dated 1981
Santa sails away in a red hot air balloon.
Caption: "Merry Christmas 1981."
☐ Purchased 19___ Pd $_______ MIB NB DB BNT
☐ Want Orig. Ret. $13.00 **NB** $175 **MIB** Sec. Mkt. **$225-$235**

QX 812-2 SANTA'S COMING
Comments: White Satin Ball, 3-1/4" dia., Dated 1981
Mrs. Santa makes sure Santa is ready for his trip and reindeer fly through a moonlit night. Caption: "Christmas 1981" and "Hustle, Bustle, Hurry, Scurry, Santa's Coming.. Never Worry."
☐ Purchased 19___ Pd $_______ MIB NB DB BNT
☐ Want Orig. Ret. $4.50 **NB** $16 **MIB** Sec. Mkt. **$24-$28**

QX 815-5 SANTA'S SURPRISE
Comments: White Satin Ball, 3-1/4" dia., Dated 1981
Santa uses the stars from the sky to decorate a small evergreen. Caption: "Twinkle, Glimmer, Sparkle, Shimmer... Let The Christmas Season Shine" and "Christmas 1981."
☐ Purchased 19___ Pd $_______ MIB NB DB BNT
☐ Want Orig. Ret. $4.50 **NB** $14 **MIB** Sec. Mkt. **$22-$25**

QX 436-2 SNOOPY AND FRIENDS
Comments: **Third in Series,** Handcrafted Panorama Ball 3-1/4" dia. Dated 1981. A "birdsled" pulls Snoopy past a snow Snoopy. **Artist:** John Francis (Collin)
☐ Purchased 19___ Pd $_______ MIB NB DB BNT
☐ Want Orig. Ret. $12.00 **NB** $65 **MIB** Sec. Mkt. **$95-$100**

QX 606-2 SON
Comments: White Satin Ball, 3-1/4" dia., Dated 1981
A variety of Christmas scenes are shown in various colored squares. Caption: "Christmas 1981" and "A Son Puts The Merry In Christmas."
☐ Purchased 19___ Pd $_______ MIB NB DB BNT
☐ Want Orig. Ret. $4.50 **NB** $14 **MIB** Sec. Mkt. **$28-$30**

QX 430-2 SPACE SANTA
Comments: Handcrafted, 3" tall, Dated 1981
Santa flies in a silver space suit.
☐ Purchased 19___ Pd $_______ MIB NB DB BNT
☐ Want Orig. Ret. $6.50 **NB** $85 **MIB** Sec. Mkt. **$105-$110**

QX 446-2 ST. NICHOLAS
Comments: Pressed Tin, 4-3/8" tall
Traditional European St. Nicholas carries a lantern to light his way.
Artist: Linda Sickman
☐ Purchased 19___ Pd $_______ MIB NB DB BNT
☐ Want Orig. Ret. $5.50 **NB-P** $38 **MIB** Sec. Mkt. **$45-$52**

QX 421-5 STAR SWING
Comments: Brass & Handcrafted, 3-5/8" tall, Dated 1981
A little girl swings from a chrome-plated brass star.
Artist: Linda Sickman
☐ Purchased 19___ Pd $_______ MIB NB DB BNT
☐ Want Orig. Ret. $5.50 **NB** $25 **MIB** Sec. Mkt. **$30-$32**

QX 800-2 TEACHER
Comments: White Satin Ball, 3-1/4" dia., Dated 1981
Multi-colored stocking in white oval, red background. Caption: "For A Special Teacher 1981."
☐ Purchased 19___ Pd $_______ MIB NB DB BNT
☐ Want Orig. Ret. $4.50 **NB** $8 **MIB** Sec. Mkt. **$14-$16**

QX 413-5 THIMBLE SERIES: ANGEL
Comments: **Fourth in Series**, Handcrafted, 1-1/2" dia.
Flying angel with white wings carries a tree that is potted in a thimble. HARD TO FIND!
☐ Purchased 19___ Pd $_______ MIB NB DB BNT
☐ Want Orig. Ret. $4.50 **NB** $90 **MIB** Sec. Mkt. **$140-$150**

QX 429-5 TOPSY-TURVY TUNES
Comments: Handcrafted, 3" tall
An opossum hangs by his tail while a redbird sits on his book of Carols. **Artist:** Donna Lee
☐ Purchased 19___ Pd $_______ MIB NB DB BNT
☐ Want Orig. Ret. $7.50 **NB** $65 **MIB** Sec. Mkt. **$78-$80**

QX 801-5 TRADITIONAL (BLACK SANTA)
Comments: RARE! White Satin Ball, 3-1/4" dia., Dated 1981
A black Santa feeds the animals in the forest. Caption: "It's Christmas. It's Time For Sharing... And Dreaming, And Caring And Merry Gift Bearing..."
☐ Purchased 19___ Pd $_______ MIB NB DB BNT
☐ Want Orig. Ret. $4.50 **NB** $68 **MIB** Sec. Mkt. **$80-$85**

QX 504-2 TWENTY-FIFTH CHRISTMAS TOGETHER
Comments: Clear Acrylic, 4-1/2" tall
Two wedding bells with frosted border designs have caption in silver foil. "25 Years Together, Christmas 1981."
☐ Purchased 19___ Pd $_______ MIB NB DB BNT
☐ Want Orig. Ret. $5.50 **NB** $18 **MIB** Sec. Mkt. **$22-$25**

QX 707-5 TWENTY-FIFTH CHRISTMAS TOGETHER
Comments: White Glass Ball, 3-1/4" dia.
White bells on a background of red ribbon and Christmas greenery. Caption: "25 Years Together, Christmas 1981" and "Christmas Season Of The Heart, Time Of Sweet Remembrance."
☐ Purchased 19___ Pd $_______ MIB NB DB BNT
☐ Want Orig. Ret. $4.50 **NB** $12 **MIB** Sec. Mkt. **$18-$20**

QX 162-1 YARN & FABRIC ORNAMENT ANGEL
Comments: Yarn with lace and felt accents, 5" tall
Reissued from 1980.
☐ Purchased 19___ Pd $_______ MIB NB DB BNT
☐ Want Orig. Ret. $3.00 Sec. Mkt. **$10-$12**

QX 161-4 YARN & FABRIC ORNAMENT SANTA
Comments: Yarn with lace and felt accents, 5" tall
Reissued from 1980.
☐ Purchased 19___ Pd $_______ MIB NB DB BNT
☐ Want Orig. Ret. $3.00 Sec. Mkt. **$10-$12**

QX 163-4 YARN & FABRIC ORNAMENT SNOWMAN
Comments: Yarn with lace and felt accents, 5" tall
Reissued from 1980.
☐ Purchased 19___ Pd $_______ MIB NB DB BNT
☐ Want Orig. Ret. $3.00 Sec. Mkt. **$10-$12**

QX 164-1 YARN & FABRIC ORNAMENT SOLDIER
Comments: Yarn with lace and felt accents, 5" tall
Reissued from 1980.
☐ Purchased 19___ Pd $_______ MIB NB DB BNT
☐ Want Orig. Ret. $3.00 Sec. Mkt. **$10-$12**

Buy - Sell - Trade Hallmark Ornaments across the U.S.A. with your "Voice Ad™" on Rosie's collector advertising line!
Call 1-900-740-7575
$2.00 per minute. Touch-tone phone required.
Must be 18 years of age.

1982 Collection

QX 300-3 ARCTIC PENGUIN
Comments: Clear Acrylic, 1-1/2" tall
Penguin molded to resemble an Ice Sculpture.
☐ Purchased 19___ Pd $_______ MIB NB DB BNT
☐ Want Orig. Ret. $4.00 **NB** $10 **MIB** Sec. Mkt. **$18-$20**

QX 455-3 BABY'S FIRST CHRISTMAS
Comments: Handcrafted, 3" tall, Dated 1982
Baby's rattle with panorama window. Caption: "Baby's First Christmas." **Artist:** Ed Seale
☐ Purchased 19___ Pd $_______ MIB NB DB BNT
☐ Want Orig. Ret. $13.00 **NB** $25 **MIB** Sec. Mkt. **$48-$50**

QMB 900-7 BABY'S FIRST CHRISTMAS
Comments: Musical, Classic Shape, 4-1/2" tall, Dated 1982
Caption: "First Christmas 1982." Plays Brahms' Lullaby.
☐ Purchased 19___ Pd $_______ MIB NB DB BNT
☐ Want Orig. Ret. $16.00 **NB** $55 **MIB** Sec. Mkt. **$75-$80**

QX 216-3 BABY'S FIRST CHRISTMAS (BOY)
Comments: Light Blue Satin Ball, 3-1/4" dia., Dated 1982
Design was hand-embroidered, then photographed. Caption: "Baby's First Christmas 1982" and "A Baby Boy Is A Precious Gift – A Blessing From Above."
☐ Purchased 19___ Pd $_______ MIB NB DB BNT
☐ Want Orig. Ret. $4.50 **NB** $12 **MIB** Sec. Mkt. **$22-$25**

QX 207-3 BABY'S FIRST CHRISTMAS (GIRL)
Comments: Light Pink Satin Ball, 3-1/4" dia., Dated 1982
Embroidered toys form a quilt. Caption: "Baby's First Christmas 1982" and "A Baby Girl Is The Sweetest Gift A Lifetime Can Provide."
☐ Purchased 19___ Pd $_______ MIB NB DB BNT
☐ Want Orig. Ret. $4.50 **NB** $12 **MIB** Sec. Mkt. **$25-$30**

QX 312-6 BABY'S FIRST CHRISTMAS: PHOTOHOLDER
Comments: Acrylic, 4-1/4" tall, Dated 1982
A stocking filled with toys. Caption: "Baby's First Christmas 1982" and "Oh What Joy And Sweet Surprise Christmas Brings To Little Eyes."
☐ Purchased 19___ Pd $_______ MIB NB DB BNT
☐ Want Orig. Ret. $6.50 **NB** $20 **MIB** Sec. Mkt. **$25-$30**

QX 302-3 BABY'S FIRST CHRISTMAS
Comments: Acrylic, 3-17/32" tall
Teddy Bear in frosted acrylic with block. Caption: "Baby's First Christmas 1982." **Artist:** Ed Seale
☐ Purchased 19___ Pd $_______ MIB NB DB BNT
☐ Want Orig. Ret. $5.50 **NB** $20 **MIB** Sec. Mkt. **$35-$40**

QX 456-6 BAROQUE ANGEL
Comments: Brass & Handcrafted, 4-7/16" tall
A cherub flies with a brass banner. Caption: "Joyeux Noel."
Artist: Donna Lee
☐ Purchased 19___ Pd $_______ MIB NB DB BNT
☐ Want Orig. Ret. $15.00 **NB** $125 **MIB** Sec. Mkt. **$140-$150**

QX 455-6 BELLRINGER, THE: ANGEL
Comments: **Fourth in Series,** Handcrafted, 2-27/32" tall
Dated 1982. The clapper is a red and green wreath with an angel in its center. **Artist:** Donna Lee
☐ Purchased 19___ Pd $_______ MIB NB DB BNT
☐ Want Orig. Ret. $15.00 **NB** $80 **MIB** Sec. Mkt. **$95-$100**

QX 305-6 BETSEY CLARK
Comments: Blue Cameo, 3-3/8" dia.
Angel decorates a tree on a cloud. Caption: "Christmas 1982" and "'Tis The Season For Trimming Trees And Making Merry Memories."
☐ Purchased 19___ Pd $_______ MIB NB DB BNT
☐ Want Orig. Ret. $8.50 **NB** $20 **MIB** Sec. Mkt. **$25-$28**

QX 215-6 BETSEY CLARK SERIES
Comments: **Tenth in Series,** White Satin Ball, 3-1/4" dia.
Three children share a bedtime story. Caption: "Christmas 1982" and "The Joys Of Christmas Are Multiplied When Shared With Those We Love."
☐ Purchased 19___ Pd $_______ MIB NB DB BNT
☐ Want Orig. Ret. $4.50 **NB** $18 **MIB** Sec. Mkt. **$28-$35**

QX 460-6 BRASS BELL
Comments: Polished Brass, 2-11/32" tall
Design of holly leaves and berries are stamped into the bell. Red ribbon and bow for hanging. **Artist:** Donna Lee
☐ Purchased 19___ Pd $_______ MIB NB DB BNT
☐ Want Orig. Ret. $12.00 **NB** $12 **MIB** Sec. Mkt. **$20-$22**

No Number **BRASS PROMOTIONAL ORNAMENT**
Comments: Dimensional Brass, 2-3/8" tall
24 k. gold tone coating. Victorian couple in sleigh are shown in front of a sleeping village.
☐ Purchased 19___ Pd $_______ MIB NB DB BNT
☐ Want Orig. Ret. $3.50 **NB** $35 **MIB** Sec. Mkt. **$40-$50**

QX 478-3 CARROUSEL
Comments: **Fifth in Series**, Handcrafted, 3" tall, Dated 1982
Snowmen on skates. Caption: "Merry Christmas 1982" on snow-covered top. **Artist:** Ed Seale
☐ Purchased 19___ Pd $_______ MIB NB DB BNT
☐ Want Orig. Ret. $10.00 **NB** $80 **MIB** Sec. Mkt. **$100-$110**

QX 220-6 CHRISTMAS ANGEL
Comments: Gold Glass Ball, 3-1/4" dia., Dated 1982
Angel shelters the flame of a glowing candle. Caption: "From Heaven Above The Light Of Love Shines Into Our Hearts At Christmas."
☐ Purchased 19___ Pd $_______ MIB NB DB BNT
☐ Want Orig. Ret. $4.50 **NB** $10 **MIB** Sec. Mkt. **$22-$25**

QX 155-4 CHRISTMAS FANTASY
Comments: Brass and Handcrafted, 3-3/4" long
Reissued from 1981.
☐ Purchased 19___ Pd $_______ MIB NB DB BNT
☐ Want Orig. Ret. $13.00 **NB** $60 **MIB** Sec. Mkt. **$85-$88**

QX 311-6 CHRISTMAS MEMORIES
Comments: Acrylic, 4-1/8" tall, Dated 1982
Square white photoholder with green holly leaves and red bow. Caption: "How Bright The Joys Of Christmas, How Warm The Memories." **Artist:** Linda Sickman
☐ Purchased 19___ Pd $_______ MIB NB DB BNT
☐ Want Orig. Ret. $6.50 **NB** $12 **MIB** Sec. Mkt. **$18-$20**

QX 145-4 CLOISONNÉ ANGEL
Comments: Cloisonné, 2-21/32" tall
An angel flies in the center of an open heart. Caption: "Peace, Love, Joy."
☐ Purchased 19___ Pd $_______ MIB NB DB BNT
☐ Want Orig. Ret. $12.00 **NB** $70 **MIB** Sec. Mkt. **$90-$95**

QX 458-3 CLOTHESPIN SOLDIER: BRITISH
Comments: ***FIRST IN SERIES***, Handcrafted, 3-5/32" tall
This soldier has a black mustache, tall black hat and red/white/blue uniform and carries a black baton. **Artist:** Linda Sickman
☐ Purchased 19___ Pd $_______ MIB NB DB BNT
☐ Want Orig. Ret. $5.00 **NB** $100 **MIB** Sec. Mkt. **$125-$130**

QX 308-6 COLORS OF CHRISTMAS: SANTA'S FLIGHT
Comments: Acrylic, 4-1/4" tall, Dated Christmas 1982
Stained glass look, Santa in a hot air balloon.
☐ Purchased 19___ Pd $_______ MIB NB DB BNT
☐ Want Orig. Ret. $4.50 **NB** $25 **MIB** Sec. Mkt. **$40-$45**

QX 308-3 COLORS OF CHRISTMAS: NATIVITY
Comments: Acrylic, 4" tall, Stained glass look
Traditional view of the Holy Family.
☐ Purchased 19___ Pd $_______ MIB NB DB BNT
☐ Want Orig. Ret. $4.50 **NB** $38 **MIB** Sec. Mkt. **$45-$52**

QX 480-6 COWBOY SNOWMAN
Comments: Handcrafted, 2-27/32" tall
Snowman is dressed in red scarf, boots and hat with a candy cane "pistol."
☐ Purchased 19___ Pd $_______ MIB NB DB BNT
☐ Want Orig. Ret. $8.00 **NB** $45 **MIB** Sec. Mkt. **$55-$60**

QX 201-3 CURRIER & IVES
Comments: White Porcelain Glass Ball, 3-1/4" dia.
Reproduction of "The Road-Winter." Caption: "Christmas 1982" and "The Road – Winter" and "Currier and Ives." This print was "registered according to an Act of Congress in 1853."
☐ Purchased 19___ Pd $_______ MIB NB DB BNT
☐ Want Orig. Ret. $4.50 **NB** $10 **MIB** Sec. Mkt. **$20-$22**

QX 435-5 CYCLING SANTA
Comments: Handcrafted, 4-3/8" tall, Reissued in 1983.
Santa rides an old "velocipede" with his pack on the back. The wheels turn and three brass bells attached to his pack jingle.
☐ Purchased 19___ Pd $_______ MIB NB DB BNT
☐ Want Orig. Ret. $20.00 **NB** $125 **MIB** Sec. Mkt. **$150-$155**

QX 204-6 DAUGHTER
Comments: Ecru Soft-Sheen Satin Ball, 3-1/4" dia.
Dated 1982 A selection of Christmas goodies are displayed. Caption: "A Daughter's Love Makes Christmas Special."
☐ Purchased 19___ Pd $_______ MIB NB DB BNT
☐ Want Orig. Ret. $4.50 **NB** $20 **MIB** Sec. Mkt. **$25-$30**

QX 217-3 DISNEY
Comments: White Satin Ball, 3-1/4" dia., Dated 1982
Seven Dwarfs prepare for Christmas. Caption: "Christmas... Time For Surprises -- In All Shapes And Sizes."
☐ Purchased 19___ Pd $_______ MIB NB DB BNT
☐ Want Orig. Ret. $4.50 **NB** $22 **MIB** Sec. Mkt. **$30-$35**

QX 425-5 DIVINE MISS PIGGY, THE™
Comments: Handcrafted, 4" long
Reissued from 1981. **Artist:** John Francis (Collin)
☐ Purchased 19___ Pd $_______ MIB NB DB BNT
☐ Want Orig. Ret. $12.00 **NB** $65 **MIB** Sec. Mkt. **$95-$105**

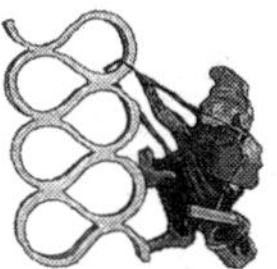

QX 457-3 ELFIN ARTIST
Comments: Handcrafted, 3" tall
Bearded elf paints the stripes on ribbon candy while hanging onto his paint bucket. **Artist:** Linda Sickman
☐ Purchased 19___ Pd $_______ MIB NB DB BNT
☐ Want Orig. Ret. $9.00 **NB** $40 **MIB** Sec. Mkt. **$50-$55**

QX 494-6 EMBROIDERED TREE
Comments: Fabric, 4-9/16" tall
Green fabric tree is decorated with embroidered flowers and trimmed in red braided cord.
☐ Purchased 19___ Pd $_______ MIB NB DB BNT
☐ Want Orig. Ret. $6.50 Sec. Mkt. **$32-$35**

QX 205-6 FATHER
Comments: Ecru Soft-Sheen Satin Ball, 3-1/4" dia.
Woodcut style. Caption: "Christmas 1982" and "A Father's Love Brightens The Season." **Artist:** Linda Sickman
☐ Purchased 19___ Pd $_______ MIB NB DB BNT
☐ Want Orig. Ret. $4.50 **NB** $8 **MIB** Sec. Mkt. **$12-$18**

QX 212-3 FIFTIETH CHRISTMAS TOGETHER
Comments: Gold Glass Ball, 3-1/4" dia., Dated 1982
Burgundy lettering, highlighted with white. Caption: "50th Christmas Together 1982" and "We Measure Our Time, Not By Years Alone, But By The Love And Joy We've Known."
☐ Purchased 19___ Pd $_______ MIB NB DB BNT
☐ Want Orig. Ret. $4.50 **NB** $12 **MIB** Sec. Mkt. **$18-$20**

QMB 901-9 FIRST CHRISTMAS TOGETHER
Comments: Musical, Classic Shape, 4-1/2" tall, Dated 1982
Plays "White Christmas" Caption: "First Christmas Together 1982."
☐ Purchased 19___ Pd $_______ MIB NB DB BNT
☐ Want Orig. Ret. $16.00 **NB** $65 **MIB** Sec. Mkt. **$75-$85**

QX 211-3 FIRST CHRISTMAS TOGETHER
Comments: Silver Chrome Glass Ball, 3-1/4" dia., Dated 1982
Two redbirds soar against a frosty background. Caption: "First Christmas Together 1982" and "Quiet Moments Together, Love That Lasts Forever."
☐ Purchased 19___ Pd $_______ MIB NB DB BNT
☐ Want Orig. Ret. $4.50 **NB** $20 **MIB** Sec. Mkt. **$25-$30**

QX 306-6 FIRST CHRISTMAS TOGETHER
Comments: Turquoise Cameo, 3-3/8" dia., Dated 1982
A couple ice skates. Caption: "First Christmas Together" and "Christmas Is For Sharing With The Special One You Love."
☐ Purchased 19___ Pd $_______ MIB NB DB BNT
☐ Want Orig. Ret. $8.50 **NB** $15 **MIB** Sec. Mkt. **$28-$30**

QX 456-3 FIRST CHRISTMAS TOGETHER - LOCKET
Comments: Polished Brass, 2-5/8" tall, Dated 1982
Hinged, heart-shaped locket opens with inserts for two photos. Includes brass hanger. Caption: "First Christmas Together 1982."
Artist: Ed Seale
☐ Purchased 19___ Pd $_______ MIB NB DB BNT
☐ Want Orig. Ret. $15.00 **NB** $18 **MIB** Sec. Mkt. **$24-$26**

QX 302-6 FIRST CHRISTMAS TOGETHER
Comments: Acrylic, 4-1/4" tall, Dated 1982
Tree. Caption: "First Christmas Together."
☐ Purchased 19___ Pd $_______ MIB NB DB BNT
☐ Want Orig. Ret. $5.50 **NB** $8 **MIB** Sec. Mkt. **$15-$20**

QX 208-6 FRIENDSHIP
Comments: White Satin Ball, 3-1/4" dia.
Happy animals ice skate together. Caption: "Christmas 1982" and "Hearts Are Happy When Friends Are Together."
☐ Purchased 19___ Pd $_______ MIB NB DB BNT
☐ Want Orig. Ret. $4.50 **NB** $12 **MIB** Sec. Mkt. **$18-$22**

QX 304-6 FRIENDSHIP
Comments: Acrylic, 3-1/4" tall, Dated 1982
Kitten/puppy together. Caption: "Christmas Is For Friends."
☐ Purchased 19___ Pd $_______ MIB NB DB BNT
☐ Want Orig. Ret. $5.50 **NB** $18 **MIB** Sec. Mkt. **$26-$30**

QX 452-3 FROSTY FRIENDS
Comments: **Third in Series**, Handcrafted, 4-1/8" tall
Dated 1982. A little Eskimo climbs an icicle "mountain." His Husky puppy sits at the top. Appear to be many "No Box" available. At one time, "leftover" ornaments were packaged in plastic bags; it appears this policy has been changed. **Artist:** Ed Seale
☐ Purchased 19___ Pd $_______ MIB NB DB BNT
☐ Want Orig. Ret. $8.00 **NB-P** $95 **MIB** Sec. Mkt. **$280-$285**

QX 222-6 GODCHILD
Comments: White Glass Ball, 3-1/4" dia., Dated 1982
A little angel reaches for a snowflake. Caption: "Merry Christmas To A Special Godchild."
☐ Purchased 19___ Pd $_______ MIB NB DB BNT
☐ Want Orig. Ret. $4.50 **NB** $8 **MIB** Sec. Mkt. **$18-$22**

QX 224-3 GRANDDAUGHTER
Comments: White Satin Ball, 3-1/4" dia.
Puppies, teddy bears and bunnies hold a rope of green garland. Caption: "Christmas 1982" and "A Granddaughter Has A Special Gift For Giving Special Joy."
☐ Purchased 19___ Pd $_______ MIB NB DB BNT
☐ Want Orig. Ret. $4.50 **NB** $5 **MIB** Sec. Mkt. **$18-$25**

QX 207-6 GRANDFATHER
Comments: Dark Blue Satin Ball, 3-1/4" dia.
Caption: "Grandfather... In His Strength He Teaches, In His Gentleness He Loves" and "Christmas 1982."
☐ Purchased 19___ Pd $_______ MIB NB DB BNT
☐ Want Orig. Ret. $4.50 **NB** $5 **MIB** Sec. Mkt. **$15-$18**

QX 200-3 GRANDMOTHER
Comments: Dark Pink Satin Ball, 3-1/4" dia., Dated 1982
Caption: "Christmas 1982" and "A Grandmother Is Love."
☐ Purchased 19___ Pd $_______ MIB NB DB BNT
☐ Want Orig. Ret. $4.50 **NB** $10 **MIB** Sec. Mkt. **$15-$18**

QX 214-6 GRANDPARENTS
Comments: White Glass Ball, 3-1/4" dia. , Dated 1982
Covered bridge and winter scenes. Caption: "Christmas 1982" and "With Thoughts Of Grandparents Come Thoughts Of Days The Heart Will Always Treasure."
☐ Purchased 19___ Pd $_______ MIB NB DB BNT
☐ Want Orig. Ret. $4.50 **NB** $8 **MIB** Sec. Mkt. **$15-$18**

QX 224-6 GRANDSON
Comments: White Satin Ball, 3-1/4" dia., Dated 1982
Bunnies sled in the snow. Caption: "Christmas 1982" and "A Grandson... Makes Days Bright, Hearts Light And Christmas Time A Real Delight."
☐ Purchased 19___ Pd $_______ MIB NB DB BNT
☐ Want Orig. Ret. $4.50 **NB** $15 **MIB** Sec. Mkt. **$22-$28**

QX 464-3 HERE COMES SANTA: JOLLY TROLLEY
Comments: **Fourth in Series,** Handcrafted, 3-3/8" tall
Santa's in the driver's seat of an old trolley car. Caption: "1982 Jolly Trolley." **Artist:** Linda Sickman
☐ Purchased 19___ Pd $_______ MIB NB DB BNT
☐ Want Orig. Ret. $15.00 **NB** $90 **MIB** Sec. Mkt. **$120-$125**

QX 502-6 HOLIDAY CHIMES: ANGEL CHIMES
Comments: Chrome-Plated Brass, 4-1/2" tall
Three angels, each holding a poinsettia, are suspended from a large snowflake. Collectors have not been aware of these being produced until recent years.
☐ Purchased 19___ Pd $_______ MIB NB DB BNT
☐ Want Orig. Ret. $5.50 **NB** $20 **MIB** Sec. Mkt. **$25-$30**

QX 494-3 HOLIDAY CHIMES: BELL CHIMES
Comments: Chrome-Plated Brass, 3" tall
Three stamped bells, each with different snowflake cutouts, hang from a snowflake. **Artist:** Linda Sickman
☐ Purchased 19___ Pd $_______ MIB NB DB BNT
☐ Want Orig. Ret. $5.50 **NB** $15 **MIB** Sec. Mkt. **$25-$28**

QX 484-6 HOLIDAY CHIMES: TREE CHIMES
Comments: Stamped Brass, 4-7/16" tall
Lacy, stamped brass tree has five bells and two doves incorporated into its leafy branches. **Artist:** Ed Seale
☐ Purchased 19___ Pd $_______ MIB NB DB BNT
☐ Want Orig. Ret. $5.50 **MIB** Sec. Mkt. **$50-$52**

QX 309-6 HOLIDAY HIGHLIGHTS: ANGEL
Comments: Acrylic, 3-1/2" tall
Angel plays harp. Gold Foil Caption: "Rejoice"
☐ Purchased 19___ Pd $_______ MIB NB DB BNT
☐ Want Orig. Ret. $5.50 **NB** $20 **MIB** Sec. Mkt. **$30-$35**

QX 311-3 HOLIDAY HIGHLIGHTS: CHRISTMAS MAGIC
Comments: Acrylic, 3-13/16" tall
Rabbit looks at an ornament hanging from a tree branch. Caption: "Christmas... Season Of Magical Moments."
☐ Purchased 19___ Pd $_______ MIB NB DB BNT
☐ Want Orig. Ret. $5.50 **NB** $20 **MIB** Sec. Mkt. **$28-$32**

QX 309-3 HOLIDAY HIGHLIGHTS: CHRISTMAS SLEIGH
Comments: Acrylic, 3-23/32" tall
A sleigh filled with gifts and a Christmas tree. Caption: "Christmas 1982."
☐ Purchased 19___ Pd $_______ MIB NB DB BNT
☐ Want Orig. Ret. $5.50 **NB** $60 **MIB** Sec. Mkt. **$75-$80**

QX 313-3 HOLIDAY WILDLIFE: CARDINALIS
Comments: ***FIRST IN SERIES***, Wood and Decoform, 4" dia.
Two cardinals are perched on a pine bough. Caption: "Cardinalis, Cardinalis. First In A Series, Wildlife Collection. Christmas 1982."
SCARCE!
☐ Purchased 19___ Pd $_______ MIB NB DB BNT
☐ Want Orig. Ret. $7.00 **NB** $300 **MIB** Sec. Mkt. **$350-$375**

QX 432-2 ICE SCULPTOR, THE
Comments: Handcrafted, 3-1/32" tall
Reissued from 1981.
Artist: Donna Lee
☐ Purchased 19___ Pd $_______ MIB NB DB BNT
☐ Want Orig. Ret. $8.00 **NB** $80 **MIB** Sec. Mkt. **$90-$98**

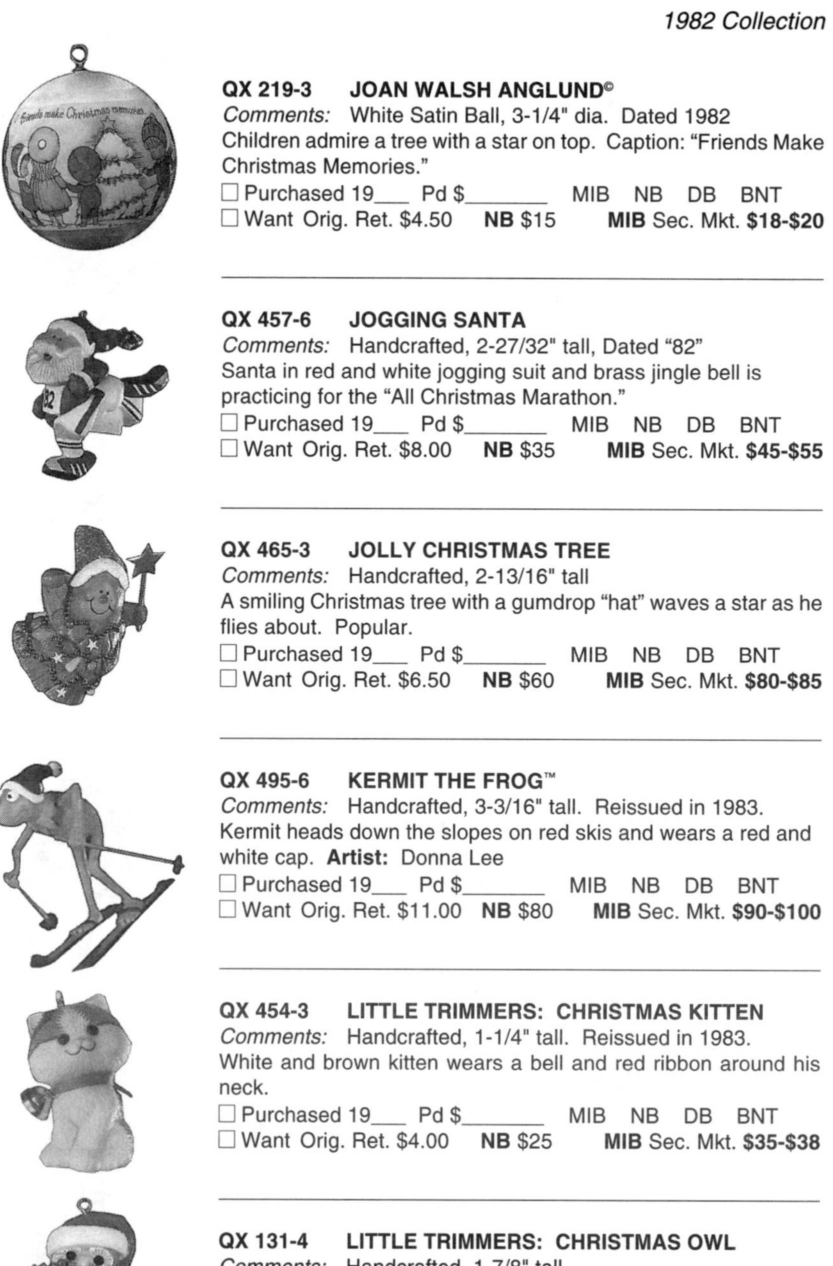

QX 219-3 JOAN WALSH ANGLUND©
Comments: White Satin Ball, 3-1/4" dia. Dated 1982
Children admire a tree with a star on top. Caption: "Friends Make Christmas Memories."
☐ Purchased 19___ Pd $_______ MIB NB DB BNT
☐ Want Orig. Ret. $4.50 **NB** $15 **MIB** Sec. Mkt. **$18-$20**

QX 457-6 JOGGING SANTA
Comments: Handcrafted, 2-27/32" tall, Dated "82"
Santa in red and white jogging suit and brass jingle bell is practicing for the "All Christmas Marathon."
☐ Purchased 19___ Pd $_______ MIB NB DB BNT
☐ Want Orig. Ret. $8.00 **NB** $35 **MIB** Sec. Mkt. **$45-$55**

QX 465-3 JOLLY CHRISTMAS TREE
Comments: Handcrafted, 2-13/16" tall
A smiling Christmas tree with a gumdrop "hat" waves a star as he flies about. Popular.
☐ Purchased 19___ Pd $_______ MIB NB DB BNT
☐ Want Orig. Ret. $6.50 **NB** $60 **MIB** Sec. Mkt. **$80-$85**

QX 495-6 KERMIT THE FROG™
Comments: Handcrafted, 3-3/16" tall. Reissued in 1983.
Kermit heads down the slopes on red skis and wears a red and white cap. **Artist:** Donna Lee
☐ Purchased 19___ Pd $_______ MIB NB DB BNT
☐ Want Orig. Ret. $11.00 **NB** $80 **MIB** Sec. Mkt. **$90-$100**

QX 454-3 LITTLE TRIMMERS: CHRISTMAS KITTEN
Comments: Handcrafted, 1-1/4" tall. Reissued in 1983.
White and brown kitten wears a bell and red ribbon around his neck.
☐ Purchased 19___ Pd $_______ MIB NB DB BNT
☐ Want Orig. Ret. $4.00 **NB** $25 **MIB** Sec. Mkt. **$35-$38**

QX 131-4 LITTLE TRIMMERS: CHRISTMAS OWL
Comments: Handcrafted, 1-7/8" tall
Reissued from 1980.
☐ Purchased 19___ Pd $_______ MIB NB DB BNT
☐ Want 1982 Retail $4.50 **NB-P** $30 **MIB** Sec. Mkt. **$45-$50**

QX 454-6 LITTLE TRIMMERS: COOKIE MOUSE
Comments: Handcrafted, 2-1/16" tall, Dated 1982
A cute white mouse sits on top of a star shaped cookie, eating one of its "points." **Artist:** Linda Sickman
☐ Purchased 19___ Pd $_______ MIB NB DB BNT
☐ Want Orig. Ret. $4.50 **NB** $40 **MIB** Sec. Mkt. **$60-$65**

QX 462-3 LITTLE TRIMMERS: DOVE LOVE
Comments: Acrylic, 2-1/16" tall
A white dove swings in the center of an open red heart.
Artist: Linda Sickman
☐ Purchased 19___ Pd $_______ MIB NB DB BNT
☐ Want Orig. Ret. $4.50 **NB** $42 **MIB** Sec. Mkt. **$55-$60**

QX 477-6 LITTLE TRIMMERS: JINGLING TEDDY
Comments: Flocked, Brass, 2-1/8" tall
A brown flocked teddy bear holds a brass bell. **Artist:** Ed Seale
☐ Purchased 19___ Pd $_______ MIB NB DB BNT
☐ Want Orig. Ret. $4.00 **NB** $27 **MIB** Sec. Mkt. **$35-$40**

QX 415-5 LITTLE TRIMMERS: MERRY MOOSE
Comments: Handcrafted, 1-3/4" tall
Young moose on ice skates.
☐ Purchased 19___ Pd $_______ MIB NB DB BNT
☐ Want Orig. Ret. $5.50 **NB** $40 **MIB** Sec. Mkt. **$50-$55**

QX 459-6 LITTLE TRIMMERS: MUSICAL ANGEL
Comments: Handcrafted, 1-15/16" tall
Tiny angel wearing a brass halo, sits on a cloud playing his lyre.
Artist: Donna Lee
☐ Purchased 19___ Pd $_______ MIB NB DB BNT
☐ Want Orig. Ret. $5.50 **NB** $70 **MIB** Sec. Mkt. **$115-$125**

QX 409-5 LITTLE TRIMMERS: PERKY PENGUIN
Comments: Handcrafted, 1-5/16" tall
Reissued from 1981.
☐ Purchased 19___ Pd $_______ MIB NB DB BNT
☐ Want 1982 Retail $4.00 **NB** $50 **MIB** Sec. Mkt. **$55-$62**

QX 209-6 LOVE
Comments: Ecru Soft-Sheen Satin Ball, 3-1/4" dia., Dated 1982
Wreaths of Christmas flowers and greenery. Caption: "Christmas 1982" and "Christmas... Season Bright With Love."
☐ Purchased 19___ Pd $_______ MIB NB DB BNT
☐ Want Orig. Ret. $4.50 **NB** $12 **MIB** Sec. Mkt. **$18-$20**

QX 304-3 LOVE
Comments: Acrylic - heart shaped, 4-1/8" tall, Dated 1982
Caption in gold foil: "Love Is Forever Between Two Hearts That Share It. 1982"
☐ Purchased 19___ Pd $_______ MIB NB DB BNT
☐ Want Orig. Ret. $5.50 **NB** $20 **MIB** Sec. Mkt. **$25-$30**

QMB 900-9 LOVE
Comments: Musical, Classic Shape, 4-1/2" tall, Dated 1982
Plays "What The World Needs Now Is Love." Caption: "Love Puts The Warmth In Christmas."
☐ Purchased 19___ Pd $_______ MIB NB DB BNT
☐ Want Orig. Ret. $16.00 **NB** $60 **MIB** Sec. Mkt. **$75-$80**

QX 217-6 MARY HAMILTON
Comments: Blue Soft-Sheen Satin Ball, 3-1/4" dia.
Dated 1982. Tiny angels ring bells and are perched on music notes as they sing. Caption: "Joy To The World."
☐ Purchased 19___ Pd $_______ MIB NB DB BNT
☐ Want Orig. Ret. $4.50 **NB** $14 **MIB** Sec. Mkt. **$20-$22**

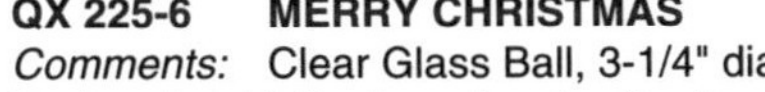

QX 225-6 MERRY CHRISTMAS
Comments: Clear Glass Ball, 3-1/4" dia.
Red and gold fired-on decal. Captions: "Merry Christmas" and "Happy New Year."
☐ Purchased 19___ Pd $_______ MIB NB DB BNT
☐ Want Orig. Ret. $4.50 **NB** $12 **MIB** Sec. Mkt. **$18-$20**

QX 218-3 MISS PIGGY & KERMIT ™
Comments: White Satin Ball, 3-1/4" dia., Dated 1982
Miss Piggy and Kermit in Christmas scenes. Caption: "Season's Greetings" and "Have Yourself A Lavish Little Christmas."
☐ Purchased 19___ Pd $_______ MIB NB DB BNT
☐ Want Orig. Ret. $4.50 **NB** $25 **MIB** Sec. Mkt. **$38-$42**

Kindness is like snow -
it beautifies everything it covers.

QX 209-3 MOMENTS OF LOVE
Comments: Blue Soft-Sheen Satin Ball, 3-1/4" dia., Dated 1982
A horse-drawn stagecoach is silhouetted in white. Caption: "Christmas 1982" and "Each Moment Of Love Lives Forever In Memory."
☐ Purchased 19___ Pd $_______ MIB NB DB BNT
☐ Want Orig. Ret. $4.50 **NB** $10 **MIB** Sec. Mkt. **$15-$20**

QX 205-3 MOTHER
Comments: White Glass Ball, 3-1/4" dia., Dated 1982
Holly and pine garland and poinsettia bouquet. Caption: "Christmas 1982" and "The Spirit Of Christmas Lives In A Mother's Loving Heart."
☐ Purchased 19___ Pd $_______ MIB NB DB BNT
☐ Want Orig. Ret. $4.50 **NB** $8 **MIB** Sec. Mkt. **$18-$20**

QX 222-3 MOTHER AND DAD
Comments: White Porcelain Glass Ball, 3-1/4" dia., Dated 1982
Holly leaves, berries and evergreens. Caption: "Christmas 1982" and "A Mother And Dad Know So Many Ways To Warm A Heart With Love."
☐ Purchased 19___ Pd $_______ MIB NB DB BNT
☐ Want Orig. Ret. $4.50 **NB** $8 **MIB** Sec. Mkt. **$15-$18**

QX 218-6 MUPPETS™ PARTY
Comments: White Satin Ball, 3-1/4" dia., Dated 1982
The whole Muppets gang is gathered for a party. Caption: "Merry Christmas 1982."
☐ Purchased 19___ Pd $_______ MIB NB DB BNT
☐ Want Orig. Ret. $4.50 **NB** $30 **MIB** Sec. Mkt. **$40-$45**

QX 212-6 NEW HOME
Comments: Dk. Blue Satin Ball, 3-1/4" dia., Dated 1982
Snow covered village homes. Caption: "Christmas Time Fills Hearts With Love And Homes With Warmth And Joy."
☐ Purchased 19___ Pd $_______ MIB NB DB BNT
☐ Want Orig. Ret. $4.50 **NB** $12 **MIB** Sec. Mkt. **$18-$20**

Oh Christmas tree,
oh Christmas tree. . .
How lovely are your branches.

QX 202-3 NORMAN ROCKWELL
Comments: Red Soft-Sheen Satin Ball, 3-1/4" dia., Dated 1982
Caption: "From The Norman Rockwell Collection 1982. Hearts Are Light, Smiles Are Bright, Child's Delight, It's Christmas."
☐ Purchased 19___ Pd $_______ MIB NB DB BNT
☐ Want Orig. Ret. $4.50 **NB** $14 **MIB** Sec. Mkt. **$25-$28**

QX 305-3 NORMAN ROCKWELL SERIES
Comments: **Third in Series**, Red Cameo, 3-3/8" dia.
Dated 1982. Caption: "Filling The Stockings. Third In A Series. The Norman Rockwell Collection. Christmas 1982."
☐ Purchased 19___ Pd $_______ MIB NB DB BNT
☐ Want Orig. Ret. $8.50 **NB** $16 **MIB** Sec. Mkt. **$20-$25**

QX 227-6 OLD FASHIONED CHRISTMAS
Comments: White Porcelain Glass Ball, 3-1/4" dia.
Reproduction of antique English greeting cards from late 1800s Caption: "Merry Christmas" and "Happy New Year."
☐ Purchased 19___ Pd $_______ MIB NB DB BNT
☐ Want Orig. Ret. $4.50 **NB** $25 **MIB** Sec. Mkt. **$40-$42**

QX 226-3 OLD WORLD ANGELS
Comments: White Porcelain Glass Ball, 3-1/4" dia.
Old-world angels hold lighted candles and float amid stars and streamers.
☐ Purchased 19___ Pd $_______ MIB NB DB BNT
☐ Want Orig. Ret. $4.50 **NB** $12 **MIB** Sec. Mkt. **$24-$28**

QX 226-6 PATTERNS OF CHRISTMAS
Comments: Gold Glass Ball, 3-1/4" dia.
Oriental designs of poinsettias and holly are highlighted in gold.
☐ Purchased 19___ Pd $_______ MIB NB DB BNT
☐ Want Orig. Ret. $4.50 **NB** $14 **MIB** Sec. Mkt. **$22-$24**

QX 200-6 PEANUTS®
Comments: Light Blue Satin Ball, 3-1/4" dia., Dated 1982
Snoopy, Woodstock and friends on a tandem bike. Caption: "Christmas 1982."
☐ Purchased 19___ Pd $_______ MIB NB DB BNT
☐ Want Orig. Ret. $4.50 **NB** $25 **MIB** Sec. Mkt. **$30-$35**

QX 419-5 PEEKING ELF
Comments: Handcrafted, 3-3/32" tall
An elf peeks over the top of a silver ball ornament tied with a red ribbon.
☐ Purchased 19___ Pd $_______ MIB NB DB BNT
☐ Want Orig. Ret. $6.50 **NB** $24 **MIB** Sec. Mkt. **$38-$42**

QX 461-3 PINECONE HOME
Comments: Handcrafted, 2-23/32" tall
A small mouse in red pajamas looks out a shuttered window of his pinecone house. **Artist:** Donna Lee
☐ Purchased 19___ Pd $_______ MIB NB DB BNT
☐ Want Orig. Ret. $8.00 **NB** $145 **MIB** Sec. Mkt. **$170-$175**

QX 479-3 RACCOON SURPRISES
Comments: Handcrafted, 3" tall
A raccoon stands on a tree branch and raids a colorful Christmas stocking. **Artist:** Donna Lee
☐ Purchased 19___ Pd $_______ MIB NB DB BNT
☐ Want Orig. Ret. $9.00 **NB** $125 **MIB** Sec. Mkt. **$145-$150**

QX 502-3 ROCKING HORSE
Comments: **Second in Series**, Handcrafted, 2" tall, Dated 1982
Black stallion with maroon saddle and rockers. Harder to find in box than no box. **Artist:** Linda Sickman
☐ Purchased 19___ Pd $_______ MIB NB DB BNT
☐ Want Orig. Ret. $10.00 **NB** $315 **MIB** Sec. Mkt. **$375-$400**

QX 221-6 SANTA
Comments: White Porcelain Glass Ball, 3-1/4" dia., Dated 1982
A close-up of Santa and Santa smoking his pipe. Caption: "Christmas 1982" and "His Eyes, How They Twinkled, His Dimples, How Merry." **Artist:** Thomas Blackshear
☐ Purchased 19___ Pd $_______ MIB NB DB BNT
☐ Want Orig. Ret. $4.50 **NB** $10 **MIB** Sec. Mkt. **$18-$20**

QX 467-6 SANTA AND REINDEER
Comments: Brass and Handcrafted, 2-9/32" tall
Santa flies in a sleigh with brass runners pulled by four stamped-brass reindeer. **Artist:** Linda Sickman
☐ Purchased 19___ Pd $_______ MIB NB DB BNT
☐ Want Orig. Ret. $9.00 **NB** $35 **MIB** Sec. Mkt. **$45-$52**

QX 148-7 SANTA BELL
Comments: Hand-decorated Porcelain, 3-11/16" tall
Santa's black boots ring the bell.
☐ Purchased 19___ Pd $_______ MIB NB DB BNT
☐ Want Orig. Ret. $15.00 **NB** $50 **MIB** Sec. Mkt. **$55-$65**

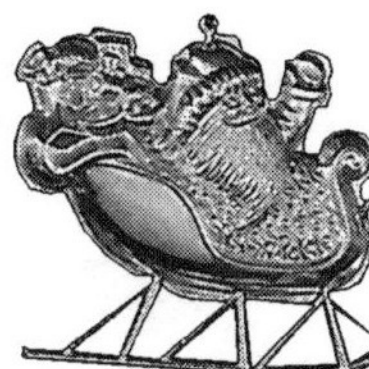

QX 478-6 SANTA'S SLEIGH
Comments: Polished Brass, 2-5/8" tall
Stamped design of Santa in a sleigh full of toys. **Artist:** Ed Seale
☐ Purchased 19___ Pd $_______ MIB NB DB BNT
☐ Want Orig. Ret. $9.00 **NB** $18 **MIB** Sec. Mkt. **$30-$35**

QX 450-3 SANTA'S WORKSHOP
Comments: Handcrafted, 3" tall. Reissued in 1983.
Santa paints a dollhouse in his snow-covered cottage. Inside of cottage can be seen from three sides. **Artist:** Donna Lee
☐ Purchased 19___ Pd $_______ MIB NB DB BNT
☐ Want Orig. Ret. $10.00 **NB** $70 **MIB** Sec. Mkt. **$80-$90**

QX 221-3 SEASON FOR CARING
Comments: Light Blue Soft-Sheen Satin Ball, 3-1/4" dia.
Dated 1982. Night scene: Bethlehem and the Star. Caption: "Christmas... Season For Caring."
☐ Purchased 19___ Pd $_______ MIB NB DB BNT
☐ Want Orig. Ret. $4.50 **NB** $12 **MIB** Sec. Mkt. **$22-$25**

QX 208-3 SISTER
Comments: White Glass Ball, 3-1/4" dia., Dated 1982
A small girl ice skates on a pond and pets a white bunny. Caption: "A Sister Brings The Beauty Of Memories And The Warmth Of Love To Christmas."
☐ Purchased 19___ Pd $_______ MIB NB DB BNT
☐ Want Orig. Ret. $4.50 **NB** $15 **MIB** Sec. Mkt. **$25-$30**

QX 480-3 SNOOPY AND FRIENDS
Comments: **Fourth in Series**, Dated 1982
Handcrafted Panorama Ball, 3-1/4" dia.
Snoopy is flying in a sleigh drawn by Woodstock and his friends.
Artist: Ed Seale
☐ Purchased 19___ Pd $_______ MIB NB DB BNT
☐ Want Orig. Ret. $13.00 **NB** $85 **MIB** Sec. Mkt. **$115-$125**

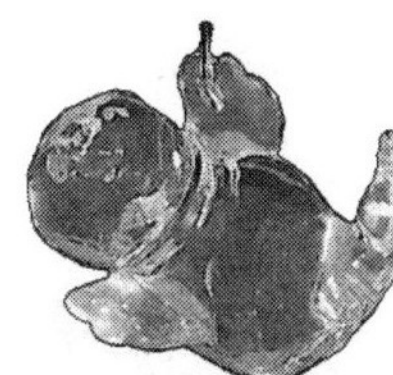

QX 300-6 SNOWY SEAL
Comments: Clear Acrylic, 1-19/32" tall
Designed to resemble an Ice Sculpture.
☐ Purchased 19___ Pd $_______ MIB NB DB BNT
☐ Want Orig. Ret. $4.00 **NB** $15 **MIB** Sec. Mkt. **$20-$22**

QX 204-3 SON
Comments: Caramel Soft-Sheen Satin Ball, 3-1/4" dia.
Marching band leads all to Christmas. Caption: "Christmas 1982" and "A Son Is The Pride Of Your Heart, The Joy Of Your Life."
☐ Purchased 19___ Pd $_______ MIB NB DB BNT
☐ Want Orig. Ret. $4.50 **NB** $15 **MIB** Sec. Mkt. **$24-$28**

QX 452-6 SPIRIT OF CHRISTMAS, THE
Comments: Handcrafted, 1-29/32" tall, Dated 1982
Santa flies in a silver and red biplane. Caption: "The Spirit Of Christmas." **Artist:** Linda Sickman
☐ Purchased 19___ Pd $_______ MIB NB DB BNT
☐ Want Orig. Ret. $10.00 **NB** $85 **MIB** Sec. Mkt. **$120-$125**

QX 228-3 STAINED GLASS
Comments: White Glass Ball, 3-1/4" dia.
Red poinsettia and green holly makes a lovely contrast with lavender, blue and green panels.
☐ Purchased 19___ Pd $_______ MIB NB DB BNT
☐ Want Orig. Ret. $4.50 **NB** $12 **MIB** Sec. Mkt. **$18-$22**

QX 214-3 TEACHER
Comments: White Glass Ball, 3-1/4" dia., Dated 1982
Elves cast shadows to spell "CHRISTMAS 1982." Caption: "To A Special Teacher."
☐ Purchased 19___ Pd $_______ MIB NB DB BNT
☐ Want Orig. Ret. $4.50 **NB** $5 **MIB** Sec. Mkt. **$10-$14**

QX 301-6 TEACHER
Comments: Acrylic Apple, 3-1/2" tall, Dated 1982
Clear with green leaves and red print: "To A Special Teacher 1982." **Artist:** Ed Seale
☐ Purchased 19___ Pd $_______ MIB NB DB BNT
☐ Want Orig. Ret. $5.50 **NB** $5 **MIB** Sec. Mkt. **$14-$18**

QX 312-3 TEACHER
Comments: Acrylic, 3-15/16" tall, Dated 1982
Snow covered red schoolhouse has a cutout for child's photo. Caption: "Merry Christmas To My Teacher."
Artist: Linda Sickman
☐ Purchased 19___ Pd $_______ MIB NB DB BNT
☐ Want Orig. Ret. $6.50 **NB** $8 **MIB** Sec. Mkt. **$15-$18**

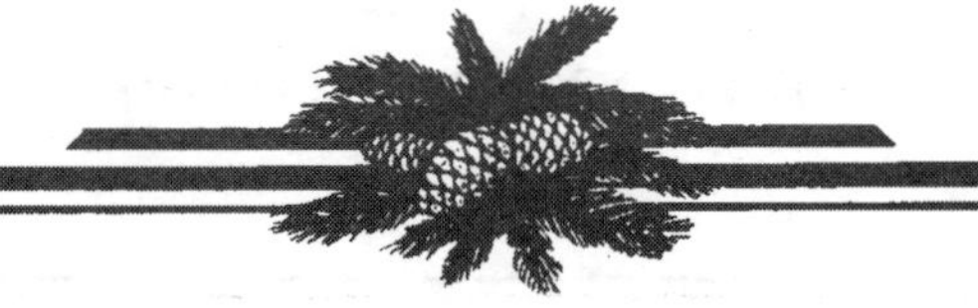

QX 451-3 THIMBLE - MOUSE
Comments: **Fifth in Series**, Handcrafted, 2-11/32" tall
Little mouse "soldier" with big ears and silver needle "baton" wears a thimble as a hat.
☐ Purchased 19___ Pd $_______ MIB NB DB BNT
☐ Want Orig. Ret. $5.00 **NB-P** $45 **MIB** Sec. Mkt. **$75-$80**

QX 307-3 THREE KINGS
Comments: Blue Cameo, 3-3/8" dia., Dated 1982
Caption: "By A Star Shining Brightly, Three Kings Set Their Course And Followed The Heavenly Light To Its Source."
Artist: Thomas Blackshear
☐ Purchased 19___ Pd $_______ MIB NB DB BNT
☐ Want Orig. Ret. $8.50 **NB** $12 **MIB** Sec. Mkt. **$22-$25**

QX 460-3 TIN LOCOMOTIVE
Comments: ***FIRST IN SERIES***, Pressed Tin, 3-5/8" tall
Dated 1982. Decorated in red, blue and silver, with a brass bell that hangs in front of the cab. This is a very popular ornament.
Artist: Linda Sickman
☐ Purchased 19___ Pd $_______ MIB NB DB BNT
☐ Want Orig. Ret. $13.00 **NB** $450 **MIB** Sec. Mkt. **$585-$600**

QX 483-6 TIN SOLDIER
Comments: Pressed Tin, 4-7/8" tall
A British soldier stands at stiff attention.
☐ Purchased 19___ Pd $_______ MIB NB DB BNT
☐ Want Orig. Ret. $6.50 **NB** $40 **MIB** Sec. Mkt. **$45-$50**

QX 203-6 TWELVE DAYS OF CHRISTMAS
Comments: White Pebbled Glass Ball, 3-1/4" dia., Dated 1982
Illustration of the verses of the Christmas carol. Caption: "The Twelve Days Of Christmas 1982."
☐ Purchased 19___ Pd $_______ MIB NB DB BNT
☐ Want Orig. Ret. $4.50 **NB** $15 **MIB** Sec. Mkt. **$25-$30**

QX 211-6 TWENTY-FIFTH CHRISTMAS TOGETHER
Comments: White Porcelain Glass Ball, 3-1/4" dia., Dated 1982
Caption: "Twenty-Fifth Christmas Together 1982" and "Christmas.. As Timeless As Snow-Fall, As Forever As Candleglow, As Always As Love."
☐ Purchased 19___ Pd $_______ MIB NB DB BNT
☐ Want Orig. Ret. $4.50 **NB** $8 **MIB** Sec. Mkt. **$14-$18**

1983 Collection

QX 220-9 1983
Comments: Raspberry Glass Ball, 3-1/4" dia.
Date is printed in gold on a narrow band. Trimmed in platinum colored stripes.
☐ Purchased 19___ Pd $_______ MIB NB DB BNT
☐ Want Orig. Ret. $4.50 **NB** $14 **MIB** Sec. Mkt. **$25-$30**

QX 217-9 AN OLD FASHIONED CHRISTMAS
Comments: Green Porcelain Glass Ball, 3-1/4" dia.
Christmas scenes reminiscent of old greeting cards.
☐ Purchased 19___ Pd $_______ MIB NB DB BNT
☐ Want Orig. Ret. $4.50 **NB** $15 **MIB** Sec. Mkt. **$22-$25**

QX 408-7 ANGEL MESSENGER
Comments: Handcrafted, 2" tall, Dated 1983
Angel wearing a blue robe carries brass date.
Artist: Ed Seale
☐ Purchased 19___ Pd $_______ MIB NB DB BNT
☐ Want Orig. Ret. $6.50 **NB** $80 **MIB** Sec. Mkt. **$95-$100**

QX 219-7 ANGELS
Comments: Clear Glass Ball, 3-1/4" dia.
The inside of the ball has a gold tinsel starburst. Design is of old world angels in soft pastels.
☐ Purchased 19___ Pd $_______ MIB NB DB BNT
☐ Want Orig. Ret. $5.00 **NB** $12 **MIB** Sec. Mkt. **$24-$26**

QX 216-7 ANNUNCIATION, THE
Comments: White Porcelain Glass Ball, 3-1/4" dia.
Reproduction of Fra Filippo Filippi of "The Annunciation."
Caption from Luke 1:35 (RSVB).
☐ Purchased 19___ Pd $_______ MIB NB DB BNT
☐ Want Orig. Ret. $4.50 **NB** $14 **MIB** Sec. Mkt. **$25-$28**

QX 301-9 BABY'S FIRST CHRISTMAS
Comments: Red Cameo, 3-3/4" wide, Dated 1983
Old fashioned rocking horse. Caption: "Baby's First Christmas 1983" and "A Baby Fills Each Day With Joy By Filling Hearts With Love." **Artist:** Linda Sickman
☐ Purchased 19___ Pd $_______ MIB NB DB BNT
☐ Want Orig. Ret. $7.50 **NB** $10 **MIB** Sec. Mkt. **$16-$18**

QX 402-7 BABY'S FIRST CHRISTMAS
Comments: Handcrafted, 3-5/32" tall, Dated 1983
Cradle painted in folk art motif. Caption: "Baby's First Christmas."
Artist: Donna Lee
☐ Purchased 19___ Pd $_______ MIB NB DB BNT
☐ Want Orig. Ret. $14.00 **NB** $28 **MIB** Sec. Mkt. **$38-$42**

QMB 903-9 BABY'S FIRST CHRISTMAS
Comments: Musical, Classic Shape, 4-1/2" tall, Dated 1983
Babies crawl up and down the candy cane letters that form the caption: "Baby's First Christmas." Plays "Schubert's Lullaby."
☐ Purchased 19___ Pd $_______ MIB NB DB BNT
☐ Want Orig. Ret. $16.00 **NB** $50 **MIB** Sec. Mkt. **$85-$90**

QX 200-9 BABY'S FIRST CHRISTMAS - BOY
Comments: Light Blue Soft-Sheen Satin Ball, 3-1/4" dia.
Dated 1983. Six tumbling teddy bears. Caption: "Baby's First Christmas 1983" and "A Baby Boy Is Love And Joy... And Pride That Lasts A Lifetime."
☐ Purchased 19___ Pd $_______ MIB NB DB BNT
☐ Want Orig. Ret. $4.50 **NB** $14 **MIB** Sec. Mkt. **$24-$28**

QX 200-7 BABY'S FIRST CHRISTMAS - GIRL
Comments: White Soft-Sheen Satin Ball, 3-1/4" dia., Dated 1983
Red dress with white polka dots and pinafore. Caption: "Baby's First Christmas 1983" and "A Baby Girl Is A Special Gift Of Love."
☐ Purchased 19___ Pd $_______ MIB NB DB BNT
☐ Want Orig. Ret. $4.50 **NB** $15 **MIB** Sec. Mkt. **$24-$28**

QX 302-9 BABY'S FIRST CHRISTMAS - PHOTOHOLDER
Comments: Acrylic, 3-7/8" tall, Dated 1983
An open baby book. Caption: "Baby's First Christmas 1983" and "A Baby Is A Dream Fulfilled, A Treasure To Hold Dear -- A Baby Is A Love That Grows More Precious Every Year."
☐ Purchased 19___ Pd $_______ MIB NB DB BNT
☐ Want Orig. Ret. $7.00
NB $12 **MIB** Sec. Mkt. **$22-$28**

QX 226-7 BABY'S SECOND CHRISTMAS
Comments: White Soft-Sheen Satin Ball, 3-1/4" dia.
Dated 1983. Caption: "Baby's Second Christmas 1983" and "A child knows such special ways to jolly up the holidays!"
☐ Purchased 19___ Pd $_______ MIB NB DB BNT
☐ Want Orig. Ret. $4.50 **NB** $16 **MIB** Sec. Mkt. **$32-$35**

QX 422-9 BAROQUE ANGELS
Comments: Handcrafted, 2-1/2" tall
Two angels with white wings with rose banners.
Artist: Donna Lee
☐ Purchased 19___ Pd $_______ MIB NB DB BNT
☐ Want Orig. Ret. $13.00 **NB** $50 **MIB** Sec. Mkt. **$75-$85**

QX 420-9 BELL WREATH
Comments: Brass, 3-13/16" tall
Holly wreath of solid brass has seven small bells.
Artist: Linda Sickman
☐ Purchased 19___ Pd $_______ MIB NB DB BNT
☐ Want Orig. Ret. $6.50 **NB** $20 **MIB** Sec. Mkt. **$30-$35**

QX 403-9 BELLRINGER, THE
Comments: **Fifth in Series,** Porcelain and Handcrafted 2-27/32" tall, Dated 1983. Cute brown teddy bear holding a gold star rings a porcelain bell decorated with holly and fir.
☐ Purchased 19___ Pd $_______ MIB NB DB BNT
☐ Want Orig. Ret. $15.00 **NB** $100 **MIB** Sec. Mkt. **$130-$138**

QX 440-1 BETSEY CLARK
Comments: Porcelain, 3-1/2" tall
Betsey Clark angel on cloud has caught a star.
☐ Purchased 19___ Pd $_______ MIB NB DB BNT
☐ Want Orig. Ret. $9.00 **NB** $18 **MIB** Sec. Mkt. **$34-$38**

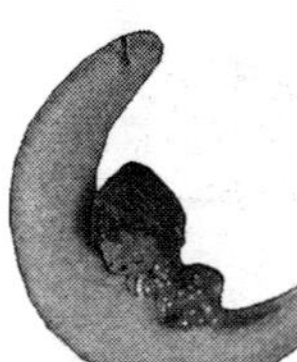

QX 404-7 BETSEY CLARK
Comments: Handcrafted, 3" tall
A child in blue sleeper is napping on a yellow flocked moon.
Artist: Ed Seale
☐ Purchased 19___ Pd $_______ MIB NB DB BNT
☐ Want Orig. Ret. $6.50 **NB** $15 **MIB** Sec. Mkt. **$30-$35**

QX 211-9 BETSEY CLARK SERIES
Comments: **Eleventh in Series,** White Glass Ball, 3-1/4" dia. Dated 1983. Boys and girls ride a carousel. Caption: "Christmas Happiness Is Found... Wherever Good Friends Gather Round."
☐ Purchased 19___ Pd $_______ MIB NB DB BNT
☐ Want Orig. Ret. $4.50 **NB** $18 **MIB** Sec. Mkt. **$30-$35**

QX 423-9 BRASS SANTA
Comments: Brass, 4" tall
Front and back views of Santa's head have been created in polished stamped brass and protectively coated.
Artist: Ed Seale
☐ Purchased 19___ Pd $_______ MIB NB DB BNT
☐ Want Orig. Ret. $9.00 **NB** $14 **MIB** Sec. Mkt. **$22-$25**

QX 411-7 CAROLING OWL
Comments: Handcrafted, 2-9/32" tall
Small white owl holding a book of carols is perched on a brass ring. **Artist:** Ed Seale
☐ Purchased 19___ Pd $_______ MIB NB DB BNT
☐ Want Orig. Ret. $4.50 **NB** $32 **MIB** Sec. Mkt. **$35-$42**

QX 401-9 CARROUSEL: SANTA & FRIENDS
Comments: **Sixth in Series**, Handcrafted, 3-3/32" tall
Santa leads a marching band of children with their trumpets. Caption: "Christmas 1983." **Artist:** Linda Sickman
☐ Purchased 19___ Pd $_______ MIB NB DB BNT
☐ Want Orig. Ret. $11.00 **NB** $38 **MIB** Sec. Mkt. **$50-$55**

QX 226-9 CHILD'S THIRD CHRISTMAS
Comments: White Satin Piqué Ball, 3-1/4" dia., Dated 1983
Caption: "To Celebrate A Child's Third Christmas. How Merry The Season, How Happy The Day When Santa Brings Christmas Surprises Your Way."
☐ Purchased 19___ Pd $_______ MIB NB DB BNT
☐ Want Orig. Ret. $4.50 **NB** $12 **MIB** Sec. Mkt. **$24-$26**

QX 216-9 CHRISTMAS JOY
Comments: Ecru Soft-Sheen Satin Ball, 3-1/4" dia., Dated 1983
Caption: "May All The Joy You Give Away... Return To You On Christmas Day."
☐ Purchased 19___ Pd $_______ MIB NB DB BNT
☐ Want Orig. Ret. $4.50 **NB** $16 **MIB** Sec. Mkt. **$28-$32**

QX 454-3 CHRISTMAS KITTEN
Comments: Handcrafted, 1-1/4" tall
Reissued from 1982. Little Trimmers: Christmas Kitten
☐ Purchased 19___ Pd $_______ MIB NB DB BNT
☐ Want Orig. Ret. $4.00 **NB** $25 **MIB** Sec. Mkt. **$35-$38**

QX 419-9 CHRISTMAS KOALA
Comments: Handcrafted, 2-3/16" tall
A flocked koala bear holds a sprig of evergreen. **Artist:** Ed Seale
☐ Purchased 19___ Pd $_______ MIB NB DB BNT
☐ Want Orig. Ret. $4.00 **NB** $20 **MIB** Sec. Mkt. **$32-$35**

QX 221-9 CHRISTMAS WONDERLAND
Comments: Clear Glass Ball, 3-1/4" dia., RARE!
The animals celebrate Christmas in the forest. Another scene inside the ball may be seen through a "peek through" area of the design.
☐ Purchased 19___ Pd $_______ MIB NB DB BNT
☐ Want Orig. Ret. $4.50 **NB** $70 **MIB** Sec. Mkt. **$95-$100**

QX 402-9 CLOTHESPIN SOLDIER: EARLY AMERICAN
Comments: **Second in Series**, Handcrafted, 2-7/16" tall
American Revolutionary soldier beats his bass drum with arms that move. **Artist:** Linda Sickman
☐ Purchased 19___ Pd $_______ MIB NB DB BNT
☐ Want Orig. Ret. $5.00 **NB** $40 **MIB** Sec. Mkt. **$50-$65**

QX 311-9 CROWN CLASSICS: ENAMELED CHRISTMAS WREATH
Comments: Enameled, 2-3/4" tall, Dated 1983
Enameled patchwork wreath with a bezel of solid brass. Caption: "Each Moment Of The Season Has Beauty All Its Own. Christmas 1983."
☐ Purchased 19___ Pd $_______ MIB NB DB BNT
☐ Want Orig. Ret. $9.00 NB $5 **MIB** Sec. Mkt. **$15-$18**

QX 303-7 CROWN CLASSICS: MEMORIES TO TREASURE
Comments: Acrylic, 4-1/4" tall, Dated 1983
Santa's beard holds your favorite photograph.
Caption: "Holiday Fun Times Make Memories To Treasure."
☐ Purchased 19___ Pd $_______ MIB NB DB BNT
☐ Want Orig. Ret. $7.00 **NB** $15 **MIB** Sec. Mkt. **$20-$22**

QX 302-7 CROWN CLASSICS: MOTHER & CHILD
Comments: Blue Oval Cameo, 3-3/4" tall
Madonna and Child design with a translucent appearance. Caption: "Come Let Us Celebrate His Love For This Is The Season Of Rejoicing."
☐ Purchased 19___ Pd $_______ MIB NB DB BNT
☐ Want Orig. Ret. $7.50 **NB** $21 **MIB** Sec. Mkt. **$38-$42**

QX 215-9 CURRIER & IVES
Comments: White Porcelain Glass Ball, 3-1/4" dia., Dated 1983
Caption: "Christmas 1983, Central Park Winter, The Skating Pond, Currier and Ives."
☐ Purchased 19___ Pd $_______ MIB NB DB BNT
☐ Want Orig. Ret. $4.50 **NB** $12 **MIB** Sec. Mkt. **$16-$19**

QX 435-5 CYCLING SANTA
Comments: Handcrafted, 4-3/8" tall
Reissued from 1982.
☐ Purchased 19___ Pd $_______ MIB NB DB BNT
☐ Want Orig. Ret. $20.00 **NB** $125 **MIB** Sec. Mkt. **$150-$155**

QX 203-7 DAUGHTER
Comments: Pink Glass Ball, 3-1/4" dia., Dated 1983
Ribbons and pearls on lace and velvet form a lovely background for the caption: "A Daughter's Love Makes Christmas Beautiful. 1983"
☐ Purchased 19___ Pd $_______ MIB NB DB BNT
☐ Want Orig. Ret. $4.50 **NB** $20 **MIB** Sec. Mkt. **$40-$45**

QX 423-7 DIANA DOLL
Comments: Porcelain Doll, 4-1/4" tall
In the style of an antique doll, Diana's face is handpainted porcelain. **Artist:** Donna Lee
☐ Purchased 19___ Pd $_______ MIB NB DB BNT
☐ Want Orig. Ret. $9.00 **NB** $15 **MIB** Sec. Mkt. **$28-$32**

QX 212-9 DISNEY
Comments: Chrome Glass Ball, 3-1/4" dia., Dated 1983
Mickey's face is framed by a green wreath.
☐ Purchased 19___ Pd $_______ MIB NB DB BNT
☐ Want Orig. Ret. $4.50 **NB** $30 **MIB** Sec. Mkt. **$48-$55**

QX 421-7 EMBROIDERED HEART
Comments: Fabric, 4-13/16" tall, Reissued in 1984
Trimmed with a green cord, this red heart has poinsettia and holly embroidery.
☐ Purchased 19___ Pd $_______ MIB NB DB BNT
☐ Want Orig. Ret. $6.50 **NB** $12 **MIB** Sec. Mkt. **$24-$26**

Happy Holidays

QX 479-6 EMBROIDERED STOCKING
Comments: Fabric, 3-1/4" tall, Reissued in 1984.
Quilted red stocking, accented with embroidery, is trimmed in lace and filled with toys. **Artist:** Linda Sickman
☐ Purchased 19___ Pd $_______ MIB NB DB BNT
☐ Want Orig. Ret. $6.50 **NB** $10 **MIB** Sec. Mkt. **$20-$22**

QX 306-9 FIRST CHRISTMAS TOGETHER
Comments: Acrylic, 4-1/4" tall, Dated 1983
Bell shape design with caption: "First Christmas Together 1983."
☐ Purchased 19___ Pd $_______ MIB NB DB BNT
☐ Want Orig. Ret. $6.00 **NB** $14 **MIB** Sec. Mkt. **$22-$24**

QX 301-7 FIRST CHRISTMAS TOGETHER
Comments: Dark Blue Cameo, 3-3/4" wide, Dated 1983
Couple on sleigh ride. Caption: "First Christmas Together 1983."
☐ Purchased 19___ Pd $_______ MIB NB DB BNT
☐ Want Orig. Ret. $7.50 **NB** $12 **MIB** Sec. Mkt. **$18-$22**

QX 432-9 FIRST CHRISTMAS TOGETHER
Comments: Polished Brass, 2-5/8" tall, Dated 1983
Locket opens; space for two photos. Caption: "First Christmas Together 1983." **Artist:** Ed Seale
☐ Purchased 19___ Pd $_______ MIB NB DB BNT
☐ Want Orig. Ret. $15.00 **NB** $25 **MIB** Sec. Mkt. **$35-$38**

QX 310-7 FIRST CHRISTMAS TOGETHER
Comments: Classic Shape, 3-1/4" dia., Dated 1983
Winter forest scene. Caption: "First Christmas Together 1983" and "All The World Is Beautiful When Seen Through Eyes Of Love."
☐ Purchased 19___ Pd $_______ MIB NB DB BNT
☐ Want Orig. Ret. $6.00 **NB** $18 **MIB** Sec. Mkt. **$38-$40**

QX 208-9 FIRST CHRISTMAS TOGETHER
Comments: White Glass Ball, 3-1/4" dia., Dated 1983
Candy canes form hearts which surround the caption and the date. The design is printed directly on the ball. Caption: "First Christmas Together." **Artist:** Linda Sickman
☐ Purchased 19___ Pd $_______ MIB NB DB BNT
☐ Want Orig. Ret. $4.50 **NB** $16 **MIB** Sec. Mkt. **$26-$30**

QX 207-7 FRIENDSHIP
Comments: White Classic Glass, 3-1/4" dia., Dated 1983
Eskimo in Christmas scenes. Caption: "Christmas 1983" and "Friendship Is A Special Gift That Gives Your Heart A Happy Lift."
☐ Purchased 19___ Pd $_______ MIB NB DB BNT
☐ Want Orig. Ret. $4.50 **NB** $10 **MIB** Sec. Mkt. **$18-$22**

QX 305-9 FRIENDSHIP
Comments: Acrylic, Classic shape, 5" tall, Dated 1983
Caption: "Christmas 1983" and "Friendship Grows More Beautiful With Each Passing Season."
☐ Purchased 19___ Pd $_______ MIB NB DB BNT
☐ Want Orig. Ret. $6.00 **NB** $10 **MIB** Sec. Mkt. **$18-$22**

QMB 904-7 FRIENDSHIP
Comments: Musical, Classic Shape, 4-1/2" tall
Muffin Celebrates Christmas. Caption: "It's Song-in-the-Air Time, Lights-Everywhere Time, Good Fun-to-Share Time, It's Christmas." Plays *We Wish You A Merry Christmas.*
☐ Purchased 19___ Pd $_______ MIB NB DB BNT
☐ Want Orig. Ret. $16.00 **NB** $75 **MIB** Sec. Mkt. **$125-$130**

QX 400-7 FROSTY FRIENDS
Comments: **Fourth in Series,** Handcrafted, 1-59/64" tall
Dated 1983. Eskimo plays with a baby seal on an iceberg. Caption: "Merry Christmas 1983." **Artist:** Ed Seale
☐ Purchased 19___ Pd $_______ MIB NB DB BNT
☐ Want Orig. Ret. $8.00 **NB** $225 **MIB** Sec. Mkt. **$280-$285**

QX 201-7 GODCHILD
Comments: White Classical Glass, 3-1/4" dia., Dated 1983
Angel and red bird sing a duet. Caption: "To Wish A Special Godchild A Very Merry Christmas."
☐ Purchased 19___ Pd $_______ MIB NB DB BNT
☐ Want Orig. Ret. $4.50 **NB** $8 **MIB** Sec. Mkt. **$15-$18**

QX 430-9 GRANDCHILD'S FIRST CHRISTMAS
Comments: Handcrafted, 3-3/4" long, Dated 1983
Baby rides in a white, wicker-look buggy. Caption: "Grandchild's First Christmas 1983."
☐ Purchased 19___ Pd $_______ MIB NB DB BNT
☐ Want Orig. Ret. $14.00 **NB** $20 **MIB** Sec. Mkt. **$35-$40**

QX 312-9 GRANDCHILD'S FIRST CHRISTMAS
Comments: White Classic Shape, 3-1/4" dia., Dated 1983
A baby and its toys. Caption: "Grandchild's First Christmas 1983" and "A Grandchild Is A Special Reason Why Christmas Is Such A Merry Season."
☐ Purchased 19___ Pd $_______ MIB NB DB BNT
☐ Want Orig. Ret. $6.00 **NB** $12 **MIB** Sec. Mkt. **$20-$24**

QX 202-7 GRANDDAUGHTER
Comments: White Porcelain Glass Ball, 3-1/4" dia., Dated 1983
Artwork from the Hallmark Historical Collection. Caption: "A Granddaughter Brings Beautiful Moments And Memories To Treasure" and "Christmas 1983."
☐ Purchased 19___ Pd $_______ MIB NB DB BNT
☐ Want Orig. Ret. $4.50 **NB** $10 **MIB** Sec. Mkt. **$28-$30**

QX 205-7 GRANDMOTHER
Comments: White Porcelain Glass Ball, 3-1/4" dia., Dated 1983
Family in a horse-drawn sleigh with fenced farm house in the background. Caption: "Over The River And Through The Woods To Grandmother's House We Go... Christmas 1983."
☐ Purchased 19___ Pd $_______ MIB NB DB BNT
☐ Want Orig. Ret. $4.50 **NB** $10 **MIB** Sec. Mkt. **$20-$22**

QX 429-9 GRANDPARENTS
Comments: Ceramic, 3" tall, Dated 1983
White Bell. Caption: "Grandparents Are Love."
☐ Purchased 19___ Pd $_______ MIB NB DB BNT
☐ Want Orig. Ret. $6.50 **NB** $15 **MIB** Sec. Mkt. **$20-$24**

QX 201-9 GRANDSON
Comments: Ecru Soft-Sheen Satin Ball, 3-1/4" dia., Dated 1983
Kitten plays with a red ornament. Caption: "Christmas 1983" and "A Grandson, Like Christmas, Brings Joy To The Heart."
☐ Purchased 19___ Pd $_______ MIB NB DB BNT
☐ Want Orig. Ret. $4.50 **NB** $16 **MIB** Sec. Mkt. **$28-$32**

QX 217-7 HERE COMES SANTA
Comments: Red Glass Ball, 3-1/4" dia., Dated 1983
Four views of Santa's face. Caption: "Merry Christmas 1983."
☐ Purchased 19___ Pd $_______ MIB NB DB BNT
☐ Want Orig. Ret. $4.50 **NB** $15 **MIB** Sec. Mkt. **$35-$40**

QX 403-7 HERE COMES SANTA: SANTA EXPRESS
Comments : **Fifth in Series,** Handcrafted, 3-7/16" tall, Dated 1983.
Santa pumps a "wooden" railroad car with gifts. The wheels turn.
Artist: Donna Lee
☐ Purchased 19___ Pd $_______ MIB NB DB BNT
☐ Want Orig. Ret. $13.00 **NB** $225 **MIB** Sec. Mkt. **$280-290**

QX 424-7 HITCHHIKING SANTA
Comments: Handcrafted, 2-21/32" tall
Santa in sunglasses and white shorts is holding a sign that reads "Goin' South" as he "thumbs" a ride. **Artist:** Ed Seale
☐ Purchased 19___ Pd $_______ MIB NB DB BNT
☐ Want Orig. Ret. $8.00 **NB** $30 **MIB** Sec. Mkt. **$42-$45**

QX 303-9 HOLIDAY HIGHLIGHTS: CHRISTMAS STOCKING
Comments: Acrylic, 4" tall, Dated 1983
"Etched" argyle Christmas stocking is filled with gifts and toys. Caption: "Merry Christmas 1983."
☐ Purchased 19___ Pd $_______ MIB NB DB BNT
☐ Want Orig. Ret. $6.00 **NB** $25 **MIB** Sec. Mkt. **$40-$45**

QX 304-7 HOLIDAY HIGHLIGHTS: STAR OF PEACE
Comments: Acrylic, 4" tall, A four-pointed star with "reflections" is centered in an oval shape. Caption: "Peace." **Artist:** Ed Seale
☐ Purchased 19___ Pd $_______ MIB NB DB BNT
☐ Want Orig. Ret. $6.00 **NB** $10 **MIB** Sec. Mkt. **$15-$18**

QX 307-7 HOLIDAY HIGHLIGHTS: TIME FOR SHARING
Comments: Acrylic, 4" tall, Dated 1983
Mary Hamilton scene of a little girl tying a scarf around a kitten's neck. Caption: "Christmas Is A Time For Sharing, Smiling, Loving, Giving, Caring."
☐ Purchased 19___ Pd $_______ MIB NB DB BNT
☐ Want Orig. Ret. $6.00 **NB** $25 **MIB** Sec. Mkt. **$40-$42**

QX 412-7 HOLIDAY PUPPY
Comments: Handcrafted, 1-19/32" tall
Cute brown and white puppy with black nose and ears has a red fabric bow around its neck.
☐ Purchased 19___ Pd $_______ MIB NB DB BNT
☐ Want Orig. Ret. $3.50 **NB** $18 **MIB** Sec. Mkt. **$25-$30**

QX 307-9 HOLIDAY SCULPTURE: HEART
Comments: Translucent Acrylic, 2" tall
Red, three-dimensional heart. **Artist:** Linda Sickman
☐ Purchased 19___ Pd $_______ MIB NB DB BNT
☐ Want Orig. Ret. $4.00 **NB** $32 **MIB** Sec. Mkt. **$42-$46**

QX 308-7 HOLIDAY SCULPTURE: SANTA
Comments: Translucent Red Acrylic
Three-dimensional Santa.
☐ Purchased 19___ Pd $_______ MIB NB DB BNT
☐ Want Orig. Ret. $4.00 **NB** $18 **MIB** Sec. Mkt. **$30-$35**

QX 309-9 HOLIDAY WILDLIFE: CHICKADEE
Comments: **Second in Series,** Decoform and Wood, 3" dia.
Dated 1983. Porcelain look insert of a chickadee on a branch. Caption: "Black-Capped Chickadees, Parus Atricapillus" and "Second In A Series, Wildlife Collection - Christmas 1983."
☐ Purchased 19___ Pd $_______ MIB NB DB BNT
☐ Want Orig. Ret. $7.00 **NB** $55 **MIB** Sec. Mkt. **$78-$80**

QX 407-9 JACK FROST
Comments: Handcrafted, 3-3/4" tall
Jack Frost is painting beautiful scrolls of frost on the windowpanes.
☐ Purchased 19___ Pd $_______ MIB NB DB BNT
☐ Want Orig. Ret. $9.00 **NB** $45 **MIB** Sec. Mkt. **$55-$60**

QX 425-9 JOLLY SANTA
Comments: Handcrafted, 1-15/16" tall
Merry Santa is posing with his pack of toys.
☐ Purchased 19___ Pd $_______ MIB NB DB BNT
☐ Want Orig. Ret. $3.50 **NB** $14 **MIB** Sec. Mkt. **$35-$40**

QX 495-6 KERMIT THE FROG™
Comments: Handcrafted, 3-9/16" tall
Reissued from 1982. **Artist:** Donna Lee
☐ Purchased 19___ Pd $_______ MIB NB DB BNT
☐ Want Orig. Ret. $11.00 **NB** $80 **MIB** Sec. Mkt. **$90-$100**

QX 207-9 LOVE
Comments: Lt. Green Glass Ball, 3-1/4" dia., Dated 1983
Woodland snow scene. Caption: "Love Makes Each Day A Joy, Each Moment A Memory" And "Christmas 1983."
☐ Purchased 19___ Pd $_______ MIB NB DB BNT
☐ Want Orig. Ret. $4.50 **NB** $12 **MIB** Sec. Mkt. **$22-$24**

QX 310-9 LOVE
Comments: Red Classic Shape Ball, 3-1/4" dia., Dated 1983
Reproduced from needlework in sampler style. Caption: "Christmas 1983" and "Love, The Spirit Which Enhances All The Seasons Of Our Lives."
☐ Purchased 19___ Pd $_______ MIB NB DB BNT
☐ Want Orig. Ret. $6.00 **NB** $20 **MIB** Sec. Mkt. **$38-$40**

QX 305-7 LOVE
Comments: Acrylic, 4" tall, Dated 1983
Skaters form the word "Love" on this heart-shaped ornament. Caption: "Christmas 1983."
☐ Purchased 19___ Pd $_______ MIB NB DB BNT
☐ Want Orig. Ret. $6.00 **NB** $12 **MIB** Sec. Mkt. **$20-$22**

QX 422-7 LOVE
Comments: Porcelain, 3-1/8" tall, Dated 1983
A small red heart hangs in the center of a larger open white heart. Caption: "Love." **Artist:** Linda Sickman
☐ Purchased 19___ Pd $_______ MIB NB DB BNT
☐ Want Orig. Ret. $13.00 **NB** $20 **MIB** Sec. Mkt. **$30-$35**

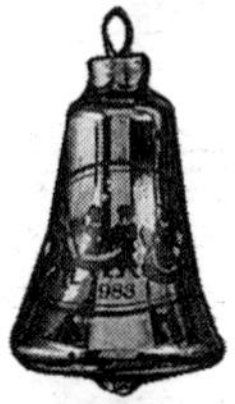

QX 223-9 LOVE IS A SONG
Comments: Silver Glass Bell, 2-1/2" tall, Dated 1983
Dickens' characters are silhouetted in red, green and white. Caption: "Christmas Is A Song Of Love For Every Heart To Sing."
☐ Purchased 19___ Pd $_______ MIB NB DB BNT
☐ Want Orig. Ret. $4.50 **NB** $18 **MIB** Sec. Mkt. **$26-$30**

QX 428-7 MADONNA AND CHILD
Comments: Porcelain, 3-1/16" tall
Madonna in blue and white holds the Christ Child.
☐ Purchased 19___ Pd $_______ MIB NB DB BNT
☐ Want Orig. Ret. $12.00 **NB** $35 **MIB** Sec. Mkt. **$42-$45**

QX 415-7 MAILBOX KITTEN
Comments: Handcrafted, 1-9/16" tall, Dated 1983
A kitten with letters in its paws peeks out of a red mailbox reading "1983 Peppermint Lane."
☐ Purchased 19___ Pd $_______ MIB NB DB BNT
☐ Want Orig. Ret. $6.50 **NB** $40 **MIB** Sec. Mkt. **$55-$62**

QX 213-7 MARY HAMILTON
Comments: White Classical Glass, 3-1/2" tall, Dated 1983
A little girl prays with forest creatures. Caption: "A Wee Little, Warm Little Christmas Time Prayer-May God Bless Us Always With Friendships To Share."
☐ Purchased 19___ Pd $_______ MIB NB DB BNT
☐ Want Orig. Ret. $4.50 **NB** $18 **MIB** Sec. Mkt. **$30-$35**

QX 405-7 MISS PIGGY™
Comments: Handcrafted, 4-9/16" tall
Dressed in a lavender skating costume, Miss Piggy makes a graceful leap on her ice skates.
☐ Purchased 19___ Pd $_______ MIB NB DB BNT
☐ Want Orig. Ret. $13.00 **NB** $185 **MIB** Sec. Mkt. **$215-$225**

QX 429-7 MOM & DAD
Comments: Ceramic Bell, 3" tall, Dated 1983
Fired-on decals of poinsettias and holly frame the captions: "Mom and Dad" and "Christmas 1983." **Artist:** Sharon Pike
☐ Purchased 19___ Pd $_______ MIB NB DB BNT
☐ Want Orig. Ret. $6.50 **NB** $15 **MIB** Sec. Mkt. **$24-$26**

QX 306-7 MOTHER
Comments: Acrylic, 4" tall, Dated 1983. Heart-shaped design with white "etched" border carries the caption: "Mother... Always Caring, Always Sharing, Always There To Love."
☐ Purchased 19___ Pd $_______ MIB NB DB BNT
☐ Want Orig. Ret. $6.00 **NB** $12 **MIB** Sec. Mkt. **$18-$20**

MDQ 340-7 MOTHER'S DAY – A MOTHER'S LOVE
Comments: Musical; White Glass Classical Ball
Plays *Swan Lake.*
☐ Purchased 19___ Pd $_______ MIB NB DB BNT
☐ Want Orig. Ret. $14.00 **NB** $60 **MIB** Sec. Mkt. **$85-$90**

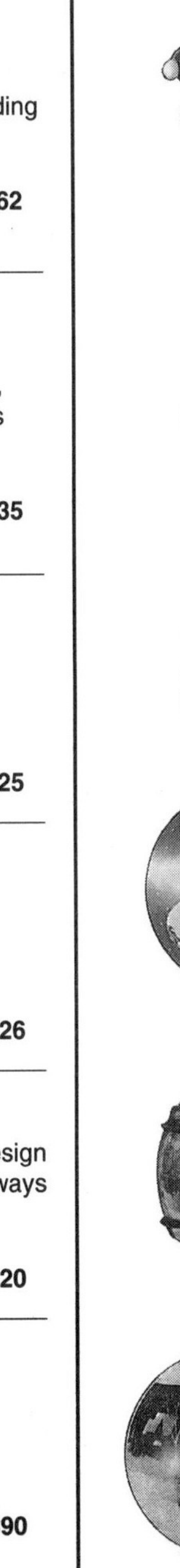

QX 407-7 MOUNTAIN CLIMBING SANTA
Comments: Handcrafted, 2-13/32" tall, Reissued in 1984.
Santa climbs a mountain with a real rope. **Artist:** Ed Seale
☐ Purchased 19___ Pd $_______ MIB NB DB BNT
☐ Want Orig. Ret. $6.50 **NB** $18 **MIB** Sec. Mkt. **$38-$42**

QX 419-7 MOUSE IN BELL
Comments: Handcrafted-Glass, 4" tall
A cute mouse with a leather tail and a brass ring in the top of his stocking cap is the "clapper" for this clear glass bell.
☐ Purchased 19___ Pd $_______ MIB NB DB BNT
☐ Want Orig. Ret. $10.00 **NB** $50 **MIB** Sec. Mkt. **$62-$68**

QX 413-7 MOUSE ON CHEESE
Comments: Handcrafted, 2-37/64" tall
An adorable grey mouse enjoys the gift-wrapped cheese on which he's sitting.
Artist: Linda Sickman
☐ Purchased 19___ Pd $_______ MIB NB DB BNT
☐ Want Orig. Ret. $6.50 **NB** $35 **MIB** Sec. Mkt. **$50-$55**

QX 214-7 MUPPETS™, THE
Comments: Lt. Blue Satin Ball, 3-1/4" dia., Dated 1983
Kermit and Miss Piggy are in a biplane skywriting "Merry Christmas" and Fozzie floats in a hot air balloon.
☐ Purchased 19___ Pd $_______ MIB NB DB BNT
☐ Want Orig. Ret. $4.50 **NB** $40 **MIB** Sec. Mkt. **$50-$55**

QMB 904-9 NATIVITY
Comments: Musical, Classic Shape, Dark Blue, 4-1/2" tall
Three Kings bring gifts for the Holy Child. Caption: "The Star Shone Bright With A Holy Light As Heaven Came To Earth That Night." Plays *Silent Night.*
☐ Purchased 19___ Pd $_______ MIB NB DB BNT
☐ Want Orig. Ret. $16.00 **NB** $30 **MIB** Sec. Mkt. **$45-$50**

QX 210-7 NEW HOME
Comments: White Soft-Sheen Satin Ball, 3-1/4" dia.
Dated 1983. Carolers on a snowy night.
Caption: "Christmas Is The Perfect Way Of Rounding Out Each Year, For Every Heart And Home's Aglow With Love And Warmth And Cheer."
☐ Purchased 19___ Pd $_______ MIB NB DB BNT
☐ Want Orig. Ret. $4.50 **NB** $12 **MIB** Sec. Mkt. **$24-$28**

QX 215-7 NORMAN ROCKWELL
Comments: Light Green Glass Ball, 3-1/4" dia., Dated 1983
Caption: "Things Are Humming, Santa's Coming, Hearts Are Full Of Cheer. Lights Are Gleaming, Kids Are Dreaming... Christmas Time Is Here. From the Norman Rockwell Collection."
☐ Purchased 19___ Pd $_______ MIB NB DB BNT
☐ Want Orig. Ret. $4.50 **NB** $35 **MIB** Sec. Mkt. **$45-$50**

QX 300-7 NORMAN ROCKWELL SERIES
Comments: **Fourth in Series**, Dark Blue Cameo, 3" dia.
Dated 1983. Caption: "Dress Rehearsal. Fourth In A Series. Christmas 1983. The Norman Rockwell Collection."
☐ Purchased 19___ Pd $_______ MIB NB DB BNT
☐ Want Orig. Ret. $7.50 **NB** $21 **MIB** Sec. Mkt. **$30-$35**

QX 409-9 OLD-FASHIONED SANTA
Comments: Handcrafted, 5-9/64" tall
Jointed, realistic interpretation. Santa wears knee-length red suit with red and white striped hose. His arms and legs are movable.
Artist: Linda Sickman
☐ Purchased 19___ Pd $_______ MIB NB DB BNT
☐ Want Orig. Ret. $11.00 **NB** $55 **MIB** Sec. Mkt. **$65-$70**

QX 218-7 ORIENTAL BUTTERFLIES
Comments: Turquoise Glass Ball, 3-1/4" dia.
Eight colorful butterflies; reproduced from original stitchery.
☐ Purchased 19___ Pd $_______ MIB NB DB BNT
☐ Want Orig. Ret. $4.50 **NB** $18 **MIB** Sec. Mkt. **$24-$28**

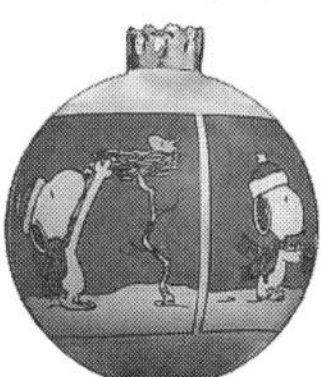

QX 212-7 PEANUTS®
Comments: White Soft-Sheen Satin Ball, 3-1/4" dia.
Dated 1983. Comic strip panels show Snoopy bringing Woodstock and his friends out of the cold. Caption: "Christmas 1983" and "May The Joy Of The Season Warm Every Heart."
☐ Purchased 19___ Pd $_______ MIB NB DB BNT
☐ Want Orig. Ret. $4.50 **NB** $18 **MIB** Sec. Mkt. **$25-$30**

QX 408-9 PEPPERMINT PENGUIN
Comments: Handcrafted, 2-3/4" tall
A red capped penguin pedals his "peppermint candy" unicycle.
☐ Purchased 19___ Pd $_______ MIB NB DB BNT
☐ Want Orig. Ret. $6.50 **NB** $24 **MIB** Sec. Mkt. **$45-$50**

QX 428-9 PORCELAIN BEAR: CINNAMON TEDDY
Comments: ***FIRST IN SERIES,*** Porcelain, 2-15/64" tall
Made of fine porcelain and hand painted. Prices up from '95.
Artist: Peter Dutkin
☐ Purchased 19___ Pd $_______ MIB NB DB BNT
☐ Want Orig. Ret. $7.00 **NB-P** $50 **MIB** Sec. Mkt. **$52-$58**

QX 416-7 RAINBOW ANGEL
Comments: Handcrafted, 2-15/16" tall
Angel with a brass halo slides down a rainbow. Trading increase seen with this ornament. **Artist:** Donna Lee
☐ Purchased 19___ Pd $_______ MIB NB DB BNT
☐ Want Orig. Ret. $5.50 **NB** $65 **MIB** Sec. Mkt. **$120-$130**

QX 417-7 ROCKING HORSE
Comments: **Third in Series,** Handcrafted, 2-7/8" tall
Dated 1983. Russet horse with green rockers.
Artist: Linda Sickman
☐ Purchased 19___ Pd $_______ MIB NB DB BNT
☐ Want Orig. Ret. $10.00 **NB** $250 **MIB** Sec. Mkt. **$285-$295**

QX 311-7 SANTA'S MANY FACES
Comments: Red Classic Shape Ball, 3-1/4" dia., Dated 1983
Six Santa scenes circle the center. Caption: "Merry Christmas."
☐ Purchased 19___ Pd $_______ MIB NB DB BNT
☐ Want Orig. Ret. $6.00 **NB** $20 **MIB** Sec. Mkt. **$30-$35**

QX 426-9 SANTA'S ON HIS WAY
Comments: Handcrafted, 3" tall, Four handcrafted openings show Santa in three-dimensional, handpainted scenes.
☐ Purchased 19___ Pd $_______ MIB NB DB BNT
☐ Want Orig. Ret. $10.00 **NB** $20 **MIB** Sec. Mkt. **$32-$35**

QX 450-3 SANTA'S WORKSHOP
Comments: Handcrafted, 3" tall. Reissued from 1982.
Artist: Donna Lee
☐ Purchased 19___ Pd $_______ MIB NB DB BNT
☐ Want Orig. Ret. $10.00 **NB** $70 **MIB** Sec. Mkt. **$80-$90**

QX 424-9 SCRIMSHAW REINDEER
Comments: Handcrafted, 3-3/4" tall
The leaping reindeer was created with the look of handcarved ivory scrimshaw accented in brown. **Artist:** Ed Seale
☐ Purchased 19___ Pd $_______ MIB NB DB BNT
☐ Want Orig. Ret. $8.00 **NB** $22 **MIB** Sec. Mkt. **$32-$35**

QX 219-9 SEASON'S GREETINGS
Comments: Chrome Glass Ball, 3-1/4" dia.
The caption, "Season's Greetings" is formed with neon lettering on a dark background.
☐ Purchased 19___ Pd $_______ MIB NB DB BNT
☐ Want Orig. Ret. $4.50 **NB** $12 **MIB** Sec. Mkt. **$22-$25**

QX 214-9 SHIRT TALES™
Comments: White Classical Glass, 3-1/2" tall, Dated 1983
A walrus, penguin and polar bear wear t-shirts that say, "Deck the Halls" and "Fa La-La-La-La" Caption: "Christmas 1983" and "Tis The Season To Be Jolly."
☐ Purchased 19___ Pd $_______ MIB NB DB BNT
☐ Want Orig. Ret. $4.50 **NB** $14 **MIB** Sec. Mkt. **$22-$24**

OX 110-9 SILVER BELL
Comments: Silverplate
Came with red ribbon; made for J. C. Penney.
☐ Purchased 19___ Pd $_______ MIB NB DB BNT
☐ Want Orig. Ret. $12.00 **NB** $20 **MIB** Sec. Mkt. **$40-$42**

QX 206-9 SISTER
Comments: White Classical Glass, 3-1/4" dia., Dated 1983
Wreath frames the caption: "A Sister Is A Forever Friend."
☐ Purchased 19___ Pd $_______ MIB NB DB BNT
☐ Want Orig. Ret. $4.50 **NB** $14 **MIB** Sec. Mkt. **$18-$20**

QX 409-7 SKATING RABBIT
Comments: Handcrafted, 3-1/4" tall
This happy rabbit has a real cotton tail and a specially designed stocking cap which covers each ear separately.
☐ Purchased 19___ Pd $_______ MIB NB DB BNT
☐ Want Orig. Ret. $8.00 **NB** $35 **MIB** Sec. Mkt. **$50-$55**

QX 418-7 SKI LIFT SANTA
Comments: Handcrafted-Brass, 3-7/8" tall, Dated 1983
Santa waves as he rides the ski lift. A brass bell is the pompon for his hat. Date is on his ski lift ticket.
☐ Purchased 19___ Pd $_______ MIB NB DB BNT
☐ Want Orig. Ret. $8.00 **NB** $50 **MIB** Sec. Mkt. **$65-$70**

QX 420-7 SKIING FOX
Comments: Handcrafted, 2-5/32" tall
A fox with a green muffler is showing great form as he races downhill. **Artist:** Donna Lee
☐ Purchased 19___ Pd $_______ MIB NB DB BNT
☐ Want Orig. Ret. $8.00 **NB** $28 **MIB** Sec. Mkt. **$40-$45**

QX 400-9 SNEAKER MOUSE
Comments: Handcrafted, 1-11/16" tall
A cute white mouse has made his bed in a red and white sneaker. **Artist:** Ed Seale
☐ Purchased 19___ Pd $_______ MIB NB DB BNT
☐ Want Orig. Ret. $4.50 **NB-P** $22 **MIB** Sec. Mkt. **$38-$42**

QX 416-9 SNOOPY AND FRIENDS
Comments: **Fifth in Series,** Handcrafted Panorama Ball 3-1/4" dia., Dated 1983. Snoopy is dressed as Santa and delivers a bag of gifts to Woodstock. **Artist:** Linda Sickman
☐ Purchased 19___ Pd $_______ MIB NB DB BNT
☐ Want Orig. Ret. $13.00 **NB** $60 **MIB** Sec. Mkt. **$85-$90**

QX 202-9 SON
Comments: Deep Blue Satin Ball, 3-1/4" dia., Dated 1983
A little boy, house, Christmas trees, and a snowman riding a snowhorse are depicted. Caption: "A Son Brings A Bit Of Christmas Cheer To Every Day Throughout The Year."
☐ Purchased 19___ Pd $_______ MIB NB DB BNT
☐ Want Orig. Ret. $4.50 **NB** $16 **MIB** Sec. Mkt. **$32-$35**

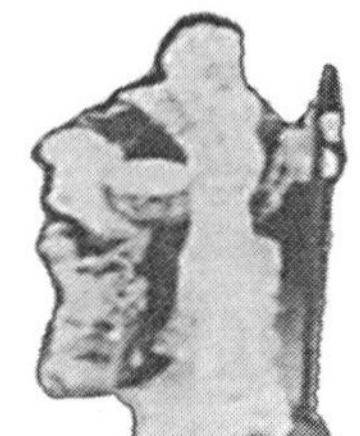

QHD 406-9 ST. NICHOLAS
Comments: Porcelain Table Decoration
An Old-World Santa makes his rounds on Christmas Eve with his pack of toys and a walking stick.
☐ Purchased 19___ Pd $_______ MIB NB DB BNT
☐ Want Orig. Ret. $27.50 **NB** $75 **MIB** Sec. Mkt. **$88-$92**

QX 224-9 TEACHER
Comments: Silver Glass Bell, 2-1/2" tall, Dated 1983
Schoolhouse and red and green lettering are bordered with green bands. Caption: "For A Special Teacher At Christmas."
☐ Purchased 19___ Pd $_______ MIB NB DB BNT
☐ Want Orig. Ret. $4.50 **NB** $12 **MIB** Sec. Mkt. **$18-$20**

QX 304-9 TEACHER
Comments: Acrylic, 3-3/4" tall, Dated 1983
A classic shape design shows a raccoon writing the caption: "Merry Christmas, Merry Christmas, Merry Christmas, Teacher!"
☐ Purchased 19___ Pd $_______ MIB NB DB BNT
☐ Want Orig. Ret. $6.00 **NB** $6 **MIB** Sec. Mkt. **$14-$16**

QX 430-7 TENTH CHRISTMAS TOGETHER
Comments: Ceramic Bell, 3" tall, Dated 1983
White ceramic bell is decorated with a golden French horn and hung with red fabric ribbon. Caption: "Tenth Christmas Together 1983."
☐ Purchased 19___ Pd $_______ MIB NB DB BNT
☐ Want Orig. Ret. $6.50 **NB** $10 **MIB** Sec. Mkt. **$22-$25**

QX 401-7 THIMBLE SERIES: THIMBLE ELF
Comments: **Sixth in Series,** Handcrafted, 1-15/16" tall
A little elf is licking his lips over a cherry-topped treat served in a thimble.
☐ Purchased 19___ Pd $_______ MIB NB DB BNT
☐ Want Orig. Ret. $5.00 **NB-P** $15 **MIB** Sec. Mkt. **$34-$38**

QX 404-9 TIN LOCOMOTIVE
Comments: **Second in Series**, Pressed Tin, 3" tall, Dated 1983
This early locomotive is lithographed in red and green and trimmed in gold. **Artist:** Linda Sickman
☐ Purchased 19___ Pd $_______ MIB NB DB BNT
☐ Want Orig. Ret. $13.00 **NB** $240 **MIB** Sec. Mkt. **$265-$280**

QX 414-9 TIN ROCKING HORSE
Comments: Pressed Tin, 3-11/64" tall. This three-dimensional lithographed tin rocking horse is a dappled gray and resembles an Early American nursery toy. **Artist:** Linda Sickman
☐ Purchased 19___ Pd $_______ MIB NB DB BNT
☐ Want Orig. Ret. $6.50 **NB** $35 **MIB** Sec. Mkt. **$42-$48**

QMB 415-9 TWELVE DAYS OF CHRISTMAS MUSICAL
Comments: Musical, Handcrafted, 3-3/4" tall. Reissued in 1984
Blue and white motifs of the song. Plays *Twelve Days of Christmas.* **Artist:** Ed Seale
☐ Purchased 19___ Pd $_______ MIB NB DB BNT
☐ Want Orig. Ret. $15.00 **NB** $65 **MIB** Sec. Mkt. **$85-$90**

QX 224-7 TWENTY-FIFTH CHRISTMAS TOGETHER
Comments: Silver Glass Bell, 2-1/2" tall, Dated 1983
Bell with red print and white snowflakes. Caption: "25th Christmas Together."
☐ Purchased 19___ Pd $_______ MIB NB DB BNT
☐ Want Orig. Ret. $4.50 **NB** $15 **MIB** Sec. Mkt. **$20-$22**

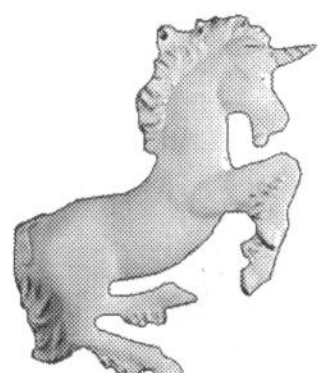

QX 426-7 UNICORN
Comments: Porcelain, 4" tall
Beautiful white porcelain prancing unicorn has hand painted gold trim. Don't confuse this with QX 429-3, 1986 Magical Unicorn.
☐ Purchased 19___ Pd $_______ MIB NB DB BNT
☐ Want Orig. Ret. $10.00 **NB** $50 **MIB** Sec. Mkt. **$65-$70**

QX 220-7 WISE MEN, THE
Comments: Gold Glass Ball, 3-1/4" dia.
Three kings raise their gifts to the star leading them.
☐ Purchased 19___ Pd $_______ MIB NB DB BNT
☐ Want Orig. Ret. $4.50 **NB** $25 **MIB** Sec. Mkt. **$40-$42**

1984 Collection

QX 246-1 A CHRISTMAS PRAYER
Comments: Blue Satin Ball, 2-7/8" dia.
Mary Hamilton's angels chase stars. Caption: "Little Prayer Be On Your Way... Bless Our Friends On Christmas Day."
☐ Purchased 19___ Pd $_______ MIB NB DB BNT
☐ Want Orig. Ret. $4.50 **NB** $15 **MIB** Sec. Mkt. **$20-$25**

QX 260-4 A GIFT OF FRIENDSHIP
Comments: Peach Glass Ball, 3" dia.
Scenes of Muffin and her kitten. Caption: "Friendship Is The Happiest Gift Of All."
☐ Purchased 19___ Pd $_______ MIB NB DB BNT
☐ Want Orig. Ret. $4.50 **NB** $12 **MIB** Sec. Mkt. **$22-$25**

QX 254-1 A SAVIOR IS BORN
Comments: Purple Glass Ball, 2-7/8" dia.
The Nativity flanks the caption which is printed in large gold lettering: "For Unto You Is Born This Day In The City Of David A Savior Which Is Christ The Lord. Luke 2:11."
☐ Purchased 19___ Pd $_______ MIB NB DB BNT
☐ Want Orig. Ret. $4.50 **NB** $15 **MIB** Sec. Mkt. **$28-$35**

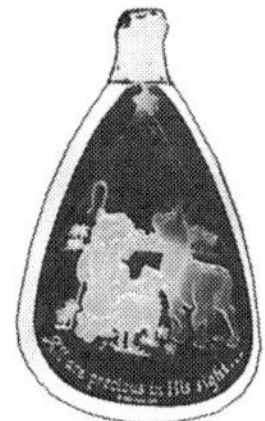

QLX 704-4 ALL ARE PRECIOUS
Comments: Lighted Acrylic, 4" tall, Reissued in 1985
A shepherd, lamb and donkey watch the star. Caption in gold foil stamp: "All Are Precious In His Sight..."
☐ Purchased 19___ Pd $_______ MIB NB DB BNT
☐ Want Orig. Ret. $8.00 **NB** $18 **MIB** Sec. Mkt. **$22-$26**

QX 452-1 ALPINE ELF
Comments: Handcrafted, 3-1/2" wide
A little elf dressed in a red coat and hat, plays a long curved horn.
Artist: Ed Seale
☐ Purchased 19___ Pd $_______ MIB NB DB BNT
☐ Want Orig. Ret. $6.00 **NB** $25 **MIB** Sec. Mkt. **$35-$42**

QX 432-1 AMANDA DOLL
Comments: Fabric, Handpainted Porcelain, 4-3/4" tall
This doll is wearing a bright green ruffled dress and bonnet.
☐ Purchased 19___ Pd $_______ MIB NB DB BNT
☐ Want Orig. Ret. $9.00 **NB** $20 **MIB** Sec. Mkt. **$25-$29**

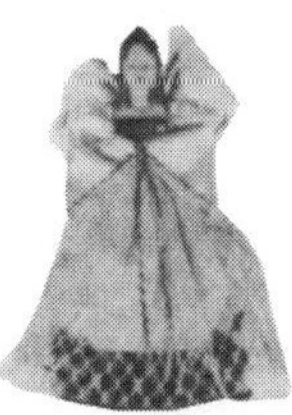

QTT 710-1 ANGEL TREE TOPPER
Comments: Fabric and Porcelain.
Golden accents on her wings and gown add to the charm of this lovely angel.
☐ Purchased 19___ Pd $_______ MIB NB DB BNT
☐ Want Orig. Ret. $24.50 **NB** $30 **MIB** Sec. Mkt. **$35-$42**

QX 349-4 ART MASTERPIECE
Comments: ***FIRST IN SERIES,*** Bezeled Satin, 2-3/4" dia.
Classic oil painting reproduced on padded satin. "Giuliano Bugiardini, *Madonna And Child And St. John,* (ca. 1505) The Nelson-Atkins Museum Of Art, Kansas City, Missouri (Nelson Fund)." **Artist:** Diana McGehee
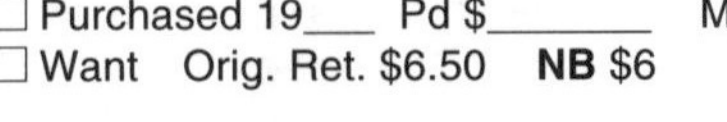
☐ Purchased 19___ Pd $_______ MIB NB DB BNT
☐ Want Orig. Ret. $6.50 **NB** $6 **MIB** Sec. Mkt. **$18-$20**

QX 340-1 BABY'S FIRST CHRISTMAS
Comments: Acrylic, 3-3/4" tall, Dated 1984
This etched teddy bear is holding a toy-filled stocking. Caption: "Baby's First Christmas."
☐ Purchased 19___ Pd $_______ MIB NB DB BNT
☐ Want Orig. Ret. $6.00 **NB** $30 **MIB** Sec. Mkt. **$38-$40**

QX 240-4 BABY'S FIRST CHRISTMAS - BOY
Comments: White Satin Ball, 2-7/8" dia., Dated 1984
A handcrafted mouse sits on top of the ornament. Caption: "Baby's First Christmas" and "A Baby Boy Is A Bundle Of Pleasure To Fill Every Day With Love Beyond Measure."
☐ Purchased 19___ Pd $_______ MIB NB DB BNT
☐ Want Orig. Ret. $4.50 **NB** $10 **MIB** Sec. Mkt. **$24-$28**

QX 240-1 BABY'S FIRST CHRISTMAS - GIRL
Comments: Cream Satin Ball, 2-7/8" dia., Dated 1984
A parade of little girls, animals and toys. Caption: "A Baby Girl Is Love That Grows In The Warmth Of Caring Hearts. Baby's First Christmas."
☐ Purchased 19___ Pd $_______ MIB NB DB BNT
☐ Want Orig. Ret. $4.50 **NB** $10 **MIB** Sec. Mkt. **$24-$28**

QX 438-1 BABY'S FIRST CHRISTMAS
Comments: Handcrafted, 3-1/2" wide, Dated 1984
A brown bear rides a sled full of toys. Caption: "Baby's First Christmas."
☐ Purchased 19___ Pd $_______ MIB NB DB BNT
☐ Want Orig. Ret. $14.00 **NB** $30 **MIB** Sec. Mkt. **$48-$52**

QX 904-1 BABY'S FIRST CHRISTMAS
Comments: Musical, Classic Shape, 4-1/4" tall, Dated 1984
"A Baby Is... Happiness, Pleasure, A Gift From Above... A Wonderful, Magical Treasure Of Love. Baby's First Christmas."
Plays *Babes in Toyland*. **Artist:** Donna Lee

☐ Purchased 19___ Pd $_______ MIB NB DB BNT
☐ Want Orig. Ret. $16.00 **NB** $22 **MIB** Sec. Mkt. **$38-$42**

QX 300-1 BABY'S FIRST CHRISTMAS PHOTOHOLDER
Comments: Fabric, 3-1/4" dia., Dated 1984
Embroidered holly sprigs with a white fabric photoholder. Caption: "Baby's First Christmas" and "A Baby Is A Special Dream Come True."
☐ Purchased 19___ Pd $_______ MIB NB DB BNT
☐ Want Orig. Ret. $7.00 **NB** $14 **MIB** Sec. Mkt. **$18-$22**

QX 241-1 BABY'S SECOND CHRISTMAS
Comments: White Satin Ball, 2-7/8" dia., Dated 1984
Pooh Bear and his friends share Christmas. A gold crown tops the ornament. Caption: "Children And Christmas Are Joys That Go Together. Baby's Second Christmas."
☐ Purchased 19___ Pd $_______ MIB NB DB BNT
☐ Want Orig. Ret. $4.50 **NB** $5 **MIB** Sec. Mkt. **$15-$18**

QX 253-1 BABY-SITTER
Comments: Green Glass Ball, 3" dia.
A group of mice have fun with their baby-sitter. Caption: "Thank Heaven For Baby-Sitters Like You."
☐ Purchased 19___ Pd $_______ MIB NB DB BNT
☐ Want Orig. Ret. $4.50 **NB** $8 **MIB** Sec. Mkt. **$14-$16**

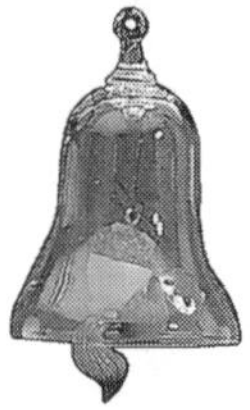

QX 443-1 BELL RINGER SQUIRREL
Comments: Glass, Handcrafted, 4" tall
A handcrafted squirrel and acorn form the clapper for this clear glass bell. **Artist:** Ed Seale
☐ Purchased 19___ Pd $_______ MIB NB DB BNT
☐ Want Orig. Ret. $10.00 **NB** $18 **MIB** Sec. Mkt. **$38-$42**

QX 438-4 BELLRINGER, THE: ELFIN ARTIST
Comments: **Sixth and Final in Series,** Dated Christmas 1984
Porcelain, 3-1/2" tall. An artistic elf has lettered his Christmas message on the bell in red paint.
☐ Purchased 19___ Pd $_______ MIB NB DB BNT
☐ Want Orig. Ret. $15.00 **NB** $25 **MIB** Sec. Mkt. **$42-$45**

QX 249-4 BETSEY CLARK
Comments: **Twelfth in Series,** Dated Christmas 1984
White Frosted Glass, 3-1/4" Children decorate their homes for the holidays. Caption: "Days Are Merry, Hearts Are Light, And All The World's A Lovely Sight."
☐ Purchased 19___ Pd $_______ MIB NB DB BNT
☐ Want Orig. Ret. $5.00 **NB** $15 **MIB** Sec. Mkt. **$32-$35**

QX 462-4 BETSEY CLARK ANGEL
Comments: Porcelain, 3-1/2" tall
Hand painted angel is dressed in a pink dress and white pinafore and plays a mandolin.
☐ Purchased 19___ Pd $_______ MIB NB DB BNT
☐ Want Orig. Ret. $9.00 **NB** $15 **MIB** Sec. Mkt. **$30-$35**

QLX 707-1 BRASS CAROUSEL
Comments: Lighted, Etched Brass, 3" tall, RARE!
Santa rides the carousel in his sleigh, pulled by one of his reindeer.
☐ Purchased 19___ Pd $_______ MIB NB DB BNT
☐ Want Orig. Ret. $9.00 **NB** $65 **MIB** Sec. Mkt. **$90-$99**

QX 451-4 CHICKADEE
Comments: Handpainted Porcelain, 3-1/4" wide
Chickadee carries a sprig of mistletoe and has a clip to fasten him to the tree. **Artist:** Linda Sickman
☐ Purchased 19___ Pd $_______ MIB NB DB BNT
☐ Want Orig. Ret. $6.00 **NB** $25 **MIB** Sec. Mkt. **$38-$42**

QX 261-1 CHILD'S THIRD CHRISTMAS
Comments: Ecru Satin Ball, 2-7/8" dia., Dated 1984
A small mouse sits on top of the ornament while teddy bears decorate for Christmas. Caption: "A Child's Third Christmas. Christmas Is A Time For Fun And Wonderful Surprises."
☐ Purchased 19___ Pd $_______ MIB NB DB BNT
☐ Want Orig. Ret. $4.50 **NB** $12 **MIB** Sec. Mkt. **$18-$22**

QLX 703-4 CHRISTMAS IN THE FOREST
Comments: Lighted Silver Classic Shape, 3-7/8" dia.
Lit from within, a moonlit night in a snowy forest is portrayed.
☐ Purchased 19___ Pd $_______ MIB NB DB BNT
☐ Want Orig. Ret. $8.00 **NB** $14 **MIB** Sec. Mkt. **$18-$20**

QX 300-4 CHRISTMAS MEMORIES PHOTOHOLDER
Comments: Fabric, 3" dia., Dated 1984
Red, white and green holiday fabrics are stitched to create a charming photo wreath.
☐ Purchased 19___ Pd $_______ MIB NB DB BNT
☐ Want Orig. Ret. $6.50 **NB** $14 **MIB** Sec. Mkt. **$24-$28**

QX 444-1 CHRISTMAS OWL
Comments: Handcrafted, Acrylic, 3-3/4" tall
A cute little owl, wearing a Santa cap, sits on an acrylic moon. His "stocking" hangs on the tip. **Artist:** Ed Seale
☐ Purchased 19___ Pd $_______ MIB NB DB BNT
☐ Want Orig. Ret. $6.00 **NB** $18 **MIB** Sec. Mkt. **$30-$35**

QLX 701-4 CITY LIGHTS
Comments: Lighted, Handcrafted, 3-1/2" tall
Santa and a squirrel are perched atop a four-way signal light which illuminates an animal. **Artist:** Bob Siedler
☐ Purchased 19___ Pd $_______ MIB NB DB BNT
☐ Want Orig. Ret. $10.00 **NB** $30 **MIB** Sec. Mkt. **$52-$55**

QX 459-1 CLASSICAL ANGEL
Comments: Limited Edition. 24,700, Handpainted Porcelain 5" tall, Wood display stand, Dated 1984
In a gown of pink, yellow and white, this angel carries a chain of brass bells. **Artist:** Donna Lee
☐ Purchased 19___ Pd $_______ MIB NB DB BNT
☐ Want Orig. Ret. $27.50 **NB/No Stand** $45
MIB Sec. Mkt. **$98-$105**

QX 447-1 CLOTHESPIN SOLDIER: CANADIAN MOUNTIE
Comments: **Third in Series,** Handcrafted, 2-1/2" tall
Dressed in a red and black uniform, this little soldier carries a holiday flag. **Artist:** Linda Sickman
☐ Purchased 19___ Pd $_______ MIB NB DB BNT
☐ Want Orig. Ret. $5.00 **NB** $15 **MIB** Sec. Mkt. **$28-$30**

QX 455-1 CUCKOO CLOCK
Comments: Handcrafted, 3-1/4" tall
This intricately detailed clock, complete with pinecone pendulums, has a brass face with "Merry Christmas" for the "time."
Artist: Donna Lee
☐ Purchased 19___ Pd $_______ MIB NB DB BNT
☐ Want Orig. Ret. $10.00 **NB** $35 **MIB** Sec. Mkt. **$48-$52**

QX 250-1 CURRIER & IVES
Comments: White Blown Glass Ball, 2-7/8" dia., Dated 1984
Caption: "American Winter Scenes, Evening, Christmas 1984."
☐ Purchased 19___ Pd $_______ MIB NB DB BNT
☐ Want Orig. Ret. $4.50 **NB** $15 **MIB** Sec. Mkt. **$20-$25**

QX 244-4 DAUGHTER
Comments: Gold Glass Classic, 3" dia., Dated 1984
Caption: "A Daughter Is Joy That Grows Deeper, Pride That Grows Stronger, Love That Touches Your Heart Every Day. Christmas 1984"
☐ Purchased 19___ Pd $_______ MIB NB DB BNT
☐ Want Orig. Ret. $4.50 **NB** $14 **MIB** Sec. Mkt. **$28-$34**

QX 250-4 DISNEY
Comments: White Glass Ball, 2-7/8" dia., Dated 1984
The whole Disney gang sends Christmas greetings: "Friends Put The Merry In Christmas."
☐ Purchased 19___ Pd $_______ MIB NB DB BNT
☐ Want Orig. Ret. $4.50 **NB** $18 **MIB** Sec. Mkt. **$32-$38**

QX 421-7 EMBROIDERED HEART
Comments: Hand-Embroidered Fabric, 4-3/4" tall
Reissued from 1983.
☐ Purchased 19___ Pd $_______ MIB NB DB BNT
☐ Want Orig. Ret. $6.50 **NB** $12 **MIB** Sec. Mkt. **$24-$26**

QX 479-6 EMBROIDERED STOCKING
Comments: Hand-Embroidered Fabric, 3-1/4" tall
Reissued from 1983. **Artist:** Linda Sickman
☐ Purchased 19___ Pd $_______ MIB NB DB BNT
☐ Want Orig. Ret. $6.50 **NB** $10 **MIB** Sec. Mkt. **$20-$22**

QX 257-1 FATHER
Comments: Acrylic, 3-1/4" wide, Dated Christmas 1984
Classic shape with musical instruments and holly at the top.
Caption: "A Father Has A Special Gift Of Giving Of Himself."
☐ Purchased 19___ Pd $_______ MIB NB DB BNT
☐ Want Orig. Ret. $6.00 **NB** $12 **MIB** Sec. Mkt. **$18-$20**

QX 342-1 FIRST CHRISTMAS TOGETHER
Comments: Acrylic, 3-5/8" dia., Dated 1984
Two doves are perched on a holly branch. Caption in silver foil: "First Christmas Together."
☐ Purchased 19___ Pd $_______ MIB NB DB BNT
☐ Want Orig. Ret. $6.00 **NB** $12 **MIB** Sec. Mkt. **$18-$21**

QX 436-4 FIRST CHRISTMAS TOGETHER
Comments: Brushed Brass, 2-1/2" tall, Dated 1984
Oval locket opens to hold two photos. Caption: "First Christmas Together" framed by hearts. **Artist:** Ed Seale
☐ Purchased 19___ Pd $_______ MIB NB DB BNT
☐ Want Orig. Ret. $15.00 **NB** $10 **MIB** Sec. Mkt. **$24-$30**

Make just one person happy this holiday - give them a Hallmark ornament.

QX 340-4 FIRST CHRISTMAS TOGETHER
Comments: Cameo, 3-1/4" dia., Dated 1984
A couple waltz against a blue background. Caption: "Each Moment Spent Together Is A Special Celebration" and "First Christmas Together." **Artist:** Diana McGehee
☐ Purchased 19___ Pd $_______ MIB NB DB BNT
☐ Want Orig. Ret. $7.50 **NB** $10 **MIB** Sec. Mkt. **$20-$25**

QX 904-4 FIRST CHRISTMAS TOGETHER
Comments: Musical, Classic Shape, 4" tall, Dated 1984
Reindeer prance across a deep blue background to the tune of *Lara's Theme.* Caption: "First Christmas Together."
Artist: Diana McGehee
☐ Purchased 19___ Pd $_______ MIB NB DB BNT
☐ Want Orig. Ret. $16.00 **NB** $18 **MIB** Sec. Mkt. **$30-$35**

QX 245-1 FIRST CHRISTMAS TOGETHER
Comments: Silver Glass Ball, 3" dia., Dated 1984
Holiday birds, flowers and greenery create a contemporary pattern. Caption: "Love... A Joy For All Seasons. First Christmas Together."
☐ Purchased 19___ Pd $_______ MIB NB DB BNT
☐ Want Orig. Ret. $4.50 **NB** $14 **MIB** Sec. Mkt. **$20-$22**

QX 256-4 FLIGHTS OF FANTASY
Comments: Blue Glass Ball, 2-7/8" dia., Dated 1984
Beautiful birds are taking the elves on a flight. A ribbon banner says "Christmas 1984."
☐ Purchased 19___ Pd $_______ MIB NB DB BNT
☐ Want Orig. Ret. $4.50 **NB** $9 **MIB** Sec. Mkt. **$16-$18**

QX 452-4 FORTUNE COOKIE ELF
Comments: Handcrafted, 2-1/2" tall
A little elf paints the fortune for the fortune cookie. Caption: "May Your Christmas Be Merry." **Artist:** Linda Sickman
☐ Purchased 19___ Pd $_______ MIB NB DB BNT
☐ Want Orig. Ret. $4.50 **NB** $30 **MIB** Sec. Mkt. **$35-$40**

QX 248-1 FRIENDSHIP
Comments: Blue-Green Glass Ball, 2-7/8" dia., Dated 1984 Silhouettes of carolers against the snow. Caption: "Let Us Sing A Christmas Song Of Friendship, Joy And Cheer."
☐ Purchased 19___ Pd $_______ MIB NB DB BNT
☐ Want Orig. Ret. $4.50 **NB** $7 **MIB** Sec. Mkt. **$18-$20**

QX 444-4 FRISBEE® PUPPY
Comments: Handcrafted, 2-3/4" tall
This animated puppy has caught a holiday frisbee with a flying leap. "Merry Christmas" is written on the frisbee.
☐ Purchased 19___ Pd $_______ MIB NB DB BNT
☐ Want Orig. Ret. $5.00 **NB** $30 **MIB** Sec. Mkt. **$48-$50**

QX 248-4 FROM OUR HOME TO YOURS
Comments: Green Glass Ball, 2-7/8" dia., Dated 1984
Sampler design of a family and home in winter. Caption: "The Spirit Of Christmas Adorns A Home With Love. Christmas 1984."
☐ Purchased 19___ Pd $_______ MIB NB DB BNT
☐ Want Orig. Ret. $4.50 **NB** $15 **MIB** Sec. Mkt. **$24-$28**

QX 437-1 FROSTY FRIENDS
Comments: **Fifth in Series**, Handcrafted, 2-1/2" tall
Dated 1984. A little Eskimo and his penguin pal have gone ice fishing and have caught a gift. **Artist:** Ed Seale
☐ Purchased 19___ Pd $_______ MIB NB DB BNT
☐ Want Orig. Ret. $8.00 **NB** $50 **MIB** Sec. Mkt. **$85-$90**

QX 343-1 FUN OF FRIENDSHIP, THE
Comments: Acrylic, 3-3/4" tall, Dated 1984
Cute etched bell shows two arctic friends. Caption: "A Friend Is A Partner In Life's Merry Moments."
☐ Purchased 19___ Pd $_______ MIB NB DB BNT
☐ Want Orig. Ret. $6.00 **NB** $22 **MIB** Sec. Mkt. **$35-$38**

QX 451-1 GIFT OF MUSIC
Comments: Musical, Handcrafted, 3" tall
Tying his Christmas gift with red ribbon is a colorful, bearded elf. The tag reads "Jolly Holidays!" Plays *Jingle Bells.*
Artist: Ed Seale
☐ Purchased 19___ Pd $_______ MIB NB DB BNT
☐ Want Orig. Ret. $15.00 **NB** $75 **MIB** Sec. Mkt. **$95-$100**

QX 242-1 GODCHILD
Comments: Gold Glass Ball, 3" dia., Dated 1984
Elf children are painting the holly berries red.
☐ Purchased 19___ Pd $_______ MIB NB DB BNT
☐ Want Orig. Ret. $4.50 **NB** $12 **MIB** Sec. Mkt. **$18-$20**

QX 257-4 GRANDCHILD'S FIRST CHRISTMAS
Comments: Green Satin Ball, 2-7/8" dia., Dated 1984
A "torn paper" scene of Santa loading toys into his bag. Hand' crafted mouse sits atop the ornament. Caption: "A Baby Makes Christmas Delightfully Bright. Grandchild's First Christmas."
☐ Purchased 19___ Pd $_______ MIB NB DB BNT
☐ Want Orig. Ret. $4.50 **NB** $8 **MIB** Sec. Mkt. **$16-$18**

QX 460-1 GRANDCHILD'S FIRST CHRISTMAS
Comments: Handcrafted, 3-3/8" tall, Dated 1984
A flocked white lamb stands on a colorful pull toy. Caption: "Grandchild's First Christmas."
☐ Purchased 19___ Pd $_______ MIB NB DB BNT
☐ Want Orig. Ret. $11.00 **NB** $15 **MIB** Sec. Mkt. **$25-$28**

QX 243-1 GRANDDAUGHTER
Comments: Green Glass Ball, 2-7/8" dia., Dated 1984
Caption is written in a sampler design: "A Granddaughter Is Warmth, Hope And Promise. Christmas 1984."
☐ Purchased 19___ Pd $_______ MIB NB DB BNT
☐ Want Orig. Ret. $4.50 **NB** $12 **MIB** Sec. Mkt. **$25-$28**

QX 244-1 GRANDMOTHER
Comments: Lt. Blue Glass Ball, 2-7/8" dia., Dated 1984
Pastel flowers frame the caption: "There's A Special Kind Of Beauty In A Grandmother's Special Love. Christmas 1984."
☐ Purchased 19___ Pd $_______ MIB NB DB BNT
☐ Want Orig. Ret. $4.50 **NB** $12 **MIB** Sec. Mkt. **$16-$18**

QX 256-1 GRANDPARENTS
Comments: French Blue Glass Ball, 2-7/8" dia., Dated 1984
"Stitched" snow scene. Caption: "Grandparents... Wherever They Are, There Is Love. Christmas 1984."
☐ Purchased 19___ Pd $_______ MIB NB DB BNT
☐ Want Orig. Ret. $4.50 **NB** $8 **MIB** Sec. Mkt. **$15-$18**

QX 242-4 GRANDSON
Comments: Blue Glass Ball, 3" dia., Dated Christmas 1984
A polar bear family enjoys Christmas together. Caption: "A Grandson Has A Wonderful Way Of Adding Love To Every Day."
☐ Purchased 19___ Pd $_______ MIB NB DB BNT
☐ Want Orig. Ret. $4.50 **NB** $12 **MIB** Sec. Mkt. **$24-$28**

QX 344-4 GRATITUDE
Comments: Acrylic, Teardrop shape, 4-1/2" tall
Ribbon and sleigh bells. Caption: "The Spirit Of Christmas Lives In Every Heart That Gives."
☐ Purchased 19___ Pd $_______ MIB NB DB BNT
☐ Want Orig. Ret. $6.00 **NB** $8 **MIB** Sec. Mkt. **$10-$12**

QX 443-4 HEARTFUL OF LOVE
Comments: Bone China, 3-3/4" wide, Dated 1984
White heart with pink roses. Caption: "Love... the Most Beautiful Treasure Of Christmas."
☐ Purchased 19___ Pd $_______ MIB NB DB BNT
☐ Want Orig. Ret. $10.00 **NB** $30 **MIB** Sec. Mkt. **$45-$48**

QX 432-4 HERE COMES SANTA -SANTA'S DELIVERIES
Comments: **Sixth in Series**, Handcrafted, 3-1/4" tall, Dated 1984
"S. Claus Free Delivery" carries a load of Christmas trees. License plate: "1984." **Artist:** Linda Sickman
☐ Purchased 19___ Pd $_______ MIB NB DB BNT
☐ Want Orig. Ret. $13.00 **NB** $75 **MIB** Sec. Mkt. **$85-$90**

QX 445-1 HOLIDAY FRIENDSHIP
Comments: Peek-Through Ball, 3-1/4" dia.
A little girl and boy wave to each other through a frosty window as each hides gifts from the other.
☐ Purchased 19___ Pd $_______ MIB NB DB BNT
☐ Want Orig. Ret. $13.00 **NB** $20 **MIB** Sec. Mkt. **$28-$32**

QX 437-4 HOLIDAY JESTER
Comments: Handcrafted, 5-1/4" tall
With movable arms and legs, this jester wears the traditional black and white costume. **Artist:** Linda Sickman
☐ Purchased 19___ Pd $_______ MIB NB DB BNT
☐ Want Orig. Ret. $11.00 **NB** $22 **MIB** Sec. Mkt. **$35-$40**

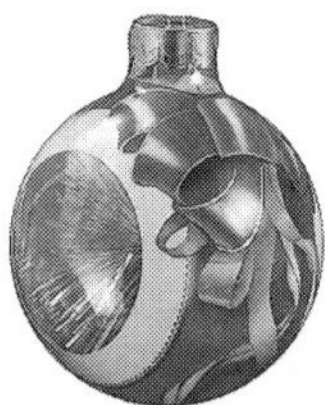

QX 253-4 HOLIDAY STARBURST
Comments: Clear Glass Ball, 2-7/8" dia., Dated 1984
Red, green and blue ribbons on the outside of this clear glass ball accent a silver starburst inside. Caption: "Christmas 1984."
☐ Purchased 19___ Pd $_______ MIB NB DB BNT
☐ Want Orig. Ret. $5.00 **NB** $12 **MIB** Sec. Mkt. **$18-$20**

QX 347-4 HOLIDAY WILDLIFE: PHEASANTS
Comments: **Third in Series,** 3" dia., Dated 1984
Caption: "Ring-Necked Pheasant, Phasianus Torquatus, Third In A Series, Wildlife Collection, Christmas 1984."
☐ Purchased 19___ Pd $_______ MIB NB DB BNT
☐ Want Orig. Ret. $7.25 **NB** $18 **MIB** Sec. Mkt. **$30-$32**

QX 463-1 KATYBETH
Comments: Handpainted Porcelain, 2-1/4" tall
This freckle-faced angel holds a friendly, happy star.
☐ Purchased 19___ Pd $_______ MIB NB DB BNT
☐ Want Orig. Ret. $9.00 **NB** $12 **MIB** Sec. Mkt. **$28-$35**

QX 453-4 KIT
Comments: Handcrafted, 2-3/4" tall
Known for his green cap, Muffin's friend Kit brings a candy cane to you.
☐ Purchased 19___ Pd $_______ MIB NB DB BNT
☐ Want Orig. Ret. $5.50 **NB** $16 **MIB** Sec. Mkt. **$25-$28**

QX 255-4 LOVE
Comments: Chrome Glass Ball, 2-7/8" dia., Dated 1984
Classic mimes share thoughts of love. Caption: "Love Can Say The Special Things That Words Alone Cannot. Christmas 1984."
☐ Purchased 19___ Pd $_______ MIB NB DB BNT
☐ Want Orig. Ret. $4.50 **NB** $12 **MIB** Sec. Mkt. **$22-$26**

QX 247-4 LOVE... THE SPIRIT OF CHRISTMAS
Comments: Chrome Glass Ball, 2-7/8" dia., Dated 1984
A bright fruit and flower design on a black band resembles a lacquer appearance. Caption: "Love, Which Is The Spirit And The Heart Of Christmas, Blossoms All Year Through."
☐ Purchased 19___ Pd $_______ MIB NB DB BNT
☐ Want Orig. Ret. $4.50 **NB** $12 **MIB** Sec. Mkt. **$30-$32**

QX 344-1 MADONNA & CHILD
Comments: Acrylic, 4" tall
This acrylic ornament features a beautifully etched design of the Holy Child cradled in the arms of the Madonna. Gold foil stamped caption: "All Is Calm, All Is Bright..." **Artist:** Don Palmiter
☐ Purchased 19___ Pd $_______ MIB NB DB BNT
☐ Want Orig. Ret. $6.00 **NB** $15 **MIB** Sec. Mkt. **$35-$40**

QX 456-4 MARATHON SANTA
Comments: Handcrafted, 2-1/4" tall, Dated 1984
Santa is a gold medalist as he runs with the Olympic torch!
Artist: Ed Seale
☐ Purchased 19___ Pd $_______ MIB NB DB BNT
☐ Want Orig. Ret. $8.00 **NB** $22 **MIB** Sec. Mkt. **$40-$42**

QX 342-4 MIRACLE OF LOVE, THE
Comments: Acrylic, 4" tall, Dated Christmas 1984
Heart etched with festive ribbon and holly design. Gold foil Caption: "Love... A Miracle Of The Heart."
☐ Purchased 19___ Pd $_______ MIB NB DB BNT
☐ Want Orig. Ret. $6.00 **NB** $18 **MIB** Sec. Mkt. **$30-$35**

QX 343-4 MOTHER
Comments: Acrylic, 3-1/4" wide, Dated 1984
Etched fir branches help to highlight the caption: "A Mother Has A Beautiful Way Of Adding Love To Every Day."
☐ Purchased 19___ Pd $_______ MIB NB DB BNT
☐ Want Orig. Ret. $6.00 **NB** $8 **MIB** Sec. Mkt. **$15-$18**

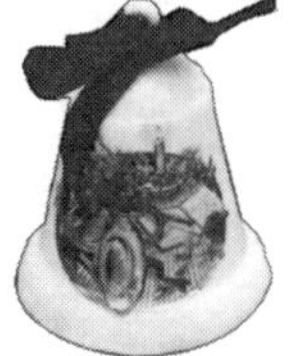

QX 258-1 MOTHER & DAD
Comments: Bone China Bell, 3" tall, Dated Christmas 1984
White bell has decal of Christmas design motifs.
☐ Purchased 19___ Pd $_______ MIB NB DB BNT
☐ Want Orig. Ret. $6.50 **NB** $15 **MIB** Sec. Mkt. **$22-$25**

QX 407-7 MOUNTAIN CLIMBING SANTA
Comments: Handcrafted, 2-1/2" tall
Reissued from 1983. **Artist:** Ed Seale
☐ Purchased 19___ Pd $_______ MIB NB DB BNT
☐ Want Orig. Ret. $6.50 **NB** $18 **MIB** Sec. Mkt. **$38-$42**

QX 442-1 MUFFIN
Comments: Handcrafted, 2-3/4" tall
Muffin wearing her trademark red, knitted cap holds a gift behind her back. **Artist:** Donna Lee
☐ Purchased 19___ Pd $_______ MIB NB DB BNT
☐ Want Orig. Ret. $5.50 **NB** $18 **MIB** Sec. Mkt. **$30-$34**

QX 251-4 MUPPETS™, THE
Comments: Chrome Glass Ball, 2-7/8" dia.
Kermit dons a Santa cap to wish us "Hoppy, Hoppy Holidays!" as Miss Piggy says, "Merry Kissmas!" Both are framed in wreaths.
☐ Purchased 19___ Pd $_______ MIB NB DB BNT
☐ Want Orig. Ret. $4.50 **NB** $20 **MIB** Sec. Mkt. **$30-$35**

QX 434-4 MUSICAL ANGEL
Comments: Handcrafted, 1-1/4" tall.
This cute little angel, caught up by the hem of her dress, is playing a tune on her brass horn. The banner hanging from her horn says "Noel." **Artist:** Donna Lee
☐ Purchased 19___ Pd $_______ MIB NB DB BNT
☐ Want Orig. Ret. $5.50 **NB** $45 **MIB** Sec. Mkt. **$65-$70**

QX 435-1 NAPPING MOUSE
Comments: Handcrafted, 1-3/4" tall
Sleeping soundly in a walnut shell, a little white mouse holds tightly onto his "teddy mouse."
☐ Purchased 19___ Pd $_______ MIB NB DB BNT
☐ Want Orig. Ret. $5.50 **NB** $32 **MIB** Sec. Mkt. **$48-$50**

QLX 700-1 NATIVITY
Comments: Lighted Panorama Ball, 3-1/2" dia.
A beautiful vision of Bethlehem at night as seen by the Three Wise Men. Caption: "Christmas...Light Through The Darkness... Love Through The Ages." **Artist:** Ed Seale
☐ Purchased 19___ Pd $_______ MIB NB DB BNT
☐ Want Orig. Ret. $12.00 **NB** $20 **MIB** Sec. Mkt. **$30-$35**

QX 459-4 NEEDLEPOINT WREATH
Comments: Needlepoint-Fabric, 3-1/2" dia.
Bright holiday poinsettias have been stitched into a lovely wreath. **Artist:** Sharon Pike
☐ Purchased 19___ Pd $_______ MIB NB DB BNT
☐ Want Orig. Ret. $6.50 **NB** $8 **MIB** Sec. Mkt. **$14-$16**

QX 245-4 NEW HOME
Comments: Pearl Blue Glass Ball, 2-7/8" dia., Dated 1984
Village holiday snow scene. Caption: "Home Is Where The Heart Is And A New Home Always Seems The Happiest Of Places, For It Is Filled With All Your Dreams. Christmas 1984."
☐ Purchased 19___ Pd $_______ MIB NB DB BNT
☐ Want Orig. Ret. $4.50 **NB** $35 **MIB** Sec. Mkt. **$45-$50**

QX 251-1 NORMAN ROCKWELL
Comments: Gold Glass Ball, 2-7/8" dia., Dated 1984
Dickens' Christmas characters. "Good Friends, Good Times, Good Health, Good Cheer And Happy Holidays Throughout The Year. From the Norman Rockwell Collection 1984."
Artist: Diana McGehee
☐ Purchased 19___ Pd $_______ MIB NB DB BNT
☐ Want Orig. Ret. $4.50 **NB** $10 **MIB** Sec. Mkt. **$20-$25**

QX 341-1 NORMAN ROCKWELL: CAUGHT NAPPING
Comments: **Fifth in Series**, Cameo, 3" dia., Dated 1984
"Caught Napping, Fifth In A Series, The Norman Rockwell Collection, Christmas 1984." **Artist:** Diana McGehee
☐ Purchased 19___ Pd $_______ MIB NB DB BNT
☐ Want Orig. Ret. $7.50 **NB** $20 **MIB** Sec. Mkt. **$32-$35**

QX 448-1 NOSTALGIC HOUSES AND SHOPS: VICTORIAN DOLLHOUSE
Comments: ***FIRST IN SERIES,*** Handcrafted, 3-1/4" tall
Fully decorated interior is complete with wallpaper, furniture, Christmas tree and a miniature dollhouse. **Artist:** Donna Lee
☐ Purchased 19___ Pd $_______ MIB NB DB BNT
☐ Want Orig. Ret. $13.00 **NB** $185 **MIB** Sec. Mkt. **$205-$210**

QX 442-4 NOSTALGIC SLED
Comments: Handcrafted, 3-1/2" wide, Reissued in 1985.
Classic-style sled with real string rope and metal runners. Caption: "Season's Greetings." **Artist:** Linda Sickman
☐ Purchased 19___ Pd $_______ MIB NB DB BNT
☐ Want Orig. Ret. $6.00 **NB** $10 **MIB** Sec. Mkt. **$25-$30**

QX 346-4 OLD FASHIONED ROCKING HORSE
Comments: Brass, Acrylic, 3-1/4" dia.
A finely-etched brass rocking horse is embedded in acrylic.
☐ Purchased 19___ Pd $_______ MIB NB DB BNT
☐ Want Orig. Ret. $7.50 **NB** $12 **MIB** Sec. Mkt. **$18-$20**

QX 341-4 PEACE ON EARTH
Comments: Red Oval Cameo, 3" tall
A beautiful old-world ivory angel plays a harp.
Caption: "Peace On Earth."
☐ Purchased 19___ Pd $_______ MIB NB DB BNT
☐ Want Orig. Ret. $7.50 **NB** $12 **MIB** Sec. Mkt. **$22-$28**

QX 252-1 PEANUTS®
Comments: Light Blue Soft-Sheen Satin Ball, 2-7/8" dia. Dated 1984. Woodstock and his friends build a gallery of snowmen as Snoopy watches. His red banner says, "Merry Christmas."
☐ Purchased 19___ Pd $_______ MIB NB DB BNT
☐ Want Orig. Ret. $4.50 **NB** $22 **MIB** Sec. Mkt. **$34-$35**

QX 456-1 PEPPERMINT 1984
Comments: Handcrafted, 2-3/4" wide, Dated 1984
The year 1984 is designed from peppermint candy. Two birds sit atop the "9." **Artist:** Donna Lee
☐ Purchased 19___ Pd $_______ MIB NB DB BNT
☐ Want Orig. Ret. $4.50 **NB** $40 **MIB** Sec. Mkt. **$50-$55**

QX 430-1 POLAR BEAR DRUMMER
Comments: Handcrafted, 2-1/4" tall
A white polar bear plays his red drum. **Artist:** Ed Seale
☐ Purchased 19___ Pd $_______ MIB NB DB BNT
☐ Want Orig. Ret. $4.50 **NB** $10 **MIB** Sec. Mkt. **$28-$30**

QX 454-1 PORCELAIN BEAR
Comments: **Second in Series**, Porcelain, 2-1/2" tall
Handpainted Cinnamon Bear holds a gold jingle bell with a red bow.
☐ Purchased 19___ Pd $_______ MIB NB DB BNT
☐ Want Orig. Ret. $7.00 **NB** $15 **MIB** Sec. Mkt. **$48-$52**

QX 447-4 RACCOON'S CHRISTMAS
Comments: Handcrafted, 2-3/4" tall
A raccoon and his neighbor have hung their Christmas stockings outside their "homes." **Artist:** Ed Seale
☐ Purchased 19___ Pd $_______ MIB NB DB BNT
☐ Want Orig. Ret. $9.00 **NB $40** **MIB** Sec. Mkt. **$55-$58**

QX 254-4 REINDEER RACETRACK
Comments: Red Glass Ball, 3" dia.
The race has started and they're off! Santa shouts his encouragement from the stands: "On Comet! On Cupid! On Donder! On Blitzen!"
☐ Purchased 19___ Pd $_______ MIB NB DB BNT
☐ Want Orig. Ret. $4.50 **NB** $10 **MIB** Sec. Mkt. **$18-$20**

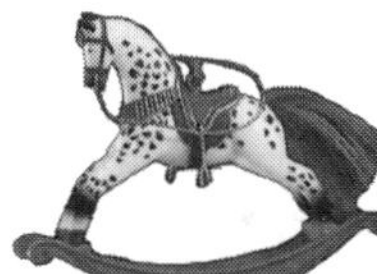

QX 435-4 ROCKING HORSE
Comments: **Fourth in Series,** Handcrafted, 4" wide
Dated 1984. Blue and red saddle and rockers are a striking contrast to this black and white Appaloosa with gray mane and tail.
☐ Purchased 19___ Pd $_______ MIB NB DB BNT
☐ Want Orig. Ret. $10.00 **NB** $50 **MIB** Sec. Mkt. **$75-$80**

QX 457-1 ROLLER SKATING RABBIT
Comments: Handcrafted, 2-1/2" wide, Reissued in 1985.
A white bunny has snuggled down in a green and white roller skate shoe for a fun ride. The red wheels really turn!
Artist: Ed Seale
☐ Purchased 19___ Pd $_______ MIB NB DB BNT
☐ Want Orig. Ret. $5.00 **NB** $18 **MIB** Sec. Mkt. **$32-$35**

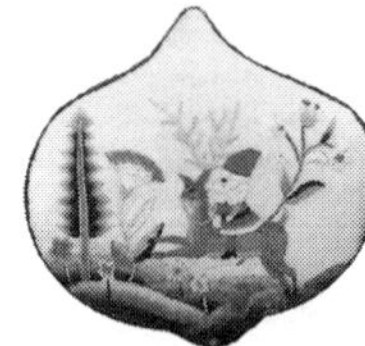

QX 458-4 SANTA
Comments: Hand-embroidered Fabric, 4" tall
Santa rides a reindeer over lush green hillsides filled with blooming flowers.
☐ Purchased 19___ Pd $_______ MIB NB DB BNT
☐ Want Orig. Ret. $7.50 **NB** $10 **MIB** Sec. Mkt. **$18-$20**

QX 433-4 SANTA MOUSE
Comments: Handcrafted, 2" tall
A cute little mouse has dressed up as Santa, complete with a furry "beard." **Artist:** Bob Siedler
☐ Purchased 19___ Pd $_______ MIB NB DB BNT
☐ Want Orig. Ret. $4.50 **NB** $40 **MIB** Sec. Mkt. **$45-$50**

QX 450-4 SANTA STAR
Comments: Handcrafted, 3-1/2" tall
Santa is designed in the shape of a five-pointed star!
☐ Purchased 19___ Pd $_______ MIB NB DB BNT
☐ Want Orig. Ret. $5.50 **NB** $30 **MIB** Sec. Mkt. **$40-$45**

QX 436-1 SANTA SULKY DRIVER
Comments: Etched Brass, 1-3/4" tall
Santa races along in his brass sulky rig. A banner reads "Season's Greetings."
☐ Purchased 19___ Pd $_______ MIB NB DB BNT
☐ Want Orig. Ret. $9.00 **NB** $19 **MIB** Sec. Mkt. **$32-$35**

QLX 702-4 SANTA'S ARRIVAL
Comments: Lighted Peek-Through Ball, 3-1/2" dia.
Santa looks through a bedroom window to see a small child sleeping soundly. **Artist:** Donna Lee
☐ Purchased 19___ Pd $_______ MIB NB DB BNT
☐ Want Orig. Ret. $13.00 **NB** $50 **MIB** Sec. Mkt. **$65-$70**

QLX 700-4 SANTA'S WORKSHOP
Comments: Lighted Peek-Through Ball, 3-1/2" dia.
Reissued in 1985. Looking through the window into Santa's workshop, one can see him giving a toy bunny to the rabbit visiting outside.
☐ Purchased 19___ Pd $_______ MIB NB DB BNT
☐ Want Orig. Ret. $13.00 **NB** $45 **MIB** Sec. Mkt. **$60-$65**

QX 252-4 SHIRT TALES
Comments: Aqua-Blue Satin Ball, 2-7/8" dia.
It's a snowball fight with all the Shirt-Tales joining in on the fun! Caption: "Joy Is In The Air, Good Time To Share -- Christmas, Christmas Everywhere."
☐ Purchased 19___ Pd $_______ MIB NB DB BNT
☐ Want Orig. Ret. $4.50 **NB** $10 **MIB** Sec. Mkt. **$15-$20**

QX 259-4 SISTER
Comments: Bone China Bell, 3" tall, Dated Christmas 1984
A basket of poinsettias are cheerful and bright against a dark blue background. Caption: "For A Wonderful Sister."
☐ Purchased 19___ Pd $_______ MIB NB DB BNT
☐ Want Orig. Ret. $6.50 **NB** $15 **MIB** Sec. Mkt. **$22-$25**

QX 439-1 SNOOPY® & WOODSTOCK
Comments: Handcrafted, 4-1/4" wide
Snoopy and Woodstock take to the slopes in their matching blue and green caps. **Artist:** Ed Seale
☐ Purchased 19___ Pd $_______ MIB NB DB BNT
☐ Want Orig. Ret. $7.50 **NB** $70 **MIB** Sec. Mkt. **$85-$90**

QX 431-4 SNOWMOBILE SANTA
Comments: Handcrafted, 2-3/4" wide
Santa enjoys himself in a shiny silver snowmobile.
☐ Purchased 19___ Pd $_______ MIB NB DB BNT
☐ Want Orig. Ret. $6.50 **NB** $15 **MIB** Sec. Mkt. **$33-$37**

QX 453-1 SNOWSHOE PENGUIN
Comments: Handcrafted, 3" tall. Santa's neighbor has donned his snowshoes and is on his way to deliver a present.
Artist: Linda Sickman
☐ Purchased 19___ Pd $_______ MIB NB DB BNT
☐ Want Orig. Ret. $6.50 **NB** $35 **MIB** Sec. Mkt. **$45-$50**

QX 450-1 SNOWY SEAL
Comments: Handcrafted, 1-1/2" wide, Reissued in 1985.
Dressed in a red fabric ribbon, this flocked white seal is ready for Christmas. **Artist:** Ed Seale
☐ Purchased 19___ Pd $_______ MIB NB DB BNT
☐ Want Orig. Ret. $4.00 **NB** $10 **MIB** Sec. Mkt. **$20-$24**

QX 243-4 SON
Comments: White Glass Ball, 3" dia., Dated Christmas 1984
Cute Christmas designs form letters to spell "Merry Christmas." Caption: "For A Wonderful Son."
☐ Purchased 19___ Pd $_______ MIB NB DB BNT
☐ Want Orig. Ret. $4.50 **NB** $16 **MIB** Sec. Mkt. **$24-$26**

QLX 703-1 STAINED GLASS
Comments: Lighted, Golden Classic Shape, 3-7/8" dia.
Old-fashioned stained glass design glows like a beautiful stained-glass window when lit.
☐ Purchased 19___ Pd $_______ MIB NB DB BNT
☐ Want Orig. Ret. $8.00 **NB** $12 **MIB** Sec. Mkt. **$18-$22**

QLX 701-1 SUGARPLUM COTTAGE
Comments: Lighted, Handcrafted, 3" tall
Reissued in 1985 and 1986. Sugarcoated gumdrops, lollipops and peppermint candy canes... mmm' good!
☐ Purchased 19___ Pd $_______ MIB NB DB BNT
☐ Want Orig. Ret. $11.00 **NB** $22 **MIB** Sec. Mkt. **$45-$50**

QX 249-1 TEACHER
Comments: White Glass Ball, 3" dia., Dated 1984
Elves deliver a large apple to the teacher. Caption: "Merry Christmas, Teacher."
☐ Purchased 19___ Pd $_______ MIB NB DB BNT
☐ Want Orig. Ret. $4.50 **NB** $6 **MIB** Sec. Mkt. **$14-$16**

Living in the past has its advantage - it's cheaper.

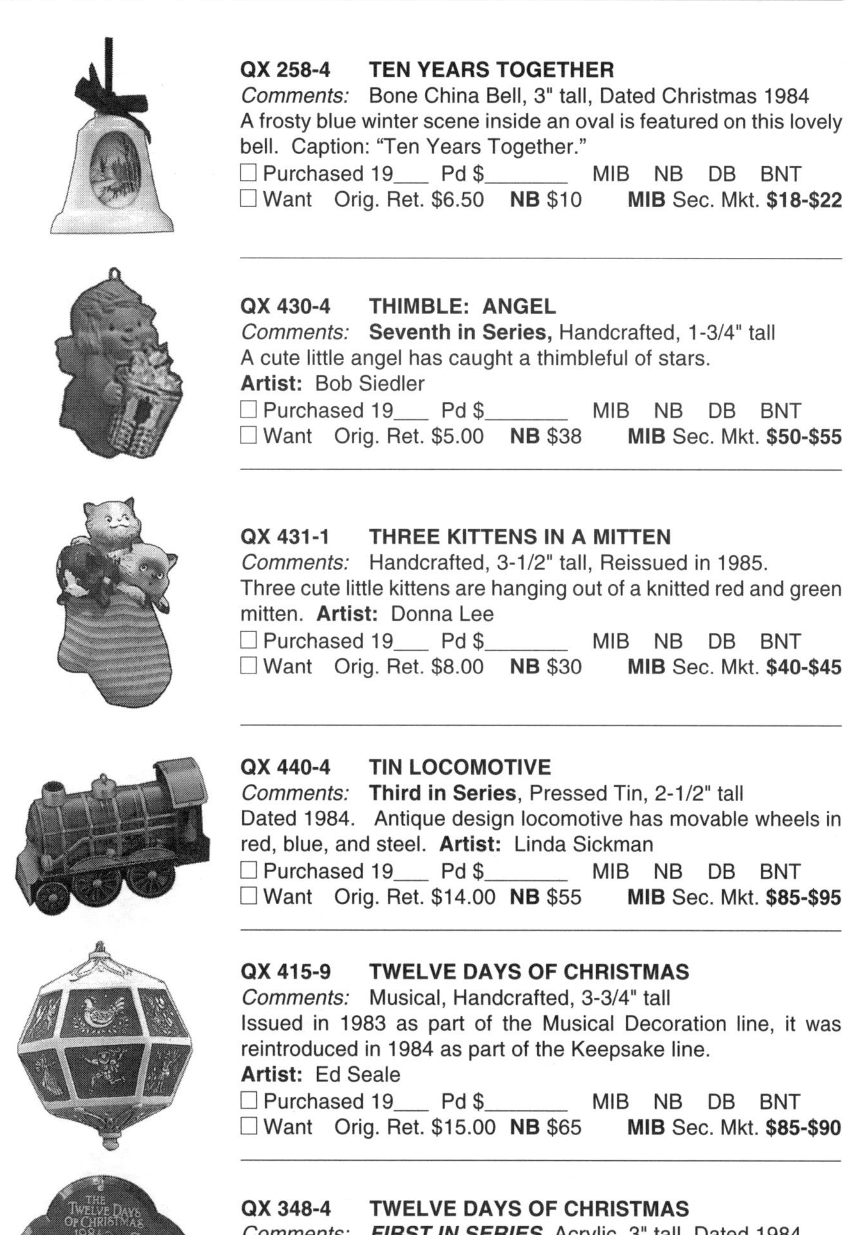

QX 258-4 TEN YEARS TOGETHER
Comments: Bone China Bell, 3" tall, Dated Christmas 1984
A frosty blue winter scene inside an oval is featured on this lovely bell. Caption: "Ten Years Together."
☐ Purchased 19___ Pd $_______ MIB NB DB BNT
☐ Want Orig. Ret. $6.50 **NB** $10 **MIB** Sec. Mkt. **$18-$22**

QX 430-4 THIMBLE: ANGEL
Comments: **Seventh in Series,** Handcrafted, 1-3/4" tall
A cute little angel has caught a thimbleful of stars.
Artist: Bob Siedler
☐ Purchased 19___ Pd $_______ MIB NB DB BNT
☐ Want Orig. Ret. $5.00 **NB** $38 **MIB** Sec. Mkt. **$50-$55**

QX 431-1 THREE KITTENS IN A MITTEN
Comments: Handcrafted, 3-1/2" tall, Reissued in 1985.
Three cute little kittens are hanging out of a knitted red and green mitten. **Artist:** Donna Lee
☐ Purchased 19___ Pd $_______ MIB NB DB BNT
☐ Want Orig. Ret. $8.00 **NB** $30 **MIB** Sec. Mkt. **$40-$45**

QX 440-4 TIN LOCOMOTIVE
Comments: **Third in Series**, Pressed Tin, 2-1/2" tall
Dated 1984. Antique design locomotive has movable wheels in red, blue, and steel. **Artist:** Linda Sickman
☐ Purchased 19___ Pd $_______ MIB NB DB BNT
☐ Want Orig. Ret. $14.00 **NB** $55 **MIB** Sec. Mkt. **$85-$95**

QX 415-9 TWELVE DAYS OF CHRISTMAS
Comments: Musical, Handcrafted, 3-3/4" tall
Issued in 1983 as part of the Musical Decoration line, it was reintroduced in 1984 as part of the Keepsake line.
Artist: Ed Seale
☐ Purchased 19___ Pd $_______ MIB NB DB BNT
☐ Want Orig. Ret. $15.00 **NB** $65 **MIB** Sec. Mkt. **$85-$90**

QX 348-4 TWELVE DAYS OF CHRISTMAS
Comments: ***FIRST IN SERIES,*** Acrylic, 3" tall, Dated 1984
Etched partridge in a pear tree. Gold foil lettering: "The Twelve Days Of Christmas" and "... And A Partridge In A Pear Tree."
☐ Purchased 19___ Pd $_______ MIB NB DB BNT
☐ Want Orig. Ret. $6.00 **NB** $245 **MIB** Sec. Mkt. **$275-$285**

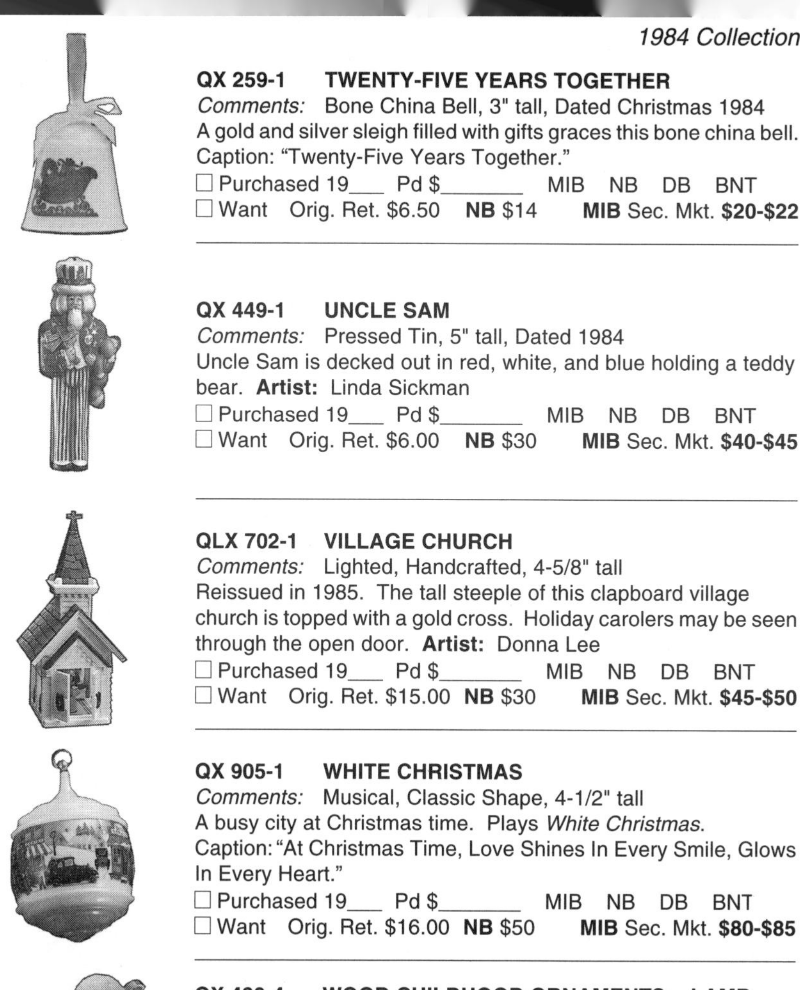

QX 259-1 TWENTY-FIVE YEARS TOGETHER
Comments: Bone China Bell, 3" tall, Dated Christmas 1984
A gold and silver sleigh filled with gifts graces this bone china bell. Caption: "Twenty-Five Years Together."
☐ Purchased 19___ Pd $_______ MIB NB DB BNT
☐ Want Orig. Ret. $6.50 **NB** $14 **MIB** Sec. Mkt. **$20-$22**

QX 449-1 UNCLE SAM
Comments: Pressed Tin, 5" tall, Dated 1984
Uncle Sam is decked out in red, white, and blue holding a teddy bear. **Artist:** Linda Sickman
☐ Purchased 19___ Pd $_______ MIB NB DB BNT
☐ Want Orig. Ret. $6.00 **NB** $30 **MIB** Sec. Mkt. **$40-$45**

QLX 702-1 VILLAGE CHURCH
Comments: Lighted, Handcrafted, 4-5/8" tall
Reissued in 1985. The tall steeple of this clapboard village church is topped with a gold cross. Holiday carolers may be seen through the open door. **Artist:** Donna Lee
☐ Purchased 19___ Pd $_______ MIB NB DB BNT
☐ Want Orig. Ret. $15.00 **NB** $30 **MIB** Sec. Mkt. **$45-$50**

QX 905-1 WHITE CHRISTMAS
Comments: Musical, Classic Shape, 4-1/2" tall
A busy city at Christmas time. Plays *White Christmas.*
Caption: "At Christmas Time, Love Shines In Every Smile, Glows In Every Heart."
☐ Purchased 19___ Pd $_______ MIB NB DB BNT
☐ Want Orig. Ret. $16.00 **NB** $50 **MIB** Sec. Mkt. **$80-$85**

QX 439-4 WOOD CHILDHOOD ORNAMENTS: LAMB
Comments: ***FIRST IN SERIES,*** Wood, Handcrafted, 2-1/4" tall
A little wooden lamb has red wheels and a fabric bow around its neck.
☐ Purchased 19___ Pd $_______ MIB NB DB BNT
☐ Want Orig. Ret. $6.50 **NB** $22 **MIB** Sec. Mkt. **$45-$50**

1985 Collection

QLX 704-4 ALL ARE PRECIOUS
Comments: Lighted Acrylic, 4" tall
Reissued from 1984.
☐ Purchased 19___ Pd $_______ MIB NB DB BNT
☐ Want Orig. Ret. $8.00 **NB** $18 **MIB** Sec. Mkt. **$22-$26**

QX 377-2 ART MASTERPIECE
Comments: **Second in Series,** Bezeled Satin, 2-3/4" dia.
Caption: "Madonna Of The Pomegranate (ca. 1487), The Uffizi Gallery, Florence, Italy." **Artist:** Diana McGehee
☐ Purchased 19___ Pd $_______ MIB NB DB BNT
☐ Want Orig. Ret. $6.75 **NB** $10 **MIB** Sec. Mkt. **$15-$18**

QX 401-2 BABY LOCKET
Comments: Textured Brass, 2-1/4" dia.
Embossed toys and the word "Baby" decorate the locket. There is space for personalizing, as well as baby's photo.
Artist: Diana McGehee
☐ Purchased 19___ Pd $_______ MIB NB DB BNT
☐ Want Orig. Ret. $16.00 **NB** $14 **MIB** Sec. Mkt. **$22-$24**

QX 370-2 BABY'S FIRST CHRISTMAS
Comments: Acrylic, 3-3/4" tall, Dated 1985
Baby cup, filled with toys, carries the caption: "Baby's First Christmas." **Artist:** Donna Lee
☐ Purchased 19___ Pd $_______ MIB NB DB BNT
☐ Want Orig. Ret. $5.75 **NB** $12 **MIB** Sec. Mkt. **$18-$20**

QX 260-2 BABY'S FIRST CHRISTMAS
Comments: Green Soft-Sheen Satin Ball, 2-7/8" dia.
Dated 1985. Topped with a handcrafted mouse.
Caption: "A Baby Keeps The Season Bright And Warms The Heart With Sweet Delight. Baby's First Christmas."
☐ Purchased 19___ Pd $_______ MIB NB DB BNT
☐ Want Orig. Ret. $5.00 **NB** $14 **MIB** Sec. Mkt. **$20-$22**

QX 478-2 BABY'S FIRST CHRISTMAS
Comments: Embroidered Fabric, 4-1/2" tall, Dated 1985
Decorated with ribbon and lace, this hand embroidered tree says "Baby's First Christmas." **Artist:** LaDene Votruba
☐ Purchased 19___ Pd $_______ MIB NB DB BNT
☐ Want Orig. Ret. $7.00 **NB** $10 **MIB** Sec. Mkt. **$15-$18**

QLX 700-5 BABY'S FIRST CHRISTMAS
Comments: Lighted, Handcrafted-Acrylic, 4" tall
This cute carousel features teddy bears riding their frosted acrylic ponies. **Artist:** Ed Seale
☐ Purchased 19___ Pd $_______ MIB NB DB BNT
☐ Want Orig. Ret. $16.50 **NB** $30 **MIB** Sec. Mkt. **$40-$45**

QX 499-5 BABY'S FIRST CHRISTMAS
Comments: Musical, Fabric, 3-1/4" tall, Dated 1985
Embroidered satin baby block. Plays Schubert's Lullaby.
Caption: "Baby's First Christmas."
☐ Purchased 19___ Pd $_______ MIB NB DB BNT
☐ Want Orig. Ret. $16.00 **NB** $20 **MIB** Sec. Mkt. **$40-$45**

QX 499-2 BABY'S FIRST CHRISTMAS
Comments: Handcrafted, 3-3/4" tall, Dated 1985
"Baby's First Christmas" is delightful in a rattan look stroller with lace trim and a red bow.
☐ Purchased 19___ Pd $_______ MIB NB DB BNT
☐ Want Orig. Ret. $15.00 **NB** $35 **MIB** Sec. Mkt. **$50-$55**

QX 478-5 BABY'S SECOND CHRISTMAS
Comments: Handcrafted, 3-1/2' tall, Dated 1985
Brown teddy in yellow t-shirt is riding his stick horse. Caption: "Baby's Second Christmas."
☐ Purchased 19___ Pd $_______ MIB NB DB BNT
☐ Want Orig. Ret. $6.00 **NB** $20 **MIB** Sec. Mkt. **$32-$35**

QX 264-2 BABY-SITTER
Comments: Green Glass Ball, 3" dia.
Panda bears are preparing for Christmas.
Caption: "A Baby-Sitter Is A Special Kind Of Friend. Christmas 1985."
Artist: Michele Pyda-Sevcik
☐ Purchased 19___ Pd $_______ MIB NB DB BNT
☐ Want Orig. Ret. $4.75 **NB** $5 **MIB** Sec. Mkt. **$12-$16**

QX 491-2 BAKER ELF
Comments: Handcrafted, 3" tall, Dated 1985
A cute elf uses red and green "icing" to decorate the bell-shaped cookie he has baked. **Artist:** Ed Seale
☐ Purchased 19___ Pd $_______ MIB NB DB BNT
☐ Want Orig. Ret. $5.75 **NB** $20 **MIB** Sec. Mkt. **$28-$32**

QX 480-5 BEARY SMOOTH RIDE
Comments: Handcrafted, 1-3/4" tall, Reissued in 1986
Teddy rides around on a colorful tricycle. **Artist:** Linda Sickman
☐ Purchased 19___ Pd $_______ MIB NB DB BNT
☐ Want Orig. Ret. $6.50 **NB** $10 **MIB** Sec. Mkt. **$22-$24**

QX 263-2 BETSEY CLARK
Comments: **Thirteenth and Final in Series**
White Glass Ball, 3-1/4" dia., Dated 1985
Angelic children dust the stars and play on the clouds. Caption: "Christmas Brings A Special Kind Of Feeling."
Artist: Sharon Pike
☐ Purchased 19___ Pd $_______ MIB NB DB BNT
☐ Want Orig. Ret. $5.00 **NB** $15 **MIB** Sec. Mkt. **$28-$32**

QX 508-5 BETSEY CLARK
Comments: Handpainted Porcelain, 2-1/2" tall
Little boy angel is holding a little lamb.
☐ Purchased 19___ Pd $_______ MIB NB DB BNT
☐ Want Orig. Ret. $8.50 **NB** $12 **MIB** Sec. Mkt. **$25-$28**

QX 481-5 BOTTLECAP FUN BUNNIES
Comments: Handcrafted, 2-1/4" tall
Mama and baby bunny go riding in a metal bottle cap from the "Santa Soda, North Pole Bottling Co." **Artist:** Bob Siedler
☐ Purchased 19___ Pd $_______ MIB NB DB BNT
☐ Want Orig. Ret. $7.75 **NB** $20 **MIB** Sec. Mkt. **$35-$38**

QX 374-2 CANDLE CAMEO
Comments: Bezeled Cameo, 3" tall, Dated 1985
Traditional ivory Christmas symbols against a red cameo. Caption: "Christmas... The Season That Brightens The World."
Artist: Sharon Pike
☐ Purchased 19___ Pd $_______ MIB NB DB BNT
☐ Want Orig. Ret. $6.75 **NB** $12 **MIB** Sec. Mkt. **$14-$16**

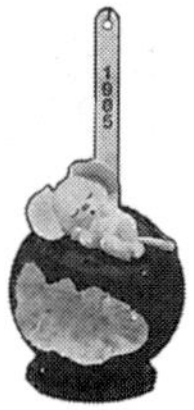

QX 470-5 CANDY APPLE MOUSE
Comments: Handcrafted, 3-3/4" tall, Dated 1985
A white mouse is sleeping on a red candy apple.
Artist: Linda Sickman
☐ Purchased 19___ Pd $_______ MIB NB DB BNT
☐ Want Orig. Ret. $6.50 **NB** $42 **MIB** Sec. Mkt. **$55-$60**

QX 512-5 CHARMING ANGEL: HEIRLOOM COLLECTION
Comments: Fabric, 3-3/4" tall
This angel has yarn hair, sheer net wings and is wearing a hand-sewn lace dress. **Artist:** Michele Pyda-Sevcik
☐ Purchased 19___ Pd $_______ MIB NB DB BNT
☐ Want Orig. Ret. $9.75 **NB** $14 **MIB** Sec. Mkt. **$22-$25**

QX 475-5 CHILD'S THIRD CHRISTMAS
Comments: Handcrafted, 2-1/4" tall, Dated 1985
A red and white sneaker with green laces holds a brown teddy bear. Caption: "A Child's Third Christmas '85."
Artist: Ed Seale
☐ Purchased 19___ Pd $_______ MIB NB DB BNT
☐ Want Orig. Ret. $6.00 **NB** $15 **MIB** Sec. Mkt. **$28-$32**

QX 490-5 CHILDREN IN THE SHOE
Comments: Handcrafted, 3-1/4" tall
This old shoe with a snow-capped roof has children everywhere; depicts the nursery rhyme. **Artist:** Ed Seale
☐ Purchased 19___ Pd $_______ MIB NB DB BNT
☐ Want Orig. Ret. $9.50 **NB** $30 **MIB** Sec. Mkt. **$48-$52**

QLX 703-2 CHRIS MOUSE
Comments: ***FIRST IN SERIES,*** Lighted, 3-7/8" tall, Dated 1985
This ornament attaches to the tree with a clip and shows Chris, dressed for bed, sitting in the base of a candle, reading a story.
Artist: Bob Siedler
☐ Purchased 19___ Pd $_______ MIB NB DB BNT
☐ Want Orig. Ret. $12.50 **NB-P** $45 **MIB** Sec. Mkt. **$90-$95**

QLX 710-5 CHRISTMAS EVE VISIT
Comments: Lighted, Etched Brass, 2" tall
Santa and his reindeer make their rounds on Christmas Eve. First stop - a brightly lit house.
☐ Purchased 19___ Pd $_______ MIB NB DB BNT
☐ Want Orig. Ret. $12.00 **NB** $15 **MIB** Sec. Mkt. **$25-$33**

QX 507-5 CHRISTMAS TREATS
Comments: Bezeled Glass, 3-1/4" tall
Colorful candy canes and Christmas candies on white makes a stained glass effect.
☐ Purchased 19___ Pd $_______ MIB NB DB BNT
☐ Want Orig. Ret. $5.50 **NB** $10 **MIB** Sec. Mkt. **$16-$20**

QX 471-5 CLOTHESPIN SOLDIER: SCOTTISH
Comments: **Fourth in Series,** Handcrafted, 2-1/2" tall
The Scottish Highlander is dressed in a colorful fabric kilt with a blue pom-pom on his red tam. **Artist:** Linda Sickman
☐ Purchased 19___ Pd $_______ MIB NB DB BNT
☐ Want Orig. Ret. $5.50 **NB** $17 **MIB** Sec. Mkt. **$24-$28**

QX 518-5 COUNTRY GOOSE
Comments: Wood, 3" dia.
A goose with a Christmas wreath around its neck graces this wood ornament. Caption: "This Original Design, Styled In The American Country Tradition, Has Been Printed On Hardwood."
Artist: Michele Pyda-Sevcik
☐ Purchased 19___ Pd $_______ MIB NB DB BNT
☐ Want Orig. Ret. $7.75 **NB** $8 **MIB** Sec. Mkt. **$12-$14**

QX 477-2 DAPPER PENGUIN
Comments: Handcrafted, 2-1/4" tall
This cute little fellow is all decked out with a red top hat, green bow tie and gold cane. **Artist:** Ed Seale
☐ Purchased 19___ Pd $_______ MIB NB DB BNT
☐ Want Orig. Ret. $5.00 **NB** $15 **MIB** Sec. Mkt. **$25-$30**

QX 503-2 DAUGHTER
Comments: Wood, 3-1/4" dia., Dated Christmas 1985
"Silk-screened" design in an embroidery hoop. Caption: "A Daughter Decorates The Holidays With Love."
☐ Purchased 19___ Pd $_______ MIB NB DB BNT
☐ Want Orig. Ret. $5.50 **NB** $8 **MIB** Sec. Mkt. **$14-$15**

QX 271-2 DISNEY CHRISTMAS
Comments: Pearl Blue Glass, 3" dia., Dated 1985
Mice hang their stockings for Christmas as Mickey dons a Santa suit.
☐ Purchased 19___ Pd $_______ MIB NB DB BNT
☐ Want Orig. Ret. $4.75 **NB** $18 **MIB** Sec. Mkt. **$25-$30**

QX 481-2 DO NOT DISTURB BEAR
Comments: Handcrafted, 3" wide, Reissued in 1986
A flocked bear snoozes comfortably in his hollow log with his "Do Not Disturb 'Til Christmas" sign. **Artist:** Ed Seale
☐ Purchased 19___ Pd $_______ MIB NB DB BNT
☐ Want Orig. Ret. $7.75 **NB** $18 **MIB** Sec. Mkt. **$25-$30**

QX 474-2 DOGGY IN A STOCKING
Comments: Handcrafted, 3" tall
A cute tan terrier is poking his head out of the red and green striped stocking.
☐ Purchased 19___ Pd $_______ MIB NB DB BNT
☐ Want Orig. Ret. $5.50 **NB** $20 **MIB** Sec. Mkt. **$35-$38**

QX 473-5 ENGINEERING MOUSE
Comments: Handcrafted, 2" tall
Designed to look like a windup toy, a little white mouse engineers a red and green locomotive. **Artist:** Bob Siedler
☐ Purchased 19___ Pd $_______ MIB NB DB BNT
☐ Want Orig. Ret. $5.50 **NB** $12 **MIB** Sec. Mkt. **$18-$25**

QX 376-2 FATHER
Comments: Wood, 3" dia., Dated Christmas 1985
Printed on wood to resemble hand painting is an old-fashioned sleigh filled with gifts and a Christmas tree, Caption: "A Father Sees Through The Eyes Of Love And Listens With His Heart."
Artist: LaDene Votruba
☐ Purchased 19___ Pd $_______ MIB NB DB BNT
☐ Want Orig. Ret. $6.50 **NB** $2 **MIB** Sec. Mkt. **$10-$11**

QX 370-5 FIRST CHRISTMAS TOGETHER
Comments: Acrylic, 3-1/2" wide, Dated 1985
Doves carry a banner with the caption: "First Christmas Together." Framed in brass.
☐ Purchased 19___ Pd $_______ MIB NB DB BNT
☐ Want Orig. Ret. $6.75 **NB** $4 **MIB** Sec. Mkt. **$16-$18**

QX 261-2 FIRST CHRISTMAS TOGETHER
Comments: Lt. Blue Glass Ball, 2-7/8" dia., Dated 1985
Silhouettes of a couple at Christmas are shown in heart frames tied with red ribbons. Caption: "Love Is A Gift From Heart To Heart. First Christmas Together."
☐ Purchased 19___ Pd $_______ MIB NB DB BNT
☐ Want Orig. Ret. $4.75 **NB** $10 **MIB** Sec. Mkt. **$18-$20**

QX 507-2 FIRST CHRISTMAS TOGETHER
Comments: Fabric and Wood, 2-1/2" tall, Dated 1985
Red and white hearts are woven in a wooden frame.
Caption: "First Christmas Together."
☐ Purchased 19___ Pd $_______ MIB NB DB BNT
☐ Want Orig. Ret. $8.00 **NB** $3 **MIB** Sec. Mkt. **$14-$16**

QX 400-5 FIRST CHRISTMAS TOGETHER
Comments: Polished Brass, 2-1/2" tall, Dated 1985
Embossed hearts surround the caption: "First Christmas Together." Locket holds two photos. **Artist:** Ed Seale
☐ Purchased 19___ Pd $_______ MIB NB DB BNT
☐ Want Orig. Ret. $16.75 **NB** $10 **MIB** Sec. Mkt. **$24-$28**

QX 493-5 FIRST CHRISTMAS TOGETHER
Comments: Porcelain, 2" tall, Dated 1985
Red porcelain hearts are the clappers of this pale green porcelain bisque bell. Caption: "First Christmas Together."
Artist: Linda Sickman
☐ Purchased 19___ Pd $_______ MIB NB DB BNT
☐ Want Orig. Ret. $13.00 **NB** $15 **MIB** Sec. Mkt. **$24-$26**

QX 265-5 FRAGGLE ROCK™ HOLIDAY
Comments: Lt. Blue Glass Ball, 3" dia., Dated 1985
Sprocket, the dog, looks on at the Christmas activities of the Fraggle Rock gang. Caption: "Happy Holidays 1985."
☐ Purchased 19___ Pd $_______ MIB NB DB BNT
☐ Want Orig. Ret. $4.75 **NB** $10 **MIB** Sec. Mkt. **$18-$22**

QX 378-5 FRIENDSHIP
Comments: Bezeled Satin, 3" tall, Dated 1985
Christmas time in an early American village. Printed on padded satin and framed with a chrome bezel. Caption: "Christmas... Season Bright With Friendship." **Artist:** Michele Pyda-Sevcik
☐ Purchased 19___ Pd $_______ MIB NB DB BNT
☐ Want Orig. Ret. $6.75 **NB** $8 **MIB** Sec. Mkt. **$15-$18**

QX 506-2 FRIENDSHIP
Comments: Embroidered Satin, 2" tall, Dated 1985
A pine branch and snowflakes are embroidered on Oriental red satin. Includes gift card. Caption: "Christmas... A Special Time For Friendship." **Artist:** Joyce Pattee
☐ Purchased 19___ Pd $_______ MIB NB DB BNT
☐ Want Orig. Ret. $7.75 **NB** $5 **MIB** Sec. Mkt. **$12-$14**

QX 520-2 FROM OUR HOUSE TO YOURS
Comments: Needlepoint-Fabric, 4" tall, Dated 1985
Caption: "A Happy Home Reflects The Joy Of Christmas All Year Round." **Artist:** Joyce Pattee
☐ Purchased 19___ Pd $_______ MIB NB DB BNT
☐ Want Orig. Ret. $7.75 **NB** $3 **MIB** Sec. Mkt. **$8-$10**

QX 482-2 FROSTY FRIENDS
Comments: **Sixth in Series,** Handcrafted, 2" tall, Dated 1985
The little Eskimo and friend are paddling a red dated kayak.
Artist: Ed Seale
☐ Purchased 19___ Pd $_______ MIB NB DB BNT
☐ Want Orig. Ret. $8.50 **NB** $50 **MIB** Sec. Mkt. **$68-$70**

QX 380-2 GODCHILD
Comments: Bezeled Satin, 2-3/4" dia., Dated Christmas 1985
From Hallmark's Antique Greeting Card Collection. Caption: "A Godchild Is A Loving Gift To Treasure Through The Years."
Artist: Diana McGehee
☐ Purchased 19___ Pd $_______ MIB NB DB BNT
☐ Want Orig. Ret. $6.75 **NB** $4 **MIB** Sec. Mkt. **$10-$12**

QX 265-2 GOOD FRIENDS
Comments: White Frosted Glass, 3" dia., Dated 1985
Penguins play in the snow. Caption: "Good Times With Good Friends Make Life's Merriest Moments."
☐ Purchased 19___ Pd $_______ MIB NB DB BNT
☐ Want Orig. Ret. $4.75 **NB** $10 **MIB** Sec. Mkt. **$22-$24**

QX 260-5 GRANDCHILD'S FIRST CHRISTMAS
Comments: Ecru Satin Ball, 2-7/8" dia., Dated 1985
Elves keep busy making Christmas toys, while Santa holds a baby on his lap. Handcrafted mouse sits at the top of the ornament. Caption: "Baby's First Christmas."
☐ Purchased 19___ Pd $_______ MIB NB DB BNT
☐ Want Orig. Ret. $5.00 **NB** $8 **MIB** Sec. Mkt. **$13-$15**

QX 495-5 GRANDCHILD'S FIRST CHRISTMAS
Comments: Handcrafted, 3-1/4" tall, Dated 1985
White knitted baby bootie holds baby's block and other toys. Caption: "Baby's First Christmas." **Artist:** LaDene Votruba
☐ Purchased 19___ Pd $_______ MIB NB DB BNT
☐ Want Orig. Ret. $11.00 **NB** $10 **MIB** Sec. Mkt. **$15-$22**

QX 263-5 GRANDDAUGHTER
Comments: Ivory Glass Ball, 2-7/8" dia., Dated 1985
Caption: "There's Nothing Like A Granddaughter To Warm The World At Christmas."
☐ Purchased 19___ Pd $_______ MIB NB DB BNT
☐ Want Orig. Ret. $4.75 **NB** $12 **MIB** Sec. Mkt. **$22-$25**

QX 262-5 GRANDMOTHER
Comments: Red Glass Ball, 3" dia., Dated Christmas 1985
Floral design with scroll banner decorates this red transparent ball. Caption: "A Grandmother Gives The Gift Of Love."
Artist: Joyce Pattee
☐ Purchased 19___ Pd $_______ MIB NB DB BNT
☐ Want Orig. Ret. $4.75 **NB** $3 **MIB** Sec. Mkt. **$15-$18**

QX 380-5 GRANDPARENTS
Comments: Bezeled Lacquer-Look, 2-3/4" wide, Dated 1985
A white poinsettia against a red background is framed in brass and accented with gold. Caption: "Grandparents Have Beautiful Ways Of Adding Love To The Holidays. Christmas 1985."
Artist: Sharon Pike
☐ Purchased 19___ Pd $_______ MIB NB DB BNT
☐ Want Orig. Ret. $7.00 **NB** $2 **MIB** Sec. Mkt. **$10-$12**

QX 262-2 GRANDSON
Comments: Green Glass Ball, 2-7/8" dia., Dated 1985
A bright red, green and yellow train circles the ball. Caption: "A Grandson Makes Holiday Joys Shine Even Brighter! Christmas 1985." **Artist:** LaDene Votruba
☐ Purchased 19___ Pd $_______ MIB NB DB BNT
☐ Want Orig. Ret. $4.75 **NB** $12 **MIB** Sec. Mkt. **$25-$29**

QX 378-2 HEART FULL OF LOVE
Comments: Bezeled Satin, 3" tall, Dated Christmas 1985
Winter scene is framed with a chrome ring. Caption: "The World Is Full Of Beauty When Hearts Are Full Of Love."
☐ Purchased 19___ Pd $_______ MIB NB DB BNT
☐ Want Orig. Ret. $6.75 **NB** $5 **MIB** Sec. Mkt. **$16-$18**

QX 405-2 HEAVENLY TRUMPETER
Comments: Porcelain, 5" tall, Limited Edition. 24,700
On her wooden display stand, this handpainted porcelain angel blows her golden trumpet.
☐ Purchased 19___ Pd $_______ MIB NB DB BNT
☐ Want Orig. Ret. $27.50 **NB** $65 **MIB** Sec. Mkt. **$95-$100**

QX 496-5 HERE COMES SANTA: SANTA'S FIRE ENGINE
Comments: **Seventh in Series**, Handcrafted, 3" tall
Dated 1985. Santa's Fire Engine from the North Pole Fire Department has Santa in the driver's seat once again.
Artist: Linda Sickman
☐ Purchased 19___ Pd $_______ MIB NB DB BNT
☐ Want Orig. Ret. $14.00 **NB** $45 **MIB** Sec. Mkt. **$58-$60**

QX 498-2 HOLIDAY HEART
Comments: Porcelain, 2" tall
Christmas greenery decorates a white porcelain puffed heart.
Caption: "Love."
☐ Purchased 19___ Pd $_______ MIB NB DB BNT
☐ Want Orig. Ret. $8.00 **NB** $10 **MIB** Sec. Mkt. **$18-$22**

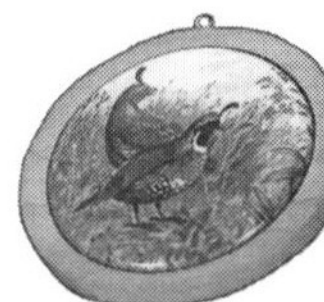

QX 376-5 HOLIDAY WILDLIFE: PARTRIDGE
Comments: **Fourth in Series,** Wood, 3" dia.
Caption: "California Partridge, Lophortyx Californica, Fourth In A Series, Wildlife Collection, Christmas 1985."
☐ Purchased 19___ Pd $_______ MIB NB DB BNT
☐ Want Orig. Ret. $7.50 **NB** $15 **MIB** Sec. Mkt. **$25-$30**

QX 271-5 HUGGA BUNCH™
Comments: Lt. Blue Glass Ball, 2-7/8" dia.
Children share hugs and Christmas fun.
Caption: "Huggy Holidays!"
☐ Purchased 19___ Pd $_______ MIB NB DB BNT
☐ Want Orig. Ret. $5.00 **NB** $10 **MIB** Sec. Mkt. **$22-$25**

QX 476-5 ICE-SKATING OWL
Comments: Handcrafted, 2" tall
White owl with a red and white hat, tries out his ice skates.
Artist: Bob Siedler
☐ Purchased 19___ Pd $_______ MIB NB DB BNT
☐ Want Orig. Ret. $5.00 **NB** $10 **MIB** Sec. Mkt. **$20-$22**

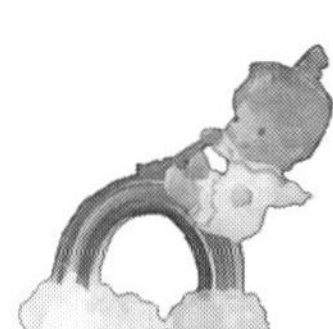

QLX 710-2 KATYBETH
Comments: Lighted, Handcrafted-Acrylic, 3-5/8" tall
Katybeth is busy painting the rainbow on which she is sitting. The rainbow and clouds light up.
☐ Purchased 19___ Pd $_______ MIB NB DB BNT
☐ Want Orig. Ret. $10.75 **NB** $28 **MIB** Sec. Mkt. **$40-$45**

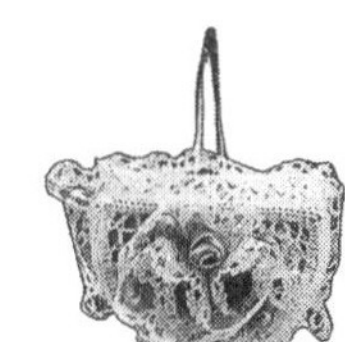

QX 514-5 KEEPSAKE BASKET: HEIRLOOM COLLECTION
Comments: Fabric, 2-1/2" tall
A rose-scented sachet is enclosed in a hand-crocheted basket trimmed with satin and lace. **Artist:** Sharon Pike
☐ Purchased 19___ Pd $_______ MIB NB DB BNT
☐ Want Orig. Ret. $15.00 **NB** $10 **MIB** Sec. Mkt. **$18-$20**

QX 484-5 KIT THE SHEPHERD
Comments: Handcrafted, 2-1/2" tall
Kit has traded in his green cap for a shepherd's headdress for the Christmas play. **Artist:** Bob Siedler
☐ Purchased 19___ Pd $_______ MIB NB DB BNT
☐ Want Orig. Ret. $5.75 **NB** $15 **MIB** Sec. Mkt. **$24-$26**

QX 474-5 KITTY MISCHIEF
Comments: Handcrafted, 2" tall, Reissued in 1986.
A ball of real yarn is used with this yellow and white kitten.
Artist: Peter Dutkin
☐ Purchased 19___ Pd $_______ MIB NB DB BNT
☐ Want Orig. Ret. $5.00 **NB** $14 **MIB** Sec. Mkt. **$20-$24**

QX 511-2 LACY HEART: HEIRLOOM COLLECTION
Comments: Fabric, 3" tall
A padded white satin heart is trimmed with lace.
Scented with a rose sachet.
☐ Purchased 19___ Pd $_______ MIB NB DB BNT
☐ Want Orig. Ret. $8.75 **NB** $10 **MIB** Sec. Mkt. **$20-$22**

QX 480-2 LAMB IN LEGWARMERS
Comments: Handcrafted, 3" tall
Green, red and white crocheted legwarmers adorn this little flocked lamb.
☐ Purchased 19___ Pd $_______ MIB NB DB BNT
☐ Want Orig. Ret. $7.00 **NB** $12 **MIB** Sec. Mkt. **$20-$24**

QLX 711-2 LITTLE RED SCHOOLHOUSE
Comments: Lighted, Handcrafted 2-5/8" tall
Inside, three parents watch the children perform in a school Christmas pageant. There is a great amount of detail on this ornament. **Artist:** Donna Lee
☐ Purchased 19___ Pd $_______ MIB NB DB BNT
☐ Want Orig. Ret. $15.75 **NB** $75 **MIB** Sec. Mkt. **$90-$95**

QX 371-5 LOVE AT CHRISTMAS
Comments: Acrylic, 3-1/4" wide
This acrylic heart is raining red foil hearts. Caption: "The Spirit Of Christmas Is Love." **Artist:** Diana McGehee
☐ Purchased 19___ Pd $_______ MIB NB DB BNT
☐ Want Orig. Ret. $5.75 **NB** $25 **MIB** Sec. Mkt. **$35-$40**

QLX 702-5 LOVE WREATH
Comments: Lighted, Acrylic, 3-1/2" tall
A wreath, hearts and ribbon is etched in clear acrylic. Caption: "Christmas Happens In The Heart." **Artist:** LaDene Votruba
☐ Purchased 19___ Pd $_______ MIB NB DB BNT
☐ Want Orig. Ret. $8.50 **NB** $20 **MIB** Sec. Mkt. **$30-$32**

QX 403-2 MERRY MOUSE
Comments: Handcrafted, 2-1/2" tall, Reissued in 1986
This happy little fellow wears a Santa hat. His tail is made of leather. **Artist:** Peter Dutkin
☐ Purchased 19___ Pd $_______ MIB NB DB BNT
☐ Want Orig. Ret. $4.50 **NB** $15 **MIB** Sec. Mkt. **$25-$30**

QX 267-2 MERRY SHIRT TALES™
Comments: Lt. Blue Glass, 3" dia., Dated Christmas 1985
The Shirt Tales gang is sledding, skating and skiing. Caption: "Every Day's A Holiday When Good Friends Get Together."
☐ Purchased 19___ Pd $_______ MIB NB DB BNT
☐ Want Orig. Ret. $4.75 **NB** $12 **MIB** Sec. Mkt. **$20-$22**

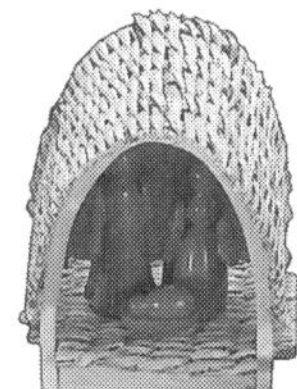

QX 482-5 MINIATURE CRECHE
Comments: ***FIRST IN SERIES,*** Wood and Straw, 3-1/2" tall
Wooden figures of the Holy Family grace the straw "stable."
Artist: Ed Seale
☐ Purchased 19___ Pd $_______ MIB NB DB BNT
☐ Want Orig. Ret. $8.75 **NB** $18 **MIB** Sec. Mkt. **$35-$40**

QX 372-2 MOTHER
Comments: Acrylic, 3-3/8" tall, Dated Christmas 1985
Acrylic teardrop framed in gold, has a caption which reads: "Mother Is The Heart Of Our Happiest Holiday Memories."
Artist: Sharon Pike
☐ Purchased 19___ Pd $_______ MIB NB DB BNT
☐ Want Orig. Ret. $6.75 **NB** $10 **MIB** Sec. Mkt. **$12-$14**

QX 509-2 MOTHER & DAD
Comments: Porcelain Bell, 3" tall, Dated Christmas 1985
White porcelain bell has a bas relief paisley design. Caption in soft blue: "Mother and Dad." **Artist:** LaDene Votruba
☐ Purchased 19___ Pd $_______ MIB NB DB BNT
☐ Want Orig. Ret. $7.75 **NB** $12 **MIB** Sec. Mkt. **$22-$24**

QX 476-2 MOUSE WAGON
Comments: Handcrafted, 2" tall, Dated 1985
Little white mouse rides his little red wagon bearing a gift of cheese.
☐ Purchased 19___ Pd $_______ MIB NB DB BNT
☐ Want Orig. Ret. $5.75 **NB** $40 **MIB** Sec. Mkt. **$60-$65**

QLX 705-2 MR. AND MRS. SANTA
Comments: Lighted, Handcrafted, 3" tall, Reissued in 1986.
Mrs. Santa decorates her Christmas tree while Santa waves to people passing by.
☐ Purchased 19___ Pd $_______ MIB NB DB BNT
☐ Want Orig. Ret. $14.50 **NB** $60 **MIB** Sec. Mkt. **$85-$90**

QX 483-5 MUFFIN THE ANGEL
Comments: Handcrafted, 2-1/2" tall
Muffin is dressed as an angel and is ready for the Christmas play.
Artist: Bob Siedler
☐ Purchased 19___ Pd $_______ MIB NB DB BNT
☐ Want Orig. Ret. $5.75 **NB** $18 **MIB** Sec. Mkt. **$24-$28**

QLX 700-1 NATIVITY
Comments: Lighted Panorama Ball, 3-1/2" dia.
Reissued from 1984. **Artist:** Ed Seale
☐ Purchased 19___ Pd $_______ MIB NB DB BNT
☐ Want Orig. Ret. $12.00 **NB** $20 **MIB** Sec. Mkt. **$30-$35**

QX 264-5 NATIVITY SCENE
Comments: Lt. Blue Glass Ball, 3" dia., Dated Christmas 1985
HARD TO FIND! Little angels welcome the Christ Child. Caption: "O Come, All Ye Faithful... Christmas 1985."
☐ Purchased 19___ Pd $_______ MIB NB DB BNT
☐ Want Orig. Ret. $4.75 **NB** $12 **MIB** Sec. Mkt. **$25-$30**

QX 269-5 NEW HOME
Comments: Blue Glass Ball, 3" dia., Dated Christmas 1985
Victorian homes, decorated for Christmas, circle this blue tear-drop ball. Caption: "New Home, New Joys, New Memories To Cherish." **Artist:** Michele Pyda-Sevcik
☐ Purchased 19___ Pd $_______ MIB NB DB BNT
☐ Want Orig. Ret. $4.75 **NB** $8 **MIB** Sec. Mkt. **$25-$30**

QX 520-5 NIECE
Comments: Acrylic, 3-3/4" tall, Dated Christmas 1985
Caption stamped in silver foil on teardrop shape: "A Niece Fills Hearts With A Special Kind Of Love."
☐ Purchased 19___ Pd $_______ MIB NB DB BNT
☐ Want Orig. Ret. $5.75 **NB** $5 **MIB** Sec. Mkt. **$8-$12**

QX 449-4 NIGHT BEFORE CHRISTMAS
Comments: Panorama Ball, 3-1/4" dia.
Push the button and the pages of this favorite Christmas story flip over (30 pages). Comes with special stand for off-tree display.
Artist: Ed Seale
☐ Purchased 19___ Pd $_______ MIB NB DB BNT
☐ Want Orig. Ret. $13.00 **NB** $35 **MIB** Sec. Mkt. **$42-$44**

QX 266-2 NORMAN ROCKWELL
Comments: White Glass Ball, 2-7/8" dia., Dated 1985
Caption: "... He Was Chubby And Plump, A Right Jolly Old Elf, And I Laughed When I Saw Him, In Spite Of Myself... C.C. Moore From The Norman Rockwell Collection 1985."
Artist: Diana McGehee
☐ Purchased 19___ Pd $_______ MIB NB DB BNT
☐ Want Orig. Ret. $4.75 **NB** $15 **MIB** Sec. Mkt. **$25-$35**

QX 374-5 NORMAN ROCKWELL: JOLLY POSTMAN
Comments: **Sixth in Series**, Light Green Cameo, 3" dia.
Dated 1985. Caption: "Jolly Postman, Sixth In A Series, Christmas 1985, The Norman Rockwell Collection."
Artist: Diana McGehee
☐ Purchased 19___ Pd $_______ MIB NB DB BNT
☐ Want Orig. Ret. $7.50 **NB** $10 **MIB** Sec. Mkt. **$30-$32**

"We Wish You A Merry Christmas and A Happy New Year"

QX 497-5 NOSTALGIC HOUSES AND SHOPS: TOY SHOP
Comments: **Second in Series**, Handcrafted, 2-1/2" tall
Dated 1985. This Old-Fashioned Toy Shop boasts a counter, cash register, dollhouse and toy truck downstairs and the owner's furnished apartment upstairs.
Artist: Donna Lee
☐ Purchased 19___ Pd $_______ MIB NB DB BNT
☐ Want Orig. Ret. $13.75 **NB** $85 **MIB** Sec. Mkt. **$105-$110**

QX 442-4 NOSTALGIC SLED
Comments: Handcrafted, 3-1/2" wide
Reissued from 1984. **Artist:** Linda Sickman
☐ Purchased 19___ Pd $_______ MIB NB DB BNT
☐ Want Orig. Ret. $6.00 **NB** $10 **MIB** Sec. Mkt. **$25-$30**

QX 519-5 OLD-FASHIONED DOLL ORNAMENT
Comments: Porcelain/Fabric, 5-1/2" tall
Dressed in a red dress and green apron, this Colonial doll is porcelain and fabric.
☐ Purchased 19___ Pd $_______ MIB NB DB BNT
☐ Want Orig. Ret. $14.50 **NB** $20 **MIB** Sec. Mkt. **$30-$32**

QX 373-5 OLD-FASHIONED WREATH
Comments: Acrylic, Etched Brass, 3-1/4" dia.
Dated Christmas 1985. Etched brass toys make up a wreath in acrylic. Gold foil caption.
☐ Purchased 19___ Pd $_______ MIB NB DB BNT
☐ Want Orig. Ret. $7.50 **NB** $10 **MIB** Sec. Mkt. **$16-$20**

QX 373-2 PEACEFUL KINGDOM
Comments: Acrylic, 3" wide, Dated Christmas 1985
The lion and lamb are etched into clear acrylic. Caption: "...And Peace Will Reign In The Kingdom..." **Artist:** Sharon Pike
☐ Purchased 19___ Pd $_______ MIB NB DB BNT
☐ Want Orig. Ret. $5.75 **NB** $8 **MIB** Sec. Mkt. **$20-$25**

QX 266-5 PEANUTS®
Comments: Blue Glass Ball, 3" dia., Dated 1985
Snoopy directs a "Christmas tree" chorus made up of Woodstock and his friends. Caption: "Sing A Song Of Christmas Joy!"
☐ Purchased 19___ Pd $_______ MIB NB DB BNT
☐ Want Orig. Ret. $4.75 **NB** $17 **MIB** Sec. Mkt. **$25-$26**

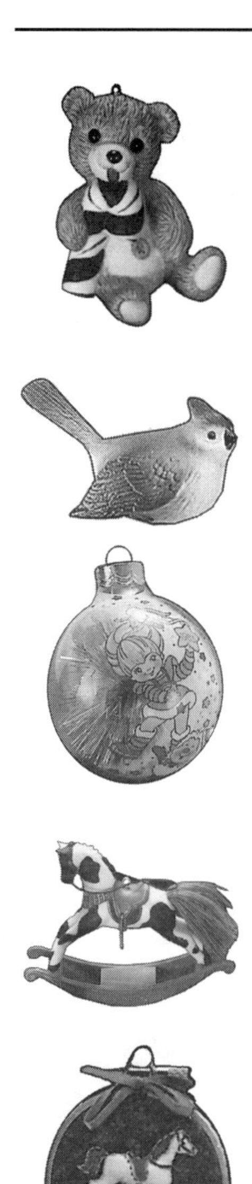

QX 479-2 PORCELAIN BEAR
Comments: **Third in Series**, Porcelain, 2-1/4" tall
This hand-painted cinnamon bear is enjoying the taste of a candy cane. **Artist:** Peter Dutkin
☐ Purchased 19___ Pd $_______ MIB NB DB BNT
☐ Want Orig. Ret. $7.50 **NB** $40 **MIB** Sec. Mkt. **$55-$60**

QX 479-5 PORCELAIN BIRD: TUFTED TITMOUSE
Comments: Porcelain, 2" tall
This hand-painted porcelain bird clips onto the tree.
Artist: Linda Sickman
☐ Purchased 19___ Pd $_______ MIB NB DB BNT
☐ Want Orig. Ret. $6.50 **NB** $18 **MIB** Sec. Mkt. **$30-$35**

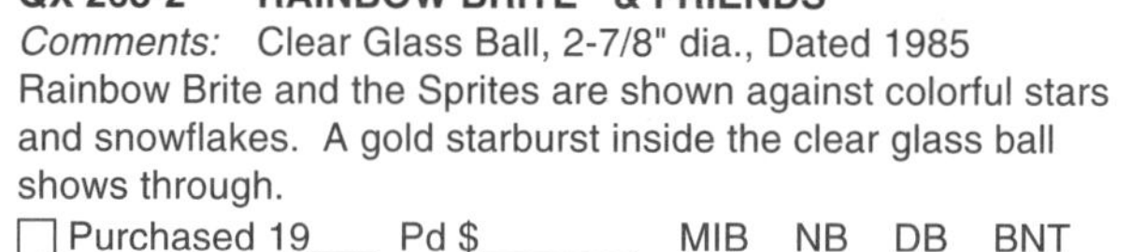

QX 268-2 RAINBOW BRITE™ & FRIENDS
Comments: Clear Glass Ball, 2-7/8" dia., Dated 1985
Rainbow Brite and the Sprites are shown against colorful stars and snowflakes. A gold starburst inside the clear glass ball shows through.
☐ Purchased 19___ Pd $_______ MIB NB DB BNT
☐ Want Orig. Ret. $4.75 **NB** $12 **MIB** Sec. Mkt. **$20-$24**

QX 493-2 ROCKING HORSE
Comments: **Fifth in Series**, Handcrafted, 4" wide, Dated 1985
A brown and white pinto with green saddle rides on blue rockers.
Artist: Linda Sickman
☐ Purchased 19___ Pd $_______ MIB NB DB BNT
☐ Want Orig. Ret. $10.75 **NB** $45 **MIB** Sec. Mkt. **$62-$65**

QX 518-2 ROCKING HORSE MEMORIES
Comments: Wood/Fabric, 3-1/4" dia., Dated Christmas 1985
A silk-screen rocking horse is appliqued against a holly pattern and is framed in a wooden embroidery hoop.
Artist: LaDene Votruba
☐ Purchased 19___ Pd $_______ MIB NB DB BNT
☐ Want Orig. Ret. $10.00 **NB** $8 **MIB** Sec. Mkt. **$12-$14**

QX 457-1 ROLLER SKATING RABBIT
Comments: Handcrafted, 2-1/2" wide
Reissued from 1984. **Artist:** Ed Seale
☐ Purchased 19___ Pd $_______ MIB NB DB BNT
☐ Want Orig. Ret. $5.00 **NB** $18 **MIB** Sec. Mkt. **$32-$35**

QX 300-5 SANTA CLAUS - THE MOVIE™: SANTA CLAUS
Comments: Lacquer-Look, 3-1/2" tall
Santa holds the reins of a sleigh overflowing with toys. "Elfmade" emblem foil stamped on the back. These ornaments, taken from the movie, went over like a lead balloon, in my opinion.
☐ Purchased 19___ Pd $_______ MIB NB DB BNT
☐ Want Orig. Ret. $6.75 **NB** $2 **MIB** Sec. Mkt. **$5-$8**

QX 300-2 SANTA CLAUS - THE MOVIE™ SANTA'S VILLAGE
Comments: Lacquer-Look, 2-1/4" tall
A portrait of Santa's magical village is set in a brass bezel. Caption: "Merry, Merry Christmas." "Elfmade" emblem foil stamped on the back.
☐ Purchased 19___ Pd $_______ MIB NB DB BNT
☐ Want Orig. Ret. $6.75 **NB** $2 **MIB** Sec. Mkt. **$5-$8**

QX 494-2 SANTA PIPE
Comments: Handcrafted, 4-1/2" tall
This pipe, with the look of carved antique meerschaum depicts Santa and the reindeer on Christmas eve.
Artist: Peter Dutkin
☐ Purchased 19___ Pd $_______ MIB NB DB BNT
☐ Want Orig. Ret. $9.50 **NB** $15 **MIB** Sec. Mkt. **$22-$24**

QX 496-2 SANTA'S SKI TRIP
Comments: Handcrafted, 3-3/4" tall, Dated 1985
Santa rides a green cable car to the top of the mountain. "Snowflake Mountain No. 1985." **Artist:** Ed Seale
☐ Purchased 19___ Pd $_______ MIB NB DB BNT
☐ Want Orig. Ret. $12.00 **NB** $48 **MIB** Sec. Mkt. **$60-$65**

QLX 700-4 SANTA'S WORKSHOP
Comments: Lighted, Peek-Through Ball, 3-1/2" dia.
Reissued from 1984.
☐ Purchased 19___ Pd $_______ MIB NB DB BNT
☐ Want Orig. Ret. $13.00 **NB** $45 **MIB** Sec. Mkt. **$60-$65**

QLX 712-2 SEASON OF BEAUTY
Comments: Lighted, Red and Gold Classic Shape, 3-1/4" dia.
A wintry scene reflects peace and beauty. Caption: "May Joy Come Into Your World As Christmas Comes Into Your Heart."
Artist: Joyce A. Lyle
☐ Purchased 19___ Pd $_______ MIB NB DB BNT
☐ Want Orig. Ret. $8.00 **NB** $12 **MIB** Sec. Mkt. **$24-$28**

QX 379-5 SEWN PHOTOHOLDER
Comments: Embroidered Fabric, 3-1/4" dia.
Dated Christmas 1985. Red fabric photoholder is embroidered with holiday designs and hearts. Caption: "Cherished Times That Mean The Most Are Kept In Memory Ever Close."
Artist: Sharon Pike
☐ Purchased 19___ Pd $_______ MIB NB DB BNT
☐ Want Orig. Ret. $7.00 **NB** $10 **MIB** Sec. Mkt. **$24-$28**

QX 517-5 SHEEP AT CHRISTMAS
Comments: Handcrafted, 3-1/4" tall, Dated 1985
This wood-look sheep wears a bell. Caption: "Season's Greetings." **Artist:** Linda Sickman
☐ Purchased 19___ Pd $_______ MIB NB DB BNT
☐ Want Orig. Ret. $8.25 **NB** $12 **MIB** Sec. Mkt. **$22-$28**

QX 506-5 SISTER
Comments: Porcelain, 2-3/4" tall, Dated Christmas 1985
White porcelain bell with red ribbon is designed with hearts and holly. Caption: "For Sister, With Love." **Artist:** Joyce Pattee
☐ Purchased 19___ Pd $_______ MIB NB DB BNT
☐ Want Orig. Ret. $7.25 **NB** $9 **MIB** Sec. Mkt. **$18-$20**

QX 473-2 SKATEBOARD RACCOON
Comments: Handcrafted, 2-1/2" tall, Reissued in 1986
A flocked raccoon is riding a red skateboard with green moveable wheels. **Artist:** Peter Dutkin
☐ Purchased 19___ Pd $_______ MIB NB DB BNT
☐ Want Orig. Ret. $6.50 **NB** $20 **MIB** Sec. Mkt. **$28-$30**

QX 491-5 SNOOPY® AND WOODSTOCK
Comments: Handcrafted, 1-3/4" tall
Snoopy and Woodstock are practicing their hockey moves.
Artist: Bob Siedler
☐ Purchased 19___ Pd $_______ MIB NB DB BNT
☐ Want Orig. Ret. $7.50 **NB** $40 **MIB** Sec. Mkt. **$50-$55**

QX 470-2 SNOW-PITCHING SNOWMAN
Comments: Handcrafted, 2" tall, Reissued in 1986
A cute little snowman, dressed in a red and green baseball cap, is captured in the middle of pitching his snowball.
Artist: Donna Lee
☐ Purchased 19___ Pd $_______ MIB NB DB BNT
☐ Want Orig. Ret. $4.50 **NB** $14 **MIB** Sec. Mkt. **$20-$24**

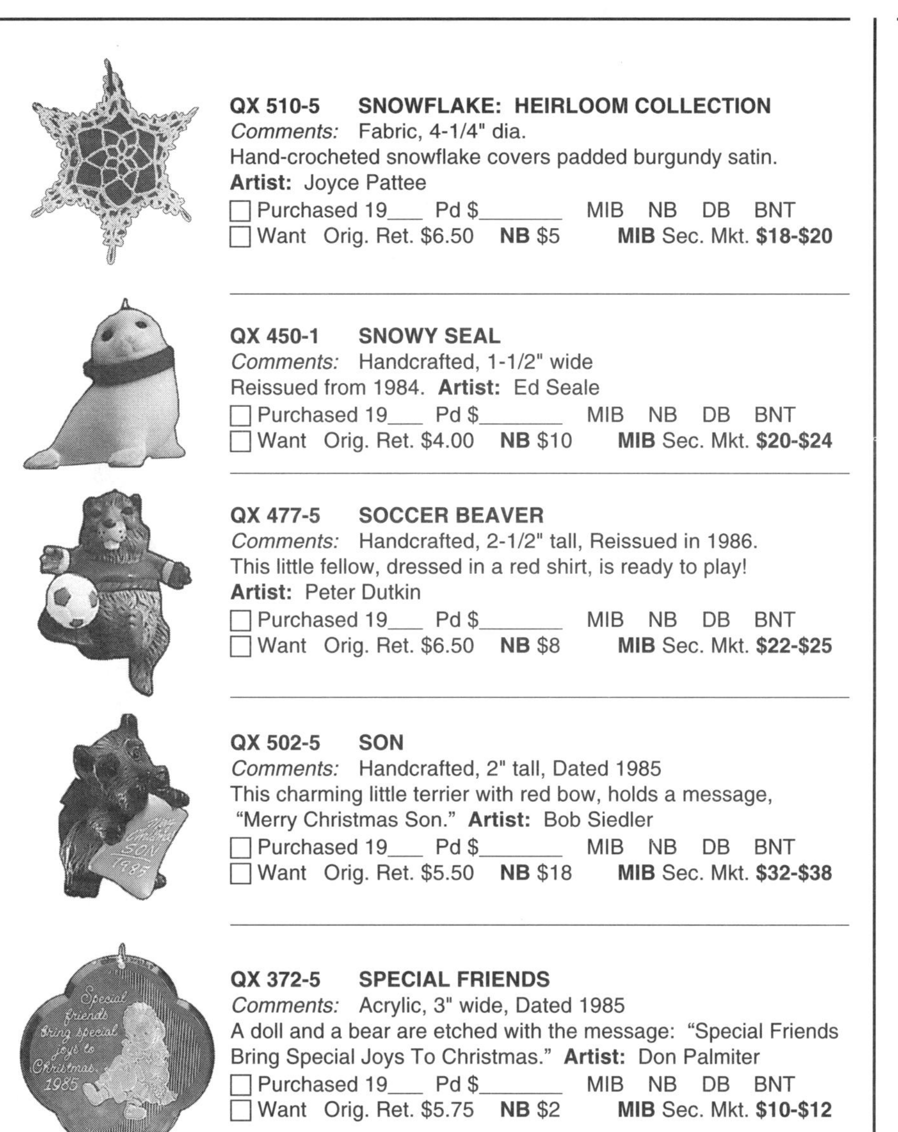

QX 510-5 SNOWFLAKE: HEIRLOOM COLLECTION
Comments: Fabric, 4-1/4" dia.
Hand-crocheted snowflake covers padded burgundy satin.
Artist: Joyce Pattee
☐ Purchased 19___ Pd $_______ MIB NB DB BNT
☐ Want Orig. Ret. $6.50 **NB** $5 **MIB** Sec. Mkt. **$18-$20**

QX 450-1 SNOWY SEAL
Comments: Handcrafted, 1-1/2" wide
Reissued from 1984. **Artist:** Ed Seale
☐ Purchased 19___ Pd $_______ MIB NB DB BNT
☐ Want Orig. Ret. $4.00 **NB** $10 **MIB** Sec. Mkt. **$20-$24**

QX 477-5 SOCCER BEAVER
Comments: Handcrafted, 2-1/2" tall, Reissued in 1986.
This little fellow, dressed in a red shirt, is ready to play!
Artist: Peter Dutkin
☐ Purchased 19___ Pd $_______ MIB NB DB BNT
☐ Want Orig. Ret. $6.50 **NB** $8 **MIB** Sec. Mkt. **$22-$25**

QX 502-5 SON
Comments: Handcrafted, 2" tall, Dated 1985
This charming little terrier with red bow, holds a message, "Merry Christmas Son." **Artist:** Bob Siedler
☐ Purchased 19___ Pd $_______ MIB NB DB BNT
☐ Want Orig. Ret. $5.50 **NB** $18 **MIB** Sec. Mkt. **$32-$38**

QX 372-5 SPECIAL FRIENDS
Comments: Acrylic, 3" wide, Dated 1985
A doll and a bear are etched with the message: "Special Friends Bring Special Joys To Christmas." **Artist:** Don Palmiter
☐ Purchased 19___ Pd $_______ MIB NB DB BNT
☐ Want Orig. Ret. $5.75 **NB** $2 **MIB** Sec. Mkt. **$10-$12**

QX 498-5 SPIRIT OF SANTA CLAUS, THE
Comments: Special Ed., Handcrafted, 4-3/4" tall
This elaborate reindeer and sleigh with Santa at the reins is beautiful! Came with a wishbone-shaped hanger.
Artist: Donna Lee
☐ Purchased 19___ Pd $_______ MIB NB DB BNT
☐ Want Orig. Ret. $22.50 **NB** $80 **MIB** Sec. Mkt. **$95-$100**

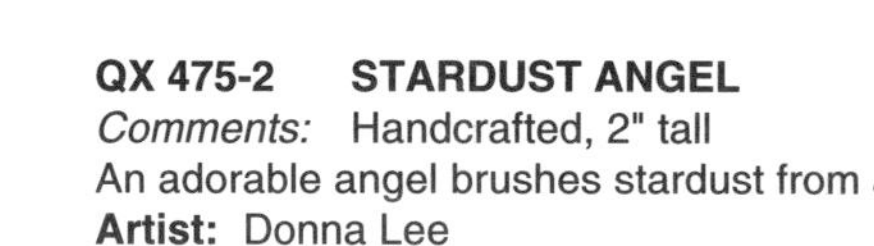

QX 475-2 STARDUST ANGEL
Comments: Handcrafted, 2" tall
An adorable angel brushes stardust from a star.
Artist: Donna Lee
☐ Purchased 19___ Pd $_______ MIB NB DB BNT
☐ Want Orig. Ret. $5.75 **NB** $22 **MIB** Sec. Mkt. **$35-$38**

QLX 701-1 SUGARPLUM COTTAGE
Comments: Lighted, Handcrafted, 3" tall
Issued in 1984, 1985 and 1986.
☐ Purchased 19___ Pd $_______ MIB NB DB BNT
☐ Want Orig. Ret. $11.00 **NB** $22 **MIB** Sec. Mkt. **$45-$50**

QX 492-2 SUN & FUN SANTA
Comments: Handcrafted, 2-3/4" tall, Dated 1985
Santa's ready for the beach with his reindeer inner tube and bathing cap. **Artist:** Bob Siedler
☐ Purchased 19___ Pd $_______ MIB NB DB BNT
☐ Want Orig. Ret. $7.75 **NB** $25 **MIB** Sec. Mkt. **$35-$40**

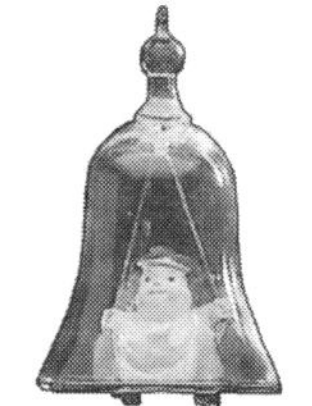

QX 492-5 SWINGING ANGEL BELL
Comments: Handcrafted/Glass, 3-3/4" tall
An angel is the clapper of this clear glass bell.
Artist: Bob Siedler
☐ Purchased 19___ Pd $_______ MIB NB DB BNT
☐ Want Orig. Ret. $11.00 **NB** $25 **MIB** Sec. Mkt. **$35-$38**

QLX 706-5 SWISS CHEESE LANE
Comments: Lighted, Handcrafted, 2-5/8" tall, Dated 1985
"Swiss Cheese Lane" turns a wedge of cheese into a comfortable home for a pair of mice. The brightly lit interior shows the details of the home.
☐ Purchased 19___ Pd $_______ MIB NB DB BNT
☐ Want Orig. Ret. $13.00 **NB** $35 **MIB** Sec. Mkt. **$48-$52**

QX 505-2 TEACHER - OWL
Comments: Handcrafted, 3" tall, "School Days 1985"
An owl sits atop a slate reading a book. The slate reads "Merry Christmas To A Grade A Teacher." May be personalized on the back of the slate.
☐ Purchased 19___ Pd $_______ MIB NB DB BNT
☐ Want Orig. Ret. $6.00 **NB** $5 **MIB** Sec. Mkt. **$18-$20**

QX 472-5 THIMBLE SERIES: SANTA
Comments: **Eighth in Series**, Handcrafted, 2-3/8" tall
Santa carries a thimble "backpack" with a Christmas tree.
Artist: Bob Siedler
☐ Purchased 19___ Pd $_______ MIB NB DB BNT
☐ Want Orig. Ret. $5.50 **NB** $18 **MIB** Sec. Mkt. **$32-$36**

QX 431-1 THREE KITTENS IN A MITTEN
Comments: Handcrafted, 3-1/2" tall
Reissued from 1984. **Artist:** Donna Lee
☐ Purchased 19___ Pd $_______ MIB NB DB BNT
☐ Want Orig. Ret. $8.00 **NB** $30 **MIB** Sec. Mkt. **$40-$45**

QX 497-2 TIN LOCOMOTIVE
Comments: **Fourth in Series**, 3-1/2" tall, Dated 1985
This black locomotive is embellished with colors and designs and a jingle bell. **Artist:** Linda Sickman
☐ Purchased 19___ Pd $_______ MIB NB DB BNT
☐ Want Orig. Ret. $14.75 **NB** $60 **MIB** Sec. Mkt. **$75-$82**

QX 471-2 TRUMPET PANDA
Comments: Handcrafted, 2" tall
A flocked panda plays a red trumpet. **Artist:** Ed Seale
☐ Purchased 19___ Pd $_______ MIB NB DB BNT
☐ Want Orig. Ret. $4.50 **NB** $12 **MIB** Sec. Mkt. **$18-$22**

QX 371-2 TWELVE DAYS OF CHRISTMAS
Comments: **Second in Series**, Acrylic, 3" tall, Dated 1985
Two turtle doves are represented for the Second Day of Christmas. Caption: "...Two Turtle Doves." **Artist:** Sharon Pike
☐ Purchased 19___ Pd $_______ MIB NB DB BNT
☐ Want Orig. Ret. $6.50 **NB** $35 **MIB** Sec. Mkt. **$50-$55**

QX 500-5 TWENTY-FIVE YEARS TOGETHER
Comments: Porcelain, 3-1/4" dia., Dated 1985
A white porcelain plate is decorated with a blue, silver and gold wreath of holly and firs. Caption: "Twenty-Five Years Together."
☐ Purchased 19___ Pd $_______ MIB NB DB BNT
☐ Want Orig. Ret. $8.00 **NB** $8 **MIB** Sec. Mkt. **$18-$22**

Happiness - A perfume you can't pour on others without spilling a little on yourself.

QX 513-2 VICTORIAN LADY
Comments: Porcelain/Fabric, 3-3/4" tall
A hand-painted porcelain doll wears a dress of burgundy satin and lace trim.
☐ Purchased 19___ Pd $_______ MIB NB DB BNT
☐ Want Orig. Ret. $9.50 **NB** $15 **MIB** Sec. Mkt. **$23-$27**

QLX 702-1 VILLAGE CHURCH
Comments: Lighted, Handcrafted, 4-5/8" tall
Reissued from 1984. **Artist:** Donna Lee
☐ Purchased 19___ Pd $_______ MIB NB DB BNT
☐ Want Orig. Ret. $15.00 **NB** $30 **MIB** Sec. Mkt. **$45-$50**

QX 519-2 WHIRLIGIG SANTA
Comments: Wood, 4" tall
Modeled after a Colonial toy, this Santa has arms that move in a whirligig fashion.
☐ Purchased 19___ Pd $_______ MIB NB DB BNT
☐ Want Orig. Ret. $12.50 **NB** $12 **MIB** Sec. Mkt. **$24-$26**

QX 490-2 WINDOWS OF THE WORLD: MEXICAN
Comments: ***FIRST IN SERIES***, Handcrafted, 3" tall, Dated 1985
A little Mexican boy sits in a brick and stucco window and plays. Caption: "Feliz Navidad." **Artist:** Donna Lee
☐ Purchased 19___ Pd $_______ MIB NB DB BNT
☐ Want Orig. Ret. $9.75 **NB** $80 **MIB** Sec. Mkt. **$100-$110**

QX 375-2 WITH APPRECIATION
Comments: Acrylic, 3-1/2" tall, Dated 1985
Silver foil snowflakes and gold caption: "Christmas... A Time When We Think Of Those Who Have Given Us So Much." Framed in brass.
☐ Purchased 19___ Pd $_______ MIB NB DB BNT
☐ Want Orig. Ret. $6.75 **NB** $2 **MIB** Sec. Mkt. **$10-$12**

QX 472-2 WOODEN CHILDHOOD SERIES: TRAIN
Comments: **Second in Series**, Wood, 3-1/2" wide
Handpainted locomotive carries a log car. Has a real pull string and wheels that turn. **Artist:** Peter Dutkin
☐ Purchased 19___ Pd $_______ MIB NB DB BNT
☐ Want Orig. Ret. $7.00 **NB** $25 **MIB** Sec. Mkt. **$45-$48**

1986 Collection

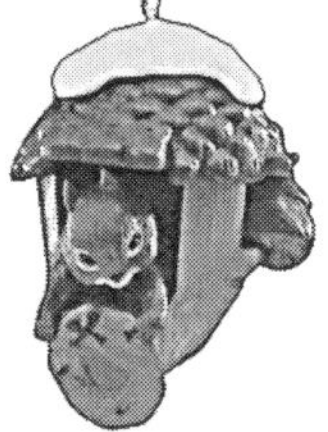

QX 424-3 ACORN INN
Comments: Handcrafted, 2" tall
Using a green wreath a squirrel decorates his snow-capped inn.
Artist: Duane Unruh
☐ Purchased 19___ Pd $_______ MIB NB DB BNT
☐ Want Orig. Ret. $8.50 **NB** $20 **MIB** Sec. Mkt. **$28-$32**

QX 350-6 ART MASTERPIECE: MADONNA & CHILD
Comments: **Third and Final in Series,** Bezeled Satin, 3-1/4" tall
Caption: "Lorenzo Di Cridi, Madonna And Child With The InfantSt. John, The Nelson-Atkins Museum Of Art, Kansas City, MO (Nelson Fund)." **Artist:** Diana McGehee
☐ Purchased 19___ Pd $_______ MIB NB DB BNT
☐ Want Orig. Ret. $6.75 **NB** $12 **MIB** Sec. Mkt. **$25-$30**

QX 412-3 BABY LOCKET
Comments: Textured Brass, 2-1/4" dia., Dated 1986
This brass locket includes embossed lettering and baby toy designs. Opens for Baby's photo and personalizing. Caption: "Baby." **Artist:** Diana McGehee
☐ Purchased 19___ Pd $_______ MIB NB DB BNT
☐ Want Orig. Ret. $16.00 **NB** $12 **MIB** Sec. Mkt. **$24-$28**

QX 271-3 BABY'S FIRST CHRISTMAS
Comments: Ecru Satin Ball 2-7/8" dia., Dated 1986
Caption: "A Baby's A Bundle Of Hope And Joy" and "Baby's First Christmas."
☐ Purchased 19___ Pd $_______ MIB NB DB BNT
☐ Want Orig. Ret. $5.50 **NB** $15 **MIB** Sec. Mkt. **$22-$25**

QLX 710-3 BABY'S FIRST CHRISTMAS
Comments: Lighted Panorama Ball, 3-5/8" tall
Baby's First Christmas 1986. Caption: "There's Someone New On Santa's List, Someone Small And Dear, Someone Santa's Sure To Love And Visit Every Year!" **Artist:** Ken Crow
☐ Purchased 19___ Pd $_______ MIB NB DB BNT
☐ Want Orig. Ret. $19.50 **NB** $32 **MIB** Sec. Mkt. **$45-$50**

QX 412-6 BABY'S FIRST CHRISTMAS
Comments: Handcrafted, 3-1/2" tall, Dated 1986
Miniature mobile has a duck, Santa, teddy bear and stocking hanging from an acrylic cloud and star with the caption: "Baby's First Christmas." **Artist:** Linda Sickman
☐ Purchased 19___ Pd $_______ MIB NB DB BNT
☐ Want Orig. Ret. $9.00 **NB** $24 **MIB** Sec. Mkt. **$38-$40**

QX 380-3 BABY'S FIRST CHRISTMAS
Comments: Acrylic, 3-3/4" tall, Dated 1986
A lamb with curly etched "wool" carries a stocking for "Baby's First Christmas." **Artist:** Don Palmiter
☐ Purchased 19___ Pd $_______ MIB NB DB BNT
☐ Want Orig. Ret. $6.00 **NB** $5 **MIB** Sec. Mkt. **$22-$25**

QX 379-2 BABY'S FIRST CHRISTMAS PHOTOHOLDER
Comments: Fabric, 3-3/4" tall, Dated 1986
Green and white gingham photoholder. Caption: "Baby's First Christmas" and "A Baby Puts Special Magic In Holiday Moments." **Artist:** Joyce Pattee
☐ Purchased 19___ Pd $_______ MIB NB DB BNT
☐ Want Orig. Ret. $8.00 **NB** $20 **MIB** Sec. Mkt. **$24-$28**

QX 413-3 BABY'S SECOND CHRISTMAS
Comments: Handcrafted, 1-3/4" tall, Dated 1986
A little mouse with a diaper delivers a stocking that says "Baby's 2nd Christmas." **Artist:** Bob Siedler
☐ Purchased 19___ Pd $_______ MIB NB DB BNT
☐ Want Orig. Ret. $6.50 **NB** $15 **MIB** Sec. Mkt. **$25-$30**

QX 275-6 BABY-SITTER
Comments: Gold Glass Ball, 3" dia., Dated Christmas 1986
Antique toys circle the ball. Caption: "For Being The Best Friend A Child Could Ever Have." Baby sitter ornaments usually never go up on the Sec. Market.
☐ Purchased 19___ Pd $_______ MIB NB DB BNT
☐ Want Orig. Ret. $4.75 **NB** $4 **MIB** Sec. Mkt. **$8-$10**

QX 480-5 BEARY SMOOTH RIDE
Comments: Handcrafted, 1-3/4" tall
Reissued from 1985. **Artist:** Linda Sickman
☐ Purchased 19___ Pd $_______ MIB NB DB BNT
☐ Want Orig. Ret. $6.50 **NB** $10 **MIB** Sec. Mkt. **$22-$24**

QX 277-6 BETSEY CLARK: HOME FOR CHRISTMAS
Comments: ***FIRST IN SERIES***, Pink Glass Ball, 2-7/8" dia. Dated 1986. Betsey and her friends are busy decorating. Caption: "May Christmas Love Fill Every Little Corner Of Your World." **Artist:** Sharon Pike
☐ Purchased 19___ Pd $_______ MIB NB DB BNT
☐ Want Orig. Ret. $5.00 **NB** $12 **MIB** Sec. Mkt. **$25-$30**

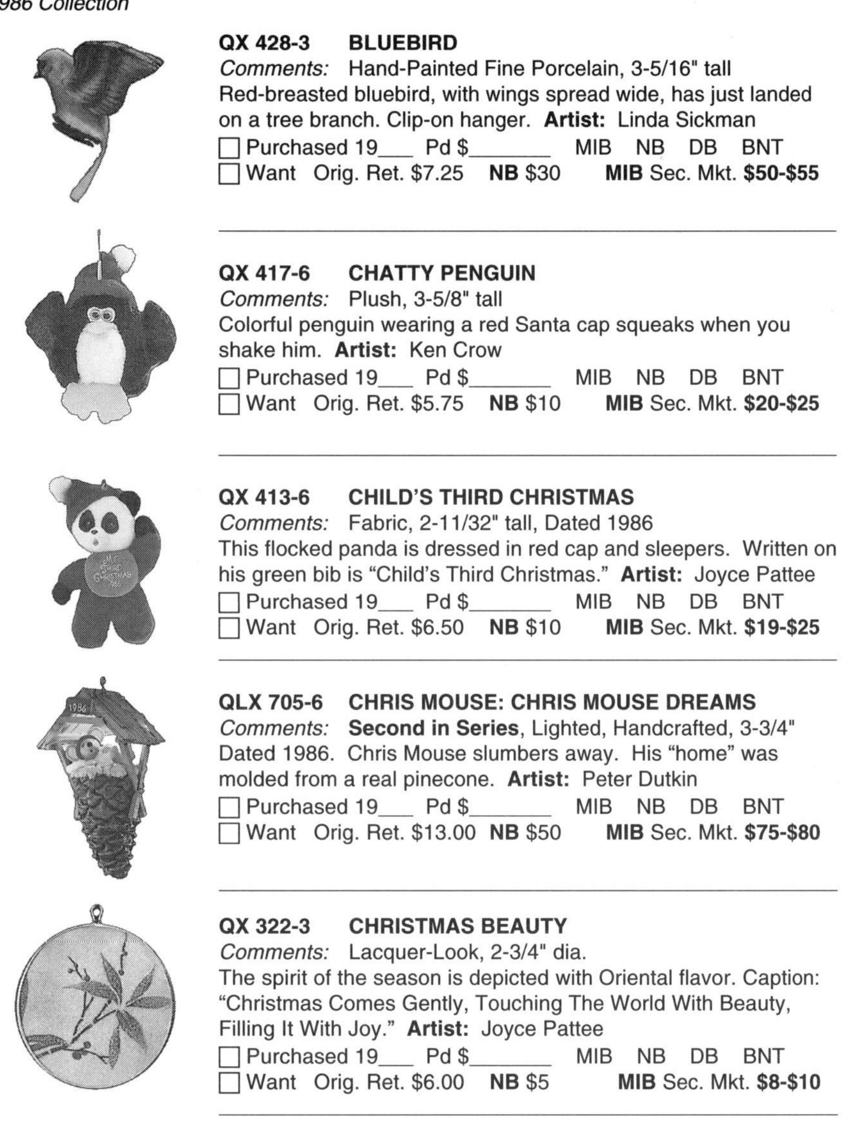

QX 428-3 BLUEBIRD
Comments: Hand-Painted Fine Porcelain, 3-5/16" tall
Red-breasted bluebird, with wings spread wide, has just landed on a tree branch. Clip-on hanger. **Artist:** Linda Sickman
☐ Purchased 19___ Pd $_______ MIB NB DB BNT
☐ Want Orig. Ret. $7.25 **NB** $30 **MIB** Sec. Mkt. **$50-$55**

QX 417-6 CHATTY PENGUIN
Comments: Plush, 3-5/8" tall
Colorful penguin wearing a red Santa cap squeaks when you shake him. **Artist:** Ken Crow
☐ Purchased 19___ Pd $_______ MIB NB DB BNT
☐ Want Orig. Ret. $5.75 **NB** $10 **MIB** Sec. Mkt. **$20-$25**

QX 413-6 CHILD'S THIRD CHRISTMAS
Comments: Fabric, 2-11/32" tall, Dated 1986
This flocked panda is dressed in red cap and sleepers. Written on his green bib is "Child's Third Christmas." **Artist:** Joyce Pattee
☐ Purchased 19___ Pd $_______ MIB NB DB BNT
☐ Want Orig. Ret. $6.50 **NB** $10 **MIB** Sec. Mkt. **$19-$25**

QLX 705-6 CHRIS MOUSE: CHRIS MOUSE DREAMS
Comments: **Second in Series**, Lighted, Handcrafted, 3-3/4" Dated 1986. Chris Mouse slumbers away. His "home" was molded from a real pinecone. **Artist:** Peter Dutkin
☐ Purchased 19___ Pd $_______ MIB NB DB BNT
☐ Want Orig. Ret. $13.00 **NB** $50 **MIB** Sec. Mkt. **$75-$80**

QX 322-3 CHRISTMAS BEAUTY
Comments: Lacquer-Look, 2-3/4" dia.
The spirit of the season is depicted with Oriental flavor. Caption: "Christmas Comes Gently, Touching The World With Beauty, Filling It With Joy." **Artist:** Joyce Pattee
☐ Purchased 19___ Pd $_______ MIB NB DB BNT
☐ Want Orig. Ret. $6.00 **NB** $5 **MIB** Sec. Mkt. **$8-$10**

QLX 704-3 CHRISTMAS CLASSICS: NUTCRACKER BALLET
Comments: ***FIRST IN SERIES***, Lighted, Handcrafted, 4-1/2" Dated 1986. Crafted in shimmering pastels, a ballerina strikes a classic pose, waiting for the ballet to begin. "Sugarplum Fairy."
☐ Purchased 19___ Pd $_______ MIB NB DB BNT
☐ Want Orig. Ret. $17.50 **NB** $60 **MIB** Sec. Mkt. **$80-$85**

QX 512-6 CHRISTMAS GUITAR
Comments: Handcrafted, 3" tall, Dated 1986
This miniature guitar is decorated with green and red holly. Hangs from fabric guitar strap. **Artist:** Duane Unruh
☐ Purchased 19___ Pd $_______ MIB NB DB BNT
☐ Want Orig. Ret. $7.00 **NB** $12 **MIB** Sec. Mkt. **$18-$24**

QLX 701-2 CHRISTMAS SLEIGH RIDE
Comments: Light and Motion, Handcrafted, 3-3/4" tall
A couple rides in a horse-drawn sleigh. The clear dome is sprinkled with "snow." Caption: "Love's Precious Moments Shine Forever In The Heart." Price is up from '95! **Artist:** Ed Seal
☐ Purchased 19___ Pd $_______ MIB NB DB BNT
☐ Want Orig. Ret. $24.50 **NB** $100 **MIB** Sec. Mkt. **$145-$150**

QX 406-3 CLOTHESPIN SOLDIERS: FRENCH OFFICER
Comments: **Fifth in Series,** Handcrafted, 1-27/32" tall
Dressed in the style of Napoleon, this officer carries a telescope and is dressed in red and green. **Artist:** LInda Sickman
☐ Purchased 19___ Pd $_______ MIB NB DB BNT
☐ Want Orig. Ret. $5.50 **NB** $15 **MIB** Sec. Mkt. **$25-$30**

QXO279-6 COCA-COLA SANTA: OPEN HOUSE ORN.
Comments: Porcelain White Glass Ball, 2-7/8" dia.
Three nostalgic paintings of Santa. Special offering for dealers' "Open House" events.
☐ Purchased 19___ Pd $_______ MIB NB DB BNT
☐ Want Orig. Ret. $4.75 **NB** $6 **MIB** Sec. Mkt. **$18-$20**

QX 414-6 COOKIES FOR SANTA
Comments: Handcrafted, 2-3/4" dia., Dated 1986
A plate carries a sign "For Santa" and holds a star shaped cookie and a gingerbread man. **Artist:** Diana McGehee
☐ Purchased 19___ Pd $_______ MIB NB DB BNT
☐ Want Orig. Ret. $4.50 **NB** $12 **MIB** Sec. Mkt. **$22-$25**

QX 511-3 COUNTRY SLEIGH
Comments: Handcrafted, 2" tall, Dated 1986
This red and gold sleigh was modeled after an antique sleigh and holds a plaid fabric blanket. **Artist:** Linda Sickman
☐ Purchased 19___ Pd $_______ MIB NB DB BNT
☐ Want Orig. Ret. $10.00 **NB** $12 **MIB** Sec. Mkt. **$22-$24**

Friendship is the cement that holds the world together.

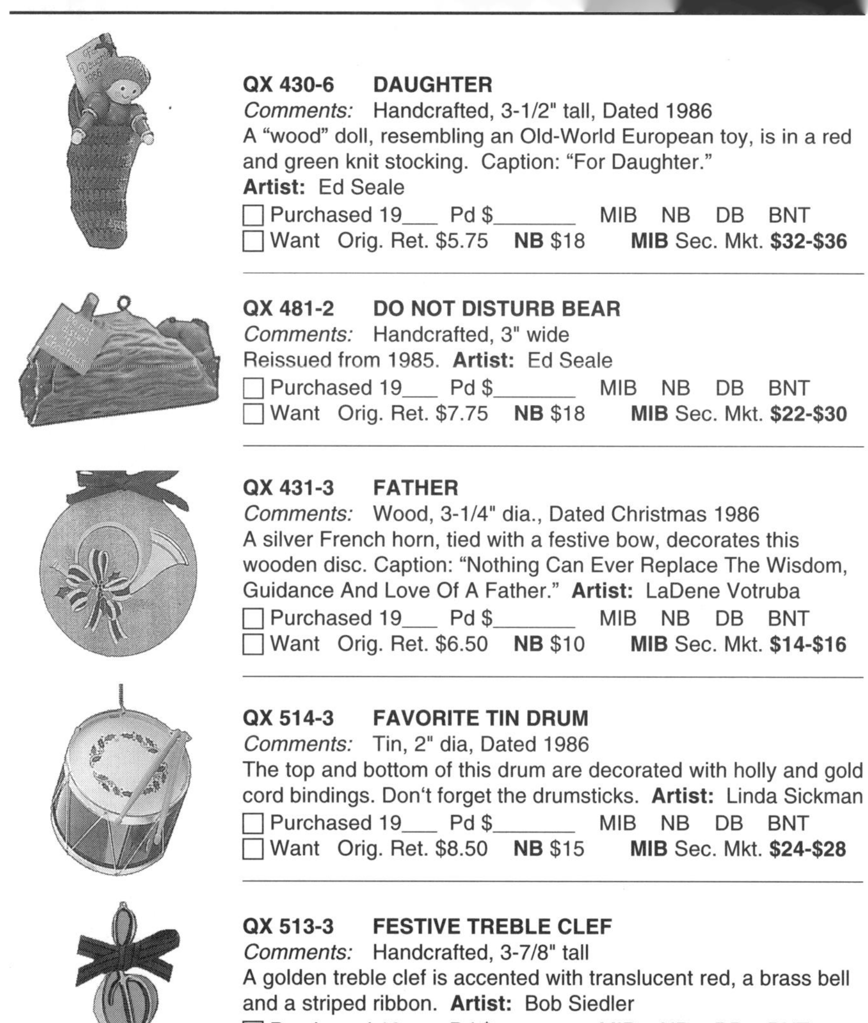

QX 430-6 DAUGHTER
Comments: Handcrafted, 3-1/2" tall, Dated 1986
A "wood" doll, resembling an Old-World European toy, is in a red and green knit stocking. Caption: "For Daughter."
Artist: Ed Seale
☐ Purchased 19___ Pd $_______ MIB NB DB BNT
☐ Want Orig. Ret. $5.75 **NB** $18 **MIB** Sec. Mkt. **$32-$36**

QX 481-2 DO NOT DISTURB BEAR
Comments: Handcrafted, 3" wide
Reissued from 1985. **Artist:** Ed Seale
☐ Purchased 19___ Pd $_______ MIB NB DB BNT
☐ Want Orig. Ret. $7.75 **NB** $18 **MIB** Sec. Mkt. **$22-$30**

QX 431-3 FATHER
Comments: Wood, 3-1/4" dia., Dated Christmas 1986
A silver French horn, tied with a festive bow, decorates this wooden disc. Caption: "Nothing Can Ever Replace The Wisdom, Guidance And Love Of A Father." **Artist:** LaDene Votruba
☐ Purchased 19___ Pd $_______ MIB NB DB BNT
☐ Want Orig. Ret. $6.50 **NB** $10 **MIB** Sec. Mkt. **$14-$16**

QX 514-3 FAVORITE TIN DRUM
Comments: Tin, 2" dia, Dated 1986
The top and bottom of this drum are decorated with holly and gold cord bindings. Don't forget the drumsticks. **Artist:** Linda Sickman
☐ Purchased 19___ Pd $_______ MIB NB DB BNT
☐ Want Orig. Ret. $8.50 **NB** $15 **MIB** Sec. Mkt. **$24-$28**

QX 513-3 FESTIVE TREBLE CLEF
Comments: Handcrafted, 3-7/8" tall
A golden treble clef is accented with translucent red, a brass bell and a striped ribbon. **Artist:** Bob Siedler
☐ Purchased 19___ Pd $_______ MIB NB DB BNT
☐ Want Orig. Ret. $8.75 **NB** $12 **MIB** Sec. Mkt. **$20-$28**

QX 400-6 FIFTY YEARS TOGETHER
Comments: Fine Porcelain, 3-13/32" tall
Dated Christmas 1986. White porcelain bell has a bas-relief holly design and a sculpted "50" as the handle. Caption: "Fifty Years Together."
☐ Purchased 19___ Pd $_______ MIB NB DB BNT
☐ Want Orig. Ret. $10.00 **NB** $14 **MIB** Sec. Mkt. **$18-$22**

Love is a game two can play and both can win.

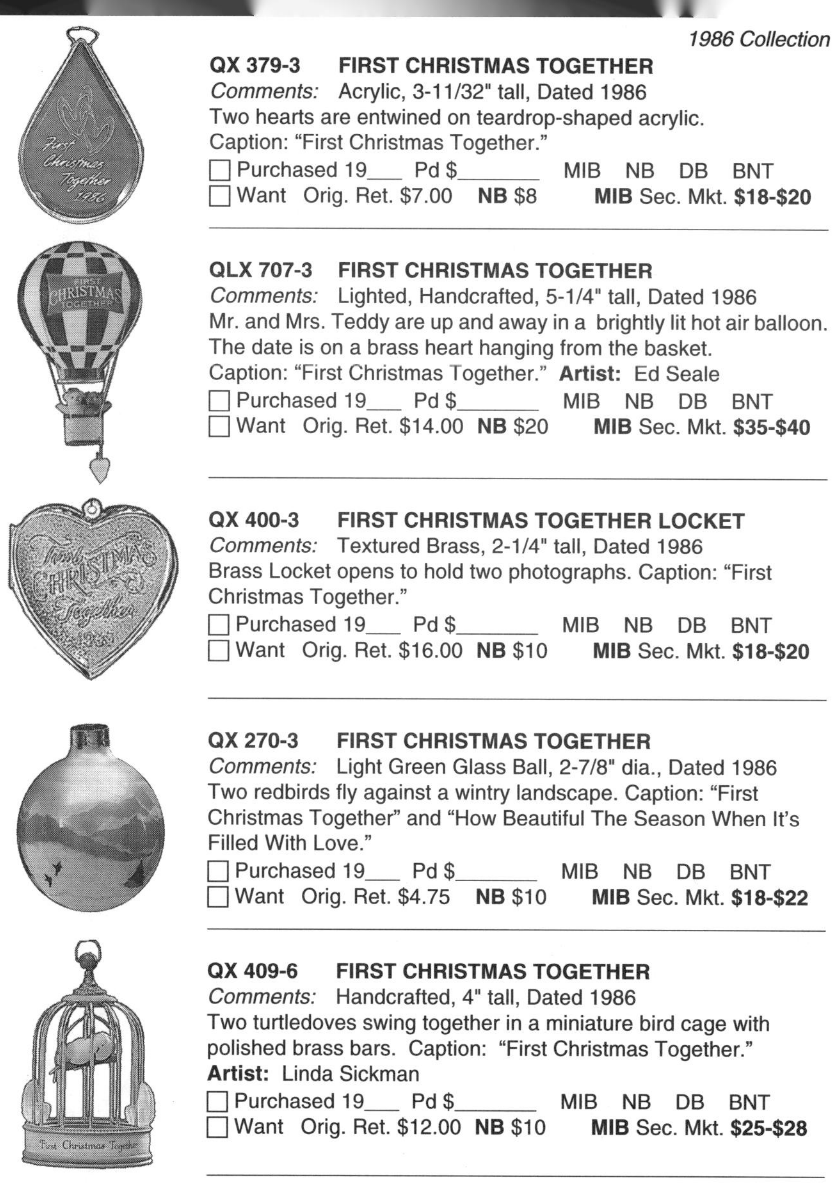

QX 379-3 FIRST CHRISTMAS TOGETHER
Comments: Acrylic, 3-11/32" tall, Dated 1986
Two hearts are entwined on teardrop-shaped acrylic.
Caption: "First Christmas Together."
☐ Purchased 19___ Pd $_______ MIB NB DB BNT
☐ Want Orig. Ret. $7.00 **NB** $8 **MIB** Sec. Mkt. **$18-$20**

QLX 707-3 FIRST CHRISTMAS TOGETHER
Comments: Lighted, Handcrafted, 5-1/4" tall, Dated 1986
Mr. and Mrs. Teddy are up and away in a brightly lit hot air balloon. The date is on a brass heart hanging from the basket.
Caption: "First Christmas Together." **Artist:** Ed Seale
☐ Purchased 19___ Pd $_______ MIB NB DB BNT
☐ Want Orig. Ret. $14.00 **NB** $20 **MIB** Sec. Mkt. **$35-$40**

QX 400-3 FIRST CHRISTMAS TOGETHER LOCKET
Comments: Textured Brass, 2-1/4" tall, Dated 1986
Brass Locket opens to hold two photographs. Caption: "First Christmas Together."
☐ Purchased 19___ Pd $_______ MIB NB DB BNT
☐ Want Orig. Ret. $16.00 **NB** $10 **MIB** Sec. Mkt. **$18-$20**

QX 270-3 FIRST CHRISTMAS TOGETHER
Comments: Light Green Glass Ball, 2-7/8" dia., Dated 1986
Two redbirds fly against a wintry landscape. Caption: "First Christmas Together" and "How Beautiful The Season When It's Filled With Love."
☐ Purchased 19___ Pd $_______ MIB NB DB BNT
☐ Want Orig. Ret. $4.75 **NB** $10 **MIB** Sec. Mkt. **$18-$22**

QX 409-6 FIRST CHRISTMAS TOGETHER
Comments: Handcrafted, 4" tall, Dated 1986
Two turtledoves swing together in a miniature bird cage with polished brass bars. Caption: "First Christmas Together."
Artist: Linda Sickman
☐ Purchased 19___ Pd $_______ MIB NB DB BNT
☐ Want Orig. Ret. $12.00 **NB** $10 **MIB** Sec. Mkt. **$25-$28**

QX 272-3 FRIENDS ARE FUN
Comments: Light Blue Glass Ball, 2-7/8" dia.
Dated Christmas 1986. Eskimo children are riding their dog sled through the snow. Caption: "It's Fun Having Friends To Go 'Round With." **Artist:** Ken Crow
☐ Purchased 19___ Pd $_______ MIB NB DB BNT
☐ Want Orig. Ret. $4.75 **NB** $18 **MIB** Sec. Mkt. **$32-$35**

QX 427-3 FRIENDSHIP GREETING
Comments: Fabric, 2-3/4" tall, Dated 1986
Silk-screened fabric is stitched to create a colorful envelope ornament. Enclosed card reads: "Friends Are Forever." Back of envelope says "Merry Christmas."
☐ Purchased 19___ Pd $_______ MIB NB DB BNT
☐ Want Orig. Ret. $8.00 **NB** $5 **MIB** Sec. Mkt. **$12-$15**

QX 381-6 FRIENDSHIP'S GIFT
Comments: Acrylic, 3" tall, Dated Christmas 1986
A little mouse helps Santa deliver a gift. Caption: "Friendship Is A Gift."
☐ Purchased 19___ Pd $_______ MIB NB DB BNT
☐ Want Orig. Ret. $6.00 **NB** $5 **MIB** Sec. Mkt. **$12-$14**

QX 383-3 FROM OUR HOME TO YOURS
Comments: Acrylic, 3-1/4" tall, Dated Christmas 1986
A fruit-filled wicker basket graces this teardrop shaped ornament. Caption: "From Our Home To Yours."
☐ Purchased 19___ Pd $_______ MIB NB DB BNT
☐ Want Orig. Ret. $6.00 **NB** $8 **MIB** Sec. Mkt. **$15-$17**

QX 405-3 FROSTY FRIENDS
Comments: **Seventh in Series**, Handcrafted, 2-1/4" tall Dated 1986. A flocked baby reindeer and the cute little Eskimo sit on an acrylic ice flow. **Artist:** Bob Siedler
☐ Purchased 19___ Pd $_______ MIB NB DB BNT
☐ Want Orig. Ret. $8.50 **NB** $45 **MIB** Sec. Mkt. **$65-$70**

QLX 705-3 GENERAL STORE
Comments: Lighted, Handcrafted, 2-11/16" tall
The store is bright with light and open for holiday business as it advertises "Christmas Trees 50¢." **Artist:** Donna Lee
☐ Purchased 19___ Pd $_______ MIB NB DB BNT
☐ Want Orig. Ret. $15.75 **NB** $50 **MIB** Sec. Mkt. **$60-$65**

QLX 708-3 GENTLE BLESSINGS
Comments: Lighted Panorama Ball, 3-5/8" tall
A glowing light shines on the Christ Child as the animals in the stable watch over Him. **Artist:** Linda Sickman
☐ Purchased 19___ Pd $_______ MIB NB DB BNT
☐ Want Orig. Ret. $15.00 **NB** $100 **MIB** Sec. Mkt. **$170-$175**

QX 428-6 GLOWING CHRISTMAS TREE
Comments: Embedded Acrylic, 3-1/4," Dated 1986
A brass Christmas tree, complete with colorful stars, is embedded in teardrop shaped acrylic. **Artist:** Joyce Pattee
☐ Purchased 19___ Pd $_______ MIB NB DB BNT
☐ Want Orig. Ret. $7.00 **NB** $10 **MIB** Sec. Mkt. **$12-$15**

QX 271-6 GODCHILD
Comments: White Satin Ball, 2-7/8" dia.
Dated Christmas 1986. Colorful teddy bears circle the ornament capped with a gold crown. Caption: "A Godchild Is A Very Special Someone."
☐ Purchased 19___ Pd $_______ MIB NB DB BNT
☐ Want Orig. Ret. $4.75 **NB** $8 **MIB** Sec. Mkt. **$14-$16**

QX 411-6 GRANDCHILD'S FIRST CHRISTMAS
Comments: Handcrafted, 2-1/4" tall, Dated 1986
A flocked bear is sound asleep in a basket ready for "Baby's First Christmas."
☐ Purchased 19___ Pd $_______ MIB NB DB BNT
☐ Want Orig. Ret. $10.00 **NB** $10 **MIB** Sec. Mkt. **$14-$16**

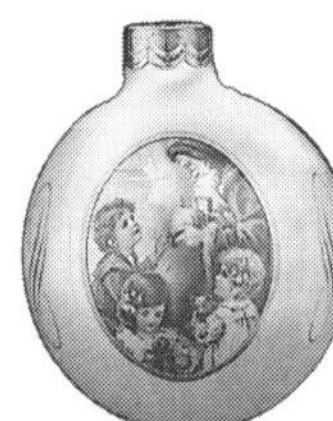

QX 273-6 GRANDDAUGHTER
Comments: White Glass Ball, 2-7/8" dia.
Dated Christmas 1986. Old-fashioned scenes of children and Christmas. Caption: "Season After Season, A Granddaughter Grows Dearer And Dearer." **Artist:** Joyce Lyle
☐ Purchased 19___ Pd $_______ MIB NB DB BNT
☐ Want Orig. Ret. $4.75 **NB** $10 **MIB** Sec. Mkt. **$22-$24**

QX 274-3 GRANDMOTHER
Comments: Ivory Satin Ball, 2-7/8" dia.
Dated Christmas 1986. A country quilt design of Christmas trees carry the message: "A Grandmother's Love Is For Always."
Artist: Joyce Pattee
☐ Purchased 19___ Pd $_______ MIB NB DB BNT
☐ Want Orig. Ret. $4.75 **NB** $8 **MIB** Sec. Mkt. **$14-$16**

QX 432-3 GRANDPARENTS
Comments: Porcelain, 5-1/2" tall, Dated Christmas 1986
Two doves in a Christmas stitch design decorate a white porcelain bell. Caption: "Grandparents Are Never Far From Thought... Ever Near In Love."
☐ Purchased 19___ Pd $_______ MIB NB DB BNT
☐ Want Orig. Ret. $7.50 **NB** $10 **MIB** Sec. Mkt. **$18-$22**

QX 273-3 GRANDSON
Comments: Blue Glass Ball, 3" dia., Dated Christmas 1986
Forest animals enjoy Christmas. "A Grandson Is A Bringer Of A Very Special Kind Of Love." **Artist:** LaDene Votruba
☐ Purchased 19___ Pd $_______ MIB NB DB BNT
☐ Want Orig. Ret. $4.75 **NB** $10 **MIB** Sec. Mkt. **$22-$24**

QX 432-6 GRATITUDE
Comments: Satin and Wood, 5" tall, Dated 1986
A bright red cardinal sits on a branch of holly, framed in an embroidery hoop. Caption: "Especially To Thank You... Especially at Christmas." **Artist:** Sharon Pike
☐ Purchased 19___ Pd $_______ MIB NB DB BNT
☐ Want Orig. Ret. $6.00 **NB** $8 **MIB** Sec. Mkt. **$10-$12**

QX 418-3 HAPPY CHRISTMAS TO OWL
Comments: Handcrafted, 3" tall
Owl reads "Christmas Stories" to a small friend, "I Heard Him Exclaim, Ere He Drove Out Of Sight, Happy Christmas To Owl, And To Owl A Good-Nite." **Artist** Duane Unruh
☐ Purchased 19___ Pd $_______ MIB NB DB BNT
☐ Want Orig. Ret. $6.00 **NB** $10 **MIB** Sec. Mkt. **$18-$20**

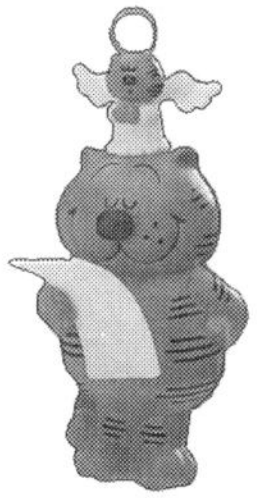

QX 436-3 HEATHCLIFF
Comments: Handcrafted, 3-3/32" tall
Heathcliff has his own little angel reminding him to be good. His letter reads: "Dear Santa, I've Been Exceptional. Heathcliff." **Artist:** Ed Seale
☐ Purchased 19___ Pd $_______ MIB NB DB BNT
☐ Want Orig. Ret. $7.50 **NB** $12 **MIB** Sec. Mkt. **$22-$25**

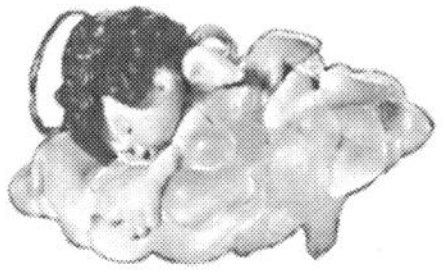

QX 417-3 HEAVENLY DREAMER
Comments: Handcrafted, 1-3/8" tall
A little angel, wearing a brass halo, has fallen asleep on a billowy acrylic cloud. **Artist:** Donna Lee
☐ Purchased 19___ Pd $_______ MIB NB DB BNT
☐ Want Orig. Ret. $5.75 **NB** $18 **MIB** Sec. Mkt. **$30-$35**

QX 515-3 HEIRLOOM SNOWFLAKE
Comments: Fabric, 4-3/4" tall
Lavender-blue padded satin is covered with lacy, hand-crocheted snowflakes. **Artist:** Joyce Pattee
☐ Purchased 19___ Pd $_______ MIB NB DB BNT
☐ Want Orig. Ret. $6.75 **NB** $10 **MIB** Sec. Mkt. **$20-$22**

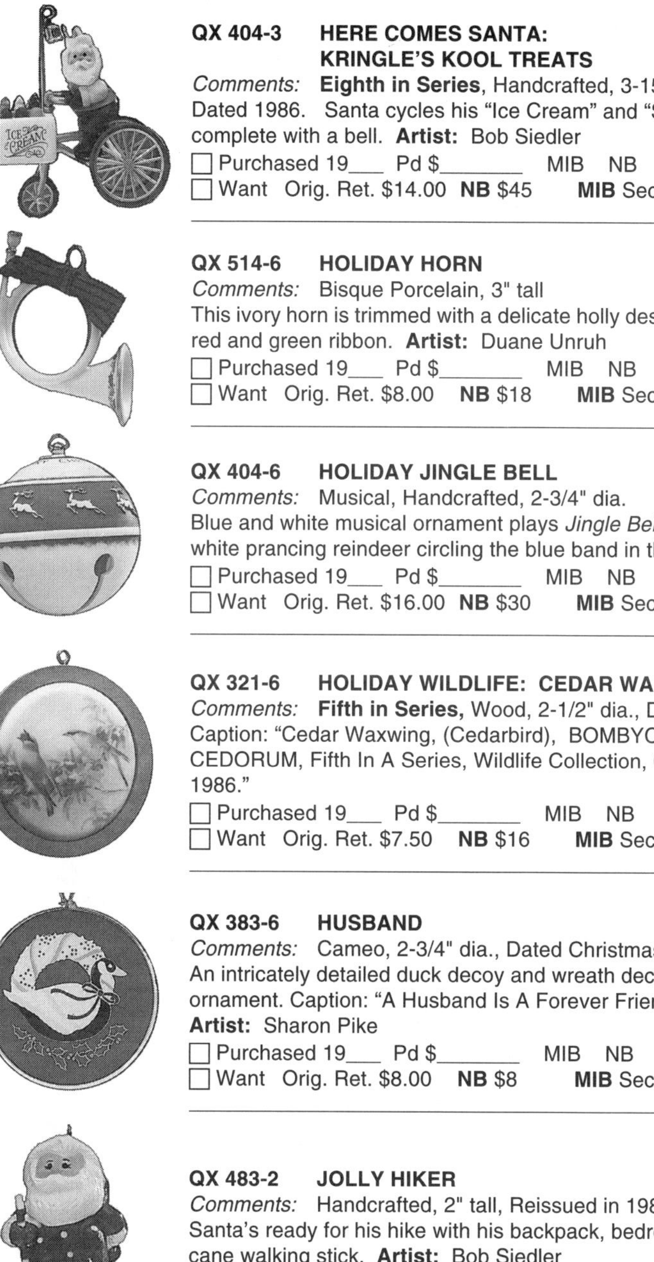

QX 404-3 HERE COMES SANTA: KRINGLE'S KOOL TREATS
Comments: **Eighth in Series**, Handcrafted, 3-15/18" tall Dated 1986. Santa cycles his "Ice Cream" and "Snow Cones" complete with a bell. **Artist:** Bob Siedler
☐ Purchased 19___ Pd $_______ MIB NB DB BNT
☐ Want Orig. Ret. $14.00 **NB** $45 **MIB** Sec. Mkt. **$60-$65**

QX 514-6 HOLIDAY HORN
Comments: Bisque Porcelain, 3" tall
This ivory horn is trimmed with a delicate holly design and tied with red and green ribbon. **Artist:** Duane Unruh
☐ Purchased 19___ Pd $_______ MIB NB DB BNT
☐ Want Orig. Ret. $8.00 **NB** $18 **MIB** Sec. Mkt. **$32-$35**

QX 404-6 HOLIDAY JINGLE BELL
Comments: Musical, Handcrafted, 2-3/4" dia.
Blue and white musical ornament plays *Jingle Bells* and has white prancing reindeer circling the blue band in the center.
☐ Purchased 19___ Pd $_______ MIB NB DB BNT
☐ Want Orig. Ret. $16.00 **NB** $30 **MIB** Sec. Mkt. **$40-$45**

QX 321-6 HOLIDAY WILDLIFE: CEDAR WAXWING
Comments: **Fifth in Series,** Wood, 2-1/2" dia., Dated 1986
Caption: "Cedar Waxwing, (Cedarbird), BOMBYCILLA CEDORUM, Fifth In A Series, Wildlife Collection, Christmas 1986."
☐ Purchased 19___ Pd $_______ MIB NB DB BNT
☐ Want Orig. Ret. $7.50 **NB** $16 **MIB** Sec. Mkt. **$28-$30**

QX 383-6 HUSBAND
Comments: Cameo, 2-3/4" dia., Dated Christmas 1986
An intricately detailed duck decoy and wreath decorate this ornament. Caption: "A Husband Is A Forever Friend." **Artist:** Sharon Pike
☐ Purchased 19___ Pd $_______ MIB NB DB BNT
☐ Want Orig. Ret. $8.00 **NB** $8 **MIB** Sec. Mkt. **$14-$16**

QX 483-2 JOLLY HIKER
Comments: Handcrafted, 2" tall, Reissued in 1987.
Santa's ready for his hike with his backpack, bedroll, and candy cane walking stick. **Artist:** Bob Siedler
☐ Purchased 19___ Pd $_______ MIB NB DB BNT
☐ Want Orig. Ret. $5.00 **NB** $10 **MIB** Sec. Mkt. **$20-$24**

QX 429-6 JOLLY ST. NICK
Comments: Hand-Painted Fine Porcelain, 5-1/2" tall
Special Edition. Crafted from a Thomas Nast St. Nicholas introduced in the 1800s. **Artist:** Duane Unruh
☐ Purchased 19___ Pd $_______ MIB NB DB BNT
☐ Want Orig. Ret. $22.50 **NB** $45 **MIB** Sec. Mkt. **$65-$72**

QX 382-3 JOY OF FRIENDS
Comments: Bezeled Satin, 2-3/4" tall
Ice skaters printed on padded satin, resemble American folk art. Framed in chrome. Caption: "Friends Make The Heart Warmer, The Day Merrier, The Season More Memorable."
Artist: Joyce Pattee
☐ Purchased 19___ Pd $_______ MIB NB DB BNT
☐ Want Orig. Ret. $6.75 **NB** $10 **MIB** Sec. Mkt. **$15-$18**

QX 513-6 JOYFUL CAROLERS
Comments: Handcrafted, 3-1/4" dia., Dated 1986
Designed similar to the Nostalgia ornaments, carolers dressed in Dickens' style share their joy. Caption: "Joy To The World."
Artist: Linda Sickman
☐ Purchased 19___ Pd $_______ MIB NB DB BNT
☐ Want Orig. Ret. $9.75 **NB** $24 **MIB** Sec. Mkt. **$32-$35**

QX 435-3 KATYBETH WITH STAR
Comments: Hand-Painted Fine Porcelain, 2-19/32" tall
Katybeth plays with a star that is passing by.
☐ Purchased 19___ Pd $_______ MIB NB DB BNT
☐ Want Orig. Ret. $7.00 **NB** $12 **MIB** Sec. Mkt. **$22-$25**

QLX 707-6 KEEP ON GLOWIN'!
Comments: Lighted, Handcrafted, 2-7/16" tall
Reissued in 1987. This bright icicle proves a source of fun for one of Santa's elves. **Artist:** Ken Crow
☐ Purchased 19___ Pd $_______ MIB NB DB BNT
☐ Want Orig. Ret. $10.00 **NB** $38 **MIB** Sec. Mkt. **$42-$46**

QX 474-5 KITTY MISCHIEF
Comments: Handcrafted, 2" tall
Reissued from 1985. **Artist:** Peter Dutkin
☐ Purchased 19___ Pd $_______ MIB NB DB BNT
☐ Want Orig. Ret. $5.00 **NB** $14 **MIB** Sec. Mkt. **$20-$24**

QX 419-3 LI'L JINGLER
Comments: Handcrafted, 2" tall, Reissued in 1987
A cute little raccoon in a red bow-tie hangs onto a stringer of brass jingle bells. Cute piece! **Artist:** Ed Seale
☐ Purchased 19___ Pd $_______ MIB NB DB BNT
☐ Want Orig. Ret. $6.75 **NB** $28 **MIB** Sec. Mkt. **$38-$42**

QX 511-6 LITTLE DRUMMERS
Comments: Handcrafted, 4" tall, Real Drumming Motion
Three little drummer boys play their drums when you tap or shake their platform. **Artist:** Ken Crow
☐ Purchased 19___ Pd $_______ MIB NB DB BNT
☐ Want Orig. Ret. $12.50 **NB** $14 **MIB** Sec. Mkt. **$22-$30**

QX 409-3 LOVING MEMORIES
Comments: Handcrafted, 5-1/4" tall, Dated 1986
A heart-shaped shadow box holds a brass bell, teddy bear and Christmas gift. **Artist:** Ed Seale
☐ Purchased 19___ Pd $_______ MIB NB DB BNT
☐ Want Orig. Ret. $9.00 **NB** $15 **MIB** Sec. Mkt. **$30-$35**

QX 272-6 MAGI , THE
Comments: Gold Glass Teardrop Ball, 3" dia.
Dated Christmas 1986. The Magi bring their gifts to the Child. Caption: "O Come Let Us Adore Him." **Artist:** Sharon Pike
☐ Purchased 19___ Pd $_______ MIB NB DB BNT
☐ Want Orig. Ret. $4.75 **NB** $10 **MIB** Sec. Mkt. **$15-$18**

QX 429-3 MAGICAL UNICORN
Comments: Limited Edition 24,700, Wooden Display Stand Hand-Painted Fine Porcelain, 4-1/2" tall. White porcelain unicorn has hand-painted pastel flowers and pastel ribbons.
Artist: Duane Unruh
☐ Purchased 19___ Pd $_______ MIB NB DB BNT
☐ Want Orig. Ret. $27.50 **NB** $75 **MIB** Sec. Mkt. **$85-$90**

QX 402-3 MARIONETTE ANGEL
Comments: Handcrafted, 3-9/16" tall, ***VERY RARE!***
This whimsical little angel has authentic marionette features. Appeared in retailers' catalogs but was pulled from production.
☐ Purchased 19___ Pd $_______ MIB NB DB BNT
☐ Want Orig. Ret. $8.50 **NB** $325 **MIB** Sec. Mkt. **$400-$410**

QX 275-2 MARY EMMERLING: AMERICAN COUNTRY COLLECTION
Comments: Glass Balls, 2-7/8" dia., Set of 4
These four blue and white glass balls feature motifs from 19th Century American homes.
☐ Purchased 19___ Pd $_______ MIB NB DB BNT
☐ Want Orig. Ret. $7.95 **NB** $12 **MIB** Sec. Mkt. **$24-$26**

QX 427-6 MEMORIES TO CHERISH: PHOTOHOLDER
Comments: Ceramic, 3-1/8" tall, Dated Christmas 1986
A white, braided wreath sports holly and a big red bow. Caption: "A Memory To Cherish."
☐ Purchased 19___ Pd $_______ MIB NB DB BNT
☐ Want Orig. Ret. $7.50 **NB** $15 **MIB** Sec. Mkt. **$25-$28**

QLX 709-3 MERRY CHRISTMAS BELL
Comments: Lighted Acrylic, 5-9/16" tall
Bell-shaped acrylic has etched Christmas flowers. Caption: "Merry Christmas." **Artist:** LaDene Votruba
☐ Purchased 19___ Pd $_______ MIB NB DB BNT
☐ Want Orig. Ret. $8.50 **NB** $12 **MIB** Sec. Mkt. **$25-$28**

QX 415-3 MERRY KOALA
Comments: Handcrafted, 2" tall, Reissued in 1987
Flocked koala is wearing an oversized Santa cap.
Artist: Linda Sickman
☐ Purchased 19___ Pd $_______ MIB NB DB BNT
☐ Want Orig. Ret. $5.00 **NB** $10 **MIB** Sec. Mkt. **$18-$22**

QX 403-2 MERRY MOUSE
Comments: Handcrafted, 2-1/2" tall
Reissued from 1985. **Artist:** Peter Dutkin
☐ Purchased 19___ Pd $_______ MIB NB DB BNT
☐ Want Orig. Ret. $4.50 **NB** $15 **MIB** Sec. Mkt. **$25-$30**

QX 407-6 MINIATURE CRECHE
Comments: **Second in Series,** Fine Porcelain, 3-3/4" tall
Porcelain bisque figures of the Holy Family is set off beautifully with the graceful arch and brass star shining brightly above.
Artist: Ed Seale
☐ Purchased 19___ Pd $_______ MIB NB DB BNT
☐ Want Orig. Ret. $9.00 **NB** $45 **MIB** Sec. Mkt. **$60-$65**

When embracing opportunity, give it a big hug.

QX 382-6 MOTHER
Comments: Acrylic, 2-3/4" dia., Dated 1986
A brass bezel frames this ornament with a heart etched in the center with the caption: "A Mother's Love Reflects The Warmth Of Christmas All Year Through."
☐ Purchased 19___ Pd $_______ MIB NB DB BNT
☐ Want Orig. Ret. $7.00 **NB** $12 **MIB** Sec. Mkt. **$18-$22**

QX 431-6 MOTHER AND DAD
Comments: Fine Porcelain, 5-1/2" tall, Dated Christmas 1986
Brilliant, colorful candles make a striking contrast on this white bell tied up in red ribbon. Caption: "For A Mother And Dad Who Are Warmly Loved." **Artist:** Michele Pyda-Sevcik
☐ Purchased 19___ Pd $_______ MIB NB DB BNT
☐ Want Orig. Ret. $7.50 **NB** $12 **MIB** Sec. Mkt. **$20-$22**

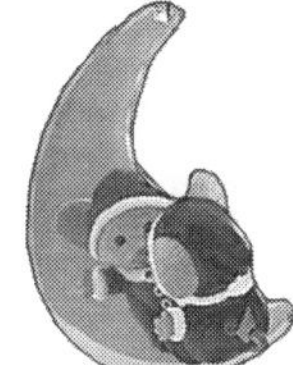

QX 416-6 MOUSE IN THE MOON
Comments: Handcrafted, 2-3/4" tall, Reissued in 1987
This cute little mouse, dressed in red sleepers, likes his reflection shown in the mirrored moon.
Artist: Ed Seale
☐ Purchased 19___ Pd $_______ MIB NB DB BNT
☐ Want Orig. Ret. $5.50 **NB** $12 **MIB** Sec. Mkt. **$20-$25**

QX 402-6 MR. AND MRS. CLAUS: MERRY MISTLETOE TIME
Comments: ***FIRST IN SERIES***, Handcrafted, 3-7/16" tall
Dated 1986. Mrs. Claus gives Santa a big kiss as he stands under the mistletoe she's holding. **Artist:** Duane Unruh
☐ Purchased 19___ Pd $_______ MIB NB DB BNT
☐ Want Orig. Ret. $13.00 **NB** $65 **MIB** Sec. Mkt. **$105-$110**

QLX 705-2 MR. AND MRS. SANTA
Comments: Lighted, Handcrafted, 3" tall
Reissued from 1985.
☐ Purchased 19___ Pd $_______ MIB NB DB BNT
☐ Want Orig. Ret. $14.50 **NB** $60 **MIB** Sec. Mkt. **$85-$90**

QX 381-3 NEPHEW
Comments: Bezeled Lacquer-Look, 2-3/4" dia., Dated 1986
A white snowman, accented with a red scarf, contrasts vividly against the sky. Caption: "To Wish A Special Nephew A Happy Holiday Season!"
☐ Purchased 19___ Pd $_______ MIB NB DB BNT
☐ Want Orig. Ret. $6.25 **NB** $6 **MIB** Sec. Mkt. **$10-$14**

QX 274-6 NEW HOME
Comments: White Glass Ball, 3" dia., Dated 1986
Gingerbread people and animals run through a neighborhood of sweets. Caption: "Christmas Is So Special When It's Spent In A New Home." **Artist:** Ken Crow
☐ Purchased 19___ Pd $_______ MIB NB DB BNT
☐ Want Orig. Ret. $4.75 **NB** $18 **MIB** Sec. Mkt. **$30-$32**

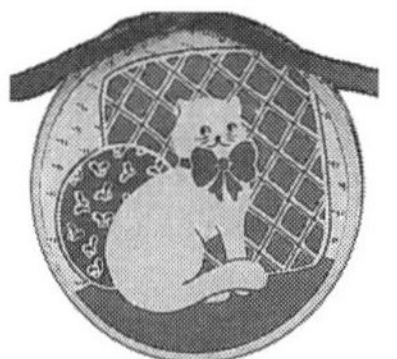

QX 426-6 NIECE
Comments: Fabric and Wood, 4-1/2" tall
Dated Christmas 1986. A white cat with a big red bow around its neck sits on red and green cushions. Caption: "Nieces Give The Nicest Gifts... Beauty, Joy And Love."
☐ Purchased 19___ Pd $_______ MIB NB DB BNT
☐ Want Orig. Ret. $6.00 **NB** $5 **MIB** Sec. Mkt. **$8-$12**

QX 276-3 NORMAN ROCKWELL
Comments: Green Glass Ball, 2-7/8" dia.
Christmas scenes reflect the excitement of Christmas. Caption: "Christmas Time Is Filled With Joy And Glad Anticipation, And All The Loving Reasons For A Happy Celebration."
☐ Purchased 19___ Pd $_______ MIB NB DB BNT
☐ Want Orig. Ret. $4.75 **NB** $12 **MIB** Sec. Mkt. **$25-$30**

QX 321-3 NORMAN ROCKWELL: CHECKING UP
Comments: **Seventh in Series**, Red Cameo, 3-1/4" dia.
Caption: "Checking Up, Seventh In A Series, Christmas 1986, The Norman Rockwell Collection." **Artist:** Sharon Pike
☐ Purchased 19___ Pd $_______ MIB NB DB BNT
☐ Want Orig. Ret. $7.75 **NB** $12 **MIB** Sec. Mkt. **$20-$25**

QX 403-3 NOSTALGIC HOUSES AND SHOPS: CHRISTMAS CANDY SHOPPE
Comments: **Third in Series**, Handcrafted, 4-5/16" tall
Dated 1986. The baking is done upstairs and the candies are sold downstairs. Very popular ornament. Harder to find than the 1985 issue. **Artist:** Donna Lee
☐ Purchased 19___ Pd $_______ MIB NB DB BNT
☐ Want Orig. Ret. $13.75 **NB** $185 **MIB** Sec. Mkt. **$260-$270**

QX 512-3 NUTCRACKER SANTA
Comments: Handcrafted, 3-3/8" tall
Crafted to look like a nutcracker, Santa's mouth pops open when you lift the tassel on his cap. **Artist:** Duane Unruh
☐ Purchased 19___ Pd $_______ MIB NB DB BNT
☐ Want Orig. Ret. $10.00 **NB** $35 **MIB** Sec. Mkt. **$48-$55**

QXO440-3 OLD-FASHIONED SANTA: OPEN HOUSE ORN.
Comments: Handcrafted, 4-1/2" tall
Old World Santa, looking like hand-carved wood, carries a bag of toys. Special offering for dealers' "Open House" events.
Artist: Linda Sickman
☐ Purchased 19___ Pd $_______ MIB NB DB BNT
☐ Want Orig. Ret. $12.75 **NB** $40 **MIB** Sec. Mkt. **$48-$55**

QSP 420-1 ON THE RIGHT TRACK: GOLD CROWN ORN.
Comments: Hand-Painted Fine Porcelain, 4-3/4" tall
The artist signed his name to this special promotional Santa. Santa, in his shirt sleeves, puts the finishing touches on a locomotive. **Artist:** Peter Dutkin
☐ Purchased 19___ Pd $_______ MIB NB DB BNT
☐ Want Orig. Ret. $15.00 **NB** $30 **MIB** Sec. Mkt. **$38-$45**

QX 422-6 OPEN ME FIRST
Comments: Handcrafted, 2-15/16" tall, Dated 1986
A child is delighted with the kitten inside a gift box titled "Open Me First."
☐ Purchased 19___ Pd $_______ MIB NB DB BNT
☐ Want Orig. Ret. $7.25 **NB** $15 **MIB** Sec. Mkt. **$25-$32**

QX 435-6 PADDINGTON™ BEAR
Comments: Handcrafted, 2-9/16" tall
This favorite bear is dressed in a bright blue coat, and yellow hat and carries a jar of honey. **Artist:** Bob Siedler
☐ Purchased 19___ Pd $_______ MIB NB DB BNT
☐ Want Orig. Ret. $6.00 **NB** $24 **MIB** Sec. Mkt. **$35-$42**

QX 276-6 PEANUTS®
Comments: Blue Glass Ball, 3" dia., Dated 1986
Snoopy, Woodstock and his feathered friends go ice skating. Caption: "Merry Christmas."
☐ Purchased 19___ Pd $_______ MIB NB DB BNT
☐ Want Orig. Ret. $4.75 **NB** $20 **MIB** Sec. Mkt. **$30-$35**

QX 425-3 PLAYFUL POSSUM
Comments: Handcrafted/Glass, 3-23/32" tall
An opossum is the clapper in a clear glass bell.
Artist: Ken Crow
☐ Purchased 19___ Pd $_______ MIB NB DB BNT
☐ Want Orig. Ret. $11.00 **NB** $18 **MIB** Sec. Mkt. **$25-$30**

QX 421-3 POPCORN MOUSE
Comments: Handcrafted, 2-1/2" tall, Dated 1986
A cute white mouse sits atop a spool of red thread and strings popcorn and cranberries.
Artist: Linda Sickman
☐ Purchased 19___ Pd $_______ MIB NB DB BNT
☐ Want Orig. Ret. $6.75 **NB** $30 **MIB** Sec. Mkt. **$42-$50**

QX 405-6 PORCELAIN BEAR
Comments: **Fourth in Series,** Porcelain, 2-11/16" tall
Cinnamon bear has a slight grin because of the wrapped gift he's hiding behind his back.
☐ Purchased 19___ Pd $_______ MIB NB DB BNT
☐ Want Orig. Ret. $7.75 **NB** $22 **MIB** Sec. Mkt. **$35-$40**

QX 420-3 PUPPY'S BEST FRIEND
Comments: Handcrafted, 2-1/4" tall
A little elf sitting on puppy's head has brought him a bone for Christmas. **Artist:** Duane Unruh
☐ Purchased 19___ Pd $_______ MIB NB DB BNT
☐ Want Orig. Ret. $6.50 **NB** $12 **MIB** Sec. Mkt. **$20-$28**

QX 421-6 RAH RAH RABBIT
Comments: Handcrafted, 2-1/2" tall, Dated 1986
This cute white bunny from "North Pole High" is cheering on her team with her megaphone and her real pompon.
Artist: Ken Crow
☐ Purchased 19___ Pd $_______ MIB NB DB BNT
☐ Want Orig. Ret. $7.00 **NB** $16 **MIB** Sec. Mkt. **$30-$35**

QX 422-3 REINDEER CHAMPS: DASHER
Comments: ***FIRST IN SERIES***, Handcrafted, 2-7/8" tall
Dated '86 "Dasher 86" is ready to run in his red, white and green shirt, shorts and sneakers. **Artist:** Bob Siedler
☐ Purchased 19___ Pd $_______ MIB NB DB BNT
☐ Want Orig. Ret. $7.50 **NB** $110 **MIB** Sec. Mkt. **$145-$155**

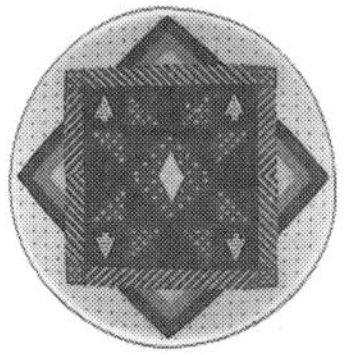

QX 510-6 REMEMBERING CHRISTMAS
Comments: Fine Porcelain, 3-1/4" dia, Dated 1986
Features a bright country quilt pattern. Caption: "Christmas Memories Are Keepsakes Of The Heart." Plate stand included.
☐ Purchased 19___ Pd $_______ MIB NB DB BNT
☐ Want Orig. Ret. $8.75 **NB** $12 **MIB** Sec. Mkt. **$24-$28**

QX 401-6 ROCKING HORSE
Comments: **Sixth in Series**, Handcrafted, 4" wide
Dated 1986. A golden palomino rides into the holidays on green rockers. Some collectors found this ornament with the number "QX 436-6." Others have found a gold sticker on the box stating "Made in Macau." **Artist:** Linda Sickman
☐ Purchased 19___ Pd $_______ MIB NB DB BNT
☐ Want Orig. Ret. $10.75 **NB-P** $40 **MIB** Sec. Mkt. **$60-$65**

QXO440-6 SANTA & HIS REINDEER: OPEN HOUSE ORN.
Comments: Handcrafted, 2" tall and 14" wide
Two reindeer pull Santa in his sleigh full of toys. Special offering for "Open House" events.
☐ Purchased 19___ Pd $_______ MIB NB DB BNT
☐ Want Orig. Ret. $9.75 **NB** $22 **MIB** Sec. Mkt. **$30-$35**

QLX 703-3 SANTA & SPARKY
Comments: ***FIRST IN SERIES,*** Light and Motion Handcrafted, 4-1/16" tall, Dated 1986
Santa lights the Christmas tree and moves back as Sparky penguin watches with excitement.
☐ Purchased 19___ Pd $_______ MIB NB DB BNT
☐ Want Orig. Ret. $22.00 **NB** $65 **MIB** Sec. Mkt. **$90-$95**

QT 700-6 SANTA TREE TOPPER
Comments: Open House, Fabric
This whimsical Santa is all set in his red and white suit and green mittens. He holds a gold wand.
☐ Purchased 19___ Pd $_______ MIB NB DB BNT
☐ Want Orig. Ret. $18.00 **NB** $28 **MIB** Sec. Mkt. **$40-$42**

QX 426-3 SANTA'S HOT TUB
Comments: Handcrafted, 3" tall
Santa and one of his reindeer are enjoying themselves in a hot tub from the "Polar Barrel Hot Tub Co."
Artist: Ed Seale
☐ Purchased 19___ Pd $_______ MIB NB DB BNT
☐ Want Orig. Ret. $12.00 **NB** $30 **MIB** Sec. Mkt. **$50-$56**

QLX 711-5 SANTA'S ON HIS WAY
Comments: Light and Hologram Panorama Ball, 3-5/8" tall
Laser photography creates a three-dimensional effect of Santa and his reindeer flying above the city.
Artist: Duane Unruh
☐ Purchased 19___ Pd $_______ MIB NB DB BNT
☐ Want Orig. Ret. $15.00 **NB** $50 **MIB** Sec. Mkt. **$70-$75**

QXO 441-3 SANTA'S PANDA PAL: OPEN HOUSE ORN.
Comments: Handcrafted, 2-1/4" tall
Cute flocked panda wears a Santa hat. Special offering for dealers' "Open House" events.
☐ Purchased 19___ Pd $_______ MIB NB DB BNT
☐ Want Orig. Ret. $5.00 **NB** $10 **MIB** Sec. Mkt. **$20-$25**

QLX 706-6 SANTA'S SNACK
Comments: Lighted, Handcrafted, 2-15/16" tall
Santa's midnight snack is a "mile-high" sandwich. Santa is dressed in reindeer slippers and a green striped nightshirt.
Artist: Ken Crow
☐ Purchased 19___ Pd $_______ MIB NB DB BNT
☐ Want Orig. Ret. $10.00 **NB** $45 **MIB** Sec. Mkt. **$58-$60**

QX 270-6 SEASON OF THE HEART
Comments: Red Glass Ball, 2-7/8" dia.
A family enjoys a ride through the snow-covered countryside in a horse-drawn sleigh. Caption: "Christmas... Season Of The Heart, Time Of Fond Remembrance."
☐ Purchased 19___ Pd $_______ MIB NB DB BNT
☐ Want Orig. Ret. $4.75 **NB** $5 **MIB** Sec. Mkt. **$14-$18**

QLX 706-3 SHARING FRIENDSHIP
Comments: Lighted Acrylic, 5-5/16" tall, Dated 1986
A poinsettia etched into clear acrylic accents the caption: "Friendship Is A Special Kind Of Sharing."
Artist: LaDene Votruba
☐ Purchased 19___ Pd $_______ MIB NB DB BNT
☐ Want Orig. Ret. $8.50 **NB** $12 **MIB** Sec. Mkt. **$25-$30**

QLT 709-6 SHINING STAR TREE TOPPER
Comments: Lighted, Acrylic
A partridge graces the center of this five-pointed star. Each of the five points include a design of a pear and leaf.
☐ Purchased 19___ Pd $_______ MIB NB DB BNT
☐ Want Orig. Ret. $17.50 **NB** $18 **MIB** Sec. Mkt. **$25-$30**

QX 277-3 SHIRT TALES™ PARADE
Comments: Gold Glass Ball, 2-7/8" dia.
The Shirt Tales Band parades around the ball. Caption: "Here Comes Christmas!" and "Merriment Is All Around Whenever Christmas Comes To Town!"
☐ Purchased 19___ Pd $_______ MIB NB DB BNT
☐ Want Orig. Ret. $4.75 **NB** $8 **MIB** Sec. Mkt. **$16-$18**

QX 380-6 SISTER
Comments: Bezeled Satin, 2-3/4" dia., Dated 1986
Red padded satin carries a design of a grapevine wreath entwined with holly and ribbon, with a teddy bear for company. Caption: "With Every Christmas, Every Year, A Sister Grows More Loved... More Dear." **Artist:** LaDene Votruba
☐ Purchased 19___ Pd $_______ MIB NB DB BNT
☐ Want Orig. Ret. $6.75 **NB** $12 **MIB** Sec. Mkt. **$15-$17**

QX 473-2 SKATEBOARD RACCOON
Comments: Handcrafted, 2-1/2" tall
Reissued from 1985. **Artist:** Peter Dutkin
☐ Purchased 19___ Pd $_______ MIB NB DB BNT
☐ Want Orig. Ret. $6.50 **NB** $20 **MIB** Sec. Mkt. **$28-$30**

QX 420-6 SKI TRIPPER
Comments: Handcrafted, 2-1/8" tall
A young skier is ready for the slopes with her red jumpsuit and skis in hand. **Artist:** Bob Siedler
☐ Purchased 19___ Pd $_______ MIB NB DB BNT
☐ Want Orig. Ret. $6.75 **NB** $10 **MIB** Sec. Mkt. **$20-$24**

QX 438-3 SNOOPY® AND WOODSTOCK
Comments: Handcrafted, 1-3/4" tall
These two friends enjoy their saucer ride down the hill on the "Beagle Express." **Artist:** Bob Siedler
☐ Purchased 19___ Pd $_______ MIB NB DB BNT
☐ Want Orig. Ret. $8.00 **NB** $32 **MIB** Sec. Mkt. **$40-$45**

QX 423-6 SNOW BUDDIES
Comments: Handcrafted, 2-1/4" tall
A little mouse has created a "snowmouse" complete with a fabric muffler. His arms are molded from real sticks.
Artist: Peter Dutkin
☐ Purchased 19___ Pd $_______ MIB NB DB BNT
☐ Want Orig. Ret. $8.00 **NB** $21 **MIB** Sec. Mkt. **$35-$38**

Smiles never go up in price nor down in value.

QX 470-2 SNOW-PITCHING SNOWMAN
Comments: Handcrafted, 2" tall
Reissued from 1985. **Artist:** Donna Lee
☐ Purchased 19___ Pd $_______ MIB NB DB BNT
☐ Want Orig. Ret. $4.50 **NB** $14 **MIB** Sec. Mkt. **$20-$24**

QX 477-5 SOCCER BEAVER
Comments: Handcrafted, 2-1/2" tall
Reissued from 1985. **Artist:** Peter Dutkin
☐ Purchased 19___ Pd $_______ MIB NB DB BNT
☐ Want Orig. Ret. $6.50 **NB** $8 **MIB** Sec. Mkt. **$22-$25**

QX 430-3 SON
Comments: Handcrafted, 4" tall, Dated 1986
A wooden boy toy is poking out of the top of a red and green striped knit stocking "For Son."
Artist: Ed Seale
☐ Purchased 19___ Pd $_______ MIB NB DB BNT
☐ Want Orig. Ret. $5.75 **NB** $15 **MIB** Sec. Mkt. **$33-$38**

QX 415-6 SPECIAL DELIVERY
Comments: Handcrafted, 2" tall
This little penguin is on his way to deliver a gift of sardines to one of his friends. **Artist:** Bob Siedler
☐ Purchased 19___ Pd $_______ MIB NB DB BNT
☐ Want Orig. Ret. $5.00 **NB** $12 **MIB** Sec. Mkt. **$20-$24**

QX 322-6 STAR BRIGHTENERS
Comments: Acrylic, 2-3/4" dia., Dated 1986
Two etched angels are polishing a star. Caption: "Joy At Christmas." **Artist:** LaDene Votruba
☐ Purchased 19___ Pd $_______ MIB NB DB BNT
☐ Want Orig. Ret. $6.00 **NB** $6 **MIB** Sec. Mkt. **$12-$15**

QX 384-3 STATUE OF LIBERTY, THE
Comments: Acrylic, 3-9/16" tall, Dated 1986
This special commemorative shows "The Lady" etched in clear acrylic and was created in honor of the statue's 100th birthday. Caption: "1886 Centennial 1986." **Artist:** Michele Pyda-Sevcik
☐ Purchased 19___ Pd $_______ MIB NB DB BNT
☐ Want Orig. Ret. $6.00 **NB** $11 **MIB** Sec. Mkt. **$24-$28**

QLX 701-1 SUGARPLUM COTTAGE
Comments: Lighted, Handcrafted, 3" tall
Issued in 1984, 1985, and 1986.
☐ Purchased 19___ Pd $_______ MIB NB DB BNT
☐ Want Orig. Ret. $11.00 **NB** $22 **MIB** Sec. Mkt. **$45-$50**

QX 408-6 SWEETHEART
Comments: Handcrafted, 3-1/2" tall, Dated Christmas 1986
An ivory gazebo with red shingled roof has a Christmas tree in the center and two squirrels sitting on the railing. Sign reads, "To My Sweetheart With Love." May be personalized.
Artist: Joyce Pattee
☐ Purchased 19___ Pd $_______ MIB NB DB BNT
☐ Want Orig. Ret. $11.00 **NB** $25 **MIB** Sec. Mkt. **$42-$50**

QX 275-3 TEACHER
Comments: White Glass Ball, 2-7/8" dia., Dated Christmas 1986
A little mouse sits next to a bright red apple, from which he has nibbled a star. Caption: "For My Teacher."
☐ Purchased 19___ Pd $_______ MIB NB DB BNT
☐ Want Orig. Ret. $4.75 **NB** $8 **MIB** Sec. Mkt. **$12-$14**

QX 401-3 TEN YEARS TOGETHER
Comments: Fine Porcelain, 3" tall, Dated 1986
Roses and holly, accented with gold, create a cloisonne look. Caption: "Ten Years Together" and "More Than Yesterday... Less Than Tomorrow."
☐ Purchased 19___ Pd $_______ MIB NB DB BNT
☐ Want Orig. Ret. $7.50 **NB** $10 **MIB** Sec. Mkt. **$22-$25**

QX 406-6 THIMBLE SERIES: PARTRIDGE
Comments: **Ninth in Series**, Handcrafted, 1-21/32" tall
A sweet little partridge has made its nest in a thimble full of greenery and fruit.
☐ Purchased 19___ Pd $_______ MIB NB DB BNT
☐ Want Orig. Ret. $5.75 **NB** $12 **MIB** Sec. Mkt. **$22-$26**

QX 379-6 TIMELESS LOVE
Comments: Acrylic, 3" tall, Dated Christmas 1986
Caption in gold foil: "Love... Comes Not In Moments Of Time But In Timeless Moments." **Artist:** LaDene Votruba
☐ Purchased 19___ Pd $_______ MIB NB DB BNT
☐ Want Orig. Ret. $6.00 **NB** $6 **MIB** Sec. Mkt. **$24-$26**

QX 403-6 TIN LOCOMOTIVE
Comments: **Fifth in Series,** Pressed Tin, 3-17/32" tall
Dated 1986. A stenciled holly design adorns the yellow and red cab of this locomotive. **Artist:** Linda Sickman
☐ Purchased 19___ Pd $_______ MIB NB DB BNT
☐ Want Orig. Ret. $14.75 **NB** $55 **MIB** Sec. Mkt. **$70-$78**

QX 418-6 TIPPING THE SCALES
Comments: Handcrafted, 2-11/16" tall, Dated 1986
Santa, in his red monogrammed robe, checks out his weight... "1986" while holding a cookie. **Artist:** Peter Dutkin
☐ Purchased 19___ Pd $_______ MIB NB DB BNT
☐ Want Orig. Ret. $6.75 **NB** $15 **MIB** Sec. Mkt. **$22-$28**

QX 423-3 TOUCHDOWN SANTA
Comments: Handcrafted, 2-15/16" tall, Dated 1986
Santa's sure to make a touchdown in his red jersey and white pants as he runs with the ball! **Artist:** Peter Dutkin
☐ Purchased 19___ Pd $_______ MIB NB DB BNT
☐ Want Orig. Ret. $8.00 **NB** $21 **MIB** Sec. Mkt. **$34-$38**

QX 425-6 TREETOP TRIO/BLUEBIRDS
Comments: Handcrafted, 2" tall, Reissued in 1987
The bluebird trio is chirping out a Christmas carol in a nest of real straw. **Artist:** Donna Lee
☐ Purchased 19___ Pd $_______ MIB NB DB BNT
☐ Want Orig. Ret. $11.00 **NB** $16 **MIB** Sec. Mkt. **$30-$34**

QX 378-6 TWELVE DAYS OF CHRISTMAS: THREE FRENCH HENS
Comments: **Third in Series**, Acrylic, 3-3/8" tall, Dated 1986
This acrylic teardrop has captions in gold and three hens on holly leaves. **Artist:** LaDene Votruba
☐ Purchased 19___ Pd $_______ MIB NB DB BNT
☐ Want Orig. Ret. $6.50 **NB** $15 **MIB** Sec. Mkt. **$38-$45**

QX 410-3 TWENTY-FIVE YEARS TOGETHER
Comments: Fine Porcelain Plate, 3-1/4" tall
Dated Christmas 1986. Blue and silver bells tied up with ribbon and holly. Comes with acrylic stand. Caption: "Twenty-Five Years Together" and "Love Lights All The Seasons Of Our Years." **Artist:** LaDene Votruba
☐ Purchased 19___ Pd $_______ MIB NB DB BNT
☐ Want Orig. Ret. $8.00 **NB** $10 **MIB** Sec. Mkt. **$24-$28**

QLX 707-2 VILLAGE EXPRESS
Comments: Light/Motion, Handcrafted, 3-1/2" tall
Reissued in 1987. A train chugs through a peaceful mountain village and a tunnel. Price up from '95. **Artist:** Linda Sickman
☐ Purchased 19___ Pd $_______ MIB NB DB BNT
☐ Want Orig. Ret. $24.50 **NB** $60 **MIB** Sec. Mkt. **$115-$120**

QX 419-6 WALNUT SHELL RIDER
Comments: Handcrafted, 1-3/4" tall, Reissued in 1987
An elf dressed in blue rides downhill in his walnut shell sled.
Artist: Ed Seale
☐ Purchased 19___ Pd $_______ MIB NB DB BNT
☐ Want Orig. Ret. $6.00 **NB** $12 **MIB** Sec. Mkt. **$20-$24**

QX 510-3 WELCOME, CHRISTMAS
Comments: Handcrafted, 2-5/8" tall, Dated 1986
A precious little angel dangles inside a wooden heart with holly and heart stencils. Caption: "Welcome, Christmas!"
Artist: Ken Crow
☐ Purchased 19___ Pd $_______ MIB NB DB BNT
☐ Want Orig. Ret. $8.25 **NB** $12 **MIB** Sec. Mkt. **$25-$30**

QX 408-3 WINDOWS OF THE WORLD: DUTCH
Comments: **Second in Series**, Handcrafted, 3" tall
Dated 1986. A little Dutch girl looks through the top half of the door of her home. Caption: "Vrolyk Kerstfeest." **Artist:** Bob Siedler
☐ Purchased 19___ Pd $_______ MIB NB DB BNT
☐ Want Orig. Ret. $10.00 **NB** $30 **MIB** Sec. Mkt. **$55-$60**

QX 407-3 WOOD CHILDHOOD: REINDEER
Comments: **Third in Series,** Wood, 2-1/2" tall, Dated 1986
This cute hand-painted wooden reindeer makes a galloping motion as he rolls along on his wagon. **Artist:** Ken Crow
☐ Purchased 19___ Pd $_______ MIB NB DB BNT
☐ Want Orig. Ret. $7.50 **NB** $14 **MIB** Sec. Mkt. **$25-$30**

QX 424-6 WYNKEN, BLYNKEN AND NOD
Comments: Handcrafted, 2-7/8" tall
The nursery rhyme has come to life as the three set sail in a small boat with silver nets. **Artist:** Donna Lee
☐ Purchased 19___ Pd $_______ MIB NB DB BNT
☐ Want Orig. Ret. $9.75 **NB** $35 **MIB** Sec. Mkt. **$42-$45**

Peace
on
Earth

1987 Collection

QLX 711-3 ANGELIC MESSENGERS
Comments: Light and Changing Scene Panorama Ball, 3-5/8" Angels suddenly appear before the shepherds. Caption: "Love Came Down At Christmas, Love All Lovely, Love Divine. Love Was Born At Christmas, Star And Angels Gave The Sign." **Artist:** Duane Unruh
☐ Purchased 19___ Pd $_______ MIB NB DB BNT
☐ Want Orig. Ret. $18.75 **NB** $45 **MIB** Sec. Mkt. **$60-$65**

QX 461-7 BABY LOCKET
Comments: Textured Metal, 2-1/4" dia., Dated 1987
This silvery locket has a space for baby's photo and for personalization. Has a wishbone hanger.
☐ Purchased 19___ Pd $_______ MIB NB DB BNT
☐ Want Orig. Ret. $15.00 **NB** $15 **MIB** Sec. Mkt. **$25-$28**

QLX 704-9 BABY'S FIRST CHRISTMAS
Comments: Lighted, Handcrafted, 3-3/4" tall, Dated 1987
Teddy paints "Baby's First Christmas" on the nursery window.
☐ Purchased 19___ Pd $_______ MIB NB DB BNT
☐ Want Orig. Ret. $13.50 **NB** $25 **MIB** Sec. Mkt. **$34-$38**

QX 461-9 BABY'S FIRST CHRISTMAS PHOTOHOLDER
Comments: Ecru Fabric, 3-1/4" dia., Dated 1987
Caption: "Baby's First Christmas" and "Welcome To Christmas, Baby Dear. Everyone Is Glad You're Here."
☐ Purchased 19___ Pd $_______ MIB NB DB BNT
☐ Want Orig. Ret. $7.50 **NB** $18 **MIB** Sec. Mkt. **$28-$32**

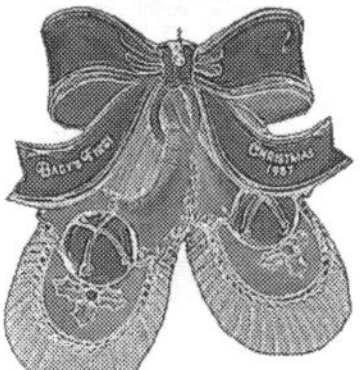

QX 372-9 BABY'S FIRST CHRISTMAS
Comments: Acrylic, 3-1/2" tall, Dated 1987
Hand-etched acrylic baby booties are decorated with jingle bells. Caption: "Baby's First Christmas."
☐ Purchased 19___ Pd $_______ MIB NB DB BNT
☐ Want Orig. Ret. $6.00 **NB** $8 **MIB** Sec. Mkt. **$18-$22**

QX 274-9 BABY'S FIRST CHRISTMAS: BABY BOY
Comments: White Satin Ball, 2-7/8" dia., Dated 1987
Baby's blocks spell "Baby Boy." Caption: "A Baby Boy, So Darling And Dear, Makes Christmas Extra Special This Year. Baby's First Christmas." **Artist:** Joyce Pattee
☐ Purchased 19___ Pd $_______ MIB NB DB BNT
☐ Want Orig. Ret. $4.75 **NB** $12 **MIB** Sec. Mkt. **$25-$28**

QX 274-7 BABY'S FIRST CHRISTMAS: BABY GIRL
Comments: White Satin Ball, 2-7/8" dia., Dated 1987
Caption: "A Baby Girl, So Dear And Sweet, Makes Your Christmas Joy Complete. Baby's First Christmas." More "girls" than "boys." **Artist:** Joyce Pattee
☐ Purchased 19___ Pd $_______ MIB NB DB BNT
☐ Want Orig. Ret. $4.75 **NB** $8 **MIB** Sec. Mkt. **$15-$20**

QX 411-3 BABY'S FIRST CHRISTMAS
Comments: Handcrafted, 4-1/4" tall, Dated 1987
Baby has lots of fun in this real spring seat. Caption: "Baby's First Christmas." **Artist:** Donna Lee
☐ Purchased 19___ Pd $_______ MIB NB DB BNT
☐ Want Orig. Ret. $9.75 **NB** $20 **MIB** Sec. Mkt. **$28-$35**

QX 460-7 BABY'S SECOND CHRISTMAS
Comments: Handcrafted, 2-3/4" tall, Dated 1987
A "Clown-in-the-Box" greets "Baby's 2nd Christmas." Attaches to the tree with a clip. **Artist:** Donna Lee
☐ Purchased 19___ Pd $_______ MIB NB DB BNT
☐ Want Orig. Ret. $5.75 **NB** $15 **MIB** Sec. Mkt. **$28-$33**

QX 279-7 BABYSITTER
Comments: Porcelain White Glass Ball, 3" dia., Dated 1987
Caption: "For Bringing Children Such Special Gifts... Gentleness, Caring, And Love. Merry Christmas." **Artist:** Sharon Pike
☐ Purchased 19___ Pd $_______ MIB NB DB BNT
☐ Want Orig. Ret. $4.75 **NB** $8 **MIB** Sec. Mkt. **$12-$14**

QX 455-7 BEARY SPECIAL
Comments: Handcrafted, 2-1/2" tall
A flocked brown bear reaches up to hang an ornament on the tree — it has his picture on it! **Artist:** Bob Siedler
☐ Purchased 19___ Pd $_______ MIB NB DB BNT
☐ Want Orig. Ret. $4.75 **NB** $8 **MIB** Sec. Mkt. **$20-$22**

QX 272-7 BETSEY CLARK: HOME FOR CHRISTMAS
Comments: **Second in Series,** Gold Glass Ball, 2-7/8" dia. Dated 1987. Betsey and her friends add final holiday decorating touches. Captions: "There's No Place Like Christmas" and "Noel." **Artist:** Sharon Pike
☐ Purchased 19___ Pd $_______ MIB NB DB BNT
☐ Want Orig. Ret. $5.00 **NB** $14 **MIB** Sec. Mkt. **$22-$26**

QX 473-7 BRIGHT CHRISTMAS DREAMS
Comments: Handcrafted 4" tall, Dated Christmas 1987
Four white mice with brightly colored nightcaps have fallen asleep in a box of Crayola Crayons. The Crayola series began in '88. **Artist:** Bob Siedler
☐ Purchased 19___ Pd $_______ MIB NB DB BNT
☐ Want Orig. Ret. $7.25 **NB** $75 **MIB** Sec. Mkt. **$98-$110**

QLX 705-9 BRIGHT NOEL
Comments: Lighted Acrylic, 5-1/2" tall
An outline of an acrylic star is the framework for a bright red Noel in the center. **Artist:** LaDene Votruba
☐ Purchased 19___ Pd $_______ MIB NB DB BNT
☐ Want Orig. Ret. $7.00 **NB** $20 **MIB** Sec. Mkt. **$30-$35**

QXC 581-7 CAROUSEL REINDEER: CHARTER CLUB MEMBERSHIP ORN.
Comments: Handcrafted, 3-3/4" tall, Dated 1987
A prancing reindeer rides a brass post inside a hoop. Caption: "1987 Charter Member." Club logo is printed in gold on bottom of hoop. **Artist:** Linda Sickman
☐ Purchased 19___ Pd $_______ MIB NB DB BNT
☐ Want Orig. Ret. $8.00 **NB** $50 **MIB** Sec. Mkt. **$65-$70**

QX 459-9 CHILD'S THIRD CHRISTMAS
Comments: Handcrafted, 3" tall, Dated 1987
A child dressed in red, rides a reindeer (which makes a galloping motion when it is tapped). Caption: "My 3rd Christmas."
Artist: Ken Crow
☐ Purchased 19___ Pd $_______ MIB NB DB BNT
☐ Want Orig. Ret. $5.75 **NB** $14 **MIB** Sec. Mkt. **$25-$30**

QX 456-7 CHOCOLATE CHIPMUNK
Comments: Handcrafted, 2" tall
This cute little fellow sits happily on a chocolate chip cookie and holds a chip in his paws. **Artist:** Ed Seale
☐ Purchased 19___ Pd $_______ MIB NB DB BNT
☐ Want Orig. Ret. $6.00 **NB** $26 **MIB** Sec. Mkt. **$40-$45**

QLX 705-7 CHRIS MOUSE GLOW
Comments: **Third in Series**, Lighted, Handcrafted, 4-1/8" Dated 1987. In a blue nightshirt and red cap, Chris Mouse swings happily from his "stained glass" lamp. **Artist:** Bob Siedler
☐ Purchased 19___ Pd $_______ MIB NB DB BNT
☐ Want Orig. Ret. $11.00 **NB** $45 **MIB** Sec. Mkt. **$55-$60**

QLX 702-9 CHRISTMAS CLASSICS: A CHRISTMAS CAROL
Comments: **Second in Series**, Lighted, Handcrafted, 4-3/16" Dated 1987. In this scene, Scrooge gives gifts to Tiny Tim while his parents look on. Setting is a stage draped in elegant curtains.
☐ Purchased 19___ Pd $_______ MIB NB DB BNT
☐ Want Orig. Ret. $16.00 **NB** $35 **MIB** Sec. Mkt. **$48-$55**

QX 453-7 CHRISTMAS CUDDLE
Comments: Handcrafted, 2-3/4" tall
A kitten and a white mouse, in matching Santa caps, snuggle together.
☐ Purchased 19___ Pd $_______ MIB NB DB BNT
☐ Want Orig. Ret. $5.75 **NB** $16 **MIB** Sec. Mkt. **$32-$35**

QX 467-9 CHRISTMAS FUN PUZZLE
Comments: Handcrafted, 2-1/2" dia.
A Santa, mouse and reindeer take on new shapes and designs as this ornament is rotated to mix or match the characters.
Artist: Donna Lee
☐ Purchased 19___ Pd $_______ MIB NB DB BNT
☐ Want Orig. Ret. $8.00 **NB** $12 **MIB** Sec. Mkt. **$18-$25**

QX 444-9 CHRISTMAS IS GENTLE
Comments: Limited Edition 24,700, Hand numbered Handpainted Bone China, 3" tall. Two lambs sit peacefully in a basket edged with gold. **Artist:** Ed Seale
☐ Purchased 19___ Pd $_______ MIB NB DB BNT
☐ Want Orig. Ret. $17.50 **NB** $30 **MIB** Sec. Mkt. **$80-$85**

QX 473-9 CHRISTMAS KEYS
Comments: Handcrafted, 2" tall
An ivory upright piano is decorated with sprigs of bright green holly and red berries. **Artist:** Duane Unruh
☐ Purchased 19___ Pd $_______ MIB NB DB BNT
☐ Want Orig. Ret. $5.75 **NB** $15 **MIB** Sec. Mkt. **$25-$30**

QLX 701-3 CHRISTMAS MORNING
Comments: Light and Motion, Handcrafted, 4-5/16" tall Reissued in 1988. Two children slide down the banister in anticipation of their Christmas gifts. **Artist:** Ken Crow
☐ Purchased 19___ Pd $_______ MIB NB DB BNT
☐ Want Orig. Ret. $24.50 **NB** $28 **MIB** Sec. Mkt. **$35-$40**

QX 442-9 CHRISTMAS TIME MIME
Comments: Limited Edition 24,700 w/stand
Hand-Painted Fine Porcelain, 2-1/2" tall. The mime shares Christmas with a teddy bear. He wears a Santa cap and beard; his bag is filled with stars. **Artist:** Duane Unruh
☐ Purchased 19___ Pd $_______ MIB NB DB BNT
☐ Want Orig. Ret. $27.50 **NB** $30 **MIB** Sec. Mkt. **$45-$50**

QX 480-7 CLOTHESPIN SOLDIER: SAILOR
Comments: **Sixth and Final in Series,** Handcrafted, 2-1/4" tall
"Christmas is here," this sailor seems to be saying as he waves his red flags with bright green trees. **Artist:** Linda Sickman
☐ Purchased 19___ Pd $_______ MIB NB DB BNT
☐ Want Orig. Ret. $5.50 **NB** $15 **MIB** Sec. Mkt. **$22-$25**

QX 481-7 COLLECTOR'S PLATE: LIGHT SHINES AT CHRISTMAS
Comments: ***FIRST IN SERIES***, Fine Porcelain, 3-1/4" dia. Dated 1987. Three children happily decorate their Christmas tree in anticipation of Christmas. **Artist:** LaDene Votruba
☐ Purchased 19___ Pd $_______ MIB NB DB BNT
☐ Want Orig. Ret. $8.00 **NB** $45 **MIB** Sec. Mkt. **$75-$80**

QX 377-7 CONSTITUTION, THE
Comments: Acrylic, 2-1/2" tall, Dated
Oval acrylic features gold foil lettering and a brass frame. Caption: "We The People, The Constitution Of The United States, 200 Years, 1787-1987." A quill is etched in the acrylic.
Artist: Joyce Pattee
☐ Purchased 19___ Pd $_______ MIB NB DB BNT
☐ Want Orig. Ret. $6.50 **NB** $8 **MIB** Sec. Mkt. **$15-$20**

QX 470-9 COUNTRY WREATH
Comments: Wood and Straw, 4-3/4" tall
This straw wreath is tied with red yarn and is decorated with wooden shapes. **Artist:** Michele Pyda-Sevcik
☐ Purchased 19___ Pd $_______ MIB NB DB BNT
☐ Want Orig. Ret. $5.75 **NB** $15 **MIB** Sec. Mkt. **$20-$22**

QX 282-9 CURRIER & IVES: AMERICAN FARM SCENE
Comments: Porcelain White Glass Ball, 2-7/8" dia., Dated 1987
The farm on a wintry morning is portrayed in this design. Caption: "Christmas 1987. American Farm Scene, Currier & Ives."
Artist: Joyce Lyle
☐ Purchased 19___ Pd $_______ MIB NB DB BNT
☐ Want Orig. Ret. $4.75 **NB** $10 **MIB** Sec. Mkt. **$22-$25**

QX 462-9 DAD
Comments: Handcrafted, 3" tall, Dated Christmas 1987
This polar bear papa may be living at the North Pole, but his new tie is from the South Pacific. Caption: "For Dad."
Artist: Bob Siedler
☐ Purchased 19___ Pd $_______ MIB NB DB BNT
☐ Want Orig. Ret. $6.00 **NB** $21 **MIB** Sec. Mkt. **$35-$42**

QX 463-7 DAUGHTER
Comments: Handcrafted, 1-1/4" tall, Dated 1987
A graceful swan sleigh is pulled by two reindeer. Caption: "Daughter." Looks like wood. **Artist:** Linda Sickman
☐ Purchased 19___ Pd $_______ MIB NB DB BNT
☐ Want Orig. Ret. $5.75 **NB** $14 **MIB** Sec. Mkt. **$22-$26**

QX 448-7 DECEMBER SHOWERS
Comments: Handcrafted, 2-1/2" tall
A little angel dressed in pink, checks out from under her umbrella to see if the rain has quit. **Artist:** Donna Lee
☐ Purchased 19___ Pd $_______ MIB NB DB BNT
☐ Want Orig. Ret. $5.50 **NB** $14 **MIB** Sec. Mkt. **$20-$24**

QX 467-7 DOC HOLIDAY
Comments: Handcrafted, 4" tall
"Doc Holiday," as noted on his shirt, rides a spring-powered mechanical reindeer. Giddyap!
Artist: Ed Seale
☐ Purchased 19___ Pd $_______ MIB NB DB BNT
☐ Want Orig. Ret. $8.00 **NB** $24 **MIB** Sec. Mkt. **$32-$38**

QX 278-3 DR. SEUSS: THE GRINCH'S CHRISTMAS
Comments: Glass Ball, 2-7/8" dia.
A happy grinch smiles inside a green wreath as the Whos sing carols around him. Caption: "A Very Merry Wish For A Merry, Merry Christmas."
☐ Purchased 19___ Pd $_______ MIB NB DB BNT
☐ Want Orig. Ret. $4.75 **NB** $24 **MIB** Sec. Mkt. **$40-$45**

QSP 930-9 ELVES - EMIL PAINTER ELF - FIGURINE
Comments: Hand-Painted Porcelain
☐ Purchased 19___ Pd $_______ MIB NB DB BNT
☐ Want Orig. Ret. $10.00
NB $22 **MIB** Sec. Mkt. **$32-$38**

QSP 930-7 ELVES - HANS CARPENTER ELF - FIGURINE
Comments: Hand-Painted Porcelain
☐ Purchased 19___ Pd $_______ MIB NB DB BNT
☐ Want Orig. Ret. $10.00 **NB** $22 **MIB** Sec. Mkt. **$32-$38**

QSP 931-7 ELVES - KURT BLUE PRINT ELF - FIGURINE
Comments: Hand-Painted Porcelain
☐ Purchased 19___ Pd $_______ MIB NB DB BNT
☐ Want Orig. Ret. $10.00 **NB** $22 **MIB** Sec. Mkt. **$32-$38**

QX 445-7 FAVORITE SANTA
Comments: Special Edition
Hand-Painted Fine Porcelain, 5-1/2" tall
A "Jolly Old Elf" indeed — Santa carries a long green, patched stocking full of gifts. **Artist:** Peter Dutkin
☐ Purchased 19___ Pd $_______ MIB NB DB BNT
☐ Want Orig. Ret. $22.50 **NB** $15 **MIB** Sec. Mkt. **$28-$35**

QX 443-7 FIFTY YEARS TOGETHER
Comments: Fine Porcelain, 5" tall, Dated Christmas 1987
This lovely bell shows off a bas relief poinsettia and is rimmed in gold. Caption: "Fifty Years Together." Handle is a sculpted "50."
Artist: Ed Seale
☐ Purchased 19___ Pd $_______ MIB NB DB BNT
☐ Want Orig. Ret. $8.00 **NB** $10 **MIB** Sec. Mkt. **$22-$25**

QX 272-9 FIRST CHRISTMAS TOGETHER
Comments: White Glass Ball, 2-7/8" dia., Dated 1987
This ornament has a delicate design of lovebirds in a garden of pastel poinsettias. Caption: "First Christmas Together" and "To All Who Love, Love Is All The World." **Artist:** Joyce A. Lyle
☐ Purchased 19___ Pd $_______ MIB NB DB BNT
☐ Want Orig. Ret. $4.75 **NB** $12 **MIB** Sec. Mkt. **$20-$25**

Small opportunities are often
the beginning of great achievements.

QX 371-9 FIRST CHRISTMAS TOGETHER
Comments: Acrylic, 2-1/2" tall, Dated 1987
Two etched swans glide gracefully among the tall grasses. Caption: "First Christmas Together."
☐ Purchased 19___ Pd $_______ MIB NB DB BNT
☐ Want Orig. Ret. $6.50 **NB** $8 **MIB** Sec. Mkt. **$16-$20**

QX 446-9 FIRST CHRISTMAS TOGETHER
Comments: Textured Brass, 2-1/4" tall, Dated 1987
Heart-shaped brass locket is decorated with embossed lovebirds and caption.
☐ Purchased 19___ Pd $_______ MIB NB DB BNT
☐ Want Orig. Ret. $15.00 **NB** $15 **MIB** Sec. Mkt. **$25-$30**

QLX 708-7 FIRST CHRISTMAS TOGETHER
Comments: Lighted, Handcrafted, 2-5/8" tall, Dated 1987
Two polar bears celebrate Christmas in their snow-capped igloo.
☐ Purchased 19___ Pd $_______ MIB NB DB BNT
☐ Want Orig. Ret. $11.50 **NB** $35 **MIB** Sec. Mkt. **$40-$45**

QX 445-9 FIRST CHRISTMAS TOGETHER
Comments: Handcrafted, 2-1/2" tall, Dated 1987
Two raccoons "share" a red fabric sweatshirt. Caption: "First Christmas Together."
☐ Purchased 19___ Pd $_______ MIB NB DB BNT
☐ Want Orig. Ret. $8.00 **NB** $15 **MIB** Sec. Mkt. **$25-$35**

QX 446-7 FIRST CHRISTMAS TOGETHER
Comments: Handcrafted, 3" tall, Dated 1987
Just add an attic and a roof to the heart and you have a cozy cottage for two! Sampler inside reads "Love, Sweet Love."
Artist: Donna Lee
☐ Purchased 19___ Pd $_______ MIB NB DB BNT
☐ Want Orig. Ret. $9.50 **NB** $15 **MIB** Sec. Mkt. **$25-$30**

QX 474-9 FOLK ART SANTA
Comments: Handcrafted, 4" tall
This Old-World Santa has been painted and antiqued to resemble folk art. His coat is accented with gold. **Artist:** Linda Sickman
☐ Purchased 19___ Pd $_______ MIB NB DB BNT
☐ Want Orig. Ret. $5.25 **NB** $20 **MIB** Sec. Mkt. **$30-$35**

QX 279-9 FROM OUR HOME TO YOURS
Comments: White Glass Ball, 3" dia., Dated 1987
Holiday decorated doorways circle this frosted ball ornament. Caption: "From Our Home... To Yours... At Christmas."
Artist: Michele Pyda-Sevcik
☐ Purchased 19___ Pd $_______ MIB NB DB BNT
☐ Want rig. Ret. $4.75 **NB** $8 **MIB** Sec. Mkt. **$18-$22**

QX 440-9 FROSTY FRIENDS
Comments: **Eighth in Series,** Handcrafted, 2" tall, Dated 1987
The little Eskimo is receiving a bright red gift from a flocked seal who has jumped up through the ice.
Artist: Ed Seale
☐ Purchased 19___ Pd $_______ MIB NB DB BNT
☐ Want Orig. Ret. $8.50 **NB** $40 **MIB** Sec. Mkt. **$55-$60**

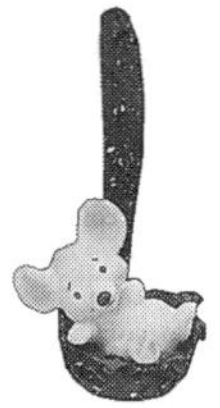

QX 449-7 FUDGE FOREVER
Comments: Handcrafted, 3" tall
A little white mouse has filled his tummy with the fudge in this blue spatterware ladle. **Artist:** Peter Dutkin
☐ Purchased 19___ Pd $_______ MIB NB DB BNT
☐ Want Orig. Ret. $5.00 **NB** $20 **MIB** Sec. Mkt. **$32-$38**

QX 276-7 GODCHILD
Comments: Blue Glass Ball, 2-7/8" dia., Dated 1987
A contemporary green tree with red balls and gold star are painted against a "snowy" blue ball. Caption: "A Godchild Makes Christmas Glow A Little Brighter." **Artist:** Michele Pyda-Sevcik
☐ Purchased 19___ Pd $_______ MIB NB DB BNT
☐ Want Orig. Ret. $4.75 **NB** $12 **MIB** Sec. Mkt. **$16-$20**

QX 464-9 GOLDFINCH
Comments: Hand-Painted Fine Porcelain, 2-1/2" tall
Poised in flight, this goldfinch is so realistically painted, you'd think it could fly away. Has a hook.
Artist: Linda Sickman
☐ Purchased 19___ Pd $_______ MIB NB DB BNT
☐ Want Orig. Ret. $7.00 **NB** $24 **MIB** Sec. Mkt. **$70-$75**

QLX 704-6 GOOD CHEER BLIMP
Comments: Blinking Lights, Handcrafted, 3-1/16" tall
Santa leans over the side of his gondola to see where his next stop will be. **Artist:** Linda Sickman
☐ Purchased 19___ Pd $_______ MIB NB DB BNT
☐ Want Orig. Ret. $16.00 **NB** $30 **MIB** Sec. Mkt. **$45-$52**

QX 460-9 GRANDCHILD'S FIRST CHRISTMAS
Comments: Handcrafted, 1-3/4" tall, Dated 1987
A teddy bear sits on a red and green quilt inside a Jenny Lind style playpen. "Grandchild's First Christmas" is on the blanket over the side. **Artist:** Ed Seale
☐ Purchased 19___ Pd $_______ MIB NB DB BNT
☐ Want Orig. Ret. $9.00 **NB** $12 **MIB** Sec. Mkt. **$20-$25**

QX 374-7 GRANDDAUGHTER
Comments: Bezeled Satin, 2-3/4" dia., Dated Christmas 1987
A snowy background holds a sleigh full of toys. Caption: "A Granddaughter Makes Each Day A Holiday In The Heart."
Artist: LaDene Votruba
☐ Purchased 19___ Pd $_______ MIB NB DB BNT
☐ Want Orig. Ret. $6.00 **NB** $5 **MIB** Sec. Mkt. **$18-$20**

QX 277-9 GRANDMOTHER
Comments: Pink Glass Ball, 3" dia., Dated Christmas 1987
Roses and carnations add a delicate touch. Caption: "Grandmothers, Like Flowers, Fill The World With Beauty, The Heart With Joy."
☐ Purchased 19___ Pd $_______ MIB NB DB BNT
☐ Want Orig. Ret. $4.75 **NB** $8 **MIB** Sec. Mkt. **$12-$15**

QX 277-7 GRANDPARENTS
Comments: Porcelain White Glass Ball, 2-7/8" dia.
Dated 1987. Children are depicted in winter activities. Caption: "Grandparents... So Warm, So Loving, So Like The Christmas Season." **Artist:** Sharon Pike
☐ Purchased 19___ Pd $_______ MIB NB DB BNT
☐ Want Orig. Ret. $4.75 **NB** $8 **MIB** Sec. Mkt. **$15-$18**

QX 276-9 GRANDSON
Comments: Blue Glass Ball, 3" dia., Dated Christmas 1987
A marching band parades around the center of this ball. Caption: "Grandsons Have A Talent For Making Wonderful Memories."
Artist: LaDene Votruba
☐ Purchased 19___ Pd $_______ MIB NB DB BNT
☐ Want Orig. Ret. $4.75 **NB** $10 **MIB** Sec. Mkt. **$18-$22**

EPCA HALLIS STAR - ORNAMENT TREE TOPPER
Comments: Acrylic, 9-7/8" tall
☐ Purchased 19___ Pd $_______ MIB NB DB BNT
☐ Want Orig. Ret. Unknown **NB** $25 **MIB** Sec. Mkt. **$35-$40**

QX 471-7 HAPPY HOLIDATA
Comments: Handcrafted, 1-1/2" tall, Reissued in 1988.
Two white mice send their message, "Happy Holidata," on this computer which flashes the words and background in alternating colors. **Artist:** Bob Siedler
☐ Purchased 19___ Pd $_______ MIB NB DB BNT
☐ Want Orig. Ret. $6.50 **NB** $18 **MIB** Sec. Mkt. **$25-$30**

QX 456-9 HAPPY SANTA
Comments: Handcrafted, 2-1/2" tall
Santa hangs onto the tree branch with his candy cane. He also holds a gold jingle bell. **Artist:** Ken Crow
☐ Purchased 19___ Pd $_______ MIB NB DB BNT
☐ Want Orig. Ret. $4.75 **NB** $15 **MIB** Sec. Mkt. **$25-$30**

QX 372-7 HEART IN BLOSSOM
Comments: Acrylic, 2-3/4" tall, Dated Christmas 1987
An acrylic etched rose is growing around the edge of the heart' shaped ornament and blooming into the center. "Love Is The Heart In Blossom." **Artist:** LaDene Votruba
☐ Purchased 19___ Pd $_______ MIB NB DB BNT
☐ Want Orig. Ret. $6.00 **NB** $12 **MIB** Sec. Mkt. **$22-$24**

QX 465-9 HEAVENLY HARMONY
Comments: Musical, Handcrafted, 4-1/4" tall
A little angel rings out *Joy To The World* as she pulls the rope to the bell tower. A key at the back activates the music.
Artist: Ken Crow
☐ Purchased 19___ Pd $_______ MIB NB DB BNT
☐ Want Orig. Ret. $15.00 **NB** $24 **MIB** Sec. Mkt. **$32-$38**

QX 484-7 HERE COMES SANTA: SANTA'S WOODY
Comments: **Ninth in Series,** Handcrafted, 2" tall, Dated 1987
Santa's new car sports whitewall tires, custom paneling and a license plate that says "JOY-2-U." **Artist:** Ken Crow
☐ Purchased 19___ Pd $_______ MIB NB DB BNT
☐ Want Orig. Ret. $14.00 **NB** $30 **MIB** Sec. Mkt. **$55-$60**

QX 375-7 HOLIDAY GREETINGS
Comments: Bezeled Foil, 2-3/4" dia., Dated 1987
A silver tree and lettering against blue foil. Caption: "Season's Greetings" and "Wishing You Happiness At This Beautiful Time Of Year."
☐ Purchased 19___ Pd $_______ MIB NB DB BNT
☐ Want Orig. Ret. $6.00 **NB** $8 **MIB** Sec. Mkt. **$12-$14**

QX 485-7 HOLIDAY HEIRLOOM
Comments: Limited Edition 34,600, Dated 1987
Lead Crystal, Silver Plating, 3-1/4" tall
Hanging in the center of a silver-plated wreath is this clear crystal bell with bow and ribbon. Many were "bought up" in 1987 for the secondary market. **Artist:** Duane Unruh
☐ Purchased 19___ Pd $_______ MIB NB DB BNT
☐ Want Orig. Ret. $25.00 **NB** $20 **MIB** Sec. Mkt. **$35-$38**

QX 470-7 HOLIDAY HOURGLASS
Comments: Handcrafted, 3" tall
This snowman changes holidays as you turn him over - "Merry Christmas" and "Happy New Year." **Artist:** Duane Unru
☐ Purchased 19___ Pd $_______ MIB NB DB BNT
☐ Want Orig. Ret. $8.00 **NB** $10 **MIB** Sec. Mkt. **$23-$25**

QX 371-7 HOLIDAY WILDLIFE: SNOW GOOSE
Comments: **Sixth in Series**, Wood, 2-1/2" dia.
Caption: "Snow Goose, CHEN HYPERBOREA, Sixth In A Series, Wildlife Collection, Christmas 1987."
Artist: LaDene Votruba
☐ Purchased 19___ Pd $_______ MIB NB DB BNT
☐ Want Orig. Ret. $7.50 **NB** $10 **MIB** Sec. Mkt. **$15-$20**

QX 471-9 HOT DOGGER
Comments: Handcrafted, 2-1/2" tall
Santa's a real "hot dogger" in his red ski suit, and has proven that he is a real champion. **Artist:** Duane Unruh
☐ Purchased 19___ Pd $_______ MIB NB DB BNT
☐ Want Orig. Ret. $6.50 **NB** $12 **MIB** Sec. Mkt. **$15-$22**

QX 373-9 HUSBAND
Comments: Blue Cameo, 3-1/4" dia., Dated 1987
A couple sit together in an ivory sleigh. Caption: "For My Husband" and "The Nicest Part Of Christmas Is Sharing It With You." **Artist:** LaDene Votruba
☐ Purchased 19___ Pd $_______ MIB NB DB BNT
☐ Want Orig. Ret. $7.00 **NB** $6 **MIB** Sec. Mkt. **$10-$12**

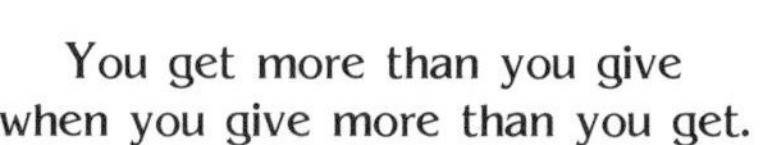

QX 278-9 I REMEMBER SANTA
Comments: Porcelain White Glass Ball, 2-7/8" dia.
Dated 1987. Three antique postcard reproductions of Santa are captured on this porcelain ball. Caption: "At Christmastime, Especially, Those Magic Memories Start... Those Memories Of Yesterday That So Delight The Heart." **Artist:** Joyce A. Lyle
☐ Purchased 19___ Pd $_______ MIB NB DB BNT
☐ Want Orig. Ret. $4.75 **NB** $12 **MIB** Sec. Mkt. **$20-$24**

QX 450-9 ICY TREAT
Comments: Handcrafted, 2-1/4" tall
A penguin in a green stocking cap is enjoying his icy cherry treat.
Artist: Bob Siedler
☐ Purchased 19___ Pd $_______ MIB NB DB BNT
☐ Want Orig. Ret. $4.50 **NB** $10 **MIB** Sec. Mkt. **$16-$22**

QX 469-7 IN A NUTSHELL
Comments: Handcrafted, 1-1/2" tall, Reissued in 1988
Open the walnut and inside are detailed Christmas scenes.
Artist: Duane Unruh
☐ Purchased 19___ Pd $_______ MIB NB DB BNT
☐ Want Orig. Ret. $5.50 **NB** $10 **MIB** Sec. Mkt. **$22-$28**

QX 449-9 JACK FROSTING
Comments: Handcrafted, 2-1/2" tall
Jack brushes a glittery frost onto each leaf to make Christmas season sparkle. **Artist:** Ed Seale
☐ Purchased 19___ Pd $_______ MIB NB DB BNT
☐ Want Orig. Ret. $7.00 **NB** $32 **MIB** Sec. Mkt. **$45-$50**

QX 283-9 JAMMIE PIES™
Comments: Porcelain White Glass Ball, 2-7/8" dia., Dated 1987
A child waits for the swan; it is bringing a visitor who knows many stories. Caption: "When Jammie Pies Are Close To You, All Your Christmas Dreams Come True."
☐ Purchased 19___ Pd $_______ MIB NB DB BNT
☐ Want Orig. Ret. $4.75 **NB** $5 **MIB** Sec. Mkt. **$11-$15**

QX 457-7 JOGGING THROUGH THE SNOW
Comments: Handcrafted, 3" tall, Dated 1987
This perky rabbit is wearing his jogging shirt and shorts and has his radio and earphones on.
Artist: Peter Dutkin
☐ Purchased 19___ Pd $_______ MIB NB DB BNT
☐ Want Orig. Ret. $7.25 **NB** $10 **MIB** Sec. Mkt. **$18-$22**

QX 466-9 JOLLY FOLLIES
Comments: Handcrafted, 2" tall
When you pull the string three penguins in top hats, spats and red bow ties dance at the "Jolly Follies."
Artist: Ken Crow
☐ Purchased 19___ Pd $_______ MIB NB DB BNT
☐ Want Orig. Ret. $8.50 **NB** $15 **MIB** Sec. Mkt. **$28-$32**

QX 483-2 JOLLY HIKER
Comments: Handcrafted, 2" tall
Reissued from 1986. **Artist:** Bob Siedler
☐ Purchased 19___ Pd $_______ MIB NB DB BNT
☐ Want Orig. Ret. $5.00 **NB** $10 **MIB** Sec. Mkt. **$20-$24**

QX 440-7 JOY RIDE
Comments: Handcrafted, 3-1/2" tall, Dated 1987
Santa's taking one of his reindeer for a ride on his new green motorcycle. The front fender says "Joy Ride."
☐ Purchased 19___ Pd $_______ MIB NB DB BNT
☐ Want Orig. Ret. $11.50 **NB** $40 **MIB** Sec. Mkt. **$50-$55**

QX 465-7 JOYOUS ANGELS
Comments: Handcrafted, 4" tall
A trio of angels dance beneath a brass star. The trim on their gowns and their halos are gold.
Artist: Ed Seale
☐ Purchased 19___ Pd $_______ MIB NB DB BNT
☐ Want Orig. Ret. $7.75 **NB** $10 **MIB** Sec. Mkt. **$20-$24**

QLX 707-6 KEEP ON GLOWIN'!
Comments: Lighted, Handcrafted, 2-7/16" tall
Reissued from 1986. **Artist:** Ken Crow
☐ Purchased 19___ Pd $_______ MIB NB DB BNT
☐ Want Orig. Ret. $10.00 **NB** $38 **MIB** Sec. Mkt. **$42-$46**

QLX 704-7 KEEPING COZY
Comments: Lighted, Handcrafted, 2-1/2" tall
Santa in his flocked long johns is joined at the potbelly stove by a little mouse. **Artist:** Ken Crow
☐ Purchased 19___ Pd $_______ MIB NB DB BNT
☐ Want Orig. Ret. $11.75 **NB** $20 **MIB** Sec. Mkt. **$30-$35**

QLX 709-7 LACY BRASS SNOWFLAKE
Comments: Lighted, Brass, 2-1/2" tall
Two snowflakes, one solid with an etched design and one a lacy filigree, reflect lights to create a sparkling snowflake.
☐ Purchased 19___ Pd $_______ MIB NB DB BNT
☐ Want Orig. Ret. $11.50 **NB** $12 **MIB** Sec. Mkt. **$23-$25**

QX 458-9 LET IT SNOW
Comments: Handcrafted, 3" tall
Christmas is for children, and this little one is ready for winter weather. He's wearing a green and red stocking cap, coat, mittens and knit muffler.
☐ Purchased 19___ Pd $_______ MIB NB DB BNT
☐ Want Orig. Ret. $6.50 **NB** $12 **MIB** Sec. Mkt. **$18-$25**

QX 419-3 LI'L JINGLER
Comments: Handcrafted, 2" tall
Reissued from 1986. **Artist:** Ed Seale
☐ Purchased 19___ Pd $_______ MIB NB DB BNT
☐ Want Orig. Ret. $6.75 **NB** $25 **MIB** Sec. Mkt. **$38-$42**

QX 469-9 LITTLE WHITTLER
Comments: Handcrafted, 3" tall
With the look of hand-carved wood, this Santa is happy with the reindeer toy he is carving. **Artist:** Peter Dutkin
☐ Purchased 19___ Pd $_______ MIB NB DB BNT
☐ Want Orig. Ret. $6.00 **NB** $18 **MIB** Sec. Mkt. **$28-$32**

QX 278-7 LOVE IS EVERYWHERE
Comments: Chrome and Frosted Blue Glass Ball, 2-7/8" dia.
Dated 1987. Two redbirds against a wintry landscape.
Caption: "Beautifully, Peacefully, Christmas Touches Our Lives... Love Is Everywhere." **Artist:** Joyce A. Lyle
☐ Purchased 19___ Pd $_______ MIB NB DB BNT
☐ Want

QLX 701-6 LOVING HOLIDAY
Comments: Light and Motion, Handcrafted, 3-5/8" tall
A couple move out of the house and meet under the clock in this reproduction of an old-fashioned glockenspiel. Caption: "Precious Times Are Spent With Those We Love."
Artist: Ed Seale
☐ Purchased 19___ Pd $_______ MIB NB DB BNT
☐ Want Orig. Ret. $22.00 **NB** $24 **MIB** Sec. Mkt. **$45-$50**

QLX 706-7 MEMORIES ARE FOREVER PHOTOHOLDER
Comments: Lighted, Handcrafted, 3-7/8" tall
The design of this ornament illuminates your favorite photo. Caption: "Memory Keeps Each Christmas Forever Warm And Bright." **Artist:** Ed Seale
☐ Purchased 19___ Pd $_______ MIB NB DB BNT
☐ Want Orig. Ret. $8.50 **NB** $15 **MIB** Sec. Mkt. **$28-$32**

QLX 708-9 MEOWY CHRISTMAS
Comments: Lighted, Handcrafted, 2-1/2" tall
Two kittens play with the white fabric bow on a glowing red heart. **Artist:** Sharon Pike
☐ Purchased 19___ Pd $_______ MIB NB DB BNT
☐ Want Orig. Ret. $10.00 **NB** $42 **MIB** Sec. Mkt. **$58-$60**

QX 415-3 MERRY KOALA
Comments: Handcrafted, 2" tall
Reissued from 1986. **Artist:** Linda Sickman
☐ Purchased 19___ Pd $_______ MIB NB DB BNT
☐ Want Orig. Ret. $5.00 **NB** $10 **MIB** Sec. Mkt. **$18-$22**

QX 481-9 MINIATURE CRECHE
Comments: **Third in Series**, Multi-plated Brass, 3-1/2" tall
Etched brass, washed in nickel, gold and copper, form a beautiful Nativity. **Artist:** Ed Seale
☐ Purchased 19___ Pd $_______ MIB NB DB BNT
☐ Want Orig. Ret. $9.00 **NB** $14 **MIB** Sec. Mkt. **$28-$32**

QX 468-7 MISTLETOAD
Comments: Handcrafted, 3-3/4" tall, Reissued in 1988
This little green fellow croaks when you pull his cord. His red hat has his name. **Artist:** Ken Crow
☐ Purchased 19___ Pd $_______ MIB NB DB BNT
☐ Want Orig. Ret. $7.00 **NB** $18 **MIB** Sec. Mkt. **$28-$30**

QX 373-7 MOTHER
Comments: Acrylic, 3-1/2" tall, Dated Christmas 1987
Caption: "Mother Is Another Word For Love" is etched in acrylic with a beveled edge.
Artist: Sharon Pike
☐ Purchased 19___ Pd $_______ MIB NB DB BNT
☐ Want Orig. Ret. $6.50 **NB** $8 **MIB** Sec. Mkt. **$16-$18**

QX 462-7 MOTHER & DAD
Comments: Porcelain, 4-3/4" tall, Dated Christmas 1987
This deep blue bell features a Christmas tree with two gifts and two red hearts. Caption: "For A Mother And Dad Who Give The Gift Of Love." **Artist:** Sharon Pike
☐ Purchased 19___ Pd $_______ MIB NB DB BNT
☐ Want Orig. Ret. $7.00 **NB** $15 **MIB** Sec. Mkt. **$20-$22**

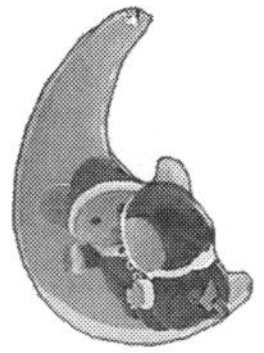

QX 416-6 MOUSE IN THE MOON
Comments: Handcrafted, 2-3/4" tall
Reissued from 1986. **Artist:** Ed Seale
☐ Purchased 19___ Pd $_______ MIB NB DB BNT
☐ Want Orig. Ret. $5.50 **NB** $12 **MIB** Sec. Mkt. **$20-$25**

QX 483-7 MR. AND MRS. CLAUS: HOME COOKING
Comments: **Second in Series**, Handcrafted, 3" tall
Dated 1987 Dec. 24. Mrs. Claus won't let Santa leave on his journey without a plate of cookies (chocolate chip, probably).
Artist: Duane Unruh
☐ Purchased 19___ Pd $_______ MIB NB DB BNT
☐ Want Orig. Ret. $13.25 **NB** $40 **MIB** Sec. Mkt. **$55-$60**

QX 273-9 NATURE'S DECORATIONS
Comments: Blue Glass Ball, 2-7/8" dia., Dated 1987
Forest animals enjoy the winter season. Caption: "The Nicest Christmas Decorations Start With Nature's Own Creations."
Artist: LaDene Votruba
☐ Purchased 19___ Pd $_______ MIB NB DB BNT
☐ Want Orig. Ret. $4.75 **NB** $8 **MIB** Sec. Mkt. **$28-$30**

QX 376-7 NEW HOME
Comments: Mirrored Acrylic, 2-3/4" dia.
Dated Christmas 1987. Caption: "A New Home Is A Wonderful Beginning To Wonderful Memories."
Artist: Joyce Pattee
☐ Purchased 19___ Pd $_______ MIB NB DB BNT
☐ Want Orig. Ret. $6.00 **NB** $14 **MIB** Sec. Mkt. **$28-$30**

QX 275-9 NIECE
Comments: Turquoise Blue Glass Ball, 3" dia., Dated 1987
White fluffy sheep, accented in red, frolic around the ball. Caption: "Christmas Is Happier... Merrier... Cheerier... Because Of A Niece's Love."
☐ Purchased 19___ Pd $_______ MIB NB DB BNT
☐ Want Orig. Ret. $4.75 **NB** $6 **MIB** Sec. Mkt. **$12-$14**

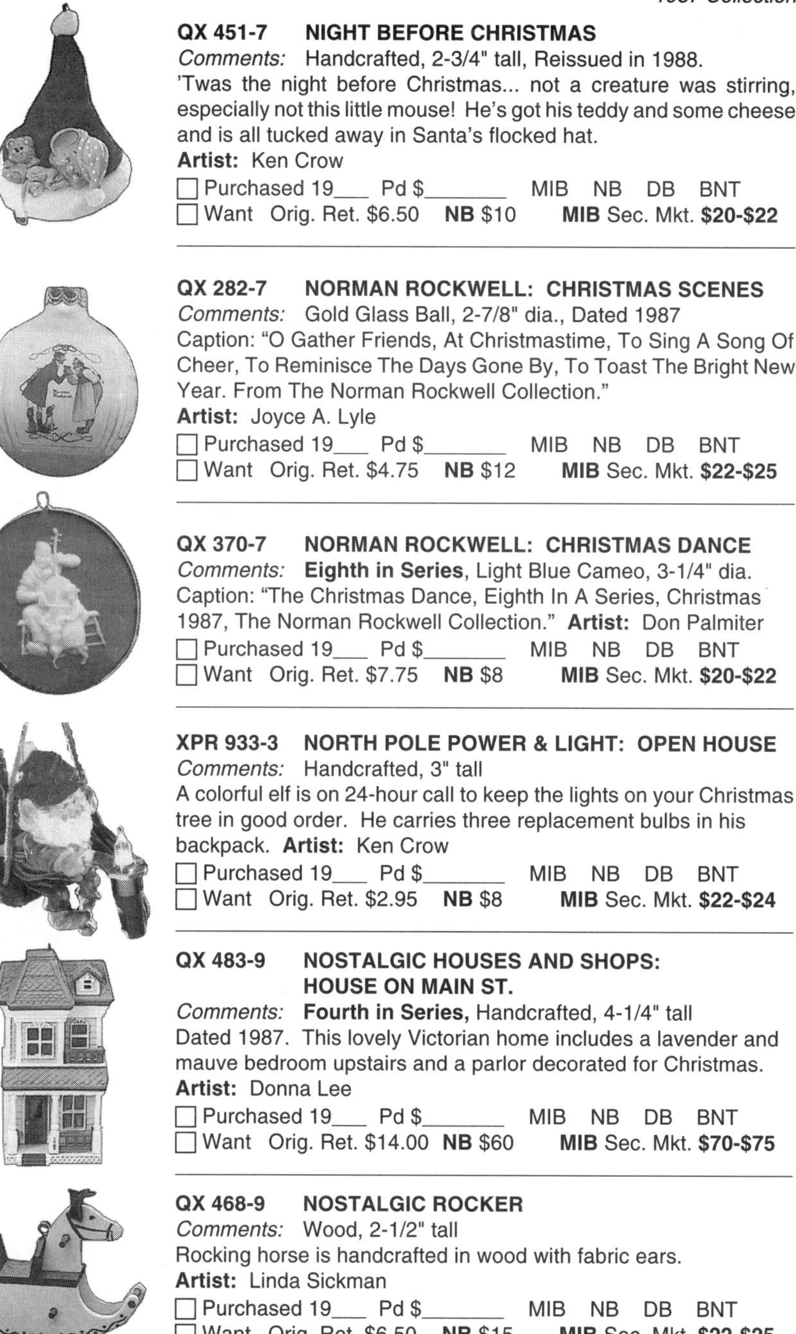

QX 451-7 NIGHT BEFORE CHRISTMAS
Comments: Handcrafted, 2-3/4" tall, Reissued in 1988.
'Twas the night before Christmas... not a creature was stirring, especially not this little mouse! He's got his teddy and some cheese and is all tucked away in Santa's flocked hat.
Artist: Ken Crow
☐ Purchased 19___ Pd $_______ MIB NB DB BNT
☐ Want Orig. Ret. $6.50 **NB** $10 **MIB** Sec. Mkt. **$20-$22**

QX 282-7 NORMAN ROCKWELL: CHRISTMAS SCENES
Comments: Gold Glass Ball, 2-7/8" dia., Dated 1987
Caption: "O Gather Friends, At Christmastime, To Sing A Song Of Cheer, To Reminisce The Days Gone By, To Toast The Bright New Year. From The Norman Rockwell Collection."
Artist: Joyce A. Lyle
☐ Purchased 19___ Pd $_______ MIB NB DB BNT
☐ Want Orig. Ret. $4.75 **NB** $12 **MIB** Sec. Mkt. **$22-$25**

QX 370-7 NORMAN ROCKWELL: CHRISTMAS DANCE
Comments: **Eighth in Series**, Light Blue Cameo, 3-1/4" dia.
Caption: "The Christmas Dance, Eighth In A Series, Christmas 1987, The Norman Rockwell Collection." **Artist:** Don Palmiter
☐ Purchased 19___ Pd $_______ MIB NB DB BNT
☐ Want Orig. Ret. $7.75 **NB** $8 **MIB** Sec. Mkt. **$20-$22**

XPR 933-3 NORTH POLE POWER & LIGHT: OPEN HOUSE
Comments: Handcrafted, 3" tall
A colorful elf is on 24-hour call to keep the lights on your Christmas tree in good order. He carries three replacement bulbs in his backpack. **Artist:** Ken Crow
☐ Purchased 19___ Pd $_______ MIB NB DB BNT
☐ Want Orig. Ret. $2.95 **NB** $8 **MIB** Sec. Mkt. **$22-$24**

QX 483-9 NOSTALGIC HOUSES AND SHOPS: HOUSE ON MAIN ST.
Comments: **Fourth in Series,** Handcrafted, 4-1/4" tall
Dated 1987. This lovely Victorian home includes a lavender and mauve bedroom upstairs and a parlor decorated for Christmas.
Artist: Donna Lee
☐ Purchased 19___ Pd $_______ MIB NB DB BNT
☐ Want Orig. Ret. $14.00 **NB** $60 **MIB** Sec. Mkt. **$70-$75**

QX 468-9 NOSTALGIC ROCKER
Comments: Wood, 2-1/2" tall
Rocking horse is handcrafted in wood with fabric ears.
Artist: Linda Sickman
☐ Purchased 19___ Pd $_______ MIB NB DB BNT
☐ Want Orig. Ret. $6.50 **NB** $15 **MIB** Sec. Mkt. **$22-$25**

QX 455-9 "OWLIDAY" WISH
Comments: Handcrafted, 2" tall Reissued in 1988
This cute white owl in spectacles is pointing to the holiday message written on the eye chart: "Seasons Greetings To You."
Artist: Sharon Pike
☐ Purchased 19___ Pd $_______ MIB NB DB BNT
☐ Want Orig. Ret. $6.50 **NB** $10 **MIB** Sec. Mkt. **$20-$22**

QX 472-7 PADDINGTON™ BEAR
Comments: Handcrafted, 3" tall
Paddington wears a red apron and white chef's cap. On his hat is a tag that says, "Please Look After This Bear. Thank You."
Artist: Sharon Pike
☐ Purchased 19___ Pd $_______ MIB NB DB BNT
☐ Want Orig. Ret. $5.50 **NB** $15 **MIB** Sec. Mkt. **$24-$28**

QX 281-9 PEANUTS®
Comments: Chrome Glass Ball, 3" dia., Dated 1987
"Everyone's Cool At Christmastime!" is depicted by Snoopy, Woodstock and his friends, as well as one snowman, all wearing their "shades."
☐ Purchased 19___ Pd $_______ MIB NB DB BNT
☐ Want Orig. Ret. $4.75 **NB** $18 **MIB** Sec. Mkt. **$28-$32**

QX 442-7 PORCELAIN BEAR
Comments: **Fifth in Series,** Fine Porcelain, 2-1/8" tall
This hand-painted Cinnamon Bear is searching for something in the toe of his red stocking.
☐ Purchased 19___ Pd $_______ MIB NB DB BNT
☐ Want Orig. Ret. $7.75 **NB** $12 **MIB** Sec. Mkt. **$22-$25**

QX 448-9 PRETTY KITTY
Comments: Handcrafted/Glass, 3-1/2" tall
A clear glass bell is a perfect display for a little kitten tangled in a red bead garland. **Artist:** Ken Crow
☐ Purchased 19___ Pd $_______ MIB NB DB BNT
☐ Want Orig. Ret. $11.00 **NB** $12 **MIB** Sec. Mkt. **$22-$25**

QX 374-9 PROMISE OF PEACE
Comments: Acrylic, 2-3/4" dia., Framed in brass
A dove with a gold foil olive branch. The caption, "A Season Of Hope, A Reminder Of Miracles, A Promise Of Peace," is etched in the bevel in the front. **Artist:** Ken Crow
☐ Purchased 19___ Pd $_______ MIB NB DB BNT
☐ Want Orig. Ret. $11.00 **NB** $11 **MIB** Sec. Mkt. **$20-$22**

QX 458-7 RACCOON BIKER
Comments: Handcrafted, 3" tall, Dated 1987
This little raccoon is pedaling his bicycle to deliver his special Christmas present. **Artist:** Bob Siedler
☐ Purchased 19___ Pd $_______ MIB NB DB BNT
☐ Want Orig. Ret. $7.00 **NB** $12 **MIB** Sec. Mkt. **$24-$28**

QX 480-9 REINDEER CHAMPS: DANCER
Comments: **Second in Series,** Handcrafted, 3-1/2" tall Dated 1987. Dancer is a vision of loveliness as she ice skates her way into the hearts and homes of collectors.
Artist: Bob Siedler
☐ Purchased 19___ Pd $_______ MIB NB DB BNT
☐ Want Orig. Ret. $7.50 **NB** $35 **MIB** Sec. Mkt. **$52-$55**

QX 452-7 REINDOGGY
Comments: Handcrafted, 2-3/4" tall, Reissued in 1988
This puppy is wearing antlers fashioned from real sticks, tied to his head with red satin ribbon.
Artist: Bob Siedler
☐ Purchased 19___ Pd $_______ MIB NB DB BNT
☐ Want Orig. Ret. $5.75 **NB** $20 **MIB** Sec. Mkt. **$30-$32**

QX 482-9 ROCKING HORSE
Comments: **Seventh in Series,** Handcrafted, 3-3/4" wide Dated 1987. A white charger on purple rockers makes a fine steed for any boy or girl.
Artist: Linda Sickman
☐ Purchased 19___ Pd $_______ MIB NB DB BNT
☐ Want Orig. Ret. $10.75 **NB** $40 **MIB** Sec. Mkt. **$60-$65**

QLX 701-9 SANTA & SPARKY: PERFECT PORTRAIT
Comments: **Second in Series,** Light and Motion, Dated 1987 Handcrafted, 4-1/16" tall. Sparky has sculpted a perfect likeness of Santa in ice. He moves forward to light the statue.
☐ Purchased 19___ Pd $_______ MIB NB DB BNT
☐ Want Orig. Ret. $19.50 **NB** $45 **MIB** Sec. Mkt. **$60-$65**

QX 457-9 SANTA AT THE BAT
Comments: Handcrafted, 3-1/4" tall, Dated 1987
Wearing a uniform for the "North Pole Nicks 87," Santa swings and hits the snowball. Highs and lows out there on this one.
☐ Purchased 19___ Pd $_______ MIB NB DB BNT
☐ Want Orig. Ret. $7.75 **NB** $12 **MIB** Sec. Mkt. **$20-$22**

QLX 706-9 SEASON FOR FRIENDSHIP
Comments: Lighted Acrylic, 5-5/16" tall
Christmas greenery is etched above the caption: "How Lovely The Season When It's Filled With Friendship." Bevels in the teardrop reflect light.
☐ Purchased 19___ Pd $_______ MIB NB DB BNT
☐ Want Orig. Ret. $8.50 **NB** $10 **MIB** Sec. Mkt. **$20-$22**

QX 454-9 SEASONED GREETINGS
Comments: Handcrafted, 2" tall
A little elf does his job very well. He salts all the holiday pretzels from a silvery shaker which is labeled, "Seasoned Greetings SALT." **Artist:** Ed Seale
☐ Purchased 19___ Pd $_______ MIB NB DB BNT
☐ Want Orig. Ret. $6.25 **NB** $10 **MIB** Sec. Mkt. **$18-$22**

QX 474-7 SISTER
Comments: Wood, 2-3/4" tall, Dated Christmas 1987
This wooden heart has a basket of brightly stenciled poinsettias on the front. Caption: "A Sister Brings Happiness Wrapped In Love." **Artist:** Linda Sickman
☐ Purchased 19___ Pd $_______ MIB NB DB BNT
☐ Want Orig. Ret. $6.00 **NB** $5 **MIB** Sec. Mkt. **$12-$15**

QX 450-7 SLEEPY SANTA
Comments: Handcrafted, 2-3/4" tall
Santa relaxes in his favorite chair and soaks his feet — it's Dec. 26 and he deserves his rest!
Artist: Ken Crow
☐ Purchased 19___ Pd $_______ MIB NB DB BNT
☐ Want Orig. Ret. $6.25 **NB** $22 **MIB** Sec. Mkt. **$35-$38**

QX 472-9 SNOOPY & WOODSTOCK
Comments: Handcrafted, 2-1/2" tall
Woodstock plays "Angel" and perches on the top of Snoopy's bottle-brush tree.
Artist: Bob Siedler
☐ Purchased 19___ Pd $_______ MIB NB DB BNT
☐ Want Orig. Ret. $7.25 **NB** $20 **MIB** Sec. Mkt. **$35-$39**

QX 463-9 SON
Comments: Handcrafted, 1" tall, Dated Christmas 1987
Hanging from a red cord is an old-fashioned toy train with the words "For Son" painted in bright colors.
Artist: Linda Sickman
☐ Purchased 19___ Pd $_______ MIB NB DB BNT
☐ Want Orig. Ret. $5.75 **NB** $20 **MIB** Sec. Mkt. **$35-$40**

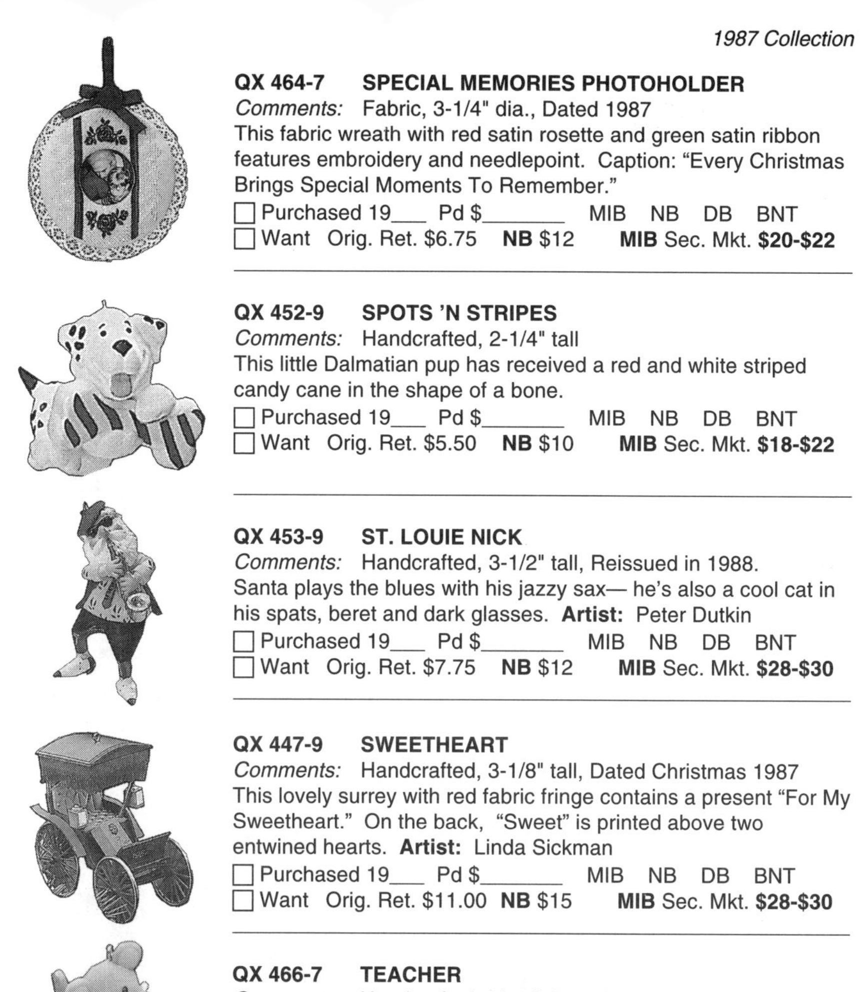

QX 464-7 SPECIAL MEMORIES PHOTOHOLDER
Comments: Fabric, 3-1/4" dia., Dated 1987
This fabric wreath with red satin rosette and green satin ribbon features embroidery and needlepoint. Caption: "Every Christmas Brings Special Moments To Remember."
☐ Purchased 19___ Pd $_______ MIB NB DB BNT
☐ Want Orig. Ret. $6.75 **NB** $12 **MIB** Sec. Mkt. **$20-$22**

QX 452-9 SPOTS 'N STRIPES
Comments: Handcrafted, 2-1/4" tall
This little Dalmatian pup has received a red and white striped candy cane in the shape of a bone.
☐ Purchased 19___ Pd $_______ MIB NB DB BNT
☐ Want Orig. Ret. $5.50 **NB** $10 **MIB** Sec. Mkt. **$18-$22**

QX 453-9 ST. LOUIE NICK
Comments: Handcrafted, 3-1/2" tall, Reissued in 1988.
Santa plays the blues with his jazzy sax— he's also a cool cat in his spats, beret and dark glasses. **Artist:** Peter Dutkin
☐ Purchased 19___ Pd $_______ MIB NB DB BNT
☐ Want Orig. Ret. $7.75 **NB** $12 **MIB** Sec. Mkt. **$28-$30**

QX 447-9 SWEETHEART
Comments: Handcrafted, 3-1/8" tall, Dated Christmas 1987
This lovely surrey with red fabric fringe contains a present "For My Sweetheart." On the back, "Sweet" is printed above two entwined hearts. **Artist:** Linda Sickman
☐ Purchased 19___ Pd $_______ MIB NB DB BNT
☐ Want Orig. Ret. $11.00 **NB** $15 **MIB** Sec. Mkt. **$28-$30**

QX 466-7 TEACHER
Comments: Handcrafted, 2" tall, Dated 1987
Teddy has taken time to write a Christmas greeting: "Merry Christmas Teacher From (name)"
Artist: Bob Siedler
☐ Purchased 19___ Pd $_______ MIB NB DB BNT
☐ Want Orig. Ret. $5.75 **NB** $12 **MIB** Sec. Mkt. **$18-$20**

QX 444-7 TEN YEARS TOGETHER
Comments: Porcelain/Bell, 4-3/4" tall, Dated Christmas 1987
A heart-shaped green wreath decorated with red ribbon, berries and flowers frames the words "Ten Years Together." Tied with satin ribbon. **Artist:** LaDene Votruba
☐ Purchased 19___ Pd $_______ MIB NB DB BNT
☐ Want Orig. Ret. $7.00 **NB** $16 **MIB** Sec. Mkt. **$22-$25**

QX 441-9 THIMBLE SERIES: DRUMMER
Comments: **Tenth in Series,** 2" tall
A brown bunny with a fluffy pom-pom tail plays his thimble drum.
Artist: Bob Siedler
☐ Purchased 19___ Pd $_______ MIB NB DB BNT
☐ Want Orig. Ret. $5.75 **NB** $18 **MIB** Sec. Mkt. **$28-$30**

QX 454-7 THREE MEN IN A TUB
Comments: Handcrafted, 3" tall
The butcher, the baker and the candlestick maker all are sitting in a small tub which says "Rub A Dub Dub." **Artist:** Donna Lee
☐ Purchased 19___ Pd $_______ MIB NB DB BNT
☐ Want Orig. Ret. $8.00 **NB** $12 **MIB** Sec. Mkt. **$22-$28**

QX 280-7 TIME FOR FRIENDS
Comments: Red Glass Ball, 3" dia., Dated Christmas 1987
Two white mice decorate with a green holly garland. Caption: "When Good Friends Meet, Good Times Are Complete!"
Artist: LaDene Votruba
☐ Purchased 19___ Pd $_______ MIB NB DB BNT
☐ Want Orig. Ret. $4.75 **NB** $8 **MIB** Sec. Mkt. **$18-$22**

QX 484-9 TIN LOCOMOTIVE
Comments: **Sixth in Series,** Pressed Tin, 3-1/2" tall, Dated 1987
With red wheels that really roll and a brass bell that rings, this locomotive is a delight for collectors of all ages.
Artist: Linda Sickman
☐ Purchased 19___ Pd $_______ MIB NB DB BNT
☐ Want Orig. Ret. $14.75 **NB** $50 **MIB** Sec. Mkt. **$60-$65**

QLX 703-9 TRAIN STATION
Comments: Lighted, Handcrafted, 3-3/16" tall
The Merriville station is open for business. A mother and child are waiting for the next train to arrive and a ticket taker stands at his station. **Artist:** Donna Lee
☐ Purchased 19___ Pd $_______ MIB NB DB BNT
☐ Want Orig. Ret. $12.75 **NB** $25 **MIB** Sec. Mkt. **$45-$48**

QX 459-7 TREETOP DREAMS
Comments: Handcrafted, 3" tall, Reissued in 1988.
This little squirrel will find a pleasant surprise when he wakes. Santa has left an acorn in his green stocking. His bed is a vine wreath.
Artist: Ed Seale
☐ Purchased 19___ Pd $_______ MIB NB DB BNT
☐ Want Orig. Ret. $6.75 **NB** $15 **MIB** Sec. Mkt. **$28-$30**

QX 425-6 TREETOP TRIO/BLUEBIRDS
Comments: Handcrafted, 2" tall
Reissued from 1986. **Artist:** Donna Lee
☐ Purchased 19___ Pd $_______ MIB NB DB BNT
☐ Want Orig. Ret. $11.00 **NB** $16 **MIB** Sec. Mkt. **$30-$34**

QX 370-9 TWELVE DAYS OF CHRISTMAS: FOUR COLLY BIRDS
Comments: **Fourth in Series,** Acrylic, 4" tall, Dated 1987
The diamond acrylic shape features four etched colly birds in the center, with gold foil captions. **Artist:** Sharon Pike
☐ Purchased 19___ Pd $_______ MIB NB DB BNT
☐ Want Orig. Ret. $6.50 **NB** $20 **MIB** Sec. Mkt. **$35-$38**

QX 443-9 TWENTY-FIVE YEARS TOGETHER
Comments: Porcelain Plate, 3-1/4" dia., Acrylic stand
Dated Christmas 1987. Two bright red cardinals perch on a pine branch above silver lettering "25 Years Together." Caption: "Love Is For Always."
☐ Purchased 19___ Pd $_______ MIB NB DB BNT
☐ Want Orig. Ret. $7.50 **NB** $16 **MIB** Sec. Mkt. **$28-$30**

QLX 707-2 VILLAGE EXPRESS
Comments: Light and Motion, Handcrafted, 3-1/2" tall
Reissued from 1986.
Artist: Linda Sickman
☐ Purchased 19___ Pd $_______ MIB NB DB BNT
☐ Want Orig. Ret. $24.50 **NB** $60 **MIB** Sec. Mkt. **$115-$120**

QX 419-6 WALNUT SHELL RIDER
Comments: Handcrafted, 1-3/4" tall
Reissued from 1986. **Artist:** Ed Seale
☐ Purchased 19___ Pd $_______ MIB NB DB BNT
☐ Want Orig. Ret. $6.00 **NB** $12 **MIB** Sec. Mkt. **$20-$24**

Ruth Moody's Santa sends Holiday Greetings!

QX 375-9 WARMTH OF FRIENDSHIP
Comments: Acrylic, 3-3/4" tall, Dated 1987
Ornament-shaped acrylic features the caption in gold foil calligraphy: "As Christmas Warms The World, Friendship Warms Our Hearts."
☐ Purchased 19___ Pd $_______ MIB NB DB BNT
☐ Want Orig. Ret. $6.00 **NB** $7 **MIB** Sec. Mkt. **$12-$15**

QX 451-9 WEE CHIMNEY SWEEP
Comments: Handcrafted, 3" tall
This little white mouse is cleaning the chimneys so Santa won't get soot all over himself when he makes his rounds Christmas Eve. **Artist:** Ed Seale
☐ Purchased 19___ Pd $_______ MIB NB DB BNT
☐ Want Orig. Ret. $6.25 **NB** $12 **MIB** Sec. Mkt. **$22-$24**

QX 482-7 WINDOWS OF THE WORLD: HAWAIIAN
Comments: **Third in Series**, Handcrafted, 3" tall, Dated 1987
A little Hawaiian girl sits in the comfort of her thatched hut strumming her ukulele. Caption: "Mele Kalikimaka." Easily found.
Artist: Donna Lee
☐ Purchased 19___ Pd $_______ MIB NB DB BNT
☐ Want Orig. Ret. $10.00 **NB** $15 **MIB** Sec. Mkt. **$20-$25**

QX 441-7 WOOD CHILDHOOD: HORSE
Comments: **Fourth in Series**, Wood, 2-1/4" tall, Dated 1987
This little horse, with a plush mane and yarn tail, is standing on a cart with wheels that turn. He sports a handpainted red and green saddle. **Artist:** Bob Siedler
☐ Purchased 19___ Pd $_______ MIB NB DB BNT
☐ Want Orig. Ret. $7.50 **NB** $10 **MIB** Sec. Mkt. **$22-$25**

QX 447-7 WORD OF LOVE
Comments: Porcelain, 2-1/8" tall, Dated Christmas 1987
The word "Love" is sculpted into a contemporary design. A small red heart dangles inside the "o."
☐ Purchased 19___ Pd $_______ MIB NB DB BNT
☐ Want Orig. Ret. $8.00 **NB** $8 **MIB** Sec. Mkt. **$18-$22**

QXC 580-9 WREATH OF MEMORIES CHARTER CLUB MEMBERSHIP ORN.
Comments: Handcrafted, 3-1/8" tall, Dated 1987
This detailed green wreath is decorated with Hallmark ornaments. Caption: "1987 Charter Member." Club logo is engraved in brass.
Artist: Duane Unruh
☐ Purchased 19___ Pd $_______ MIB NB DB BNT
☐ Want Orig. Ret.: Gift to Charter Members.
NB $35 **MIB** Sec. Mkt. **$55-$60**

CHRISTMAS...
Hallmark Style!

☜ Ruth A. Davey's plush animals enjoy Hallmark ornaments, too!

Betty Willing places a train around the base of her tree. ☞

1988 Collection

QX 482-1 A KISS™ FROM SANTA
Comments: Handcrafted, 3-1/4" tall
A "chocolate" Santa holds a Hershey's Kiss. His hat is red with a silvery trim. **Artist:** Duane Unruh
☐ Purchased 19___ Pd $_______ MIB NB DB BNT
☐ Want Orig. Ret. $4.50 **NB** $14 **MIB** Sec. Mkt. **$25-$28**

QX 488-1 AMERICANA DRUM
Comments: Tin, 2" dia., Dated 1988
An American eagle and banner design is portrayed against a vivid blue background. Caption: "Merry Christmas U.S.A."
Artist: Linda Sickman
☐ Purchased 19___ Pd $_______ MIB NB DB BNT
☐ Want Orig. Ret. $7.75 **NB** $10 **MIB** Sec. Mkt. **$25-$28**

QX 408-4 ANGELIC MINSTREL: KEEPSAKE CLUB
Comments: Limited Edition, 49,900, Wood Display Stand
Hand-Painted Fine Porcelain, 5" tall
This blue gowned angel plays a golden lyre. Offered only to members of the Hallmark Keepsake Ornament Club. Some say this was overproduced for a Limited Edition. **Artist:** Donna Lee
☐ Purchased 19___ Pd $_______ MIB NB DB BNT
☐ Want Orig. Ret. $29.50 **NB** $25 **MIB** Sec. Mkt. **$32-$35**

QX 472-1 ARCTIC TENOR
Comments: Handcrafted, 1-3/4" tall
This penguin is in great voice for his solo. He's wearing spats and a green bow tie and has his song book of "Arctic Arias" open.
Artist: Bob Siedler
☐ Purchased 19___ Pd $_______ MIB NB DB BNT
☐ Want Orig. Ret. $4.00 **NB** $8 **MIB** Sec. Mkt. **$15-$20**

QX 410-1 BABY REDBIRD
Comments: Handcrafted, 2-5/8" tall
This baby resembles the cardinals who feast throughout the winter at bird feeders. **Artist:** Robert Chad
☐ Purchased 19___ Pd $_______ MIB NB DB BNT
☐ Want Orig. Ret. $5.00 **NB** $7 **MIB** Sec. Mkt. **$14-$18**

QX 272-1 BABY'S FIRST CHRISTMAS: BOY
Comments: White Satin Ball, 2-7/8" dia., Dated 1988
Caption: "From The Moment A New Baby Boy Arrives, He's The Love Of Your Heart, The Light In Your Eyes. Baby's First Christmas."
☐ Purchased 19___ Pd $_______ MIB NB DB BNT
☐ Want Orig. Ret. $4.75 **NB** $8 **MIB** Sec. Mkt. **$20-$23**

QX 272-4 BABY'S FIRST CHRISTMAS: GIRL
Comments: White Satin Ball, 2-7/8" dia., Dated 1988
Caption: "A Sweet Baby Girl, So Tiny And New, Is A Bundle Of Joy And A Dream Come True. Baby's First Christmas."
☐ Purchased 19___ Pd $_______ MIB NB DB BNT
☐ Want Orig. Ret. $4.75 **NB** $6 **MIB** Sec. Mkt. **$18-$22**

QLX 718-4 BABY'S FIRST CHRISTMAS
Comments: Light and Motion, Handcrafted, 4" tall, Dated 1988
A carousel of prancing horses under a blue and white canopy celebrates Baby's First Christmas. **Artist:** Ed Seale
☐ Purchased 19___ Pd $_______ MIB NB DB BNT
☐ Want Orig. Ret. $24.00 **NB** $25 **MIB** Sec. Mkt. **$48-$52**

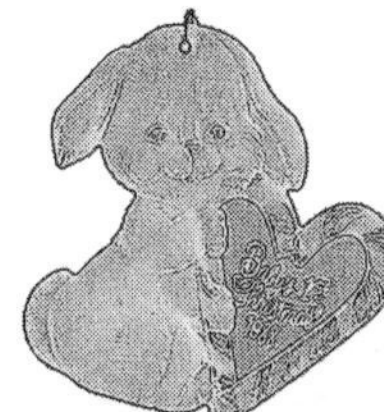

QX 372-1 BABY'S FIRST CHRISTMAS
Comments: Acrylic, 4" tall, Dated 1988
Baby's First Christmas in gold foil letters is framed by a heart made from two candy canes and is held by an intricately etched bunny. **Artist:** Sharon Pike
☐ Purchased 19___ Pd $_______ MIB NB DB BNT
☐ Want Orig. Ret. $6.00 **NB** $12 **MIB** Sec. Mkt. **$20-$22**

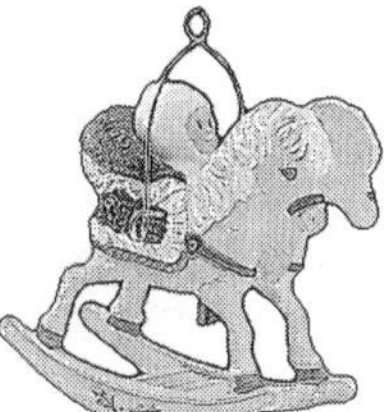

QX 470-1 BABY'S FIRST CHRISTMAS
Comments: Handcrafted, 3-5/8" tall, Dated 1988
Baby's all wrapped up in white bunting and a green blanket trimmed with lace for a ride in a cute rocking horse trimmed in red and green. **Artist:** Ken Crow
☐ Purchased 19___ Pd $_______ MIB NB DB BNT
☐ Want Orig. Ret. $9.75 **NB** $20 **MIB** Sec. Mkt. **$40-$42**

QX 470-4 BABY'S FIRST CHRISTMAS PHOTOHOLDER
Comments: Fabric, 5" tall, Dated 1988
Embroidered angels and holly decorate this heart-shaped photo holder. Caption: "Baby's First Christmas" and "A Baby Is A Gift Of Joy, A Gift Of Love At Christmas."
☐ Purchased 19___ Pd $_______ MIB NB DB BNT
☐ Want Orig. Ret. $7.50 **NB** $14 **MIB** Sec. Mkt. **$25-$28**

QX 471-1 BABY'S SECOND CHRISTMAS
Comments: Handcrafted, 1-3/4" tall, Dated 1988
A flocked bear enjoys pounding the blocks on a child's toy. "Baby's 2nd Christmas" on side. **Artist:** Sharon Pike
☐ Purchased 19___ Pd $_______ MIB NB DB BNT
☐ Want Orig. Ret. $6.00 **NB** $20 **MIB** Sec. Mkt. **$30-$34**

QX 279-1 BABYSITTER
Comments: Green Glass Ball, 2-7/8" dia., Dated 1988
Childlike drawings portray winter fun in the snow. Caption: "May The Love You Show Children Return To You This Holiday."
Artist: Linda Sickman
☐ Purchased 19___ Pd $_______ MIB NB DB BNT
☐ Want Orig. Ret. $4.75 **NB** $6 **MIB** Sec. Mkt. **$10-$12**

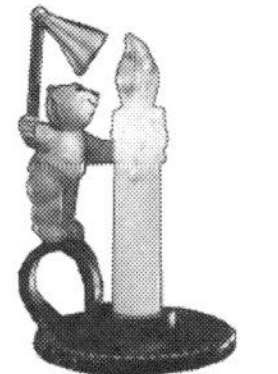

QLX 715-1 BEARLY REACHING
Comments: Light, Handcrafted, 4" tall
This tiny little bear must stand on the candle holder with his candle snuffer in hand to put out the candle at night. **Artist:** Linda Sickman
☐ Purchased 19___ Pd $_______ MIB NB DB BNT
☐ Want Orig. Ret. $9.50 **NB** $14 **MIB** Sec. Mkt. **$38-$40**

QX 271-4 BETSEY CLARK: HOME FOR CHRISTMAS
Comments: **Third in Series,** Light Blue Glass Ball, 2-7/8" dia. Dated 1988. Betsey and her friends show love: pressing a stocking, baking cookies and stitching a quilt. Caption: "A Homemade Touch Can Do So Much To Make Each Christmas Special." **Artist:** Sharon Pike
☐ Purchased 19___ Pd $_______ MIB NB DB BNT
☐ Want Orig. Ret. $5.00 **NB** $12 **MIB** Sec. Mkt. **$20-$24**

QX 471-4 CHILD'S THIRD CHRISTMAS
Comments: Handcrafted, 2-1/2" tall, Dated 1988
Riding a red reindeer bounce ball is a lot of fun for this tyke. Ball says "My 3rd Christmas."
Artist: Robert Chad
☐ Purchased 19___ Pd $_______ MIB NB DB BNT
☐ Want Orig. Ret. $6.00 **NB** $12 **MIB** Sec. Mkt. **$28-$30**

QLX 715-4 CHRIS MOUSE STAR
Comments: **Fourth in Series,** Light, Handcrafted, 2-1/2" tall Dated 1988. Chris, in his red nightcap and blue nightshirt, is shining and cleaning a golden star.
Artist: Bob Siedler
☐ Purchased 19___ Pd $_______ MIB NB DB BNT
☐ Want Orig. Ret. $8.75 **NB** $40 **MIB** Sec. Mkt. **$58-$60**

QX 494-1 CHRISTMAS CARDINAL
Comments: Handcrafted, 2-7/8" tall
A little cardinal suspended from golden beads twirls inside an outline of an evergreen.
Artist: Anita Marra Rogers
☐ Purchased 19___ Pd $_______ MIB NB DB BNT
☐ Want Orig. Ret. $4.75 **NB** $8 **MIB** Sec. Mkt. **$15-$18**

QLX 716-1 CHRISTMAS CLASSICS: NIGHT BEFORE CHRISTMAS
Comments: **Third in Series.** Light, Handcrafted, 4-1/2" tall Dated 1988. While everyone sleeps snugly upstairs, Santa is filling the stockings in the decorated living room downstairs. No series number on this ornament. **Artist:** Donna Lee
☐ Purchased 19___ Pd $_______ MIB NB DB BNT
☐ Want Orig. Ret. $15.00 **NB** $20 **MIB** Sec. Mkt. **$30-$34**

QX 480-1 CHRISTMAS CUCKOO
Comments: Handcrafted, 4-7/8" tall
Tap the pendulum and watch for two surprises. The clock changes from 12:00 to 3:00 and the little door opens to show a blue bird inside. **Artist:** Ken Crow
☐ Purchased 19___ Pd $_______ MIB NB DB BNT
☐ Want Orig. Ret. $8.00 **NB** $15 **MIB** Sec. Mkt. **$28-$30**

QLX 717-1 CHRISTMAS IS MAGIC
Comments: Light, Handcrafted, 3-1/4" tall
Santa uses the light from a table lantern and his puppy's bones to create a reindeer silhouette on the window. "Christmas Is Magic!" **Artist:** Ken Crow
☐ Purchased 19___ Pd $_______ MIB NB DB BNT
☐ Want Orig. Ret. $12.00 **NB** $35 **MIB** Sec. Mkt. **$50-$55**

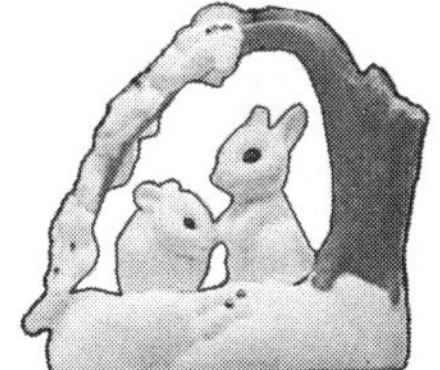

QX 407-1 CHRISTMAS IS SHARING: KEEPSAKE CLUB
Comments: Limited Edition, 49,900, Hand Numbered Hand-Painted Bone China, 2-1/4" tall
Two little rabbits sit in the arch of a tree bowed down with the weight of the snowfall. **Artist:** Ed Seale
☐ Purchased 19___ Pd $_______ MIB NB DB BNT
☐ Want Orig. Ret. $17.50 **NB** $22 **MIB** Sec. Mkt. **$38-$40**

QX 372-4 CHRISTMAS MEMORIES PHOTOHOLDER
Comments: Acrylic, 3-3/4" tall, Dated 1988
This acrylic wreath is circled with silver foil snowflakes. Caption: "Christmas Is More Than A Day In December... It's The Magic And Love We'll Always Remember." **Artist:** Joyce Pattee
☐ Purchased 19___ Pd $_______ MIB NB DB BNT
☐ Want Orig. Ret. $6.50 **NB** $10 **MIB** Sec. Mkt. **$22-$24**

QLX 701-3 CHRISTMAS MORNING
Comments: Light and Motion, Handcrafted, 4-5/16" tall Reissued from 1987.
Artist: Ken Crow
☐ Purchased 19___ Pd $_______ MIB NB DB BNT
☐ Want Orig. Ret. $24.50 **NB** $28 **MIB** Sec. Mkt. **$35-$40**

QLX 712-4 CIRCLING THE GLOBE
Comments: Light, Handcrafted, 2-3/4" tall
Santa is charting his delivery route by using a large lighted globe.
Artist: Ken Crow
☐ Purchased 19___ Pd $_______ MIB NB DB BNT
☐ Want Orig. Ret. $10.50 **NB** $25 **MIB** Sec. Mkt. **$40-$42**

QX 406-1 COLLECTOR'S PLATE: WAITING FOR SANTA
Comments: **Second in Series,** Fine Porcelain, 3-1/4" dia. Dated 1988. A brother and sister have fallen asleep in the chair as they watch for Santa. **Artist:** LaDene Votruba
☐ Purchased 19___ Pd $_______ MIB NB DB BNT
☐ Want Orig. Ret. $8.00 **NB** $35 **MIB** Sec. Mkt. **$48-$50**

QX 487-4 COOL JUGGLER
Comments: Handcrafted, 4-3/4" tall
This fellow has it all figured out -- juggling, that is. Just tap the snowball below and watch the snowman's arms move as he juggles three snowballs. **Artist:** Ken Crow
☐ Purchased 19___ Pd $_______ MIB NB DB BNT
☐ Want Orig. Ret. $6.50 **NB** $12 **MIB** Sec. Mkt. **$20-$22**

QLX 721-1 COUNTRY EXPRESS
Comments: Light and Motion, Handcrafted, 3-1/2" tall
An engine, boxcar and caboose travel round and round a country village as it travels over a trestle and through a mountain tunnel.
Artist: Linda Sickman
☐ Purchased 19___ Pd $_______ MIB NB DB BNT
☐ Want Orig. Ret. $24.50 **NB** $50 **MIB** Sec. Mkt. **$68-$70**

QX 411-1 CYMBALS OF CHRISTMAS
Comments: Handcrafted, 2-1/8" tall
This little angel is so happy, she's letting everyone know. She's made cymbals from two gold stars she's pulled from the sky.
Artist: Donna Lee
☐ Purchased 19___ Pd $_______ MIB NB DB BNT
☐ Want Orig. Ret. $5.50 **NB** $14 **MIB** Sec. Mkt. **$28-$30**

QX 414-1 DAD
Comments: Handcrafted, 2-3/4" tall, Dated 1988
The gift box "For Dad" held new socks. Hey, these red and green ones are really warm! **Artist:** Bob Siedler
☐ Purchased 19___ Pd $_______ MIB NB DB BNT
☐ Want Orig. Ret. $7.00 **NB** $12 **MIB** Sec. Mkt. **$22-$25**

QX 415-1 DAUGHTER
Comments: Handcrafted, 3-5/8" tall, Dated 1988
A cookie girl has baked up a batch of even more cookies for "Daughter." **Artist:** Joyce Pattee
☐ Purchased 19___ Pd $_______ MIB NB DB BNT
☐ Want Orig. Ret. $5.75 **NB** $40 **MIB** Sec. Mkt. **$50-$55**

QX 416-1 FELIZ NAVIDAD
Comments: Handcrafted, 2-7/8" tall
This little gray burro in a Mexican sombrero, carries a wrapped package and a bottle brush tree in his saddlebags. "Feliz Navidad!" **Artist:** Duane Unruh
☐ Purchased 19___ Pd $_______ MIB NB DB BNT
☐ Want Orig. Ret. $6.75 **NB** $15 **MIB** Sec. Mkt. **$25-$28**

QLX 720-4 FESTIVE FEEDER
Comments: Light, Handcrafted, 3" tall
These birds will be well-fed all winter with their bird feeder full of food. Red and green Christmas lights shine on the top.
Artist: Linda Sickman
☐ Purchased 19___ Pd $_______ MIB NB DB BNT
☐ Want Orig. Ret. $11.50 **NB** $32 **MIB** Sec. Mkt. **$48-$50**

QX 374-1 FIFTY YEARS TOGETHER
Comments: Acrylic, 3-1/8" tall, Dated Christmas 1988
"50 Years Together" caption is stamped in gold foil. Brass frame accents the design.
☐ Purchased 19___ Pd $_______ MIB NB DB BNT
☐ Want Orig. Ret. $6.75 **NB** $12 **MIB** Sec. Mkt. **$18-$21**

QX 419-1 FILLED WITH FUDGE
Comments: Handcrafted, 3-3/8" tall
A little mouse has found the tastiest treat in the house. It's a cone filled with chocolate fudge. **Artist:** Ed Seale
☐ Purchased 19___ Pd $_______ MIB NB DB BNT
☐ Want Orig. Ret. $4.75 **NB** $12 **MIB** Sec. Mkt. **$28-$30**

QX 373-1 FIRST CHRISTMAS TOGETHER
Comments: Acrylic, 4" tall, Dated 1988
A brass frame and art nouveau design make this acrylic ornament a lovely ornament. Caption: "Our First Christmas Together." **Artist:** LaDene Votruba
☐ Purchased 19___ Pd $_______ MIB NB DB BNT
☐ Want Orig. Ret. $6.75 **NB** $20 **MIB** Sec. Mkt. **$25-$28**

QX 274-1 FIRST CHRISTMAS TOGETHER
Comments: Sparkling Glass Ball, 2-7/8" dia., Dated 1988
Two cardinals against a snow-covered scene.
Caption: "Beauty Is Found In Many Things, But Most Of All In Love. Our First Christmas Together."
☐ Purchased 19___ Pd $_______ MIB NB DB BNT
☐ Want Orig. Ret. $4.75 **NB** $12 **MIB** Sec. Mkt. **$20-$22**

QX 489-4 FIRST CHRISTMAS TOGETHER
Comments: Handcrafted, 3-1/4" tall, Dated 1988
Two bears with heart-shaped gifts behind their backs stand in the center of an open heart. Caption: "First Christmas Together."
Artist: Sharon Pike
☐ Purchased 19___ Pd $_______ MIB NB DB BNT
☐ Want Orig. Ret. $9.00 **NB** $14 **MIB** Sec. Mkt. **$22-$25**

QLX 702-7 FIRST CHRISTMAS TOGETHER
Comments: Lighted, Handcrafted, 3" tall, Dated 1988
Two white mice sit in the center of a colorful candy wreath.
Caption: "Our First Christmas Together 1988."
☐ Purchased 19___ Pd $_______ MIB NB DB BNT
☐ Want Orig. Ret. $12.00 **NB** $22 **MIB** Sec. Mkt. **$38-$40**

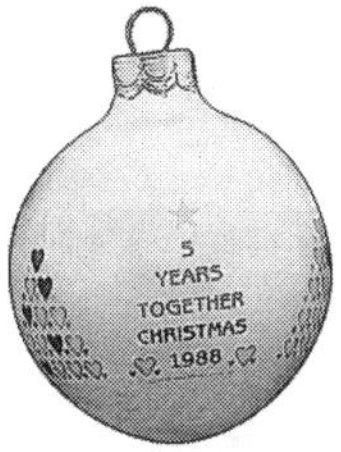

QX 274-4 FIVE YEARS TOGETHER
Comments: White Glass Ball, 2-7/8" dia.
Dated Christmas 1988. Five Christmas trees, composed of green and red hearts, circle the ball. Caption: "5 Years Together."
Artist: Diana McGehee
☐ Purchased 19___ Pd $_______ MIB NB DB BNT
☐ Want Orig. Ret. $4.75 **NB** $10 **MIB** Sec. Mkt. **$20-$22**

QX 279-4 FROM OUR HOME TO YOURS
Comments: Sparkling Glass Ball, 2-7/8" dia., Dated 1988
Homes and happy snow-people are alternated around this sparkling ball. Caption: "Merry Christmas From Our Home To Yours." **Artist:** Joyce Pattee
☐ Purchased 19___ Pd $_______ MIB NB DB BNT
☐ Want Orig. Ret. $4.75 **NB** $10 **MIB** Sec. Mkt. **$15-$18**

QX 403-1 FROSTY FRIENDS
Comments: **Ninth in Series,** Handcrafted, 3-3/8" tall
Dated 1988. Our Arctic friends are having fun decorating the North Pole with red fabric ribbon.
Artist: Ed Seale
☐ Purchased 19___ Pd $_______ MIB NB DB BNT
☐ Want Orig. Ret. $8.75 **NB** $40 **MIB** Sec. Mkt. **$60-$65**

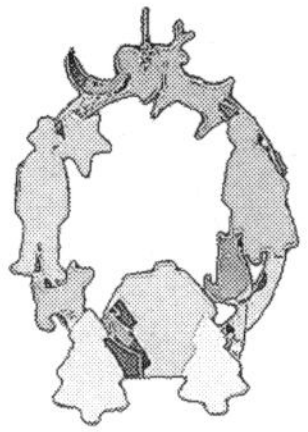

QX 492-1 GLOWING WREATH
Comments: Dimensional Brass, 3-1/2" tall
Starting with a simple brass circle, a house and a heart, nine additional design shapes are added to achieve a layered appearance. **Artist:** Joyce Pattee
☐ Purchased 19___ Pd $_______ MIB NB DB BNT
☐ Want Orig. Ret. $6.00 **NB** $10 **MIB** Sec. Mkt. **$15-$17**

QX 417-4 GO FOR THE GOLD
Comments: Handcrafted, 3-1/2" tall, Dated 1988
Santa's dressed in a red, white and blue jogging suit and he's carrying the Olympic torch. Look for the '96 Summer Olympic ornaments to debut. **Artist:** Bob Siedler
☐ Purchased 19___ Pd $_______ MIB NB DB BNT
☐ Want Orig. Ret. $8.00 **NB** $14 **MIB** Sec. Mkt. **$25-$28**

QX 278-4 GODCHILD
Comments: Gold Glass Ball, 2-7/8" dia., Dated 1988
Three children are caroling, carrying a bell, a song book and an old-fashioned lamp. Caption: "A Godchild Brings Joy To The World... Especially At Christmas."
☐ Purchased 19___ Pd $_______ MIB NB DB BNT
☐ Want Orig. Ret. $4.75 **NB** $12 **MIB** Sec. Mkt. **$18-$20**

QX 476-4 GOIN' CROSS COUNTRY
Comments: Handcrafted, 3-1/4" tall
This white bear, dressed in a bright red hat and colorful muffler, is traveling via his red skis.
Artist: Linda Sickman
☐ Purchased 19___ Pd $_______ MIB NB DB BNT
☐ Want Orig. Ret. $8.50 **NB** $14 **MIB** Sec. Mkt. **$22-$25**

QX 479-4 GONE FISHING
Comments: Handcrafted, 2-1/2" tall
Santa caught a blue fish. He's dressed in wading bibs and carries a flexible rod with nylon line. Price down from 1995.
Artist: Bob Siedler
☐ Purchased 19___ Pd $_______ MIB NB DB BNT
☐ Want Orig. Ret. $5.00 **NB** $12.50 **MIB** Sec. Mkt. **$17-$22**

QX 277-4 GRANDDAUGHTER
Comments: Red/White Glass Ball, 2-7/8" dia.
Dated Christmas 1988. An angel catches a star.
Caption: "A Granddaughter Is A Delight To Love!"
Artist: LaDene Votruba
☐ Purchased 19___ Pd $_______ MIB NB DB BNT
☐ Want Orig. Ret. $4.75 **NB** $12 **MIB** Sec. Mkt. **$20-$22**

QX 276-4 GRANDMOTHER
Comments: Gold Glass Ball, 2-7/8" dia., Dated 1988
With the look of crewel embroidery, the caption is bordered with the partridge and pear tree theme.
Caption: "Grandmother Makes Love A Christmas Tradition."
☐ Purchased 19___ Pd $_______ MIB NB DB BNT
☐ Want Orig. Ret. $4.75 **NB** $10 **MIB** Sec. Mkt. **$15-$18**

QX 277-1 GRANDPARENTS
Comments: Red Glass Ball, 2-7/8" dia., Dated Christmas 1988
A cozy Christmas scene with a tree and a cat napping on a rug. Caption: "Grandparents Are The Heart Of So Many Treasured Memories." **Artist:** Joyce Pattee
☐ Purchased 19___ Pd $_______ MIB NB DB BNT
☐ Want Orig. Ret. $4.75 **NB** $8 **MIB** Sec. Mkt. **$16-$18**

QX 278-1 GRANDSON
Comments: Green/White Glass Ball, 2-7/8" tall, Dated 1988
Santa's catching snowflakes! Caption: "A Grandson Makes Christmas Merry!" **Artist:** LaDene Votruba
☐ Purchased 19___ Pd $_______ MIB NB DB BNT
☐ Want Orig. Ret. $4.75 **NB** $10 **MIB** Sec. Mkt. **$18-$20**

QX 375-4 GRATITUDE
Comments: Acrylic, 3-3/8" tall, Dated 1988
A snow-covered evergreen tree and snowflakes. Caption: "Christmas Fills Our Hearts With Thoughts Of Those Who Care."
Artist: Joyce Pattee
☐ Purchased 19___ Pd $_______ MIB NB DB BNT
☐ Want Orig. Ret. $6.00 **NB** $6 **MIB** Sec. Mkt. **$12-$14**

QX 471-4 HAPPY HOLIDATA
Comments: Handcrafted, 1-1/2" tall
Artist: Bob Siedler
☐ Purchased 19___ Pd $_______ MIB NB DB BNT
☐ Want Orig. Ret. $6.50 **NB** $18 **MIB** Sec. Mkt. **$25-$30**

QLX 711-4 HEAVENLY GLOW
Comments: Light, Brass, 3" tall
A delicately etched brass angel holds a Christmas star. Lighted from within. **Artist:** Michele Pyda-Sevcik
☐ Purchased 19___ Pd $_______ MIB NB DB BNT
☐ Want Orig. Ret. $11.75 **NB** $15 **MIB** Sec. Mkt. **$22-$25**

QX 400-1 HERE COMES SANTA: KRINGLE KOACH
Comments: **Tenth in Series**, Handcrafted, 3-1/4" tall
Dated 1988. Santa's delivering presents by way of the "Kringle Koach." He's wearing a ten-gallon hat and carrying a teddy bear passenger. **Artist:** Ken Crow
☐ Purchased 19___ Pd $_______ MIB NB DB BNT
☐ Want Orig. Ret. $14.00 **NB** $30 **MIB** Sec. Mkt. **$40-$46**

QX 422-1 HOE-HOE-HOE!
Comments: Handcrafted, 2-3/8" tall
Santa's all ready to work in the garden. He's wearing a red visor and green coveralls.
Artist: Bob Siedler
☐ Purchased 19___ Pd $_______ MIB NB DB BNT
☐ Want Orig. Ret. $5.00 **NB** $10 **MIB** Sec. Mkt. **$12-$18**

QX 406-4 HOLIDAY HEIRLOOM: KEEPSAKE CLUB
Comments: **Second in Series,** Limited Edition 34,600
Lead Crystal/Silver Plating, 3-1/2" tall, Dated 1988
The second crystal bell has two angels in flight holding a silver-plated star. Offered only to Club Members.
Artist: Duane Unruh
☐ Purchased 19___ Pd $_______ MIB NB DB BNT
☐ Want Orig. Ret. $25.00 **NB** $18 **MIB** Sec. Mkt. **$28-$32**

QX 423-1 HOLIDAY HERO
Comments: Handcrafted, 2-5/8" tall
S. Claus is number "1" on the football field and off. He's ready to pass the football for a win! **Artist:** Bob Siedler
☐ Purchased 19___ Pd $_______ MIB NB DB BNT
☐ Want Orig. Ret. $5.00 **NB** $10 **MIB** Sec. Mkt. **$12-$18**

QX 371-1 HOLIDAY WILDLIFE: PURPLE FINCH
Comments: **Seventh and Final in Series,** Wood, 2-1/2" dia.
Dated Christmas 1988. Caption: "Purple Finch, CARPODACUS PURPUREUS, Seventh In A Series, Wildlife Collection."
☐ Purchased 19___ Pd $_______ MIB NB DB BNT
☐ Want Orig. Ret. $7.75 **NB** $8.50 **MIB** Sec. Mkt. **$15-$24**

QX 469-7 IN A NUTSHELL
Comments: Handcrafted, 1-1/2" tall, Reissued from 1987.
Artist: Duane Unruh
☐ Purchased 19___ Pd $_______ MIB NB DB BNT
☐ Want Orig. Ret. $5.50 **NB** $10 **MIB** Sec. Mkt. **$18-$28**

QX 477-4 JINGLE BELL CLOWN
Comments: Musical/Handcrafted, 3" tall, Dated 1988
This happy clown likes to ring his brass jingle bell as he rides along in his reindeer cart. Tune: "Jingle Bells."
☐ Purchased 19___ Pd $_______ MIB NB DB BNT
☐ Want Orig. Ret. $15.00 **NB** $14 **MIB** Sec. Mkt. **$22-$25**

QX 473-1 JOLLY WALRUS
Comments: Handcrafted, 1-7/8" tall
This cute walrus has quite a toothy smile. He has a green foil wreath tied with red satin ribbon.
Artist: Anita Marra Rogers
☐ Purchased 19___ Pd $_______ MIB NB DB BNT
☐ Want Orig. Ret. $4.50 **NB** $8 **MIB** Sec. Mkt. **$20-$24**

QX 486-1 KISS THE CLAUS
Comments: Handcrafted, 2-3/4" tall
Santa's apron says to "Kiss the Claus." But he's serving up cheeseburgers right now.
Artist: Duane Unruh
☐ Purchased 19___ Pd $_______ MIB NB DB BNT
☐ Want Orig. Ret. $5.00 **NB** $10 **MIB** Sec. Mkt. **$12-$15**

QLX 716-4 KITTY CAPERS
Comments: Blinking Lights, Handcrafted, 1-1/2" tall
Kitty has gotten himself all tangled up in the Christmas tree lights. Fastens with a clip. **Artist:** Sharon Pike
☐ Purchased 19___ Pd $_______ MIB NB DB BNT
☐ Want Orig. Ret. $13.00 **NB** $22 **MIB** Sec. Mkt. **$42-$45**

QX 495-1 KRINGLE MOON
Comments: Handcrafted, 3-3/8" tall
Santa has been sculpted in the shape of a quarter moon. He's napping away with a brass jingle bell at the top of his hat.
Artist: Anita Marra Rogers
☐ Purchased 19___ Pd $_______ MIB NB DB BNT
☐ Want Orig. Ret. $5.50 **NB** $22 **MIB** Sec. Mkt. **$30-$35**

QX 421-4 KRINGLE PORTRAIT
Comments: Handcrafted, 3-1/4" tall
Santa's face and beard is circled by a wreath. His sleigh, along with a tree and teddy bear are sculpted on the back. Some color differences have been noted.
☐ Purchased 19___ Pd $_______ MIB NB DB BNT
☐ Want Orig. Ret. $7.50 **NB** $18 **MIB** Sec. Mkt. **$24-$28**

QX 495-4 KRINGLE TREE
Comments: Handcrafted, 3-3/8" tall
Resembling an Old World carving is the Kringle Tree -- it's Santa in green, sculpted to look like a Christmas tree!
☐ Purchased 19___ Pd $_______ MIB NB DB BNT
☐ Want Orig. Ret. $6.50 **NB** $32 **MIB** Sec. Mkt. **$38-$40**

QLX 701-7 KRINGLE'S TOY SHOP
Comments: Open House Ornament, Light/Motion, Handcrafted Reissued in 1989. Two children stand outside the large picture window and watch Santa's elves making the toys he will deliver on Christmas Eve. **Artist:** Ed Seale
☐ Purchased 19___ Pd $_______ MIB NB DB BNT
☐ Want Orig. Ret. $24.50 **NB** $45 **MIB** Sec. Mkt. **$55-$60**

QLX 718-1 LAST-MINUTE HUG
Comments: Light and Motion, Handcrafted, 3-1/2" tall
As Santa heads out one door for his annual flight, Mrs. Claus hurries out the other to give him one last hug.
Artist: Duane Unruh
☐ Purchased 19___ Pd $_______ MIB NB DB BNT
☐ Want Orig. Ret. $22.00 **NB** $36 **MIB** Sec. Mkt. **$48-$52**

QX 408-1 LITTLE JACK HORNER
Comments: Handcrafted, 2-1/2" tall
The nursery rhyme says, "He stuck in his thumb and pulled out a plum." His name is on his hat.
Artist: Bob Siedler
☐ Purchased 19___ Pd $_______ MIB NB DB BNT
☐ Want Orig. Ret. $8.00 **NB** $15 **MIB** Sec. Mkt. **$20-$22**

QX 374-4 LOVE FILLS THE HEART
Comments: Acrylic, 3" tall
Two birds perch on the border of holly leaves and berries. Caption: "Love Fills The Heart Forever."
Artist: LaDene Votruba
☐ Purchased 19___ Pd $_______ MIB NB DB BNT
☐ Want Orig. Ret. $6.00 **NB** $12 **MIB** Sec. Mkt. **$20-$22**

QX 275-4 LOVE GROWS
Comments: Chrome Glass Ball, 2-7/8" dia.
Dated Christmas 1988. To achieve a rich lacquered look, bright large blossoms have been printed against a black background. Caption: "Patiently, Joyfully, Beautifully, Love Grows."
☐ Purchased 19___ Pd $_______ MIB NB DB BNT
☐ Want Orig. Ret. $4.75 **NB** $14 **MIB** Sec. Mkt. **$22-$25**

QX 486-4 LOVE SANTA
Comments: Handcrafted, 2-1/2" tall
Santa is in great form as he volleys the tennis ball (pom-pom) back and forth.
Artist: Bob Siedler
☐ Purchased 19___ Pd $_______ MIB NB DB BNT
☐ Want Orig. Ret. $5.00 **NB** $10 **MIB** Sec. Mkt. **$18-$20**

QX 493-4 LOVING BEAR
Comments: Handcrafted, 3-1/4" tall
A teddy bear with his heart showing on his fur twirls inside a wreath of hearts. Handpainted.
Artist: Anita Marra Rogers
☐ Purchased 19___ Pd $_______ MIB NB DB BNT
☐ Want Orig. Ret. $4.75 **NB** $6 **MIB** Sec. Mkt. **$12-$18**

QX 407-4 MARY'S ANGELS: BUTTERCUP
Comments: ***FIRST IN SERIES***, 2-1/4" tall
Redheaded Buttercup is dressed in yellow and is napping on a frosted acrylic cloud. **Artist:** Robert Chad
☐ Purchased 19___ Pd $_______ MIB NB DB BNT
☐ Want Orig. Ret. $5.00 **NB** $25 **MIB** Sec. Mkt. **$40-$45**

QX 423-4 MERRY-MINT UNICORN
Comments: Hand-Painted Fine Porcelain, 3-3/4" tall
This lovely white unicorn has a red and white striped horn and is balancing on a peppermint candy.
Artist: Anita Marra Rogers
☐ Purchased 19___ Pd $_______ MIB NB DB BNT
☐ Want Orig. Ret. $8.50 **NB** $12 **MIB** Sec. Mkt. **$20-$23**

QX 410-4 MIDNIGHT SNACK
Comments: Handcrafted, 2-1/2" tall
Donuts make the perfect nighttime snack and this little white mouse agrees as he nibbles away.
Artist: Bob Siedler
☐ Purchased 19___ Pd $_______ MIB NB DB BNT
☐ Want Orig. Ret. $6.00 **NB** $15 **MIB** Sec. Mkt. **$18-$22**

QX 403-4 MINIATURE CRECHE
Comments: **Fourth in Series,** Acrylic, 2-3/4" tall
The Holy Family is depicted in frosted acrylic which has been set in a clear acrylic star. The edges of the star are faceted and painted gold. Spring sales of $10 reported.
Artist: Duane Unruh
☐ Purchased 19___ Pd $_______ MIB NB DB BNT
☐ Want Orig. Ret. $8.50 **NB** $8.50 **MIB** Sec. Mkt. **$15-$20**

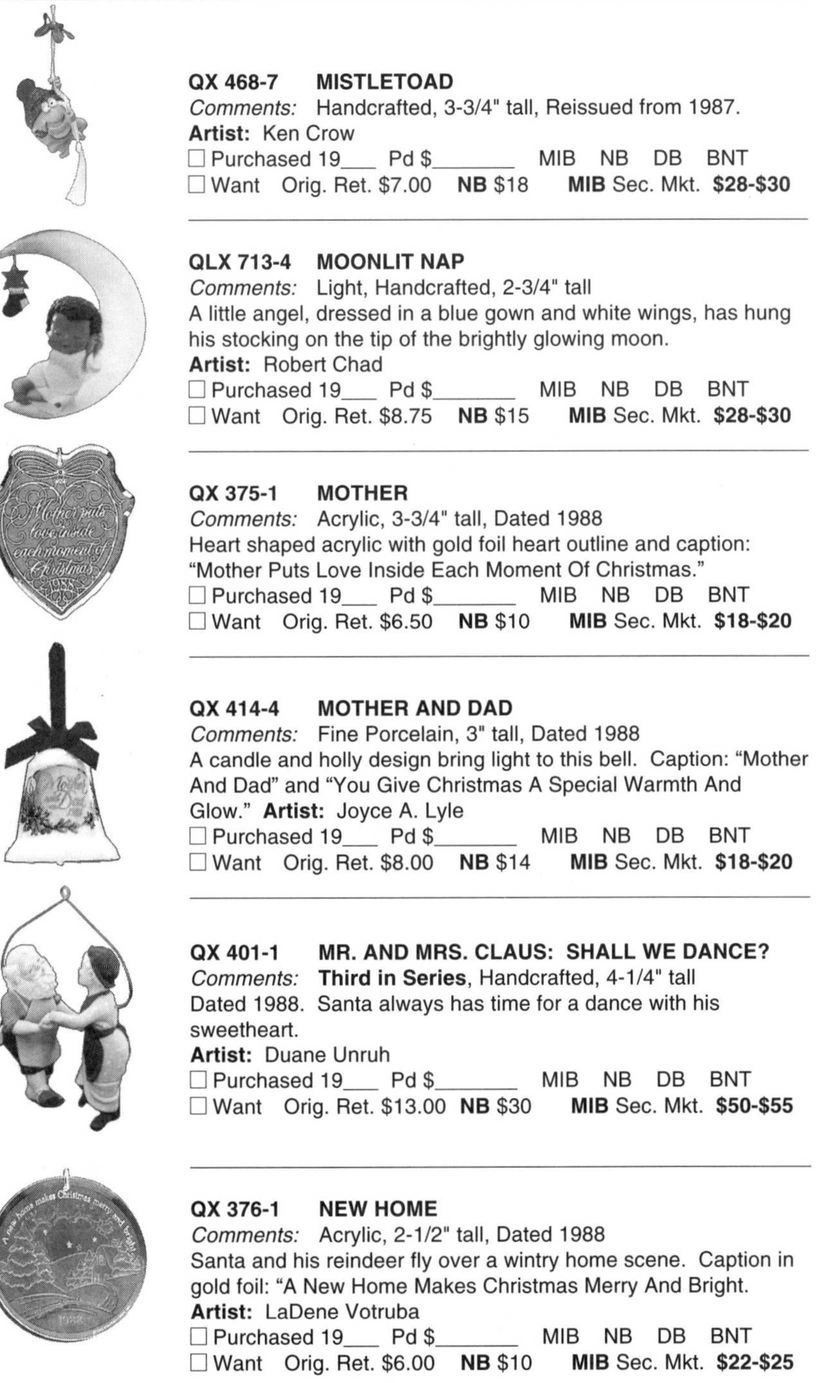

QX 468-7 MISTLETOAD
Comments: Handcrafted, 3-3/4" tall, Reissued from 1987.
Artist: Ken Crow
☐ Purchased 19___ Pd $_______ MIB NB DB BNT
☐ Want Orig. Ret. $7.00 **NB** $18 **MIB** Sec. Mkt. **$28-$30**

QLX 713-4 MOONLIT NAP
Comments: Light, Handcrafted, 2-3/4" tall
A little angel, dressed in a blue gown and white wings, has hung his stocking on the tip of the brightly glowing moon.
Artist: Robert Chad
☐ Purchased 19___ Pd $_______ MIB NB DB BNT
☐ Want Orig. Ret. $8.75 **NB** $15 **MIB** Sec. Mkt. **$28-$30**

QX 375-1 MOTHER
Comments: Acrylic, 3-3/4" tall, Dated 1988
Heart shaped acrylic with gold foil heart outline and caption: "Mother Puts Love Inside Each Moment Of Christmas."
☐ Purchased 19___ Pd $_______ MIB NB DB BNT
☐ Want Orig. Ret. $6.50 **NB** $10 **MIB** Sec. Mkt. **$18-$20**

QX 414-4 MOTHER AND DAD
Comments: Fine Porcelain, 3" tall, Dated 1988
A candle and holly design bring light to this bell. Caption: "Mother And Dad" and "You Give Christmas A Special Warmth And Glow." **Artist:** Joyce A. Lyle
☐ Purchased 19___ Pd $_______ MIB NB DB BNT
☐ Want Orig. Ret. $8.00 **NB** $14 **MIB** Sec. Mkt. **$18-$20**

QX 401-1 MR. AND MRS. CLAUS: SHALL WE DANCE?
Comments: **Third in Series**, Handcrafted, 4-1/4" tall
Dated 1988. Santa always has time for a dance with his sweetheart.
Artist: Duane Unruh
☐ Purchased 19___ Pd $_______ MIB NB DB BNT
☐ Want Orig. Ret. $13.00 **NB** $30 **MIB** Sec. Mkt. **$50-$55**

QX 376-1 NEW HOME
Comments: Acrylic, 2-1/2" tall, Dated 1988
Santa and his reindeer fly over a wintry home scene. Caption in gold foil: "A New Home Makes Christmas Merry And Bright.
Artist: LaDene Votruba
☐ Purchased 19___ Pd $_______ MIB NB DB BNT
☐ Want Orig. Ret. $6.00 **NB** $10 **MIB** Sec. Mkt. **$22-$25**

QX 422-4 NICK THE KICK
Comments: Handcrafted, 2-1/4" tall
Santa's playing soccer for the "Blizzard" team. The number on the back of his shirt is "OO." **Artist:** Bob Siedler
☐ Purchased 19___ Pd $_______ MIB NB DB BNT
☐ Want Orig. Ret. $5.00 **NB** $12 **MIB** Sec. Mkt. **$18-$20**

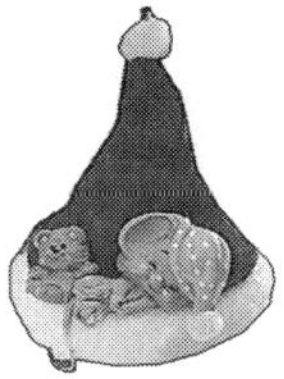

QX 451-7 NIGHT BEFORE CHRISTMAS
Comments: Handcrafted, 2-3/4" tall. Reissued from 1987.
Artist: Ken Crow
☐ Purchased 19___ Pd $_______ MIB NB DB BNT
☐ Want Orig. Ret. $6.50 **NB** $10 **MIB** Sec. Mkt. **$20-$22**

QX 490-4 NOAH'S ARK
Comments: Pressed Tin, 2-1/8" tall
Similar to antique pull toys with wheels that turn and a metallic pull cord. This vessel is also filled with passengers. Tin ornaments are popular. **Artist:** Linda Sickman
☐ Purchased 19___ Pd $_______ MIB NB DB BNT
☐ Want Orig. Ret. $8.50 **NB** $22 **MIB** Sec. Mkt. **$38-$40**

QX 273-1 NORMAN ROCKWELL: CHRISTMAS SCENES
Comments: White Glass Ball, 2-7/8" dia., Dated 1988
Caption: "Christmas.. The Season That Blesses The World" and "Christmas...The Season That Touches The Heart. From the Norman Rockwell Collection." **Artist:** Joyce A. Lyle
☐ Purchased 19___ Pd $_______ MIB NB DB BNT
☐ Want Orig. Ret. $4.75 **NB** $12 **MIB** Sec. Mkt. **$22-$24**

QX 370-4 NORMAN ROCKWELL: AND TO ALL A GOOD NIGHT
Comments: **Ninth and Final in Series,** Red Cameo, 3-1/4" dia.
Caption: "And To All A Good Night, Ninth In A Series, Christmas 1988, The Norman Rockwell Collection."
☐ Purchased 19___ Pd $_______ MIB NB DB BNT
☐ Want Orig. Ret. $7.75 **NB** $12 **MIB** Sec. Mkt. **$18-$20**

QX 401-4 NOSTALGIC HOUSES AND SHOPS: HALL BRO'S CARD SHOP
Comments: **Fifth in Series**, 4-1/4" tall, Dated 1988
An old-fashioned cash register sits on a counter in this card shop and a greeting card display is nearby. The second floor is an artist's studio. **Artist:** Donna Lee
☐ Purchased 19___ Pd $_______ MIB NB DB BNT
☐ Want Orig. Ret. $14.50 **NB** $35 **MIB** Sec. Mkt. **$50-$55**

QX 498-1 OLD-FASHIONED CHURCH
Comments: Wood, 4-1/2" tall
In American country motif, this small white church boasts a steeple with a cross at the top.
Artist: Linda Sickman
☐ Purchased 19___ Pd $_______ MIB NB DB BNT
☐ Want Orig. Ret. $4.00 **NB** $10 **MIB** Sec. Mkt. **$18-$20**

QX 497-1 OLD-FASHIONED SCHOOLHOUSE
Comments: Wood, 3" tall
The little red schoolhouse is reminiscent of early country with its flag and bell tower.
Artist: Linda Sickman
☐ Purchased 19___ Pd $_______ MIB NB DB BNT
☐ Want Orig. Ret. $4.00 **NB** $10 **MIB** Sec. Mkt. **$18-$20**

QX 481-4 OREO®
Comments: Handcrafted, 1-7/8" dia.
Cookie opens to show frosting inside. Santa's face is part of the frosting. "Ho Ho Ho!"
Artist: Duane Unruh
☐ Purchased 19___ Pd $_______ MIB NB DB BNT
☐ Want Orig. Ret. $4.00 **NB** $8 **MIB** Sec. Mkt. **$14-$18**

QXC 580-4 OUR CLUBHOUSE: KEEPSAKE CLUB
Comments: Handcrafted, 2-1/2" tall, Dated 1988
"For Club Members Only" is a cute little clubhouse with a mouse inside. He's decorated the inside for Christmas. The Club logo is on the bottom. **Artist:** Bob Siedler
☐ Purchased 19___ Pd $_______ MIB NB DB BNT
☐ Want Price: Came with Club Membership of $15.00_______
NB $30 **MIB** Sec. Mkt. **$45-$48**

QX 455-9 "OWLIDAY" WISH
Comments: Handcrafted, 2" tall. Reissued from 1987.
Artist: Sharon Pike
☐ Purchased 19___ Pd $_______ MIB NB DB BNT
☐ Want Orig. Ret. $6.50 **NB** $10 **MIB** Sec. Mkt. **$20-$22**

QX 479-1 PAR FOR SANTA
Comments: Handcrafted, 2-5/8" tall
Santa's waiting for the St. Nick Open to begin and he's ready to tee off.
Artist: Bob Siedler
☐ Purchased 19___ Pd $_______ MIB NB DB BNT
☐ Want Orig. Ret. $5.00 **NB** $10 **MIB** Sec. Mkt. **$15-$20**

QLX 719-4 PARADE OF THE TOYS
Comments: Light and Motion, Handcrafted, 3-1/2" tall
The toys are on parade. A toy soldier pulls a red wagon with a jack-in-the-box which pops up and down, a doll pushes a baby carriage and three ducks all circle a lighted Christmas tree.
Artist: Linda Sickman
☐ Purchased 19___ Pd $_______ MIB NB DB BNT
☐ Want Orig. Ret. $24.50 **NB** $25 **MIB** Sec. Mkt. **$40-$50**

QX 476-1 PARTY LINE
Comments: Handcrafted, 1-3/4" tall
Two little raccoons have solved their communication problems; they've created their own telephone from two miniature cans of "Campbell's Chicken Noodle Soup." Campbell's Collectibles are very popular. **Artist:** Sharon Pike
☐ Purchased 19___ Pd $_______ MIB NB DB BNT
☐ Want Orig. Ret. $8.75 **NB** $18 **MIB** Sec. Mkt. **$28-$30**

QX 280-1 PEANUTS®
Comments: Blue Glass Ball, 2-7/8" dia., Dated Christmas 1988
Santa Snoopy flies across the sky on a sled loaded with gifts, and pulled by Woodstock and his friends.
☐ Purchased 19___ Pd $_______ MIB NB DB BNT
☐ Want Orig. Ret. $4.75 **NB** $18 **MIB** Sec. Mkt. **$28-$30**

QX 487-1 PEEK-A-BOO KITTIES
Comments: Handcrafted, 5" tall
While a kitten plays with a ball of yarn, two more peek out of the basket when you pull the string.
Artist: Ken Crow
☐ Purchased 19___ Pd $_______ MIB NB DB BNT
☐ Want Orig. Ret. $7.50 **NB** $15 **MIB** Sec. Mkt. **$20-$23**

QX 478-4 POLAR BOWLER
Comments: Handcrafted, 2-1/4" tall
Santa shows great form with his polished green bowling ball at the "North Pole Bowl."
Artist: Bob Siedler
☐ Purchased 19___ Pd $_______ MIB NB DB BNT
☐ Want Orig. Ret. $5.00 **NB** $10 **MIB** Sec. Mkt. **$15-$18**

QX 404-4 PORCELAIN BEAR
Comments: **Sixth in Series,** Fine Porcelain, 2-1/4" tall
This year's cinnamon bear is thrilled with his gift! It's wrapped inside a red heart-shaped box with a green bow.
Artist: Sharon Pike
☐ Purchased 19___ Pd $_______ MIB NB DB BNT
☐ Want Orig. Ret. $8.00 **NB** $22 **MIB** Sec. Mkt. **$32-$38**

QX 474-4 PURRFECT SNUGGLE
Comments: Handcrafted, 2" tall
A gray and white striped kitten has found a new friend - a brown teddy bear with a holiday bow.
Artist: Anita Marra Rogers
☐ Purchased 19___ Pd $_______ MIB NB DB BNT
☐ Want Orig. Ret. $6.25 **NB** $15 **MIB** Sec. Mkt. **$25-$28**

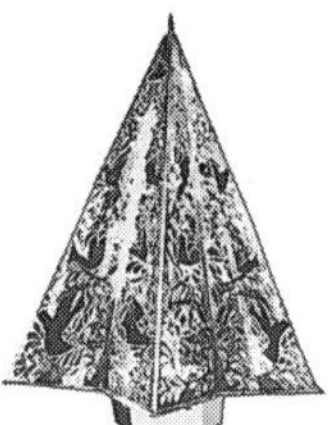

QLX 712-1 RADIANT TREE
Comments: Light, Brass, 3-1/4" tall
Ten cutout triangular panels form this brass tree which radiates light from all sides.
Artist: Joyce A. Lyle
☐ Purchased 19___ Pd $_______ MIB NB DB BNT
☐ Want Orig. Ret. $11.75 **NB** $12 **MIB** Sec. Mkt. **$18-$22**

QX 405-1 REINDEER CHAMPS: PRANCER
Comments: **Third in Series**, Handcrafted, 3-1/2" tall, Dated
"Prancer 88" is a basketball champion with his white sport shoes and shooting technique.
Artist: Bob Siedler
☐ Purchased 19___ Pd $_______ MIB NB DB BNT
☐ Want Orig. Ret. $7.50 **NB** $22 **MIB** Sec. Mkt. **$35-$38**

QX 452-7 REINDOGGY
Comments: Handcrafted,2-3/4" tall, Reissued from 1987.
Artist: Bob Siedler
☐ Purchased 19___ Pd $_______ MIB NB DB BNT
☐ Want Orig. Ret. $5.75 **NB** $20 **MIB** Sec. Mkt. **$30-$32**

QX 402-4 ROCKING HORSE
Comments: **Eighth in Series**, 3-1/4" wide, Dated 1988
A dapple gray pony is accented with red, green and gold trappings, and is seated on bright red and green rockers.
Artist: Linda Sickman
☐ Purchased 19___ Pd $_______ MIB NB DB BNT
☐ Want Orig. Ret. $10.75 **NB** $28 **MIB** Sec. Mkt. **$50-$55**

QX 491-1 SAILING! SAILING!
Comments: Pressed Tin, 2-7/8" tall
A red and white hoisted sail sets off this sailboat. A sailor enjoys the day as water laps against the sides of his boat.
Artist: Linda Sickman
☐ Purchased 19___ Pd $_______ MIB NB DB BNT
☐ Want Orig. Ret. $8.50 **NB** $16 **MIB** Sec. Mkt. **$25-$28**

QLX 719-1 SANTA & SPARKY: ON WITH THE SHOW
Comments: **Third in Series**, Light and Motion, Handcrafted, 4" Dated 1988. Santa steps forward and waves his magic wand and presto! A penguin pops out of his hat!
☐ Purchased 19___ Pd $_______ MIB NB DB BNT
☐ Want Orig. Ret. $19.50 **NB** $28 **MIB** Sec. Mkt. **$35-$42**

QX 483-4 SANTA FLAMINGO
Comments: Handcrafted, 5-1/2" tall
This pink flamingo stands tall among others due to his long legs (which really move). He wears a red fabric Santa hat with furry white trim. **Artist:** Michele Pyda-Sevcik
☐ Purchased 19___ Pd $_______ MIB NB DB BNT
☐ Want Orig. Ret. $4.75 **NB** $14 **MIB** Sec. Mkt. **$25-$28**

QX 492-4 SHINY SLEIGH
Comments: Dimensional Brass, 1-3/8" tall
The multidimensional design of Santa and his reindeer has been achieved by bending and shaping one continuous piece of brass. **Artist:** Joyce Pattee
☐ Purchased 19___ Pd $_______ MIB NB DB BNT
☐ Want Orig. Ret. $5.75 **NB** $12 **MIB** Sec. Mkt. **$18-$20**

QX 499-4 SISTER
Comments: Fine Porcelain Bell, 3" tall, Dated 1988
A little girl placing a star on the top of her Christmas tree. Caption: "Sisters Know So Many Ways To Brighten Up The Holidays!"
Artist: LaDene Votruba
☐ Purchased 19___ Pd $_______ MIB NB DB BNT
☐ Want Orig. Ret. $8.00 **NB** $12 **MIB** Sec. Mkt. **$24-$26**

QLX 720-1 SKATER'S WALTZ
Comments: Light and Motion, Handcrafted, 3-1/2" tall
Two Victorian couples ice skate around snow covered evergreens and a lamppost. **Artist:** Duane Unruh
☐ Purchased 19___ Pd $_______ MIB NB DB BNT
☐ Want Orig. Ret. $24.50 **NB** $35 **MIB** Sec. Mkt. **$55-$58**

QXC 580-1 SLEIGHFUL OF DREAMS: KEEPSAKE CLUB
Comments: Handcrafted, 2-1/8" tall, Dated 1988
Designed to resemble an old-fashioned wooden sleigh, this creation features bas relief designs of favorite past Keepsake ornaments. **Artist:** Linda Sickman
☐ Purchased 19___ Pd $_______ MIB NB DB BNT
☐ Want Orig. Ret. $8.00 **NB** $42 **MIB** Sec. Mkt. **$62-$65**

QX 472-4 SLIPPER SPANIEL
Comments: Handcrafted, 3" tall
This little brown and white puppy has fallen asleep in a red flocked slipper. **Artist:** Ken Crow
☐ Purchased 19___ Pd $_______ MIB NB DB BNT
☐ Want Orig. Ret. $4.25 **NB** $7 **MIB** Sec. Mkt. **$16-$18**

QX 474-1 SNOOPY® AND WOODSTOCK
Comments: Handcrafted, 2-3/8" tall
These two friends have tucked themselves into a red and white knit stocking which includes a bone with a green bow.
Artist: Duane Unruh
☐ Purchased 19___ Pd $_______ MIB NB DB BNT
☐ Want Orig. Ret. $6.00 **NB** $20 **MIB** Sec. Mkt. **$30-$35**

QX 475-1 SOFT LANDING
Comments: Handcrafted, 3" tall
If Santa falls down on his ice skates, he won't get hurt -- he's tied a green pillow to his waist.
Artist: Robert Chad
☐ Purchased 19___ Pd $_______ MIB NB DB BNT
☐ Want Orig. Ret. $7.00 **NB** $12 **MIB** Sec. Mkt. **$22-$24**

QX 415-4 SON
Comments: Handcrafted, 3-5/8" tall, Dated 1988
Similar to the Daughter ornament, a cookie boy is carrying a cookie sheet full of more cookies.
Artist: Joyce Pattee
☐ Purchased 19___ Pd $_______ MIB NB DB BNT
☐ Want Orig. Ret. $5.75 **NB** $31 **MIB** Sec. Mkt. **$38-$42**

QLX 711-1 SONG OF CHRISTMAS
Comments: Light, Acrylic, 3-1/2" tall
The beveled, faceted edge sets off the exquisite etched cardinal. Caption: "Song Of Christmas."
☐ Purchased 19___ Pd $_______ MIB NB DB BNT
☐ Want Orig. Ret. $8.50 **NB** $15 **MIB** Sec. Mkt. **$24-$26**

QX 493-1 SPARKLING TREE
Comments: Dimensional Brass, 3-3/8" tall
A brass Christmas tree is layered with brass silhouettes of a home, reindeer, doves, heart and star. There are also cutouts in the tree. **Artist:** Joyce Pattee
☐ Purchased 19___ Pd $_______ MIB NB DB BNT
☐ Want Orig. Ret. $6.00 **NB** $12 **MIB** Sec. Mkt. **$18-$20**

QX 276-1 SPIRIT OF CHRISTMAS
Comments: Chrome Glass Ball, 2-7/8" dia., Christmas 1988
Silhouettes of children from other nations circle a teardrop ball. Caption: "Love Begins Changing The World By Awakening One Heart At A Time." **Artist:** Joyce A. Lyle
☐ Purchased 19___ Pd $_______ MIB NB DB BNT
☐ Want Orig. Ret. $4.75 **NB** $10 **MIB** Sec. Mkt. **$18-$20**

QX 475-4 SQUEAKY CLEAN
Comments: Handcrafted, 2-3/8" tall
This little mouse is sure to be clean for Christmas as he bathes in his walnut shell bath and shower.
Artist: Sharon Pike
☐ Purchased 19___ Pd $_______ MIB NB DB BNT
☐ Want Orig. Ret. $6.75 **NB** $15 **MIB** Sec. Mkt. **$18-$24**

QX 453-9 ST. LOUIE NICK
Comments: Handcrafted, 3-1/2" tall
Reissued from 1987.
Artist: Peter Dutkin
☐ Purchased 19___ Pd $_______ MIB NB DB BNT
☐ Want Orig. Ret. $7.75 **NB** $12 **MIB** Sec. Mkt. **$28-$30**

QX 494-4 STARRY ANGEL
Comments: Handcrafted, 2-7/8" tall
The white-robed angel twirls inside an open star decorated with red and green design. **Artist:** Anita Marra Rogers
☐ Purchased 19___ Pd $_______ MIB NB DB BNT
☐ Want Orig. Ret. $4.75 **NB** $10 **MIB** Sec. Mkt. **$18-$20**

QX 418-4 SWEET STAR
Comments: Handcrafted, 1-3/4" tall
A little squirrel nibbles the cherry he found on top of the star-shaped cookie. Clips on the tree.
Artist: Ed Seale
☐ Purchased 19___ Pd $_______ MIB NB DB BNT
☐ Want Orig. Ret. $5.00 **NB** $14 **MIB** Sec. Mkt. **$24-$26**

QX 490-1 SWEETHEART
Comments: Handcrafted, 3-3/8" tall, Dated Christmas 1988
A swan sleigh in pearly colors holds a single rose inside. May be personalized on the bottom: "For __, Love ___." Caption: "Sweetheart." Easily found. **Artist:** Duane Unruh
☐ Purchased 19___ Pd $_______ MIB NB DB BNT
☐ Want Orig. Ret. $9.75 **NB** $10 **MIB** Sec. Mkt. **$15-$18**

QX 417-1 TEACHER
Comments: Handcrafted, 2-1/4" tall, Dated 1988
This flocked bunny has created a card for his favorite teacher at Christmas. Caption: "For Teacher" and "Merry Christmas 1988."
Artist: Sharon Pike
☐ Purchased 19___ Pd $_______ MIB NB DB BNT
☐ Want Orig. Ret. $6.25 **NB** $10 **MIB** Sec. Mkt. **$18-$20**

QX 418-1 TEENY TASTER
Comments: Handcrafted, 4-3/8" tall. Reissued in 1989
This cute little chipmunk can't wait until everything is done-- he's got a big red spoonful of batter to taste now!
Artist: Ed Seale
☐ Purchased 19___ Pd $_______ MIB NB DB BNT
☐ Want Orig. Ret. $4.75 **NB** $12 **MIB** Sec. Mkt. **$16-$20**

QX 275-1 TEN YEARS TOGETHER
Comments: White Glass Ball, 2-7/8" dia.
Dated Christmas 1988. A gentle snowfall gives a peaceful appearance as two deer stand on a hill. Caption: "Love Warms Every Moment, Brightens Every Day. Ten Years Together."
☐ Purchased 19___ Pd $_______ MIB NB DB BNT
☐ Want Orig. Ret. $4.75 **NB** $10 **MIB** Sec. Mkt. **$15-$18**

QX 405-4 THIMBLE SNOWMAN
Comments: **Eleventh in Series,** 2-3/8" tall
The silvery thimble makes a perfect hat for this jolly snowman with red scarf and green mittens.
Artist: Bob Siedler
☐ Purchased 19___ Pd $_______ MIB NB DB BNT
☐ Want Orig. Ret. $5.75 **NB** $10 **MIB** Sec. Mkt. **$18-$24**

QX 400-4 TIN LOCOMOTIVE
Comments: **Seventh in Series**, Pressed Tin, 3" tall
Dated 1988. This bright blue locomotive features a pierced tin cowcatcher.
Artist: Linda Sickman
☐ Purchased 19___ Pd $_______ MIB NB DB BNT
☐ Want Orig. Ret. $14.75 **NB** $28 **MIB** Sec. Mkt. **$48-$55**

QX 473-4 TOWN CRIER, THE
Comments: Handcrafted, 2-1/4" tall
This little rabbit, dressed in Colonial style, rings his bell and makes his announcement: "Hear Ye! Hear Ye! Christmas Joy Is Always Near Ye!" **Artist:** Ed Seale
☐ Purchased 19___ Pd $_______ MIB NB DB BNT
☐ Want Orig. Ret. $5.50 **NB** $10 **MIB** Sec. Mkt. **$18-$22**

QX 477-1 TRAVELS WITH SANTA
Comments: Handcrafted, 2" tall
Santa's license plate proclaims "B MERRY" to all who pass him in his shiny travel trailer. Look through the picture window and you'll see his TV and bottlebrush Christmas tree.
Artist: Donna Lee
☐ Purchased 19___ Pd $_______ MIB NB DB BNT
☐ Want Orig. Ret. $10.00 **NB** $18 **MIB** Sec. Mkt. **$32-$38**

QLX 710-4 TREE OF FRIENDSHIP
Comments: Lighted Acrylic, 4-1/4" tall
This tree-shaped acrylic has beveled edges and etched snowflakes and caption: "Friends Decorate The Holiday With Love."
☐ Purchased 19___ Pd $_______ MIB NB DB BNT
☐ Want Orig. Ret. $8.50 **NB** $12 **MIB** Sec. Mkt. **$22-$24**

QX 459-7 TREETOP DREAMS
Comments: Handcrafted, 3" tall
Reissued from 1987. **Artist:** Ed Seale
☐ Purchased 19___ Pd $_______ MIB NB DB BNT
☐ Want Orig. Ret. $6.75 **NB** $15 **MIB** Sec. Mkt. **$28-$30**

QX 371-4 TWELVE DAYS OF CHRISTMAS: FIVE GOLDEN RINGS
Comments: **Fifth in Series**, Acrylic, 3" tall, Dated 1988
With gold foil captions, a design of five rings is etched into this quatrefoil designed acrylic.
Artist: Sharon Pike
☐ Purchased 19___ Pd $_______ MIB NB DB BNT
☐ Want Orig. Ret. $6.50 **NB** $15 **MIB** Sec. Mkt. **$22-$25**

QX 373-4 TWENTY-FIVE YEARS TOGETHER
Comments: Acrylic, 3-1/8" tall, Dated Christmas 1988
The caption, "25 Years Together" is stamped in silver foil on a silver bezeled acrylic ornament.
Artist: Joyce Pattee
☐ Purchased 19___ Pd $_______ MIB NB DB BNT
☐ Want Orig. Ret. $6.75 **NB** $12 **MIB** Sec. Mkt. **$18-$20**

QX 488-4 UNCLE SAM NUTCRACKER
Comments: Handcrafted, 5-1/4" tall, Dated 1988
When you lift Uncle Sam's ponytail, his mouth moves in real nutcracker fashion. **Artist:** Donna Lee
☐ Purchased 19___ Pd $_______ MIB NB DB BNT
☐ Want Orig. Ret. $7.00
NB $14 **MIB** Sec. Mkt. **$28-$32**

QX 409-1 VERY STRAWBEARY
Comments: Handcrafted, 2-1/4" tall
This flocked teddy bear has a special treat - a strawberry snow-cone. Includes the artist's initials, "PDII"
Artist: Peter Dutkin
☐ Purchased 19___ Pd $_______ MIB NB DB BNT
☐ Want Orig. Ret. $4.75 **NB** $8 **MIB** Sec. Mkt. **$15-$18**

QX 402-1 WINDOWS OF THE WORLD: FRENCH
Comments: **Fourth in Series,** Handcrafted, 3-1/2" tall
Dated 1988. A little boy plays with his poodle near a fireplace waiting for Santa. A banner overhead proclaims "Joyeux Noel."
Artist: Donna Lee
☐ Purchased 19___ Pd $_______ MIB NB DB BNT
☐ Want Orig. Ret. $10.00 **NB** $14 **MIB** Sec. Mkt. **$22-$24**

QX 478-1 WINTER FUN
Comments: Handcrafted, 2" tall
Three children are racing downhill on a fast toboggan. One child faces backwards. **Artist:** Robert Chad
☐ Purchased 19___ Pd $_______ MIB NB DB BNT
☐ Want Orig. Ret. $8.50 **NB** $14 **MIB** Sec. Mkt. **$22-$26**

QX 411-4 WONDERFUL SANTACYCLE, THE
Comments: Special Edition, Handcrafted, 4-1/4" tall
Santa's fancy three-wheeler has replaced the normal seat and handlebars with a rocking horse! Includes golden spoked wheels. Easily found. **Artist:** Ed Seale
☐ Purchased 19___ Pd $_______ MIB NB DB BNT
☐ Want Orig. Ret. $22.50 **NB** $24 **MIB** Sec. Mkt. **$38-$42**

QX 404-1 WOOD CHILDHOOD: AIRPLANE
Comments: **Fifth in Series,** Wood, 1-5/8" tall, Dated 1988
This toy wooden airplane is painted red and green and has a cord to pull it along. **Artist:** Peter Dutkin
☐ Purchased 19___ Pd $_______ MIB NB DB BNT
☐ Want Orig. Ret. $7.50 **NB** $12 **MIB** Sec. Mkt. **$20-$22**

QX 416-4 YEAR TO REMEMBER
Comments: Ceramic, 3-3/4" tall, Dated 1988
The year date has been designed in ivory ceramic and incorporates holly, berries and an oval frame. It is tied with a red satin ribbon.
☐ Purchased 19___ Pd $_______ MIB NB DB BNT
☐ Want Orig. Ret. $7.00 **NB** $12 **MIB** Sec. Mkt. **$18-$20**

1989 Collection

QX 482-1 A KISS™ FROM SANTA
Comments: Handcrafted, 3-1/4" tall
Reissued from 1988. **Artist:** Duane Unruh
☐ Purchased 19___ Pd $_______ MIB NB DB BNT
☐ Want Orig. Ret. $4.50 **NB** $14 **MIB** Sec. Mkt. **$25-$28**

QLX 720-2 ANGEL MELODY
Comments: Lighted Acrylic, 5-7/16" tall
Etched and faceted to reflect the light, an angel in the center joyfully plays her trumpet.
Artist: LaDene Votruba
☐ Purchased 19___ Pd $_______ MIB NB DB BNT
☐ Want Orig. Ret. $9.50 **NB** $15 **MIB** Sec. Mkt. **$22-$24**

QLX 723-2 ANIMALS SPEAK, THE
Comments: Lighted Panorama Ball, 3-5/8" tall
The story of Christmas is illustrated. Caption: "The Animals Rejoiced And Spoke, The Star Shone Bright Above, For On This Day A Child Was Born To Touch The World With Love."
Artist: John Francis (Collin)
☐ Purchased 19___ Pd $_______ MIB NB DB BNT
☐ Want Orig. Ret. $13.50 **NB** $85 **MIB** Sec. Mkt. **$115-$125**

QX 452-5 BABY PARTRIDGE
Comments: Handcrafted, 2-3/4" tall
This sweet little bird attaches to your tree with a special clip.
Artist: John Francis (Collin)
☐ Purchased 19___ Pd $_______ MIB NB DB BNT
☐ Want Orig. Ret. $6.75 **NB** $10 **MIB** Sec. Mkt. **$14-$16**

QX 272-5 BABY'S FIRST CHRISTMAS: BOY
Comments: Blue Satin Ball, 2-7/8" dia., Dated 1989
Caption: "A New Baby Boy To Love. Baby's First Christmas."
Artist: LaDene Votruba
☐ Purchased 19___ Pd $_______ MIB NB DB BNT
☐ Want Orig. Ret. $4.75 **NB** $6 **MIB** Sec. Mkt. **$16-$18**

QX 272-2 BABY'S FIRST CHRISTMAS: GIRL
Comments: Pink Satin Ball, 2-7/8" dia., Dated 1989
Caption: "A New Baby Girl To Love. Baby's First Christmas."
Artist: LaDene Votruba
☐ Purchased 19___ Pd $_______ MIB NB DB BNT
☐ Want Orig. Ret. $4.75 **NB** $5 **MIB** Sec. Mkt. **$16-$18**

QX 381-5 BABY'S FIRST CHRISTMAS
Comments: Acrylic, 3-7/16" tall, Dated '89
An etched reindeer holds a stocking full of toys for baby. "Baby's First Christmas" in gold foil. **Artist:** John Francis (Collin)
☐ Purchased 19___ Pd $_______ MIB NB DB BNT
☐ Want Orig. Ret. $6.75 **NB** $9 **MIB** Sec. Mkt. **$16-$18**

QX 449-2 BABY'S FIRST CHRISTMAS
Comments: Handcrafted, 2-5/8" tall, Dated 1989
A flocked teddy bear wearing a green bow and red Santa cap holds a candy cane "1." Hat says "Baby's 1st Christmas."
Artist: Robert Chad
☐ Purchased 19___ Pd $_______ MIB NB DB BNT
☐ Want Orig. Ret. $7.25 **NB** $40 **MIB** Sec. Mkt. **$55-$60**

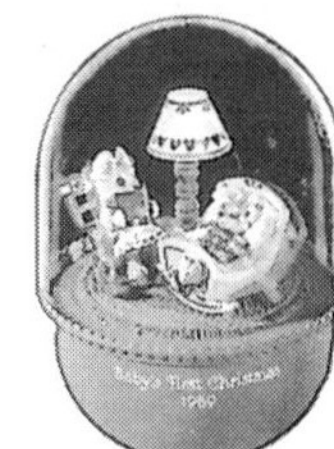

QLX 727-2 BABY'S FIRST CHRISTMAS
Comments: Light, Motion and Music, Handcrafted, 4-1/2" tall
Dated 1989. Mama mouse rocks baby's cradle as she rocks back and forth. Caption: "Baby's First Christmas" and "Christmas And Babies Fill A Home With Love." Plays *Brahms' Lullaby.*
Artist: Ed Seale
☐ Purchased 19___ Pd $_______ MIB NB DB BNT
☐ Want Orig. Ret. $30.00 **NB** $50 **MIB** Sec. Mkt. **$62-$65**

QX 468-2 BABY'S FIRST CHRISTMAS PHOTOHOLDER
Comments: Handcrafted, 3-3/4" tall, Dated 1989
Caption: "A New Star On The Family Tree!" says it all! Decorated with colorful toys. **Artist:** LaDene Votruba
☐ Purchased 19___ Pd $_______ MIB NB DB BNT
☐ Want Orig. Ret. $6.25 **NB** $20 **MIB** Sec. Mkt. **$40-$45**

QX 449-5 BABY'S SECOND CHRISTMAS
Comments: Handcrafted, 2-13/16" tall, Dated '89
"Baby's 2nd Christmas" is celebrated by a cute polar bear holding a red, white and green "2." **Artist:** John Francis (Collin)
☐ Purchased 19___ Pd $_______ MIB NB DB BNT
☐ Want Orig. Ret. $6.75 **NB** $20 **MIB** Sec. Mkt. **$28-$30**

QLX 721-5 BACKSTAGE BEAR
Comments: Lighted, Handcrafted, 3-3/8" tall
A teddy checks his appearance in the lighted mirror before a performance. Caption: "Beary Christmas!" and on the script: "Beary Christmas To All And To All A Good Night." A mold production sample was found at a garage sale!
Artist: Bob Siedler
☐ Purchased 19___ Pd $_______ MIB NB DB BNT
☐ Want Orig. Ret. $13.50 **NB** $15 **MIB** Sec. Mkt. **$32-$35**

QX 489-5 BALANCING ELF
Comments: Handcrafted, 4-3/8" tall
One of Santa's elves stands in the center of a big brass ring and holds two brass bells.
Artist: Robert Chad
☐ Purchased 19___ Pd $_______ MIB NB DB BNT
☐ Want Orig. Ret. $6.75 **NB** $16 **MIB** Sec. Mkt. **$22-$25**

QX 454-2 BEAR-I-TONE
Comments: Handcrafted, 2-1/4" tall
An adorable flocked bear plays a real metal triangle in the Christmas band.
Artist: Bob Siedler
☐ Purchased 19___ Pd $_______ MIB NB DB BNT
☐ Want Orig. Ret. $4.75 **NB** $10 **MIB** Sec. Mkt. **$16-$20**

QX 230-2 BETSEY CLARK: HOME FOR CHRISTMAS
Comments: **Fourth in Series**, 2-7/8" dia., Dated 1989
Betsey and her friends remember the animals outdoors at Christmas. Caption: "Fun And Friendship Are The Things The Christmas Season Always Brings!"
☐ Purchased 19___ Pd $_______ MIB NB DB BNT
☐ Want Orig. Ret. $5.00 **NB** $14 **MIB** Sec. Mkt. **$25-$30**

QX 445-2 BROTHER
Comments: Handcrafted, 3-1/4" tall, Dated 1989
A puppy has jumped into this red and white high-top tennis shoe and is playing with the green laces. Caption: "Brother" and "No One Else Can Fill Your Shoes!" **Artist:** Joyce A. Lyle
☐ Purchased 19___ Pd $_______ MIB NB DB BNT
☐ Want Orig. Ret. $7.25 **NB** $10 **MIB** Sec. Mkt. **$18-$20**

QLX 724-5 BUSY BEAVER
Comments: Light, Handcrafted, 2-7/8" tall
A beaver warms his paws over a fire in a barrel on a cold night. He's selling "Fresh Cut Trees."
Artist: Donna Lee
☐ Purchased 19___ Pd $_______ MIB NB DB BNT
☐ Want Orig. Ret. $17.50 **NB** $40 **MIB** Sec. Mkt. **$50-$55**

QX 411-2 CACTUS COWBOY
Comments: Handcrafted, 3-1/2" tall, Dated 1989
Not an easy ornament to locate. A smiling green cactus is wrapped up in red lights and wears a red cowboy hat. Not easy to locate. **Artist:** Peter Dutkin
☐ Purchased 19___ Pd $_______ MIB NB DB BNT
☐ Want Orig. Ret. $6.75 **NB** $30 **MIB** Sec. Mkt. **$40-$45**

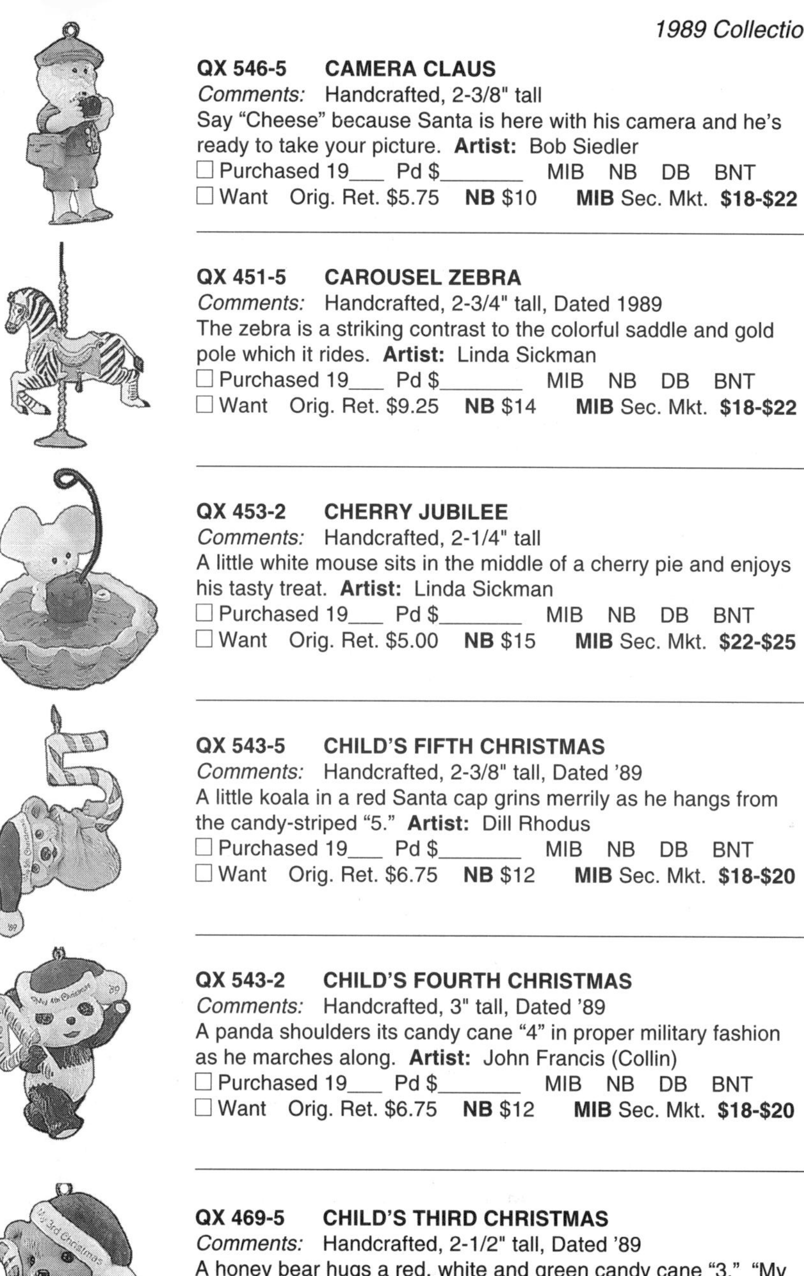

QX 546-5 CAMERA CLAUS
Comments: Handcrafted, 2-3/8" tall
Say "Cheese" because Santa is here with his camera and he's ready to take your picture. **Artist:** Bob Siedler
☐ Purchased 19___ Pd $_______ MIB NB DB BNT
☐ Want Orig. Ret. $5.75 **NB** $10 **MIB** Sec. Mkt. **$18-$22**

QX 451-5 CAROUSEL ZEBRA
Comments: Handcrafted, 2-3/4" tall, Dated 1989
The zebra is a striking contrast to the colorful saddle and gold pole which it rides. **Artist:** Linda Sickman
☐ Purchased 19___ Pd $_______ MIB NB DB BNT
☐ Want Orig. Ret. $9.25 **NB** $14 **MIB** Sec. Mkt. **$18-$22**

QX 453-2 CHERRY JUBILEE
Comments: Handcrafted, 2-1/4" tall
A little white mouse sits in the middle of a cherry pie and enjoys his tasty treat. **Artist:** Linda Sickman
☐ Purchased 19___ Pd $_______ MIB NB DB BNT
☐ Want Orig. Ret. $5.00 **NB** $15 **MIB** Sec. Mkt. **$22-$25**

QX 543-5 CHILD'S FIFTH CHRISTMAS
Comments: Handcrafted, 2-3/8" tall, Dated '89
A little koala in a red Santa cap grins merrily as he hangs from the candy-striped "5." **Artist:** Dill Rhodus
☐ Purchased 19___ Pd $_______ MIB NB DB BNT
☐ Want Orig. Ret. $6.75 **NB** $12 **MIB** Sec. Mkt. **$18-$20**

QX 543-2 CHILD'S FOURTH CHRISTMAS
Comments: Handcrafted, 3" tall, Dated '89
A panda shoulders its candy cane "4" in proper military fashion as he marches along. **Artist:** John Francis (Collin)
☐ Purchased 19___ Pd $_______ MIB NB DB BNT
☐ Want Orig. Ret. $6.75 **NB** $12 **MIB** Sec. Mkt. **$18-$20**

QX 469-5 CHILD'S THIRD CHRISTMAS
Comments: Handcrafted, 2-1/2" tall, Dated '89
A honey bear hugs a red, white and green candy cane "3." "My 3rd Christmas" is on his Santa hat.
Artist: John Francis (Collin)
☐ Purchased 19___ Pd $_______ MIB NB DB BNT
☐ Want Orig. Ret. $6.75 **NB** $15 **MIB** Sec. Mkt. **$20-$23**

QLX 722-5 CHRIS MOUSE COOKOUT
Comments: **Fifth in Series**, Handcrafted, 4-1/2" tall
Dated 1989. Chris, dressed in a red nightcap and green night shirt, toasts his marshmallow. **Artist:** Anita Marra Rogers
☐ Purchased 19___ Pd $_______ MIB NB DB BNT
☐ Want Orig. Ret. $9.50 **NB** $45 **MIB** Sec. Mkt. **$58-$62**

XPR 972-1 CHRISTMAS CAROUSEL HORSE COLLECTION: GINGER
Comments: Special Offer, Handcrafted/Brass, 3-3/16" tall
Dated 1989. Palomino with white mane and tail. Caption: "Ginger, 4 In A Collection Of Four." **Artist:** Julia Lee
☐ Purchased 19___ Pd $_______ MIB NB DB BNT
☐ Want Orig. Ret. $3.95 w/$10 Hallmark purchase.
NB $15 **MIB** Sec. Mkt. **$20-$22**

XPR 972-2 CHRISTMAS CAROUSEL HORSE COLLECTION: HOLLY
Comments: Special Offer, Handcrafted/Brass, 3-3/16" tall
Dated 1989. Gray horse with red, gold and green saddle.
Caption: "Holly, 2 In A Collection Of Four." **Artist:** Julia Lee
☐ Purchased 19___ Pd $_______ MIB NB DB BNT
☐ Want Orig. Ret. $3.95 w/$10 Hallmark purchase.
NB $15 **MIB** Sec. Mkt. **$20-$22**

XPR 971-9 CHRISTMAS CAROUSEL HORSE COLLECTION: SNOW *(Most Popular)*
Comments: Special Offer, Handcrafted/Brass, 3-3/16" tall
Dated 1989. White horse with golden mane and tail.
Caption: "Snow, 1 In A Collection Of Four." **Artist:** Julia Lee
☐ Purchased 19___ Pd $_______ MIB NB DB BNT
☐ Want Orig. Ret. $3.95 w/$10 Hallmark purchase.
NB $25 **MIB** Sec. Mkt. **$28-$32**

XPR 972-0 CHRISTMAS CAROUSEL HORSE COLLECTION: STAR
Comments: Special Offer, Handcrafted/Brass, 3-3/16" tall
Dated 1989. Brown horse with white mane and tail.
Caption: "Star, 3 In A Collection Of Four." **Artist:** Julia Lee
☐ Purchased 19___ Pd $_______ MIB NB DB BNT
☐ Want Orig. Ret. $3.95 w/$10 Hallmark purchase.
NB $15 **MIB** Sec. Mkt. **$20-$22**

XPR 972-3 CHRISTMAS CAROUSEL HORSE COLLECTION: CAROUSEL DISPLAY STAND
Comments: Special Offer, Handcrafted/Brass, 4-5/8" tall
Dated 1989. Brass pole w/red and green ribbons in center.
Stand did not include horses.
☐ Purchased 19___ Pd $_______ MIB NB DB BNT
☐ Want Orig. Ret. $1.00 w/any Hallmark purchase.
NB $8 **MIB** Sec. Mkt. **$15**

QLX 724-2 CHRISTMAS CLASSICS: LITTLE DRUMMER BOY
Comments: **Fourth in Series**, Lighted, 3-1/4" tall, Dated 1989
A little drummer boy kneels beside the manger to play his drum for the Baby. **Artist:** Donna Lee
☐ Purchased 19___ Pd $_______ MIB NB DB BNT
☐ Want Orig. Ret. $13.50 **NB** $28 **MIB** Sec. Mkt. **$38-$42**

QXC 451-2 CHRISTMAS IS PEACEFUL: KEEPSAKE CLUB
Comments: Limited Edition 49,900, Bone China, 2-1/2" tall
Two owls are perched on a snowy branch of a tree. Trimmed with gold. Hand numbered.
Artist: Ed Seale
☐ Purchased 19___ Pd $_______ MIB NB DB BNT
☐ Want Orig. Ret. $18.50 **NB** $20 **MIB** Sec. Mkt. **$35-$40**

QX 544-5 CHRISTMAS KITTY
Comments: ***FIRST IN SERIES***, Fine Porcelain, 3-3/16" tall
This cute little kitty is wearing a light green dress with a red-trimmed white collar and apron. She carries a basket of poinsettias. Plentiful. **Artist:** Anita Marra Rogers
☐ Purchased 19___ Pd $_______ MIB NB DB BNT
☐ Want Orig. Ret. $14.75 **NB** $15 **MIB** Sec. Mkt. **$28-$32**

QX 488-5 CLAUS CONSTRUCTION
Comments: Handcrafted, 4-3/4" tall. Reissued in 1990
Santa wears a personalized belt (Nick) and a hard hat as he balances on the big metal beam.
Artist: Ed Seale
☐ Purchased 19___ Pd $_______ MIB NB DB BNT
☐ Want Orig. Ret. $7.75 **NB** $15 **MIB** Sec. Mkt. **$28-$32**

QXC 428-5 COLLECT A DREAM: KEEPSAKE CLUB
Comments: Handcrafted, 1-3/4" tall, Dated 1989
A mouse has laid down his "Keepsake Ornament Treasury" book and has fallen asleep in his leafy hammock. Offered to Keepsake Members only. Plentiful! **Artist:** Sharon Pike
☐ Purchased 19___ Pd $_______ MIB NB DB BNT
☐ Want Orig. Ret. $9.00 **NB** $25 **MIB** Sec. Mkt. **$35-$40**

QX 461-2 COLLECTOR'S PLATE: MORNING OF WONDER
Comments: **Third in Series,** Fine Porcelain, 3-1/4" dia.
Dated 1989. Christmas morning is always a delight for children when they see their gifts. **Artist:** LaDene Votruba
☐ Purchased 19___ Pd $_______ MIB NB DB BNT
☐ Want Orig. Ret. $8.25 **NB** $22 **MIB** Sec. Mkt. **$28-$32**

QX 487-5 COOL SWING
Comments: Handcrafted/Acrylic, 3-1/2" tall
A penguin in a red stocking cap has fun swinging on his ice cube which says "Have A Cool Christmas."
Artist: Ken Crow
☐ Purchased 19___ Pd $_______ MIB NB DB BNT
☐ Want Orig. Ret. $6.25 **NB** $22 **MIB** Sec. Mkt. **$35-$40**

QX 467-2 COUNTRY CAT
Comments: Handcrafted, 2-1/4" tall
This black and white fat cat is ready to ride. He's seated in an old-fashioned red wagon.
Artist: Michele Pyda-Sevcik
☐ Purchased 19___ Pd $_______ MIB NB DB BNT
☐ Want Orig. Ret. $6.25 **NB** $14 **MIB** Sec. Mkt. **$16-$18**

QX 426-2 CRANBERRY BUNNY
Comments: Handcrafted, 2-5/8" tall
This cute white flocked bunny is wearing a green stocking hat and is stringing cranberries.
Artist: Anita Marra Rogers
☐ Purchased 19___ Pd $_______ MIB NB DB BNT
☐ Want Orig. Ret. $5.75 **NB** $10 **MIB** Sec. Mkt. **$16-$18**

QX 435-2 CRAYOLA® CRAYON: BRIGHT JOURNEY
Comments: ***FIRST IN SERIES***, Handcrafted, 3" tall, Dated 1989
Bear has built a raft with a sail made from a Crayola crayon box. Nice series... many first editions were bought up for secondary market. **Artist:** Linda Sickman
☐ Purchased 19___ Pd $_______ MIB NB DB BNT
☐ Want Orig. Ret. $8.75 **NB** $30 **MIB** Sec. Mkt. **$45-$52**

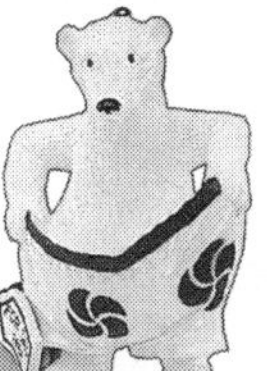

QX 441-2 DAD
Comments: Handcrafted, 2-7/8" tall, Dated 1989
Dad's red and white shorts are just a wee bit big.
Captioned: "For Dad." **Artist:** Julia Lee
☐ Purchased 19___ Pd $_______ MIB NB DB BNT
☐ Want Orig. Ret. $7.25 **NB** $8 **MIB** Sec. Mkt. **$14-$16**

QX 443-2 DAUGHTER
Comments: Handcrafted, 3" tall, Dated Christmas 1989
This little wood-look doll is dressed in bright red and carries a hat box for "Daughter." **Artist:** Linda Sickman
☐ Purchased 19___ Pd $_______ MIB NB DB BNT
☐ Want Orig. Ret. $6.25 **NB** $10 **MIB** Sec. Mkt. **$18-$20**

QX 426-5 DEER DISGUISE
Comments: Handcrafted, 1-3/4" tall
Two children peek out from under their reindeer costume to see where they're going. **Artist:** Bob Siedler
☐ Purchased 19___ Pd $_______ MIB NB DB BNT
☐ Want Orig. Ret. $5.75 **NB** $12 **MIB** Sec. Mkt. **$20-$24**

QX 439-2 FELIZ NAVIDAD
Comments: Handcrafted, 2" tall
Resembling a piñata, this colorful bull carries the Spanish Christmas greeting. Tail is real yarn. Feliz Navidad ornaments are collected exclusively by many.
Artist: Michele Pyda-Sevcik
☐ Purchased 19___ Pd $_______ MIB NB DB BNT
☐ Want Orig. Ret. $6.75 **NB** $18 **MIB** Sec. Mkt. **$25-$28**

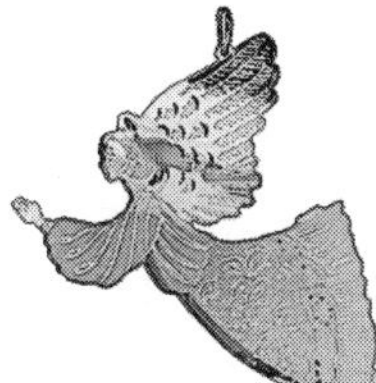

QX 463-5 FESTIVE ANGEL
Comments: Dimensional Brass, 3-5/16" tall
This beautiful angel is created from etched layers of brass; her wings are arched together.
☐ Purchased 19___ Pd $_______ MIB NB DB BNT
☐ Want Orig. Ret. $6.75 **NB** $14 **MIB** Sec. Mkt. **$18-$22**

QX 384-2 FESTIVE YEAR
Comments: Acrylic, 2-13/16" tall, Dated 1989
The date is captured in silver foil in the center of this ornament resembling stained glass. **Artist:** LaDene Votruba
☐ Purchased 19___ Pd $_______ MIB NB DB BNT
☐ Want Orig. Ret. $7.75 **NB** $10 **MIB** Sec. Mkt. **$18-$20**

QX 486-2 FIFTY YEARS TOGETHER PHOTOHOLDER
Comments: Porcelain, 3-3/4" tall, Dated Christmas 1989
A lovely white wreath, accented with green holly and red berries, holds a photo. Caption: "50 Years Together."
Artist: Anita Marra Rogers
☐ Purchased 19___ Pd $_______ MIB NB DB BNT
☐ Want Orig. Ret. $8.75 **NB** $10 **MIB** Sec. Mkt. **$18-$20**

QX 547-5 FIRST CHRISTMAS, THE
Comments: Blue Cameo, 3-1/8" tall,
Caption: "For Unto You Is Born This Day In The City Of David A Saviour, Which Is Christ The Lord."
☐ Purchased 19___ Pd $_______ MIB NB DB BNT
☐ Want Orig. Ret. $7.75 **NB** $8 **MIB** Sec. Mkt. **$14-$16**

QX 383-2 FIRST CHRISTMAS TOGETHER
Comments: Acrylic, 2-7/16" tall, Dated 1989
Etched deer in the forest make a lovely ornament; gold foil lettering "Our First Christmas." **Artist:** Dill Rhodus
☐ Purchased 19___ Pd $_______ MIB NB DB BNT
☐ Want Orig. Ret. $6.75 **NB** $16 **MIB** Sec. Mkt. **$22-$25**

QLX 734-2 FIRST CHRISTMAS TOGETHER
Comments: Light, Handcrafted, 3-3/4" tall, Dated 1989
The flickering light from the fireplace casts a warm glow for the "First Christmas Together." **Artist:** Donna Lee
☐ Purchased 19___ Pd $_______ MIB NB DB BNT
☐ Want Orig. Ret. $17.50 **NB** $22 **MIB** Sec. Mkt. **$40-$45**

QX 485-2 FIRST CHRISTMAS TOGETHER
Comments: Handcrafted, 3-1/2" tall, Dated 1989
A heart-shaped wreath decorated with holly, berries and red hearts makes the perfect support for a swing for these loving chipmunks. **Artist:** Anita Marra Rogers
☐ Purchased 19___ Pd $_______ MIB NB DB BNT
☐ Want Orig. Ret. $9.75 **NB** $16 **MIB** Sec. Mkt. **$24-$26**

QX 273-2 FIRST CHRISTMAS TOGETHER
Comments: White Glass Ball, 2-7/8" dia., Dated '89
Mr. Polar Bear holds a sprig of mistletoe over his sweetheart's head as they rub noses. Caption: "Our First Christmas Together" and "Tis The Season To Be Cuddly."
☐ Purchased 19___ Pd $_______ MIB NB DB BNT
☐ Want Orig. Ret. $4.75 **NB** $12 **MIB** Sec. Mkt. **$18-$22**

QX 273-5 FIVE YEARS TOGETHER
Comments: Blue/Green Glass, 2-7/8" dia.
Dated Christmas 1989. Caption: "Five Years Together" and "Love Makes The World A Beautiful Place To Be."
☐ Purchased 19___ Pd $_______ MIB NB DB BNT
☐ Want Orig. Ret. $4.75 **NB** $12 **MIB** Sec. Mkt. **$20-$22**

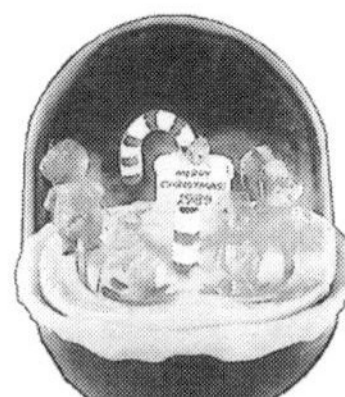

QLX 728-2 FOREST FROLICS
Comments: ***FIRST IN SERIES,*** Light and Motion, Dated 1989 Handcrafted, 4-7/16" tall. A candy cane in the center has a sign that reads "Merry Christmas" while forest animals ski the trail that circles it. **Artist:** Sharon Pike
☐ Purchased 19___ Pd $_______ MIB NB DB BNT
☐ Want Orig. Ret. $24.50 **NB** $60 **MIB** Sec. Mkt. **$85-$90**

QX 545-2 FORTY YEARS TOGETHER PHOTOHOLDER
Comments: Porcelain, 3-3/4" tall, Dated Christmas 1989
White wreath with green holly and red berries holds a couple's favorite photo. Caption: "40 Years Together."
Artist: Anita Marra Rogers
☐ Purchased 19___ Pd $_______ MIB NB DB BNT
☐ Want Orig. Ret. $8.75 **NB** $12 **MIB** Sec. Mkt. **$16-$18**

QX 413-2 FRIENDSHIP TIME
Comments: Handcrafted, 2-1/2" tall, Dated Christmas 1989
Two delightful mice, in red and green, take time out to chat in a teacup. Caption: "... Always Time For Friendship."
Artist: Julia Lee
☐ Purchased 19___ Pd $_______ MIB NB DB BNT
☐ Want Orig. Ret. $9.75 **NB** $21 **MIB** Sec. Mkt. **$28-$32**

QX 384-5 FROM OUR HOME TO YOURS
Comments: Acrylic, 3-1/2" tall, Dated 1989
A beautifully detailed mailbox full of gifts is etched onto oval acrylic. Caption: "From Our Home To Yours At Christmas."
☐ Purchased 19___ Pd $_______ MIB NB DB BNT
☐ Want Orig. Ret. $6.25 **NB** $8 **MIB** Sec. Mkt. **$14-$16**

QX 457-2 FROSTY FRIENDS
Comments: **Tenth in Series**, Handcrafted, 2-1/2" tall
Dated 1989. The little Eskimo and his husky puppy are rushing over the ice to deliver a gift.
Artist: Ed Seale
☐ Purchased 19___ Pd $_______ MIB NB DB BNT
☐ Want Orig. Ret. $9.25 **NB** $28 **MIB** Sec. Mkt. **$44-$48**

QX 548-5 GENTLE FAWN
Comments: Handcrafted, 2-5/16" tall
This flocked fawn has large shiny eyes that tug at your heart. He wears holly in his ribbon.
☐ Purchased 19___ Pd $_______ MIB NB DB BNT
☐ Want Orig. Ret. $7.75 **NB** $10 **MIB** Sec. Mkt. **$15-$18**

QX 386-2 GEORGE WASHINGTON BICENTENNIAL
Comments: Acrylic, 3-9/16" tall, Dated
The likeness of George Washington is etched into clear acrylic. Caption: "1789-1989 American Bicentennial, George Washington, First Presidential Inauguration."
☐ Purchased 19___ Pd $_______ MIB NB DB BNT
☐ Want Orig. Ret. $6.25 **NB** $6 **MIB** Sec. Mkt. **$16-$18**

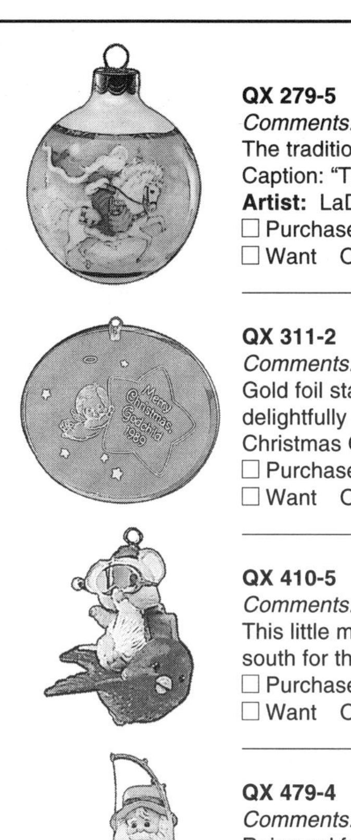

QX 279-5 GIFT BRINGERS, THE: ST. NICHOLAS
Comments: ***FIRST IN SERIES***, White Glass Ball, 2-7/8" dia.
The tradition of St. Nicholas is captured on this ball.
Caption: "The Gift Bringers, St. Nicholas, Christmas 1989."
Artist: LaDene Votruba
☐ Purchased 19___ Pd $_______ MIB NB DB BNT
☐ Want Orig. Ret. $5.00 **NB** $8 **MIB** Sec. Mkt. **$16-$18**

QX 311-2 GODCHILD
Comments: Acrylic, 2-3/4" tall, Dated 1989
Gold foil stars and a gold foil halo and caption add to this delightfully etched cherub who carries her message: "Merry Christmas Godchild." **Artist:** John Francis (Collin)
☐ Purchased 19___ Pd $_______ MIB NB DB BNT
☐ Want Orig. Ret. $6.25 **NB** $7 **MIB** Sec. Mkt. **$10-$12**

QX 410-5 GOIN' SOUTH
Comments: Handcrafted, 1-7/8" tall
This little mouse has hitched a ride with a redbird and is headed south for the winter. **Artist:** Ken Crow
☐ Purchased 19___ Pd $_______ MIB NB DB BNT
☐ Want Orig. Ret. $4.25 **NB** $15 **MIB** Sec. Mkt. **$22-$26**

QX 479-4 GONE FISHING
Comments: Handcrafted, 2-1/2" tall
Reissued from 1988.
Artist: Bob Siedler
☐ Purchased 19___ Pd $_______ MIB NB DB BNT
☐ Want Orig. Ret. $5.75 **NB** $12.50 **MIB** Sec. Mkt. **$17-$22**

QX 464-2 GRACEFUL SWAN
Comments: Dimensional Brass, 2-1/4" tall
With its elaborate etching and detail, this swan is quite elegant and graceful.
☐ Purchased 19___ Pd $_______ MIB NB DB BNT
☐ Want Orig. Ret. $6.75 **NB** $14 **MIB** Sec. Mkt. **$18-$20**

QX 278-2 GRANDDAUGHTER
Comments: White and Green Glass Ball, 2-7/8" dia.
Dated 1989. The forest animals all have fun as they skate on a frozen pond. Caption: "A Granddaughter Makes Christmastime One Of The Best Times Of All!"
☐ Purchased 19___ Pd $_______ MIB NB DB BNT
☐ Want Orig. Ret. $4.75 **NB** $8.50 **MIB** Sec. Mkt. **$18-$20**

QX 382-2 GRANDDAUGHTER'S FIRST CHRISTMAS
Comments: Acrylic, 4-1/4" tall, Dated 1989
A kitten in a stocking cap likes to play in this etched stocking. "Granddaughter's First Christmas" is stamped in gold foil.
Artist: John Francis (Collin)
☐ Purchased 19___ Pd $_______ MIB NB DB BNT
☐ Want Orig. Ret. $6.75 **NB** $10 **MIB** Sec. Mkt. **$16-$20**

QX 277-5 GRANDMOTHER
Comments: Tan Glass Ball, 2-7/8" dia.
Dated Christmas 1989. A stencil-look garland of ribbon, pine cones and poinsettias frames the caption: "A Grandmother Is Thought About Often... And Always With Love."
Artist: Joyce A. Lyle
☐ Purchased 19___ Pd $_______ MIB NB DB BNT
☐ Want Orig. Ret. $4.75 **NB** $6 **MIB** Sec. Mkt. **$15-$18**

QX 277-2 GRANDPARENTS
Comments: Peach Glass Ball, 2-7/8" dia., Dated 1989
The caption is printed against a frosty winter scene: "Grandparents Make Christmas Welcome In Their Home And In Their Hearts." **Artist:** Joyce A. Lyle
☐ Purchased 19___ Pd $_______ MIB NB DB BNT
☐ Want Orig. Ret. $4.75 **NB** $7 **MIB** Sec. Mkt. **$14-$16**

QX 278-5 GRANDSON
Comments: Periwinkle Blue Glass, 2-7/8" dia., Dated 1989
Santa climbs into a chimney; his bag of toys is nearby. Caption: "A Grandson Brings Joy To Everyone.. Just Like Christmas!"
☐ Purchased 19___ Pd $_______ MIB NB DB BNT
☐ Want Orig. Ret. $4.75 **NB** $6 **MIB** Sec. Mkt. **$16-$20**

QX 382-5 GRANDSON'S FIRST CHRISTMAS
Comments: Acrylic, 4-1/4" tall, Dated 1989
An etched puppy hides inside an acrylic stocking. "Grandson's First Christmas" in gold. **Artist:** John Francis (Collin)
☐ Purchased 19___ Pd $_______ MIB NB DB BNT
☐ Want Orig. Ret. $6.75 **NB** $12 **MIB** Sec. Mkt. **$15-$18**

QX 385-2 GRATITUDE
Comments: Acrylic, 2-3/4" dia., Dated 1989
A green etched sprig of holly with a red ribbon is lovely on this bezeled ornament. Caption: "Thankful Feelings Flow From Heart To Heart At Christmas." **Artist:** LaDene Votruba
☐ Purchased 19___ Pd $_______ MIB NB DB BNT
☐ Want Orig. Ret. $6.75 **NB** $8 **MIB** Sec. Mkt. **$12-$14**

QX 418-5 GYM DANDY
Comments: Handcrafted, 2-1/2" tall
Kringle's Gym finds Santa in red and gray sweats working out with dumbbells. **Artist:** Bob Siedler
☐ Purchased 19___ Pd $_______ MIB NB DB BNT
☐ Want Orig. Ret. $5.75 **NB** $10 **MIB** Sec. Mkt. **$15-$18**

QX 430-5 HANG IN THERE
Comments: Handcrafted, 3" tall
A little mouse is hanging on to his red Santa cap, even though it's too big for him. He has a green ribbon tied to his leather tail.
Artist: Ken Crow
☐ Purchased 19___ Pd $_______ MIB NB DB BNT
☐ Want Orig. Ret. $5.25 **NB** $24 **MIB** Sec. Mkt. **$34-$36**

QX 455-5 HARK! IT'S HERALD
Comments: ***FIRST IN SERIES,*** Handcrafted, 2" tall, Dated 1989
Herald, dressed in a green jacket and red hat, plays his xylophone.
Artist: Ken Crow
☐ Purchased 19___ Pd $_______ MIB NB DB BNT
☐ Want Orig. Ret. $6.75 **NB** $12 **MIB** Sec. Mkt. **$25-$30**

QX 458-5 HERE COMES SANTA: CHRISTMAS CABOOSE
Comments: **Eleventh in Series**, Handcrafted, 3-1/2" tall
Dated 1989. This delightful caboose has movable wheels and shows Santa leaning out the window to wave at everyone as he passes. **Artist:** Ken Crow
☐ Purchased 19___ Pd $_______ MIB NB DB BNT
☐ Want Orig. Ret. $14.75 **NB** $25 **MIB** Sec. Mkt. **$45-$50**

QX 545-5 HERE'S THE PITCH
Comments: Handcrafted, 2-3/8" tall
Santa's playing the majors in his red baseball cap, cleated shoes and uniform. His name and number: "Santa 1." What else?!
Artist: Bob Siedler
☐ Purchased 19___ Pd $_______ MIB NB DB BNT
☐ Want Orig. Ret. $5.75 **NB** $12 **MIB** Sec. Mkt. **$16-$20**

QLX 722-2 HOLIDAY BELL
Comments: Lighted, Lead Crystal, 3-1/2" tall, Dated 1989
With a specially designed brass cap, the many facets give this bell the look of hand-cut glass.
☐ Purchased 19___ Pd $_______ MIB NB DB BNT
☐ Want Orig. Ret. $17.50 **NB** $21 **MIB** Sec. Mkt. **$34-$36**

QXC 460-5 HOLIDAY HEIRLOOM: KEEPSAKE CLUB
Comments: **Third and Final in Series**, Limited Edition 34,600
Lead Crystal/Silver Plating, 2-1/2" tall, Dated 1989. A crystal bell hangs from a tree surrounded by old-fashioned toys. Offered only to Keepsake Club Members. **Artist:** Duane Unruh
☐ Purchased 19___ Pd $_______ MIB NB DB BNT
☐ Want Orig. Ret. $25.00 **NB** $18 **MIB** Sec. Mkt. **$33-$35**

QX 469-2 HOPPY HOLIDAYS
Comments: Handcrafted, 2-3/4" tall, Dated 1989
This little flocked bunny has hopped right into a shopping cart. He has two gifts in his red cart.
Artist: Bob Siedler
☐ Purchased 19___ Pd $_______ MIB NB DB BNT
☐ Want Orig. Ret. $7.75 **NB** $12 **MIB** Sec. Mkt. **$20-$23**

QX 463-2 HORSE WEATHERVANE
Comments: Handcrafted, 3" tall
A white and brown horse, galloping into the wind, has been designed to resemble carved wood.
Artist: Linda Sickman
☐ Purchased 19___ Pd $_______ MIB NB DB BNT
☐ Want Orig. Ret. $5.75 **NB** $10 **MIB** Sec. Mkt. **$15-$18**

QX 437-2 JOYFUL TRIO
Comments: Handcrafted, 2-1/4" tall
Holding a blue banner proclaiming "Joy To You," this delightful trio of angels sing out for peace and harmony.
Artist: John Francis (Collin)
☐ Purchased 19___ Pd $_______ MIB NB DB BNT
☐ Want Orig. Ret. $9.75 **NB** $10 **MIB** Sec. Mkt. **$16-$18**

QLX 729-5 JOYOUS CAROLERS
Comments: Light, Motion and Music, Handcrafted, 4-11/16" tall
Victorian carolers sing under a lamppost to the melody of a violin. Plays *We Wish You A Merry Christmas.* **Artist:** Duane Unruh
☐ Purchased 19___ Pd $_______ MIB NB DB BNT
☐ Want Orig. Ret. $30.00 **NB** $45 **MIB** Sec. Mkt. **$65-$70**

QLX 701-7 KRINGLE'S TOY SHOP
Comments: Light and Motion, Handcrafted, 3-5/8" tall
Reissued from 1988.
Artist: Ed Seale
☐ Purchased 19___ Pd $_______ MIB NB DB BNT
☐ Want Orig. Ret. $24.50 **NB** $45 **MIB** Sec. Mkt. **$55-$60**

QX 424-5 KRISTY CLAUS
Comments: Handcrafted, 2-15/16" tall
Wearing green earmuffs, Santa's lovely wife is ready to show her grace and style on the ice.
Artist: Bob Siedler
☐ Purchased 19___ Pd $_______ MIB NB DB BNT
☐ Want Orig. Ret. $5.75 **NB** $8 **MIB** Sec. Mkt. **$14-$16**

QX 383-5 LANGUAGE OF LOVE
Comments: Acrylic, 3" tall, Dated 1989
The etched outline of poinsettias is lovely on this heart-shaped ornament. Caption: "Together... The Most Caring Word In The Language Of Love."
☐ Purchased 19___ Pd $_______ MIB NB DB BNT
☐ Want Orig. Ret. $6.25 **NB** $9 **MIB** Sec. Mkt. **$18-$22**

QX 488-2 LET'S PLAY
Comments: Handcrafted, 2-3/4" tall, Dated 1989
Tap this ornament and the puppy and kitten play and move. Kitten sits on the pup's red doghouse.
Artist: Ken Crow
☐ Purchased 19___ Pd $_______ MIB NB DB BNT
☐ Want Orig. Ret. $7.25 **NB** $12 **MIB** Sec. Mkt. **$28-$32**

QLX 726-2 LOVING SPOONFUL
Comments: Light and Motion, Handcrafted, 3-1/2" tall
Two little mice have turned the teaspoon at the sugar bowl into a seesaw. Caption: "Sugar."
Artist: Bob Siedler
☐ Purchased 19___ Pd $_______ MIB NB DB BNT
☐ Want Orig. Ret. $19.50 **NB** $25 **MIB** Sec. Mkt. **$38-$40**

QX 452-2 MAIL CALL
Comments: Handcrafted, 3" tall
A raccoon mail carrier delivers mail from the "Branch Office" to a redbird's "branch." **Artist:** Ed Seale
☐ Purchased 19___ Pd $_______ MIB NB DB BNT
☐ Want Orig. Ret. $8.75 **NB** $10 **MIB** Sec. Mkt. **$18-$20**

QX 454-5 MARY'S ANGELS: BLUEBELL
Comments: **Second in Series**, Handcrafted/Acrylic, 3" tall
Bluebell kneels in prayer on a frosted acrylic cloud. She has a light blue gown. Plentiful! **Artist:** Robert Chad
☐ Purchased 19___ Pd $_______ MIB NB DB BNT
☐ Want Orig. Ret. $5.75 **NB** $35 **MIB** Sec. Mkt. **$48-$52**

QX 447-2 MERRY-GO-ROUND UNICORN
Comments: Hand-Painted Porcelain, 2-11/16" tall
This sweet little unicorn with a red and white striped horn and golden hooves rides up and down on a candy-striped pole.
Artist: Anita Marra Rogers
☐ Purchased 19___ Pd $_______ MIB NB DB BNT
☐ Want Orig. Ret. $10.75 **NB** $12 **MIB** Sec. Mkt. **$18-$20**

QLX 727-5 METRO EXPRESS
Comments: Light and Motion, Handcrafted, 3-1/2" tall
Two trains on separate tracks race around the skyscrapers in this busy city. Two more trains may be seen in the tunnels at the bottom. **Artist:** Linda Sickman
☐ Purchased 19___ Pd $_______ MIB NB DB BNT
☐ Want Orig. Ret. $28.00 **NB** $55 **MIB** Sec. Mkt. **$75-$80**

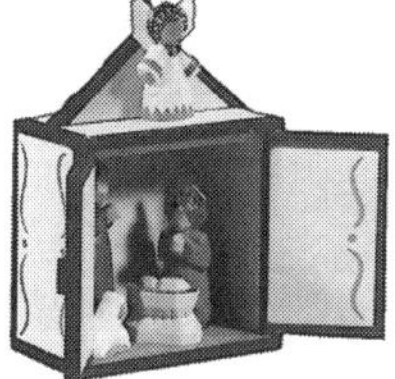

QX 459-2 MINIATURE CRECHE
Comments: **Fifth and Final in Series,** Handcrafted, 3" tall
The *retablo,* or double-door design to the final nativity in this series is designed in the style of Southwestern art.
Artist: Anita Marra Rogers
☐ Purchased 19___ Pd $_______ MIB NB DB BNT
☐ Want Orig. Ret. $9.25 **NB** $12 **MIB** Sec. Mkt. **$22-$25**

QX 442-5 MOM AND DAD
Comments: Handcrafted, 2-3/8" tall, Dated 1989
Ice skating hand in hand two penguins are identified by their sweaters, "Mom" and "Dad"!
Artist: Sharon Pike
☐ Purchased 19___ Pd $_______ MIB NB DB BNT
☐ Want Orig. Ret. $9.75 **NB** $12 **MIB** Sec. Mkt. **$22-$25**

QLX 713-4 MOONLIT NAP
Comments: Handcrafted, 2-3/4" tall, Reissued from 1988.
Artist: Robert Chad
☐ Purchased 19___ Pd $_______ MIB NB DB BNT
☐ Want Orig. Ret. $8.75 **NB** $15 **MIB** Sec. Mkt. **$28-$30**

QX 440-5 MOTHER
Comments: Fine Porcelain, 2-1/2" tall, Dated 1989 Tied with red ribbon, this heart shaped porcelain plate has a border of holiday designs and caption: "Mother Is The Heart Of The Family."
☐ Purchased 19___ Pd $_______ MIB NB DB BNT
☐ Want Orig. Ret. $9.75 **NB** $16 **MIB** Sec. Mkt. **$24-$26**

QX 457-5 MR. AND MRS. CLAUS: HOLIDAY DUET
Comments: **Fourth in Series**, Handcrafted, 3-1/4" tall
Dated 1989. Santa and his wife sing "We Wish You A Merry Christmas And A Happy New Year."
Artist: Duane Unruh
☐ Purchased 19___ Pd $_______ MIB NB DB BNT
☐ Want Orig. Ret. $13.25 **NB** $35 **MIB** Sec. Mkt. **$45-$50**

QX 275-5 NEW HOME
Comments: Lavender and White Glass Ball, 2-7/8" dia.
Dated Christmas 1989. A home is nestled among the trees in a wintry landscape. Caption: "Love Is The Light In The Window Of Your New Home." **Artist:** LaDene Votruba
☐ Purchased 19___ Pd $_______ MIB NB DB BNT
☐ Want Orig. Ret. $4.75 **NB** $10 **MIB** Sec. Mkt. **$20-$22**

QXC 448-3 NOELLE: KEEPSAKE CLUB
Comments: Limited Edition 49,900, Fine Porcelain, 3-3/4"
This elegant cat has a red bow with a jingle bell and sprig of holly. Comes with wooden display stand. Available to Club Members only. **Artist:** Duane Unruh
☐ Purchased 19___ Pd $_______ MIB NB DB BNT
☐ Want Orig. Ret. $19.75 **NB** $20 **MIB** Sec. Mkt. **$35-$38**

QX 276-2 NORMAN ROCKWELL
Comments: Gold Glass Ball, 2-7/8" dia., Dated 1989
"Norman Rockwell, Famous Holiday Covers From *The Saturday Evening Post*" - "Santa's Seen In The Smiles The Whole World Is Sharing, He's Found Where There's Friendship And Loving And Caring." **Artist:** Joyce A. Lyle
☐ Purchased 19___ Pd $_______ MIB NB DB BNT
☐ Want Orig. Ret. $4.75 **NB** $10 **MIB** Sec. Mkt. **$18-$20**

QX 546-2 NORTH POLE JOGGER
Comments: Handcrafted, 2-1/4" tall
Santa in his jogging suit that reads "North Pole 1K." Santa jogs along while he listens to his favorite music. **Artist:** Bob Siedler
☐ Purchased 19___ Pd $_______ MIB NB DB BNT
☐ Want Orig. Ret. $5.75 **NB** $10 **MIB** Sec. Mkt. **$18-$22**

QX 458-2 NOSTALGIC HOUSES AND SHOPS: U.S. POST OFFICE
Comments: **Sixth in Series**, Handcrafted, 4-1/4" tall
Dated 1989. Designed as a red brick building.
The upstairs has a furnished office.
Artist: Donna Lee
☐ Purchased 19___ Pd $_______ MIB NB DB BNT
☐ Want Orig. Ret. $14.25 **NB** $35 **MIB** Sec. Mkt. **$58-$62**

QX 466-5 NOSTALGIC LAMB
Comments: Handcrafted, 1-3/4" tall
This lamb has been sculpted to show its curly wool. He rides in a red wagon with wheels that turn.
Artist: Michele Pyda-Sevcik
☐ Purchased 19___ Pd $_______ MIB NB DB BNT
☐ Want Orig. Ret. $6.75 **NB** $10 **MIB** Sec. Mkt. **$14-$16**

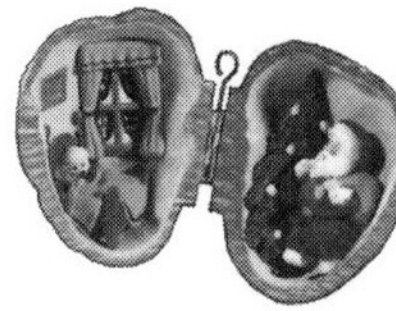

QX 465-5 NUTSHELL DREAMS
Comments: Handcrafted, 1-1/2" tall
A child sleeping in his bedroom dreams of the toys Santa will leave; in another room, Santa motions quiet so as not to wake the child. **Artist:** Robert Chad
☐ Purchased 19___ Pd $_______ MIB NB DB BNT
☐ Want Orig. Ret. $5.75 **NB** $15 **MIB** Sec. Mkt. **$20-$22**

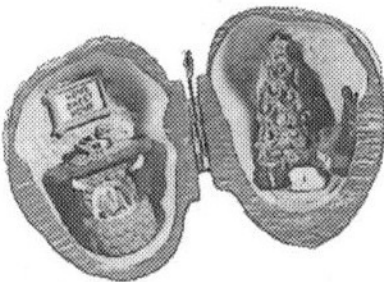

QX 465-2 NUTSHELL HOLIDAY
Comments: Handcrafted, 1-1/2" tall. Reissued in 1990
Open this tiny nutshell and you will find a home decorated and waiting for Santa's arrival.
Artist: Anita Marra Rogers
☐ Purchased 19___ Pd $_______ MIB NB DB BNT
☐ Want Orig. Ret. $5.75 **NB** $15 **MIB** Sec. Mkt. **$24-$28**

QX 487-2 NUTSHELL WORKSHOP
Comments: Handcrafted, 1-1/2" tall
Santa's elves keep busy building new toys in the tiny workshop inside. **Artist:** Robert Chad
☐ Purchased 19___ Pd $_______ MIB NB DB BNT
☐ Want Orig. Ret. $5.75 **NB** $15 **MIB** Sec. Mkt. **$20-$22**

QX 434-5 OLD WORLD GNOME
Comments: Handcrafted, 3-1/4" tall
This friendly gnome has been created to resemble a European wood carving.
☐ Purchased 19___ Pd $_______ MIB NB DB BNT
☐ Want Orig. Ret. $7.75 **NB** $18 **MIB** Sec. Mkt. **$24-$28**

QX 419-2 ON THE LINKS
Comments: Handcrafted, 2-1/2" tall
Santa's golf swing is perfect. He's wearing red slacks and sunshade and a green shirt.
Artist: Bob Siedler
☐ Purchased 19___ Pd $_______ MIB NB DB BNT
☐ Want Orig. Ret. $5.75 **NB** $12 **MIB** Sec. Mkt. **$18-$22**

QX 481-4 OREO® COOKIE
Comments: Handcrafted, 1-7/8" dia.
Reissued from 1988.
Artist: Duane Unruh
☐ Purchased 19___ Pd $_______ MIB NB DB BNT
☐ Want Orig. Ret. $4.00 **NB** $8 **MIB** Sec. Mkt. **$14-$18**

QX 580-5 ORNAMENT EXPRESS, THE
Comments: Special Edition, Handcrafted, Dated 1989
Locomotive, 2-1/4"; Coal Car, 1-3/4"; Caboose, 2-1/8" tall.
May be displayed separately or together. All have revolving wheels and caption. Coal car holds a bag of miniature reproductions of prior years' ornaments. Caboose wishes everyone "Merry Christmas." **Artist:** Linda Sickman
☐ Purchased 19___ Pd $_______ MIB NB DB BNT
☐ Want Orig. Ret. $22.00 **NB** $30 **MIB** Sec. Mkt. **$44-$48**

QX 436-5 OWLIDAY GREETINGS
Comments: Handcrafted, 1-1/2' tall
This white owl has textured feathers and carries a red banner which says "Owliday Greetings"! **Artist:** Sharon Pike
☐ Purchased 19___ Pd $_______ MIB NB DB BNT
☐ Want Orig. Ret. $4.00 **NB** $8 **MIB** Sec. Mkt. **$18-$20**

QX 429-2 PADDINGTON™ BEAR
Comments: Handcrafted, 4-1/4" tall
Paddington marches along in his red raincoat and green hat playing his drum. Gift tag reads: "Please Look After This Bear. Thank You." **Artist:** John Francis (Collin)
☐ Purchased 19___ Pd $_______ MIB NB DB BNT
☐ Want Orig. Ret. $5.75 **NB** $14 **MIB** Sec. Mkt. **$18-$20**

QX 476-1 PARTY LINE
Comments: Handcrafted, 1-3/4" tall
Reissued from 1988.
Artist: Sharon Pike
☐ Purchased 19___ Pd $_______ MIB NB DB BNT
☐ Want Orig. Ret. $8.75 **NB** $18 **MIB** Sec. Mkt. **$28-$30**

QX 276-5 PEANUTS®: A CHARLIE BROWN CHRISTMAS
Comments: Blue Glass Ball, 2-7/8" dia., Dated
Caption: "A Charlie Brown Christmas Television Special, Happy 25th Anniversary 1965-1989" and "Christmas... Season Of Love."
☐ Purchased 19___ Pd $_______ MIB NB DB BNT
☐ Want Orig. Ret. $4.75 **NB** $25 **MIB** Sec. Mkt. **$40-$45**

QX 487-1 PEEK-A-BOO KITTIES
Comments: Handcrafted, 5" tall
Reissued from 1988.
Artist: Ken Crow
☐ Purchased 19___ Pd $_______ MIB NB DB BNT
☐ Want Orig. Ret. $7.50 **NB** $15 **MIB** Sec. Mkt. **$20-$23**

QX 450-5 PEPPERMINT CLOWN
Comments: Hand-Painted Fine Porcelain, 5-1/32" tall
This hand-painted porcelain clown rides a peppermint unicycle.
Artist: Peter Dutkin
☐ Purchased 19___ Pd $_______ MIB NB DB BNT
☐ Want Orig. Ret. $24.75 **NB** $20 **MIB** Sec. Mkt. **$28-$30**

QX 453-5 PLAYFUL ANGEL
Comments: Handcrafted/Acrylic, 3-1/8" tall
A little angel plays in a swing attached to an acrylic cloud. She wears a brass halo. **Artist:** Donna Lee
☐ Purchased 19___ Pd $_______ MIB NB DB BNT
☐ Want Orig. Ret. $6.75 **NB** $18 **MIB** Sec. Mkt. **$23-$25**

QX 478-4 POLAR BOWLER
Comments: Handcrafted, 2-1/4" tall
Reissued from 1988.
Artist: Bob Siedler
☐ Purchased 19___ Pd $_______ MIB NB DB BNT
☐ Want 1989 Retail $5.75 **NB** $10 **MIB** Sec. Mkt. **$15-$18**

QX 461-5 PORCELAIN BEAR
Comments: **Seventh in Series**, Fine Porcelain, 2" tall
This hand-painted cinnamon bear is enjoying his special treat from Santa - a bag of candy! **Artist:** Sharon Pike
☐ Purchased 19___ Pd $_______ MIB NB DB BNT
☐ Want Orig. Ret. $8.75 **NB** $12 **MIB** Sec. Mkt. **$18-$22**

QX 456-2 REINDEER CHAMPS: VIXEN
Comments: **Fourth in Series**, Handcrafted, 3-1/4" tall
Dated '89. "Vixen" wears a sporty tennis outfit in red and white and a green visor. **Artist:** Bob Siedler
☐ Purchased 19___ Pd $_______ MIB NB DB BNT
☐ Want Orig. Ret. $7.75 **NB** $14 **MIB** Sec. Mkt. **$22-$25**

QX 462-2 ROCKING HORSE
Comments: **Ninth in Series**, Handcrafted, 4" wide
Dated 1989. A russet and black bay horse is fitted with brass stirrups and red yarn rein. **Artist:** Linda Sickman
☐ Purchased 19___ Pd $_______ MIB NB DB BNT
☐ Want Orig. Ret. $10.75 **NB** $25 **MIB** Sec. Mkt. **$40-$45**

QX 407-2 RODNEY REINDEER
Comments: Handcrafted, 5" tall, Dated 89
Rodney is checking the route for Christmas Eve on his "Reindeer Route 89." He's made of a flexible material which allows him to be bent into many positions. **Artist:** Bob Siedler
☐ Purchased 19___ Pd $_______ MIB NB DB BNT
☐ Want Orig. Ret. $6.75 **NB** $7 **MIB** Sec. Mkt. **$14-$16**

QX 467-5 ROOSTER WEATHERVANE
Comments: Handcrafted, 3-1/2" tall
With the design of American folk art, this bright, colorful rooster is crowing good morning to everyone.
☐ Purchased 19___ Pd $_______ MIB NB DB BNT
☐ Want Orig. Ret. $5.75 **NB** $6 **MIB** Sec. Mkt. **$14-$16**

QLX 725-2 RUDOLPH THE RED-NOSED REINDEER
Comments: Lighted, Handcrafted, 2-1/2" tall
Rudolph's nose glows to light Santa's way, in addition to the blinking lights on Santa's sleigh.
Artist: Robert Chad
☐ Purchased 19___ Pd $_______ MIB NB DB BNT
☐ Want Orig. Ret. $19.50 **NB** $50 **MIB** Sec. Mkt. **$65-$72**

QX 415-2 SEA SANTA
Comments: Handcrafted, 2-1/2" tall
Santa's ready to do some diving for underwater treasure in his scuba gear. Caption: "Sea Santa."
Artist: Bob Siedler
☐ Purchased 19___ Pd $_______ MIB NB DB BNT
☐ Want Orig. Ret. $5.75 **NB** $12 **MIB** Sec. Mkt. **$20-$22**

QX 279-2 SISTER
Comments: Porcelain White Glass Ball, 2-7/8" dia.
Dated Christmas 1989. Caption: "Having A Sister Means Happiness. Loving A Sister Means Joy."
☐ Purchased 19___ Pd $_______ MIB NB DB BNT
☐ Want Orig. Ret. $4.75 **NB** $9 **MIB** Sec. Mkt. **$15-$18**

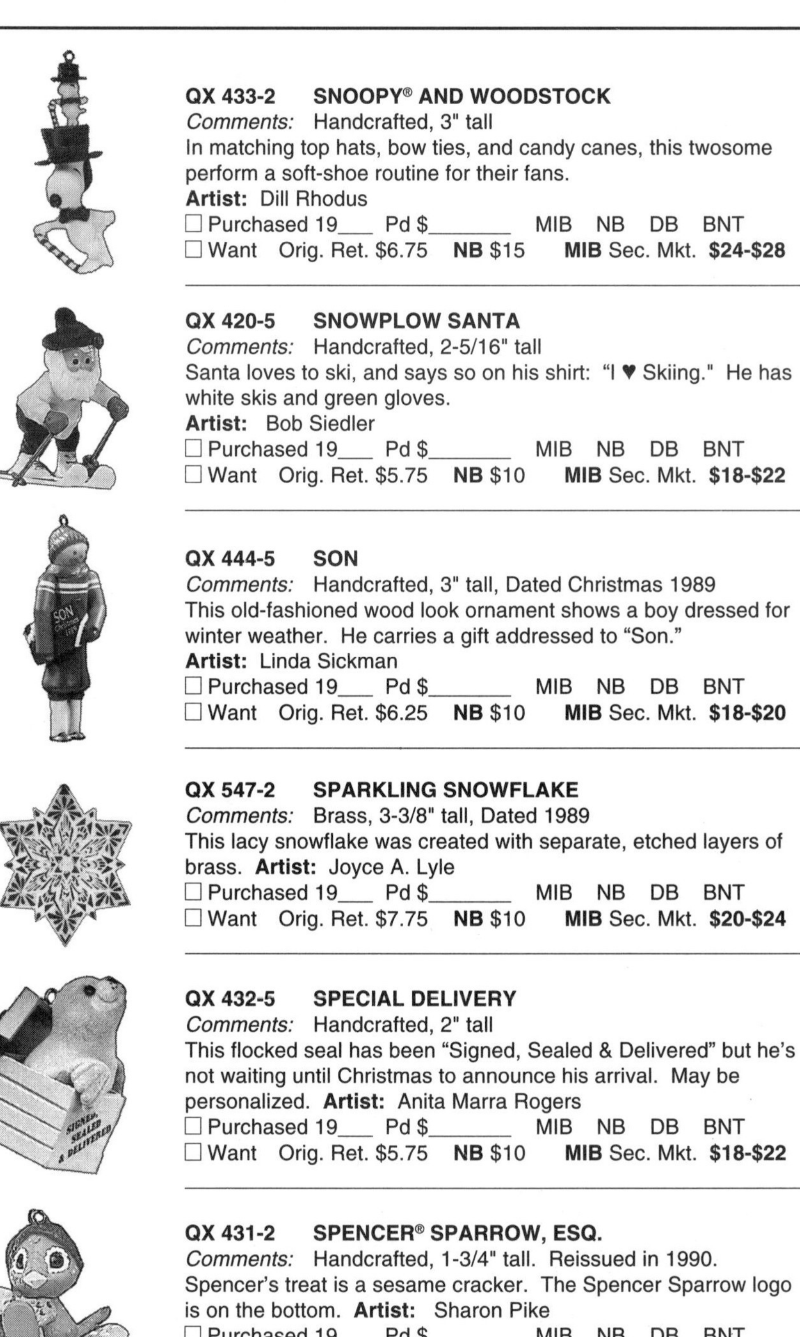

QX 433-2 SNOOPY® AND WOODSTOCK
Comments: Handcrafted, 3" tall
In matching top hats, bow ties, and candy canes, this twosome perform a soft-shoe routine for their fans.
Artist: Dill Rhodus
☐ Purchased 19___ Pd $_______ MIB NB DB BNT
☐ Want Orig. Ret. $6.75 **NB** $15 **MIB** Sec. Mkt. **$24-$28**

QX 420-5 SNOWPLOW SANTA
Comments: Handcrafted, 2-5/16" tall
Santa loves to ski, and says so on his shirt: "I ♥ Skiing." He has white skis and green gloves.
Artist: Bob Siedler
☐ Purchased 19___ Pd $_______ MIB NB DB BNT
☐ Want Orig. Ret. $5.75 **NB** $10 **MIB** Sec. Mkt. **$18-$22**

QX 444-5 SON
Comments: Handcrafted, 3" tall, Dated Christmas 1989
This old-fashioned wood look ornament shows a boy dressed for winter weather. He carries a gift addressed to "Son."
Artist: Linda Sickman
☐ Purchased 19___ Pd $_______ MIB NB DB BNT
☐ Want Orig. Ret. $6.25 **NB** $10 **MIB** Sec. Mkt. **$18-$20**

QX 547-2 SPARKLING SNOWFLAKE
Comments: Brass, 3-3/8" tall, Dated 1989
This lacy snowflake was created with separate, etched layers of brass. **Artist:** Joyce A. Lyle
☐ Purchased 19___ Pd $_______ MIB NB DB BNT
☐ Want Orig. Ret. $7.75 **NB** $10 **MIB** Sec. Mkt. **$20-$24**

QX 432-5 SPECIAL DELIVERY
Comments: Handcrafted, 2" tall
This flocked seal has been "Signed, Sealed & Delivered" but he's not waiting until Christmas to announce his arrival. May be personalized. **Artist:** Anita Marra Rogers
☐ Purchased 19___ Pd $_______ MIB NB DB BNT
☐ Want Orig. Ret. $5.75 **NB** $10 **MIB** Sec. Mkt. **$18-$22**

QX 431-2 SPENCER® SPARROW, ESQ.
Comments: Handcrafted, 1-3/4" tall. Reissued in 1990.
Spencer's treat is a sesame cracker. The Spencer Sparrow logo is on the bottom. **Artist:** Sharon Pike
☐ Purchased 19___ Pd $_______ MIB NB DB BNT
☐ Want Orig. Ret. $6.75 **NB** $12 **MIB** Sec. Mkt. **$18-$22**

QLX 728-5 SPIRIT OF ST. NICK
Comments: Light and Motion, Handcrafted, 4" tall
Early barnstorming days are recalled as Santa demonstrates his flying expertise. A banner reads "Spirit of St. Nick" and a message in the snow proclaims "Merry Christmas!"
Artist: Ed Seale
☐ Purchased 19___ Pd $_______ MIB NB DB BNT
☐ Want Orig. Ret. $24.50 **NB** $55 **MIB** Sec. Mkt. **$70-$75**

QX 456-5 STOCKING KITTEN
Comments: Handcrafted, 2-3/4" tall. Reissued in 1990.
A sweet kitten is having fun playing in a bright red, flocked stocking with a green pom-pom. **Artist:** Sharon Pike
☐ Purchased 19___ Pd $_______ MIB NB DB BNT
☐ Want Orig. Ret. $6.75 **NB** $9 **MIB** Sec. Mkt. **$15-$18**

QX 438-5 SWEET MEMORIES PHOTOHOLDER
Comments: Handcrafted, 3-1/16" tall, Dated 1989
A candy-cane striped wreath is decorated with a large red fabric bow and green holly. Caption: "Christmas Is The Perfect Time For Making Sweet Memories."
☐ Purchased 19___ Pd $_______ MIB NB DB BNT
☐ Want Orig. Ret. $6.75 **NB** $10 **MIB** Sec. Mkt. **$20-$22**

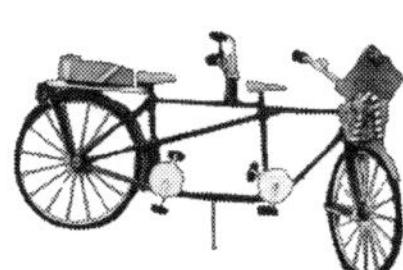

QX 486-5 SWEETHEART
Comments: Handcrafted, 4-5/8" wide, Dated 1989
This red tandem bicycle has a gift in the basket that says "Merry Christmas Sweetheart."
Artist: Linda Sickman
☐ Purchased 19___ Pd $_______ MIB NB DB BNT
☐ Want Orig. Ret. $9.75 **NB** $18 **MIB** Sec. Mkt. **$34-$38**

QX 412-5 TEACHER
Comments: Handcrafted, 2-1/4" tall, Dated Christmas 1989
This little mouse is a pleasant student. Inside his book he's written "For A Nice Teacher."
☐ Want ☐ Own: MIB NB DB BNT Paid $________
Orig. Ret. $5.75 **NB** $10 **MIB** Sec. Mkt. **$18-$22**

ERROR: *The words on the book are turned around, facing the reader, rather than the mouse writing the words.*
NB $25 **MIB** Sec. Mkt. **$28-$32**

QX 418-1 TEENY TASTER
Comments: Handcrafted, 4-3/8" tall
Reissued from 1988. **Artist:** Ed Seale
☐ Purchased 19___ Pd $_______ MIB NB DB BNT
☐ Want Orig. Ret. $4.75 **NB** $12 **MIB** Sec. Mkt. **$16-$20**

QX 274-2 TEN YEARS TOGETHER
Comments: White Glass Ball, 2-7/8" dia.
Dated Christmas 1989. A couple rides in a horse-drawn sleigh. Caption: "There's Joy In Each Season When There's Love In Our Hearts" and "Ten Years Together." **Artist:** Joyce A. Lyle
☐ Purchased 19___ Pd $_______ MIB NB DB BNT
☐ Want Orig. Ret. $4.75 **NB** $10 **MIB** Sec. Mkt. **$18-$22**

QX 455-2 THIMBLE SERIES: PUPPY
Comments: **Twelfth and Final in Series,** Handcrafted, 1-3/4"
This adorable puppy with a big red bow, captures everyone's attention as he sits inside a thimble.
Artist: Anita Marra Rogers
☐ Purchased 19___ Pd $_______ MIB NB DB BNT
☐ Want Orig. Ret. $5.75 **NB** $12 **MIB** Sec. Mkt. **$22-$24**

QX 460-2 TIN LOCOMOTIVE
Comments: **Eighth and Final in Series**, Dated 1989
Pressed Tin, 3-3/16" tall. The last locomotive in the series is also one of the most complex. A brass bell jingles as the wheels turn.
Artist: Linda Sickman
☐ Purchased 19___ Pd $_______ MIB NB DB BNT
☐ Want Orig. Ret. $14.75 **NB** $40 **MIB** Sec. Mkt. **$50-$55**

QLX 717-4 TINY TINKER
Comments: Light and Motion, Handcrafted, 3" tall
This little elf is burning the midnight oil to repair a shoe. A toy locomotive also waits for repair. **Artist:** Ken Crow
☐ Purchased 19___ Pd $_______ MIB NB DB BNT
☐ Want Orig. Ret. $19.50 **NB** $35 **MIB** Sec. Mkt. **$45-$50**

QX 409-2 TV BREAK
Comments: Handcrafted, 3" tall
Santa watches his favorite TV programs while relaxing in his hammock.
Artist: Donna Lee
☐ Purchased 19___ Pd $_______ MIB NB DB BNT
☐ Want Orig. Ret. $6.25 **NB** $10 **MIB** Sec. Mkt. **$18-$22**

QX 381-2 TWELVE DAYS OF CHRISTMAS: SIX GEESE-A-LAYING SIXTH SERIES
Comments: **Sixth in Series,** Acrylic, 3" tall, Dated 1989
Six geese are etched into heart-shaped acrylic. Captions in gold foil.
☐ Purchased 19___ Pd $_______ MIB NB DB BNT
☐ Want Orig. Ret. $6.75 **NB** $10 **MIB** Sec. Mkt. **$18-$22**

QX 485-5 TWENTY-FIVE YEARS TOGETHER PHOTOHOLDER
Comments: Porcelain, 3-3/4" tall, Dated Christmas 1989
A wreath decorated with holly and berries carries the silver caption: "25 Years Together." **Artist:** Anita Marra Rogers
☐ Purchased 19___ Pd $_______ MIB NB DB BNT
☐ Want Orig. Ret. $8.75 **NB** $7 **MIB** Sec. Mkt. **$15-$18**

QLX 723-5 UNICORN FANTASY
Comments: Lighted, Handcrafted, 4-1/2" tall
A shimmering unicorn prances inside a lighted, crystal gazebo.
Artist: Dill Rhodus
☐ Purchased 19___ Pd $_______ MIB NB DB BNT
☐ Want Orig. Ret. $9.50 **NB** $12 **MIB** Sec. Mkt. **$23-$25**

QXC 580-2 VISIT FROM SANTA: KEEPSAKE CLUB
Comments: Handcrafted, 4" tall, Dated 1989
Santa with toys and "personalized" sled or "Merry Christmas." Sled was personalized with the name of the Club member. Personalized ornaments are selling for less than the Merry Christmas verse. **Artist:** Ken Crow
☐ Purchased 19___ Pd $_______ MIB NB DB BNT
☐ Want Price: Came with Club Membership of $_______
NB $20 **MIB** Sec. Mkt. **$35-$40**

QX 489-2 WIGGLY SNOWMAN
Comments: Handcrafted, 4-3/4" tall
This pearly snowman wiggles and jiggles his head for you when you tap him. What fun!
Artist: Dill Rhodus
☐ Purchased 19___ Pd $_______ MIB NB DB BNT
☐ Want Orig. Ret. $6.75 **NB** $16 **MIB** Sec. Mkt. **$22-$25**

QX 462-5 WINDOWS OF WORLD: GERMAN
Comments: **Fifth in Series**, Handcrafted, 3-3/4" tall
Dated 1989. Caption: "Frohliche Weihnachten." A little German boy sits near his Christmas tree in his Alpine cottage, playing his concertina. **Artist:** Donna Lee
☐ Purchased 19___ Pd $_______ MIB NB DB BNT
☐ Want Orig. Ret. $10.75 **NB** $20 **MIB** Sec. Mkt. **$26-$30**

QX 427-2 WINTER SURPRISE
Comments: ***FIRST IN SERIES,*** Handcrafted, 3-1/4" tall
Dated 1989. Inside an egg-shaped peek-through ornament, two penguins decorate their white frosted Christmas tree with tiny ornaments. Series ended in 1992.
☐ Purchased 19___ Pd $_______ MIB NB DB BNT
☐ Want Orig. Ret. $10.75 **NB** $15 **MIB** Sec. Mkt. **$22-$26**

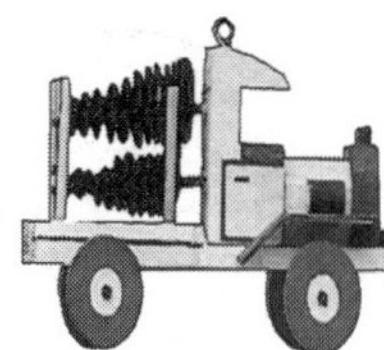

QX 459-5 WOOD CHILDHOOD: TRUCK
Comments: **Sixth and Final in Series**, Wood, 2" tall
Dated 1989. This truck is hauling a cargo of Christmas trees as it rolls along on movable wheels.
☐ Purchased 19___ Pd $_______ MIB NB DB BNT
☐ Want Orig. Ret. $7.75 **NB** $12 **MIB** Sec. Mkt. **$18-$24**

QX 274-5 WORLD OF LOVE
Comments: Silver Blue Glass Ball, 2-7/8" dia., Dated 1989
Children from around the world enjoy the holiday season.
Caption: "Christmas Is Here, And The Sound Of Love Echoes All Over The World."
☐ Purchased 19___ Pd $_______ MIB NB DB BNT
☐ Want Orig. Ret. $4.75 **NB** $15 **MIB** Sec. Mkt. **$25-$28**

1990 Collection

QX 317-3 ACROSS THE MILES
Comments: Acrylic, 3-1/2" tall
Etched into this oval acrylic a happy raccoon carries a large poinsettia. Caption: "Christmas Smiles Across The Miles."
Artist: LaDene Votruba
☐ Purchased 19___ Pd $_______ MIB NB DB BNT
☐ Want Orig. Ret. $6.75 **NB** $10 **MIB** Sec. Mkt. **$14-$16**

QX 474-6 ANGEL KITTY
Comments: Handcrafted, 2-9/16" tall, Dated '90
The artist used her own cat as the model for this ornament, dressed in a blue dress and slippers with sparkling net wings, a brass halo and brass star wand. **Artist:** Michele Pyda-Sevcik
☐ Purchased 19___ Pd $_______ MIB NB DB BNT
☐ Want Orig. Ret. $8.75 **NB** $14 **MIB** Sec. Mkt. **$24-$28**

QXC 445-3 ARMFUL OF JOY: KEEPSAKE CLUB
Comments: Handcrafted, 2-13/16" tall, Dated
This wide-eyed elf has quite a job. He's trying to balance a stack of colorful gifts. Top box is labeled "1990 Membership Kit." Club logo is on the elf's shopping bag. Available to Club Members only. **Artist:** John Francis (Collin)
☐ Purchased 19___ Pd $_______ MIB NB DB BNT
☐ Want Orig. Ret. $9.75 **NB** $20 **MIB** Sec. Mkt. **$35-$40**

School days can be the happiest days of your life, provided the children are old enough to go.

QX 548-6 BABY UNICORN
Comments: Fine Porcelain, 2" tall
This iridescent unicorn watches from large, dark eyes. His horn and hooves are painted gold. **Artist:** Anita Marra Rogers
☐ Purchased 19___ Pd $_______ MIB NB DB BNT
☐ Want Orig. Ret. $9.75 **NB** $12 **MIB** Sec. Mkt. **$18-$22**

QX 303-6 BABY'S FIRST CHRISTMAS
Comments: Acrylic, 4-7/32" tall, Dated 1990
A fluffy etched puppy takes a ride in a hot air balloon.
Caption: "Baby's First Christmas" **Artist:** Anita Marra Rogers
☐ Purchased 19___ Pd $_______ MIB NB DB BNT
☐ Want Orig. Ret. $6.75 **NB** $15 **MIB** Sec. Mkt. **$20-$22**

QX 485-6 BABY'S FIRST CHRISTMAS
Comments: Handcrafted, 2-3/8" tall, Dated '90
A baby bear dreams sweetly, with candy cane in hand, on a green leaf. "Baby's First Christmas" **Artist:** John Francis (Collin)
☐ Purchased 19___ Pd $_______ MIB NB DB BNT
☐ Want Orig. Ret. $7.75 **NB** $20 **MIB** Sec. Mkt. **$32-$35**

QLX 724-6 BABY'S FIRST CHRISTMAS
Comments: Light and Motion, Handcrafted, 3-3/4" tall
Dated 1990. The stork flies with his precious bundle above the snow-covered village. Caption: "Baby's First Christmas."
Artist: Don Palmiter
☐ Purchased 19___ Pd $_______ MIB NB DB BNT
☐ Want Orig. Ret. $28.00 **NB** $40 **MIB** Sec. Mkt. **$58-$62**

QX 206-3 BABY'S FIRST CHRISTMAS: BABY BOY
Comments: Blue Satin Ball, 2-7/8" dia., Dated 1990
Caption: "Baby's First Christmas" and "Joy Comes Into Your Heart When A Baby Boy Comes Into Your World." Usually harder to locate the boy than the girl.
☐ Purchased 19___ Pd $_______ MIB NB DB BNT
☐ Want Orig. Ret. $4.75 **NB** $12 **MIB** Sec. Mkt. **$18-$22**

QX 206-6 BABY'S FIRST CHRISTMAS: BABY GIRL
Comments: Pink Satin Ball, 2-7/8" dia., Dated 1990
Caption: "Baby's First Christmas" and "Joy Comes Into Your Heart When A Baby Girl Comes Into Your World."
☐ Purchased 19___ Pd $_______ MIB NB DB BNT
☐ Want Orig. Ret. $4.75 **NB** $12 **MIB** Sec. Mkt. **$18-$22**

QX 484-3 BABY'S FIRST CHRISTMAS PHOTOHOLDER
Comments: Fabric, 3-1/2" dia., Dated 1990
Embroidered bunnies scamper among the holly. Caption: "Baby's First Christmas" and "There Are So Many Moments To Cherish With A Beautiful Baby To Love."
☐ Purchased 19___ Pd $_______ MIB NB DB BNT
☐ Want Orig. Ret. $7.75 **NB** $15 **MIB** Sec. Mkt. **$25-$30**

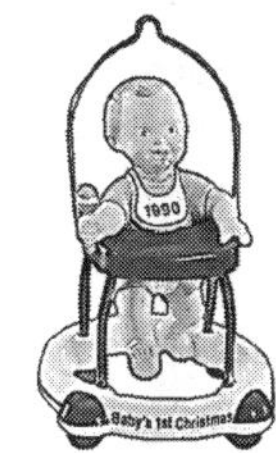

QX 485-3 BABY'S FIRST CHRISTMAS
Comments: Handcrafted, 3-3/8" tall, Dated 1990
This little baby is sure to keep happy in his red and white baby-walker. "Baby's 1st Christmas"
Artist: John Francis (Collin)
☐ Purchased 19___ Pd $_______ MIB NB DB BNT
☐ Want Orig. Ret. $9.75 **NB** $14 **MIB** Sec. Mkt. **$18-$22**

QX 486-3 BABY'S SECOND CHRISTMAS
Comments: Handcrafted, 2-3/16" tall, Dated '90
Identical to 1989; only date has changed.
Artist: John Francis (Collin)
☐ Purchased 19___ Pd $_______ MIB NB DB BNT
☐ Want Orig. Ret. $6.75 **NB** $20 **MIB** Sec. Mkt. **$28-$30**

QX 548-3 BEARBACK RIDER
Comments: Handcrafted, 3-1/4" tall, Dated 1990
A perky penguin with a red hat is riding "bear-back" on a polar bear on red and white rockers.
Artist: Ken Crow
☐ Purchased 19___ Pd $_______ MIB NB DB BNT
☐ Want Orig. Ret. $9.75 **NB** $14 **MIB** Sec. Mkt. **$22-$26**

QX 473-3 BEARY GOOD DEAL
Comments: Handcrafted, 2" tall
This cute flocked bear is playing with "Santa" cards and he must have a good hand by the smile on his face.
Artist: Bob Siedler
☐ Purchased 19___ Pd $_______ MIB NB DB BNT
☐ Want Orig. Ret. $6.75 **NB** $10 **MIB** Sec. Mkt. **$14-$16**

QLX 732-6 BEARY SHORT NAP
Comments: Lighted, Handcrafted, 2-3/8" tall, Dated
Tomorrow is Dec. 25 so this Santa bear cannot nap too long. A little mouse also naps in a drawer of his desk.
Artist: Bob Siedler
☐ Purchased 19___ Pd $_______ MIB NB DB BNT
☐ Want Orig. Ret. $10.00 **NB** $18 **MIB** Sec. Mkt. **$25-$30**

QX 203-3 BETSEY CLARK- HOME FOR CHRISTMAS
Comments: **Fifth in Series,** Pink Glass Ball, 2-7/8" dia. Dated 1990. Betsey's children are making holiday music. Caption: "Merry Christmas" and "Tis The Season When Hearts Are Singing!"
☐ Purchased 19___ Pd $_______ MIB NB DB BNT
☐ Want Orig. Ret. $5.00 **NB** $10 **MIB** Sec. Mkt. **$20-$22**

QX 519-6 BILLBOARD BUNNY
Comments: Handcrafted, 2-3/8" tall
The Easter bunny is wearing a bright red sandwich board proclaiming his thoughts about the Christmas season: "Bah Hum Bug" and "Ban Fruit Cake."
Artist: Julia Lee
☐ Purchased 19___ Pd $_______ MIB NB DB BNT
☐ Want Orig. Ret. $7.75 **NB** $12 **MIB** Sec. Mkt. **$15-$18**

QLX 736-3 BLESSINGS OF LOVE
Comments: Lighted Panorama Ball, 4-3/4" tall
The barn animals watch the Baby Jesus sleeping in the manger. Caption: "His Humble Birth Blessed All The Earth With Love And Joy Forever."
☐ Purchased 19___ Pd $_______ MIB NB DB BNT
☐ Want Orig. Ret. $14.00 **NB** $25 **MIB** Sec. Mkt. **$45-$50**

QX 504-3 BORN TO DANCE
Comments: Handcrafted, 2-9/16" tall
This little ballerina mouse is wearing a pink lacy tutu and is very flexible. She may be bent into various dance positions.
Artist: Sharon Pike
☐ Purchased 19___ Pd $_______ MIB NB DB BNT
☐ Want Orig. Ret. $7.75 **NB** $12 **MIB** Sec. Mkt. **$18-$22**

QX 449-3 BROTHER
Comments: Handcrafted, 2-3/16" tall, Dated 1990
The baseball glove claims "M.V.B. Most Valuable Brother" and the puppy sitting in the middle of the glove thinks so, too.
Artist: Bob Siedler
☐ Purchased 19___ Pd $_______ MIB NB DB BNT
☐ Want Orig. Ret. $5.75 **NB** $8 **MIB** Sec. Mkt. **$12-$14**

QX 316-6 CHILD CARE GIVER
Comments: Acrylic, 3" tall, Dated Christmas 1990
Etched onto this quatrefoil shaped ornament is a teddy bear hugging a bunny. Gold foil caption: "A Special Person Like You Is Every Child's Dream."
☐ Purchased 19___ Pd $_______ MIB NB DB BNT
☐ Want Orig. Ret. $6.75 **NB** $8 **MIB** Sec. Mkt. **$12-$15**

QX 487-6 CHILD'S FIFTH CHRISTMAS
Comments: Handcrafted, 2-3/8" tall, Dated '90
Identical to 1989; only date has changed.
Artist: Dill Rhodus
☐ Purchased 19___ Pd $_______ MIB NB DB BNT
☐ Want Orig. Ret. $6.75 **NB** $12 **MIB** Sec. Mkt. **$18-$20**

QX 487-3 CHILD'S FOURTH CHRISTMAS
Comments: Handcrafted, 3" tall, Dated '90
Identical to 1989; only date has changed.
Artist: John Francis (Collin)
☐ Purchased 19___ Pd $_______ MIB NB DB BNT
☐ Want Orig. Ret. $6.75 **NB** $12 **MIB** Sec. Mkt. **$18-$20**

QX 486-6 CHILD'S THIRD CHRISTMAS
Comments: Handcrafted, 2-1/2" tall, Dated '90
Identical to 1989; only date has changed.
Artist: John Francis (Collin)
☐ Purchased 19___ Pd $_______ MIB NB DB BNT
☐ Want Orig. Ret. $6.75 **NB** $15 **MIB** Sec. Mkt. **$20-$23**

QLX 724-3 CHILDREN'S EXPRESS
Comments: Light and Motion, Handcrafted, 3-3/4" tall
Two children have fun playing with a train set. The little boy swings his legs and moves his head back and forth as he watches the train. **Artist:** Linda Sickman
☐ Purchased 19___ Pd $_______ MIB NB DB BNT
☐ Want Orig. Ret. $28.00 **NB** $50 **MIB** Sec. Mkt. **$65-$70**

QX 436-6 CHIMING IN
Comments: Handcrafted/Brass, 5" tall, Dated 1990
A little squirrel is standing on top of the chimes waiting for his cue to ring the chimes with his candy cane mallet.
Artist: Sharon Pike
☐ Purchased 19___ Pd $_______ MIB NB DB BNT
☐ Want Orig. Ret. $9.75 **NB** $12 **MIB** Sec. Mkt. **$20-$24**

QLX 729-6 CHRIS MOUSE WREATH
Comments: **Sixth in Series**, Handcrafted, 4-1/2" tall
Dated 1990. Chris lights the candle inside a lovely green wreath decorated with gold balls.
Artist: Anita Marra Rogers
☐ Purchased 19___ Pd $_______ MIB NB DB BNT
☐ Want Orig. Ret. $10.00 **NB** $22 **MIB** Sec. Mkt. **$40-$45**

A husband who shops with his wife is a wait-watcher.

QLX 730-3 CHRISTMAS CLASSICS: THE LITTLEST ANGEL

Comments: **Fifth in Series**, Lighted, Handcrafted, 4-1/2" Dated 1990. The Littlest Angel kneels in awe as his gift to the Child is transformed into the Star of Bethlehem. Caption: "The Littlest Angel." **Artist:** John Francis (Collin)

☐ Purchased 19___ Pd $_______ MIB NB DB BNT
☐ Want Orig. Ret. $14.00 **NB** $30 **MIB** Sec. Mkt. **$38-$42**

QX 437-3 CHRISTMAS CROC

Comments: Handcrafted, 1-1/18" tall
This bright green crocodile wears a Christmas red smile and a fabric muffler to match. Twist the tip of his tail and he'll open his mouth for you. **Artist:** Michele Pyda-Sevcik

☐ Purchased 19___ Pd $_______ MIB NB DB BNT
☐ Want Orig. Ret. $7.75 **NB** $12 **MIB** Sec. Mkt. **$18-$20**

QX 450-6 CHRISTMAS KITTY

Comments: **Second in Series**, Fine Porcelain, 3" tall
This hand-painted grey kitten is lovely in her pale blue and white coat, hat and muff with sprigs of holly.
Artist: Anita Marra Rogers

☐ Purchased 19___ Pd $_______ MIB NB DB BNT
☐ Want Orig. Ret. $14.75 **NB** $18 **MIB** Sec. Mkt. **$30-$34**

QXC 476-6 CHRISTMAS LIMITED: KEEPSAKE CLUB

Comments: Limited Edition 38,700, Wood Display Stand Cast Metal, 2-5/8" tall. This blue and red, brass-trimmed locomotive has a brass bell that rings and wheels that turn. Available to Members only. **Artist:** Linda Sickman

☐ Purchased 19___ Pd $_______ MIB NB DB BNT
☐ Want Orig. Ret. $19.75 **NB** $85 **MIB** Sec. Mkt. **$95-$100**

QLX 727-6 CHRISTMAS MEMORIES

Comments: Light and Motion, Handcrafted, 4-1/4" tall
A Clydesdale horse pulls a family in a sleigh as they bring home their Christmas tree. Caption: "The Joy Is In Remembering..."
Artist: Duane Unruh

☐ Purchased 19___ Pd $_______ MIB NB DB BNT
☐ Want Orig. Ret. $25.00 **NB** $40 **MIB** Sec. Mkt. **$50-$55**

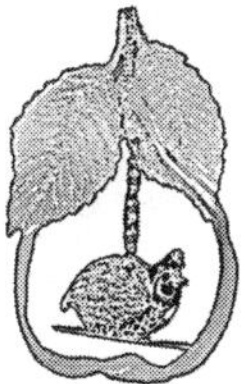

QX 524-6 CHRISTMAS PARTRIDGE

Comments: Dimensional Brass, 3-1/4" tall
A delicately etched partridge dangles inside the silhouette of a pear with large etched leaves.
Artist: Linda Sickman

☐ Purchased 19___ Pd $_______ MIB NB DB BNT
☐ Want Orig. Ret. $7.75 **NB** $10 **MIB** Sec. Mkt. **$15-$20**

QX 488-5 CLAUS CONSTRUCTION

Comments: Handcrafted, 4-3/4" tall
Reissued from 1989.
Artist: Ed Seale

☐ Purchased 19___ Pd $_______ MIB NB DB BNT
☐ Want Orig. Ret. $7.75 **NB** $15 **MIB** Sec. Mkt. **$28-$32**

QXC 445-6 CLUB HOLLOW: KEEPSAKE CLUB

Comments: Handcrafted, 1-7/8" tall, Dated
This feathered owl is reading "Whoo's Whoo" in the "Courier 1990," snug inside his snow-capped home. "Collectors Club + Me" is carved in the back of the tree. Club logo on the bottom.
Artist: Ken Crow

☐ Purchased 19___ Pd $_______ MIB NB DB BNT
☐ Want Price: Came with Club Membership of $_______
NB $20 **MIB** Sec. Mkt. **$30-$35**

QX 443-6 COLLECTOR'S PLATE: COOKIES FOR SANTA

Comments: **Fourth in Series**, Fine Porcelain, 3-1/4" dia. Dated 1990. Two children have set out a plate of cookies and are writing their wish list for Santa. Caption "Cookies For Santa" on back. **Artist:** LaDene Votruba

☐ Purchased 19___ Pd $_______ MIB NB DB BNT
☐ Want Orig. Ret. $8.75 **NB** $18 **MIB** Sec. Mkt. **$28-$32**

QX 448-6 COPY OF CHEER

Comments: Handcrafted, 2-1/16" tall, Dated 1990
A little mouse is making copies of his "Merry Christmas" message to distribute to everyone! **Artist:** Bob Siedler

☐ Purchased 19___ Pd $_______ MIB NB DB BNT
☐ Want Orig. Ret. $7.75 **NB** $10 **MIB** Sec. Mkt. **$16-$18**

QX 504-6 COUNTRY ANGEL

Comments: Handcrafted, Limited amount of trading reported. Sculpted to resemble hand-carved wood, the Country Angel was pulled from the line due to production problems. The only pieces produced were the retailers' display items.

☐ Purchased 19___ Pd $_______ MIB NB DB BNT
☐ Want Orig. Ret. $6.75 **NB** $75 **MIB** Sec. Mkt. **$125-$150**

QX 499-3 COYOTE CAROLS

Comments: Handcrafted, 3" tall
These coyotes love to howl a few bars of their favorite Christmas carols. Could it be "Home on the Range at Christmas"?
Artist: Julia Lee

☐ Purchased 19___ Pd $_______ MIB NB DB BNT
☐ Want Orig. Ret. $8.75 **NB** $14 **MIB** Sec. Mkt. **$20-$25**

QX 496-6 COZY GOOSE
Comments: Handcrafted, 3-1/8" tall
This goose wants to make sure he's warm throughout the holidays in his goose-down vest.
Artist: Sharon Pike
☐ Purchased 19___ Pd $_______ MIB NB DB BNT
☐ Want Orig. Ret. $5.75 **NB** $8 **MIB** Sec. Mkt. **$14-$16**

QX 458-6 CRAYOLA® CRAYON: BRIGHT MOVING COLORS
Comments: **Second in Series**, Handcrafted, 2-1/4" tall
This little white mouse has ingeniously crafted a sled using red and blue crayon runners and the box forms the sled.
Artist: Ken Crow
☐ Purchased 19___ Pd $_______ MIB NB DB BNT
☐ Want Orig. Ret. $8.75 **NB** $30 **MIB** Sec. Mkt. **$40-$45**

QX 453-3 DAD
Comments: Handcrafted, 2-1/2" tall, Dated 1990
Dad is one happy king, whether of forest or home in his oversized sweater. **Artist:** Julia Lee
☐ Purchased 19___ Pd $_______ MIB NB DB BNT
☐ Want Orig. Ret. $6.75 **NB** $8 **MIB** Sec. Mkt. **$15-$18**

QX 491-3 DAD-TO-BE
Comments: Handcrafted, 3" tall, Dated Christmas 1990
A proud papa to be is ready with suitcase in hand and a book of instructions, "Tips for Dads." **Artist:** Bob Siedler
☐ Purchased 19___ Pd $_______ MIB NB DB BNT
☐ Want Orig. Ret. $5.75 **NB** $14 **MIB** Sec. Mkt. **$20-$22**

QX 449-6 DAUGHTER
Comments: Handcrafted, 2-1/4" tall, Dated 1990
This snow "Daughter" shows graceful form on her ice skates. Red skirt and tam, green muffler. **Artist:** Bob Siedler
☐ Purchased 19___ Pd $_______ MIB NB DB BNT
☐ Want Orig. Ret. $5.75 **NB** $10 **MIB** Sec. Mkt. **$16-$20**

QLX 721-3 DEER CROSSING
Comments: Blinking Lights, Handcrafted, 3-15/16" tall
Just in case you miss the blinking red lights on this "Deer Crossing" sign, a little beaver with a Stop sign will remind you to watch for the deer. **Artist:** Bob Siedler
☐ Purchased 19___ Pd $_______ MIB NB DB BNT
☐ Want Orig. Ret. $18.00 **NB** $30 **MIB** Sec. Mkt. **$45-$50**

QX 505-6 DICKENS CAROLER BELL: MR. ASHBOURNE
Comments: Fine Porcelain, 4-1/4" tall, Dated 1990
FIRST IN COLLECTION. Special Edition. This bell combines the look of a figurine with the charm of a bell. Mr. Ashbourne opens his song book and sings. His jacket is trimmed in gold.
Artist: Robert Chad
☐ Purchased 19___ Pd $_______ MIB NB DB BNT
☐ Want Orig. Ret. $21.75 **NB** $25 **MIB** Sec. Mkt. **$45-$50**

QX 482-3 DONDER'S DINER
Comments: Handcrafted, 2-3/8" tall, Dated 1990
Peek into this streetcar converted into a diner and you'll see Donder serving Santa a hamburger. Signs on the walls advertise the fare. **Artist:** Donna Lee
☐ Purchased 19___ Pd $_______ MIB NB DB BNT
☐ Want Orig. Ret. $13.75 **NB** $12 **MIB** Sec. Mkt. **$20-$22**

QXC 447-6 DOVE OF PEACE: KEEPSAKE CLUB
Comments: Limited Edition 25,400, Wood Display Stand
Hand-Painted Fine Porcelain, 2-3/8" tall
This beautiful dove in flight carries a golden brass banner with the words "Peace," "Hope" and "Love." Available to Club Members only. **Artist:** Linda Sickman
☐ Purchased 19___ Pd $_______ MIB NB DB BNT
☐ Want Orig. Ret. $24.75 **NB** $35 **MIB** Sec. Mkt. **$60-$65**

QLX 735-6 ELF OF THE YEAR
Comments: Lighted, Handcrafted, 2-15/16" tall, Dated 1990
This little elf, all dressed in green, holds a glowing red 1990 outlined in gold. **Artist:** Patricia Andrews
☐ Purchased 19___ Pd $_______ MIB NB DB BNT
☐ Want Orig. Ret. $10.00 **NB** $15 **MIB** Sec. Mkt. **$25-$30**

QLX 726-5 ELFIN WHITTLER
Comments: Light and Motion, Handcrafted, 3-1/8" tall
Listen carefully and you can hear a tapping sound as this busy little elf carves a statue of Santa. A teddy bear has been whittled on the reverse side of the same stump.
Artist: Ken Crow
☐ Purchased 19___ Pd $_______ MIB NB DB BNT
☐ Want Orig. Ret. $20.00 **NB** $35 **MIB** Sec. Mkt. **$50-$55**

If you have been going in circles, perhaps you have been cutting too many corners.

QX 446-6 FABULOUS DECADE
Comments: ***FIRST IN SERIES***, Handcrafted/Brass, 1-3/8" tall Dated 1990. A frisky squirrel holds up a brass 1990 to usher in the decade. Popular Series!
Artist: Ed Seale
☐ Purchased 19___ Pd $_______ MIB NB DB BNT
☐ Want Orig. Ret. $7.75 **NB** $25 **MIB** Sec. Mkt. **$40-$45**

QX 517-3 FELIZ NAVIDAD
Comments: Handcrafted, 3" tall, Dated 1990
A little white mouse's serape shows the year as this fellow peeks out of a bright red chili pepper. His sombrero wishes everyone "Feliz Navidad."
☐ Purchased 19___ Pd $_______ MIB NB DB BNT
☐ Want Orig. Ret. $6.75 **NB** $12 **MIB** Sec. Mkt. **$25-$28**

QX 490-6 FIFTY YEARS TOGETHER
Comments: Faceted Glass, 2-9/16" tall
Dated Christmas 1990. Gold foil lettering is lovely on this heart-shaped faceted glass border. Caption: "50 Years Together."
Artist: Joyce Pattee
☐ Purchased 19___ Pd $_______ MIB NB DB BNT
☐ Want Orig. Ret. $9.75 **NB** $12 **MIB** Sec. Mkt. **$18-$20**

QLX 725-5 FIRST CHRISTMAS TOGETHER
Comments: Lighted, Handcrafted, 3-5/8" tall, Dated 1990
When the porch light turns off, a light inside the house turns on, silhouetting a couple in the picture window. "Our First Christmas Together" **Artist:** Donna Lee
☐ Purchased 19___ Pd $_______ MIB NB DB BNT
☐ Want Orig. Ret. $18.00 **NB** $30 **MIB** Sec. Mkt. **$45-$48**

QX 488-6 FIRST CHRISTMAS TOGETHER PHOTOHOLDER
Comments: Fabric, 3-1/4" tall, Dated 1990
Caption: "First Christmas Together" and "Loving Memories Are Celebrations Of The Heart." **Artist:** LaDene Votruba
☐ Purchased 19___ Pd $_______ MIB NB DB BNT
☐ Want Orig. Ret. $7.75 **NB** $10 **MIB** Sec. Mkt. **$18-$20**

QX 213-6 FIRST CHRISTMAS TOGETHER
Comments: Light Gold Glass Ball, 2-7/8" dia., Dated 1990
Inside a cozy living room, a raccoon couple trim their tree. "Our First Christmas Together" and "Love Decorates Our Lives With Joy!" **Artist:** LaDene Votruba
☐ Purchased 19___ Pd $_______ MIB NB DB BNT
☐ Want Orig. Ret. $4.75
NB $10 **MIB** Sec. Mkt. **$16-$20**

QX 314-6 FIRST CHRISTMAS TOGETHER
Comments: Acrylic, 2-3/4" tall, Dated 1990
Two etched doves and a heart-shaped holly wreath are set off with gold foil caption: "Our First Christmas Together."
Artist: LaDene Votruba
☐ Purchased 19___ Pd $_______ MIB NB DB BNT
☐ Want Orig. Ret. $6.75 **NB** $10 **MIB** Sec. Mkt. **$20-$22**

QX 488-3 FIRST CHRISTMAS TOGETHER
Comments: Handcrafted, 1-9/16" tall, Dated 1990
Two happy foxes snuggle together inside a cozy, snow-covered log. Caption: "Our First Christmas Together" and "Isn't Love Wonderful!" **Artist:** Michele Pyda-Sevcik
☐ Purchased 19___ Pd $_______ MIB NB DB BNT
☐ Want Orig. Ret. $9.75 **NB** $12 **MIB** Sec. Mkt. **$18-$22**

What a stunning tree of all Hallmark ornaments! Paula Baldridge has decorated the area below the tree as well! Many photos of collectors' trees are published in our Ornament Collector magazine.

QX 210-3 FIVE YEARS TOGETHER
Comments: Light Silver Glass Ball, 2-7/8" dia.
Dated Christmas 1990. Two deer prance around this teardrop ball. Caption: "5 Years Together" and "Loves Makes You Happy!" **Artist:** LaDene Votruba
☐ Purchased 19___ Pd $_______ MIB NB DB BNT
☐ Want Orig. Ret. $4.75 **NB** $10 **MIB** Sec. Mkt. **$18-$20**

QLX 723-6 FOREST FROLICS
Comments: **Second in Series**, Light and Motion, Dated 1990 Handcrafted, 4-1/2" tall. The forest friends have gathered together for fun and play. Caption: "Merry Christmas 1990."
Artist: Sharon Pike
☐ Purchased 19___ Pd $_______ MIB NB DB BNT
☐ Want Orig. Ret. $25.00 **NB** $50 **MIB** Sec. Mkt. **$65-$70**

QX 490-3 FORTY YEARS TOGETHER
Comments: Faceted Glass, 2-9/16" tall
Dated Christmas 1990. The caption in this heart-shaped glass ornament is in red foil. "40 Years Together."
Artist: Joyce Pattee
☐ Purchased 19___ Pd $_______ MIB NB DB BNT
☐ Want Orig. Ret. $9.75 **NB** $10 **MIB** Sec. Mkt. **$12-$14**

QX 414-3 FRIENDSHIP KITTEN
Comments: Handcrafted, 2-3/8" tall, Dated 1990
A white kitten seals a Hallmark card addressed "To a Special Friend" and has added his own greeting, "Merry Christmas."
Artist: Dill Rhodus
☐ Purchased 19___ Pd $_______ MIB NB DB BNT
☐ Want Orig. Ret. $6.75 **NB** $10 **MIB** Sec. Mkt. **$16-$18**

QX 216-6 FROM OUR HOME TO YOURS
Comments: Periwinkle Blue Glass Ball, 2-7/8" dia.
Dated Christmas 1990. A needlepoint design shows two homes and a white picket fence. Caption: "From Our Home To Yours."
☐ Purchased 19___ Pd $_______ MIB NB DB BNT
☐ Want Orig. Ret. $4.75 **NB** $6 **MIB** Sec. Mkt. **$12-$14**

QX 439-6 FROSTY FRIENDS
Comments: **Eleventh in Series,** Handcrafted, 2-1/2" tall
Dated 1990. The little Eskimo and a flocked seal are having lots of fun sliding on the ice.
Artist: Ed Seale
☐ Purchased 19___ Pd $_______ MIB NB DB BNT
☐ Want Orig. Ret. $9.75 **NB** $15 **MIB** Sec. Mkt. **$28-$32**

QX 230-3 GARFIELD
Comments: Blue Chrome Glass Ball, 2-7/8" dia., Dated 1990
Garfield cuts a neat design on the ice.
Caption: "Merry Christmas" and "Oh Yeah -- Happy New Year, Too!"
☐ Purchased 19___ Pd $_______ MIB NB DB BNT
☐ Want Orig. Ret. $4.75 **NB** $10 **MIB** Sec. Mkt. **$14-$18**

QX 475-6 GENTLE DREAMERS
Comments: Handcrafted, 1-7/16" tall
Nestled together in the center of a large red poinsettia are these two flocked bunnies. Clip-on orn. **Artist:** John Francis (Collin)
☐ Purchased 19___ Pd $_______ MIB NB DB BNT
☐ Want Orig. Ret. $8.75 **NB** $12 **MIB** Sec. Mkt. **$24-$28**

QX 280-3 GIFT BRINGERS, THE: ST. LUCIA
Comments: **Second in Series**, White Glass Ball, 2-7/9" dia.
St. Lucia welcomes the Christmas season in a white robe and a crown of candles. Caption: "The Gift Bringers, St. Lucia, Christmas 1990." **Artist:** LaDene Votruba
☐ Purchased 19___ Pd $_______ MIB NB DB BNT
☐ Want Orig. Ret. $5.00 **NB** $7 **MIB** Sec. Mkt. **$16-$18**

QX 503-3 GINGERBREAD ELF
Comments: Handcrafted, 3-11/16" tall, Dated 1990
A rosy cheeked gingerbread baker with a flowing white beard and sparkling chef's hat has baked two reindeer cookies, now on a silver tray.
☐ Purchased 19___ Pd $_______ MIB NB DB BNT
☐ Want Orig. Ret. $5.75 **NB** $8 **MIB** Sec. Mkt. **$15-$18**

QX 317-6 GODCHILD
Comments: Acrylic, 2-5/8" tall, Dated 1990
A happy, waving koala slides down the hill on his toboggan.
Caption: "Merry Christmas, Godchild."
Artist: John Francis (Collin)
☐ Purchased 19___ Pd $_______ MIB NB DB BNT
☐ Want Orig. Ret. $6.75 **NB** $8 **MIB** Sec. Mkt. **$12-$14**

QX 496-3 GOLF'S MY BAG
Comments: Handcrafted, 3-3/4" tall
You can surely tell which clubs are Santa's by his specially designed reindeer head covers for his clubs. Bag is inscribed "Golf's My Bag! Santa." **Artist:** Julia Lee
☐ Purchased 19___ Pd $_______ MIB NB DB BNT
☐ Want Orig. Ret. $7.75 **NB** $12 **MIB** Sec. Mkt. **$18-$22**

QX 523-6 GOOSE CART
Comments: Handcrafted, 1-3/4" tall
Riding in a green cart which says "Welcome Christmas" is this goose with a red bow around its neck.
☐ Purchased 19___ Pd $_______ MIB NB DB BNT
☐ Want Orig. Ret. $7.75 **NB** $8 **MIB** Sec. Mkt. **$12-$15**

QX 228-6 GRANDDAUGHTER
Comments: Pink Glass Ball, 2-7/8" dia.
Dated Christmas 1990. Caption: "Granddaughter-- Happiness Happens Wherever She Goes!"
Artist: Joyce A. Lyle
☐ Purchased 19___ Pd $_______ MIB NB DB BNT
☐ Want Orig. Ret. $4.75 **NB** $6 **MIB** Sec. Mkt. **$14-$16**

QX 310-6 GRANDDAUGHTER'S FIRST CHRISTMAS
Comments: Acrylic, 3-9/16" tall, Dated 1990
A little mouse of frosted, textured acrylic is sitting inside a hat box. Pink foil lettering announces "Granddaughter's First Christmas."
Artist: John Francis (Collin)
☐ Purchased 19___ Pd $_______ MIB NB DB BNT
☐ Want Orig. Ret. $6.75 **NB** $8 **MIB** Sec. Mkt. **$14-$18**

QX 223-6 GRANDMOTHER
Comments: Blue/White Glass Ball, 2-7/8" dia.
Dated Christmas 1990. A little mouse writes a message: "Grandmother... You're Wonderful!" on a tall wood fence.
Artist: LaDene Votruba
☐ Purchased 19___ Pd $_______ MIB NB DB BNT
☐ Want Orig. Ret. $4.75 **NB** $8 **MIB** Sec. Mkt. **$12-$15**

QX 225-3 GRANDPARENTS
Comments: Kelly Green Glass Ball, 2-7/8" dia., Dated 1990
Garland of evergreen, holly, candy canes, poinsettia and ribbon frame two messages: "Grandparents And Christmas... Two Beautiful Ways To Say Love" and "Season's Greetings."
☐ Purchased 19___ Pd $_______ MIB NB DB BNT
☐ Want Orig. Ret. $4.75 **NB** $6 **MIB** Sec. Mkt. **$12-$14**

QX 229-3 GRANDSON
Comments: Porcelain White Glass Ball, 2-7/8" dia.
Dated 1990. Five white bears are having loads of Christmas fun! Caption: "For You" and "A Grandson Fills Christmas With Cheer!"
Artist: LaDene Votruba
☐ Purchased 19___ Pd $_______ MIB NB DB BNT
☐ Want Orig. Ret. $4.75 **NB** $6 **MIB** Sec. Mkt. **$12-$14**

QX 306-3 GRANDSON'S FIRST CHRISTMAS
Comments: Acrylic, 3-21/32" tall, Dated 1990
A baby lamb is snuggled inside a clear box. "Grandson's First Christmas" in blue foil letters. **Artist:** John Francis (Collin)
☐ Purchased 19___ Pd $_______ MIB NB DB BNT
☐ Want Orig. Ret. $6.75 **NB** $8 **MIB** Sec. Mkt. **$14-$16**

QX 465-6 GREATEST STORY
Comments: ***FIRST IN SERIES***, Bisque Porcelain/Brass, 3-3/4" Dated 1990. A porcelain nativity dangles inside a lacy brass snowflake. **Artist:** LaDene Votruba
☐ Purchased 19___ Pd $_______ MIB NB DB BNT
☐ Want Orig. Ret. $12.75 **NB** $15 **MIB** Sec. Mkt. **$26-$30**

QX 471-3 HANG IN THERE
Comments: Handcrafted, 2-1/4" tall
A charming little raccoon in his green cap is hanging on tightly to a branch so as not to miss anything.
Artist: Ed Seale
☐ Purchased 19___ Pd $_______ MIB NB DB BNT
☐ Want Orig. Ret. $6.75 **NB** $10 **MIB** Sec. Mkt. **$18-$24**

QX 464-5 HAPPY VOICES
Comments: Wood, 3-1/8" tall
A shadow box provides a perfect setting for two carolers and their dog. Caption: "Happy Voices Fill The Air!"
Artist: LaDene Votruba
☐ Purchased 19___ Pd $_______ MIB NB DB BNT
☐ Want Orig. Ret. $6.75 **NB** $8 **MIB** Sec. Mkt. **$12-$15**

QX 476-3 HAPPY WOODCUTTER
Comments: Handcrafted, 2" tall, Dated 1990
This little fellow with the big toothy smile has cut a Christmas tree for his home... with a chain saw. **Artist:** Julia Lee
☐ Purchased 19___ Pd $_______ MIB NB DB BNT
☐ Want Orig. Ret. $9.75 **NB** $14 **MIB** Sec. Mkt. **$22-$26**

QX 446-3 HARK! IT'S HERALD
Comments: **Second in Series,** Handcrafted, 2-1/8" tall
Dated 1990. A bass drum with "Hark! It's Herald."
Artist: Ken Crow
☐ Purchased 19___ Pd $_______ MIB NB DB BNT
☐ Want Orig. Ret. $6.75
NB $14 **MIB** Sec. Mkt. **$20-$24**

QX 472-6 HEART OF CHRISTMAS
Comments: ***FIRST IN SERIES***, Handcrafted, 2" tall, Dated 1990
This double-hinged heart opens to reveal Santa filling the stockings. One child watches from behind the Christmas tree and another from the stairs. "Keep The Magic Of Christmas In Your Heart." **Artist:** Ed Seale
☐ Purchased 19___ Pd $_______ MIB NB DB BNT
☐ Want Orig. Ret. $13.75 **NB** $50 **MIB** Sec. Mkt. **$65-$70**

QX 492-3 HERE COMES SANTA: FESTIVE SURREY
Comments: **Twelfth in Series**, Handcrafted, 3-1/8" tall
Dated 1990. Santa's surrey has wheels that revolve and is decorated with a wreath on the back of the seat. A bag of toys is at Santa's feet. **Artist:** Linda Sickman
☐ Purchased 19___ Pd $_______ MIB NB DB BNT
☐ Want Orig. Ret. $14.75 **NB** $30 **MIB** Sec. Mkt. **$38-$42**

QX 524-3 HOLIDAY CARDINALS
Comments: Dimensional Brass, 2-13/16" tall
Intricate detail is achieved on this ornament by etching two separate layers of brass to add depth to the cardinals sitting among greenery. **Artist:** Joyce A. Lyle
☐ Purchased 19___ Pd $_______ MIB NB DB BNT
☐ Want Orig. Ret. $7.75 **NB** $12 **MIB** Sec. Mkt. **$18-$20**

QLX 733-3 HOLIDAY FLASH
Comments: Blinking Light, Handcrafted, 3-11/16" tall
A bluebird holds a "cheese" sign, assisting this photographer elf. The flash blinks on and off.
Artist: Robert Chad
☐ Purchased 19___ Pd $_______ MIB NB DB BNT
☐ Want Orig. Ret. $18.00 **NB** $22 **MIB** Sec. Mkt. **$38-$42**

QX 518-3 HOME FOR THE OWLIDAYS
Comments: Handcrafted, 2-1/4" tall
A little owl carries his suitcase under his wing on his way home for Christmas.
☐ Purchased 19___ Pd $_______ MIB NB DB BNT
☐ Want Orig. Ret. $6.75 **NB** $8 **MIB** Sec. Mkt. **$15-$18**

QLX 735-3 HOP 'N POP POPPER
Comments: Motion, Handcrafted, 3-7/16" tall
Turn on the motion switch and the popcorn appears to pop, making a popping sound. That's good news to the bunny waiting on top of the popper with his bowl in hand. Very popular!
Artist: Bob Siedler
☐ Purchased 19___ Pd $_______ MIB NB DB BNT
☐ Want Orig. Ret. $20.00 **NB** $75 **MIB** Sec. Mkt. **$90-$100**

QX 497-6 HOT DOGGER
Comments: Handcrafted, 2-7/8" tall, Dated '90
A plump, smiling "Hot Dogger" wears a green stocking cap and reflective glasses on the ski slopes. A toasted bun completes his attire. **Artist:** Ken Crow
☐ Purchased 19___ Pd $_______ MIB NB DB BNT
☐ Want Orig. Ret. $7.75 **NB** $12 **MIB** Sec. Mkt. **$18-$20**

QX 315-6 JESUS LOVES ME
Comments: Acrylic, 2-3/4" dia.
A happy bunny shows his joy in this etched frosted design. Caption: "Jesus Loves Me." **Artist:** Joyce Pattee
☐ Purchased 19___ Pd $_______ MIB NB DB BNT
☐ Want Orig. Ret. $6.75 **NB** $10 **MIB** Sec. Mkt. **$14-$16**

QX 468-3 JOLLY DOLPHIN
Comments: Handcrafted, 3" tall
This adorable, happy creature is performing tricks for the holiday season -- he's jumping through a be-ribboned wreath!
Artist: Anita Marra Rogers
☐ Purchased 19___ Pd $_______ MIB NB DB BNT
☐ Want Orig. Ret. $6.75 **NB** $10 **MIB** Sec. Mkt. **$22-$25**

QX 550-3 JOY IS IN THE AIR
Comments: Handcrafted, 2-5/8" tall, Dated 1990
Santa parachutes to earth to deliver some toys to the boys and girls. Caption: "Joy Is In The Air!"
Artist: Ken Crow
☐ Purchased 19___ Pd $_______ MIB NB DB BNT
☐ Want Orig. Ret. $7.75 **NB** $12 **MIB** Sec. Mkt. **$24-$28**

QX 410-6 KING KLAUS
Comments: Handcrafted, 4-5/8" tall
Santa waves a Christmas greeting from the top of the Empire State Building.
Artist: Ed Seale
☐ Purchased 19___ Pd $_______ MIB NB DB BNT
☐ Want Orig. Ret. $7.75 **NB** $8 **MIB** Sec. Mkt. **$12-$16**

QX 471-6 KITTY'S BEST PAL
Comments: Handcrafted, 2-3/8" tall, Dated 1990
This adorable kitten nestled in a dated Christmas stocking snuggles against Santa's cheek.
Artist: John Francis (Collin)
☐ Purchased 19___ Pd $_______ MIB NB DB BNT
☐ Want Orig. Ret. $6.75 **NB** $10 **MIB** Sec. Mkt. **$18-$22**

QLX 722-6 LETTER TO SANTA
Comments: Light, Handcrafted, 2-1/2" tall
A pajama-clad child sends his letter to Santa by way of the computer! His message: "Dear Santa, I've Been Very, Very, Very Good!" **Artist:** Anita Marra Rogers
☐ Purchased 19___ Pd $_______ MIB NB DB BNT
☐ Want Orig. Ret. $14.00 **NB** $16 **MIB** Sec. Mkt. **$28-$30**

QX 523-3 LITTLE DRUMMER BOY
Comments: Handcrafted, 2-3/8" tall, Dated 1990
This little fellow will march straight into your heart as he beats his dated drum.
Artist: Duane Unruh
☐ Purchased 19___ Pd $_______ MIB NB DB BNT
☐ Want Orig. Ret. $7.75 **NB** $8 **MIB** Sec. Mkt. **$18-$20**

QX 470-3 LONG WINTER'S NAP
Comments: Handcrafted, 1-3/8" tall, Dated 1990
A dachshund wearing a Santa cap sleeps soundly in an open-ended gift box. He fastens to the tree with a special clip.
Artist: Anita Marra Rogers
☐ Purchased 19___ Pd $_______ MIB NB DB BNT
☐ Want Orig. Ret. $6.75 **NB** $8 **MIB** Sec. Mkt. **$18-$22**

QX 547-6 LOVABLE DEARS
Comments: Handcrafted, 2-5/16" tall
A little girl, dressed in a bright red coat and blue muffler, shares a hug with her pet fawn.
Artist: Duane Unruh
☐ Purchased 19___ Pd $_______ MIB NB DB BNT
☐ Want Orig. Ret. $8.75 **NB** $10 **MIB** Sec. Mkt. **$15-$18**

QX 442-3 MARY'S ANGELS: ROSEBUD
Comments: **Third in Series**, Handcrafted and Acrylic, 3-1/8" tall
Rosebud, in a pink gown and with wings spread, holds a candle for all to see. She stands on a frosted acrylic cloud.
Artist: Robert Chad
☐ Purchased 19___ Pd $_______ MIB NB DB BNT
☐ Want Orig. Ret. $5.75 **NB** $22 **MIB** Sec. Mkt **$35-$40**

QX 444-6 MEOW MART
Comments: Handcrafted, 1-1/4" tall
What does it take to make a playful kitten happy? Only a sack from the "Meow Mart" and a ball of red yarn! **Artist:** Sharon Pike
☐ Purchased 19___ Pd $_______ MIB NB DB BNT
☐ Want Orig. Ret. $7.75 **NB** $10 **MIB** Sec. Mkt. **$18-$20**

QX 473-6 MERRY OLDE SANTA
Comments: ***FIRST IN SERIES***, Handcrafted, 4-3/4" tall
Dated 1990. An old-fashioned German Santa has toys tucked into his pockets and carries a small Christmas tree in his hand. Many sales found.
Artist: Ed Seale
☐ Purchased 19___ Pd $_______ MIB NB DB BNT
☐ Want Orig. Ret. $14.75 **NB** $50 **MIB** Sec. Mkt. **$70-$75**

QX 459-3 MOM AND DAD
Comments: Handcrafted, 2-1/2" tall, Dated 1990
These smiling bears are mailing a Hallmark card in their mailbox which is sitting on a tree stump. Mailbox reads "Mom And Dad."
Artist: Robert Chad
☐ Purchased 19___ Pd $_______ MIB NB DB BNT
☐ Want Orig. Ret. $8.75 **NB** $12 **MIB** Sec. Mkt. **$22-$25**

QX 491-6 MOM-TO-BE
Comments: Handcrafted, 2-7/8" tall, Dated Christmas 1990
First to debut for Mom-To-Be. This Momma bunny is happily awaiting a new little bundle.
Artist: Bob Siedler
☐ Purchased 19___ Pd $_______ MIB NB DB BNT
☐ Want Orig. Ret. $5.75 **NB** $20 **MIB** Sec. Mkt. **$30-$35**

QX 493-3 MOOY CHRISTMAS
Comments: Handcrafted, 2-1/16" tall
This little holstein wears a bright red scarf with its Christmas greeting: "Mooy Christmas."
☐ Purchased 19___ Pd $_______ MIB NB DB BNT
☐ Want Orig. Ret. $6.75 **NB** $10 **MIB** Sec. Mkt. **$20-$24**

QX 453-6 MOTHER
Comments: Ceramic w/Bisque Finish, 2-7/8 dia., Dated 1990
Delicate filigree lettering confirms that "Mother Is Love."
Tied with red ribbon. **Artist:** LaDene Votruba
☐ Purchased 19___ Pd $_______ MIB NB DB BNT
☐ Want Orig. Ret. $8.75 **NB** $12 **MIB** Sec. Mkt. **$18-$22**

QX 475-3 MOUSEBOAT
Comments: Handcrafted, 3" tall, Dated 1990
A whimsical sailor mouse is headed out to sea in his walnut shell boat. The sail contains the signature of the artist, "Seale" and the date. **Artist:** Ed Seale
☐ Purchased 19___ Pd $_______ MIB NB DB BNT
☐ Want Orig. Ret. $7.75 **NB** $8 **MIB** Sec. Mkt. **$14-$16**

QX 439-3 MR. AND MRS. CLAUS: POPCORN PARTY
Comments: **Fifth in Series**, Handcrafted, 3" tall, Dated 1990
Santa and his Mrs. have popped a big pan of popcorn and are busy stringing it to put on their Christmas tree.
Artist: Duane Unruh
☐ Purchased 19___ Pd $_______ MIB NB DB BNT
☐ Want Orig. Ret. $13.75 **NB** $35 **MIB** Sec. Mkt. **$50-$55**

QLX 726-3 MRS. SANTA'S KITCHEN
Comments: Light and Motion, Handcrafted, 4-3/4" tall
Dated 1990. Mrs. Santa's gingerbread cookies dance around her kitchen to celebrate. Caption: "Christmas Cookies Dance And Play To Celebrate The Holiday!" **Artist:** Dill Rhodus
☐ Purchased 19___ Pd $_______ MIB NB DB BNT
☐ Want Orig. Ret. $25.00 **NB** $55 **MIB** Sec. Mkt. **$75-$80**

QX 434-3 NEW HOME
Comments: Handcrafted, 2-11/16" tall, Dated 1990
A three-dimensional effect has been added to this heart to portray a home, tree and snowman. Caption: "There's No Place Like.. A New Home!" **Artist:** Michele Pyda-Sevcik
☐ Purchased 19___ Pd $_______ MIB NB DB BNT
☐ Want Orig. Ret. $6.75 **NB** $12 **MIB** Sec. Mkt. **$20-$25**

QX 229-6 NORMAN ROCKWELL ART
Comments: Light Gold Glass Ball, 2-7/8" dia., Christmas 1990
"Norman Rockwell, Famous Holiday Covers From *The Saturday Evening Post.*" "Merrie Christmas, *Post* Cover: Dec. 17, 1938." "*God Bless Us Everyone,* Said Tiny Tim" "*Post* Cover: Dec. 15, 1934." "Merrie Christmas, *Post* Cover: Dec. 8, 1928."
Artist: Joyce A. Lyle
☐ Purchased 19___ Pd $_______ MIB NB DB BNT
☐ Want Orig. Ret. $4.75 **NB** $10 **MIB** Sec. Mkt. **$14-$18**

QX 469-6 NOSTALGIC HOUSES AND SHOPS: HOLIDAY HOME
Comments: **Seventh in Series,** Handcrafted, 3-7/8" tall
Dated 1990. A decorated bottlebrush tree shows through the picture window of a furnished living room.
Artist: Donna Lee
☐ Purchased 19___ Pd $_______ MIB NB DB BNT
☐ Want Orig. Ret. $14.75 **NB** $40 **MIB** Sec. Mkt. **$55-$62**

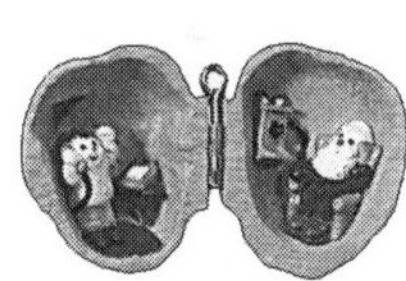

QX 519-3 NUTSHELL CHAT
Comments: Handcrafted, 1-7/16" tall
Inside a walnut shell a child is telling Santa what he wants for Christmas. Santa listens from the other half of the shell as he rests in his chair.
☐ Purchased 19___ Pd $_______ MIB NB DB BNT
☐ Want Orig. Ret. $6.75 **NB** $15 **MIB** Sec. Mkt. **$22-$24**

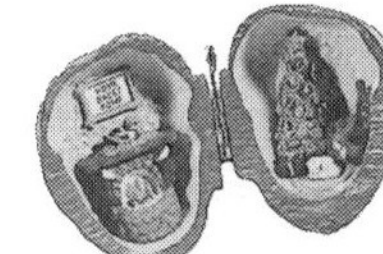

QX 465-2 NUTSHELL HOLIDAY
Comments: Handcrafted, 1-1/2" tall, Reissued from 1989.
Artist: Anita Marra Rogers
☐ Purchased 19___ Pd $_______ MIB NB DB BNT
☐ Want Orig. Ret. $5.75 **NB** $15 **MIB** Sec. Mkt. **$24-$28**

QLX 721-2 PARTRIDGES IN A PEAR
Comments: Lighted, Dimensional Brass, 3-3/4" tall
An exquisite brass pear features a filigree partridge in each section of the ornament.
Artist: Joyce A. Lyle
☐ Purchased 19___ Pd $_______ MIB NB DB BNT
☐ Want Orig. Ret. $14.00 **NB** $20 **MIB** Sec. Mkt. **$28-$32**

QX 210-6 PEACEFUL KINGDOM
Comments: Light Gold Glass Ball, 2-7/8" dia.
Dated Christmas 1990. A lion cub snuggles with a lamb. Caption: "And Peace Will Reign In The Kingdom -- The Lion Will Lie Down With The Lamb."
☐ Purchased 19___ Pd $_______ MIB NB DB BNT
☐ Want Orig. Ret. $4.75 **NB** $12 **MIB** Sec. Mkt. **$15-$20**

QX 223-3 PEANUTS®
Comments: Chrome Glass Ball, 2-7/8" dia., Dated 1990
Schroeder plays a lively Christmas melody while the rest of the gang dances merrily. Caption: "Christmas Is The Merriest, Lightest, Jolliest, Brightest, Happiest Time Of The Year!" Peanuts anniversary logo is on the box with the words "40 Years Of Happiness."
☐ Purchased 19___ Pd $_______ MIB NB DB BNT
☐ Want Orig. Ret. $4.75 **NB** $15 **MIB** Sec. Mkt. **$20-$22**

QX 497-3 PEPPERONI MOUSE
Comments: Handcrafted, 1-3/4" tall
Since mice like cheese, why not pizza!? This little mouse especially likes pepperoni pizza! **Artist:** Bob Siedler
☐ Purchased 19___ Pd $_______ MIB NB DB BNT
☐ Want Orig. Ret. $6.75 **NB** $10 **MIB** Sec. Mkt. **$15-$18**

QX 469-3 PERFECT CATCH
Comments: Handcrafted, 3-13/16" tall, Dated '90
Santa proves that he's a man for all seasons as he catches the fly ball to win the game! His team is the "North Pole Nicks." Go Santa! **Artist:** Bob Siedler
☐ Purchased 19___ Pd $_______ MIB NB DB BNT
☐ Want Orig. Ret. $7.75 **NB** $10 **MIB** Sec. Mkt. **$18-$20**

QX 466-6 POLAR JOGGER
Comments: Handcrafted, 1-5/8" tall
This chubby fellow is waddling away some extra calories. To keep warm, he's donned a red sweat shirt from "Polar College."
Artist: Bob Siedler
☐ Purchased 19___ Pd $_______ MIB NB DB BNT
☐ Want Orig. Ret. $5.75 **NB** $10 **MIB** Sec. Mkt. **$14-$18**

QX 462-6 POLAR PAIR
Comments: Handcrafted, 2" tall
What's more fun than one penguin? Why, it's two! And everywhere the parent goes, baby tags along in his own special backpack. **Artist:** Bob Siedler
☐ Purchased 19___ Pd $_______ MIB NB DB BNT
☐ Want Orig. Ret. $5.75 **NB** $8 **MIB** Sec. Mkt. **$15-$18**

QX 515-6 POLAR SPORT
Comments: Handcrafted 1-3/4" tall
Our dapper penguin draws looks from everyone around wearing a scarf and beret and driving his red convertible sports car.
Artist: Bob Siedler
☐ Purchased 19___ Pd $_______ MIB NB DB BNT
☐ Want Orig. Ret. $7.75 **NB** $10 **MIB** Sec. Mkt. **$18-$20**

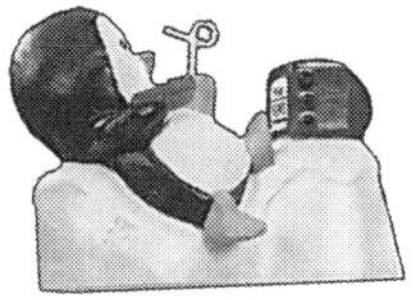

QX 516-6 POLAR TV
Comments: Handcrafted 1-5/8" tall
Life can be great! This penguin relaxes on a shimmery iceberg and sips a cool drink as he watches the "Polar News" on television. **Artist:** Bob Siedler
☐ Purchased 19___ Pd $_______ MIB NB DB BNT
☐ Want Orig. Ret. $7.75 **NB** $8 **MIB** Sec. Mkt. **$14-$18**

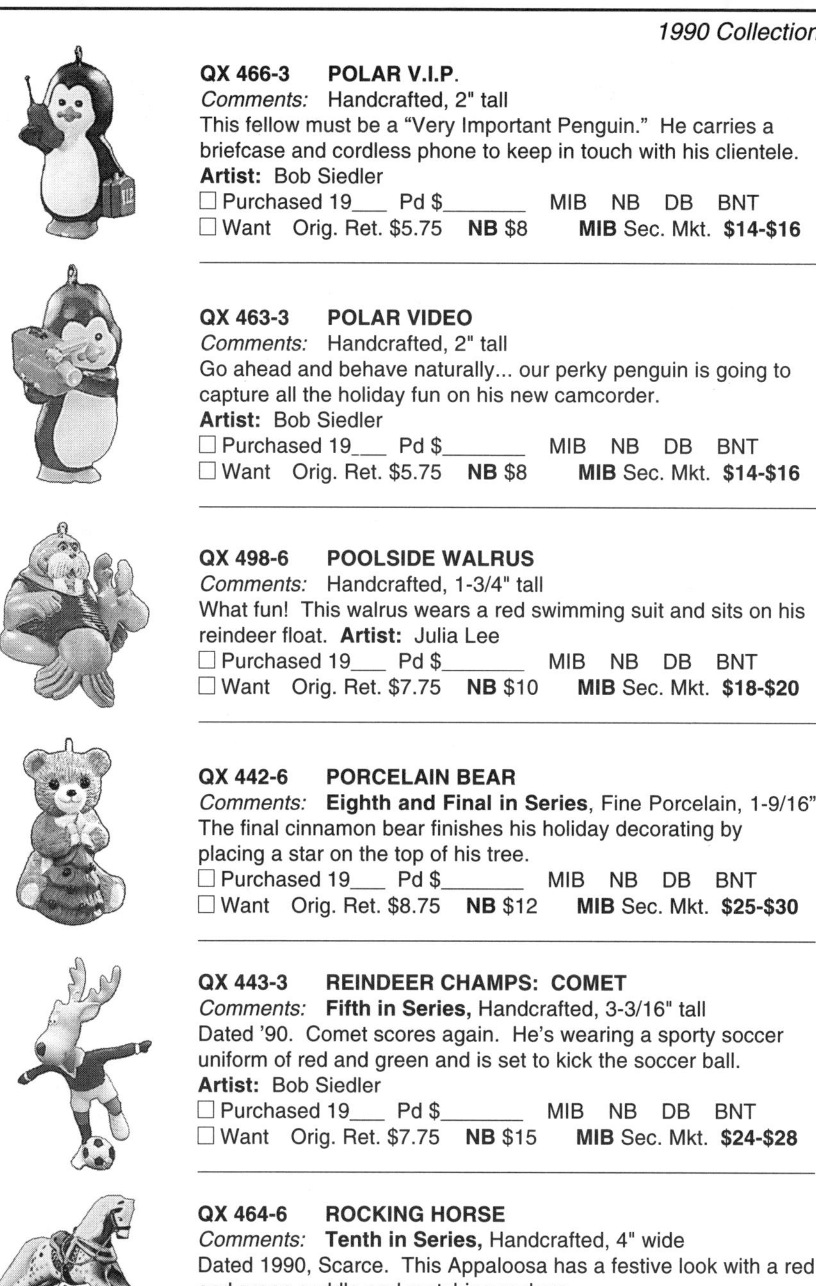

QX 466-3 POLAR V.I.P.
Comments: Handcrafted, 2" tall
This fellow must be a "Very Important Penguin." He carries a briefcase and cordless phone to keep in touch with his clientele.
Artist: Bob Siedler
☐ Purchased 19___ Pd $_______ MIB NB DB BNT
☐ Want Orig. Ret. $5.75 **NB** $8 **MIB** Sec. Mkt. **$14-$16**

QX 463-3 POLAR VIDEO
Comments: Handcrafted, 2" tall
Go ahead and behave naturally... our perky penguin is going to capture all the holiday fun on his new camcorder.
Artist: Bob Siedler
☐ Purchased 19___ Pd $_______ MIB NB DB BNT
☐ Want Orig. Ret. $5.75 **NB** $8 **MIB** Sec. Mkt. **$14-$16**

QX 498-6 POOLSIDE WALRUS
Comments: Handcrafted, 1-3/4" tall
What fun! This walrus wears a red swimming suit and sits on his reindeer float. **Artist:** Julia Lee
☐ Purchased 19___ Pd $_______ MIB NB DB BNT
☐ Want Orig. Ret. $7.75 **NB** $10 **MIB** Sec. Mkt. **$18-$20**

QX 442-6 PORCELAIN BEAR
Comments: **Eighth and Final in Series**, Fine Porcelain, 1-9/16"
The final cinnamon bear finishes his holiday decorating by placing a star on the top of his tree.
☐ Purchased 19___ Pd $_______ MIB NB DB BNT
☐ Want Orig. Ret. $8.75 **NB** $12 **MIB** Sec. Mkt. **$25-$30**

QX 443-3 REINDEER CHAMPS: COMET
Comments: **Fifth in Series,** Handcrafted, 3-3/16" tall
Dated '90. Comet scores again. He's wearing a sporty soccer uniform of red and green and is set to kick the soccer ball.
Artist: Bob Siedler
☐ Purchased 19___ Pd $_______ MIB NB DB BNT
☐ Want Orig. Ret. $7.75 **NB** $15 **MIB** Sec. Mkt. **$24-$28**

QX 464-6 ROCKING HORSE
Comments: **Tenth in Series,** Handcrafted, 4" wide
Dated 1990, Scarce. This Appaloosa has a festive look with a red and green saddle and matching rockers.
Artist: Linda Sickman
☐ Purchased 19___ Pd $_______ MIB NB DB BNT
☐ Want Orig. Ret. $10.75 **NB** $35 **MIB** Sec. Mkt. **$55-$60**

QX 468-6 S. CLAUS TAXI
Comments: Handcrafted, 2" tall, Dated 12-25-90
That Santa's taxi is in constant demand is proven by the teddy bear passenger in the front seat. The taxi's wheels revolve. License: "Santa." **Artist:** Peter Dutkin
☐ Purchased 19___ Pd $_______ MIB NB DB BNT
☐ Want Orig. Ret. $11.75 **NB** $18 **MIB** Sec. Mkt. **$28-$32**

QX 498-3 SANTA SCHNOZ
Comments: Handcrafted, 2-1/2" tall
Santa sports a phony pair of glasses, mustache and schnoz! He's hiding a gift behind his back.
Artist: Ken Crow
☐ Purchased 19___ Pd $_______ MIB NB DB BNT
☐ Want Orig. Ret. $6.75 **NB** $10 **MIB** Sec. Mkt. **$22-$26**

QLX 725-6 SANTA'S HO-HO-HOEDOWN
Comments: Light and Motion, Handcrafted, 4-3/8" tall
"Ho-Ho-Ho! Doe-See-Doe! Grab Your Partner -- And 'Round We Go!" calls Santa as four reindeer couples twirl around at the barn dance. **Artist:** Ken Crow
☐ Purchased 19___ Pd $_______ MIB NB DB BNT
☐ Want Orig. Ret. $25.00 **NB** $70 **MIB** Sec. Mkt. **$85-$90**

QX 227-3 SISTER
Comments: Porcelain White Glass Ball, 2-7/8" dia., Dated 1990
Large colorful poinsettias add charm. Caption: "A Sister Adds Her Own Special Touch To The Beauty And Joy Of Christmas."
☐ Purchased 19___ Pd $_______ MIB NB DB BNT
☐ Want Orig. Ret. $4.75 **NB** $8 **MIB** Sec. Mkt. **$12-$14**

QX 472-3 SNOOPY® AND WOODSTOCK
Comments: Handcrafted, 2-1/4" tall
Snoopy and Woodstock share a special hug between friends. The slogan "40 Years Of Happiness" appears on the ornament box. **Artist:** Dill Rhodus
☐ Purchased 19___ Pd $_______ MIB NB DB BNT
☐ Want Orig. Ret. $6.75 **NB** $12 **MIB** Sec. Mkt. **$24-$28**

QX 451-6 SON
Comments: Handcrafted, 1-7/8" tall, Dated 1990
A warmly dressed "snowboy" loves to play hockey. His cap reads "Son" and his jersey announces the year.
Artist: Bob Siedler
☐ Purchased 19___ Pd $_______ MIB NB DB BNT
☐ Want Orig. Ret. $5.75 **NB** $7 **MIB** Sec. Mkt. **$14-$16**

QLX 725-3 SONG & DANCE
Comments: Motion and Music, Handcrafted, 4-1/8" tall
A mouse couple spins around and around on a record as it plays *Jingle Bells* on the old phonograph. Caption: "Love And Christmas... Two Reasons To Celebrate!"
Artist: Anita Marra Rogers
☐ Purchased 19___ Pd $_______ MIB NB DB BNT
☐ Want Orig. Ret. $20.00 **NB** $65 **MIB** Sec. Mkt. **$85-$90**

QX 431-2 SPENCER® SPARROW, ESQ.
Comments: Handcrafted, 1-3/4" tall, Reissued from 1989.
Artist: Sharon Pike
☐ Purchased 19___ Pd $_______ MIB NB DB BNT
☐ Want Orig. Ret. $6.75 **NB** $12 **MIB** Sec. Mkt. **$18-$22**

QX 549-6 SPOON RIDER
Comments: Handcrafted, 2-2/4" tall
A couple of mischievous elves are ready to go sledding -- in a teaspoon. Where's the snow?
Artist: Patricia Andrews
☐ Purchased 19___ Pd $_______ MIB NB DB BNT
☐ Want Orig. Ret. $9.75 **NB** $12 **MIB** Sec. Mkt. **$18-$20**

QLX 730-6 STARLIGHT ANGEL
Comments: Lighted, Handcrafted, 2-3/4" tall
A sweet angel wearing a blue robe and shiny brass halo is carrying a bag full of stars.
Artist: Anita Marra Rogers
☐ Purchased 19___ Pd $_______ MIB NB DB BNT
☐ Want Orig. Ret. $14.00 **NB** $20 **MIB** Sec. Mkt. **$34-$38**

QLX 733-6 STARSHIP CHRISTMAS
Comments: Blinking Lights, Handcrafted, 2-1/4" tall
Dated 1990. Santa and one of his reindeer fly off in their "Starship Christmas S.S." to deliver a bag of toys to children in other galaxies. **Artist:** Bob Siedler
☐ Purchased 19___ Pd $_______ MIB NB DB BNT
☐ Want Orig. Ret. $18.00 **NB** $35 **MIB** Sec. Mkt. **$50-$55**

QX 518-6 STITCHES OF JOY
Comments: Handcrafted, 2-1/2" tall
A blue-gowned mama rabbit is working her needlepoint sampler with a special Christmas message: "Joy."
Artist: Julia Lee
☐ Purchased 19___ Pd $_______ MIB NB DB BNT
☐ Want Orig. Ret. $7.75 **NB** $15 **MIB** Sec. Mkt. **$22-$26**

QX 456-5 STOCKING KITTEN
Comments: Handcrafted, 2-3/4" tall
Reissued from 1989. **Artist:** Sharon Pike
☐ Purchased 19___ Pd $_______ MIB NB DB BNT
☐ Want Orig. Ret. $6.75 **NB** $9 **MIB** Sec. Mkt. **$15-$18**

QX 549-3 STOCKING PALS
Comments: Handcrafted, 3-1/4" tall, Dated 1990
A dated gift balances in the top of a knit stocking. Two koalas hold the yarn ends to the stocking.
Artist: Ed Seale
☐ Purchased 19___ Pd $_______ MIB NB DB BNT
☐ Want Orig. Ret. $10.75 **NB** $12 **MIB** Sec. Mkt. **$22-$25**

QXC 447-3 SUGAR PLUM FAIRY: KEEPSAKE CLUB
Comments: Limited Edition 25,400, Wood display stand
Hand-Painted Fine Porcelain, 5-1/2" tall
This ballerina dances gracefully on her toes in her pearly white tutu. She's a lovely addition to the Keepsake line. Available to Members only. **Artist:** Patricia Andrews
☐ Purchased 19___ Pd $_______ MIB NB DB BNT
☐ Want Orig. Ret. $27.75 **NB** $30 **MIB** Sec. Mkt. **$52-$55**

QX 489-3 SWEETHEART
Comments: Handcrafted, 3-1/8" tall, Dated 1990
Two gifts rest beside a snowy wishing well "For Sweethearts." The well is filled with acrylic "water." **Artist:** Dill Rhodus
☐ Purchased 19___ Pd $_______ MIB NB DB BNT
☐ Want Orig. Ret. $11.75 **NB** $15 **MIB** Sec. Mkt. **$25-$30**

QX 448-3 TEACHER
Comments: Handcrafted, 2-3/8" tall, Dated Dec. 25, 1990
An adorable chipmunk points to the lessons he has learned, along with a message, "We ♥ Teacher." **Artist:** Ed Seale
☐ Purchased 19___ Pd $_______ MIB NB DB BNT
☐ Want Orig. Ret. $7.75 **NB** $6 **MIB** Sec. Mkt. **$12-$15**

QX 215-3 TEN YEARS TOGETHER
Comments: White Glass Ball, 2-7/8" dia.
Dated Christmas 1990. Redbirds enjoy an early winter snowfall. Caption: "Love Wraps The World In Wonder. 10 Years Together."
Artist: Joyce A. Lyle
☐ Purchased 19___ Pd $_______ MIB NB DB BNT
☐ Want Orig. Ret. $4.75 **NB** $6 **MIB** Sec. Mkt. **$12-$14**

QX 499-6 THREE LITTLE PIGGIES
Comments: Handcrafted, 2-5/8" tall
A red and blue five-toed stocking holds these happy chaps in their colorful nightcaps.
Artist: Ken Crow
☐ Purchased 19___ Pd $_______ MIB NB DB BNT
☐ Want Orig. Ret. $7.75 **NB** $10 **MIB** Sec. Mkt. **$18-$20**

QX 213-3 TIME FOR LOVE: CARDINALS
Comments: Light Gold Glass Ball, 2-7/8" dia., Dated 1990
A pair of cardinals perch on evergreen and holly branches. Caption: "Christmas Is A Beautiful Time To Be In Love."
Artist: Joyce A. Lyle
☐ Purchased 19___ Pd $_______ MIB NB DB BNT
☐ Want Orig. Ret. $4.75 **NB** $6 **MIB** Sec. Mkt. **$14-$16**

QX 303-3 TWELVE DAYS OF CHRISTMAS: SEVEN SWANS A-SWIMMING
Comments: **Seventh in a Series**, Acrylic, 3-3/8" tall
Dated 1990. An etched swan swims on this acrylic teardrop symbolic of the gifts given on the seventh day. Captions in gold foil.
☐ Purchased 19___ Pd $_______ MIB NB DB BNT
☐ Want Orig. Ret. $6.75 **NB** $12 **MIB** Sec. Mkt. **$22-$25**

QX 489-6 TWENTY-FIVE YEARS TOGETHER
Comments: Faceted Glass , 2-9/16" tall, Dated Christmas 1990
The faceted glass heart has a silver caption: "25 Years Together." **Artist:** Joyce Pattee
☐ Purchased 19___ Pd $_______ MIB NB DB BNT
☐ Want Orig. Ret. $9.75 **NB** $10 **MIB** Sec. Mkt. **$14-$16**

QX 492-6 TWO PEAS IN A POD
Comments: Handcrafted, 3-3/4" tall
This pea pod houses two smiling peas who are looking through an opening in the pod. Tied with red satin ribbon.
Artist: Patricia Andrews
☐ Purchased 19___ Pd $_______ MIB NB DB BNT
☐ Want Orig. Ret. $4.75 **NB** $20 **MIB** Sec. Mkt. **$30-$35**

QX 477-3 WELCOME, SANTA
Comments: Handcrafted, 2-5/8" tall
Press the candle and Santa starts up the chimney. Caption: "Welcome Santa" and "With A Wink And A Grin And A Big 'Ho Ho Ho,' Santa Drops In With A Christmas Hello!" **Artist:** Ken Crow
☐ Purchased 19___ Pd $_______ MIB NB DB BNT
☐ Want Orig. Ret. $11.75 **NB** $18 **MIB** Sec. Mkt. **$25-$30**

QX 463-6 WINDOWS OF THE WORLD: IRISH
Comments: **Sixth and Final in Series,** Handcrafted, 3" tall
Dated 1990. An Irish child leans out her window to see a leprechaun holding a gift. The caption "Nollaig Shona" means Merry Christmas. **Artist:** Donna Lee
☐ Purchased 19___ Pd $_______ MIB NB DB BNT
☐ Want Orig. Ret. $10.75 **NB** $10 **MIB** Sec. Mkt. **$16-$22**

QX 444-3 WINTER SURPRISE
Comments: **Second in Series**, Handcrafted, 3-1/4" tall
Dated 1990. Two penguins ice skate on a frozen lake. The scene is completed by two bottle brush trees and a glittering blue sky.
Artist: John Francis (Collin)
☐ Purchased 19___ Pd $_______ MIB NB DB BNT
☐ Want Orig. Ret. $10.75 **NB** $12 **MIB** Sec. Mkt. **$18-$25**

Pictured above is Kurt M. Kessler's tree decorated with 556 Hallmark ornaments. Wow! It surely took more than an hour to decorate this tree!

Jody Shaffer's favorite time of the year is Christmas. Living in Las Vegas can make getting into the Christmas spirit a little bit difficult, but she said, "The day after Thanksgiving I dig into my boxes of Hallmark ornaments and begin decorating." Her tree, decorated with all Hallmark ornaments, is pictured below.

Mary Zini's Dalmatian, Ashley, sits by her tree decorated with Dalmatian ornaments and lights.

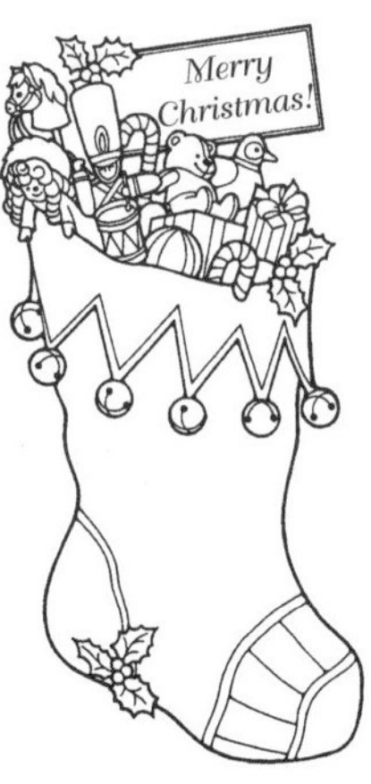

This attractively decorated miniature tree is surrounded by miniature Hallmark carousels. In the background of Lois Winter's display is a full size carousel horse! Nice!

1991 Collection

QX 488-7 A CHILD'S CHRISTMAS
Comments: Handcrafted, 2-3/8" tall, Dated 1991
Seated on a braided rug captioned "A Child's Christmas" is this wide-eyed child in a red sleeper with his old-fashioned wood-style blocks. **Artist:** John Francis (Collin)
☐ Purchased 19___ Pd $_______ MIB NB DB BNT
☐ Want Orig. Ret. $9.75 **NB** $10 **MIB** Sec. Mkt. **$14-$16**

QX 499-7 A CHRISTMAS CAROL COLLECTION: BOB CRATCHIT
Comments: Hand-Painted Fine Porcelain, 3-15/16" tall
Caption: "Bob Cratchit 1991." Holding a Ledger and quill pen, Bob Cratchit wears the dress of a Victorian bookkeeper.
Artist: Duane Unruh
☐ Purchased 19___ Pd $_______ MIB NB DB BNT
☐ Want Orig. Ret. $13.75 **NB** $16 **MIB** Sec. Mkt. **$28-$30**

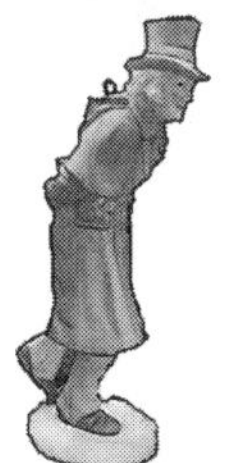

QX 498-9 A CHRISTMAS CAROL COLLECTION: EBENEZER SCROOGE
Comments: Hand-Painted Fine Porcelain, 4-1/16" tall
Caption: "Ebenezer Scrooge 1991." A content, smiling Scrooge has found the real source of happiness in giving to others.
Artist: Duane Unruh
☐ Purchased 19___ Pd $_______ MIB NB DB BNT
☐ Want Orig. Ret. $13.75 **NB** $15 **MIB** Sec. Mkt. **$35-$40**

QX 479-9 A CHRISTMAS CAROL COLLECTION: MERRY CAROLERS
Comments: Hand-Painted Fine Porcelain, 4-1/8" tall
Caption: "Merry Carolers 1991." A man and woman sing the story of Christmas. Caption on pages: "Joy To The World! The Lord Is Come." **Artist:** Duane Unruh
☐ Purchased 19___ Pd $_______ MIB NB DB BNT
☐ Want Orig. Ret. $29.75 **NB** $35 **MIB** Sec. Mkt. **$80-$85**

QX 499-9 A CHRISTMAS CAROL COLLECTION: MRS. CRATCHIT
Comments: Hand-Painted Fine Porcelain, 3-7/8" tall
Caption: "Mrs. Cratchit 1991." In a ruffled dress, Mrs. Cratchit serves a Christmas turkey provided by a generous Scrooge.
Artist: Duane Unruh
☐ Purchased 19___ Pd $_______ MIB NB DB BNT
☐ Want Orig. Ret. $13.75 **NB** $15 MIB Sec. Mkt. **$28-$32**

QX 503-7 A CHRISTMAS CAROL COLLECTION: TINY TIM
Comments: Hand-Painted Fine Porcelain, 2-1/8" tall
Caption: "Tiny Tim 1991." The child sits on a wooden bench with his crutches nearby. **Artist:** Duane Unruh
☐ Purchased 19___ Pd $_______ MIB NB DB BNT
☐ Want Orig. Ret. $10.75 **NB** $15 **MIB** Sec. Mkt. **$32-$38**

QX 315-7 ACROSS THE MILES
Comments: Acrylic, 2-5/8" tall, Dated 1991
Sparkling acrylic, framed in brass, is etched with holly leaves and ribbons. "There's No Such Thing As Far Away When Christmas Draws Us Close." **Artist:** Joyce Lyle
☐ Purchased 19___ Pd $_______ MIB NB DB BNT
☐ Want Orig. Ret. $6.75 **NB** $8 **MIB** Sec. Mkt. **$12-$14**

QX 532-9 ALL STAR
Comments: Handcrafted, 2-1/8" tall, Dated '91
This two-toned turtle is "All Star 91" as shown by his umpire's cap and his catcher's mitt. **Artist:** Bob Siedler
☐ Purchased 19___ Pd $_______ MIB NB DB BNT
☐ Want Orig. Ret. $6.75 **NB** $12 **MIB** Sec. Mkt. **$18-$20**

QLX 711-7 ARCTIC DOME
Comments: Light and Motion, Handcrafted, 2-15/16" tall
Dated 1991. Santa and his North Stars reindeer are playing the polar bear South Paws. The lines move back and forth across the field and Santa spins away from the defenders.
Artist: Ken Crow
☐ Purchased 19___ Pd $_______ MIB NB DB BNT
☐ Want Orig. Ret. $25.00 **NB** $40 **MIB** Sec. Mkt. **$48-$52**

QX 510-7 BABY'S FIRST CHRISTMAS
Comments: Silver-Plated, 2-5/8" tall, Dated 1991
An intricately sculpted bear peeks out of the top of a baby bootie. A silver tag detaches for engraving and personalization.
Artist: John Francis (Collin)
☐ Purchased 19___ Pd $_______ MIB NB DB BNT
☐ Want Orig. Ret. $17.75 **NB** $12 **MIB** Sec. Mkt. **$22-$26**

QLX 724-7 BABY'S FIRST CHRISTMAS
Comments: Lighted, Handcrafted, 4-1/2" tall, Dated 1991
Santa takes time from his busy schedule. Plays *Rock-A-Bye-Baby.* Caption: "Baby's First Christmas" and "Rock-A-Bye-Baby." **Artist:** Ed Seale
☐ Purchased 19___ Pd $_______ MIB NB DB BNT
☐ Want Orig. Ret. $30.00 **NB** $45 **MIB** Sec. Mkt. **$60-$65**

QX 488-9 BABY'S FIRST CHRISTMAS
Comments: Handcrafted, 2-1/2" tall, Dated 1991
This adorable teddy hugs his big candy cane "1." His flocked cap says "Baby's First Christmas." **Artist:** John Francis (Collin)
☐ Purchased 19___ Pd $_______ MIB NB DB BNT
☐ Want Orig. Ret. $7.75 **NB** $20 **MIB** Sec. Mkt. **$30-$35**

QX 221-7 BABY'S FIRST CHRISTMAS: BABY BOY
Comments: Blue Satin Ball, 2-7/8" dia., Dated 1991
Caption: "A Baby Boy's World... Soft With Lullabies, Sweet With Hugs, Bright With Wonder, Warm With Love. Baby's First Christmas." **Artist:** Mary Hamilton
☐ Purchased 19___ Pd $_______ MIB NB DB BNT
☐ Want Orig. Ret. $4.75 **NB** $15 **MIB** Sec. Mkt. **$18-$20**

QX 222-7 BABY'S FIRST CHRISTMAS: BABY GIRL
Comments: Pink Satin Ball, 2-7/8" dia., Dated 1991
Caption: "A Baby Girl's World... Soft With Lullabies, Sweet With Hugs, Bright With Wonder, Warm With Love. Baby's First Christmas." **Artist:** Mary Hamilton
☐ Purchased 19___ Pd $_______ MIB NB DB BNT
☐ Want Orig. Ret. $4.75 **NB** $10 **MIB** Sec. Mkt. **$15-$18**

QX 486-9 BABY'S FIRST CHRISTMAS PHOTOHOLDER
Comments: Fabric, 4-3/8" dia., Dated 1991
Embroidered teddy bears and holly frame baby's photo. Caption: "Baby's First Christmas" and "The Cutest Grins, The Brightest Eyes, Always Come In Baby Size." **Artist:** LaDene Votruba
☐ Purchased 19___ Pd $_______ MIB NB DB BNT
☐ Want Orig. Ret. $7.75 **NB** $12 **MIB** Sec. Mkt. **$20-$22**

QX 489-7 BABY'S SECOND CHRISTMAS
Comments: Handcrafted, 2-3/16" tall, Dated 1991
Identical to 1989; only date has changed.
Artist: John Francis (Collin)
☐ Purchased 19___ Pd $_______ MIB NB DB BNT
☐ Want Orig. Ret. $6.75 **NB** $20 **MIB** Sec. Mkt. **$28-$30**

QX 537-7 BASKET BELL PLAYERS
Comments: Handcrafted and Wicker, 2" tall, Dated 1991
Two adorable kittens are having fun playing with the shiny brass bell tied to the handle of their basket. **Artist:** Ed Seale
☐ Purchased 19___ Pd $_______ MIB NB DB BNT
☐ Want Orig. Ret. $7.75 **NB** $12 **MIB** Sec. Mkt. **$22-$24**

QXC 725-9 BEARY ARTISTIC: KEEPSAKE CLUB
Comments: Lighted, Handcrafted and Acrylic, 2-1/2" tall
This little bear is carving the word "JOY" from a chunk of "ice." The "O" contains the logo for the Keepsake Ornament Club. Club Members only. **Artist:** Bob Siedler
☐ Purchased 19___ Pd $_______ MIB NB DB BNT
☐ Want Orig. Ret. $10.00 **NB** $28 **MIB** Sec. Mkt. **$38-$42**

QX 210-9 BETSEY CLARK: HOME FOR CHRISTMAS
Comments: **Sixth and Final in Series,** Dated 1991
Light Blue Glass Ball, 2-7/8" dia.
Betsey and her friends love the snow! Caption: "Getting Favorite Friends Together Is Extra Fun In Frosty Weather!" The box notes a new series will begin in 1992.
☐ Purchased 19___ Pd $_______ MIB NB DB BNT
☐ Want Orig. Ret. $5.00 **NB** $10 **MIB** Sec. Mkt. **$20-$22**

QX 532-7 BIG CHEESE, THE
Comments: Handcrafted, 1-7/8" tall
Dated Merry Christmas 1991. "The Big Cheese" has stuffed himself with Swiss cheese and has curled up in the hole he has nibbled. Artist: Bob Siedler
☐ Purchased 19___ Pd $_______ MIB NB DB BNT
☐ Want Orig. Ret. $6.75 **NB** $10 **MIB** Sec. Mkt. **$18-$20**

QLX 724-9 BRINGING HOME THE TREE
Comments: Light and Motion, Handcrafted, 4-3/8" tall
Dated 1991. A man and child emerge from the forest with their tree. The door to the home swings open and they go inside, their dog following closely behind. Caption: "Merry Christmas."
Artist: Duane Unruh
☐ Purchased 19___ Pd $_______ MIB NB DB BNT
☐ Want Orig. Ret. $28.00 **NB** $40 **MIB** Sec. Mkt. **$50-$55**

QX 547-9 BROTHER
Comments: Handcrafted, 2-3/4" tall, Dated 1991
Designed especially for a "Superstar Brother" is a puppy hanging onto the rim of the basketball hoop. **Artist:** Bob Siedler
☐ Purchased 19___ Pd $_______ MIB NB DB BNT
☐ Want Orig. Ret. $6.75 **NB** $8 **MIB** Sec. Mkt. **$16-$18**

QX 490-9 CHILD'S FIFTH CHRISTMAS
Comments: Handcrafted, 2-3/8" tall, Dated 1991
Identical to 1989; only date has changed.
Artist: Dill Rhodus
☐ Purchased 19___ Pd $_______ MIB NB DB BNT
☐ Want Orig. Ret. $6.75 **NB** $12 **MIB** Sec. Mkt. **$18-$20**

QX 490-7 CHILD'S FOURTH CHRISTMAS
Comments: Handcrafted, 3" tall, Dated 1991
Identical to 1989; only date has changed.
Artist: John Francis (Collin)
☐ Purchased 19___ Pd $_______ MIB NB DB BNT
☐ Want Orig. Ret. $6.75 **NB** $12 **MIB** Sec. Mkt. **$18-$20**

QX 489-9 CHILD'S THIRD CHRISTMAS
Comments: Handcrafted, 2-1/2" tall, Dated 1991
Identical to 1989; only date has changed.
Artist: John Francis (Collin)
☐ Purchased 19___ Pd $_______ MIB NB DB BNT
☐ Want Orig. Ret. $6.75 **NB** $15 **MIB** Sec. Mkt. **$20-$23**

QX 533-9 CHILLY CHAP
Comments: Handcrafted, 3-3/4" tall, Dated 1991
This double-dip ice cream cone snowman is adorable in pearly colors. He wears a sparkly hat decorated with a dated holly leaf.
Artist: Donna Lee
☐ Purchased 19___ Pd $_______ MIB NB DB BNT
☐ Want Orig. Ret. $6.75 **NB** $8 **MIB** Sec. Mkt. **$18-$22**

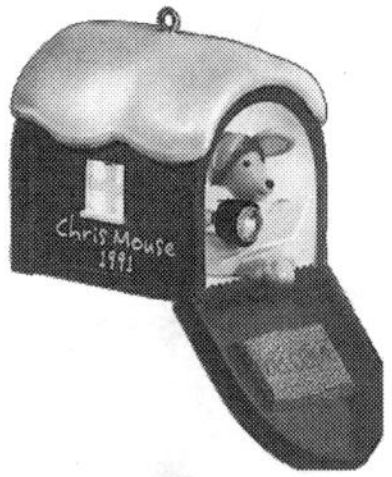

QLX 720-7 CHRIS MOUSE MAIL
Comments: **Seventh in Series**, Lighted, Handcrafted, 3" tall
Dated 1991. Chris has made a comfy home inside a red mail box. His "Welcome" mat is out and he reads a message "JOY" with a flashlight. **Artist:** Bob Siedler
☐ Purchased 19___ Pd $_______ MIB NB DB BNT
☐ Want Orig. Ret. $10.00 **NB** $18 **MIB** Sec. Mkt. **$38-$42**

QX 437-7 CHRISTMAS KITTY
Comments: **Third and Final in Series**, Fine Porcelain, 3-1/16"
Wearing a ruffled gown and carrying two red and white candy canes is this pretty hand-painted kitten. This series is not in demand.
Artist: Anita Marra Rogers
☐ Purchased 19___ Pd $_______ MIB NB DB BNT
☐ Want Orig. Ret. $14.75 **NB** $10 **MIB** Sec. Mkt. **$28-$32**

QX 529-9 CHRISTMAS WELCOME
Comments: Handcrafted, 3-3/8" tall, Dated 1991
This basket of fruit, sitting inside a ring wrapped with red "ribbon" is reminiscent of the nostalgia ornaments from 1975.
Artist: Linda Sickman
☐ Purchased 19___ Pd $_______ MIB NB DB BNT
☐ Want Orig. Ret. $9.75 **NB** $10 **MIB** Sec. Mkt. **$18-$22**

QX 431-9 CLASSIC AMERICAN CARS: 1957 CORVETTE
Comments: ***FIRST IN SERIES***, Handcrafted, 1-5/16" tall
Dated 1991. Very popular. Some are found with a green Christmas tree, some with brown. No difference in value between the two.
Artist: Don Palmiter
☐ Purchased 19___ Pd $_______ MIB NB DB BNT
☐ Want Orig. Ret. $12.75 **NB** $150 **MIB** Sec. Mkt. **$195-$210**

XPR 973-3 CLAUS & CO. R.R. ORNAMENTS: CABOOSE
Comments: Handcrafted, Dated 1991
Santa waves happily to one and all as the train passes through.
Artist: Don Palmiter
☐ Purchased 19___ Pd $_______ MIB NB DB BNT
☐ Want Orig. Ret. $3.95 w/$5 Hallmark purchase.
NB $5 **MIB** Sec. Mkt. **$14-$18**

XPR 973-1 CLAUS & CO. R.R. ORNAMENTS: GIFT CAR
Comments: Handcrafted, Dated 1991. **Artist:** Don Palmiter
This coal car carries an overflowing load of brightly wrapped gifts.
☐ Purchased 19___ Pd $_______ MIB NB DB BNT
☐ Want Orig. Ret. $3.95 w/$5 Hallmark purchase.
NB $5 **MIB** Sec. Mkt. **$14-$18**

XPR 973-0 CLAUS & CO. R.R. ORNAMENTS: LOCOMOTIVE
Comments: Handcrafted, Dated 1991. **Artist:** Don Palmiter
☐ Purchased 19___ Pd $_______ MIB NB DB BNT
☐ Want Orig. Ret. $3.95 w/$5 Hallmark purchase.
NB $8 **MIB** Sec. Mkt. **$25-$30**

XPR 973-2 CLAUS & CO. R.R. ORNAMENTS: PASSENGER CAR
Comments: Handcrafted, Dated 1991. **Artist:** Don Palmiter
☐ Purchased 19___ Pd $_______ MIB NB DB BNT
☐ Want Orig. Ret. $3.95 w/$5 Hallmark purchase.
NB $5 **MIB** Sec. Mkt. **$14-$18**

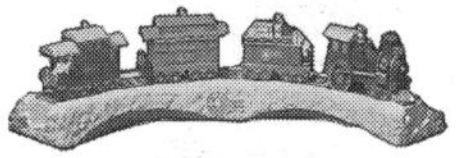

XPR 973-4 CLAUS & CO. R.R. ORNAMENTS: TRESTLE
Comments: Handcrafted, Dated 1991. **Artist:** Don Palmite
Holds four ornament cars in the series. Train cars not included.
☐ Purchased 19___ Pd $_______ MIB NB DB BNT
☐ Want Orig. Ret. $2.95 w/any Hallmark purchase
NB $5 **MIB** Sec. Mkt. **$10-$12**

QX 436-9 COLLECTOR'S PLATE: LET IT SNOW
Comments: **Fifth in Series**, Fine Porcelain, 3-1/4" dia. Dated 1991. Two children and their dog have fun on a snowy day building a snowman. **Artist:** LaDene Votruba
☐ Purchased 19___ Pd $_______ MIB NB DB BNT
☐ Want Orig. Ret. $8.75 **NB** $16 **MIB** Sec. Mkt. **$26-$30**

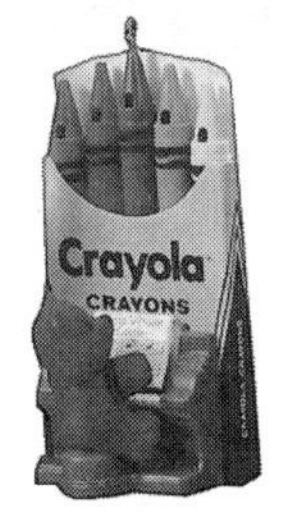

QX 421-9 CRAYOLA® CRAYON: BRIGHT VIBRANT CAROLS
Comments: **Third in Series**, Handcrafted, 3-1/4" tall Dated 1991. A red teddy bear is seated at a pipe organ created from an open box of crayons. The sheet music is titled "Bright Vibrant Carols" and the words... "Jingle Bears! Jingle Bears!" **Artist:** Ken Crow
☐ Purchased 19___ Pd $_______ MIB NB DB BNT
☐ Want Orig. Ret. $9.75 **NB** $18 **MIB** Sec. Mkt. **$38-$42**

QX 519-9 CUDDLY LAMB
Comments: Handcrafted, 1-7/8" tall
Detailed texturing and white flocking give this lamb the look and feel of wool. **Artist:** Anita Marra Rogers
☐ Purchased 19___ Pd $_______ MIB NB DB BNT
☐ Want Orig. Ret. $6.75 **NB** $8 **MIB** Sec. Mkt. **$16-$18**

QX 512-7 DAD
Comments: Handcrafted, 2-1/4" tall, Dated Dad 1991
A white polar bear dad, with wrench in hand, reads his "Easy To Assemble!" Instruction Sheet, but the directions appear to be complex. Artist: Julia Lee
☐ Purchased 19___ Pd $_______ MIB NB DB BNT
☐ Want Orig. Ret. $7.75 **NB** $10 **MIB** Sec. Mkt. **$18-$20**

QX 487-9 DAD-TO-BE
Comments: Handcrafted, 2-3/8" tall, Dated Christmas 1991
This kangaroo papa-to-be proudly announces the fact on his shirt. **Artist:** Julia Lee
☐ Purchased 19___ Pd $_______ MIB NB DB BNT
☐ Want Orig. Ret. $5.75 **NB** $8 **MIB** Sec. Mkt. **$15-$18**

QX 547-7 DAUGHTER
Comments: Handcrafted, 3-1/16" tall, Dated Daughter 1991
A little white mouse with a red hair bow snuggles peacefully in a pink slipper. **Artist:** Bob Siedler
☐ Purchased 19___ Pd $_______ MIB NB DB BNT
☐ Want Orig. Ret. $5.75 **NB** $12 **MIB** Sec. Mkt. **$24-$28**

QX 503-9 DICKENS CAROLER BELL: MRS. BEAUMONT
Comments: **Second in Collection,** Special Edition, Dated 1991 Hand-Painted Fine Porcelain, 4-1/4" tall
This lovely Victorian lady is beautifully detailed and holds an open song book. **Artist:** Robert Chad
☐ Purchased 19___ Pd $_______ MIB NB DB BNT
☐ Want Orig. Ret. $21.75 **NB** $25 **MIB** Sec. Mkt. **$45-$50**

QX 527-7 DINOCLAUS
Comments: Handcrafted, 2-5/8" tall, Dated 1991
This prehistoric fellow has a fun role at Christmas as he delivers toys and candy to all the good little cave-boys and girls.
Artist: Robert Chad
☐ Purchased 19___ Pd $_______ MIB NB DB BNT
☐ Want Orig. Ret. $7.75 **NB** $12 **MIB** Sec. Mkt. **$18-$22**

QLX 720-9 ELFIN ENGINEER
Comments: Lighted, Handcrafted, 2-3/4" tall
A whimsical elf polishes the bright red train so that it will shine brightly on Christmas day. **Artist:** Robert Chad
☐ Purchased 19___ Pd $_______ MIB NB DB BNT
☐ Want Orig. Ret. $10.00 **NB** $14 **MIB** Sec. Mkt. **$22-$26**

QX 227-9 EXTRA-SPECIAL FRIENDS
Comments: White Glass Ball, 2-7/8" dia., Dated 1991
A squirrel and raccoon chat with each other and a mouse and rabbit go sledding. Caption: "Special Friends Make Christmas Extra Special."
☐ Purchased 19___ Pd $_______ MIB NB DB BNT
☐ Want Orig. Ret. $4.75 **NB** $6 **MIB** Sec. Mkt. **$14-$16**

QX 411-9 FABULOUS DECADE
Comments: **Second in Series**, Handcrafted/Brass, 1-3/4" Dated 1991. A little raccoon holds a sparkling brass 1991.
Artist: Ed Seale
☐ Purchased 19___ Pd $_______ MIB NB DB BNT
☐ Want Orig. Ret. $7.75 **NB** $20 **MIB** Sec. Mkt. **$38-$42**

QLX 714-7 FATHER CHRISTMAS
Comments: Flickering light, Handcrafted, 4" tall, Dated 1991
An Old World Father Christmas walks through the city streets with his flickering lamp and sack full of toys for the children.
Artist: Duane Unruh
☐ Purchased 19___ Pd $_______ MIB NB DB BNT
☐ Want Orig. Ret. $14.00 **NB** $25 **MIB** Sec. Mkt. **$40-$45**

QX 527-9 FELIZ NAVIDAD
Comments: Handcrafted, 2" tall, Dated Feliz Navidad 1991
Santa's taking his afternoon siesta south of the border. He's added a sombrero and a colorful fabric serape to his traditional costume. **Artist:** Julia Lee
☐ Purchased 19___ Pd $_______ MIB NB DB BNT
☐ Want Orig. Ret. $6.75 **NB** $15 **MIB** Sec. Mkt. **$22-$25**

QLX 717-9 FESTIVE BRASS CHURCH
Comments: Lighted, Dimensional Brass, 3-1/8" tall
Light sparkles and shines from this intricately etched brass church. All the windows are trimmed with wreaths to celebrate the holidays. **Artist:** Diana McGehee
☐ Purchased 19___ Pd $_______ MIB NB DB BNT
☐ Want Orig. Ret. $14.00 **NB** $16 **MIB** Sec. Mkt. **$30-$35**

QX 438-7 FIDDLIN' AROUND
Comments: Handcrafted, 2-7/8" tall
This little fellow is multi-talented... He does a little dance while playing his fiddle. **Artist:** LaDene Votruba
☐ Purchased 19___ Pd $_______ MIB NB DB BNT
☐ Want Orig. Ret. $7.75 **NB** $10 **MIB** Sec. Mkt. **$18-$22**

QX 494-7 FIFTY YEARS TOGETHER PHOTOHOLDER
Comments: Handcrafted and Brass, 3-1/4" dia., Dated 1991
"50 Years Together" is framed with pearly white roses. Caption: "Golden Christmas Memories.. Golden Years Of Love."
Artist: LaDene Votruba
☐ Purchased 19___ Pd $_______ MIB NB DB BNT
☐ Want Orig. Ret. $8.75 **NB** $10 **MIB** Sec. Mkt. **$18-$20**

QX 491-9 FIRST CHRISTMAS TOGETHER
Comments: Handcrafted, 3-1/8" tall, Dated 1991
A twirl-about couple dances inside the center of their heart-shaped vine wreath. Caption: "Our First Christmas Together."
Artist: Linda Sickman
☐ Purchased 19___ Pd $_______ MIB NB DB BNT
☐ Want Orig. Ret. $8.75 **NB** $12 **MIB** Sec. Mkt. **$24-$28**

QX 313-9 FIRST CHRISTMAS TOGETHER
Comments: Acrylic, 3-3/16" tall, Dated 1991
A heart-shaped frosted acrylic wreath shows two sculpted doves and the caption in gold foil: "Our First Christmas Together."
Artist: Sharon Pike
☐ Purchased 19___ Pd $_______ MIB NB DB BNT
☐ Want Orig. Ret. $6.75 **NB** $10 **MIB** Sec. Mkt. **$22-$25**

QX 222-9 FIRST CHRISTMAS TOGETHER
Comments: White Glass Ball, 2-7/8" dia., Dated 1991
A romantic Victorian couple is ice skating. Caption: "Our First Christmas Together" and "Christmas Is For Sharing With The Special One You Love."
☐ Purchased 19___ Pd $_______ MIB NB DB BNT
☐ Want Orig. Ret. $4.75 **NB** $6 **MIB** Sec. Mkt. **$16-$18**

QLX 713-7 FIRST CHRISTMAS TOGETHER
Comments: Light and Motion, Handcrafted, 4-1/8" tall
Dated 1991. A large red heart proclaims "Our First Christmas Together" as a loving teddy bear couple snuggle in swan-shaped cars at the "Tunnel of Love." **Artist:** Linda Sickman
☐ Purchased 19___ Pd $_______ MIB NB DB BNT
☐ Want Orig. Ret. $25.00 **NB** $35 **MIB** Sec. Mkt. **$55-$60**

QX 491-7 FIRST CHRISTMAS TOGETHER PHOTOHOLDER
Comments: Handcrafted and Brass, 3-1/4" dia., Dated 1991
"1st Christmas Together" written on a banner is carried by two ivory doves. Caption: "Of Life's Many Treasures, The Most Beautiful Is Love." **Artist:** LaDene Votruba
☐ Purchased 19___ Pd $_______ MIB NB DB BNT
☐ Want Orig. Ret. $8.75 **NB** $8 **MIB** Sec. Mkt. **$22-$24**

QX 492-7 FIVE YEARS TOGETHER
Comments: Faceted Glass, 2-9/16" tall, Dated 1991
Caption in red foil.
☐ Purchased 19___ Pd $_______ MIB NB DB BNT
☐ Want Orig. Ret. $7.75 **NB** $8 **MIB** Sec. Mkt. **$18-$20**

QXC 315-9 FIVE YEARS TOGETHER: KEEPSAKE CLUB CHARTER MEMBER
Comments: Acrylic, 3" tall, Dated 1991
A red quatrefoil with gold lettering has the Keepsake Ornament Club logo and "Charter Member, Five Years Together."
☐ Purchased 19___ Pd $_______ MIB NB DB BNT
☐ Want Price: Free Gift to Charter Members
NB $25 **MIB** Sec. Mkt. **$50-$55**

QX 535-9 FOLK ART REINDEER
Comments: Hand Painted Wood and Brass, 2-5/16" tall
Dated 1991. This hand-carved, hand-painted reindeer is wearing a collar with the date in brass. No two ornaments will be exactly alike. **Artist:** LaDene Votruba
☐ Purchased 19___ Pd $_______ MIB NB DB BNT
☐ Want Orig. Ret. $8.75 **NB** $10 **MIB** Sec. Mkt. **$16-$20**

QLX 721-9 FOREST FROLICS
Comments: **Third in Series**, Light and Motion, Dated 1991
Handcrafted, 4-1/2" tall. As the "stage" revolves, it appears that each member of the ice show is skating in a circle. Caption: "Merry Christmas." **Artist:** Sharon Pike
☐ Purchased 19___ Pd $_______ MIB NB DB BNT
☐ Want Orig. Ret. $25.00 **NB** $45 **MIB** Sec. Mkt. **$60-$65**

QX 493-9 FORTY YEARS TOGETHER
Comments: Faceted Glass, 2-9/16" tall, Dated 1991
Identical to 1990 with date change.
☐ Purchased 19___ Pd $_______ MIB NB DB BNT
☐ Want Orig. Ret. $7.75 **NB** $10 **MIB** Sec. Mkt. **$12-$14**

QX 528-9 FRIENDS ARE FUN
Comments: Handcrafted, 2-15/16" tall
Dated Christmas 1991. Give one of these bunnies a push on the teeter-totter and they move up and down; the package moves back and forth. Caption: "Friends Are For Fun!" **Artist:** Ken Crow
☐ Purchased 19___ Pd $_______ MIB NB DB BNT
☐ Want Orig. Ret. $9.75 **NB** $12 **MIB** Sec. Mkt. **$18-$22**

QLX 716-9 FRIENDSHIP TREE
Comments: Lighted, Handcrafted, 3-1/8" tall, Dated 1991
Sharing homes in the same snow-covered tree makes it easy to exchange gifts. **Artist:** Peter Dutkin
☐ Purchased 19___ Pd $_______ MIB NB DB BNT
☐ Want Orig. Ret. $10.00 **NB** $12 **MIB** Sec. Mkt. **$22-$25**

QX 228-7 FROM OUR HOME TO YOURS
Comments: Midnight Blue and White Glass Ball, 2-7/8" dia.
Dated Christmas 1991. A bright red cardinal delivers a message of JOY from the bears to the mice. Caption: "From Our Home To Yours." **Artist:** LaDene Votruba
☐ Purchased 19___ Pd $_______ MIB NB DB BNT
☐ Want Orig. Ret. $4.75 **NB** $10 **MIB** Sec. Mkt. **$16-$18**

QX 432-7 FROSTY FRIENDS
Comments: **Twelfth in Series**, Handcrafted and Acrylic, 1-7/8"
Dated 1991. Ice hockey is fun when you have a little penguin friend to play with you. **Artist:** Sharon Pike
☐ Purchased 19___ Pd $_______ MIB NB DB BNT
☐ Want Orig. Ret. $9.75 **NB** $20 **MIB** Sec. Mkt. **$35-$40**

QXC 477-9 GALLOPING INTO CHRISTMAS: KEEPSAKE CLUB
Comments: Limited Edition 28,400, Wood Display Stand
Pressed Tin, 3" tall. A carefully painted and detailed Santa on horseback rolls along on wheels that move. Available to Members only. **Artist:** Linda Sickman
☐ Purchased 19___ Pd $_______ MIB NB DB BNT
☐ Want Orig. Ret. $19.75 **NB** $40 **MIB** Sec. Mkt. **$70-$75**

QX 517-7 GARFIELD
Comments: Handcrafted, 3-3/4" tall, Dated '91
Garfield is an angel in his brass halo and white wings. He sits on a dated star. **Artist:** Dill Rhodus
☐ Purchased 19___ Pd $_______ MIB NB DB BNT
☐ Want Orig. Ret. $7.75 **NB** $15 **MIB** Sec. Mkt. **$22-$28**

QX 211-7 GIFT BRINGERS, THE: CHRISTKINDL
Comments: **Third in Series**, White Glass Ball, 2-7/8" dia.
Christmas 1991. Symbolizing the Christ Child, Christkindl travels through the countryside on a tiny deer delivering gifts.
Artist: LaDene Votruba
☐ Purchased 19___ Pd $_______ MIB NB DB BNT
☐ Want Orig. Ret. $5.00 **NB** $10 **MIB** Sec. Mkt. **$18-$22**

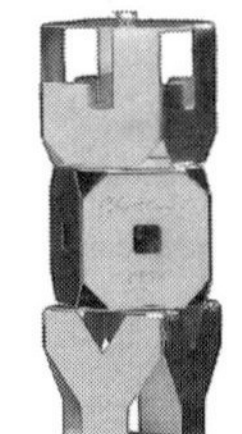

QX 531-9 GIFT OF JOY
Comments: Brass, Chrome and Copper, 4" tall, Christmas 1991
A brass "J," chrome "O," and copper "Y" in die-cut design spell JOY on all four sides. Each letter revolves.
Artist: Diana McGehee
☐ Purchased 19___ Pd $_______ MIB NB DB BNT
☐ Want Orig. Ret. $8.75 **NB** $12 **MIB** Sec. Mkt. **$20-$24**

QX 548-9 GODCHILD
Comments: Handcrafted, 2-1/16" tall, Dated 1991
A little angel in white playing her trumpet, is suspended from a golden banner which reads: "Merry Christmas, Godchild!"
Artist: Ron Bishop
☐ Purchased 19___ Pd $_______ MIB NB DB BNT
☐ Want Orig. Ret. $6.75 **NB** $8 **MIB** Sec. Mkt. **$14-$18**

QX 229-9 GRANDDAUGHTER
Comments: Porcelain White Glass Ball, 2-7/8" dia.
Dated Christmas 1991. Knit-look bunnies prance on a pink background. Caption: "A Granddaughter Is A Special Joy!"
Artist: Michele Pyda-Sevcik
☐ Purchased 19___ Pd $_______ MIB NB DB BNT
☐ Want Orig. Ret. $4.75 **NB** $10 **MIB** Sec. Mkt. **$18-$22**

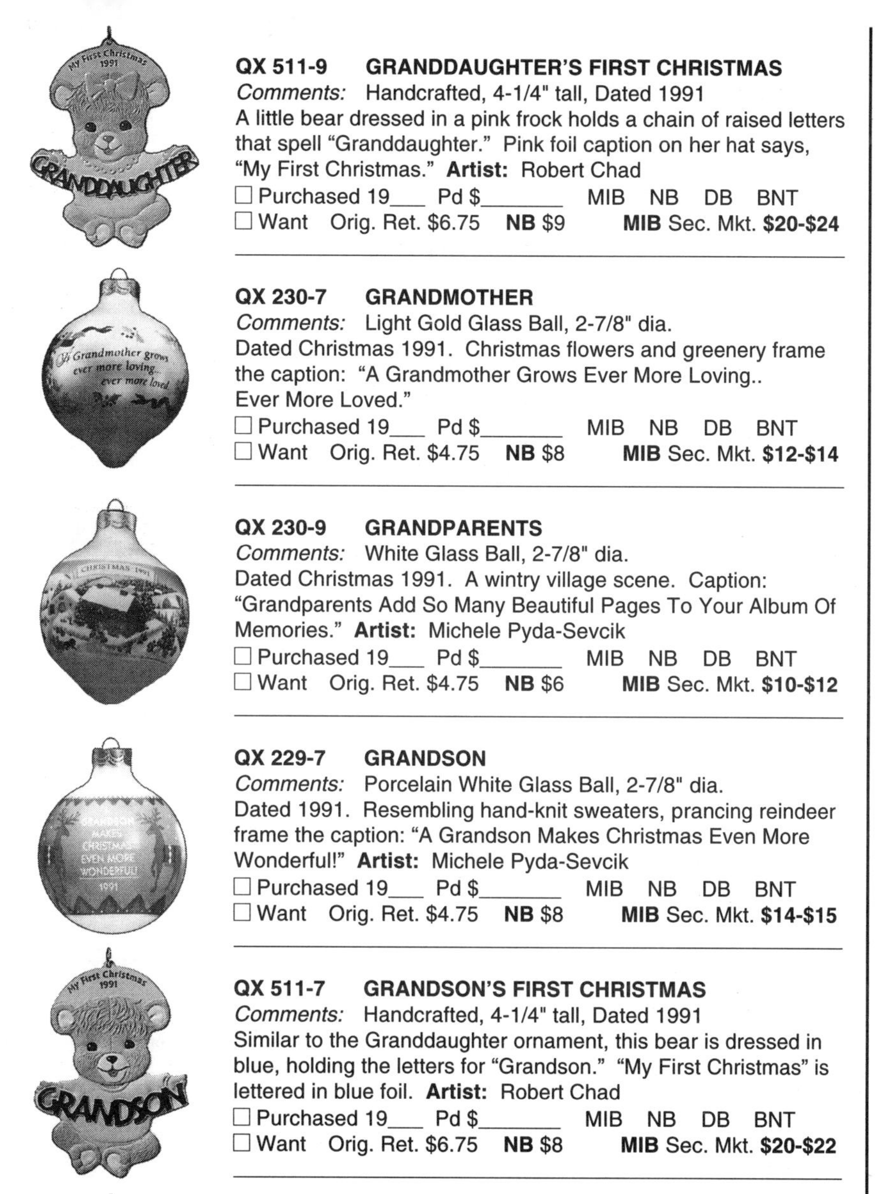

QX 511-9 GRANDDAUGHTER'S FIRST CHRISTMAS
Comments: Handcrafted, 4-1/4" tall, Dated 1991
A little bear dressed in a pink frock holds a chain of raised letters that spell "Granddaughter." Pink foil caption on her hat says, "My First Christmas." **Artist:** Robert Chad
☐ Purchased 19___ Pd $_______ MIB NB DB BNT
☐ Want Orig. Ret. $6.75 **NB** $9 **MIB** Sec. Mkt. **$20-$24**

QX 230-7 GRANDMOTHER
Comments: Light Gold Glass Ball, 2-7/8" dia.
Dated Christmas 1991. Christmas flowers and greenery frame the caption: "A Grandmother Grows Ever More Loving.. Ever More Loved."
☐ Purchased 19___ Pd $_______ MIB NB DB BNT
☐ Want Orig. Ret. $4.75 **NB** $8 **MIB** Sec. Mkt. **$12-$14**

QX 230-9 GRANDPARENTS
Comments: White Glass Ball, 2-7/8" dia.
Dated Christmas 1991. A wintry village scene. Caption: "Grandparents Add So Many Beautiful Pages To Your Album Of Memories." **Artist:** Michele Pyda-Sevcik
☐ Purchased 19___ Pd $_______ MIB NB DB BNT
☐ Want Orig. Ret. $4.75 **NB** $6 **MIB** Sec. Mkt. **$10-$12**

QX 229-7 GRANDSON
Comments: Porcelain White Glass Ball, 2-7/8" dia.
Dated 1991. Resembling hand-knit sweaters, prancing reindeer frame the caption: "A Grandson Makes Christmas Even More Wonderful!" **Artist:** Michele Pyda-Sevcik
☐ Purchased 19___ Pd $_______ MIB NB DB BNT
☐ Want Orig. Ret. $4.75 **NB** $8 **MIB** Sec. Mkt. **$14-$15**

QX 511-7 GRANDSON'S FIRST CHRISTMAS
Comments: Handcrafted, 4-1/4" tall, Dated 1991
Similar to the Granddaughter ornament, this bear is dressed in blue, holding the letters for "Grandson." "My First Christmas" is lettered in blue foil. **Artist:** Robert Chad
☐ Purchased 19___ Pd $_______ MIB NB DB BNT
☐ Want Orig. Ret. $6.75 **NB** $8 **MIB** Sec. Mkt. **$20-$22**

QX 412-9 GREATEST STORY
Comments: **Second in Series**, Dated 1991
Fine Bisque Porcelain and Brass, 3-3/4" tall
The shepherds stare in awe at the Star of Bethlehem.
Artist: LaDene Votruba
☐ Purchased 19___ Pd $_______ MIB NB DB BNT
☐ Want Orig. Ret. $12.75 **NB** $18 **MIB** Sec. Mkt. **$25-$30**

QX 437-9 HARK! IT'S HERALD
Comments: **Third in Series,** Handcrafted, 2" tall, Dated 1991
This year Herald has decided to try his musical talents with a golden fife. **Artist:** Anita Marra Rogers
☐ Purchased 19___ Pd $_______ MIB NB DB BNT
☐ Want Orig. Ret. $6.75 **NB** $9 **MIB** Sec. Mkt. **$22-$26**

QX 435-7 HEART OF CHRISTMAS
Comments: **Second in Series**, Handcrafted, 2" tall
Dated 1991. A father and son are "bringing home the tree." Mother waves as they near home. Opens locket-style.
Artist: Ed Seale
☐ Purchased 19___ Pd $_______ MIB NB DB BNT
☐ Want Orig. Ret. $13.75 **NB** $20 **MIB** Sec. Mkt. **$35-$40**

QX 436-7 HEAVENLY ANGELS
Comments: ***FIRST IN SERIES***, Handcrafted, 3-1/16" tall
Dated Christmas 1991. A bas relief, baroque style angel has been carved and antiqued. **Artist:** Joyce A. Lyle
☐ Purchased 19___ Pd $_______ MIB NB DB BNT
☐ Want Orig. Ret. $7.75 **NB** $15 **MIB** Sec. Mkt. **$35-$38**

QX 434-9 HERE COMES SANTA: SANTA'S ANTIQUE CAR
Comments: **Thirteenth in Series**, Handcrafted, 2-1/4" tall
Dated 1991. Santa's riding into Christmas in an antique car with a hood ornament resembling reindeer antlers! License plate says "SANTA." **Artist:** Linda Sickman
☐ Purchased 19___ Pd $_______ MIB NB DB BNT
☐ Want Orig. Ret. $14.75 **NB** $30 **MIB** Sec. Mkt. **$45-$50**

QXC 476-9 HIDDEN TREASURE/LI'L KEEPER: KEEPSAKE CLUB
Comments: Handcrafted: Acorn 2-1/8 tall; Squirrel 7/8" tall
Dated 1991. This be-ribboned acorn has a key that turns to reveal more surprises inside. **Artist:** Ken Crow
☐ Purchased 19___ Pd $_______ MIB NB DB BNT
☐ Want Price: Came with Club Membership of $20.00
NB $25 **MIB** Sec. Mkt. **$35-$45**

QLX 717-7 HOLIDAY GLOW
Comments: Lighted Panorama Ball, 3-3/4" tall
A puppy and kitten look inside a home decorated for Christmas. Light fills the room inside and highlights the decorations on the tree. **Artist:** Sharon Pike
☐ Purchased 19___ Pd $_______ MIB NB DB BNT
☐ Want Orig. Ret. $14.00 **NB** $18 **MIB** Sec. Mkt. **$28-$32**

QX 410-9 HOOKED ON SANTA
Comments: Handcrafted, 4" tall
Santa's hooked a big one this time... himself! His hook has gotten caught in his green waders. **Artist:** Julia Lee
☐ Purchased 19___ Pd $_______ MIB NB DB BNT
☐ Want Orig. Ret. $7.75 **NB** $12 **MIB** Sec. Mkt. **$20-$24**

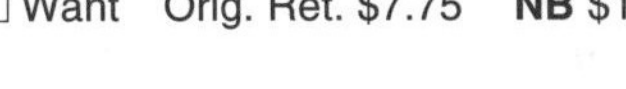

QLX 723-7 IT'S A WONDERFUL LIFE
Comments: Blinking Lights, Handcrafted, 3-3/16" tall
Dated 1991. A nostalgic movie theater is now showing a classic, *It's A Wonderful Life.* The marquee proclaims "Happy Holidays" and on a poster: "Coming Soon: A Christmas Carol."
Artist: Donna Lee
☐ Purchased 19___ Pd $_______ MIB NB DB BNT
☐ Want Orig. Ret. $20.00 **NB** $50 **MIB** Sec. Mkt. **$65-$70**

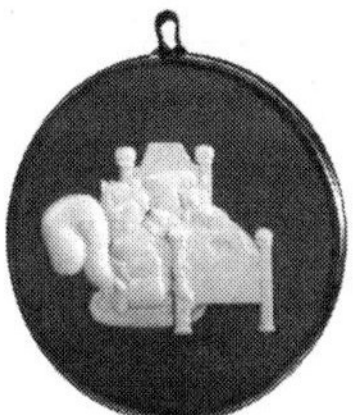

QX 314-7 JESUS LOVES ME
Comments: Blue Cameo, 2-3/4" dia., Christmas 1991
A baby squirrel kneels beside his bed to say his nighttime prayers. Caption: "Jesus Loves Me." **Artist:** Dill Rhodus
☐ Purchased 19___ Pd $_______ MIB NB DB BNT
☐ Want Orig. Ret. $7.75 **NB** $9 **MIB** Sec. Mkt. **$14-$16**

QLX 732-3 JINGLE BEARS
Comments: Light, Music and Motion, Handcrafted, 4-3/8" tall
Papa bear plays the tune *Jingle Bells* and mama sways from side to side. Caption: "Happy Family Memories Make The Season Bright." **Artist:** Julia Lee
☐ Purchased 19___ Pd $_______ MIB NB DB BNT
☐ Want Orig. Ret. $25.00 **NB** $30 **MIB** Sec. Mkt. **$45-$50**

QX 541-9 JOLLY WOLLY SANTA
Comments: Handcrafted, 3-3/4" tall, Dated 1991
With his sack of toys and jingle bells, this whimsical Santa is ready for Christmas. **Artist:** Linda Sickman
☐ Purchased 19___ Pd $_______ MIB NB DB BNT
☐ Want Orig. Ret. $7.75 **NB** $10 **MIB** Sec. Mkt. **$24-$28**

QX 542-7 JOLLY WOLLY SNOWMAN
Comments: Handcrafted, 3-3/4" tall, Dated 1991
A well-rounded fellow, for sure! The snowman design lithographed on this tin container has a corncob pipe and eyes made out of coal. **Artist:** Linda Sickman
☐ Purchased 19___ Pd $_______ MIB NB DB BNT
☐ Want Orig. Ret. $7.75 **NB** $10 **MIB** Sec. Mkt. **$20-$22**

QX 542-9 JOLLY WOLLY SOLDIER
Comments: Pressed Tin, 3-3/4" tall, Dated 1991
This tin soldier, dressed in his elaborate red and blue uniform, keeps everyone in step with the beat of his drum.
Artist: Linda Sickman
☐ Purchased 19___ Pd $_______ MIB NB DB BNT
☐ Want Orig. Ret. $7.75 **NB** $8 **MIB** Sec. Mkt. **$18-$22**

QX 536-9 JOYOUS MEMORIES PHOTOHOLDER
Comments: Hand-Painted Handcrafted, 3-3/8" dia.
Dated 1991. A bas-relief holly design sculpted and painted white on white frames a favorite photograph. Caption: "Each Joy Of Christmas Becomes A Precious Memory."
Artist: LaDene Votruba
☐ Purchased 19___ Pd $_______ MIB NB DB BNT
☐ Want Orig. Ret. $6.75 **NB** $10 **MIB** Sec. Mkt. **$20-$22**

QLX 711-9 KRINGLE'S BUMPER CARS
Comments: Blinking Lights and Motion, Handcrafted, 3-3/4" tall
Santa, one of his elves and a reindeer have a bit of fun playing in the bumper cars. **Artist:** Linda Sickman
☐ Purchased 19___ Pd $_______ MIB NB DB BNT
☐ Want Orig. Ret. $25.00 **NB** $40 **MIB** Sec. Mkt. **$45-$50**

QX 223-7 MARY ENGELBREIT
Comments: Porcelain White Glass Ball, 2-7/8" dia.
Dated Christmas 1991. Santa leads a parade of elves, dove, bunny and reindeer.
☐ Purchased 19___ Pd $_______ MIB NB DB BNT
☐ Want Orig. Ret. $4.75 **NB** $14 **MIB** Sec. Mkt. **$18-$22**

QX 427-9 MARY'S ANGELS: IRIS
Comments: **Fourth in Series**, Handcrafted and Acrylic, 2" tall
Iris sleeps comfortably on her frosted acrylic cloud. She's wearing a lavender dress. **Artist:** Robert Chad
☐ Purchased 19___ Pd $_______ MIB NB DB BNT
☐ Want Orig. Ret. $6.75 **NB** $15 **MIB** Sec. Mkt. **$32-$36**

QX 538-9 MATCHBOX MEMORIES: EVERGREEN INN
Comments: Handcrafted, 1-7/16" tall, Dated 1991
The proprietor of this country inn looks surprisingly like Santa! Caption: "Evergreen Inn 1991" **Artist:** Ed Seale
☐ Purchased 19___ Pd $_______ MIB NB DB BNT
☐ Want Orig. Ret. $8.75 **NB** $15 **MIB** Sec. Mkt. **$16-$20**

QX 539-9 MATCHBOX MEMORIES: HOLIDAY CAFE
Comments: Handcrafted, 1-7/16" tall, Dated 1991
A couple sit at a table by the window and hold hands. Lettering on the "window" is reversed. **Artist:** Ed Seale
☐ Purchased 19___ Pd $_______ MIB NB DB BNT
☐ Want Orig. Ret. $8.75 **NB** $10 **MIB** Sec. Mkt. **$14-$18**

QX 539-7 MATCHBOX MEMORIES: SANTA'S STUDIO
Comments: Handcrafted, 1-7/16" tall, Dated 1991
Santa chisels and sculpts a likeness of one of his elves. Statue has the appearance of marble. **Artist:** Ed Seale
☐ Purchased 19___ Pd $_______ MIB NB DB BNT
☐ Want Orig. Ret. $8.75 **NB** $10 **MIB** Sec. Mkt. **$16-$20**

QX 435-9 MERRY OLDE SANTA
Comments: **Second in Series**, Handcrafted, 4" tall
Dated 1991. This Old World Santa carries a walking stick with a brass bell to announce his arrival. He wears a long red coat.
Artist: Julia Lee
☐ Purchased 19___ Pd $_______ MIB NB DB BNT
☐ Want Orig. Ret. $14.75 **NB** $60 **MIB** Sec. Mkt. **$75-$82**

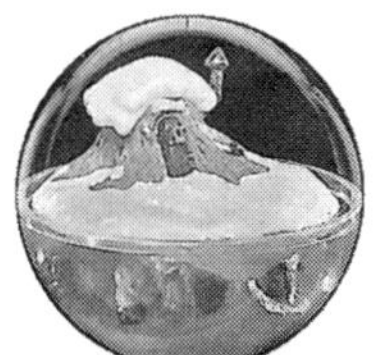

QLX 714-9 MOLE FAMILY HOME
Comments: Flickering Light, Handcrafted, 3-3/8" tall
Dated 1991. All that may be seen above ground is a snow-covered tree stump and red door, but underground mother bakes cookies while father and child read a story. **Artist:** Julia Lee
☐ Purchased 19___ Pd $_______ MIB NB DB BNT
☐ Want Orig. Ret. $20.00 **NB** $20 **MIB** Sec. Mkt. **$35-$45**

QX 546-7 MOM AND DAD
Comments: Handcrafted, 3-5/8" tall, Dated 1991
Two raccoons are snuggling together in a real knit stocking. The stocking carries the caption: "Mom And Dad."
☐ Purchased 19___ Pd $_______ MIB NB DB BNT
☐ Want Orig. Ret. $9.75 **NB** $12 **MIB** Sec. Mkt. **$20-$23**

QX 487-7 MOM-TO-BE
Comments: Handcrafted, 2-3/8" tall, Dated Christmas 1991
The lady kangaroo carries a wrapped gift in her pouch. Her sweat shirt reads "Mom-To-Be." **Artist:** Julia Lee
☐ Purchased 19___ Pd $_______ MIB NB DB BNT
☐ Want Orig. Ret. $5.75 **NB** $10 **MIB** Sec. Mkt. **$18-$20**

QX 545-7 MOTHER
Comments: Fine Porcelain, Hand-Formed Tin, 3-1/8" tall
This porcelain pendant is hung by a tin "ribbon." Caption: "Having You For A Mother Is The Nicest Gift Of All" and "Mother, Christmas 1991."
☐ Purchased 19___ Pd $_______ MIB NB DB BNT
☐ Want Orig. Ret. $9.75 **NB** $12 **MIB** Sec. Mkt. **$25-$28**

QX 433-9 MR. AND MRS. CLAUS: CHECKING HIS LIST
Comments: **Sixth in Series**, Handcrafted, 3" tall, Dated 1991
Mrs. Santa holds the list while Santa checks the items and makes sure everything is ready to go. **Artist:** Duane Unruh
☐ Purchased 19___ Pd $_______ MIB NB DB BNT
☐ Want Orig. Ret. $13.75 **NB** $20 **MIB** Sec. Mkt. **$35-$40**

QX 544-9 NEW HOME
Comments: Handcrafted, 2-1/4" tall, Dated 1991
A bright red cardinal perches on the stand outside his birdhouse. Caption: "New Home" and "Home... The Place Where Happiness Lives!" **Artist:** Ron Bishop
☐ Purchased 19___ Pd $_______ MIB NB DB BNT
☐ Want Orig. Ret. $6.75 **NB** $14 **MIB** Sec. Mkt. **$18-$24**

QX 530-7 NIGHT BEFORE CHRISTMAS
Comments: Handcrafted, 3-1/4" tall, Dated 1991
Santa turns around and around on a chimney top deciding which house is next on his stop. **Artist:** Linda Sickman
☐ Purchased 19___ Pd $_______ MIB NB DB BNT
☐ Want Orig. Ret. $9.75 **NB** $14 **MIB** Sec. Mkt. **$22-$25**

QX 486-7 NOAH'S ARK
Comments: Handcrafted, 3" tall, Dated 1991
Caption: "Joy•Love•Hope•Peace" and "Noah's Ark." Turn the knob on the side of the ark and animals move their heads; Noah raises his arm. **Artist:** Ken Crow
☐ Purchased 19___ Pd $_______ MIB NB DB BNT
☐ Want Orig. Ret. $13.75 **NB** $35 **MIB** Sec. Mkt. **$45-$50**

QX 225-9 NORMAN ROCKWELL ART
Comments: Lt. Gold Glass Ball, 2-7/8" dia., Christmas 1991
Caption: "Santa's Wee Helpers Work All Through The Year, But They're Specially Busy As Christmas Draws Near With Last Minute Touches To Finish The Toys And Make Them All Ready For Good Girls and Boys!" **Artist:** Joyce A. Lyle
☐ Purchased 19___ Pd $_______ MIB NB DB BNT
☐ Want Orig. Ret. $5.00 **NB** $10 **MIB** Sec. Mkt. **$18-$22**

QX 413-9 NOSTALGIC HOUSES AND SHOPS: FIRE STATION
Comments: **Eighth in Series**, Handcrafted, 4" tall
Dated 1991. "Fire Co. 1991" contains an old-time fire engine, Christmas tree, and two dalmatians, awaiting the return of the firemen. **Artist:** Donna Lee
☐ Purchased 19___ Pd $_______ MIB NB DB BNT
☐ Want Orig. Ret. $14.75 **NB** $35 **MIB** Sec. Mkt. **$55-$60**

QX 535-7 NOTES OF CHEER
Comments: Handcrafted, 1-3/4" tall, Dated 1991
This flocked brown bear seems to be asking "any requests?" as he plays his special keyboard. **Artist:** Bob Siedler
☐ Purchased 19___ Pd $_______ MIB NB DB BNT
☐ Want Orig. Ret. $5.75 **NB** $10 **MIB** Sec. Mkt. **$14-$16**

QX 517-6 NUTSHELL NATIVITY
Comments: Handcrafted, 1-7/16" tall
The three kings (left) kneel before the Baby in the manger (right) and present their gifts. **Artist:** Anita M. Rogers
☐ Purchased 19___ Pd $_______ MIB NB DB BNT
☐ Want Orig. Ret. $6.75 **NB** $15 **MIB** Sec. Mkt. **$24-$28**

QX 483-3 NUTTY SQUIRREL
Comments: Handcrafted, 1-3/4" tall
The detailed sculpting on this little fellow makes him a prize. He Is delivering an acorn tied with a bright red handcrafted bow.
Artist: Sharon Pike
☐ Purchased 19___ Pd $_______ MIB NB DB BNT
☐ Want Orig. Ret. $5.75 **NB** $10 **MIB** Sec. Mkt. **$14-$16**

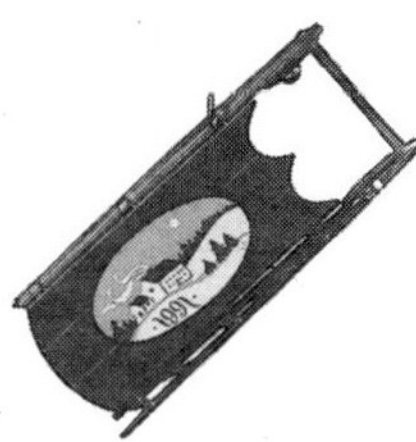

QX 431-7 OLD FASHIONED SLED
Comments: Handcrafted, 1-5/16" tall, Dated 1991
This authentically detailed sled pictures winter scenery. Tiny gold bells are on the front of the Bentwood-style runners.
Artist: Linda Sickman
☐ Purchased 19___ Pd $_______ MIB NB DB BNT
☐ Want Orig. Ret. $8.75 **NB** $9 **MIB** Sec. Mkt. **$16-$18**

QX 534-7 ON A ROLL
Comments: Handcrafted, 5" tall, Merry Christmas 1991
A little mouse swings on a strand of green fabric ribbon, scissors in hand. The red spool fastens to the tree with a wishbone hanger.
Artist: Ken Crow
☐ Purchased 19___ Pd $_______ MIB NB DB BNT
☐ Want Orig. Ret. $6.75 **NB** $12 **MIB** Sec. Mkt. **$16-$21**

QX 529-7 PARTRIDGE IN A PEAR TREE
Comments: Handcrafted, 3-5/16" tall, Dated 1991
This ornament of a partridge sitting in the top of a pear tree has the look of carved wood. **Artist:** Linda Sickman
☐ Purchased 19___ Pd $_______ MIB NB DB BNT
☐ Want Orig. Ret. $9.75 **NB** $14 **MIB** Sec. Mkt. **$18-$20**

QX 512-9 PEACE ON EARTH: ITALY
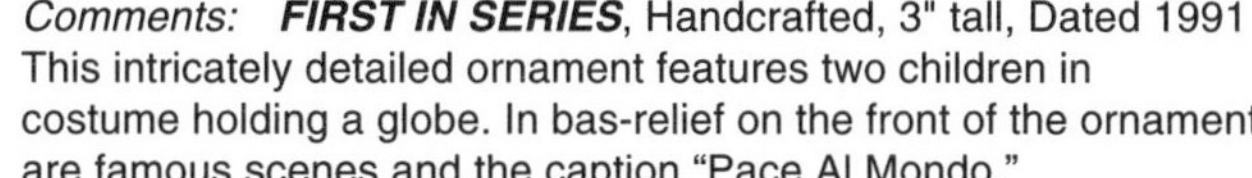
Comments: ***FIRST IN SERIES***, Handcrafted, 3" tall, Dated 1991
This intricately detailed ornament features two children in costume holding a globe. In bas-relief on the front of the ornament are famous scenes and the caption "Pace Al Mondo."
Artist: Linda Sickman
☐ Purchased 19___ Pd $_______ MIB NB DB BNT
☐ Want Orig. Ret. $11.75 **NB** $18 **MIB** Sec. Mkt. **$32-$36**

QX 225-7 PEANUTS®
Comments: Chrome Glass Ball, 2-7/8" dia., Dated 1991
The gang decorates Snoopy's doghouse. Caption: "It's The Time Of The Year For Sharing Good Cheer!"
☐ Purchased 19___ Pd $_______ MIB NB DB BNT
☐ Want Orig. Ret. $5.00 **NB** $12 **MIB** Sec. Mkt. **$20-$23**

QLX 722-9 PEANUTS®
Comments: ***FIRST IN SERIES,*** Flickering Light, Handcrafted, 3". Dated '91. Snoopy and Woodstock wait for Santa -- inside the stocking on the fireplace. The mantel holds a plate of cookies "For Santa." **Artist:** Dill Rhodus
☐ Purchased 19___ Pd $_______ MIB NB DB BNT
☐ Want Orig. Ret. $18.00 **NB** $40 **MIB** Sec. Mkt. **$60-$65**

QX 439-9 POLAR CIRCUS WAGON
Comments: Handcrafted, 2-7/8" tall, Dated 1991
The circus has come to the North Pole; a polar bear rides in a cage designed to resemble an antique pull toy.
Artist: Linda Sickman
☐ Purchased 19___ Pd $_______ MIB NB DB BNT
☐ Want Orig. Ret. $13.75 **NB** $16 **MIB** Sec. Mkt. **$25-$30**

QX 528-7 POLAR CLASSIC
Comments: Handcrafted, 3" tall, Dated '91
A white bear with a red shirt and green visor that says "Polar Classic 91" has a perfect swing. **Artist:** Bob Siedler
☐ Purchased 19___ Pd $_______ MIB NB DB BNT
☐ Want Orig. Ret. $6.75 **NB** $11 **MIB** Sec. Mkt. **$18-$22**

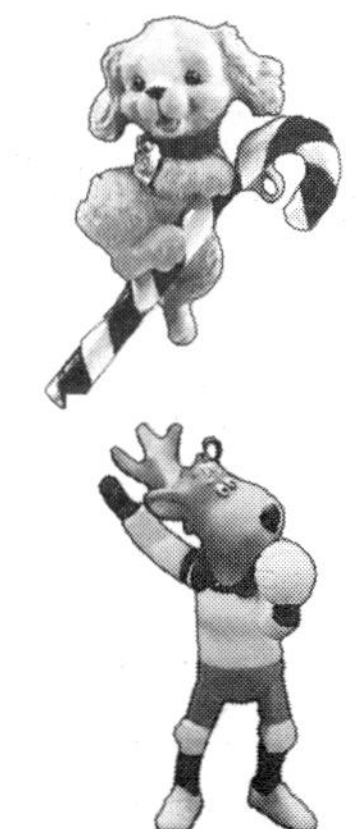

QX 537-9 PUPPY LOVE
Comments: ***FIRST IN SERIES***, Handcrafted and Brass 3-1/8" tall, Dated '91. A golden cocker spaniel rides a candy cane. He wears a brass identification tag on a red ribbon around his neck. **Artist:** Anita Marra Rogers
☐ Purchased 19___ Pd $_______ MIB NB DB BNT
☐ Want Orig. Ret. $7.75 **NB** $22 **MIB** Sec. Mkt. **$45-$48**

QX 434-7 REINDEER CHAMPS: CUPID
Comments: **Sixth in Series,** Handcrafted, 3-1/8" tall Dated '91. Cupid serves on the volleyball court with style and grace. Her name is on her shirt. **Artist:** Bob Siedler
☐ Purchased 19___ Pd $_______ MIB NB DB BNT
☐ Want Orig. Ret. $7.75 **NB** $15 **MIB** Sec. Mkt. **$30-$35**

QX 414-7 ROCKING HORSE
Comments: **Eleventh in Series**, Handcrafted, 4" wide Dated 1991. A buckskin wears a patterned saddle that resembles hand-tooled leather with shiny brass stirrups. His mane and tail are black. **Artist:** Linda Sickman
☐ Purchased 19___ Pd $_______ MIB NB DB BNT
☐ Want Orig. Ret. $10.75 **NB** $20 **MIB** Sec. Mkt. **$32-$38**

QLX 727-3 SALVATION ARMY BAND
Comments: Light, Motion and Music, Handcrafted, 4-5/8" tall Standing on a brick street beneath a lighted lamp a band plays *Joy To The World.* Includes the familiar kettle and sign: "The Salvation Army®, Sharing Is Caring." **Artist:** Duane Unruh
☐ Purchased 19___ Pd $_______ MIB NB DB BNT
☐ Want Orig. Ret. $30.00 **NB** $55 **M IB** Sec. Mkt. **$75-$80**

QX 438-9 SANTA SAILOR
Comments: Handcrafted and Metal, 3-3/8" tall, Dated '91 Santa's dressed in nautical dress blues and stands with his pack of toys on a metal anchor. **Artist:** Ed Seale
☐ Purchased 19___ Pd $_______ MIB NB DB BNT
☐ Want Orig. Ret. $9.75 **NB** $12 **MIB** Sec. Mkt. **$22-$25**

QLX 716-7 SANTA SPECIAL
Comments: Light, Motion and Sound, Handcrafted, 3-1/8" tall This locomotive looks, acts and sounds like a real train. The headlight is lighted; it whistles and chugs. The wheels and drive rods turn. Engineer Santa waves. Reissued in 1992.
Artist: Ed Seale
☐ Purchased 19___ Pd $_______ MIB NB DB BNT
☐ Want Orig. Ret. $40.00 **NB** $60 **MIB** Sec. Mkt. **$75-$80**

QLX 715-9 SANTA'S HOT LINE
Comments: Blinking Lights, Handcrafted, 3-7/8" tall Dated 1991. A busy elf answers calls on this old-fashioned switchboard and adds to his list: "Sara - Train, Paul - Puppy."
Artist: Ken Crow
☐ Purchased 19___ Pd $_______ MIB NB DB BNT
☐ Want Orig. Ret. $18.00 **NB** $25 **MIB** Sec. Mkt. **$40-$45**

QX 523-7 SANTA'S PREMIERE: GOLD CROWN ORN.
Comments: Hand-Painted Fine Porcelain, 3-1/4" tall Dated 1991. The handle of this gold-rimmed porcelain bell is a finely crafted Santa in a long red coat. Caption: "Hallmark Keepsake Ornament Premiere, Gold Crown Exclusive."
☐ Purchased 19___ Pd $_______ MIB NB DB BNT
☐ Want Orig. Ret. $10.75 **NB** $25 **MIB** Sec. Mkt. **$38-$42**

QXC 479-7 SECRETS FOR SANTA: KEEPSAKE CLUB
Comments: Limited Edition 28,700, Wood Display Stand Hand-Painted, Handcrafted, 3-1/2" tall
A child seated on Santa's lap whispers a wish in his ear. Available to Club Members only. **Artist:** Anita Marra Rogers
☐ Purchased 19___ Pd $_______ MIB NB DB BNT
☐ Want Orig. Ret. $23.75 **NB** $30 **MIB** Sec. Mkt. **$50-$55**

QX 548-7 SISTER
Comments: Handcrafted, 3-3/4" tall, Dated 1991
This cookie angel has been lavishly decorated with pearly "icing" to serve up a lovely treat for "Sister," as noted on the star she is holding. **Artist:** Joyce A. Lyle
☐ Purchased 19___ Pd $_______ MIB NB DB BNT
☐ Want Orig. Ret. $6.75 **NB** $12 **MIB** Sec. Mkt. **$18-$22**

QX 544-7 SKI LIFT BUNNY
Comments: Handcrafted, 2-3/4" tall, Dated 1991
With a white pom-pom tail, this colorfully dressed bunny loves to ride the ski lift. **Artist:** Julia Lee
☐ Purchased 19___ Pd $_______ MIB NB DB BNT
☐ Want Orig. Ret. $6.75 **NB** $12 **MIB** Sec. Mkt. **$18-$20**

QLX 726-6 SKI TRIP
Comments: Light and Motion, Handcrafted, 4-1/4" tall
In this snow-covered village, skiers ride the ski lift to the top of the hill then glide down the slopes. Lights shine through the lodge's windows. **Artist:** Ed Seale
☐ Purchased 19___ Pd $_______ MIB NB DB BNT
☐ Want Orig. Ret. $28.00 **NB** $48 **MIB** Sec. Mkt. **$55-$60**

QX 519-7 SNOOPY® AND WOODSTOCK
Comments: Handcrafted, 2-1/8" tall, Dated 1991
Snoopy and Woodstock enjoy a Christmas meal of pepperoni pizza and "Root Beer." **Artist:** Dill Rhodus
☐ Purchased 19___ Pd $_______ MIB NB DB BNT
☐ Want Orig. Ret. $6.75 **NB** $15 **MIB** Sec. Mkt. **$25-$30**

QX 526-9 SNOWY OWL
Comments: Handcrafted, 3" tall
The distinctive markings for this wide-eyed bird make it very impressive as well as beautiful. **Artist:** Linda Sickman
☐ Purchased 19___ Pd $_______ MIB NB DB BNT
☐ Want Orig. Ret. $7.75 **NB** $12 **MIB** Sec. Mkt. **$18-$20**

QX 546-9 SON
Comments: Handcrafted, 3-3/16" tall, Dated Son 1991
This flocked red slipper holds a flocked white mouse, fast asleep on a green pillow. **Artist:** Bob Siedler
☐ Purchased 19___ Pd $_______ MIB NB DB BNT
☐ Want Orig. Ret. $5.75 **NB** $10 **MIB** Sec. Mkt. **$15-$18**

QLX 715-7 SPARKLING ANGEL
Comments: Blinking Lights, Handcrafted, 3-13/16" tall
The stars on this little angel's glittering gold tinsel garland twinkle off and on. **Artist:** Robert Chad
☐ Purchased 19___ Pd $_______ MIB NB DB BNT
☐ Want Orig. Ret. $18.00 **NB** $24 **MIB** Sec. Mkt. **$28-$32**

QLX 719-9 STARSHIP ENTERPRISE
Comments: Blinking Lights, Handcrafted, 1-5/8" tall
Dated 1991. Commemorating the 25th anniversary of the television series *Star Trek*. Many *Star Trek* collectors were unaware of its debut. Production was much less than 92's Shuttlecraft Galileo, which was abundant. ('93 ornament is now somewhat hard to find.) **Artist:** Lynn Norton
☐ Purchased 19___ Pd $_______ MIB NB DB BNT
☐ Want Orig. Ret. $20.00 **Lights Not Working** $100
NB $280 **MIB** Sec. Mkt. **$300-$325**

QX 536-7 SWEET TALK
Comments: Handcrafted, 2-1/8" tall
A little girl's love for her pony is evident by the look on her face... and the candy cane in her hand. **Artist:** Duane Unruh
☐ Purchased 19___ Pd $_______ MIB NB DB BNT
☐ Want Orig. Ret. $8.75 **NB** $10 **MIB** Sec. Mkt. **$18-$20**

QX 495-7 SWEETHEART
Comments: Fine Porcelain, 2-1/2" tall, Dated 1991
An old-fashioned sleigh ride has been reproduced on a heart-shaped porcelain ornament. Caption: "Merry Christmas, Sweetheart" and "Gently Comes The Season Of Love."
☐ Purchased 19___ Pd $_______ MIB NB DB BNT
☐ Want Orig. Ret. $9.75 **NB** $14 **MIB** Sec. Mkt. **$22-$25**

QX 228-9 TEACHER
Comments: Porcelain White Glass Ball, 2-7/8" dia.
Dated Christmas 1991. With the look of a child's drawing "For My Teacher," this ball shows a tree with gifts and a wreath.
Artist: Anita Marra Rogers
☐ Purchased 19___ Pd $_______ MIB NB DB BNT
☐ Want Orig. Ret. $4.75 **NB** $7 **MIB** Sec. Mkt. **$10-$12**

QX 492-9 TEN YEARS TOGETHER
Comments: Faceted Glass, 2-9/16" tall, Dated 1991
Caption in red foil.
☐ Purchased 19___ Pd $_______ MIB NB DB BNT
☐ Want Orig. Ret. $7.75 **NB** $10 **MIB** Sec. Mkt. **$15-$20**

QX 533-7 TENDER TOUCHES COLLECTION: FANFARE BEAR
Comments: Hand-Painted and Handcrafted, 2-7/16" tall
Dated 1991. The "Little Drummer Bear" plays his drum with real wooden drumsticks. **Artist:** Ed Seale
☐ Purchased 19___ Pd $_______ MIB NB DB BNT
☐ Want Orig. Ret. $8.75 **NB** $12 **MIB** Sec. Mkt. **$18-$22**

QX 496-9 TENDER TOUCHES COLLECTION: GLEE CLUB BEARS
Comments: Hand-Painted and Handcrafted, 2" tall, Dated 1991
Three brown bears in ivory choir robes sing carols from their "Deck the Halls" song book. **Artist:** Ed Seale
☐ Purchased 19___ Pd $_______ MIB NB DB BNT
☐ Want Orig. Ret. $8.75 **NB** $15 **MIB** Sec. Mkt. **$18-$22**

QX 495-9 TENDER TOUCHES COLLECTION: LOOK OUT BELOW
Comments: Hand-Painted and Handcrafted, 1-3/4" tall
Dated 1991. A little grey mouse waves to his friends as he sleds down the hill. **Artist:** Ed Seale
☐ Purchased 19___ Pd $_______ MIB NB DB BNT
☐ Want Orig. Ret. $8.75 **NB** $15 **MIB** Sec. Mkt. **$18-$22**

QX 498-7 TENDER TOUCHES COLLECTION: LOVING STITCHES

Comments: Hand-Painted and Handcrafted, 2-1/4" tall
Dated 1991. A darling chipmunk rocks in her high-back rocking chair and stitches a heart sampler for a special friend.
Artist: Ed Seale
☐ Purchased 19___ Pd $_______ MIB NB DB BNT
☐ Want Orig. Ret. $8.75 **NB** $22 **MIB** Sec. Mkt. **$30-$35**

QX 497-7 TENDER TOUCHES COLLECTION: PLUM DELIGHTFUL

Comments: Hand-Painted and Handcrafted, 2-1/4" tall
Dated 1991. Mrs. Raccoon has prepared a delicious plum pudding to serve her Christmas guests. Her white lace apron has a dated heart. **Artist:** Ed Seale
☐ Purchased 19___ Pd $_______ MIB NB DB BNT
☐ Want Orig. Ret. $8.75 **NB** $12 **MIB** Sec. Mkt. **$18-$21**

QX 497--9 TENDER TOUCHES COLLECTION: SNOW TWINS

Comments: Hand-Painted and Handcrafted, 2-1/8" tall
Dated '91. Don't all snowmen have long ears and a carrot for a nose? The little fellow in the red suit thinks so.
Artist: Ed Seale
☐ Purchased 19___ Pd $_______ MIB NB DB BNT
☐ Want Orig. Ret. $8.75 **NB** $12 **MIB** Sec. Mkt. **$18-$21**

QX 496-7 TENDER TOUCHES COLLECTION: YULE LOGGER

Comments: Hand-Painted and Handcrafted, 2" tall, Dated '91
This adorable beaver in his red sweater, jeans and yellow muffler, has cut his own tree. **Artist:** Ed Seale
☐ Purchased 19___ Pd $_______ MIB NB DB BNT
☐ Want Orig. Ret. $8.75 **NB** $18 **MIB** Sec. Mkt. **$25-$28**

QX 530-9 TERRIFIC TEACHER

Comments: Handcrafted, 2-1/4" tall, Dated Christmas 1991
This cute little owl has a special rubber stamp created for his Terrific Teacher. **Artist:** Linda Sickman
☐ Purchased 19___ Pd $_______ MIB NB DB BNT
☐ Want Orig. Ret. $6.75 **NB** $8 **MIB** Sec. Mkt. **$14-$16**

QLX 712-9 TOYLAND TOWER

Comments: Motion, Handcrafted, 3-13/16" tall
A teddy bear sits and beats a drum at the gate entrance as a colorful soldier guards the tower. **Artist:** Ken Crow
☐ Purchased 19___ Pd $_______ MIB NB DB BNT
☐ Want Orig. Ret. $20.00 **NB** $27 **MIB** Sec. Mkt. **$38-$42**

QX 439-7 TRAMP AND LADDIE

Comments: Handcrafted, 2-11/16" tall
Laddie doesn't want anything to happen to his kitten friend so he carries it safely in a basket.
Artist: John Francis (Collin)
☐ Purchased 19___ Pd $_______ MIB NB DB BNT
☐ Want Orig. Ret. $7.75 **NB** $15 **MIB** Sec. Mkt. **$24-$28**

QX 308-9 TWELVE DAYS OF CHRISTMAS: EIGHT MAIDS A-MILKING

Comments: **Eighth in Series,** Acrylic, 3-7/8" tall, Dated 1991
A sweet maiden milks her cow which is wearing a holly garland and bell.
☐ Purchased 19___ Pd $_______ MIB NB DB BNT
☐ Want Orig. Ret. $6.75 **NB** $12 **MIB** Sec. Mkt. **$22-$25**

QX 493-7 TWENTY-FIVE YEARS TOGETHER PHOTOHOLDER

Comments: Handcrafted and Chrome, 3-1/4" dia., Dated 1991
Caption is on a blue banner with swans: "25 Years Together" and "Silver Christmas Memories... Silver Years Of Love."
Artist: LaDene Votruba
☐ Purchased 19___ Pd $_______ MIB NB DB BNT
☐ Want Orig. Ret. $8.75 **NB** $12 **MIB** Sec. Mkt. **$18-$20**

QX 494-9 UNDER THE MISTLETOE

Comments: Handcrafted, 2-3/8" tall, Dated 1991
A little tan rabbit holds a sprig of mistletoe and sneaks a kiss from his sweetheart. **Artist:** Sharon Pike
☐ Purchased 19___ Pd $_______ MIB NB DB BNT
☐ Want Orig. Ret. $8.75 **NB** $14 **MIB** Sec. Mkt. **$18-$22**

QX 504-7 UP 'N' DOWN JOURNEY

Comments: Handcrafted, 3-3/8" Tall, Merry Christmas 1991
Tap the sleigh and Santa rocks back and forth waving to every-one and the reindeer prances. **Artist:** Ken Crow
☐ Purchased 19___ Pd $_______ MIB NB DB BNT
☐ Want Orig. Ret. $9.75 **NB** $18 **MIB** Sec. Mkt. **$28-$30**

QX 557-9 WINNIE-THE-POOH COLLECTION: CHRISTOPHER ROBIN

Comments: Handcrafted, 4-3/4" tall
Christopher Robin is wearing red shoes and scarf and is bringing home the Christmas tree. **Artist:** Bob Siedler
☐ Purchased 19___ Pd $_______ MIB NB DB BNT
☐ Want Orig. Ret. $9.75 **NB** $22 **MIB** Sec. Mkt. **$34-$38**

QX 561-7 WINNIE-THE-POOH COLLECTION: KANGA AND ROO

Comments: Handcrafted, 3-1/4" tall
Mother Kanga shows baby Roo a string of cranberries to decorate the Christmas tree. **Artist:** Bob Siedler
☐ Purchased 19___ Pd $_______ MIB NB DB BNT
☐ Want Orig. Ret. $9.75 **NB** $35 **MIB** Sec. Mkt. **$48-$52**

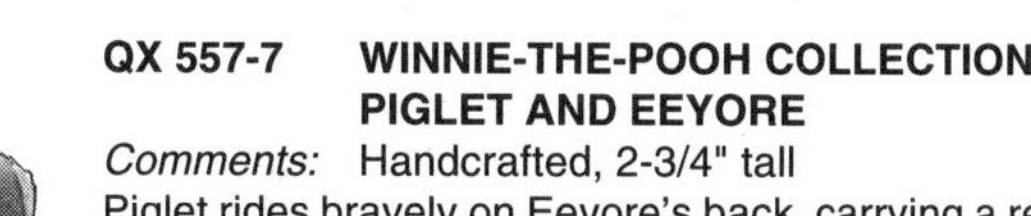

QX 557-7 WINNIE-THE-POOH COLLECTION: PIGLET AND EEYORE

Comments: Handcrafted, 2-3/4" tall
Piglet rides bravely on Eeyore's back, carrying a red ornament for the tree. Eeyore wears a pink ribbon tied on his tail.
Artist: Bob Siedler
☐ Purchased 19___ Pd $_______ MIB NB DB BNT
☐ Want Orig. Ret. $9.75 **NB** $35 **MIB** Sec. Mkt. **$45-$50**

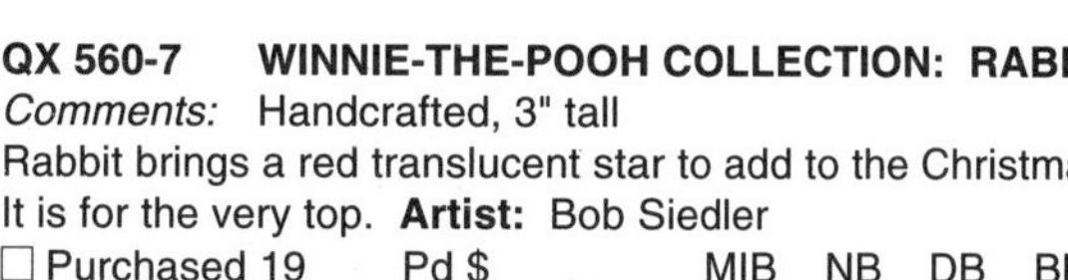

QX 560-7 WINNIE-THE-POOH COLLECTION: RABBIT

Comments: Handcrafted, 3" tall
Rabbit brings a red translucent star to add to the Christmas tree. It is for the very top. **Artist:** Bob Siedler
☐ Purchased 19___ Pd $_______ MIB NB DB BNT
☐ Want Orig. Ret. $9.75 **NB** $22 **MIB** Sec. Mkt. **$30-$32**

QX 560-9 WINNIE-THE-POOH COLLECTION: TIGGER

Comments: Handcrafted, 3-1/2" tall
Tigger springs into Christmas carrying a brightly wrapped gift. He's proof that "tiggers" truly are wonderful things. This ornament was more popular, or less produced than others, thus the value has increased. **Artist:** Bob Siedler
☐ Purchased 19___ Pd $_______ MIB NB DB BNT
☐ Want Orig. Ret. $9.75 **NB** $85 **MIB** Sec. Mkt. **$100-$110**

QX 556-9 WINNIE-THE-POOH COLLECTION: WINNIE-THE-POOH

Comments: Handcrafted, 3" tall
Pooh's idea of the perfect gift is a jar of "Hunny" tied with a big red bow. **Artist:** Bob Siedler
☐ Purchased 19___ Pd $_______ MIB NB DB BNT
☐ Want Orig. Ret. $9.75 **NB** $35 **MIB** Sec. Mkt. **$52-$58**

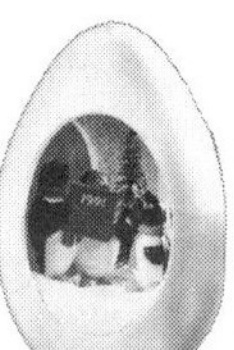

QX 427-7 WINTER SURPRISE

Comments: **Third in Series**, Handcrafted, 3-1/4" tall
Dated 1991. A penguin trio sings from "Polar Carols 1991" as they stand beside a snow-covered tree.
Artist: Joyce A. Lyle
☐ Purchased 19___ Pd $_______ MIB NB DB BNT
☐ Want Orig. Ret. $10.75 **NB** $15 **MIB** Sec. Mkt. **$22-$25**

1992 Collection

QX 457-4 A CHILD'S CHRISTMAS

Comments: Handcrafted, 2-3/4" tall, Dated 1992
A teddy bear sleeps peacefully on a rocking lamb's back. May be personalized six ways with inserts for Niece, Nephew, Granddaughter, Grandson, Great-Grandchild or A Child's Christmas.
Artist: John Francis (Collin)
☐ Purchased 19___ Pd $_______ MIB NB DB BNT
☐ Want Orig. Ret. $9.75 **NB** $12 **MIB** Sec. Mkt. **$18-$22**

QX 599-1 A SANTA-FULL!

Comments: Handcrafted Peek-Through, 3" tall, Dated 1992
Santa is stuffed! Really! You can see the cookies inside his see-through belly! **Artist:** Julia Lee
☐ Purchased 19___ Pd $_______ MIB NB DB BNT
☐ Want Orig. Ret. $9.75 **NB** $18 **MIB** Sec. Mkt. **$35-$38**

QX 304-4 ACROSS THE MILES

Comments: Acrylic, 3-3/8" dia., Dated 1992
A lovely winter country scene is etched in clear acrylic inside a frosted acrylic wreath. Caption: "Merry Christmas Across The Miles." **Artist:** Dill Rhodus
☐ Purchased 19___ Pd $_______ MIB NB DB BNT
☐ Want Orig. Ret. $6.75 **NB** $8 **MIB** Sec. Mkt. **$12-$14**

QLX 723-9 ANGEL OF LIGHT

Comments: Lighted Tree Topper, 10-1/4" tall
This delicate angel in a flowing gown of blue and white, carries a brightly lit acrylic star.
☐ Purchased 19___ Pd $_______ MIB NB DB BNT
☐ Want Orig. Ret. $30.00 **NB** $30 **MIB** Sec. Mkt. **$35-$45**

QX 485-1 ANNIVERSARY YEAR PHOTOHOLDER

Comments: Brass and Chrome, Dated 1992
Caption: "Loving Moments Together.. Loving Memories Forever." Personalize to mark the 5th, 10th, 25th, 30th, 35th, 40th or 50th anniversary. **Artist:** Duane Unruh
☐ Purchased 19___ Pd $_______ MIB NB DB BNT
☐ Want Orig. Ret. $9.75 **NB** $16 **MIB** Sec. Mkt. **$20-$24**

QX 464-4 BABY'S FIRST CHRISTMAS
Comments: Handcrafted, 2-1/8" tall, Dated 1992
This cute light brown bear holds a red, white and green striped candy-cane "1" in celebration of its first Christmas.
Artist: John Francis (Collin)
☐ Purchased 19___ Pd $_______ MIB NB DB BNT
☐ Want Orig. Ret. $7.75 **NB** $16 **MIB** Sec. Mkt. **$22-$26**

QX 458-1 BABY'S FIRST CHRISTMAS
Comments: Hand-Painted Fine Porcelain, 3-1/2" tall
Dated 1992. A tiny baby sleeps soundly in a wicker-look basket tied with pale green ribbon. **Artist:** Trish Andrews
☐ Purchased 19___ Pd $_______ MIB NB DB BNT
☐ Want Orig. Ret. $18.75 **NB** $22 **MIB** Sec. Mkt. **$35-$40**

QLX 728-1 BABY'S FIRST CHRISTMAS
Comments: Light and Music, Handcrafted, 3-7/16" tall
Dated 1992. Baby sleeps soundly in this white, lace-trimmed crib. Plays *Silent Night.* **Artist:** Ken Crow
☐ Purchased 19___ Pd $_______ MIB NB DB BNT
☐ Want Orig. Ret. $22.00 **NB** $60 **MIB** Sec. Mkt. **$80-$85**

QX 219-1 BABY'S FIRST CHRISTMAS - BABY BOY
Comments: Blue Satin Ball, 2-7/8" dia.
Dated 1992. Forest animals decorate a Christmas tree.
Caption: "To Love, Spoil, Play With, Adore -- That's What Baby Boys Are For!" **Artist:** LaDene Votruba
☐ Purchased 19___ Pd $_______ MIB NB DB BNT
☐ Want Orig. Ret. $4.75 **NB** $6 **MIB** Sec. Mkt. **$12-$14**

QX 220-4 BABY'S FIRST CHRISTMAS - BABY GIRL
Comments: Pink Satin Ball, 2-7/8" dia.
Dated 1992. Forest animals decorate a Christmas tree.
Caption: "To Love, Spoil, Play With, Adore -- That's What Baby Girls Are For!" **Artist:** LaDene Votruba
☐ Purchased 19___ Pd $_______ MIB NB DB BNT
☐ Want Orig. Ret. $4.75 **NB** $6 **MIB** Sec. Mkt. **$10-$14**

QX 464-1 BABY'S FIRST CHRISTMAS PHOTOHOLDER
Comments: Embroidered Fabric, 3-3/16" tall, Dated 1992
White eyelet lace and embroidered designs frame baby's photo.
Caption: "With Every Small Discovery, Baby Makes A Merry Memory." **Artist:** LaDene Votruba
☐ Purchased 19___ Pd $_______ MIB NB DB BNT
☐ Want Orig. Ret. $7.75 **NB** $14 **MIB** Sec. Mkt. **$18-$20**

QX 465-1 BABY'S SECOND CHRISTMAS
Comments: Handcrafted, 2-3/16" tall, Dated 1992
Identical to 1989, only date has changed.
Artist: John Francis (Collin)
☐ Purchased 19___ Pd $_______ MIB NB DB BNT
☐ Want Orig. Ret. $6.75 **NB** $10 **MIB** Sec. Mkt. **$12-$14**

QX 507-1 BEAR BELL CHAMP
Comments: Handcrafted, 2-3/16" tall, Dated 1992
This champion lifts real bells -- jingle bells, that is!
1992 Commemorative. **Artist:** Ed Seale
☐ Purchased 19___ Pd $_______ MIB NB DB BNT
☐ Want Orig. Ret. $7.75 **NB** $10 **MIB** Sec. Mkt. **$16-$18**

QX 210-4 BETSEY'S COUNTRY CHRISTMAS
Comments: ***FIRST IN SERIES***, Aqua Teardrop Ball, 2-7/8"
Dated 1992. Caption: "Christmas Sets Our Hearts A-Dancing!"
☐ Purchased 19___ Pd $_______ MIB NB DB BNT
☐ Want Orig. Ret. $5.00 **NB** $15 **MIB** Sec. Mkt. **$23-$25**

QX 468-4 BROTHER
Comments: Handcrafted, 4-1/8" tall, Dated 1992
Pull the ball on this ornament and the drummer beats a rhythm on his drum. **Artist:** Ken Crow
☐ Purchased 19___ Pd $_______ MIB NB DB BNT
☐ Want Orig. Ret. $6.75 **NB** $10 **MIB** Sec. Mkt. **$12-$14**

QX 515-4 CHEERFUL SANTA
Comments: Handcrafted, 3-1/8" tall, Dated 1992
Bearing the date on his pack, this Black Santa waves a very merry Christmas to all. Heavy trading in '94 **Artist:** Duane Unruh
☐ Purchased 19___ Pd $_______ MIB NB DB BNT
☐ Want Orig. Ret. $9.75 **NB** $18 **MIB** Sec. Mkt. **$32-$35**

QX 466-4 CHILD'S FIFTH CHRISTMAS
Comments: Handcrafted, 2-3/8" tall, Dated 1992
Identical to 1989, only date has changed.
Artist: Dill Rhodus
☐ Purchased 19___ Pd $_______ MIB NB DB BNT
☐ Want Orig. Ret. $6.75 **NB** $12 **MIB** Sec. Mkt. **$18-$20**

QX 466-1 CHILD'S FOURTH CHRISTMAS
Comments: Handcrafted, 3" tall, Dated 1992
Identical to 1989, only date has changed.
Artist: John Francis (Collin)
☐ Purchased 19___ Pd $_______ MIB NB DB BNT
☐ Want Orig. Ret. $6.75 **NB** $10 **MIB** Sec. Mkt. **$20-$22**

QX 465-4 CHILD'S THIRD CHRISTMAS
Comments: Handcrafted, 2-1/2" tall, Dated 1992
Identical to 1989, only date has changed.
Artist: John Francis (Collin)
☐ Purchased 19___ Pd $_______ MIB NB DB BNT
☐ Want Orig. Ret. $6.75 **NB** $10 **MIB** Sec. Mkt. **$17-$20**

QLX 707-4 CHRIS MOUSE TALES
Comments: **Eighth in Series,** Light, Handcrafted, 3-9/16" tall Dated 1992. Chris Mouse opens the shutters of his brightly lit shoe-house. A "Chris Mouse Tales" story book forms the roof for his "house." **Artist:** Anita Marra Rogers
☐ Purchased 19___ Pd $_______ MIB NB DB BNT
☐ Want Orig. Ret. $12.00 **NB** $22 **MIB** Sec. Mkt. **$30-$32**

QLX 727-1 CHRISTMAS PARADE
Comments: Light and Motion, Handcrafted, 3-3/8" tall, Dated '92 It's Christmas time in the city as evidenced by the decorations atop the skyscrapers and the parade marching 'round the city.
Artist: Linda Sickman
☐ Purchased 19___ Pd $_______ MIB NB DB BNT
☐ Want Orig. Ret. $30.00 **NB** $48 **MIB** Sec. Mkt. **$60-$65**

QX 532-1 CHRISTMAS SKY LINE COLLECTION: CABOOSE
Comments: Die Cast Metal, 2" tall, Dated 1992
The traditional red caboose brings up the tail of the Christmas Sky Line Collection. May be displayed hanging or standing.
Artist: Linda Sickman
☐ Purchased 19___ Pd $_______ MIB NB DB BNT
☐ Want Orig. Ret. $9.75 **NB** $18 **MIB** Sec. Mkt. **$25-$28**

QX 540-1 CHRISTMAS SKY LINE COLLECTION: COAL CAR
Comments: Die Cast Metal, 1-7/8" tall, Dated 1992
"Christmas Sky Line" proudly proclaims the name of the line on the side of the coal car. **Artist:** Linda Sickman
☐ Purchased 19___ Pd $_______ MIB NB DB BNT
☐ Want Orig. Ret. $9.75 **NB** $15 **MIB** Sec. Mkt. **$20-$22**

QX 531-1 CHRISTMAS SKY LINE COLLECTION: LOCOMOTIVE
Comments: Die Cast Metal, 1-3/4" tall, Dated 1992
This cheery locomotive is bright blue with red wheels and a red cabin. **Artist:** Linda Sickman
☐ Purchased 19___ Pd $_______ MIB NB DB BNT
☐ Want Orig. Ret. $9.75 **NB** $30 **MIB** Sec. Mkt. **$40-$45**

QX 531-4 CHRISTMAS SKY LINE COLLECTION: STOCK CAR
Comments: Die Cast Metal, 1-7/8" tall, Dated 1992
The stock car is painted a bright yellow with black stripes.
Artist: Linda Sickman
☐ Purchased 19___ Pd $_______ MIB NB DB BNT
☐ Want Orig. Ret. $9.75 **NB** $15 **MIB** Sec. Mkt. **$20-$22**

QXC 546-4 CHRISTMAS TREASURES: KEEPSAKE CLUB
Comments: Limited Edition 15,500, Handcrafted, Dated 1992 Chest 1-3/16" tall. A chest of Christmas Treasures holds three dated miniature ornaments: an ice skate, a horse on wheels, and a Santa jack-in-the box.
Artist: Robert Chad
☐ Purchased 19___ Pd $_______ MIB NB DB BNT
☐ Want Orig. Ret. $22.00 **NB** $120 **MIB** Sec. Mkt. **$150-$165**

QX 428-4 CLASSIC AMERICAN CARS: 1966 MUSTANG
Comments: **Second in Series**, Handcrafted, 1-1/4" tall Dated 1992. White mustang convertible with a " tree" and gift-wrapped packages. **Artist:** Don Palmiter
☐ Purchased 19___ Pd $_______ MIB NB DB BNT
☐ Want Orig. Ret. $12.75 **NB** $30 **MIB** Sec. Mkt. **$48-$55**

QX 446-1 COLLECTOR'S PLATE: SWEET HOLIDAY HARMONY
Comments: **Sixth and Final Edition**, Porcelain, 3-1/4" dia. Dated 1992, includes Acrylic Display Stand. This brother and sister duet becomes a trio when their puppy joins his voice with theirs. **Artist:** LaDene Votruba
☐ Purchased 19___ Pd $_______ MIB NB DB BNT
☐ Want Orig. Ret. $8.75 **NB** $18 **MIB** Sec. Mkt. **$26-$30**

QLX 726-4 CONTINENTAL EXPRESS
Comments: Light and Motion, Handcrafted, 3-3/4" tall Dated 1992. Two trains circle a village going in opposite directions.
Artist: Linda Sickman
☐ Purchased 19___ Pd $_______ MIB NB DB BNT
☐ Want Orig. Ret. $32.00 **NB** $55 **MIB** Sec. Mkt. **$68-$70**

QX 547-4 COOL FLIERS
Comments: Handcrafted, 3-1/2" tall, Dated 1992
These two can really swing! A snowman and snow woman on trapezes may be hung on separate branches; their hands interlock to complete their act. **Artist:** Julia Lee
☐ Purchased 19___ Pd $_______ MIB NB DB BNT
☐ Want Orig. Ret. $10.75 **NB** $14 **MIB** Sec. Mkt. **$22-$26**

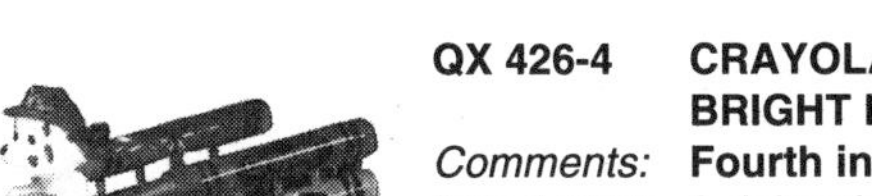

QX 426-4 CRAYOLA® CRAYON: BRIGHT BLAZING COLORS
Comments: **Fourth in Series**, Handcrafted, 2-1/8" tall Dated 1992. A dalmatian, wearing a bright red fireman's helmet, races to the rescue. **Artist:** Ken Crow
☐ Purchased 19___ Pd $_______ MIB NB DB BNT
☐ Want Orig. Ret. $9.75 **NB** $21 **MIB** Sec. Mkt. **$32-$36**

QX 467-4 DAD
Comments: Handcrafted, 2-5/16" tall, Dated 1992
It's official! "Dad's A Winner!" Dad naps comfortably in his recliner with a smile on his face as the newspaper declares that it's been a "Banner Year For Dad!" **Artist:** Bob Siedler
☐ Purchased 19___ Pd $_______ MIB NB DB BNT
☐ Want Orig. Ret. $7.75 **NB** $14 **MIB** Sec. Mkt. **$18-$20**

QX 461-1 DAD-TO-BE
Comments: Handcrafted, 2-3/8" tall, Dated 1992
Dad rooster crows out the good news -- he'll be a father soon!
Artist: Julia Lee
☐ Purchased 19___ Pd $_______ MIB NB DB BNT
☐ Want Orig. Ret. $6.75 **NB** $12 **MIB** Sec. Mkt. **$18-$20**

QLX 726-1 DANCING NUTCRACKER, THE
Comments: Light, Motion and Music, Handcrafted, 3-1/4" tall Dated 1992. As the music plays the Overture to Tchaikovsky's *Nutcracker,* the Nutcracker dances for you. "Wide" range of reported sales on this one. **Artist:** LaDene Votruba
☐ Purchased 19___ Pd $_______ MIB NB DB BNT
☐ Want Orig. Ret. $30.00 **NB** $35 **MIB** Sec. Mkt. **$52-$55**

QX 503-1 DAUGHTER
Comments: Handcrafted, 2-1/8" tall, Dated 1992
This girl squirrel is flying high in her pink and silver airplane. Wearing a turquoise sweater, she waves happily.
Artist: John Francis (Collin)
☐ Purchased 19___ Pd $_______ MIB NB DB BNT
☐ Want Orig. Ret. $6.75 **NB** $12 **MIB** Sec. Mkt. **$18-$22**

QX 520-4 DECK THE HOGS
Comments: Handcrafted, 3-1/8" tall, Dated 1992
"Deck The Hogs With Boughs Of Holly" sings a happy fellow decorated with red ribbon and holly.
Artist: John Francis (Collin)
☐ Purchased 19___ Pd $_______ MIB NB DB BNT
☐ Want Orig. Ret. $8.75 **NB** $12 **MIB** Sec. Mkt. **$18-$20**

QX 455-4 DICKENS CAROLER BELL: LORD CHADWICK
Comments: **Third in Collection**, Hand-Painted Porcelain 4-5/8" tall. Dated 1992 inside bell. Lord Chadwick depicts a Victorian gentleman with his pale blue coat and a sprig of Christmas ivy in his hat. **Artist:** Robert Chad
☐ Purchased 19___ Pd $_______ MIB NB DB BNT
☐ Want Orig. Ret. $21.75 **NB** $28 **MIB** Sec. Mkt. **$45-$48**

QX 514-4 DOWN-UNDER HOLIDAY
Comments: Handcrafted, 2-7/8" tall, Dated '92
A koala has hopped a ride on the back of a kangaroo in his red and white sneakers. He also carries a wrapped gift in his pouch and a dated boomerang. **Artist:** Ken Crow
☐ Purchased 19___ Pd $_______ MIB NB DB BNT
☐ Want Orig. Ret. $7.75 **NB** $14 **MIB** Sec. Mkt. **$18-$22**

QX 512-1 EGG NOG NEST
Comments: Handcrafted, 2-1/2" tall, Dated 1992
A cute little bluebird has made his home in an Egg Nog carton; he's trimmed the "roof" with lights and is hanging out his stocking for Santa. "Vitamins And Cheer Added." "Enjoy By 12-25-92."
☐ Purchased 19___ Pd $_______ MIB NB DB BNT
☐ Want Orig. Ret. $7.75 **NB** $10 **MIB** Sec. Mkt. **$16-$18**

QX 593-1 ELFIN MARIONETTE
Comments: Handcrafted, 3-15/16" tall, Dated 1992
This wood-look marionette works just like the real thing! Move the crossbar and the elf moves his arms and legs.
Artist: Robert Chad
☐ Purchased 19___ Pd $_______ MIB NB DB BNT
☐ Want Orig. Ret. $11.75 **NB** $15 **MIB** Sec. Mkt. **$25-$28**

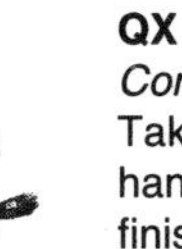

QX 562-4 ELVIS
Comments: Brass-plated, 4-1/2" tall, Dated '92
Taken from his early years, Elvis strikes a classic pose, guitar in hand. This special issue Keepsake ornament has a bronze-cast finish. Was not well received by the consumer or collector.
Artist: Dill Rhodus/Joyce A. Lyle
☐ Purchased 19___ Pd $_______ MIB NB DB BNT
☐ Want Orig. Ret. $14.75 **NB** $5 **MIB** Sec. Mkt. **$12-$15**

QLX 727-4 ENCHANTED CLOCK
Comments: Light and Motion, Handcrafted, 3-15/16" tall
Caption: "When This Enchanted Clock Strikes Twelve Each Starry Christmas Eve, The Magic Toys Will Dance And Play, If Only You Believe." Several found below retail. **Artist:** Ken Crow
☐ Purchased 19___ Pd $_______ MIB NB DB BNT
☐ Want Orig. Ret. $30.00 **NB** $35 **MIB** Sec. Mkt. **$58-$62**

QX 424-4 FABULOUS DECADE
Comments: **Third in Series,** 1-7/8" tall, Handcrafted and Brass Dated 1992. A light brown bear with a red neck ribbon holds a shiny brass "1992." **Artist:** Ed Seale
☐ Purchased 19___ Pd $_______ MIB NB DB BNT
☐ Want Orig. Ret. $7.7 **NB** $22 **MIB** Sec. Mkt. **$35-$38**

QLX 709-1 FEATHERED FRIENDS
Comments: Light, Handcrafted, 1-15/16" tall, Dated 1992
A favorite pastime for many during the winter months is to watch the birds at outdoor feeders. **Artist:** Linda Sickman
☐ Purchased 19___ Pd $_______ MIB NB DB BNT
☐ Want Orig. Ret. $14.00 **NB** $22 **MIB** Sec. Mkt. **$30-$33**

QX 518-1 FELIZ NAVIDAD
Comments: Handcrafted, 2-7/8" tall, Dated 1992
A merry mouse rides his guitar and wishes everyone "Feliz Navidad" ... *Merry Christmas!* **Artist:** Trish Andrews
☐ Purchased 19___ Pd $_______ MIB NB DB BNT
☐ Want Orig. Ret. $6.75 **NB** $12 **MIB** Sec. Mkt. **$15-$18**

QX 301-1 FIRST CHRISTMAS TOGETHER, OUR
Comments: Acrylic, 3" tall, Dated 1992
Red hearts and gold foil lettering decorate this clear acrylic heart. Caption: "Our First Christmas Together 1992."
Artist: LaDene Votruba
☐ Purchased 19___ Pd $_______ MIB NB DB BNT
☐ Want Orig. Ret. $6.75 **NB** $10 **MIB** Sec. Mkt. **$14-$18**

QX 506-1 FIRST CHRISTMAS TOGETHER, OUR
Comments: Handcrafted, 2-7/8" tall, Dated 1992
Two little mice share a sugar heart inside a silvery sugar bowl. Caption: "Our First Christmas Together 1992."
Artist: Julia Lee
☐ Purchased 19___ Pd $_______ MIB NB DB BNT
☐ Want Orig. Ret. $9.75 **NB** $12 **MIB** Sec. Mkt. **$17-$21**

QX 469-4 FIRST CHRISTMAS TOGETHER PHOTOHOLDER
Comments: Handcrafted, 3-1/2" tall, Dated 1992
Slide your favorite photo into the shutter-framed window of this snow-capped home. Captions: "Our First Christmas Together" and "Home Is Where The Heart Is." **Artist:** Ed Seale
☐ Purchased 19___ Pd $_______ MIB NB DB BNT
☐ Want Orig. Ret. $8.75 **NB** $12 **MIB** Sec. Mkt. **$22-$24**

QX 518-4 FOR MY GRANDMA PHOTOHOLDER
Comments: Embroidered Fabric, 3-1/8" tall, Dated 1992
Hearts and holly decorate this heart-shaped ivory photo holder for Grandma. Caption: "Merry Christmas -- With Love And Kisses From XOXO."
☐ Purchased 19___ Pd $_______ MIB NB DB BNT
☐ Want Orig. Ret. $7.75 **NB** $8 **MIB** Sec. Mkt. **$12-$16**

QX 484-4 FOR THE ONE I LOVE
Comments: Hand-Painted Fine Porcelain, 2-3/8" tall, Dated 1992
This ivory heart is filled with lovely pink roses in full bloom. Captions: "For The One I Love." and "Having Your Love Makes Christmas Perfect 1992." **Artist:** Joyce A. Lyle
☐ Purchased 19___ Pd $_______ MIB NB DB BNT
☐ Want Orig. Ret. $9.75 **NB** $12 **MIB** Sec. Mkt. **$18-$22**

QLX 725-4 FOREST FROLICS
Comments: **Fourth in Series,** Handcrafted, 4-1/8" tall Dated 1992. Light and Motion. Forest friends have fun together on a seesaw which moves up and down. **Artist:** Sharon Pike
☐ Purchased 19___ Pd $_______ MIB NB DB BNT
☐ Want Orig. Ret. $28.00 **NB** $38 **MIB** Sec. Mkt. **$55-$60**

QX 504-1 FRIENDLY GREETINGS
Comments: Handcrafted, 2-5/16" tall, Dated 1992
A yellow and white kitten shares "A Friendly Christmas Greeting." Caption: "Friendship -- Tis The Reason To Be Jolly!" Add your own message inside the card as well. **Artist:** Robert Chad
☐ Purchased 19___ Pd $_______ MIB NB DB BNT
☐ Want Orig. Ret. $7.75 **NB** $10 **MIB** Sec. Mkt. **$14-$16**

QX 503-4 FRIENDSHIP LINE
Comments: Handcrafted, 4-1/2" tall, Dated 1992
Two chipmunks converse gaily on a red telephone receiver.
Artist: Ed Seale
☐ Purchased 19___ Pd $_______ MIB NB DB BNT
☐ Want Orig. Ret. $9.75 **NB** $14 **MIB** Sec. Mkt. **$25-$28**

QX 213-1 FROM OUR HOME TO YOURS
Comments: White Glass Ball, 2-7/8" dia., Dated 1992
A whimsical Christmas scene of snow-capped houses decorates this glass ball. **Artist:** LaDene Votruba
☐ Purchased 19___ Pd $_______ MIB NB DB BNT
☐ Want Orig. Ret. $4.75 **NB** $6 **MIB** Sec. Mkt. **$10-$14**

QX 429-1 FROSTY FRIENDS
Comments: **Thirteenth in Series**, 2-11/16" tall, Dated 1992, Handcrafted and Acrylic. Our little Eskimo friend shares his bright red and white candy canes with his whale friend.
Artist: Julia Lee
☐ Purchased 19___ Pd $_______ MIB NB DB BNT
☐ Want Orig. Ret. $9.75 **NB** $18 **MIB** Sec. Mkt. **$28-$30**

QX 513-4 FUN ON A BIG SCALE
Comments: Handcrafted, 3-3/16" tall, Dated 1992
Fun is exactly what this little hamster is having! Press down gently on the dish of candy and the scale tips.
Artist: Ken Crow
☐ Purchased 19___ Pd $_______ MIB NB DB BNT
☐ Want Orig. Ret. $10.75 **NB** $12 **MIB** Sec. Mkt. **$22-$25**

QX 537-4 GARFIELD
Comments: Handcrafted, 2-7/16" tall, Dated '92
That cool cat is ready for bed; he's wearing a Santa nightcap, his special slippers, and has his book and blanket in hand.
Artist: Don Palmiter
☐ Purchased 19___ Pd $_______ MIB NB DB BNT
☐ Want Orig. Ret. $7.75 **NB** $12 **MIB** Sec. Mkt. **$16-$20**

QX 537-1 GENIUS AT WORK
Comments: Handcrafted, 2-3/8" tall, Dated 1992
Watch the elf work as he pounds his hammer and jiggles the wrench. **Artist:** Ken Crow
☐ Purchased 19___ Pd $_______ MIB NB DB BNT
☐ Want Orig. Ret. $10.75 **NB** $14 **MIB** Sec. Mkt. **$20-$22**

QX 212-4 GIFT BRINGERS, THE: KOLYADA
Comments: **Fourth in Series,** White Glass Ball, 2-7/8" dia. Dated Christmas 1992. The elf maiden Kolyada brings Christmas to Russian children. **Artist:** LaDene Votruba
☐ Purchased 19___ Pd $_______ MIB NB DB BNT
☐ Want Orig. Ret. $5.00 **NB** $8 **MIB** Sec. Mkt. **$18-$20**

QX 594-1 GODCHILD
Comments: Handcrafted, 1-5/8" tall, Dated 1992
The love of the Godparent and Godchild for each other is quite apparent on the faces of these sheep. **Artist:** Duane Unruh
☐ Purchased 19___ Pd $_______ MIB NB DB BNT
☐ Want Orig. Ret. $6.75 **NB** $10 **MIB** Sec. Mkt. **$16-$20**

QX 598-4 GOLF'S A BALL
Comments: Handcrafted, 3-1/2" tall, Dated 1992
This cheery snowman is fashioned from golf balls and has golf clubs for arms.
Artist: Lee Schuler
☐ Purchased 19___ Pd $_______ MIB NB DB BNT
☐ Want Orig. Ret. $6.75 **NB** $10 **MIB** Sec. Mkt. **$18-$22**

QX 517-1 GONE WISHIN'
Comments: Handcrafted, 1-11/16" tall, Dated '92
While Santa naps in his silver motorboat, he has hooked a green package on his line. **Artist:** Donna Lee
☐ Purchased 19___ Pd $_______ MIB NB DB BNT
☐ Want Orig. Ret. $8.75 **NB** $9 **MIB** Sec. Mkt. **$15-$18**

QLX 724-4 GOOD SLEDDING AHEAD
Comments: Light and Motion, Handcrafted, 3-9/16" tall Dated 1992. A dog follows closely behind as the children sled 'round and 'round their house. Many prices found below original retail! **Artist:** Don Palmiter
☐ Purchased 19___ Pd $_______ MIB NB DB BNT
☐ Want Orig. Ret. $28.00 **NB** $30 **MIB** Sec. Mkt. **$45-$50**

QX 560-4 GRANDDAUGHTER
Comments: Handcrafted, 1-3/4" tall, Dated 1992
A little mouse, with pink frock and a bow on her head, naps in the core of the red apple she has been nibbling. Caption: "Granddaughter, You're The Apple Of My Eye." **Artist:** Ed Seale
☐ Purchased 19___ Pd $_______ MIB NB DB BNT
☐ Want Orig. Ret. $6.75 **NB** $10 **MIB** Sec. Mkt. **$18-$20**

QX 463-4 GRANDDAUGHTER'S FIRST CHRISTMAS
Comments: Handcrafted, 2-3/16" tall, Dated 1992
This little girl cub loves the toys and ice skates tucked inside her Christmas bag. **Artist:** Bob Siedler
☐ Purchased 19___ Pd $_______ MIB NB DB BNT
☐ Want Orig. Ret. $6.75 **NB** $10 **MIB** Sec. Mkt. **$15-$18**

QX 201-1 GRANDMOTHER
Comments: Pink Glass Ball, 2-7/8" dia., Dated 1992
The caption: "A Grandmother's World... A World Of Love And Cherished Memories. Christmas 1992," is framed with decorative holly and Christmas memorabilia.
☐ Purchased 19___ Pd $_______ MIB NB DB BNT
☐ Want Orig. Ret. $4.75 **NB** $6 **MIB** Sec. Mkt. **$12-$14**

QX 200-4 GRANDPARENTS
Comments: Silver Glass Ball, 2-7/8" dia., Dated 1992
Christmas themes frame the caption: "Grandparents Have A Special Way Of Brightening Up The Holiday! Christmas 1992."
☐ Purchased 19___ Pd $_______ MIB NB DB BNT
☐ Want Orig. Ret. $4.75 **NB** $6 **MIB** Sec. Mkt. **$12-$14**

QX 561-1 GRANDSON
Comments: Handcrafted, 1-3/4" tall, Dated 1992
A stuffed little mouse in a blue nightshirt naps against the core of a green apple he's eaten. Caption: "Grandson, You're The Apple Of My Eye. 1992" **Artist:** Ed Seale
☐ Purchased 19___ Pd $_______ MIB NB DB BNT
☐ Want Orig. Ret. $6.75 **NB** $14 **MIB** Sec. Mkt. **$18-$20**

QX 462-1 GRANDSON'S FIRST CHRISTMAS
Comments: Handcrafted, 2-1/4" tall, Dated 1992
A little boy bear cub, wearing a red ball cap, happily opens his sack of Christmas toys. **Artist:** Bob Siedler
☐ Purchased 19___ Pd $_______ MIB NB DB BNT
☐ Want Orig. Ret. $6.75 **NB** $12 **MIB** Sec. Mkt. **$16-$20**

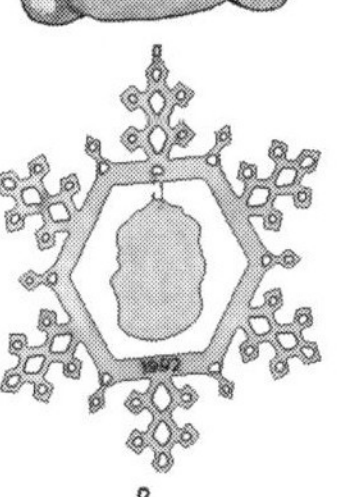

QX 425-1 GREATEST STORY
Comments: **Third and Final in Series**
Porcelain and Brass, 3-3/4" tall, Dated 1992
The traditional picture of the birth of Christ is portrayed in white porcelain. **Artist:** LaDene Votruba
☐ Purchased 19___ Pd $_______ MIB NB DB BNT
☐ Want Orig. Ret. $12.75 **NB** $15 **MIB** Sec. Mkt. **$22-$26**

QX 510-1 GREEN THUMB SANTA
Comments: Handcrafted, 2-3/16" tall, Dated '92
Santa is wearing a red visor and using a watering can dated '92. He is giving his Christmas tree a drink. **Artist:** Don Palmiter
☐ Purchased 19___ Pd $_______ MIB NB DB BNT
☐ Want Orig. Ret. $7.75 **NB** $10 **MIB** Sec. Mkt. **$15-$18**

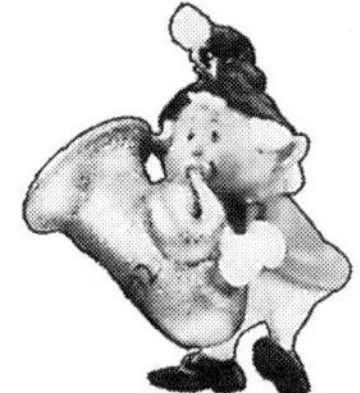

QX 446-4 HARK! IT'S HERALD
Comments: **Fourth and Final Edition,** Handcrafted, 2-1/16" tall. Dated 1992. Completing the series, Herald blows a Merry Christmas melody on his baritone. **Artist:** Julia Lee
☐ Purchased 19___ Pd $_______ MIB NB DB BNT
☐ Want Orig. Ret. $7.75 **NB** $14 **MIB** Sec. Mkt. **$20-$22**

QX 441-1 HEART OF CHRISTMAS
Comments: **Third in Series**, Handcrafted, 2" tall, Dated 1992
This heart opens to reveal a family preparing for Christmas at home. Caption: "Christmas Traditions Warm Every Heart."
Artist: Ed Seale
☐ Purchased 19___ Pd $_______ MIB NB DB BNT
☐ Want Orig. Ret. $13.75 **NB** $18 **MIB** Sec. Mkt. **$28-$30**

QX 445-4 HEAVENLY ANGELS
Comments: **Second in Series,** Handcrafted, 3" tall, Dated 1992
This lovely bas-relief angel heralds the season of Christmas.
Artist: Joyce A. Lyle
☐ Purchased 19___ Pd $_______ MIB NB DB BNT
☐ Want Orig. Ret. $7.75 **NB** $18 **MIB** Sec. Mkt. **$28-$30**

QX 514-1 HELLO-HO-HO
Comments: Handcrafted, 3-15/16" tall, Dated 1992
Santa opens the doors and comes out to greet you when you pull the ball. **Artist:** Ken Crow
☐ Purchased 19___ Pd $_______ MIB NB DB BNT
☐ Want Orig. Ret. $9.75 **NB** $14 **MIB** Sec. Mkt. **$20-$22**

QX 434-1 HERE COMES SANTA: KRINGLE TOURS
Comments: **Fourteenth in Series**, Handcrafted, 2-5/8" tall Dated 1992. Santa makes the perfect tour guide as he leads the Christmas tour. This is the longest-running Keepsake Ornament series. **Artist:** Linda Sickman
☐ Purchased 19___ Pd $_______ MIB NB DB BNT
☐ Want Orig. Ret. $14.75 **NB** $20 **MIB** Sec. Mkt. **$38-$42**

QX 504-4 HOLIDAY MEMO
Comments: Handcrafted, 2-7/16" tall, Dated 1992
This cute Christmas critter, astride a stapler, holds a message, "MEMO: Have A Very Merry Christmas... (inside) And A Terrific New Year!" **Artist:** Anita Marra Rogers
☐ Purchased 19___ Pd $_______ MIB NB DB BNT
☐ Want Orig. Ret. $7.75 **NB** $10 **MIB** Sec. Mkt. **$15-$18**

QX 543-1 HOLIDAY TEATIME
Comments: Handcrafted, 1-7/8" tall; 1/7/16" tall, Dated '92
Two clip-on mice form a teatime duet. One mouse holds a cup and saucer while the other holds the tea bag from above.
Artist: Anita Marra Rogers
☐ Purchased 19___ Pd $_______ MIB NB DB BNT
☐ Want Orig. Ret. $14.75 **NB** $18 **MIB** Sec. Mkt. **$30-$32**

QX 513-1 HOLIDAY WISHES
Comments: Handcrafted, 2-7/16" tall, Dated '92
Two little kittens are making their wishes on a giant wishbone. Caption: "Holiday Wishes." **Artist:** Sharon Pike
☐ Purchased 19___ Pd $_______ MIB NB DB BNT
☐ Want Orig. Ret. $7.75 **NB** $10 **MIB** Sec. Mkt. **$16-$18**

QX 506-4 HONEST GEORGE
Comments: Handcrafted, 2-1/2" tall, Dated 1992
Commemorating the 1992 election year is patriot George Washington with his axe and tree over his shoulder.
Artist: Julia Lee
☐ Purchased 19___ Pd $_______ MIB NB DB BNT
☐ Want Orig. Ret. $7.75 **NB** $10 **MIB** Sec. Mkt. **$18-$20**

QX 302-4 JESUS LOVES ME
Comments: Light Green Cameo, 2-7/8" dia., Dated 1992
A small child takes time from his play to pray, his stuffed bear and toys at his feet. Caption: "Jesus Loves Me. Christmas 1992."
Artist: Trish Andrews
☐ Purchased 19___ Pd $_______ MIB NB DB BNT
☐ Want Orig. Ret. $7.75 **NB** $8 **MIB** Sec. Mkt. **$12-$15**

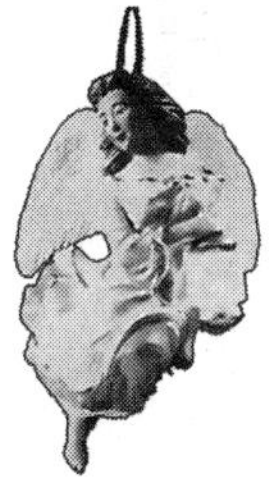

QLX 723-1 LIGHTING THE WAY
Comments: Light, Handcrafted, 3-11/16" tall
Flickering light dances on your tree from this angel's lantern. Some lighted ornaments can be found for less if "sought" after at shows, through ads, etc. **Artist:** Trish Andrews
☐ Purchased 19___ Pd $_______ MIB NB DB BNT
☐ Want Orig. Ret. $18.00 **NB** $30 **MIB** Sec. Mkt. **$40-$45**

QLX 709-4 LOOK! IT'S SANTA
Comments: Light, Handcrafted, 4-1/16" tall, Dated 1992
Excited children peer around their Christmas tree to catch a glimpse of Santa; they know he's there because they see his shadow on the wall. **Artist:** Donna Lee
☐ Purchased 19___ Pd $_______ MIB NB DB BNT
☐ Want Orig. Ret. $14.00 **NB** $25 **MIB** Sec. Mkt. **$35-$40**

QX 484-1 LOVE TO SKATE
Comments: Handcrafted, 2-5/8" tall, Dated Christmas 1992
This bear couple have eyes only for each other as they skate into the Christmas season. **Artist:** Anita Marra Rogers
☐ Purchased 19___ Pd $_______ MIB NB DB BNT
☐ Want Orig. Ret. $8.75 **NB** $12 **MIB** Sec. Mkt. **$18-$22**

QX 515-1 LOVING SHEPHERD
Comments: Handcrafted, 2-13/16" tall, Dated 1992
A content, happy lamb looks with joy to his shepherd, confident of his love and care. **Artist:** Trish Andrews
☐ Purchased 19___ Pd $_______ MIB NB DB BNT
☐ Want Orig. Ret. $7.75 **NB** $10 **MIB** Sec. Mkt. **$15-$18**

QX 427-4 MARY'S ANGELS: LILY
Comments: **Fifth in Series**, Acrylic and Handcrafted, 2-7/16" tall
Lily yawns widely and wipes her eyes as she sits sleepy-eyed on her frosted acrylic cloud. This is a popular series.
Artist: Robert Chad
☐ Purchased 19___ Pd $_______ MIB NB DB BNT
☐ Want Orig. Ret. $6.75 **NB** $35 **MIB** Sec. Mkt. **$50-$55**

QX 516-1 MEMORIES TO CHERISH PHOTOHOLDER
Comments: Fine Porcelain, 3-5/8" tall, "Merry Christmas 1992"
Frame a favorite photo in this lovely hand-painted fine porcelain ornament. **Artist:** Trish Andrews
☐ Purchased 19___ Pd $_______ MIB NB DB BNT
☐ Want Orig. Ret. $10.75 **NB** $12 **MIB** Sec. Mkt. **$18-$20**

QX 441-4 MERRY OLDE SANTA
Comments: **Third in Series**, Handcrafted, 4-1/8" tall
Dated 1992. While a teddy sits nearby on a toy drum, Santa is filling a red stocking with a horn. **Artist:** Duane Unruh
☐ Purchased 19___ Pd $_______ MIB NB DB BNT
☐ Want Orig. Ret. $14.75 **NB** $20 **MIB** Sec. Mkt. **$35-$40**

QX 511-4 MERRY "SWISS" MOUSE
Comments: Handcrafted, 1-13/16" tall, Dated 1992
This little white mouse and his all-time favorite Swiss cheese clips to your tree or wreath. **Artist:** Ed Seale
☐ Purchased 19___ Pd $_______ MIB NB DB BNT
☐ Want Orig. Ret. $7.75 **NB** $10 **MIB** Sec. Mkt. **$14-$16**

QX 516-4 MOM
Comments: Handcrafted, 2-3/8" tall, Dated 1992
Mama rabbit closes her eyes and reflects on "Mom's Christmas Memories." Sweet dreams! **Artist:** Anita Marra Rogers
☐ Purchased 19___ Pd $_______ MIB NB DB BNT
☐ Want Orig. Ret. $7.75 **NB** $10 **MIB** Sec. Mkt. **$18-$20**

QX 467-1 MOM AND DAD
Comments: Handcrafted, 1-15/16" tall, Dated 1992
Mom and Dad beavers are hanging the lights on the tree. This stringer ornament may be hung on one branch or two different branches of your tree. **Artist:** Bob Siedler
☐ Purchased 19___ Pd $_______ MIB NB DB BNT
☐ Want Orig. Ret. $9.75 **NB** $24 **MIB** Sec. Mkt. **$35-$40**

QX 461-4 MOM-TO-BE
Comments: Handcrafted, 2-5/16" tall, Dated 1992
A happy hen sits on her, as yet, unhatched egg which sports a gold bow. **Artist:** Julia Lee
☐ Purchased 19___ Pd $_______ MIB NB DB BNT
☐ Want Orig. Ret. $6.75 **NB** $12 **MIB** Sec. Mkt. **$18-$20**

QX 498-4 MOTHER GOOSE
Comments: Handcrafted, 3-1/2" tall, Dated 1992
Mother Goose reads her Nursery Rhymes while gliding on a large white goose. Swing the ornament back and forth; the head, tail and wings of the goose move up and down. Prices down from '94. **Artist:** Ken Crow
☐ Purchased 19___ Pd $_______ MIB NB DB BNT
☐ Want Orig. Ret. $13.75 **NB** $20 **MIB** Sec. Mkt. **$26-$30**

QX 429-4 MR. AND MRS. CLAUS: GIFT EXCHANGE
Comments: **Seventh in Series**, Handcrafted, 3-1/8" tall Dated 1992. Taking time out from their busy Christmas schedules, this loving couple exchange gifts. **Artist:** Duane Unruh
☐ Purchased 19___ Pd $_______ MIB NB DB BNT
☐ Want Orig. Ret. $14.75 **NB** $20 **MIB** Sec. Mkt. **$30-$35**

QX 519-1 NEW HOME
Comments: Handcrafted, 2-1/2" tall, Dated 1992
A little mouse looks out the door of his cupcake home, topped with pink frosting "snow" and a cherry. Caption: "Home Sweet Home." **Artist:** Sharon Pike
☐ Purchased 19___ Pd $_______ MIB NB DB BNT
☐ Want Orig. Ret. $8.75 **NB** $12 **MIB** Sec. Mkt. **$18-$20**

QX 222-4 NORMAN ROCKWELL ART
Comments: White Glass Ball, 2-7/8" dia., Dated 1992
Captions: "Christmas Sing Merrilie." and "In Each Of Our Hearts Lives An Ideal Christmas... A Season Of Snow-Covered Trees, Smiling Carolers, And Santa Claus, A Season Of Memories And Dreams." **Artist:** Joyce A. Lyle
☐ Purchased 19___ Pd $_______ MIB NB DB BNT
☐ Want Orig. Ret. $5.00 **NB** $ 8.50 **MIB** Sec. Mkt. **$15-$18**

QX 510-4 NORTH POLE FIRE FIGHTER
Comments: Handcrafted, 3-3/4" tall, Dated 1992
Santa is on his way to rescue Christmas as he slides down the "North Pole" with his pack on his back. **Artist:** Ed Seale
☐ Purchased 19___ Pd $_______ MIB NB DB BNT
☐ Want Orig. Ret. $9.75 **NB** $14 **MIB** Sec. Mkt. **$18-$22**

QX 524-4 NORTH POLE NUTCRACKERS: ERIC THE BAKER
Comments: Handcrafted, 4-3/8" tall, Dated on Bottom - '92
Yum! Eric's been in the kitchen again. What tasty treat is he serving today? **Artist:** Linda Sickman
☐ Purchased 19___ Pd $_______ MIB NB DB BNT
☐ Want Orig. Ret. $8.75 **NB** $10 **MIB** Sec. Mkt. **$18-$20**

QX 526-1 NORTH POLE NUTCRACKERS: FRANZ THE ARTIST
Comments: Handcrafted, 4-5/8" tall, Dated on Bottom - '92
Franz is ready to paint your portrait! He carries his brush and palette with him. **Artist:** Linda Sickman
☐ Purchased 19___ Pd $_______ MIB NB DB BNT
☐ Want Orig. Ret. $8.75 **NB** $15 **MIB** Sec. Mkt. **$22-$25**

QX 526-4 NORTH POLE NUTCRACKERS: FRIEDA THE ANIMALS' FRIEND
Comments: Handcrafted, 4-3/8" tall, Dated on Bottom - '92
The animals know of Frieda's love for them and they happily come to her. **Artist:** Linda Sickman
☐ Purchased 19___ Pd $_______ MIB NB DB BNT
☐ Want Orig. Ret. $8.75 **NB** $15 **MIB** Sec. Mkt. **$20-$24**

QX 528-1 NORTH POLE NUTCRACKERS: LUDWIG THE MUSICIAN
Comments: Handcrafted, 4-7/8" tall, Dated on Bottom - '92
Ludwig's talents are readily seen by his sheet music and French Horn. **Artist:** Linda Sickman
☐ Purchased 19___ Pd $_______ MIB NB DB BNT
☐ Want Orig. Ret. $8.75 **NB** $15 **MIB** Sec. Mkt. **$18-$20**

QX 525-1 NORTH POLE NUTCRACKERS: MAX THE TAILOR
Comments: Handcrafted, 4-3/8" tall, Dated on Bottom - '92
Max comes complete with needle and thread to stitch a torn teddy bear. **Artist:** Linda Sickman
☐ Purchased 19___ Pd $_______ MIB NB DB BNT
☐ Want Orig. Ret. $8.75 **NB** $12 **MIB** Sec. Mkt. **$18-$22**

QX 525-4 NORTH POLE NUTCRACKERS: OTTO THE CARPENTER
Comments: Handcrafted, 4-3/8" tall, Dated on Bottom - '92
Otto is ready for business with his mallet in one hand and his masterpiece in the other. **Artist:** Linda Sickman
☐ Purchased 19___ Pd $_______ MIB NB DB BNT
☐ Want Orig. Ret. $8.75 **NB** $12 **MIB** Sec. Mkt. **$20-$22**

QX 425-4 NOSTALGIC HOUSES AND SHOPS: FIVE-AND-TEN-CENT STORE
Comments: **Ninth in Series**, Handcrafted, 3-5/8" tall
Dated 1992. This old-fashioned shop recreates the original shops, down to the bubble gum machine in front of the store.
Artist: Donna Lee
☐ Purchased 19___ Pd $_______ MIB NB DB BNT
☐ Want Orig. Ret. $14.75 **NB** $25 **MIB** Sec. Mkt. **$38-$40**

QLX 708-1 NUT SWEET NUT
Comments: Light, Handcrafted, 2-1/16" tall, Dated 1992
A cute little chipmunk peeks through the door of his snow-covered walnut home. **Artist:** Ken Crow
☐ Purchased 19___ Pd $_______ MIB NB DB BNT
☐ Want Orig. Ret. $10.00 **NB** $15 **MIB** Sec. Mkt. **$20-$25**

QX 541-1 O CHRISTMAS TREE
Comments: Porcelain Bell, Dated 1992
A Christmas tree sits atop this Hallmark Keepsake Premiere Bell.
Artist: LaDene Votruba
☐ Purchased 19___ Pd $_______ MIB NB DB BNT
☐ Want Orig. Ret. $10.75 **NB** $12 **MIB** Sec. Mkt. **$25-$30**

QLX 722-1 OUR FIRST CHRISTMAS
Comments: Light, Panorama Ball, 3-5/8" tall, Dated 1992
The view inside this blue panorama ball reveals a couple enjoying a cozy, flickering fireplace. Caption: "Christmas Is A Magic Time Of Sweet, Romantic Moments." **Artist:** Robert Chad
☐ Purchased 19___ Pd $_______ MIB NB DB BNT
☐ Want Orig. Ret. $20.00 **NB** $22 **MIB** Sec. Mkt. **$42-$45**

QX 561-4 OWL
Comments: Handcrafted, 2-7/8" tall
Owl is getting ready for Christmas with his string of colored lights. An addition to the Winnie-the-Pooh collection. **Artist:** Bob Siedler
☐ Purchased 19___ Pd $_______ MIB NB DB BNT
☐ Want Orig. Ret. $9.75 **NB** $18 **MIB** Sec. Mkt. **$28-$30**

QX 454-4 OWLIVER
Comments: ***FIRST IN SERIES***, Handcrafted, 2-1/16" tall
Dated 1992. Owliver reads from a book. This first in series ornament is still not showing an increase on the secondary market.
Artist: Bob Siedler
☐ Purchased 19___ Pd $_______ MIB NB DB BNT
☐ Want Orig. Ret. $7.75 **NB** $12 **MIB** Sec. Mkt. **$18-$22**

QX 523-4 PARTRIDGE IN A PEAR TREE
Comments: Handcrafted, 4-1/8" tall, Dated '92
The pear at the top of this tree, planted in a gift box, opens to reveal an embarrassed partridge in his boxer shorts. Tree trunk is dated. **Artist:** Bob Siedler
☐ Purchased 19___ Pd $_______ MIB NB DB BNT
☐ Want Orig. Ret. $8.75 **NB** $10 **MIB** Sec. Mkt. **$18-$22**

QX 517-4 PEACE ON EARTH: SPAIN
Comments: **Second in Series,** Handcrafted, 3" dia., Dated 1992
Two Spanish children wish to all "Paz Sobre La Tierra."
Artist: Linda Sickman
☐ Purchased 19___ Pd $_______ MIB NB DB BNT
☐ Want Orig. Ret. $11.75 **NB** $14 **MIB** Sec. Mkt. **$24-$28**

QX 224-4 PEANUTS®
Comments: Chrome Ball, 2-7/8" dia., Christmas 1992
Charlie Brown, Lucy, and the rest of the Peanuts gang act out the Nativity. Caption: "... Behold, I Bring You Good Tidings Of Great Joy, Which Shall Be To All People."
☐ Purchased 19___ Pd $_______ MIB NB DB BNT
☐ Want Orig. Ret. $5.00 **NB** $11 **MIB** Sec. Mkt. **$18-$22**

QLX 721-4 PEANUTS®
Comments: **Second in Series**, Handcrafted, 3-15/16" tall Dated 1992. Lights blink merrily on the wreath as Snoopy and Woodstock sit cozily on the roof of Snoopy's doghouse. Caption: "Happy Holidays." **Artist:** Dill Rhodus
☐ Purchased 19___ Pd $_______ MIB NB DB BNT
☐ Want Orig. Ret. $18.00 **NB** $30 **MIB** Sec. Mkt. **$50-$55**

QX 529-1 PLEASE PAUSE HERE
Comments: Handcrafted, 4" tall, Dated '92
Santa's note reads, "Dear SANTA, Please Pause Here. Your PAL." Santa holds his Coca-Cola and does just that. Clips onto a tree branch or garland. **Artist:** Donna Lee
☐ Purchased 19___ Pd $_______ MIB NB DB BNT
☐ Want Orig. Ret. $14.75 **NB** $28 **MIB** Sec. Mkt. **$32-$36**

QX 491-4 POLAR POST
Comments: Handcrafted, 2-7/8" tall, Dated 1992
This polar mail carrier, dressed in a red scarf, holds a real working compass to help find the North Pole. **Artist:** Ed Seale
☐ Purchased 19___ Pd $_______ MIB NB DB BNT
☐ Want Orig. Ret. $8.75 **NB** $10 **MIB** Sec. Mkt. **$18-$20**

QX 448-4 PUPPY LOVE
Comments: **Second in Series**, 2-5/8" tall, Handcrafted/Brass Dated '92. A gray and white terrier wags a Merry Christmas from his wicker basket. **Artist:** Anita Marra Rogers
☐ Purchased 19___ Pd $_______ MIB NB DB BNT
☐ Want Orig. Ret. $7.75 **NB** $22 **MIB** Sec. Mkt. **$38-$42**

QX 509-4 RAPID DELIVERY
Comments: Handcrafted, 1-7/8" tall, Dated 1992
The Christmas deliveries must be made... and this cute little elf is braving the rapids in his blue raft. **Artist:** Don Palmiter
☐ Purchased 19___ Pd $_______ MIB NB DB BNT
☐ Want Orig. Ret. $8.75 **NB** $12 **MIB** Sec. Mkt. **$20-$22**

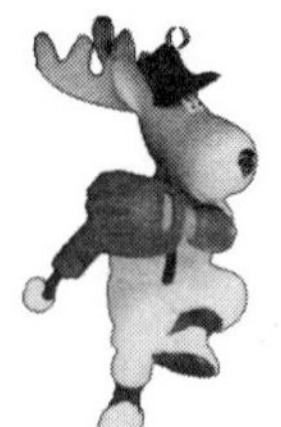

QX 528-4 REINDEER CHAMPS: DONDER
Comments: **Seventh in Series**, Handcrafted, 3-1/16" tall Dated 1992. Donder is ready to strike out the opposing team. He's wearing his team colors: white with red socks and a green shirt. **Artist:** Bob Siedler
☐ Purchased 19___ Pd $_______ MIB NB DB BNT
☐ Want Orig. Ret. $8.75 **NB** $14 **MIB** Sec. Mkt. **$28-$32**

QX 426-1 ROCKING HORSE
Comments: **Twelfth in Series,** Handcrafted, 3" tall, Dated 1992
This brown horse wears a lacy white saddle blanket with a green saddle trimmed in red. **Artist:** Linda Sickman
☐ Purchased 19___ Pd $_______ MIB NB DB BNT
☐ Want Orig. Ret. $10.75 **NB** $18 **MIB** Sec. Mkt. **$30-$35**

QXC 508-1 RODNEY TAKES FLIGHT: KEEPSAKE CLUB
Comments: Handcrafted, 1-3/4" tall, Dated 1992
Rodney is off and flying! Captions: "Rodney's Flight School Holiday Special" and "FLY WITH RODNEY Club Members Welcome." **Artist:** Donna Lee
☐ Purchased 19___ Pd $_______ MIB NB DB BNT
☐ Want Price: Came with Club Membership of $20.00
NB $18 **MIB** Sec. Mkt. **$22-$25**

QX 507-4 SANTA MARIA
Comments: Handcrafted, 3-1/8" tall, Dated 1992
Santa spies land as he stands aboard the Santa Maria, commemorating the 500th anniversary of Columbus' arrival in America. Plenty out there on the secondary market! **Artist:** Ken Crow
☐ Purchased 19___ Pd $_______ MIB NB DB BNT
☐ Want Orig. Ret. $12.75 **NB** $8 **MIB** Sec. Mkt. **$12-$18**

XPR 973-5 SANTA & HIS REINDEER COLLECTION: DASHER & DANCER (SLEIGH ON PAGE 169)
Comments: Handcrafted, 3-15/64" tall
Dasher and Dancer lead the way to Hallmark's Christmas Open House Promotional ornaments. **Artist:** Ken Crow
☐ Purchased 19___ Pd $_______ MIB NB DB BNT
☐ Want Orig. Ret. $4.95 with any $5 Hallmark purchase
NB $5 **MIB** Sec. Mkt. **$25-$28**

XPR 973-6 SANTA & HIS REINDEER COLLECTION: PRANCER & VIXEN
Comments: Handcrafted, 3-15/64" tall
Artist: Ken Crow
☐ Purchased 19___ Pd $_______ MIB NB DB BNT
☐ Want Orig. Ret. $4.95 with any $5 Hallmark purchase
NB $5 **MIB** Sec. Mkt. **$15-$18**

XPR 973-7 SANTA & HIS REINDEER COLLECTION: COMET & CUPID
Comments: Handcrafted, 3-3/64" tall
Artist: Ken Crow
☐ Purchased 19___ Pd $_______ MIB NB DB BNT
☐ Want Orig. Ret. $4.95 with any $5 Hallmark purchase
NB $5 **MIB** Sec. Mkt. **$15-$18**

XPR 973-8 SANTA & HIS REINDEER COLLECTION: DONDER & BLITZEN
Comments: Handcrafted, 3-5/32" tall
Artist: Ken Crow
☐ Purchased 19___ Pd $_______ MIB NB DB BNT
☐ Want Orig. Ret. $4.95 with any $5 Hallmark purchase
NB $5 **MIB** Sec. Mkt. **$25-$28**

XPR 973-9 SANTA & HIS REINDEER COLLECTION: SANTA & SLEIGH
Comments: Handcrafted, 2-9/16" tall, Dated 1992
Santa and his sleigh complete the Collection. All ornaments in this set link together. **Artist:** Ken Crow
☐ Purchased 19___ Pd $_______ MIB NB DB BNT
☐ Want Orig. Ret. $4.95 with any $5 Hallmark purchase
NB $5 **MIB** Sec. Mkt. **$18-$22**

QLX 716-7 SANTA SPECIAL
Comments: Light, Motion and Sound, Handcrafted, 3-1/8" tall
Reissued from 1991. **Artist:** Ed Seale
☐ Purchased 19___ Pd $_______ MIB NB DB BNT
☐ Want Orig. Ret. $40.00 **NB** $60 **MIB** Sec. Mkt. **$75-$80**

QLX 732-1 SANTA SUB
Comments: Blinking Lights, Handcrafted, 2-3/4" tall, Dated '92
Santa's safe in the USS Peppermint, red and white striped submarine. **Artist:** Ken Crow
☐ Purchased 19___ Pd $_______ MIB NB DB BNT
☐ Want Orig. Ret. $18.00 **NB** $30 **MIB** Sec. Mkt. **$38-$42**

QLX 724-1 SANTA'S ANSWERING MACHINE
Comments: Voice, Sound and Blinking Light, 1-7/8" tall
Dated 1992. Santa's not in, but when you press the button you will hear his Christmas message to you, along with the jingling of bells. **Plenty out there!** **Artist:** Julia Lee
☐ Purchased 19___ Pd $_______ MIB NB DB BNT
☐ Want Orig. Ret. $22.00 **NB** $9 MIB Sec. Mkt. **$15-$20**

QXC 729-1 SANTA'S CLUB LIST: KEEPSAKE CLUB
Comments: Members Only, Light, Handcrafted, 2-1/8" tall
Dressed as Santa, a small raccoon holds a lighted candle and reads from "Santa's Club List." **Artist:** Ed Seale
☐ Purchased 19___ Pd $_______ MIB NB DB BNT
☐ Want Orig. Ret. $15.00 **NB** $20 **MIB** Sec. Mkt. **$35-$38**

QX 543-4 SANTA'S HOOK SHOT
Comments: Handcrafted, 2" tall, Dated '92
Santa's "Hooked on Christmas!" Set of two ornaments includes Santa, wearing a green dated jersey and red shorts and a clip-on basketball hoop with basketball. **Artist:** Ed Seale
☐ Purchased 19___ Pd $_______ MIB NB DB BNT
☐ Want Orig. Ret. $12.75 **NB** $18 **MIB** Sec. Mkt. **$28-$32**

QX 508-4 SANTA'S ROUNDUP
Comments: Handcrafted, 3-3/4" tall, Dated 1992
Wearing his white-tassled cowboy hat, Santa performs the best rope tricks. His green rope is in the shape of a Christmas tree!
Artist: Julia Lee
☐ Purchased 19___ Pd $_______ MIB NB DB BNT
☐ Want Orig. Ret. $8.75 **NB** $14 **MIB** Sec. Mkt. **$20-$25**

QX 542-4 SECRET PAL
Comments: Handcrafted, 2-3/4" tall, Dated 1992
A chipper raccoon dressed in blue and red tips his hat as he delivers a gift "From Your Secret Pal."
Artist: Anita Marra Rogers
☐ Purchased 19___ Pd $_______ MIB NB DB BNT
☐ Want Orig. Ret. $7.75 **NB** $10 **MIB** Sec. Mkt. **$12-$15**

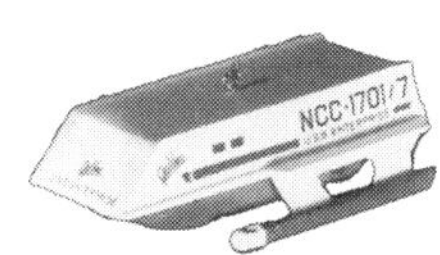

QLX 733-1 SHUTTLECRAFT GALILEO
Comments: Voice and Light, Handcrafted, Dated 1992
This Special Issue gives an authentic greeting in the voice of Mr. Spock. Many more Galileos produced than the '91 Starship Enterprise. Easily found on the secondary market. **Artist:** Dill Rhodus
☐ Purchased 19___ Pd $_______ MIB NB DB BNT
☐ Want Orig. Ret. $21.00 **NB** $14 **MIB** Sec. Mkt. **$48-$52**

QX 532-4 SILVER STAR
Comments: Die-Cast Metal, each 1-1/2" tall, Dated 1992
The sleek streamliner includes a locomotive, luggage car and dome car. May be hung on tree or displayed standing.
Artist: Linda Sickman
☐ Purchased 19___ Pd $_______ MIB NB DB BNT
☐ Want Orig. Ret. $28.00 **NB** $20 **MIB** Sec. Mkt. **$50-$60**

Give a Hallmark collectible to those you love.

QX 468-1 SISTER
Comments: Handcrafted, 4" tall, Dated 1992
When the ball is pulled gently, sister's basket opens and a little kitten peeks out. **Artist:** Ken Crow
☐ Purchased 19___ Pd $_______ MIB NB DB BNT
☐ Want Orig. Ret. $6.75 **NB** $8 **MIB** Sec. Mkt. **$14-$16**

QX 521-4 SKIING 'ROUND
Comments: Handcrafted, 3-5/8" tall, Dated '92
This fellow has gotten himself all bound up in the middle of a snowball. **Artist:** Julia Lee
☐ Purchased 19___ Pd $_______ MIB NB DB BNT
☐ Want Orig. Ret. $8.75
NB $12 **MIB** Sec. Mkt. **$18-$22**

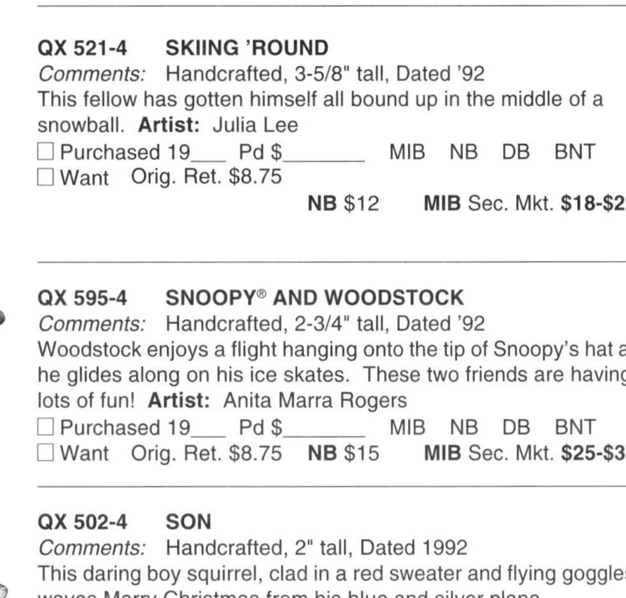

QX 595-4 SNOOPY® AND WOODSTOCK
Comments: Handcrafted, 2-3/4" tall, Dated '92
Woodstock enjoys a flight hanging onto the tip of Snoopy's hat as he glides along on his ice skates. These two friends are having lots of fun! **Artist:** Anita Marra Rogers
☐ Purchased 19___ Pd $_______ MIB NB DB BNT
☐ Want Orig. Ret. $8.75 **NB** $15 **MIB** Sec. Mkt. **$25-$30**

QX 502-4 SON
Comments: Handcrafted, 2" tall, Dated 1992
This daring boy squirrel, clad in a red sweater and flying goggles, waves Merry Christmas from his blue and silver plane.
Artist: John Francis (Collin)
☐ Purchased 19___ Pd $_______ MIB NB DB BNT
☐ Want Orig. Ret. $6.75 **NB** $10 **MIB** Sec. Mkt. **$18-$21**

QX 541-4 SPECIAL CAT PHOTOHOLDER
Comments: Handcrafted, 4-1/8" tall, Dated 1992
A little mouse takes advantage of the fact that the owner here is only a photo of the family cat. **Artist:** Robert Chad
☐ Purchased 19___ Pd $_______ MIB NB DB BNT
☐ Want Orig. Ret. $7.75 **NB** $9 **MIB** Sec. Mkt. **$16-$18**

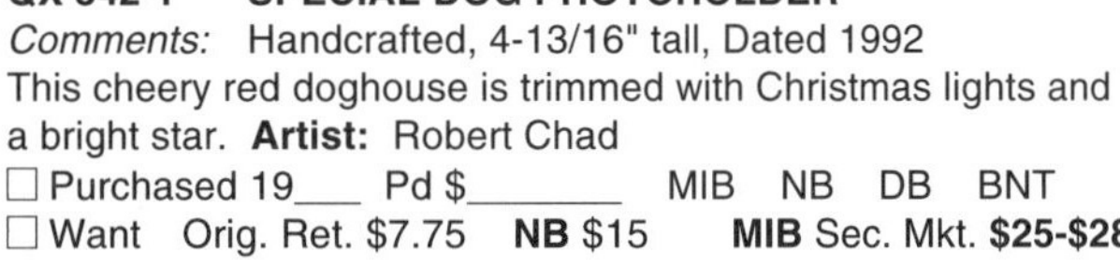

QX 542-1 SPECIAL DOG PHOTOHOLDER
Comments: Handcrafted, 4-13/16" tall, Dated 1992
This cheery red doghouse is trimmed with Christmas lights and a bright star. **Artist:** Robert Chad
☐ Purchased 19___ Pd $_______ MIB NB DB BNT
☐ Want Orig. Ret. $7.75 **NB** $15 **MIB** Sec. Mkt. **$25-$28**

QX 523-1 SPIRIT OF CHRISTMAS STRESS
Comments: Handcrafted, 3-1/2" tall
Handling all the details of what to buy for Christmas can occasionally be stressful as depicted by this Shoebox Greetings character. **Artist:** Robert Chad
☐ Purchased 19___ Pd $_______ MIB NB DB BNT
☐ Want Orig. Ret. $8.75 **NB** $14 **MIB** Sec. Mkt. **$20-$24**

QX 593-4 STOCKED WITH JOY
Comments: Pressed Tin, 4-3/4" tall, Dated 1992
A horse, checker board and other toys stuffed into a blue stocking would delight any child. Tin ornaments are becoming very popular.
Artist: Linda Sickman
☐ Purchased 19___ Pd $_______ MIB NB DB BNT
☐ Want Orig. Ret. $7.75 **NB** $12 **MIB** Sec. Mkt. **$18-$21**

QX 599-4 TASTY CHRISTMAS
Comments: Handcrafted, 2-5/16" tall
Decorated with silver garland, the shark's jaws open and close when you turn his tail. Caption: "It's Beginning To Taste A Lot Like Christmas!" **Artist:** Julia Lee
☐ Purchased 19___ Pd $_______ MIB NB DB BNT
☐ Want Orig. Ret. $9.75 **NB** $12 **MIB** Sec. Mkt. **$18-$22**

QX 226-4 TEACHER
Comments: Red Glass Ball, 2-7/8" dia., Dated Dec. 25, 1992
Costumed children spell "Christmas" with the letters on their hats. Mary Engelbreit design. Caption: "For Teacher -- Thanks For Making Learning Lots Of Fun!"
☐ Purchased 19___ Pd $_______ MIB NB DB BNT
☐ Want Orig. Ret. $4.75 **NB** $8 **MIB** Sec. Mkt. **$12-$14**

QX 489-1 TOBIN FRALEY CAROUSEL
Comments: ***FIRST IN SERIES***, Porcelain and Brass, 5-1/4" tall Dated 1992. A beautiful white horse decorated in red and green rides a brass carousel pole.
Artist: Tobin Fraley
☐ Purchased 19___ Pd $_______ MIB NB DB BNT
☐ Want Orig. Ret. $28.00 **NB** $25 **MIB** Sec. Mkt. **$35-$40**

QX 545-9 TOBOGGAN TAIL
Comments: Handcrafted, 2-1/2" tall, Dated 1992
Who needs a separate sled when you have one that's built-in? With her tail tucked beneath her, mama beaver gives her son a thrilling ride. **Artist:** Trish Andrews
☐ Purchased 19___ Pd $_______ MIB NB DB BNT
☐ Want Orig. Ret. $7.75 **NB** $14 **MIB** Sec. Mkt. **$16-$18**

QX 509-1 TREAD BEAR
Comments: Handcrafted, 2-1/4" tall, Dated 1992
Swinging happily in his tire swing, this little white bear is dressed warmly in his red scarf. Caption: "Bear Paws 1992 Road Gripper." **Artist:** Ed Seale
☐ Purchased 19___ Pd $_______ MIB NB DB BNT
☐ Want Orig. Ret. $8.75 **NB** $12 **MIB** Sec. Mkt. **$15-$20**

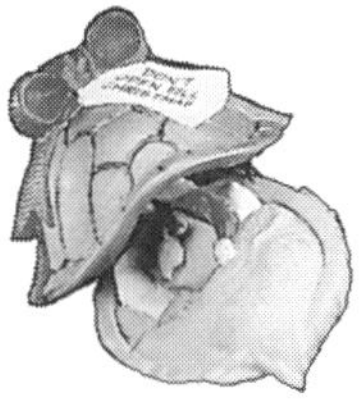

QX 499-1 TURTLE DREAMS
Comments: Handcrafted, 1-13/16" tall, Dated '92
Open the shell and find this little fellow all tucked in, complete with a red stocking cap! Caption: "Don't Open Till Christmas."
Artist: Julia Lee
☐ Purchased 19___ Pd $_______ MIB NB DB BNT
☐ Want Orig. Ret. $8.75 **NB** $14 **MIB** Sec. Mkt. **$22-$26**

QX 303-1 TWELVE DAYS OF CHRISTMAS: NINE LADIES DANCING
Comments: **Ninth in Series**, Acrylic, 3" tall, Dated 1992
A lovely maiden with holly decorations on her skirt dances on a quatrefoil shaped acrylic. This series needs a scarce one!
Artist: Michele Pyda-Sevcik
☐ Purchased 19___ Pd $_______ MIB NB DB BNT
☐ Want Orig. Ret. $6.75 **NB** $12 **MIB** Sec. Mkt. **$16-$21**

QX 500-1 UNCLE ART'S ICE CREAM
Comments: Handcrafted, 3-1/4" tall, Dated 1992
A cute little mouse seems to be having fun turning the crank on this old fashioned ice cream freezer.
Artist: Bob Siedler
☐ Purchased 19___ Pd $_______ MIB NB DB BNT
☐ Want Orig. Ret. $8.75 **NB** $14 **MIB** Sec. Mkt. **$22-$26**

QLX 732-4 UNDER CONSTRUCTION
Comments: Light, Handcrafted, 3-1/2" tall, Dated 1992
A little beaver flashes his red light to warn that you're nearing the tree-trimming zone. Caption: "Caution, Tree-Trimming Zone, 1992 Branch Under Construction." **Artist:** Don Palmiter
☐ Purchased 19___ Pd $_______ MIB NB DB BNT
☐ Want Orig. Ret. $18.00 **NB** $20 **MIB** Sec. Mkt. **$38-$42**

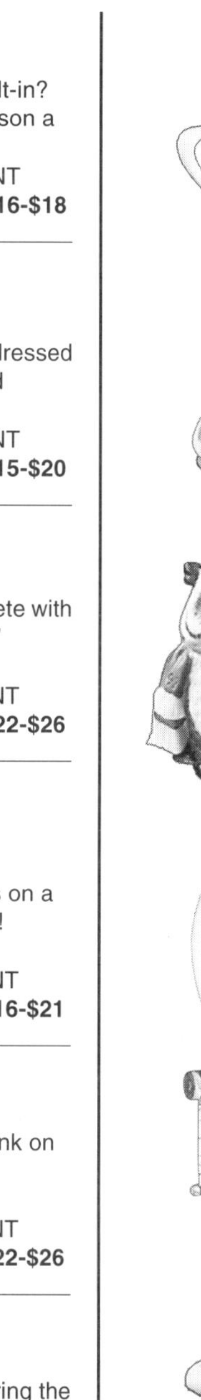

QX 505-1 V.P. OF IMPORTANT STUFF
Comments: Handcrafted, 2-1/16" tall, Dated 1992
A penguin eats his donut from inside a white coffee cup. Caption is green print. **Artist:** Bob Siedler
☐ Purchased 19___ Pd $_______ MIB NB DB BNT
☐ Want Orig. Ret. $6.75 **NB** $8 **MIB** Sec. Mkt. **$12-$16**

QXC 406-7 VICTORIAN SKATER: KEEPSAKE CLUB
Comments: Limited Edition 14,700, Wood Display Stand Dated 1992, Hand-Painted Porcelain, 3-3/4" tall
Holding her holly-trimmed muff, a Victorian skater in grey dress and pink coat glides gracefully. Dated on bottom.
Artist: Duane Unruh
☐ Purchased 19___ Pd $_______ MIB NB DB BNT
☐ Want Orig. Ret. $25.00 **NB** $35 **MIB** Sec. Mkt. **$50-$55**

QLX 708-4 WATCH OWLS
Comments: Light, Porcelain, 2-1/4" tall, Dated 1992
Two hand-painted fine porcelain owls glow with light. Wearing red and green scarves, they're ready to keep watch on your tree.
Artist: John Francis (Collin)
☐ Purchased 19___ Pd $_______ MIB NB DB BNT
☐ Want Orig. Ret. $12.00 **NB** $15 **MIB** Sec. Mkt. **$25-$28**

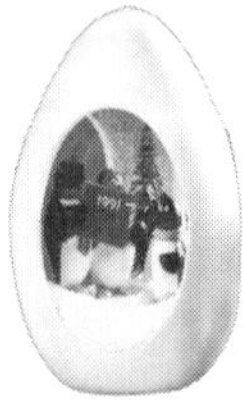

QX 427-1 WINTER SURPRISE
Comments: **Fourth and Final Edition**, 3-1/4" tall, Handcrafted, Dated 1992. Three penguin pals have fun in the snow as they build a gigantic snowman.
Artist: John Francis (Collin)
☐ Purchased 19___ Pd $_______ MIB NB DB BNT
☐ Want Orig. Ret. $11.75 **NB** $15 **MIB** Sec. Mkt. **$18-$20**

QX 505-4 WORLD-CLASS TEACHER
Comments: Handcrafted, 3-1/4" tall, Dated 1992
A lively young squirrel in a green and yellow sweater rolls down the map to show his teacher is the best in the world.
Artist: Bob Siedler
☐ Purchased 19___ Pd $_______ MIB NB DB BNT
☐ Want Orig. Ret. $7.75 **NB** $10 `**MIB** Sec. Mkt. **$18-$20**

QLX 731-4 YULETIDE RIDER
Comments: Light and Motion, Handcrafted, 3-3/8" tall Dated 1992. Santa chugs along in his convertible. Scenery, road and car wheels revolve. **Artist:** Ed Seale
☐ Purchased 19___ Pd $_______ MIB NB DB BNT
☐ Want Orig. Ret. $28.00 **NB** $35 **MIB** Sec. Mkt. **$45-$50**

1993 Collection

QX 568-2 20TH ANNIVERSARY: FROSTY FRIENDS
Comments: Handcrafted, 2-1/2" tall, Dated 1993
Frosty and his penguin pal decorate their igloo for a Merry Christmas. This anniversary edition complements the Frosty Friends Series. **Artist:** Ed Seale
☐ Purchased 19___ Pd $_______ MIB NB DB BNT
☐ Want Orig. Ret. $20.00 **NB** $35 **MIB** Sec. Mkt. **$48-$55**

QX 530-2 20TH ANNIVERSARY: GLOWING PEWTER WREATH
Comments: Fine Pewter, 3-11/16" tall, Dated 1993
Images of Santa, music instruments, a star, and a dated stocking are part of the design on this pewter wreath. Seek and ye shall find for even less.
Artist: Duane Unruh
☐ Purchased 19___ Pd $_______ MIB NB DB BNT
☐ Want Orig. Ret. $18.75 **NB** $22 **MIB** Sec. Mkt. **$34-$38**

QX 567-5 20TH ANNIVERSARY: SHOPPING WITH SANTA
Comments: Handcrafted, 3-1/2" tall, Dated 1993
Santa drives into Christmas in this vintage car. Let's go Hallmarking! This ornament complements the Here Comes Santa Series. **Artist:** Linda Sickman
☐ Purchased 19___ Pd $_______ MIB NB DB BNT
☐ Want Orig. Ret. $24.00 **NB** $22 **MIB** Sec. Mkt. **$45-$50**

QX 561-2 20TH ANNIVERSARY: TANNENBAUM'S DEPT. STORE
Comments: Handcrafted, 4-15/16" tall, Dated 1993
Tannenbaum's three-story shop complements the Nostalgic Houses and Shops Series. Artist: Donna Lee
☐ Purchased 19___ Pd $_______ MIB NB DB BNT
☐ Want Orig. Ret. $26.00 **NB** $40 **MIB** Sec. Mkt. **$50-$55**

QX 588-2 A CHILD'S CHRISTMAS
Comments: Handcrafted, 2-5/16" tall, Dated 1993
A light brown teddy has popped out of a brightly striped gift box to wish happy holidays. May be personalized for Niece, Nephew, Granddaughter, Grandson, Great-Grandchild, or A Child's Christmas." **Artist:** John Francis (Collin)
☐ Purchased 19___ Pd $_______ MIB NB DB BNT
☐ Want Orig. Ret. $9.75 **NB** $10 **MIB** Sec. Mkt. **$11-$14**

Live so that you wouldn't be afraid to sell the family parrot.

QX 591-2 ACROSS THE MILES
Comments: Handcrafted, 1-11/16" tall, Dated 1993
This white bear is sprawled on the ice reading a journal from "Across the Miles." **Artist:** John Francis (Collin)
☐ Purchased 19___ Pd $_______ MIB NB DB BNT
☐ Want Orig. Ret. $8.75 NB $10 **MIB** Sec. Mkt. **$12-$16**

QX 597-2 ANNIVERSARY YEAR PHOTOHOLDER
Comments: Brass and Chrome, 3-13/16" tall, Dated 1993
This ornate photo holder may be personalized eight ways to mark anniversaries for 5, 10, 25, 30, 35, 40, 50 and 60 years.
Artist: Joyce A. Lyle
☐ Purchased 19___ Pd $_______ MIB NB DB BNT
☐ Want Orig. Ret. $9.75 NB $11 **MIB** Sec. Mkt. **$14-$18**

QX 590-2 APPLE FOR TEACHER
Comments: Handcrafted, 2-3/8" tall, Dated 1993
Open the apple and view two mice students at their desks and a chalkboard which may be personalized. Caption: "A Is For Apple, A+ Is For Teacher." **Artist:** Ed Seale
☐ Purchased 19___ Pd $_______ MIB NB DB BNT
☐ Want Orig. Ret. $7.75 NB $8 **MIB** Sec. Mkt. **$12-$14**

QX 551-2 BABY'S FIRST CHRISTMAS
Comments: Silver plated, 3-1/16" tall, Dated 1993
This silver-plated baby rattle is all tied up in a red bow and comes with a silver tag which may be engraved for personalization.
Artist: Don Palmiter
☐ Purchased 19___ Pd $_______ MIB NB DB BNT
☐ Want Orig. Ret. $18.75 NB $19 **MIB** Sec. Mkt. **$24-$28**

QX 551-5 BABY'S FIRST CHRISTMAS
Comments: Handcrafted, 3-3/16" tall, Dated 1993
An adorable baby squirrel plays merrily in its walnut shell "swing." **Artist:** Trish Andrews
☐ Purchased 19___ Pd $_______ MIB NB DB BNT
☐ Want Orig. Ret. $10.75 **NB** $12 **MIB** Sec. Mkt. **$18-$22**

QX 552-2 BABY'S FIRST CHRISTMAS PHOTOHOLDER
Comments: Handcrafted, 4-3/4" dia., Dated 1993
Christmas and baby designs adorn this "quilted" lace-trimmed photoholder. Caption: "Christmas And Babies Fill A Home With Special Joys." **Artist:** Anita Marra Rogers
☐ Purchased 19___ Pd $_______ MIB NB DB BNT
☐ Want Orig. Ret. $7.75 **NB** $12 **MIB** Sec. Mkt. **$16-$18**

QX 552-5 BABY'S FIRST CHRISTMAS
Comments: Handcrafted, 2-3/16" dia., Dated 1993
Also known as the "Teddy Bear Years," a tan teddy holds a red stocking filled with a large cookie star, as he enjoys his pacifier.
Artist: Ken Crow
☐ Purchased 19___ Pd $_______ MIB NB DB BNT
☐ Want Orig. Ret. $7.75 **NB** $14 **MIB** Sec. Mkt. **$22-$25**

QLX 736-5 BABY'S FIRST CHRISTMAS
Comments: Light and Music, 3-7/8" tall, Dated 1993
Baby sleeps soundly in the nursery on Christmas Eve.
Plays "Brahms' Lullaby." Caption: "There's A New Little Stocking For Santa To Fill!" **Artist:** John Francis (Collin)
☐ Purchased 19___ Pd $_______ MIB NB DB BNT
☐ Want Orig. Ret. $22.00 **NB** $25 **MIB** Sec. Mkt. **$45-$48**

QX 210-5 BABY'S FIRST CHRISTMAS-BOY
Comments: Light Blue Glass Ball, 2-7/8" dia., Dated 1993
Toy animals sit side by side around this glass ball. Caption: "A Baby Boy Is A Bundle Of Delight." **Artist:** LaDene Votruba
☐ Purchased 19___ Pd $_______ MIB NB DB BNT
☐ Want Orig. Ret. $4.75 **NB** $6 **MIB** Sec. Mkt. **$10-$14**

QX 209-2 BABY'S FIRST CHRISTMAS-GIRL
Comments: Pink Glass Ball, 2-7/8" dia., Dated 1993
Toy animals sit side by side around this glass ball. Caption: "A Baby Girl Is A Bundle Of Delight." **Artist:** LaDene Votruba
☐ Purchased 19___ Pd $_______ MIB NB DB BNT
☐ Want Orig. Ret. $4.75 **NB** $5 **MIB** Sec. Mkt. **$10-$12**

QX 599-2 BABY'S SECOND CHRISTMAS
Comments: Handcrafted, 2-3/16" dia., Dated 1993
Identical to 1989 except for date. **Artist:** John Francis (Collin)
☐ Purchased 19___ Pd $_______ MIB NB DB BNT
☐ Want Orig. Ret. $6.75 **NB** **MIB** Sec. Mkt.

XPR 974-7 BEARINGERS OF VICTORIA CIRCLE: ABEARNATHY
Comments: Handcrafted
☐ Purchased 19___ Pd $_______ MIB NB DB BNT
☐ Want Orig. Ret.: $4.95 with any $5 Hallmark purchase
NB $5 **MIB** Sec. Mkt. **$8-$10**

Dad: How do you keep milk from turning sour?
Son: Keep it in the cow!

XPR 974-8 BEARINGERS OF VICTORIA CIRCLE: BEARNADETTE
Comments: Handcrafted
☐ Purchased 19___ Pd $_______ MIB NB DB BNT
☐ Want Orig. Ret. : $4.95 with any $5 Hallmark purchase
NB $5 **MIB** Sec. Mkt. **$8-$10**

XPR 974-9 BEARINGERS OF VICTORIA CIRCLE: FIREPLACE HEARTH
Comments: Handcrafted
☐ Purchased 19___ Pd $_______ MIB NB DB BNT
☐ Want Orig. Ret.: $4.95 with any Hallmark purchase
NB $5 **MIB** Sec. Mkt. **$10-$12**

XPR 974-5 BEARINGERS OF VICTORIA CIRCLE: MAMA BEARINGER
Comments: Handcrafted
☐ Purchased 19___ Pd $_______ MIB NB DB BNT
☐ Want Orig. Ret.: $4.95 with any $5 Hallmark purchase
NB $5 **MIB** Sec. Mkt. **$10-$12**

XPR 974-6 BEARINGERS OF VICTORIA CIRCLE: PAPA BEARINGER
Comments: Handcrafted
☐ Purchased 19___ Pd $_______ MIB NB DB BNT
☐ Want Orig. Ret.: $4.95 with any $5 Hallmark purchase
NB $5 **MIB** Sec. Mkt. **$8-$10**

QX 576-2 BEARY GIFTED
Comments: Handcrafted, 2-5/8" tall, Dated 1993
This little brown bear artist becomes his own "Masterpiece" inside an empty frame. **Artist:** Ken Crow
☐ Purchased 19___ Pd $_______ MIB NB DB BNT
☐ Want Orig. Ret. $7.75 **NB** $8 **MIB** Sec. Mkt. **$16-$18**

QLX 740-2 BELLS ARE RINGING
Comments: Light/Motion/Sound, 4-3/16" tall, Dated 1993
A jolly little elf pulls a rope, which causes the bell to ring as it swings back and forth. Delightful! **Artist:** Ken Crow
☐ Purchased 19___ Pd $_______ MIB NB DB BNT
☐ Want Orig. Ret. $28.00 **NB** $32 **MIB** Sec. Mkt. **$55-$60**

Bumper sticker: Beware of sudden stops...collector looking for Hallmark ornaments.

QX 206-2 BETSEY'S COUNTRY CHRISTMAS
Comments: **Second in Series,** Teardrop Ball, 2-7/8" tall, Dated 1993. Caption: "Happy Is The Memory Of Bringing Home The Christmas Tree!"
☐ Purchased 19___ Pd $_______ MIB NB DB BNT
☐ Want Orig. Ret. $5.00 **NB** $5 **MIB** Sec. Mkt. **$14-16**

QX 584-2 BIG ON GARDENING
Comments: Handcrafted, 2-1/2" tall, Dated 1993
This cute little elephant in a red gardening apron is holding a red potted flower and gardening tools. **Artist:** LaDene Votruba
☐ Purchased 19___ Pd $_______ MIB NB DB BNT
☐ Want Orig. Ret. $9.75 **NB** $10 **MIB** Sec. Mkt. **$14-18**

QX 535-2 BIG ROLLER
Comments: Handcrafted, 3-1/16" tall, Dated 1993
This little creature dressed for winter runs on a nickel-plated exercise wheel that really spins. **Artist:** Bob Siedler
☐ Purchased 19___ Pd $_______ MIB NB DB BNT
☐ Want Orig. Ret. $8.75 **NB** $9 **MIB** Sec. Mkt. **$14-$18**

QX 525-2 BIRD WATCHER
Comments: Handcrafted, 2-7/16" tall, Dated 1993
All set with his sneakers, camera and binoculars, a bluebird has its eyes on Santa and his reindeer. **Artist:** Julia Lee
☐ Purchased 19___ Pd $_______ MIB NB DB BNT
☐ Want Orig. Ret. $9.75 **NB** $14 **MIB** Sec. Mkt. **$18-22**

QX 556-5 BOWLING FOR ZZZS
Comments: Handcrafted, 1-13/16" tall, Dated 1993
A little mouse naps under a hand towel captioned Santa Claus Lanes, which is tucked inside a green bowling bag.
Artist: John Francis (Collin)
☐ Purchased 19___ Pd $_______ MIB NB DB BNT
☐ Want Orig. Ret. $7.75 **NB** $9 **MIB** Sec. Mkt. **$14-$18**

QX 554-2 BROTHER
Comments: Handcrafted, 2-3/8" tall, Dated 1993
Sporting a red, white and green football helmet, this ornament is sure to score big! **Artist:** Anita Marra Rogers
☐ Purchased 19___ Pd $_______ MIB NB DB BNT
☐ Want Orig. Ret. $6.75 **NB** $5 **MIB** Sec. Mkt. **$8-$10**

QX 578-5 CARING NURSE
Comments: Handcrafted, 1-1/4" tall, Dated 1993
This little bear nurse specializes in "TLC" as she checks her patient with a stethoscope. **Artist:** John Francis (Collin)
☐ Purchased 19___ Pd $_______ MIB NB DB BNT
☐ Want Orig. Ret. $6.75 **NB** $10 **MIB** Sec. Mkt. **$16-$20**

QX 522-2 CHILD'S FIFTH CHRISTMAS
Comments: Handcrafted, 2-3/8" tall, Dated 1993.
Identical to 1989 except for date.
Artist: Dill Rhodus
☐ Purchased 19___ Pd $_______ MIB NB DB BNT
☐ Want Orig. Ret. $6.75 **NB** $10 **MIB** Sec. Mkt. **$14-$16**

QX 521-5 CHILD'S FOURTH CHRISTMAS
Comments: Handcrafted, 3" tall, Dated 1993.
Identical to 1989 except for date.
Artist: John Francis (Collin)
☐ Purchased 19___ Pd $_______ MIB NB DB BNT
☐ Want Orig. Ret. $6.75 **NB** $10 **MIB** Sec. Mkt. **$14-$16**

QX 599-5 CHILD'S THIRD CHRISTMAS
Comments: Handcrafted, 2-1/2" tall, Dated 1993.
Identical to 1989 except for date.
Artist: John Francis (Collin)
☐ Purchased 19___ Pd $_______ MIB NB DB BNT
☐ Want Orig. Ret. $6.75 **NB** $10 **MIB** Sec. Mkt. **$14-$18**

QLX 715-2 CHRIS MOUSE FLIGHT
Comments: **Ninth in a Series**, Light, Handcrafted, 4" tall, Dated 1993. Chris Mouse flies high in his hot air teacup balloon. **Artist:** Anita Marra Rogers
☐ Purchased 19___ Pd $_______ MIB NB DB BNT
☐ Want Orig. Ret. $12.00 **NB** $14 **MIB** Sec. Mkt. **$28-$32**

QX 582-5 CHRISTMAS BREAK
Comments: Handcrafted, 3-1/16" tall, Dated 1993
With one ski in hand, Santa is wearing a cast this Christmas. Ouch! Get well soon, Santa! **Artist:** Ed Seale
☐ Purchased 19___ Pd $_______ MIB NB DB BNT
☐ Want Orig. Ret. $7.75 **NB** $8 **MIB** Sec. Mkt. **$16-$21**

QX 527-5 CLASSIC AMERICAN CARS: 1956 Ford Thunderbird

Comments: **Third in Series**, Handcrafted, 2-5/16" tall Dated 1993. This blue T-bird is guaranteed to delight car collectors of all ages! **Artist:** Don Palmiter

☐ Purchased 19___ Pd $_______ MIB NB DB BNT
☐ Want Orig. Ret. $12.75 **NB** $20 **MIB** Sec. Mkt. **$35-$40**

QX 566-2 CLEVER COOKIE

Comments: Handcrafted and Tin, 3-1/8" tall, Dated 1993 Clever is the right word, as this gingerbread cookie girl decides to leave her cutter frame. **Artist:** Linda Sickman

☐ Purchased 19___ Pd $_______ MIB NB DB BNT
☐ Want Orig. Ret. $7.75 **NB** $12 **MIB** Sec. Mkt. **$16-$20**

QX 593-5 COACH

Comments: Handcrafted, 2-1/2" tall, Dated 1993 A new commemorative ornament to the line, this penguin, wearing a red cap, holds onto his clipboard as he blows a silver whistle. **Artist:** Don Palmiter

☐ Purchased 19___ Pd $_______ MIB NB DB BNT
☐ Want Orig. Ret. $6.75 **NB** $9 **MIB** Sec. Mkt. **$10-$15**

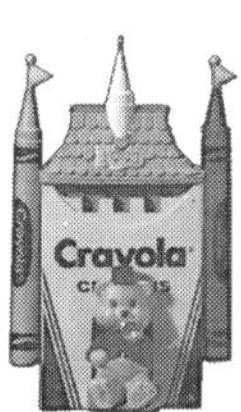

QX 442-2 CRAYOLA® CRAYON: Bright Shining Castle

Comments: **Fifth in Series**, Handcrafted, 3-5/8" tall, Dated 1993 A bear trumpeter welcomes everyone to his colorful castle. **Artist:** Ken Crow

☐ Purchased 19___ Pd $_______ MIB NB DB BNT
☐ Want Orig. Ret. $10.75 **NB** $12 **MIB** Sec. Mkt. **$28-$32**

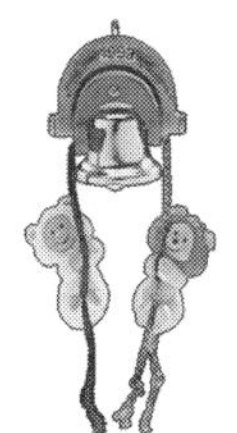

QX 528-5 CURLY 'N' KINGLY

Comments: Handcrafted, 4-1/8" tall, Dated 1993 A lion and a lamb work together to ring the bell and wish you a Merry Christmas. **Artist:** Ken Crow

☐ Purchased 19___ Pd $_______ MIB NB DB BNT
☐ Want Orig. Ret. $10.75 **NB** $12 **MIB** Sec. Mkt. **$20-$24**

QX 585-5 DAD

Comments: Handcrafted, 2-5/8" tall, Dated 1993 Dad is all set to make something special in his workshop with his saw and his tool belt. **Artist:** Julia Lee

☐ Purchased 19___ Pd $_______ MIB NB DB BNT
☐ Want Orig. Ret. $7.75 **NB** $10 **MIB** Sec. Mkt. **$16-$18**

QX 553-2 DAD-TO-BE

Comments: Handcrafted, 2-1/8" tall, Dated 1993 "Dad-To-Bee," wearing a red and white cap, is buzzing to his honey with a bouquet of flowers. **Artist:** Julia Lee

☐ Purchased 19___ Pd $_______ MIB NB DB BNT
☐ Want Orig. Ret. $6.75 **NB** $10 **MIB** Sec. Mkt. **$12-$16**

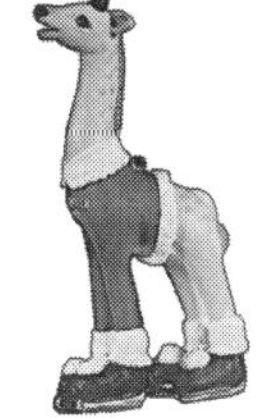

QX 587-2 DAUGHTER

Comments: Handcrafted, 4-7/16" tall, Dated 1993 This giraffe with bendable neck and legs is wearing a green sweater and red ice skates. **Artist:** LaDene Votruba

☐ Purchased 19___ Pd $_______ MIB NB DB BNT
☐ Want Orig. Ret. $6.75 **NB** $7 **MIB** Sec. Mkt. **$10-$14**

QX 550-5 DICKENS CAROLER BELL: LADY DAPHNE

Comments: **Fourth and Final in Collection**, Porcelain Bell 4-1/4" tall, Dated 1993 Lady Daphne is ready for caroling in her red and white coat and hat, songbook in hand. **Artist:** Robert Chad

☐ Purchased 19___ Pd $_______ MIB NB DB BNT
☐ Want Orig. Ret. $21.75 **NB** $24 **MIB** Sec. Mkt. **$38-$42**

QLX 717-2 DOG'S BEST FRIEND

Comments: Light, 3" tall A black and white pooch adorns a fire hydrant with Christmas lights and an acrylic star. **Artist:** Julia Lee

☐ Purchased 19___ Pd $_______ MIB NB DB BNT
☐ Want Orig. Ret. $12.00 **NB** $14 **MIB** Sec. Mkt. **$23-$28**

QLX 737-2 DOLLHOUSE DREAMS

Comments: Light, 3-5/16" tall, Dated 1993 A little girl plays with her dollhouse which is complete with a flickering fire in the hearth and lights which blink on upstairs. **Artist:** Ken Crow

☐ Purchased 19___ Pd $_______ MIB NB DB BNT
☐ Want Orig. Ret. $22.00 **NB** $30 **MIB** Sec. Mkt. **$45-$50**

QX 557-5 DUNKIN' ROO

Comments: Handcrafted, 3-7/8" tall, Dated 1993 Wearing red tennis shoes and a green shirt, this kangaroo is sure to get his ball into the basket. **Artist:** Bob Siedler

☐ Purchased 19___ Pd $_______ MIB NB DB BNT
☐ Want Orig. Ret. $7.75 **NB** $10 **MIB** Sec. Mkt. **$15-$18**

QX 447-5 FABULOUS DECADE
Comments: **Fourth in Series,** Handcrafted and Brass
1-13/16" tall, Dated 1993
A perky skunk carries a brass "1993" by its tail.
Artist: Sharon Pike
☐ Purchased 19___ Pd $_______ MIB NB DB BNT
☐ Want Orig. Ret. $7.75 **NB** $10 **MIB** Sec. Mkt. **$15-$18**

QX 578-2 FAITHFUL FIRE FIGHTER
Comments: Handcrafted, 2-3/4" tall
A little Dalmatian, in a fireman's hat and yellow raincoat is ready to go with a water hose in paw. **Artist:** LaDene Votruba
☐ Purchased 19___ Pd $_______ MIB NB DB BNT
☐ Want Orig. Ret. $8 **NB** $10 **MIB** Sec. Mkt. **$18-$21**

QX 536-5 FELIZ NAVIDAD
Comments: Handcrafted Brass, 2-15/16" tall, Dated 1993
A monk stands at the entrance of a Spanish mission, complete with a gold bell in the tower. **Artist:** Donna Lee
☐ Purchased 19___ Pd $_______ MIB NB DB BNT
☐ Want Orig. Ret. $8.75 **NB** $8 **MIB** Sec. Mkt. **$15-$20**

QX 557-2 FILLS THE BILL
Comments: Handcrafted, 3-7/8" tall, Dated 1993
Pole in hand, a pelican sitting at "Pier 93" is casting his fishing line for a Christmas nibble. **Artist:** Bob Siedler
☐ Purchased 19___ Pd $_______ MIB NB DB BNT
☐ Want Orig. Ret. $8.75 **NB** $9 **MIB** Sec. Mkt. **$14-$18**

QLX 716-5 FOREST FROLICS
Comments: **Fifth in a Series,** Light/Motion, Handcrafted, 4-3/16" tall, Dated 1993. Woodland animals scamper around a snow coated tree adorned with a lighted gold star.
Artist: Sharon Pike
☐ Purchased 19___ Pd $_______ MIB NB DB BNT
☐ Want Orig. Ret. $25.00 **NB** $35 **MIB** Sec. Mkt. **$45-$50**

QX 414-2 FROSTY FRIENDS
Comments: **Fourteenth in Series**, Handcrafted, 2-7/8" tall Dated 1993. Frosty's little husky puppy snuggles into his icy doghouse. **Artist:** Julia Lee
☐ Purchased 19___ Pd $_______ MIB NB DB BNT
☐ Want Orig. Ret. $9.75 **NB** $18 **MIB** Sec. Mkt. **$28-$32**

QXC 544-2 GENTLE TIDINGS: KEEPSAKE CLUB
Comments: Hand-painted Porcelain, 4-9/16" dia., Dated 1993
A delicate porcelain angel cradles a lamb in her arms. Available to Club Members only. **Artist:** Trish Andrews
☐ Purchased 19___ Pd $_______ MIB NB DB BNT
☐ Want Orig. Ret. $25.00 **NB** $25 **MIB** Sec. Mkt. **$38-$40**

QX 206-5 GIFT BRINGERS, THE: THE MAGI
Comments: **Fifth and Final in Series**, White Glass Ball 2-7/8" dia., Dated 1993. Three wise men from the East bring their gifts of gold, frankincense and myrrh to the Baby.
Artist: LaDene Votruba
☐ Purchased 19___ Pd $_______ MIB NB DB BNT
☐ Want Orig. Ret. $5.00 **NB** $6 **MIB** Sec. Mkt. **$14-$18**

QX 587-5 GODCHILD
Comments: Handcrafted, 2" tall, Dated 1993
A small child kneels in prayer by his pillow which reads, "Bless You, Godchild 1993." **Artist:** Robert Chad
☐ Purchased 19___ Pd $_______ MIB NB DB BNT
☐ Want Orig. Ret. $8.75 **NB** $9 **MIB** Sec. Mkt. **$14-$16**

QX 555-2 GRANDCHILD'S FIRST CHRISTMAS
Comments: Handcrafted, 1-7/8" tall, Dated 1993
With the wonder of its first Christmas, this adorable baby raccoon's eyes are aglow. **Artist:** John Francis (Collin)
☐ Purchased 19___ Pd $_______ MIB NB DB BNT
☐ Want Orig. Ret. $6.75 **NB** $7 **MIB** Sec. Mkt. **$14-$16**

QX 563-5 GRANDDAUGHTER
Comments: Handcrafted, 3-5/8" tall, Dated 1993
A little koala girl with a pink bow in her hair, waves hello from her stand on a red telephone. **Artist:** Robert Chad
☐ Purchased 19___ Pd $_______ MIB NB DB BNT
☐ Want Orig. Ret. $6.75 **NB** $6 **MIB** Sec. Mkt. **$12-$14**

QX 566-5 GRANDMOTHER
Comments: Handcrafted, 2-9/16" tall, Dated 1993
A card reading "Grandmother 1993" sits atop a lovely basket filled with poinsettias. **Artist:** Trish Andrews
☐ Purchased 19___ Pd $_______ MIB NB DB BNT
☐ Want Orig. Ret. $6.75 **NB** $6 **MIB** Sec. Mkt. **$12-$15**

QX 208-5 GRANDPARENTS
Comments: Gold Glass Ball, 2-7/8" Dia., Dated 1993
Christmas flowers and green bands against a white sleeve are graced with the words: "The Christmas Traditions, Loving And Giving Are Kept By Grandparents All Year. 1993"
Artist: LaDene Votruba
☐ Purchased 19___ Pd $_______ MIB NB DB BNT
☐ Want Orig. Ret. $4.75 **NB** $5 **MIB** Sec. Mkt. **$12-$14**

QX 563-2 GRANDSON
Comments: Handcrafted, 3-11/16" tall, Dated 1993
An active koala bear, dressed in a bright red shirt with matching cap, waves and swings on a green telephone receiver.
Artist: Robert Chad
☐ Purchased 19___ Pd $_______ MIB NB DB BNT
☐ Want Orig. Ret. $6.75 **NB** $7 **MIB** Sec. Mkt. **$12-$14**

QX 540-2 GREAT CONNECTIONS
Comments: Handcrafted, 3-5/8" tall, Dated 1993
Two little redbirds, with their blue and green ski hats, are busy making a paper chain garland for the tree. (Set of two hang-together ornaments) **Artist:** Anita Marra Rogers
☐ Purchased 19___ Pd $_______ MIB NB DB BNT
☐ Want Orig. Ret. $10.75 **NB** $14 **MIB** Sec. Mkt. **$24-$28**

QX 536-2 HE IS BORN
Comments: Handcrafted, 3-9/16" tall, Dated Christmas 1993
A touching Nativity scene is engraved on this bisque-look ornament. Caption: "For Unto Us A Child Is Born... Isaiah 9:6."
Artist: Joyce A. Lyle
☐ Purchased 19___ Pd $_______ MIB NB DB BNT
☐ Want Orig. Ret. $9.75 **NB** $15 **MIB** Sec. Mkt. **$28-$30**

QX 448-2 HEART OF CHRISTMAS
Comments: **Fourth in Series**, Handcrafted, 2" tall, Dated 1993
Open this Christmas heart and view the lovely wintry landscape inside. Caption: "Christmas Brings A Gentle Peace That Enters Every Heart." **Artist:** Ed Seale
☐ Purchased 19___ Pd $_______ MIB NB DB BNT
☐ Want Orig. Ret. $14.75 **NB** $14 **MIB** Sec. Mkt. **$28-$32**

QX 494-5 HEAVENLY ANGELS
Comments: **Third and Final in Series**, Handcrafted, 3" tall Dated 1993. An angel cradles a dove in her hands.
Artist: Joyce A. Lyle
☐ Purchased 19___ Pd $_______ MIB NB DB BNT
☐ Want Orig. Ret. $7.75 **NB** $8 **MIB** Sec. Mkt. **$18-$22**

QX 410-2 HERE COMES SANTA: HAPPY HAUL-IDAYS
Comments: **Fifteenth in Series**, Handcrafted, 2-7/8" tall Dated 1993. Santa is delivering toys rather than hauling things away in his truck. **Artist:** Linda Sickman
☐ Purchased 19___ Pd $_______ MIB NB DB BNT
☐ Want Orig. Ret. $14.75 **NB** $22 **MIB** Sec. Mkt. **$28-$34**

QX 533-2 HIGH TOP-PURR
Comments: Handcrafted, 2-3/16" tall, Dated 1993
Tucked inside a red sneaker, a little brown kitten plays with the shoe strings. **Artist:** Ed Seale
☐ Purchased 19___ Pd $_______ MIB NB DB BNT
☐ Want Orig. Ret. $8.75 **NB** $12 **MIB** Sec. Mkt. **$25-$28**

QX 572-5 HOLIDAY BARBIE™
Comments: ***FIRST IN SERIES***, Handcrafted, 3-1/2" tall Dated 1993. Patterned after 1993 Holiday Barbie doll. It is our opinion it will continue to rise as the series continues.
Artist: Trish Andrews
☐ Purchased 19___ Pd $_______ MIB NB DB BNT
☐ Want Orig. Ret. $14.75 **NB** $85 **MIB** Sec. Mkt. **$120-$130**

QX 562-2 HOLIDAY FLIERS: TIN AIRPLANE
Comments: Handcrafted, 1-5/16" tall, Dated 1993
Santa pilots a red and grey airplane with a message to all, "Season's Greetings." **Artist:** Linda Sickman
☐ Purchased 19___ Pd $_______ MIB NB DB BNT
☐ Want Orig. Ret. $7.75 **NB** $10 **MIB** Sec. Mkt. **$25-$28**

QX 562-5 HOLIDAY FLIERS: TIN BLIMP
Comments: Handcrafted, 1-11/16" tall, Dated 1993
"Happy Holidays 1993" are wished to all on the sides of his holiday decorated blimp. **Artist:** Linda Sickman
☐ Purchased 19___ Pd $_______ MIB NB DB BNT
☐ Want Orig. Ret. $7.75 **NB** $14 **MIB** Sec. Mkt. **$22-$24**

QX 561-5 HOLIDAY FLIERS: TIN HOT AIR BALLOON
Comments: Handcrafted, 2-5/8" tall, Dated 1993
A golden colored hot air balloon decorated with holly and red bows wishes everyone a "Merry Christmas."
Artist: Linda Sickman
☐ Purchased 19___ Pd $_______ MIB NB DB BNT
☐ Want Orig. Ret. $7.75 **NB** $12 **MIB** Sec. Mkt. **$16-$18**

QX 556-2 HOME FOR CHRISTMAS
Comments: Handcrafted, 1-3/4" tall, Dated 1993
A little ball player slides to home plate. Cute!
Artist: Bob Siedler
☐ Purchased 19___ Pd $_______ MIB NB DB BNT
☐ Want Orig. Ret. $7.75 **NB** $10 **MIB** Sec. Mkt. **$14-$16**

QLX 739-5 HOME ON THE RANGE
Comments: Light/Motion/Music, Handcrafted, 4-1/8" tall Dated 1993. Plays "Home On The Range." Santa's rocking horse is hitched to one cactus, and Christmas lights and star adorn another "Christmas Cactus." Santa and horse rock.
Artist: Linda Sickman
☐ Purchased 19___ Pd $_______ MIB NB DB BNT
☐ Want Orig. Ret. $32.00 **NB** $45 **MIB** Sec. Mkt. **$55-$65**

QX 525-5 HOWLING GOOD TIME
Comments: Handcrafted, 3" tall, Dated 1993
In a Texan mood, Santa in his cowboy hat sings a duet with his good pal, a brown dog. **Artist:** Anita Marra Rogers
☐ Purchased 19___ Pd $_______ MIB NB DB BNT
☐ Want Orig. Ret. $9.75 **NB** $12 **MIB** Sec. Mkt. **$16-$18**

QX 583-5 ICICLE BICYCLE
Comments: Handcrafted, 2-1/2" tall, Dated 1993
A snowman races his cool cycle with wheels that really turn.
Artist: Julia Lee
☐ Purchased 19___ Pd $_______ MIB NB DB BNT
☐ Want Orig. Ret. $9.75 **NB** $10 **MIB** Sec. Mkt. **$18-$20**

QXC 527-2 IT'S IN THE MAIL: KEEPSAKE CLUB
Comments: Handcrafted, 2-5/8" tall, Dated 1993
A little "Post Mouse" is sending you a copy of the "Collector's Courier," but only if you are a member of the Keepsake Ornament Club! **Artist:** Ed Seale
☐ Purchased 19___ Pd $_______ MIB NB DB BNT
☐ Want Orig. Ret. Comes w/Membership
NB $15 **MIB** Sec. Mkt. **$22-$25**

QX 529-5 JULIANNE AND TEDDY
Comments: Handcrafted and Fabric, 2-3/4" tall, Dated 1993
This Special Edition ornament is a dark-haired Victorian child with her favorite teddy. **Artist:** Duane Unruh
☐ Purchased 19___ Pd $_______ MIB NB DB BNT
☐ Want Orig. Ret. $21.75 **NB** $22 **MIB** Sec. Mkt. **$35-$38**

QLX 719-2 LAMPLIGHTER, THE
Comments: Light, 4-3/16" tall, Dated 1993
A little bear lights an old-fashioned street lantern to make Christmas bright for everyone. **Artist:** Don Palmiter
☐ Purchased 19___ Pd $_______ MIB NB DB BNT
☐ Want Orig. Ret. $18.00 **NB** $25 **MIB** Sec. Mkt. **$33-$36**

QLX 738-5 LAST MINUTE SHOPPING
Comments: Light/Motion, Handcrafted, 4-1/8" tall, Dated 1993
Shoppers scurry through the shops, making their last-minute purchases. **Artist:** LaDene Votruba
☐ Purchased 19___ Pd $_______ MIB NB DB BNT
☐ Want Orig. Ret. $28.00 **NB** $35 **MIB** Sec. Mkt. **$50-$55**

QX 537-2 LITTLE DRUMMER BOY
Comments: Handcrafted, 2-3/4" tall, Dated 1993
A little African-American boy merrily plays his drum.
Artist: Don Palmiter
☐ Purchased 19___ Pd $_______ MIB NB DB BNT
☐ Want Orig. Ret. $8.75 **NB** $10 **MIB** Sec. Mkt. **$16-$20**

QX 568-5 LOOK FOR THE WONDER
Comments: Handcrafted, 3-1/2" tall, Dated 1993
Designed from a Ukrainian holiday tradition, Grandma points toward heaven. This ornament may be used as an Advent calendar by sliding the angel along the window frame.
Artist: Donna Lee
☐ Purchased 19___ Pd $_______ MIB NB DB BNT
☐ Want Orig. Ret. $12.75 **NB** $16 **MIB** Sec. Mkt. **$26-$30**

QX 541-2 LOONEY TUNES COLLECTION: BUGS BUNNY
Comments: Handcrafted, 3-9/16" tall
Bugs is all set for Christmas with his bag full of his favorite holiday treat... carrots! **Artist:** Linda Sickman
☐ Purchased 19___ Pd $_______ MIB NB DB BNT
☐ Want Orig. Ret. $9.75 **NB** $14 **MIB** Sec. Mkt. **$22-$25**

QX 549-5 LOONEY TUNES COLLECTION: ELMER FUDD
Comments: Handcrafted, 2-7/8" tall
Elmer plays Santa and brings lots of goodies to the rest of the Looney Tunes family. **Artist:** Joyce A. Lyle
☐ Purchased 19___ Pd $_______ MIB NB DB BNT
☐ Want Orig. Ret. $8.75 **NB** $12 **MIB** Sec. Mkt. **$20-$22**

QX 565-2 LOONEY TUNES COLLECTION: PORKY PIG
Comments: Handcrafted, 2-9/18" tall
Santa's coming! Porky is ready for bed dressed in his nightshirt and slippers, but he's getting Santa's treats ready first!
Artist: Trish Andrews
☐ Purchased 19___ Pd $_______ MIB NB DB BNT
☐ Want Orig. Ret. $8.75 **NB** $12 **MIB** Sec. Mkt. **$18-$20**

QX 540-5 LOONEY TUNES COLLECTION: SYLVESTER AND TWEETY
Comments: Handcrafted, 3-9/16" tall
Sylvester and Tweety get into the spirit of Christmas. Tweety is wearing a red Santa cap and Sylvester is sporting antlers and sleigh bells. **Artist:** Don Palmiter
☐ Purchased 19___ Pd $_______ MIB NB DB BNT
☐ Want Orig. Ret. $9.75 **NB** $18 **MIB** Sec. Mkt. **$30-$35**

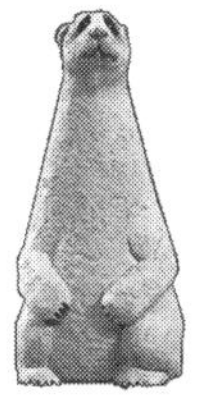

QX 574-5 LOU RANKIN POLAR BEAR
Comments: Handcrafted, 3-15/16" tall
This unique bear is sculpted after the style of artist, Lou Rankin.
Artist: Dill Rhodus
☐ Purchased 19___ Pd $_______ MIB NB DB BNT
☐ Want Orig. Ret. $9.75 **NB** $14 **MIB** Sec. Mkt. **$25-$30**

QX 532-5 MAKIN' MUSIC
Comments: Handcrafted and Brass, 2" tall
A little mouse plays his violin as he stands atop a brass music staff. **Artist:** Ed Seale
☐ Purchased 19___ Pd $_______ MIB NB DB BNT
☐ Want Orig. Ret. $9.75 **NB** $11 **MIB** Sec. Mkt. **$18-$21**

QX 577-5 MAKING WAVES
Comments: Handcrafted, 2-1/2" tall, Dated 1993
Santa and one of his reindeer are racing into Christmas in a speedboat. **Artist:** Don Palmiter
☐ Purchased 19___ Pd $_______ MIB NB DB BNT
☐ Want Orig. Ret. $9.75 **NB** $14 **MIB** Sec. Mkt. **$25-$28**

QX 207-5 MARY ENGELBREIT
Comments: Red Glass Ball, 2-7/8" dia., Dated 1993
Christmas morning is a delight for all children, as depicted on this ball ornament. Caption: "Christmas Morning 1993."
©1993 Mary Engelbreit
☐ Purchased 19___ Pd $_______ MIB NB DB BNT
☐ Want Orig. Ret. $5.00 **NB** $8 **MIB** Sec. Mkt. **$12-$14**

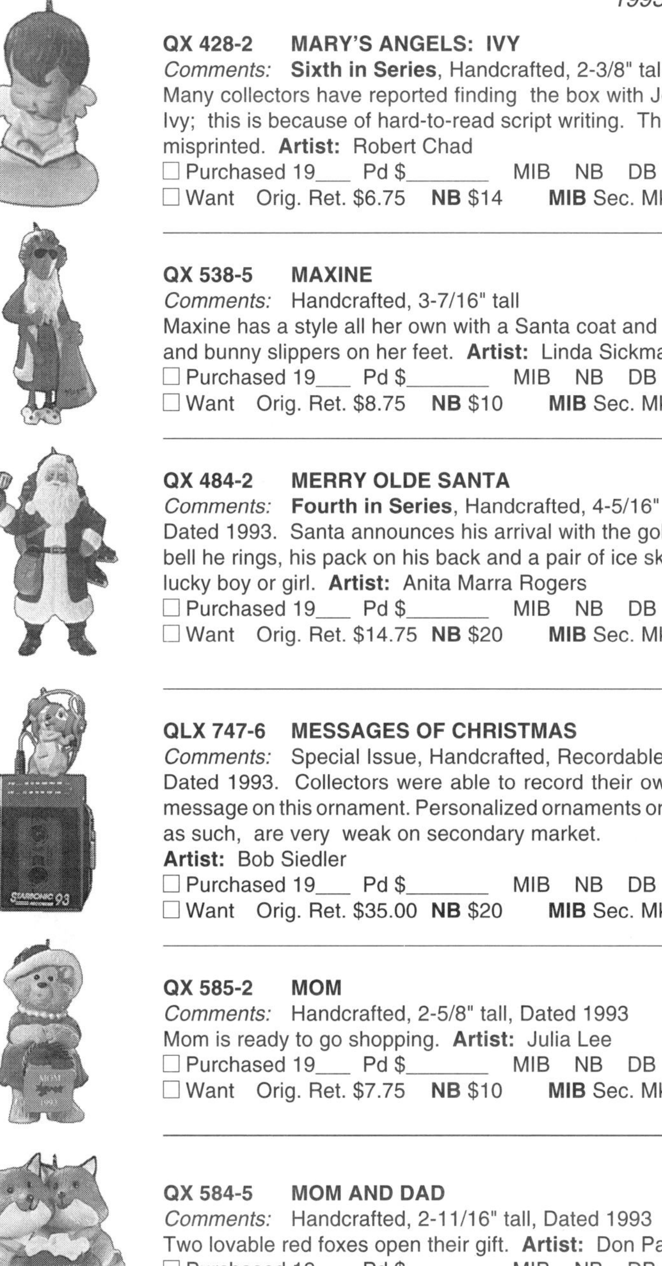

QX 428-2 MARY'S ANGELS: IVY
Comments: **Sixth in Series**, Handcrafted, 2-3/8" tall
Many collectors have reported finding the box with Joy instead of Ivy; this is because of hard-to-read script writing. The box is not misprinted. **Artist:** Robert Chad
☐ Purchased 19___ Pd $_______ MIB NB DB BNT
☐ Want Orig. Ret. $6.75 **NB** $14 **MIB** Sec. Mkt. **$20-$25**

QX 538-5 MAXINE
Comments: Handcrafted, 3-7/16" tall
Maxine has a style all her own with a Santa coat and beard and bunny slippers on her feet. **Artist:** Linda Sickman
☐ Purchased 19___ Pd $_______ MIB NB DB BNT
☐ Want Orig. Ret. $8.75 **NB** $10 **MIB** Sec. Mkt. **$18-$22**

QX 484-2 MERRY OLDE SANTA
Comments: **Fourth in Series**, Handcrafted, 4-5/16" tall
Dated 1993. Santa announces his arrival with the golden bell he rings, his pack on his back and a pair of ice skates for a lucky boy or girl. **Artist:** Anita Marra Rogers
☐ Purchased 19___ Pd $_______ MIB NB DB BNT
☐ Want Orig. Ret. $14.75 **NB** $20 **MIB** Sec. Mkt. **$30-$35**

QLX 747-6 MESSAGES OF CHRISTMAS
Comments: Special Issue, Handcrafted, Recordable, 4-1/2" tall
Dated 1993. Collectors were able to record their own Christmas message on this ornament. Personalized ornaments or mechanized as such, are very weak on secondary market.
Artist: Bob Siedler
☐ Purchased 19___ Pd $_______ MIB NB DB BNT
☐ Want Orig. Ret. $35.00 **NB** $20 **MIB** Sec. Mkt. **$38-$42**

QX 585-2 MOM
Comments: Handcrafted, 2-5/8" tall, Dated 1993
Mom is ready to go shopping. **Artist:** Julia Lee
☐ Purchased 19___ Pd $_______ MIB NB DB BNT
☐ Want Orig. Ret. $7.75 **NB** $10 **MIB** Sec. Mkt. **$18-$20**

QX 584-5 MOM AND DAD
Comments: Handcrafted, 2-11/16" tall, Dated 1993
Two lovable red foxes open their gift. **Artist:** Don Palmiter
☐ Purchased 19___ Pd $_______ MIB NB DB BNT
☐ Want Orig. Ret. $9.75 **NB** $10 **MIB** Sec. Mkt. **$14-$18**

QX 553-5 MOM-TO-BE
Comments: Handcrafted, 2-1/8" tall, Dated 1993
Mama bee is preparing for her new little one -- she's bringing in the honey pot. **Artist:** Julia Lee
☐ Purchased 19___ Pd $_______ MIB NB DB BNT
☐ Want Orig. Ret. $6.75 **NB** $8 **MIB** Sec. Mkt. **$12-$14**

QX 528-2 MOTHER GOOSE: HUMPTY DUMPTY
Comments: ***FIRST IN SERIES,*** Handcrafted, 2-1/2" tall, Dated 1993 Inspired by the nursery rhyme "Humpty Dumpty."
Artists: Ed Seale/LaDene Votruba
☐ Purchased 19___ Pd $_______ MIB NB DB BNT
☐ Want Orig. Ret. $13.75 **NB** $20 **MIB** Sec. Mkt. **$35-$40**

QX 420-2 MR. AND MRS. CLAUS: A FITTING MOMENT
Comments: **Eighth in Series,** Handcrafted, 3-1/8" tall Dated 1993. Does Santa's suit still fit?
Artist: John Francis (Collin)
☐ Purchased 19___ Pd $_______ MIB NB DB BNT
☐ Want Orig. Ret. $14.75 **NB** $18 **MIB** Sec. Mkt. **$34-$38**

QX 573-5 NEPHEW
Comments: Handcrafted, 2-1/2" tall, Dated 1993
This little fella is ready for a western Christmas.
Artist: Anita Marra Rogers
☐ Purchased 19___ Pd $_______ MIB NB DB BNT
☐ Want Orig. Ret. $6.75 **NB** $4 **MIB** Sec. Mkt. **$10-$12**

QX 590-5 NEW HOME
Comments: Enamel on Metal, 3-5/16" tall, Dated 1993
The top portion of this unique key is a house! What a novel ornament. Caption: "A New Home Opens The Door To Memories And Love." **Artist:** Don Palmiter
☐ Purchased 19___ Pd $_______ MIB NB DB BNT
☐ Want Orig. Ret. $7.75 **NB** $20 **MIB** Sec. Mkt. **$30-$35**

QX 573-2 NIECE
Comments: Handcrafted, 2-1/2" tall, Dated 1993
All set for Christmas, this little gal wears a red hat and boots, and has a dated gold star. **Artist:** Anita Marra Rogers
☐ Purchased 19___ Pd $_______ MIB NB DB BNT
☐ Want Orig. Ret. $6.75 **NB** $4 **MIB** Sec. Mkt. **$10-$12**

QX 417-5 NOSTALGIC HOUSES AND SHOPS: COZY HOME
Comments: **Tenth in Series**, Handcrafted, 3-13/16" tall Dated 1993. What a lovely home! A veranda covers the old-fashioned porch and welcomes all inside.
Artist: Donna Lee
☐ Purchased 19___ Pd $_______ MIB NB DB BNT
☐ Want Orig. Ret. $14.75 **NB** $24 **MIB** Sec. Mkt. **$35-$40**

QLX 739-2 NORTH POLE MERRYTHON
Comments: Light and Motion, 4-1/8" tall, Dated 1993
Santa and his reindeer run around the North Pole on this lighted ornament. Caption: "Go Santa 1993."
Artist: Ed Seale
☐ Purchased 19___ Pd $_______ MIB NB DB BNT
☐ Want Orig. Ret. $25.00 **NB** $40 **MIB** Sec. Mkt. **$45-$50**

QX 526-5 ON HER TOES
Comments: Handcrafted, 3-15/16" tall
A young ballerina in pastel pink twirls on one toe.
Artist: Trish Andrews
☐ Purchased 19___ Pd $_______ MIB NB DB BNT
☐ Want Orig. Ret. $8.75 **NB** $12 **MIB** Sec. Mkt. **$15-$20**

QX 534-2 ONE ELF-MARCHING BAND
Comments: Handcrafted, 2-7/8" tall, Dated 1993
A bell in one hand and baton in the other, the elf beats the drum and claps the cymbals on his back when the cord is pulled. **Artist:** Robert Chad
☐ Purchased 19___ Pd $_______ MIB NB DB BNT
☐ Want Orig. Ret. $12.75 **NB** $16 **MIB** Sec. Mkt. **$24-$28**

QX 594-2 OUR CHRISTMAS TOGETHER
Comments: Handcrafted, 4-13/16" tall, Dated 1993
Two cats cuddle together on a white swing built for two.
A Christmas wreath decorates the back of the swing.
Artist: Donna Lee
☐ Purchased 19___ Pd $_______ MIB NB DB BNT
☐ Want Orig. Ret. $10.75 **NB** $12 **MIB** Sec. Mkt. **$18-$23**

QX 589-2 OUR FAMILY PHOTOHOLDER
Comments: Handcrafted, 4-9/16" tall, Dated 1993
Insert your favorite photo in the picture window of this "house."
Caption: "Happy Holidays 1993" **Artist:** Duane Unruh
☐ Purchased 19___ Pd $_______ MIB NB DB BNT
☐ Want Orig. Ret. $7.75 **NB** $8 **MIB** Sec. Mkt. **$12-$16**

QX 595-5 OUR FIRST CHRISTMAS TOGETHER
Comments: Brass and Silver Plated, 3-1/4" tall, Dated 1993
A silver-plated man and woman dance and spin in the center of a brass heart etched with holly and "Our First Christmas 1993."
Artist: Anita Marra Rogers
☐ Purchased 19___ Pd $_______ MIB NB DB BNT
☐ Want Orig. Ret. $18.75 **NB** $20 **MIB** Sec. Mkt. **$34-$38**

QX 564-2 OUR FIRST CHRISTMAS TOGETHER
Comments: Handcrafted, 2-3/16" tall, Dated 1993
A raccoon couple celebrate their first Christmas around their Christmas tree. **Artist:** Joyce A. Lyle
☐ Purchased 19___ Pd $_______ MIB NB DB BNT
☐ Want Orig. Ret. $9.75 **NB** $10 **MIB** Sec. Mkt. **$14-$16**

QLX 735-5 OUR FIRST CHRISTMAS TOGETHER
Comments: Light, 2-3/4" tall, Dated 1993
A couple sit side by side in front of a flickering fire inside this peek-through ball. **Artist:** Robert Chad
☐ Purchased 19___ Pd $_______ MIB NB DB BNT
☐ Want Orig. Ret. $20.00 **NB** $22 **MIB** Sec. Mkt. **$38-$40**

QX 595-2 OUR FIRST CHRISTMAS TOGETHER PHOTOHOLDER
Comments: Handcrafted, 3-5/8" tall, Dated 1993
Red hearts adorn an oval green wreath for this photo frame. Caption: "Love Is The Heart's Most Cherished Treasure."
Artist: Duane Unruh
☐ Purchased 19___ Pd $_______ MIB NB DB BNT
☐ Want Orig. Ret. $8.75 **NB** $9 **MIB** Sec. Mkt. **$14-$16**

QX 301-5 OUR FIRST CHRISTMAS TOGETHER
Comments: Acrylic, 3-3/8" tall, Dated 1993
Two frosted swans snuggle together inside a frosted heart frame. **Artist:** Trish Andrews
☐ Purchased 19___ Pd $_______ MIB NB DB BNT
☐ Want Orig. Ret. $6.75 **NB** $8 **MIB** Sec. Mkt. **$14-$16**

QX 542-5 OWLIVER
Comments: **Second in Series**, Handcrafted, 2-3/8" tall Dated 1993. Owliver naps on a tree stump while a little squirrel delivers a present. **Artist:** Bob Siedler
☐ Purchased 19___ Pd $_______ MIB NB DB BNT
☐ Want Orig. Ret. $7.75 **NB** $8 **MIB** Sec. Mkt. **$15-$18**

QX 524-2 PEACE ON EARTH: POLAND
Comments: **Third and Final in Series**, Handcrafted, 3" dia. Dated 1993. Children in native dress portray a message for all mankind, one of peace. Caption: "Pokój Ludziom Dobrej Wol." **Artist:** Linda Sickman
☐ Purchased 19___ Pd $_______ MIB NB DB BNT
☐ Want Orig. Ret. $11.75 **NB** $14 **MIB** Sec. Mkt. **$20-$24**

QLX 715-5 PEANUTS®
Comments: **Third in Series**, Blinking Lights, Handcrafted, 3-1/2" tall, Dated 1993. Snoopy and Woodstock admire their Christmas tree; its lights blink off and on. **Artist:** Dill Rhodus
☐ Purchased 19___ Pd $_______ MIB NB DB BNT
☐ Want Orig. Ret. $18.00 **NB** $25 **MIB** Sec. Mkt. **$36-$40**

QX 207-2 PEANUTS®
Comments: Silver Glass Ball, 2-7/8" dia., Dated 1993
The characters from Peanuts are wishing you a Merry Christmas in Spanish, German, Italian, French and English.
☐ Purchased 19___ Pd $_______ MIB NB DB BNT
☐ Want Orig. Ret. $5.00 **NB** $8 **MIB** Sec. Mkt. **$16-$18**

QX 531-5 PEANUTS® GANG
Comments: ***FIRST IN SERIES***, Handcrafted, 2-3/8" tall, Dated 1993. Charlie Brown has a twin! It's a "snow boy" he built himself!
Artist: Dill Rhodus
☐ Purchased 19___ Pd $_______ MIB NB DB BNT
☐ Want Orig. Ret. $9.75 **NB** $20 **MIB** Sec. Mkt. **$48-$52**

QX 524-5 PEEK-A-BOO TREE
Comments: Handcrafted, 4-3/16" tall, Dated 1993
Little animals peek in and out of the tree when you turn the pinecone knob. **Artist:** Ken Crow
☐ Purchased 19___ Pd $_______ MIB NB DB BNT
☐ Want Orig. Ret. $10.75 **NB** $12 **MIB** Sec. Mkt. **$22-$25**

QX 532-2 PEEP INSIDE
Comments: Handcrafted, 2-7/16" tall, Dated 1993
A birdhouse opens to reveal mama's babies inside on the nest, waiting for their Christmas dinner.
Artist: Donna Lee
☐ Purchased 19___ Pd $_______ MIB NB DB BNT
☐ Want Orig. Ret. $13.75 **NB** $15 **MIB** Sec. Mkt. **$22-$25**

QX 593-2 PEOPLE FRIENDLY
Comments: Handcrafted, 2-5/16" tall, Dated 1993
A raccoon sits atop the keys of a computer terminal decorated with Christmas lights. Was personalized four ways: "Secretary Friendly," "Student Friendly," "VIP Friendly," or a blank which one signed. **Artist:** Ed Seale
☐ Purchased 19___ Pd $_______ MIB NB DB BNT
☐ Want Orig. Ret. $8.75 **NB** $9 **MIB** Sec. Mkt. **$14-$16**

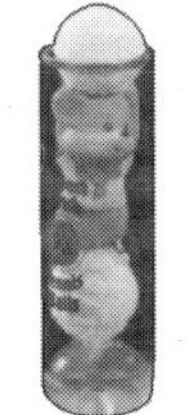

QX 577-2 PERFECT MATCH
Comments: Handcrafted, 3-1/3" tall, Dated 1993
A little bear sits between two yellow tennis balls in a canister captioned "Perfect Match Tennis Balls 93." **Artist:** Bob Siedler
☐ Purchased 19___ Pd $_______ MIB NB DB BNT
☐ Want Orig. Ret. $8.75 **NB** $10 **MIB** Sec. Mkt. **$16-$20**

QX 575-5 PINK PANTHER, THE
Comments: Handcrafted, 3" tall, Dated 1993
Dressed as Santa and carrying his pack on his back, the Pink Panther prepares to climb down the chimney.
Artist: Don Palmiter
☐ Purchased 19___ Pd $_______ MIB NB DB BNT
☐ Want Orig. Ret. $12.75 **NB** $14 **MIB** Sec. Mkt. **$18-$24**

QX 574-2 PLAYFUL PALS: COCA-COLA SANTA
Comments: Handcrafted, 3-7/8" tall, Dated 1993
A little black French poodle sits up and begs for Santa's cookie. The gift-wrapped doghouse is dated. **Artist:** Anita Marra Rogers
☐ Purchased 19___ Pd $_______ MIB NB DB BNT
☐ Want Orig. Ret. $14.75 **NB** $18 **MIB** Sec. Mkt. **$28-$30**

QX 539-2 POPPING GOOD TIMES
Comments: Handcrafted, 2" tall, Dated 1993
Two individual mice, one with a bag of popcorn and the other with a popcorn popper, create a set of hang-together ornaments.
Artist: Robert Chad
☐ Purchased 19___ Pd $_______ MIB NB DB BNT
☐ Want Orig. Ret. $14.75 **NB** $18 **MIB** Sec. Mkt. **$28-$30**

QX 504-5 PUPPY LOVE
Comments: **Third in Series**, Handcrafted, 1-9/16" tall Dated 1993. A golden retriever is enjoying a speedy trip downhill on a toboggan. **Artist:** Anita Marra Rogers
☐ Purchased 19___ Pd $_______ MIB NB DB BNT
☐ Want Orig. Ret. $7.75 **NB** $6 **MIB** Sec. Mkt. **$20-$25**

QX 579-5 PUTT-PUTT PENGUIN
Comments: Handcrafted, 3" tall, Dated 1993
A perky penguin in a blue hat rides to the next hole in his red golf cart. The words "Putt-Putt" are on both sides of the cart.
Artist: Julia Lee
☐ Purchased 19___ Pd $_______ MIB NB DB BNT
☐ Want Orig. Ret. $9.75 **NB** $8 **MIB** Sec. Mkt. **$16-$22**

QX 579-2 QUICK AS A FOX
Comments: Handcrafted, 2-5/8" tall, Dated 1993
This little postal fox handles his deliveries with speed and ingenuity. He has fastened his package to a pair of ice skate blades and rides his way into Christmas. **Artist:** Ken Crow
☐ Purchased 19___ Pd $_______ MIB NB DB BNT
☐ Want Orig. Ret. $8.75 **NB** $8 **MIB** Sec. Mkt. **$15-$18**

QLX 736-2 RADIO NEWS FLASH
Comments: Light and Sound, 3-3/16" tall, Dated 1993
A kitten listens to the sounds of Christmas on this holly trimmed old-fashioned radio. Caption: "Christmas Is In The Air!"
Artist: Donna Lee
☐ Purchased 19___ Pd $_______ MIB NB DB BNT
☐ Want Orig. Ret. $22.00 **NB** $30 **MIB** Sec. Mkt. **$42-$48**

QLX 718-5 RAIDING THE FRIDGE
Comments: Light, 3-7/16" tall, Dated 1993
Santa's catching a late-night snack. The refrigerator light is on because he has the door open. Caption: "Cold Milk And Cool Cookies For Santa!" **Artist:** Anita Marra Rogers
☐ Purchased 19___ Pd $_______ MIB NB DB BNT
☐ Want Orig. Ret. $16.00 **NB** $21 **MIB** Sec. Mkt. **$34-$36**

QX 512-4 READY FOR FUN
Comments: Handcrafted and Tin, 3-1/8" tall, Dated 1993
A gingerbread cookie boy moves out of his cookie cutter frame so that he might join in the Christmas festivities.
Artist: Joyce A. Lyle
☐ Purchased 19___ Pd $_______ MIB NB DB BNT
☐ Want Orig. Ret. $7.75 **NB** $8.50 **MIB** Sec. Mkt. **$16-$18**

QX 433-1 REINDEER CHAMPS: BLITZEN
Comments: **Eighth and Final in Series,** Handcrafted, 3-1/8" tall, Dated 1993. Blitzen scores again! Santa's reindeer team wins this football game! **Artist:** Bob Siedler
☐ Purchased 19___ Pd $_______ MIB NB DB BNT
☐ Want Orig. Ret. $8.75 **NB** $12 **MIB** Sec. Mkt. **$20-$24**

QLX 741-5 ROAD RUNNER AND WILE E. COYOTE™
Comments: Light/Motion, Handcrafted, 4-1/8" tall, Dated 1993
Wile E. Coyote will never learn as he chases the Road Runner through a cave. Caption: "Have A Dynamite Christmas!"
Artist: Robert Chad
☐ Purchased 19___ Pd $_______ MIB NB DB BNT
☐ Want Orig. Ret. $30.00 **NB** $45 **MIB** Sec. Mkt. **$65-$70**

QX 416-2 ROCKING HORSE
Comments: **Thirteenth in Series**, Handcrafted, 3" tall
Dated 1993. Dark grey with white stockings and a white star on its forehead, this horse also sports a white tail.
Artist: Linda Sickman
☐ Purchased 19___ Pd $_______ MIB NB DB BNT
☐ Want Orig. Ret. $10.75 **NB** $12 **MIB** Sec. Mkt. **$30-$38**

QX 538-2 ROOM FOR ONE MORE
Comments: Handcrafted, 3-3/16" tall, Dated 1993
How many reindeer can squeeze into the telephone booth with Santa? Count them and see! Proclaimed as a sleeper by many in '94 thus, many bought up extras. Easily found now.
Artist: Ken Crow
☐ Purchased 19___ Pd $_______ MIB NB DB BNT
☐ Want Orig. Ret. $8.75 **NB** $25 **MIB** Sec. Mkt. **$45-$50**

QLX 735-2 SANTA'S SNOW-GETTER
Comments: Light, 3-5/16" tall, Dated 1993
Santa is making his Christmas deliveries with the help of a red and white snowmobile. **Artist:** Ken Crow
☐ Purchased 19___ Pd $_______ MIB NB DB BNT
☐ Want Orig. Ret. $18.00 **NB** $22 **MIB** Sec. Mkt. **$36-$42**

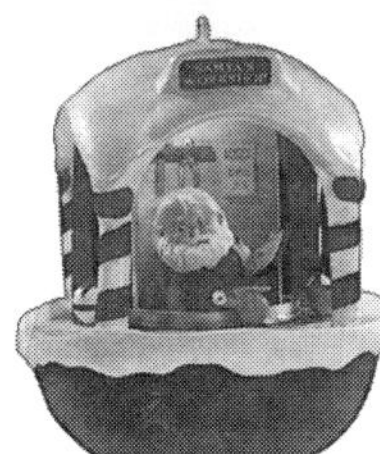

QLX 737-5 SANTA'S WORKSHOP
Comments: Light/Motion, Handcrafted, 4-1/16" tall, Dated 1993
It's December 23 and Santa is busy with last-minute toys. The ballerina twirls, the blades of the helicopter revolve, and the ball and top spin around as the toys circle on a conveyor belt.
Artist: Bob Siedler
☐ Purchased 19___ Pd $_______ MIB NB DB BNT
☐ Want Orig. Ret. $28.00 **NB** $34 **MIB** Sec. Mkt. **$50-$55**

QXC 543-5 SHARING CHRISTMAS: KEEPSAKE CLUB
Comments: Limited Edition Porcelain, 3-3/4" tall, Dated 1993
A boy and girl sit on a bench and share a Christmas gift. Delicate holly designs enhance the beauty of this ornament. Caption: "Christmas, A Beautiful Season For Sharing."
Artist: Joyce A. Lyle
☐ Purchased 19___ Pd $_______ MIB NB DB BNT
☐ Want Orig. Ret. $20.00 **NB** $18 **MIB** Sec. Mkt. **$32-$35**

QX 530-5 SILVERY NOEL
Comments: Silver-plated, 2" tall, Dated 1993
Decorative letters "N-O-E-L" make up the sides of this silver-plated block with a dated, hinged lid that opens.
Artist: Joyce A. Lyle
☐ Purchased 19___ Pd $_______ MIB NB DB BNT
☐ Want Orig. Ret. $12.75 **NB** $14 **MIB** Sec. Mkt. **$22-$25**

QX 554-5 SISTER
Comments: Handcrafted, 2-1/4" tall, Dated 1993
A Cheerleader kitten cheers for Christmas with her red and yellow pom-poms. **Artist:** Anita Marra Rogers
☐ Purchased 19___ Pd $_______ MIB NB DB BNT
☐ Want Orig. Ret. $6.75 **NB** $8 **MIB** Sec. Mkt. **$15-$18**

QX 588-5 SISTER TO SISTER
Comments: Handcrafted, 2-5/16" tall, Dated 1993
Two mice sit together in a compact. The lipstick message on the mirror reads, "Sisters Are Forever Friends!" Somewhat scarce due to production problems.
Artist: Ed Seale
☐ Purchased 19___ Pd $_______ MIB NB DB BNT
☐ Want Orig. Ret. $9.75 **NB** $28 **MIB** Sec. Mkt. **$48-$52**

QX 533-5 SMILE! IT'S CHRISTMAS PHOTOHOLDER
Comments: Handcrafted Photoholder, 4" tall, Dated 1993
A little mouse pulls on the end of the film to see what's developed! This ornament hold two photos. Caption: "Develop By December 25th, 35 mm Merry Memories (Double Exposure), CHRISTMAS COLOR, ASA 93." **Artist:** Ed Seale
☐ Purchased 19___ Pd $_______ MIB NB DB BNT
☐ Want Orig. Ret. $9.75 **NB** $12 **MIB** Sec. Mkt. **$18-$22**

Good news: You've made the '96 Olympic javelin team.
Bad news: You're the target.

QX 535-5 SNOW BEAR ANGEL
Comments: Handcrafted, 2-3/4" dia., Dated 1993
Making angels in the snow is fun! Even this bear enjoys it. Pull the snowball and the bear will move his arms and legs. Caption: "This Little Bear Has Christmas Fun By Making Angels, One By One!" Remember when we were kids? We did this too!
Artist: Julia Lee
☐ Purchased 19___ Pd $_______ MIB NB DB BNT
☐ Want Orig. Ret. $7.75 **NB** $10 **MIB** Sec. Mkt. **$15-$18**

QX 576-5 SNOWBIRD
Comments: Handcrafted, 2-5/8" tall, Dated 1993
This bird is ready for some Christmas sights. He's wearing his sunglasses and tennis shoes, and has his gift and camera handy.
Artist: Julia Lee
☐ Purchased 19___ Pd $_______ MIB NB DB BNT
☐ Want Orig. Ret. $7.75 **NB** $10 **MIB** Sec. Mkt. **$14-$16**

QX 531-2 SNOWY HIDEAWAY
Comments: Handcrafted, 3" dia., Dated 1993
A little red fox sits quietly in a snow-covered wreath.
Artist: John Francis (Collin)
☐ Purchased 19___ Pd $_______ MIB NB DB BNT
☐ Want Orig. Ret. $9.75 **NB** $10 **MIB** Sec. Mkt. **$18-$22**

QX 586-5 SON
Comments: Handcrafted, 4-7/16" tall, Dated 1993
Bendable neck and legs are a special feature of this giraffe wearing a red turtleneck sweater and blue ice skates.
Artist: LaDene Votruba
☐ Purchased 19___ Pd $_______ MIB NB DB BNT
☐ Want Orig. Ret. $6.75 **NB** $6 **MIB** Sec. Mkt. **$12-$14**

QLX 740-5 SONG OF THE CHIMES
Comments: Light and Motion, 4-1/8" tall, Dated 1993
Brass doves are set in motion by the heat of the "candle." Chimes ring as the doves circle the star.
Artists: Trish Andrews/L. N.
☐ Purchased 19___ Pd $_______ MIB NB DB BNT
☐ Want Orig. Ret. $25.00 **NB** $35 **MIB** Sec. Mkt. **$50-$55**

QX 523-5 SPECIAL CAT PHOTOHOLDER
Comments: Handcrafted and Brass, 4-1/8" tall, Dated 1993
Insert a photo of your "Classy Cat" into this photo frame designed as a cat collar. A golden bell signals that Christmas time is near. **Artist:** LaDene Votruba
☐ Purchased 19___ Pd $_______ MIB NB DB BNT
☐ Want Orig. Ret. $7.75 **NB** $8 **MIB** Sec. Mkt. **$12-$16**

QX 596-2 SPECIAL DOG PHOTOHOLDER
Comments: Handcrafted and Brass, 4-13/16" tall, Dated 1993
This photo frame is designed to resemble a dog collar, designed with bones and including a "Perfect Pooch 1993" tag.
Artist: LaDene Votruba
☐ Purchased 19___ Pd $_______ MIB NB DB BNT
☐ Want Orig. Ret. $7.75 **NB** $8 **MIB** Sec. Mkt. **$12-$15**

QX 598-2 STAR OF WONDER
Comments: Handcrafted, 3-1/4" tall, Dated 1993
Forest animals take time to gaze at the Star in the wintry sky.
Artist: Joyce A. Lyle
☐ Purchased 19___ Pd $_______ MIB NB DB BNT
☐ Want Orig. Ret. $6.75 **NB** $12 **MIB** Sec. Mkt. **$24-$29**

QX 564-5 STAR TEACHER PHOTOHOLDER
Comments: Handcrafted, 2-15/16" tall, Dated 1993
A little white bear holds up a gold star photo frame. Captions: "1993 For A Star Teacher." and "Have A Beary Merry Christmas!"
Artist: Trish Andrews
☐ Purchased 19___ Pd $_______ MIB NB DB BNT
☐ Want Orig. Ret. $5.75 **NB** $5 **MIB** Sec. Mkt. **$10-$12**

QX 596-5 STRANGE AND WONDERFUL LOVE
Comments: Handcrafted, 2-13/16" tall, Dated 1993
A porcupine cozies up to a flowering cactus. Caption: "Ours Is A Strange And Wonderful Relationship." **Artist:** Linda Sickman
☐ Purchased 19___ Pd $_______ MIB NB DB BNT
☐ Want Orig. Ret. $8.75 **NB** $10 **MIB** Sec. Mkt. **$15-$18**

QX 575-2 SUPERMAN
Comments: Handcrafted, 6" tall
Look! Up in the sky! It's a bird, it's Santa... no, it's Superman! Plenty available on secondary market.
Artist: Robert Chad
☐ Purchased 19___ Pd $_______ MIB NB DB BNT
☐ Want Orig. Ret. $12.75 **NB** $15 **MIB** Sec. Mkt. **$45-$50**

QX 539-5 SWAT TEAM, THE
Comments: Handcrafted, 1-9/16" tall, Dated 1993
Hang-together ornaments. Two white kittens play swat games with a ball of red yarn. **Artist:** Trish Andrews
☐ Purchased 19___ Pd $_______ MIB NB DB BNT
☐ Want Orig. Ret. $12.75 **NB** $14 **MIB** Sec. Mkt. **$24-$28**

QX 534-5 THAT'S ENTERTAINMENT
Comments: Handcrafted, 2-15/16" tall, Dated 1993
Watch as Santa pulls a rabbit out of his hat!
Artist: Bob Siedler
☐ Purchased 19___ Pd $_______ MIB NB DB BNT
☐ Want Orig. Ret. $8.75 **NB** $7 **MIB** Sec. Mkt. **$16-$18**

QX 555-5 TO MY GRANDMA
Comments: Handcrafted, 3-5/16" tall, Dated 1993
A red note pad acts as a photo holder. May be personalized. Captions: "To My Grandma XOXO 1993 XOXO" and "I May Be Little, But I Love You Great Big!" **Artist:** Donna Lee
☐ Purchased 19___ Pd $_______ MIB NB DB BNT
☐ Want Orig. Ret. $7.75 **NB** $8 **MIB** Sec. Mkt. **$12-$15**

QX 550-2 TOBIN FRALEY CAROUSEL
Comments: **Second in Series**, Porcelain and Brass, 5-1/4" tall Dated 1993. A white horse decorated in Christmas finery gallops into Christmas. Secondary market buyers bought less of this ornament than the first, so this is the reason for the higher value. (Supply and demand)
☐ Purchased 19___ Pd $_______ MIB NB DB BNT
☐ Want Orig. Ret. $28.00 **NB** $25 **MIB** Sec. Mkt. **$30-$35**

QX 592-5 TOP BANANA
Comments: Handcrafted, 2-7/16" tall, Dated 1993
This perky little monkey, dressed in a Santa suit and sitting on top of a bunch of bananas, is sure to perk up anyone's Christmas.
Artist: Anita Marra Rogers
☐ Purchased 19___ Pd $_______ MIB NB DB BNT
☐ Want Orig. Ret. $7.75 **NB** $9 **MIB** Sec. Mkt. **$18-$22**

QXC 543-2 TRIMMED WITH MEMORIES: KEEPSAKE CLUB ANNIVERSARY EDITION
Comments: Handcrafted, 3-7/8" tall, Dated 1993 and 1973
A blue spruce is decorated with small gold replicas of Keepsake ornaments, as well as candles and garland. **Artist:** Linda Sickman
☐ Purchased 19___ Pd $_______ MIB NB DB BNT
☐ Want Orig. Ret. $12.00 **NB** $12 **MIB** Sec. Mkt. **$24-$26**

QX 301-2 TWELVE DAYS OF CHRISTMAS: TEN LORDS A-LEAPIN
Comments: **Tenth in Series**, Acrylic, 3" tall, Dated 1993
One of the ten lords leaps among holly leaves on this heart-shaped acrylic ornament. **Artist:** Robert Chad
☐ Purchased 19___ Pd $_______ MIB NB DB BNT
☐ Want Orig. Ret. $6.75 **NB** $6 **MIB** Sec. Mkt. **$14-$16**

QX 529-2 U. S. CHRISTMAS STAMPS
Comments: ***FIRST IN SERIES***, Enamel on Copper, 2-5/16" tall Dated 1993. Inspired by a Christmas stamp issued in 1983 in Santa Claus, Indiana. Display stand included. This series ended with the 1995 ornament. **Artist:** Linda Sickman
☐ Purchased 19___ Pd $_______ MIB NB DB BNT
☐ Want Orig. Ret. $10.75 **NB** $12 **MIB** Sec. Mkt. **$20-$24**

QLX 741-2 U. S. S. ENTERPRISE™
Comments: Handcrafted, Blinking Light, Stardated 1993
This special promotional ornament was the third ornament to be produced with the Star Trek theme. This Enterprise is from Star Trek® The Next Generation™. **Artist:** Lynn Norton
☐ Purchased 19___ Pd $_______ MIB NB DB BNT
☐ Want Orig. Ret. $24.00 **NB** $30 **MIB** Sec. Mkt. **$50-$55**

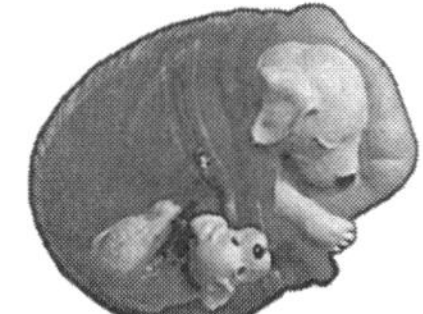

QX 526-2 WAKE-UP CALL
Comments: Handcrafted, 1-7/18" tall, Dated 1993
It's Christmas morning and junior can't wait til dad wakes up.
Artist: Duane Unruh
☐ Purchased 19___ Pd $_______ MIB NB DB BNT
☐ Want Orig. Ret. $8.75 **NB** $8 **MIB** Sec. Mkt. **$16-$18**

QX 589-5 WARM AND SPECIAL FRIENDS
Comments: Handcrafted and Stamped Metal, 2-1/8" tall Dated 1993. Two mice sit atop a can of "Hershey's Cocoa."
Artist: Linda Sickman
☐ Purchased 19___ Pd $_______ MIB NB DB BNT
☐ Want Orig. Ret. $10.75 **NB** $11 **MIB** Sec. Mkt. **$24-$26**

QX 537-5 WATER BED SNOOZE
Comments: Handcrafted, 1-3/4" tall, Dated 1993
A bear sleeping on the "Polar Water Bed" is actually sleeping on top of an ice cube tray! **Artist:** Julia Lee
☐ Purchased 19___ Pd $_______ MIB NB DB BNT
☐ Want Orig. Ret. $9.75 **NB** $10 **MIB** Sec. Mkt. **$18-$24**

QLX 742-2 WINNIE THE POOH
Comments: Voice, Handcrafted, 3-5/8" tall, Dated 1993
Pooh sits on a tree stump with his pot of "Hunny." This ornament features the voice of Sterling Holloway (who has always been the voice of Pooh and passed away in 1993.) Somewhat plentiful.
Artist: Bob Siedler
☐ Purchased 19___ Pd $_______ MIB NB DB BNT
☐ Want Orig. Ret. $24.00 **NB** $24 **MIB** Sec. Mkt. **$40-$45**

QX 571-2 WINNIE THE POOH COLLECTION: EEYORE
Comments: Handcrafted, 2" tall
Hang on Eeyore!
Artist: Bob Siedler
☐ Purchased 19___ Pd $_______ MIB NB DB BNT
☐ Want Orig. Ret. $9.75 **NB** $10 **MIB** Sec. Mkt. **$20-$22**

QX 567-2 WINNIE THE POOH COLLECTION: KANGA AND ROO
Comments: Handcrafted, 3-3/8" tall
Roo peeks out from Kanga's pouch for a better view.
Artist: Bob Siedler
☐ Purchased 19___ Pd $_______ MIB NB DB BNT
☐ Want Orig. Ret. $9.75 **NB** $10 **MIB** Sec. Mkt. **$22-$24**

QX 569-5 WINNIE THE POOH COLLECTION: OWL
Comments: Handcrafted, 3-5/8" tall
Owl stays warm in winter by strapping a hot water bottle to his stomach. **Artist:** Bob Siedler
☐ Purchased 19___ Pd $_______ MIB NB DB BNT
☐ Want Orig. Ret. $9.75 **NB** $10 **MIB** Sec. Mkt. **$20-$22**

QX 570-2 WINNIE THE POOH COLLECTION: RABBIT
Comments: Handcrafted, 3-1/2" tall
Rabbit finds that frying pans make great snowshoes!
Artist: Bob Siedler
☐ Purchased 19___ Pd $_______ MIB NB DB BNT
☐ Want Orig. Ret. $9.75 **NB** $10 **MIB** Sec. Mkt. **$20-$22**

QX 570-5 WINNIE THE POOH COLLECTION: TIGGER AND PIGLET
Comments: Handcrafted, 3-3/4" tall
As Tigger glides on his ice skates, Piglet grabs a ride on his tail.
Artist: Bob Siedler
☐ Purchased 19___ Pd $_______ MIB NB DB BNT
☐ Want Orig. Ret. $9.75 **NB** $20 **MIB** Sec. Mkt. **$40-$45**

QX 571-5 WINNIE THE POOH COLLECTION: WINNIE THE POOH
Comments: Handcrafted, 3-3/8" tall
Pooh is an expert skier!
Artist: Bob Siedler
☐ Purchased 19___ Pd $_______ MIB NB DB BNT
☐ Want Orig. Ret. $9.75 **NB** $20 **MIB** Sec. Mkt. **$35-$38**

QXC 569-2 YOU'RE ALWAYS WELCOME
Comments: Handcrafted, 2-1/2" tall, Dated 1993
A Tender Touches bear puts out her special "Welcome 1993" door mat. The Tender Touches logo and Keepsake Ornament Premiere is on the base of this ornament. Plentiful in '94 and '95!
Artist: Ed Seale
☐ Purchased 19___ Pd $_______ MIB NB DB BNT
☐ Want Orig. Ret. $9.75 **NB** $20 **MIB** Sec. Mkt. **$50-$55**

Hallmark Keepsake
Personalized Ornaments

These ornaments may not escalate in value on the secondary market unless perhaps they are personalized with a well-known name or saying. No sales on these have been reported or found advertised.

1993

QP 603-5 BABY BLOCK PHOTOHOLDER
Comments: Handcrafted Photoholder, 2-13/16" tall
A baby bear shaking its green rattle sits atop a baby block which is also a photo holder. May be personalized with a name or special message. Was special ordered through Hallmark. Reissued in 1994. **Artist:** John Francis (Collin)
☐ Purchased 19___ Pd $_______ MIB NB DB BNT
☐ Want Orig. Ret. $14.75 No Personalization
MIB Sec. Mkt. **$15-$18**

QP 605-2 COOL SNOWMAN
Comments: White Glass Ball, 2-7/8" diam.
Personalization is in the caption area above the snowman's head.
☐ Purchased 19___ Pd $_______ MIB NB DB BNT
☐ Want Orig. Ret. $8.75 No Personalization
MIB Sec. Mkt. **$5-$8**

QP 602-5 FESTIVE ALBUM PHOTOHOLDER
Comments: Handcrafted Photoholder, 7-7/16" tall
This engraved photo album holds your favorite photo inside. A little mouse swings from a ribbon. Reissued in 1994. Similiar to the '95 (premiere in July) artist photos ornament.
Artist: LaDene Votruba
☐ Purchased 19___ Pd $_______ MIB NB DB BNT
☐ Want Orig. Ret. $12.75 **MIB** Sec. Mkt. **$12-$14**

QP 604-2 FILLED WITH COOKIES
Comments: Handcrafted, 2-1/8" tall
An acorn-designed cookie jar is being raided by a little squirrel. Shh! Don't tell! Reissued in '95. **Artist:** Anita Marra Rogers
☐ Purchased 19___ Pd $_______ MIB NB DB BNT
☐ Want Orig. Ret. $12.75 **MIB** Sec. Mkt. **$10-$12**

QP 601-2 GOING GOLFIN'
Comments: Handcrafted, 2-13/16" tall
This little beaver is ready to go, golf club in hand, as he sits on a large golf ball. **Artist:** Don Palmiter
Reissued in 1994.
☐ Purchased 19___ Pd $_______ MIB NB DB BNT
☐ Want Orig. Ret. $12.75 **MIB** Sec. Mkt. **$10-$12**

QP 600-2 HERE'S YOUR FORTUNE
Comments: Handcrafted,1-13/16" tall
Fortune cookie anyone? Send your own message to someone special on the fortune cookie strip. **Artist:** Ed Seale
☐ Purchased 19___ Pd $_______ MIB NB DB BNT
☐ Want Orig. Ret. $10.75 **MIB** Sec. Mkt. **$8-$10**

QP 601-5 MAILBOX DELIVERY
Comments: Handcrafted, 1-7/8" tall
A cheery raccoon inside the red mailbox holds an envelope with the message "Merry Christmas." Reissued in 1994 and 1995.
Artist: Ken Crow
☐ Purchased 19___ Pd $_______ MIB NB DB BNT
☐ Want Orig. Ret. $14.75 **MIB** Sec. Mkt. **$10-$12**

QP 602-2 ON THE BILLBOARD
Comments: Handcrafted, 2-1/8" tall
A little elf from the "Santa Sign Co." will paint your message on the billboard. Reissued in 1994 and 1995. **Artist:** Ken Crow
☐ Purchased 19___ Pd $_______ MIB NB DB BNT
☐ Want Orig. Ret. $12.75 **MIB** Sec. Mkt. **$10-$12**

QP 604-5 PEANUTS®
Comments: White Glass Ball, 2-7/8" dia.
The Peanuts gang is here to send a special Christmas wish.
☐ Purchased 19___ Pd $_______ MIB NB DB BNT
☐ Want Orig. Ret. $9.00 **MIB** Sec. Mkt. **$8.50**

QP 603-2 PLAYING BALL
Comments: Handcrafted, 3-11/16" tall
An adorable bear cub is ready to play ball. The personalized message is written on his bat. Reissued in 1994 and 1995.
Artist: John Francis (Collin)
☐ Purchased 19___ Pd $_______ MIB NB DB BNT
☐ Want Orig. Ret. $12.75 **MIB** Sec. Mkt. **$10-$12**

QP 605-5 REINDEER IN THE SKY
Comments: White Glass Ball, 2-7/8" dia.
Santa's reindeer hold a conversation of your design!
☐ Purchased 19___ Pd $_______ MIB NB DB BNT
☐ Want Orig. Ret. $8.75 **MIB** Sec. Mkt. **$5-$8**

QP 600-5 SANTA SAYS
Comments: Handcrafted, 2-15/16" tall
What does Santa say? Pull the cord and the message pops out of the pack on his back. Reissued in 1994. **Artist:** Ed Seale
☐ Purchased 19___ Pd $_______ MIB NB DB BNT
☐ Want Orig. Ret. $12.75 **MIB** Sec. Mkt. **$12-$15**

Hallmark Keepsake Showcase Ornaments

Found at Gold Crown Stores only

Folk Art Americana - 1993

QK 105-2 ANGEL IN FLIGHT
Comments: Wood Look, 3-1/4" tall, Dated 1993
This angel appears to be hand-chiseled in wood.
Artist: Linda Sickman
☐ Purchased 19___ Pd $_______ MIB NB DB BNT
☐ Want Orig. Ret. $15.75 **NB** $20 **MIB** Sec. Mkt. **$35-$40**

QK 105-5 POLAR BEAR ADVENTURE
Comments: Wood Look, 2-15/16" tall, Dated 1993
A small elf brings home the tree. **Artist:** Linda Sickman
☐ Purchased 19___ Pd $_______ MIB NB DB BNT
☐ Want Orig. Ret. $15.00 **NB** $25 **MIB** Sec. Mkt. **$55-$60**

Hope you subscribe to *The Ornament Collector* magazine!

QK 106-5 RIDING IN THE WOODS
Comments: Wood Look, 2-13/16" tall, Dated 1993
An elf rides astride a red fox. **Artist:** Linda Sickman
☐ Purchased 19___ Pd $_______ MIB NB DB BNT
☐ Want Orig. Ret. $15.75 **NB** $35 **MIB** Sec. Mkt. **$50-$55**

QK 104-5 RIDING THE WIND
Comments: Wood Look, 2-1/16" tall, Dated 1993
An elf flies on the back of a white goose. **Artist:** Linda Sickman
☐ Purchased 19___ Pd $_______ MIB NB DB BNT
☐ Want Orig. Ret. $15.75 **NB** $25 **MIB** Sec. Mkt. **$45-$48**

QK 107-2 SANTA CLAUS
Comments: Wood Look, 4-5/8" tall, Dated 1993
Santa delivers lots of toys to children. Santa collectors love him!
Artist: Linda Sickman
☐ Purchased 19___ Pd $_______ MIB NB DB BNT
☐ Want Orig. Ret. $16.75 **NB** $120 **MIB** Sec. Mkt. **$175-$190**

Holiday Enchantment - 1993

QK 103-2 ANGELIC MESSENGERS
Comments: Porcelain, 3-1/2" tall, Dated 1993
Angels descend from heaven to relate the good news that Christ has been born in Bethlehem. **Artist:** LaDene Votruba
☐ Purchased 19___ Pd $_______ MIB NB DB BNT
☐ Want Orig. Ret. $13.75 **NB** $18 **MIB** Sec. Mkt. **$35-$40**

QK 104-2 BRINGING HOME THE TREE
Comments: Porcelain, 2-13/16" tall, Dated 1993
A couple emerge from the woods pulling their Christmas tree on a sled. **Artist:** Robert Chad
☐ Purchased 19___ Pd $_______ MIB NB DB BNT
☐ Want Orig. Ret. $13.75 **NB** $18 **MIB** Sec. Mkt. **$32-$36**

QK 101-2 JOURNEY TO THE FOREST
Comments: Porcelain, 4-1/2" tall, Dated 1993
Santa goes into the forest to check on his reindeer.
☐ Purchased 19___ Pd $_______ MIB NB DB BNT
☐ Want Orig. Ret. $13.75 **NB** $15 **MIB** Sec. Mkt. **$30-$35**

QK 102-5 MAGI, THE
Comments: Porcelain, 3-3/4" tall, Dated 1993
The wise men follow the star to Bethlehem to find the Christ child. Caption: "We Three Kings Of Orient Are, Bearing Gifts We Traverse Afar, Field And Fountain, Moor And Mountain, Following Yonder Star."
☐ Purchased 19___ Pd $_______ MIB NB DB BNT
☐ Want Orig. Ret. $13.75 **NB** $20 **MIB** Sec. Mkt. **$35-$40**

QK 100-5 VISIONS OF SUGARPLUMS
Comments: Fine Porcelain, 3-1/2" dia, Dated 1993
A child dreams of Christmas treats and toys on Christmas Eve. Caption: "The Children Were Nestled All Snug In Their Beds, While Visions Of Sugarplums Danced In Their Heads."
Artist: LaDene Votruba
☐ Purchased 19___ Pd $_______ MIB NB DB BNT
☐ Want Orig. Ret. $13.75 **NB** $20 **MIB** Sec. Mkt. **$30-$35**

Old-World Silver - 1993

QK 107-5 SILVER DOVE OF PEACE
Comments: Silver-Plated, 3-3/16" tall, Dated 1993
A dove of peace is intricately engraved on the sides of this silver ornament in European style. Caption: "Silver Dove Of Peace."
Artist: Don Palmiter
☐ Purchased 19___ Pd $_______ MIB NB DB BNT
☐ Want Orig. Ret. $24.75 **MIB** Sec. Mkt. **$32-$36**

QK 109-2 SILVER SANTA
Comments: Silver-Plated, 3-5/16" tall, Dated 1993
Santa's head is fashioned and circles the sides of this ornament.
Artist: Duane Unruh
☐ Purchased 19___ Pd $_______ MIB NB DB BNT
☐ Want Orig. Ret. $24.75 **NB** $35 **MIB** Sec. Mkt. **$55-$60**

QK 108-2 SILVER SLEIGH
Comments: Silver-Plated, 3-1/8" tall, Dated 1993
Detailed engraving on this ornament portrays a sleigh.
Artist: Don Palmiter
☐ Purchased 19___ Pd $_______ MIB NB DB BNT
☐ Want Orig. Ret. $24.75 **NB** $28 **MIB** Sec. Mkt. **$35-$40**

QK 108-5 SILVER STAR AND HOLLY
Comments: Silver-Plated, 3-1/16" tall, Dated 1993
Lavishly engraved stars and holly decorate this unique Christmas ornament. **Artist:** Don Palmiter
☐ Purchased 19___ Pd $_______ MIB NB DB BNT
☐ Want Orig. Ret. $24.75 **NB** $28 **MIB** Sec. Mkt. **$35-$40**

Portraits in Bisque - 1993

QK 115-2 CHRISTMAS FEAST
Comments: Porcelain Bisque, 3-1/2" tall, Dated 1993
Two little girls look on as mother carries the roasted turkey to the table. **Artist:** Sharon Pike
☐ Purchased 19___ Pd $_______ MIB NB DB BNT
☐ Want Orig. Ret. $15.75 **NB** $20 **MIB** Sec. Mkt. **$35-$38**

QK 114-2 JOY OF SHARING
Comments: Porcelain Bisque, 3-1/2" tall, Dated 1993
Two friends exchange Christmas gifts during this season of giving.
☐ Purchased 19___ Pd $_______ MIB NB DB BNT
☐ Want Orig. Ret. $15.75 **NB** $20 **MIB** Sec. Mkt. **$30-$35**

QK 114-5 MISTLETOE KISS
Comments: Porcelain Bisque, 3-5/6" tall
A gentleman prepares to kiss his favorite lady as he holds a sprig of mistletoe over her head. **Artist:** Sharon Pike
☐ Purchased 19___ Pd $_______ MIB NB DB BNT
☐ Want Orig. Ret. $15.75 **NB** $18 **MIB** Sec. Mkt. **$30-$35**

QK 116-2 NORMAN ROCKWELL: JOLLY POSTMAN
Comments: Porcelain Bisque, 3-1/4" tall
Children crowd around a happy postman who is delivering the Christmas mail. **Artist:** Peter Dutkin
☐ Purchased 19___ Pd $_______ MIB NB DB BNT
☐ Want Orig. Ret. $15.75 **NB** $18 **MIB** Sec. Mkt. **$35-$38**

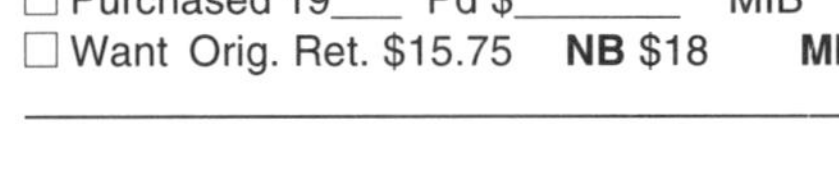

QK 115-5 NORMAN ROCKWELL: FILLING THE STOCKINGS
Comments: Porcelain Bisque, 3-9/16" tall
Santa is busy at his chores on Christmas Eve. **Artist:** Peter Dutkin
☐ Purchased 19___ Pd $_______ MIB NB DB BNT
☐ Want Orig. Ret. $15.75 **NB** $18 **MIB** Sec. Mkt. **$35-$38**

Good news: All rowers on the galley are getting an extra ratio of rum with lunch.
Bad news: After lunch, the captain wants to go water skiing.

1994 Collection

QX 581-6 A FELINE OF CHRISTMAS
Comments: Handcrafted, 3-1/16" tall, Dated 1994
Dangling from a string of lights, this silly cat, a Shoebox Greetings design, holds tightly to a Christmas tree ball ornament. **Artist:** Patricia Andrews
☐ Purchased 19___ Pd $_______ MIB NB DB BNT
☐ Want Orig. Ret. $8.95 **MIB** Sec. Mkt. **$22-$25**

QX 577-3 A SHARP FLAT
Comments: Handcrafted, 3-3/4" tall, Dated 1994
A virtuoso mouse lives in the back of this violin. His "flat" is complete with a fireplace and Christmas tree. The front of the ornament resembles a classical violin. **Artist:** Ken Crow
☐ Purchased 19___ Pd $_______ MIB NB DB BNT
☐ Want Orig. Ret. $10.95 **MIB** Sec. Mkt. **$12-$18**

QX 565-6 ACROSS THE MILES
Comments: Handcrafted, 2-9/16" tall, Dated 1994
This cheery raccoon is sending his Christmas greeting via a note in a bottle. **Artist:** Patricia Andrews
☐ Purchased 19___ Pd $_______ MIB NB DB BNT
☐ Want Orig. Ret. $8.95 **MIB** Sec. Mkt. **$12-$14**

QX 592-3 ALL PUMPED UP
Comments: Handcrafted, 2-7/16" tall, Dated 1994
A little elf sits atop an air pump; he has just filled the football for "Santa's Football League." **Artist:** Dill Rhodus
☐ Purchased 19___ Pd $_______ MIB NB DB BNT
☐ Want Orig. Ret. $8.95 **MIB** Sec. Mkt. **$16-$18**

QX 589-6 ANGEL HARE
Comments: Handcrafted/Brass Halo, 2-1/2" tall, Dated 1994
A whimsical bunny angel is putting the final touch to the Christmas tree -- Angel Hair. **Artist:** Linda Sickman
☐ Purchased 19___ Pd $_______ MIB NB DB BNT
☐ Want Orig. Ret. $8.95 **MIB** Sec. Mkt. **$18-$20**

QX 568-3 ANNIVERSARY YEAR: PHOTOHOLDER
Comments: Brass/Chrome, 3-13/16" tall, Dated 1994
Delicately etched with holly and ribbon, this photoholder may be personalized to mark 5, 10, 20, 25, 30, 35, 40, 45, 50 and 60 years. Caption: "Loving moments together... Loving memories forever." **Artist:** Ron Bishop
☐ Purchased 19___ Pd $_______ MIB NB DB BNT
☐ Want Orig. Ret. $10.95 **MIB** Sec. Mkt. **$14-$16**

QLX 738-3 AWAY IN A MANGER
Comments: Light, Handcrafted, 3-7/16" tall
Dated 1994. The star of Bethlehem is aglow and casts its light on Baby Jesus lying in his manger bed. Caption: "Away in a manger, no crib for a bed. The little Lord Jesus laid down his sweet head."
Artist: Joyce Lyle
☐ Purchased 19___ Pd $_______ MIB NB DB BNT
☐ Want Orig. Ret. $16.00 **NB** $18 **MIB** Sec. Mkt. **$30-$35**

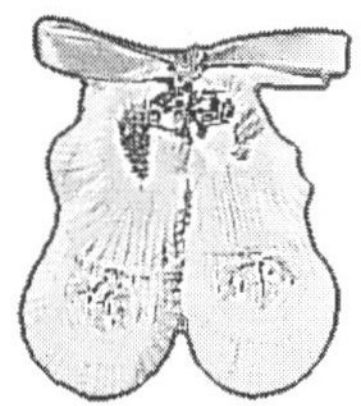

QX 563-3 BABY'S FIRST CHRISTMAS
Comments: Porcelain/Brass, 2-9/16" tall, Dated 1994
A brass tag and bell and green satin ribbon grace porcelain "knitted" booties. **Artist:** Duane Unruh
☐ Purchased 19___ Pd $_______ MIB NB DB BNT
☐ Want Orig. Ret. $18.95 **NB** $20 **MIB** Sec. Mkt. **$30-$35**

QX 574-3 BABY'S FIRST CHRISTMAS
Comments: Handcrafted, 1-7/8" tall, Dated 1994
Pull the safety pin to open the baby block; shh... a baby teddy is sound asleep inside. **Artist:** Ed Seale
☐ Purchased 19___ Pd $_______ MIB NB DB BNT
☐ Want Orig. Ret. $12.95 **NB** $15 **MIB** Sec. Mkt. **$18-22**

QLX 746-6 BABY'S FIRST CHRISTMAS
Comments: Light and Music, Handcrafted, 2-11/16" tall
Dated 1994. Mama and Papa squirrels check on their tiny infant, sound asleep in his cradle. Plays *Rock-a-Bye Baby.*
Artist: John Francis (Collin)
☐ Purchased 19___ Pd $_______ MIB NB DB BNT
☐ Want Orig. Ret. $20.00 **NB** $22 **MIB** Sec. Mkt. **$35-$40**

QX 571-3 BABY'S FIRST CHRISTMAS: TEDDY BEAR YEARS COLLECTION
Comments: Handcrafted, 2-3/16" tall, Dated 1994
Baby celebrates its first Christmas with a stocking and star-shaped Christmas cookie. Design is repeated from 1993.
Artist: Ken Crow
☐ Purchased 19___ Pd $_______ MIB NB DB BNT
☐ Want Orig. Ret. $7.95 **NB** $10 **MIB** Sec. Mkt. **$14-$16**

QX 243-6 BABY'S FIRST CHRISTMAS: BABY BOY
Comments: Blue Glass Ball, 2-7/8" dia., Dated 1994
As Santa peeks through the window, a baby boy is bouncing in his crib. Caption: "Santa's excited for he'll soon get to meet a new baby boy who's precious and sweet."
☐ Purchased 19___ Pd $_______ MIB NB DB BNT
☐ Want Orig. Ret. $7.95 **NB** $2 **MIB** Sec. Mkt. **$8-$10**

QX 243-3 BABY'S FIRST CHRISTMAS: BABY GIRL
Comments: Pink Glass Ball, 2-7/8" dia., Dated 1994
Santa peeks through a window and watches a baby girl in her crib. Caption: "Santa's excited for he'll soon get to meet a new baby girl who's precious and sweet."
☐ Purchased 19___ Pd $_______ MIB NB DB BNT
☐ Want Orig. Ret. $5.00 **NB** $2 **MIB** Sec. Mkt. **$8-$10**

QX 563-6 BABY'S FIRST CHRISTMAS PHOTOHOLDER
Comments: Handcrafted, 3-5/16" tall, Dated 1994
Baby's photo is framed appropriately with stars, a teddy bear and rocking horse. Caption: "There's a new little star on your horizon."
Artist: LaDene Votruba
☐ Purchased 19___ Pd $_______ MIB NB DB BNT
☐ Want Orig. Ret. $7.95 **NB** $8 **MIB** Sec. Mkt. **$14-$18**

QX 571-6 BABY'S SECOND CHRISTMAS: TEDDY BEAR YEARS COLLECTION
Comments: Handcrafted, 2-3/8" tall, Dated 1994
This teddy wears a red and white bow tie and holds a green Christmas stocking with a tree-shaped cookie. **Artist:** Ken Crow
☐ Purchased 19___ Pd $_______ MIB NB DB BNT
☐ Want Orig. Ret. $7.95 **NB** $5 **MIB** Sec. Mkt. **$14-$16**

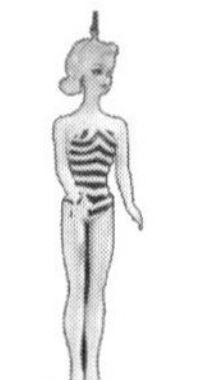

QX 500-6 BARBIE™
Comments: ***FIRST IN SERIES,*** Handcrafted, 4-7/16" tall
Dated 1994. Barbie is back in her original black and white swimsuit, marking the 35th anniversary of her debut in 1959.
☐ Purchased 19___ Pd $_______ MIB NB DB BNT
☐ Want Orig. Ret. $14.95 **MIB** Sec. Mkt. **$38-$45**

QLX 750-6 BARNEY™
Comments: Light and Motion, Handcrafted, 4-1/8" tall,
Dated 1994. Barney and his rabbit friend sled around a snowman. Caption: "Sledding is simply Stu-u-u-pendous."
☐ Purchased 19___ Pd $_______ MIB NB DB BNT
☐ Want Orig. Ret. $24.00 **NB** $28 **MIB** Sec. Mkt. **$35-$40**

QX 596-6 BARNEY™
Comments: Handcrafted, 3-15/16" tall, Dated 1994
A favorite of many small children, Barney skates into Christmas wearing a Santa cap.
☐ Purchased 19___ Pd $_______ MIB NB DB BNT
☐ Want Orig. Ret. $9.95 **NB** $10 **MIB** Sec. Mkt. **$15-$20**

QX 532-3 BASEBALL HEROES: BABE RUTH
Comments: ***FIRST IN SERIES,*** Handcrafted, 3-3/8" Dia. Dated 1994. Caption: "714 Career Home Runs, 60 Home Runs in 1927; .342 Lifetime Batting Average; Inducted into Hall of Fame 1936." This new series features baseball greats, the first of which is "The Babe." **Artist:** Dill Rhodus
☐ Purchased 19___ Pd $_______ MIB NB DB BNT
☐ Want Orig. Ret. $12.95 **NB** $35 **MIB** Sec. Mkt. **$50-$60**

QX 585-3 BATMAN
Comments: Handcrafted, 5-11/16" tall, Dated 1994. Batman swings from the Batarang. The size is complementary to Superman which was issued in 1993. **Artist:** Robert Chad
☐ Purchased 19___ Pd $_______ MIB NB DB BNT
☐ Want Orig. Ret. $12.95 **NB** $12 **MIB** Sec. Mkt. **$22-$28**

QX 537-3 BEATLES GIFT SET
Comments: Handcrafted, Dated 1994
Set includes four ornaments plus microphones, stage and drum set. An abundance is waiting to be sold on the secondary market! **Artist:** Anita Marra Rogers

A. Paul McCartney, 4-9/16"
B. John Lennon, 4-1/2"
C. George Harrison, 4-9/16"
D. Ringo Starr, 3-3/4"
E. Stand with Two Microphones, 3-15/16"
F. Drum Set, 2-3/4"
G. Floor Tom-Tom, 2-13/16"
H. Top Hat Cymbal, 2-7/16"
I. Stage, 2-3/16"

☐ Purchased 19___ Pd $_______ MIB NB DB BNT
☐ Want Orig. Ret. $48.00 **MIB** Sec. Mkt. **$70-$75**

QX 240-3 BETSEY'S COUNTRY CHRISTMAS
Comments: **Third and Final in Series,** Teardrop Ball 2-7/8" dia, Dated 1994. Betsey and her friends gather together to decorate the house for the Christmas holidays. Caption: "It's the simple joys, the simple pleasures, the heart remembers and dearly treasures."
☐ Purchased 19___ Pd $_______ MIB NB DB BNT
☐ Want Orig. Ret. $5.00 **MIB** Sec. Mkt. **$8-$10**

Doctor: Why do you have D 23650 tattooed on your back?
Patient: It's not a tattoo. That's where my wife ran into me while I was trying to open the garage door!

QX 587-3 BIG SHOT
Comments: Handcrafted, 2-7/8" tall, Dated 1994
This little fellow actually spins the basketball on his finger!
Artist: Bob Siedler
☐ Purchased 19___ Pd $_______ MIB NB DB BNT
☐ Want Orig. Ret. $7.95 **MIB** Sec. Mkt. **$12-$14**

QX 551-6 BROTHER
Comments: Handcrafted, 1-15/16" tall, Dated 1994
"Super Terrific Brother" zips around town in his sports car.
Artist: Sharon Pike
☐ Purchased 19___ Pd $_______ MIB NB DB BNT
☐ Want Orig. Ret. $6.95 **MIB** Sec. Mkt. **$10-$12**

QX 587-6 BUSY BATTER
Comments: Handcrafted, 2-5/8" tall, Dated 1994
Playing for the "Wood Sox," someone pitch the ball to this busy beaver before he chews his bat to pieces! **Artist:** Bob Siedler
☐ Purchased 19___ Pd $_______ MIB NB DB BNT
☐ Want Orig. Ret. $7.95 **MIB** Sec. Mkt. **$10-$14**

QLX 737-6 CANDY CANE LOOKOUT
Comments: Light and Voice, Handcrafted, 4-1/4" tall Dated 1994. A penguin at the top of the lighthouse keeps a lookout while Santa, Mrs. Santa and another penguin sing carols below.
Artist: John Francis (Collin)
☐ Purchased 19___ Pd $_______ MIB NB DB BNT
☐ Want Orig. Ret. $18.00 **NB** $20 **MIB** Sec. Mkt.**$35-$38**

QX 577-6 CANDY CAPER
Comments: Handcrafted, 2-11/16" tall, Dated 1994
A glass jar full of red and green peppermint candies is just too irresistible! **Artist:** Patricia Andrews
☐ Purchased 19___ Pd $_______ MIB NB DB BNT
☐ Want Orig. Ret. $8.95 **MIB** Sec. Mkt. **$14-$16**

QX 582-3 CARING DOCTOR
Comments: Handcrafted, 2-5/16" tall, Dated 1994
The doctor dates the cast on his cookie patient.
Artist: Anita Marra Rogers
☐ Purchased 19___ Pd $_______ MIB NB DB BNT
☐ Want Orig. Ret. $8.95 **MIB** Sec. Mkt. **$14-$16**

Most highways have three lanes...a left lane, a right lane and the lane you're trapped in when you finally find your exit.

QX 531-3 CAT NAPS
Comments: ***FIRST IN SERIES,*** Handcrafted, 1-15/16" tall Dated 1994. Kitty naps in her very own cookie jar.
Artist: Dill Rhodus
☐ Purchased 19___ Pd $_______ MIB NB DB BNT
☐ Want Orig. Ret. $7.75 **MIB** Sec. Mkt.**$20-$22**

QX 583-6 CHAMPION TEACHER
Comments: Handcrafted, 1-11/16" tall, Dated 1994
A cute little worm pokes his head out of a bright red apple to give his opinion of his teacher. **Artist:** Bob Siedler
☐ Purchased 19___ Pd $_______ MIB NB DB BNT
☐ Want Orig. Ret. $6.95 **MIB** Sec. Mkt. **$10-$12**

QX 579-6 CHEERS TO YOU!
Comments: Handcrafted/Brass Bell, 3-1/16" tall
"Frohliche Weihnacten," the German Merry Christmas, is inscribed on this stein. **Artist:** Ken Crow
☐ Purchased 19___ Pd $_______ MIB NB DB BNT
☐ Want Orig. Ret. $10.95 **MIB** Sec. Mkt. **$18-$22**

QX 578-6 CHEERY CYCLISTS
Comments: Handcrafted, 3-3/16" tall, Dated 1994
Santa and his reindeer are riding a motorcycle built for five!
Artist: Ken Crow
☐ Purchased 19___ Pd $_______ MIB NB DB BNT
☐ Want Orig. Ret. $12.95 **MIB** Sec. Mkt. **$25-$28**

QX 590-6 CHILD CARE GIVER
Comments: Handcrafted, 2-1/8" tall, Dated 1994
A little raccoon sits entranced by the "Holiday Stories" being read by the child care giver. **Artist:** LaDene Votruba
☐ Purchased 19___ Pd $_______ MIB NB DB BNT
☐ Want Orig. Ret. $7.95 **MIB** Sec. Mkt. **$12-$14**

QX 573-3 CHILD'S FIFTH CHRISTMAS: TEDDY BEAR YEARS COLLECTION
Comments: Handcrafted, 2-3/8" tall, Dated 1994
Design is repeated from 1993. **Artist:** Dill Rhodus
☐ Purchased 19___ Pd $_______ MIB NB DB BNT
☐ Want Orig. Ret. $6.95 **MIB** Sec. Mkt. **$10-$12**

QX 572-6 CHILD'S FOURTH CHRISTMAS: TEDDY BEAR YEARS COLLECTION
Comments: Handcrafted, 3" tall, Dated 1994
Design is repeated from 1993. **Artist:** John Francis (Collin)
☐ Purchased 19___ Pd $_______ MIB NB DB BNT
☐ Want Orig. Ret. $6.95 **MIB** Sec. Mkt. **$10-$12**

QX 572-3 CHILD'S THIRD CHRISTMAS: TEDDY BEAR YEARS COLLECTION
Comments: Handcrafted, 2-1/2" tall, Dated 1994
Design is repeated from 1993. **Artist:** John Francis (Collin)
☐ Purchased 19___ Pd $_______ MIB NB DB BNT
☐ Want Orig. Ret. $6.95 **MIB** Sec. Mkt. **$10-$12**

QLX 739-3 CHRIS MOUSE JELLY
Comments: **Tenth in Series,** Lighted, Handcrafted, 2-13/16" tall Dated 1994. Chris Mouse dips into "Lite Jelly From the Kitchen of Chris Mouse" to add a bread and jelly sandwich to his evening cheese snack. **Artist:** Anita Marra Rogers
☐ Purchased 19___ Pd $_______ MIB NB DB BNT
☐ Want Orig. Ret. $12.00 **MIB** Sec. Mkt. **$20-$25**

QX 542-2 CLASSIC AMERICAN CARS: 1957 CHEVROLET BEL AIR
Comments: **Fourth in Series,** Handcrafted, 1-3/8" tall Dated 1994. A well-liked addition to a very popular series.
Artist: Don Palmiter
☐ Purchased 19___ Pd $_______ MIB NB DB BNT
☐ Want Orig. Ret. $12.95 **MIB** Sec. Mkt. **$32-$35**

QX 593-3 COACH
Comments: Handcrafted, 3-1/8" tall, Dated 1994
A happy coach is ready to go with his green gym bag and whistle.
Artist: Duane Unruh
☐ Purchased 19___ Pd $_______ MIB NB DB BNT
☐ Want Orig. Ret. $7.95 **MIB** Sec. Mkt. **$10-$12**

Bank Robber: This is a stickup! Give me all your money or else.
Teller: Or else what?
Bank Robber: Don't confuse me, this is my first job.

QX 539-6 COCK-A-DOODLE CHRISTMAS
Comments: Handcrafted, 3-3/16" tall, Dated 1994
A rooster crows his Christmas greeting from atop a pony.
Artist: LaDene Votruba
☐ Purchased 19___ Pd $_______ MIB NB DB BNT
☐ Want Orig. Ret. $8.95 **NB** $6 **MIB** Sec. Mkt. **$14-$18**

QX 589-3 COLORS OF JOY
Comments: Handcrafted, 2-3/16" tall, Dated 1994
A little mouse stands in a tray of paints and adds his holiday sentiment to the cover. **Artist:** Ed Seale
☐ Purchased 19___ Pd $_______ MIB NB DB BNT
☐ Want Orig. Ret. $7.95 **NB** $6 **MIB** Sec. Mkt. **$15-$18**

QLX 742-6 CONVERSATIONS WITH SANTA
Comments: Motion and Voice, Handcrafted, 3-1/8" tall
Dated 1994. Santa's mouth moves as he speaks one of four messages. **Artist:** Ed Seale
☐ Purchased 19___ Pd $_______ MIB NB DB BNT
☐ Want Orig. Ret. $28.00 **NB** $20 **MIB** Sec. Mkt. **$35-$40**

QLX 741-6 COUNTRY SHOWTIME
Comments: Blinking Lights and Motion, Handcrafted 4-3/16" tall
Dated 1994. This jointed "wooden" Santa dances at center stage.
Artist: Linda Sickman
☐ Purchased 19___ Pd $_______ MIB NB DB BNT
☐ Want Orig. Ret. $22.00 **NB** $20 **MIB** Sec. Mkt. **$35-$40**

QX 527-3 CRAYOLA® CRAYON: BRIGHT PLAYFUL COLORS
Comments: **Sixth in Series,** Handcrafted, 3-3/8" tall
Dated 1994. A Teddy Bear swings while waiting for Santa. Popular series. **Artist:** Ken Crow
☐ Purchased 19___ Pd $_______ MIB NB DB BNT
☐ Want Orig. Ret. $10.95 **MIB** Sec. Mkt. **$18-$20**

QX 546-3 DAD
Comments: Handcrafted, 2-5/16" tall, Dated 1994
Dad has won a loving cup. Of course he's the "World's Greatest Dad"! **Artist:** Anita Marra Rogers
☐ Purchased 19___ Pd $_______ MIB NB DB BNT
☐ Want Orig. Ret. $7.95 **MIB** Sec. Mkt. **$10-$12**

QX 547-3 DAD-TO-BE
Comments: Handcrafted, 2-9/16" tall, Dated 1994
The soon-to-be papa, dressed in his red and white striped night shirt, holds a package entitled "All Night Takeout" in one hand and his car keys in the other. **Artist:** Sharon Pike
☐ Purchased 19___ Pd $_______ MIB NB DB BNT
☐ Want Orig. Ret. $7.95 **MIB** Sec. Mkt. **$12-$16**

QX 562-3 DAUGHTER
Comments: Handcrafted, 2-13/16" tall, Dated 1994
Daughter dinosaur is having lots of Christmas fun on her new roller blades. **Artist:** Patricia Andrews
☐ Purchased 19___ Pd $_______ MIB NB DB BNT
☐ Want Orig. Ret. $6.95 **MIB** Sec. Mkt. **$10-$12**

QX 580-6 DEAR SANTA MOUSE
Comments: Handcrafted, 2-15/16" tall, 1-11/16" tall, Dated 1994
Set of two hang-together ornaments. While one mouse holds the ink bottle, the other writes their letter, "Dear Santa, We know you're very busy and we'd help you if we could, but we really thought you'd want to hear -- this year we've been real good! X" **Artist:** Ken Crow
☐ Purchased 19___ Pd $_______ MIB NB DB BNT
☐ Want Orig. Ret. $14.95 **NB** $15 **MIB** Sec. Mkt. **$24-$28**

QX533-6 EAGER FOR CHRISTMAS
Comments: Handcrafted
The whimsical Tender Touches beaver chats happily with a little bluebird perched atop his Christmas tree. This exclusive Premiere ornament was available for purchase beginning at the Keepsake ornament premieres in July 1994. **Artist:** Ed Seale
☐ Purchased 19___ Pd $_______ MIB NB DB BNT
☐ Want Orig. Ret. $15.00 **MIB** Sec. Mkt. **$22-$25**

QLX 748-6 EAGLE HAS LANDED, THE
Comments: Light and Voice, Handcrafted, 4-1/2" tall
Dated 1994. An American astronaut places the American flag on the surface of the moon. Commemorating the 25th anniversary of the first lunar landing. Caption: "Here men from the planet earth first set foot upon the moon, July 1969 A.D. We came in peace for all mankind." Features astronaut Neil Armstrong repeating his message, "Houston, Tranquility Base here. The Eagle has landed... One small step for man, one giant leap for mankind."
Artist: Ed Seale
☐ Purchased 19___ Pd $_______ MIB NB DB BNT
☐ Want Orig. Ret. $24.00 **NB** $20 **MIB** Sec. Mkt. **$50-$55**

QX 583-3 EXTRA-SPECIAL DELIVERY
Comments: Handcrafted, 2-1/8" tall, Dated 1994
This special mail carrier truly is "First Class."
Artist: Ken Crow
☐ Purchased 19___ Pd $_______ MIB NB DB BNT
☐ Want Orig. Ret. $7.95 **NB** $6 **MIB** Sec. Mkt. **$14-$18**

QX 526-3 FABULOUS DECADE
Comments: **Fifth in Series,** Handcrafted and Brass, 2" tall Dated 1994. A white Christmas bunny heralds the year.
Artist: Ed Seale
☐ Purchased 19___ Pd $_______ MIB NB DB BNT
☐ Want Orig. Ret. $7.95 **NB** $6 **MIB** Sec. Mkt. **$18-$22**

QX 595-3 FEELIN' GROOVY
Comments: Handcrafted, 2-11/16" tall, Dated 1994
Santa is wearin' his shades and flashing a peace sign to all he meets.
☐ Purchased 19___ Pd $_______ MIB NB DB BNT
☐ Want Orig. Ret. $7.95 **NB** $6 **MIB** Sec. Mkt. **$14-$16**

QX 579-3 FELIZ NAVIDAD
Comments: Handcrafted, 2-13/16" tall, Dated 1994
A little Spanish mouse in his sombrero, awakens from his siesta and pops up from a gaily painted Mexican pot.
Artist: Anita Marra Rogers
☐ Purchased 19___ Pd $_______ MIB NB DB BNT
☐ Want Orig. Ret. $8.95 **NB** $10 **MIB** Sec. Mkt. **$20-$22**

QLX 743-3 FELIZ NAVIDAD
Comments: Motion and Music, Handcrafted, 3-1/8" tall Dated 1994. A boy taps the bell-shaped piñata with a stick and the children dance around the sombrero. Plays *Feliz Navidad.*
Artist: Linda Crow
☐ Purchased 19___ Pd $_______ MIB NB DB BNT
☐ Want Orig. Ret. $28.00 **NB** $30 **MIB** Sec. Mkt. **$45-$50**

QX 584-6 FOLLOW THE SUN
Comments: Handcrafted, 3-13/16" tall, Dated 1994
Riding a reindeer and sleigh weather vane, this bird is following "Route 94" to "Lake Wannagothere." **Artist:** Ken Crow
☐ Purchased 19___ Pd $_______ MIB NB DB BNT
☐ Want Orig. Ret. $8.95 **NB** $8 **MIB** Sec. Mkt. **$14-$16**

QX 561-3 FOR MY GRANDMA: PHOTOHOLDER
Comments: Handcrafted, 3-9/16" tall, Dated 1994
Grandma will be delighted with this brightly decorated Christmas tree photoholder. Caption: "1994 I Love you! From _______"
Artist: Donna Lee
☐ Purchased 19___ Pd $_______ MIB NB DB BNT
☐ Want Orig. Ret. $6.95 **NB** $5 **MIB** Sec. Mkt. **$12-$14**

QLX 743-6 FOREST FROLICS
Comments: **Sixth in Series,** Light and Motion, Handcrafted, 4-1/8" tall, Dated 1994. The forest animals play happily around the Christmas tree. **Artist:** Sharon Pike
☐ Purchased 19___ Pd $_______ MIB NB DB BNT
☐ Want Orig. Ret. $28.00 **NB** $28 **MIB** Sec. Mkt. **$40-$45**

QX 500-3 FRED AND BARNEY: THE FLINTSTONES®
Comments: Handcrafted, 2-5/8" tall, Dated 1994
The ever-popular duo are headed out in their Stone Age car.
Artist: Dill Rhodus
☐ Purchased 19___ Pd $_______ MIB NB DB BNT
☐ Want Orig. Ret. $14.95 **NB** $12 **MIB** Sec. Mkt. **$25-$30**

QX 568-6 FRIENDLY PUSH
Comments: Handcrafted, 3-1/8" tall, Dated 1994
As one little brown mouse sits inside an ice skate, another little gray mouse gives a friendly little push. **Artist:** Bob Seidler
☐ Purchased 19___ Pd $_______ MIB NB DB BNT
☐ Want Orig. Ret. $8.95 **NB** $9 **MIB** Sec. Mkt. **$14-$18**

QX 476-6 FRIENDSHIP SUNDAE
Comments: Handcrafted, 3-1/4" tall, Dated 1994
These two white mice must love lots of Hershey's chocolate on their ice cream! Yum, yum! **Artist:** Linda Sickman
☐ Purchased 19___ Pd $_______ MIB NB DB BNT
☐ Want Orig. Ret. $10.95 **NB** $10 **MIB** Sec. Mkt. **$22-$26**

QX 529-3 FROSTY FRIENDS
Comments: **Fifteenth in Series,** Handcrafted, 2-1/8" tall Dated 1994. Little Eskimo holds a wreath while his polar bear friend jumps through. **Artist:** Ed Seale
☐ Purchased 19___ Pd $_______ MIB NB DB BNT
☐ Want Orig. Ret. $9.95 **NB** $10 **MIB** Sec. Mkt. **$22-$24**

A well done jab - Successful acupuncture

QX 598-6 GARDEN ELVES COLLECTION: DAISY DAYS
Comments: Handcrafted, 2-7/8" tall
Summer daisies always brighten up a room, and this blonde haired lass is bringing some home to share. **Artist:** Robert Chad
☐ Purchased 19___ Pd $_______ MIB NB DB BNT
☐ Want Orig. Ret. $9.95 **NB** $5 **MIB** Sec. Mkt. **$10-$12**

QX 599-3 GARDEN ELVES COLLECTION: HARVEST JOY
Comments: Handcrafted, 2-13/16" tall
This little lad, dressed in green and tan, is bringing home the bounty of a good autumn harvest. **Artist:** Robert Chad
☐ Purchased 19___ Pd $_______ MIB NB DB BNT
☐ Want Orig. Ret. $9.95 **NB** $5 **MIB** Sec. Mkt. **$10-$12**

QX 598-3 GARDEN ELVES COLLECTION: TULIP TIME
Comments: Handcrafted, 2-5/16" tall
A pot full of red tulips testifies to this young lady's green thumb. She represents Spring. **Artist:** Robert Chad
☐ Purchased 19___ Pd $_______ MIB NB DB BNT
☐ Want Orig. Ret. $9.95 **NB** $5 **MIB** Sec. Mkt. **$10-$12**

QX 597-6 GARDEN ELVES COLLECTION: YULETIDE CHEER
Comments: Handcrafted, 2-13/16" tall
This little lad is getting ready for Christmas. He has a miniature tree in one hand and a holly leaf in the other. **Artist:** Robert Chad
☐ Purchased 19___ Pd $_______ MIB NB DB BNT
☐ Want Orig. Ret. $9.95 **NB** $5 **MIB** Sec. Mkt. **$10-$12**

QX 575-3 GARFIELD
Comments: Handcrafted, 2-1/2" tall, Dated 1994
Garfield is heading off to bed with his teddy, candle and Christmas stocking for Santa to fill.
☐ Purchased 19___ Pd $_______ MIB NB DB BNT
☐ Want Orig. Ret. $12.95 **NB** $10 **MIB** Sec. Mkt. **$18-$22**

QX 597-3 GENTLE NURSE
Comments: Handcrafted, 2-7/16" tall, Dated 1994
The nurse has her patient's complete confidence as she bandages his paw. **Artist:** Joyce Lyle
☐ Purchased 19___ Pd $_______ MIB NB DB BNT
☐ Want Orig. Ret. $6.95 **NB** $5 **MIB** Sec. Mkt. **$12-$16**

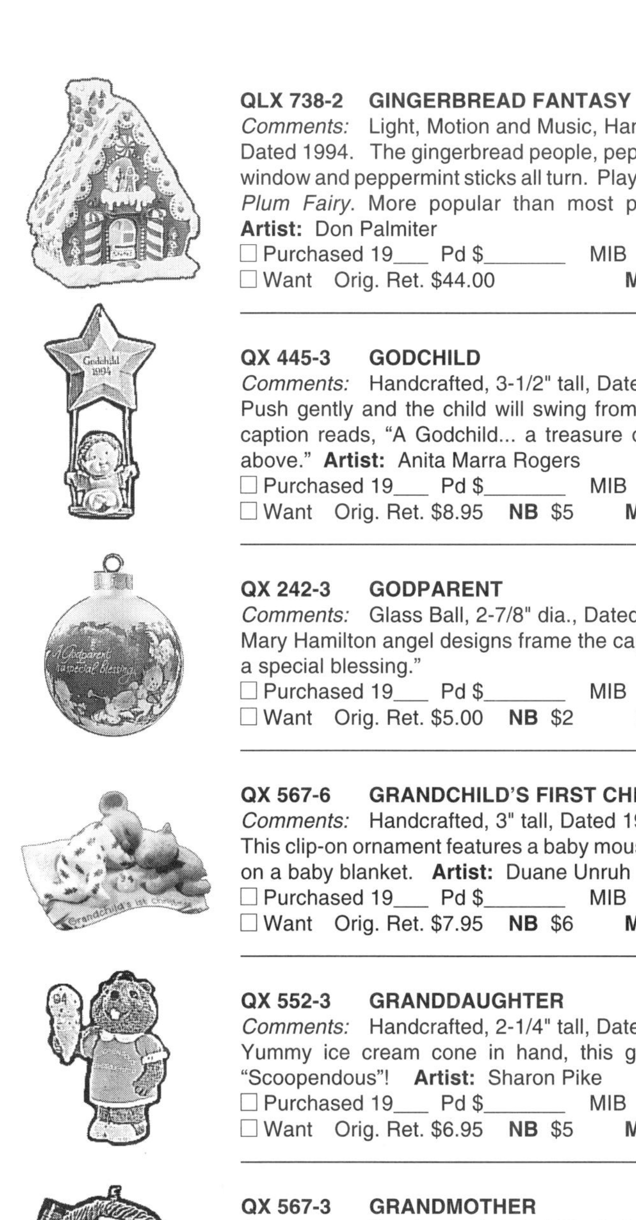

QLX 738-2 GINGERBREAD FANTASY
Comments: Light, Motion and Music, Handcrafted, 4-1/4" tall
Dated 1994. The gingerbread people, peppermint above the top window and peppermint sticks all turn. Plays *Dance Of The Sugar Plum Fairy*. More popular than most past L.M. ornaments. **Artist:** Don Palmiter
☐ Purchased 19___ Pd $_______ MIB NB DB BNT
☐ Want Orig. Ret. $44.00 **MIB** Sec. Mkt. **$85-$95**

QX 445-3 GODCHILD
Comments: Handcrafted, 3-1/2" tall, Dated 1994
Push gently and the child will swing from the golden star. The caption reads, "A Godchild... a treasure on earth from heaven above." **Artist:** Anita Marra Rogers
☐ Purchased 19___ Pd $_______ MIB NB DB BNT
☐ Want Orig. Ret. $8.95 **NB** $5 **MIB** Sec. Mkt. **$12-$14**

QX 242-3 GODPARENT
Comments: Glass Ball, 2-7/8" dia., Dated 1994
Mary Hamilton angel designs frame the caption, "A Godparent is a special blessing."
☐ Purchased 19___ Pd $_______ MIB NB DB BNT
☐ Want Orig. Ret. $5.00 **NB** $2 **MIB** Sec. Mkt. **$8-$10**

QX 567-6 GRANDCHILD'S FIRST CHRISTMAS
Comments: Handcrafted, 3" tall, Dated 1994
This clip-on ornament features a baby mouse sleeping peacefully on a baby blanket. **Artist:** Duane Unruh
☐ Purchased 19___ Pd $_______ MIB NB DB BNT
☐ Want Orig. Ret. $7.95 **NB** $6 **MIB** Sec. Mkt. **$12-$14**

QX 552-3 GRANDDAUGHTER
Comments: Handcrafted, 2-1/4" tall, Dated 1994
Yummy ice cream cone in hand, this granddaughter is truly "Scoopendous"! **Artist:** Sharon Pike
☐ Purchased 19___ Pd $_______ MIB NB DB BNT
☐ Want Orig. Ret. $6.95 **NB** $5 **MIB** Sec. Mkt. **$14-$16**

QX 567-3 GRANDMOTHER
Comments: Handcrafted, 1-13/16" tall, Dated 1994
Someone has baked a basket of sugar cookies for Grandma. The liner in the basket is fabric. **Artist:** Patricia Andrews
☐ Purchased 19___ Pd $_______ MIB NB DB BNT
☐ Want Orig. Ret. $7.95 **NB** $5 **MIB** Sec. Mkt. **$12-$14**

QX 561-6 GRANDPA
Comments: Handcrafted, 2-7/16" tall, Dated 1994
A new commemorative ornament, a Grandpa owl in striped vest and tie hugs his grandson. **Artist:** Duane Unruh
☐ Purchased 19___ Pd $_______ MIB NB DB BNT
☐ Want Orig. Ret. $7.95 **NB** $6 **MIB** Sec. Mkt. **$12-$16**

QX 242-6 GRANDPARENTS
Comments: White Glass Ball, 2-7/8" dia. Dated 1994
A red cardinal sits on a branch of bright red berries.
Caption: "Merry Christmas to very special grandparents who are very special people."
☐ Purchased 19___ Pd $_______ MIB NB DB BNT
☐ Want Orig. Ret. $5.00 **NB** $3 **MIB** Sec. Mkt. **$6-$10**

QX 552-6 GRANDSON
Comments: Handcrafted, 2-7/16" tall, Dated 1994
This "Scoopendous Grandson" is enjoying his double-scoop strawberry ice cream cone. **Artist:** Sharon Pike
☐ Purchased 19___ Pd $_______ MIB NB DB BNT
☐ Want Orig. Ret. $6.95 **NB** $3 **MIB** Sec. Mkt. **$12-$16**

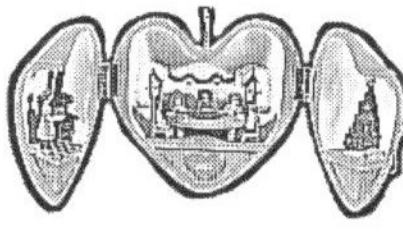

QX 542-3 HAPPY BIRTHDAY, JESUS
Comments: Handcrafted, 2-1/8" tall, Dated 1994
Clip-on ornament. An angel tends to Baby Jesus in his manger bed.
Artist: Joyce Lyle
☐ Purchased 19___ Pd $_______ MIB NB DB BNT
☐ Want Orig. Ret. $12.95 **NB** $14 **MIB** Sec. Mkt. **$18-$22**

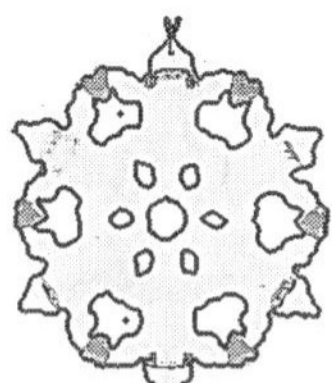

QX 526-6 HEART OF CHRISTMAS
Comments: **Fifth and Final in Series,** Handcrafted, 2" tall
Dated 1994. It's Christmas and Mama has a feast in store for her family. **Artist:** Ed Seale
☐ Purchased 19___ Pd $_______ MIB NB DB BNT
☐ Want Orig. Ret. $14.95 **NB** $15 **MIB** Sec. Mkt. **$22-$26**

QX 440-6 HEARTS IN HARMONY
Comments: Porcelain, 3" tall, Dated 1994
Boys and girls of different nationalities join hearts in unity to form a unique snowflake pattern. **Artist:** Patricia Andrews
☐ Purchased 19___ Pd $_______ MIB NB DB BNT
☐ Want Orig. Ret. $10.95 **NB** $8 **MIB** Sec. Mkt. **$12-$14**

QX 553-6 HELPFUL SHEPHERD
Comments: Handcrafted/Brass Staff, 2-11/16" tall
A shepherd carries his lamb across his shoulders.
Artist: Robert Chad
☐ Purchased 19___ Pd $_______ MIB NB DB BNT
☐ Want Orig. Ret. $8.95 **NB** $8 **MIB** Sec. Mkt. **$12-$14**

QX 529-6 HERE COMES SANTA: MAKIN' TRACTOR TRACKS
Comments: **Sixteenth in Series,** Handcrafted, 2-11/16" tall
Dated 1994. Santa plows the "back forty" with his "Reindeer" tractor. This piece is somewhat scarce. **Artist:** Linda Sickman
☐ Purchased 19___ Pd $_______ MIB NB DB BNT
☐ Want Orig. Ret. $14.95 **NB** $20 **MIB** Sec. Mkt. **$45-$50**

QX 521-6 HOLIDAY BARBIE™
Comments: **Second in Series,** Handcrafted, 3-3/8" tall
Dated 1994. Barbie glitters in her gold and ivory gown. She coordinated with the Holiday Barbie Doll which was offered in 1994 and the '95 Hallmark stocking hanger.
☐ Purchased 19___ Pd $_______ MIB NB DB BNT
☐ Want Orig. Ret. $14.95 **NB** $22 **MIB** Sec. Mkt. **$38-$45**

QX 582-6 HOLIDAY PATROL
Comments: Handcrafted, 2-1/2" tall, Dated 1994
"Stop for Christmas" is the message of this policeman.
Artist: Dill Rhodus
☐ Purchased 19___ Pd $_______ MIB NB DB BNT
☐ Want Orig. Ret. $8.95 **NB** $8 **MIB** Sec. Mkt. **$12-$14**

QXC 482-3 HOLIDAY PURSUIT: KEEPSAKE CLUB
Comments: Handcrafted, 2-7/8" tall, Dated 1994
Super sleuth Keepsake Bear is hot on the trail of the 1994 ornaments. **Artist:** John Francis (Collin)
☐ Purchased 19___ Pd $_______ MIB NB DB BNT
☐ Want Orig. Ret.: Came with Club Membership
MIB Sec. Mkt. **$18-$20**

QX 594-6 ICE SHOW
Comments: Handcrafted, 2-7/8" tall, Dated 1994
A little redbird does amazing tricks skating atop an ice cube. Many of the ice cubes are found with bubbles in them. Perfect cube with no bubble projected value of $45. **Artist:** Patricia Andrews
☐ Purchased 19___ Pd $_______ MIB NB DB BNT
☐ Want Orig. Ret. $7.95 **NB** $8 **MIB** Sec. Mkt. **$12-$16**

QX 576-3 IN THE PINK
Comments: Handcrafted, 2-3/4" tall, Dated 1994
A pink flamingo lounges in the shade of a palm tree, sipping his drink.
Artist: Patricia Andrews
☐ Purchased 19___ Pd $_______ MIB NB DB BNT
☐ Want Orig. Ret. $9.95 **NB** $8 **MIB** Sec. Mkt. **$14-$18**

QX 585-6 IT'S A STRIKE
Comments: Handcrafted, 2-13/16" tall, Dated 1994
This monkey will have a perfect score if he continues to bowl strikes at "Santa Claus Lanes." **Artist:** Bob Siedler
☐ Purchased 19___ Pd $_______ MIB NB DB BNT
☐ Want Orig. Ret. $8.95 **NB** $7 **MIB** Sec. Mkt. **$12-$16**

QX 578-3 JINGLE BELL BAND
Comments: Handcrafted, 4" tall, Dated 1994
Our musical mice in the band play the bells -- jingle bells, that is!
Artist: Ken Crow
☐ Purchased 19___ Pd $_______ MIB NB DB BNT
☐ Want Orig. Ret. $10.95 **NB** $9 **MIB** Sec. Mkt. **$22-$25**

QXC 483-3 JOLLY HOLLY SANTA: KEEPSAKE CLUB
Comments: Limited Edition, Wood Display Stand
Handcrafted/Hand Painted, 3-1/8" tall, Dated 1994
This Santa depicts the essence of a Victorian Christmas with a bag full of toys for all the girls and boys. **Artist:** Joyce A. Lyle
☐ Purchased 19___ Pd $_______ MIB NB DB BNT
☐ Want Orig. Ret. $22.00 **MIB** Sec. Mkt. **$35-$40**

QX 447-3 JOYOUS SONG
Comments: Handcrafted, 3-9/16" tall, Dated 1994
An African-American girl in a red choir robe sings a happy melody.
Artist: Patricia Andrews
☐ Purchased 19___ Pd $_______ MIB NB DB BNT
☐ Want Orig. Ret. $8.95 **NB** $7 **MIB** Sec. Mkt. **$12-$14**

QX 575-6 JUMP-ALONG JACKALOPE
Comments: Handcrafted, 3-7/16" tall, Dated 1994
The elusive jackalope has been captured in a Keepsake ornament.
Artist: John Francis (Collin)
☐ Purchased 19___ Pd $_______ MIB NB DB BNT
☐ Want Orig. Ret. $8.95 **NB** $7 **MIB** Sec. Mkt. **$14-$16**

If you love rainbows, you must be willing to put up with some rain.

QX 541-3 KEEP ON MOWIN'
Comments: Handcrafted, 3-1/8" tall, Dated 1994
Santa, in t-shirt, shorts and sandals, pushes a mower; the wheels and blades of the mower turn freely. **Artist:** Bob Siedler
☐ Purchased 19___ Pd $_______ MIB NB DB BNT
☐ Want Orig. Ret. $8.95 **NB** $7 **MIB** Sec. Mkt. **$14-$16**

QX 591-6 KICKIN' ROO
Comments: Handcrafted, 2-11/16" tall, Dated 1994
A little roo in his red and white jersey is a big hit on the soccer field.
Artist: Bob Siedler
☐ Purchased 19___ Pd $_______ MIB NB DB BNT
☐ Want Orig. Ret. $7.95 **NB** $6 **MIB** Sec. Mkt. **$12-$14**

QX 542-6 KIDDIE CAR CLASSICS: MURRAY® CHAMPION
Comments: ***FIRST IN SERIES,*** Cast Metal, 1-7/8" tall
Dated 1994. This ornament series is similar to the larger Hallmark Kiddie Car Classics. There was a first in series of same in the mini line. Very popular! **Artist:** Don Palmiter
☐ Purchased 19___ Pd $_______ MIB NB DB BNT
☐ Want Orig. Ret. $13.95 **NB** $25 **MIB** Sec. Mkt. **$48-$55**

QX 541-6 KITTY'S CATAMARAN
Comments: Handcrafted, 4-9/16" tall, Dated 1994
Kitty is taking his sailboat, the "Cat's Meow" out for a holiday ride.
Artist: Ed Seale
☐ Purchased 19___ Pd $_______ MIB NB DB BNT
☐ Want Orig. Ret. $10.95 **NB** $8 **MIB** Sec. Mkt. **$14-$18**

QLX 741-3 KRINGLE TROLLEY
Comments: Light, Handcrafted, 3-5/16" tall, Dated 1994
Santa's picking up travelers on the "Kringle Christmas Trolley" up and down the "Jingle Bell Lane Snow Express." **Artist:** Ken Crow
☐ Purchased 19___ Pd $_______ MIB NB DB BNT
☐ Want Orig. Ret. $20.00 **NB** $15 **MIB** Sec. Mkt. **$28-$32**

To err is human, but to really mess things up you need a computer.

QX 588-6 KRINGLE'S KAYAK
Comments: Handcrafted, 1-13/16" tall, Dated 1994
Some of Santa's deliveries cannot be reached by sleigh, so he takes a kayak. **Artist:** Ed Seale
☐ Purchased 19___ Pd $_______ MIB NB DB BNT
☐ Want Orig. Ret. $7.95 **NB** $8 **MIB** Sec. Mkt. **$15-$20**

QX 540-6 LION KING, THE: MUFASA AND SIMBA
Comments: Handcrafted, 3" tall
Father and son enjoy their time together, playing and learning about life in the wild.
☐ Purchased 19___ Pd $_______ MIB NB DB BNT
☐ Want Orig. Ret. $14.95 **NB** $15 **MIB** Sec. Mkt. **$28-$35**

QX 530-3 LION KING, THE: SIMBA AND NALA
Comments: Handcrafted, 2" tall, 2-3/8" tall
Set of two hang-together ornaments. The young lion prince and his best friend Nala love to play together.
☐ Purchased 19___ Pd $_______ MIB NB DB BNT
☐ Want Orig. Ret. $12.95 **MIB** Sec. Mkt. **$30-$32**

QLX 551-3 LION KING, THE: SIMBA, SARABI AND MUFASA
Comments: Light and Sound, Handcrafted, 4-1/4" tall
Mufasa's family is complete with the birth of the new prince, Simba. Plays *Circle of Life.* With Sound. **Artist:** Ken Crow
☐ Purchased 19___ Pd $_______ MIB NB DB BNT
☐ Want Orig. Ret. $32.00 **NB** $25 **MIB** Sec. Mkt. **$35-$40**

QLX 551-3 LION KING, THE: SIMBA, SARABI AND MUFASA
Comments: Light and Sound, Handcrafted, 4-1/4" tall
Mufasa's family is complete with the birth of the new prince, Simba. Plays *Circle of Life. No Sound* **Artist:** Ken Crow
☐ Purchased 19___ Pd $_______ MIB NB DB BNT
☐ Want Orig. Ret. $32.00 **NB** $50 **MIB** Sec. Mkt. **$75-$80**

QX 536-6 LION KING, THE: TIMON AND PUMBAA
Comments: Handcrafted, 2-1/4" tall
The wart hog and his little friend frolic without a care in the world.
☐ Purchased 19___ Pd $_______ MIB NB DB BNT
☐ Want Orig. Ret. $8.95 **NB** $10 **MIB** Sec. Mkt. **$22-$25**

QX 541-5 LOONEY TUNES COLLECTION: DAFFY DUCK
Comments: Handcrafted, 3" tall
Daffy is trying out an angel robe and wings. His halo is brass.
Artist: Don Palmiter
☐ Purchased 19___ Pd $_______ MIB NB DB BNT
☐ Want Orig. Ret. $8.95 **NB** $8 **MIB** Sec. Mkt. **$14-$20**

QX 560-2 LOONEY TUNES COLLECTION: ROAD RUNNER AND WILE E. COYOTE
Comments: Handcrafted, 3-1/2" tall
The crafty coyote has a special gift for the road runner. Watch out! There's a wire attached. **Artist:** Robert Chad
☐ Purchased 19___ Pd $_______ MIB NB DB BNT
☐ Want Orig. Ret. $12.95 **NB** $10 **MIB** Sec. Mkt. **$24-$28**

QX 534-3 LOONEY TUNES COLLECTION: SPEEDY GONZALES
Comments: Handcrafted, 1-5/8" tall
Speedy is hoping to get even more zip... on his red skis.
Artist: Don Palmiter
☐ Purchased 19___ Pd $_______ MIB NB DB BNT
☐ Want Orig. Ret. $8.95 **NB** $8 **MIB** Sec. Mkt. **$14-$20**

QX 560-5 LOONEY TUNES COLLECTION: TASMANIAN DEVIL
Comments: Handcrafted, 2-3/8" tall
Taz is getting ready for Christmas -- right now he's all tangled up in the lights. It was very popular with Taz collectors and sold out early. It continues to be sought after. **Artist:** Don Palmiter
☐ Purchased 19___ Pd $_______ MIB NB DB BNT
☐ Want Orig. Ret. $8.95 **NB** $30 **MIB** Sec. Mkt. **$48-$55**

QX 534-6 LOONEY TUNES COLLECTION: YOSEMITE SAM
Comments: Handcrafted, 2-7/16" tall
Yosemite Sam is jumpin' up and down with Christmas joy, a candy cane in each hand. **Artist:** Don Palmiter
☐ Purchased 19___ Pd $_______ MIB NB DB BNT
☐ Want Orig. Ret. $8.95 **NB** $8 **MIB** Sec. Mkt. **$14-$18**

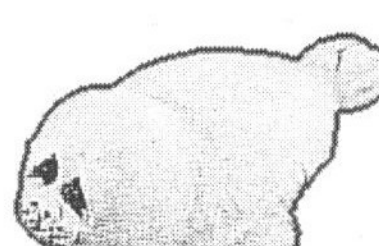

QX 545-6 LOU RANKIN SEAL
Comments: Handcrafted, 1-1/8" tall
Lou Rankin's distinctive artistry is shown in this clip-on ornament.
Artist: Ron Bishop
☐ Purchased 19___ Pd $_______ MIB NB DB BNT
☐ Want Orig. Ret. $9.95 **NB** $9 **MIB** Sec. Mkt. **$16-$20**

QX 481-3 LUCINDA AND TEDDY
Comments: Special Edition, Handcrafted/Fabric, 2-1/2" tall
Dated 1994. Lucinda shares a Christmas gift with her favorite teddy. **Artist:** Duane Unruh
☐ Purchased 19___ Pd $_______ MIB NB DB BNT
☐ Want Orig. Ret. $21.75 **NB** $18 **MIB** Sec. Mkt. **$35-$40**

QX 588-3 MAGIC CARPET RIDE
Comments: Handcrafted, 1-7/8" tall, Dated 1994
Santa with his bag of toys is making his Christmas Eve rounds without his reindeer... he's flying on a magic carpet.
Artist: Ed Seale
☐ Purchased 19___ Pd $_______ MIB NB DB BNT
☐ Want Orig. Ret. $7.95 **NB** $9 **MIB** Sec. Mkt. **$24-$26**

QXC 483-6 MAJESTIC DEER: KEEPSAKE CLUB
Comments: Limited Edition. Wood Display Stand
Hand-Painted Fine Porcelain/Pewter, 3-3/4" tall
A white deer with pewter horns leaps gracefully among the branches of your tree. Available to Club Members only.
Artist: Duane Unruh
☐ Purchased 19___ Pd $_______ MIB NB DB BNT
☐ Want Orig. Ret. $25.00 **MIB** Sec. Mkt. **$28-$30**

QX 540-3 MAKING IT BRIGHT
Comments: Handcrafted, 3-5/16" tall, Dated 1994
An squirrel paints his name in bright red on the side of a silver mail box.
Artist: Dill Rhodus
☐ Purchased 19___ Pd $_______ MIB NB DB BNT
☐ Want Orig. Ret. $8.95 **MIB** Sec. Mkt. **$10-$15**

QX 241-6 MARY ENGELBREIT
Comments: Gold Glass Ball, 2-7/8" dia., Dated 1994
Snowmen circle the ball along with the caption, "Let It Snow."
☐ Purchased 19___ Pd $_______ MIB NB DB BNT
☐ Want Orig. Ret. $5.00 **NB** $3 **MIB** Sec. Mkt. **$8-$10**

QX 527-6 MARY'S ANGELS: JASMINE
Comments: **Seventh in Series,** Handcrafted, 2-7/8" tall
A sweet angel dangles a star from her perch atop a cloud.
Artist: Robert Chad
☐ Purchased 19___ Pd $_______ MIB NB DB BNT
☐ Want Orig. Ret. $6.95 **MIB** Sec. Mkt. **$14-$18**

QLX 750-3 MAXINE
Comments: Blinking lights, Handcrafted, 4" tall
Dated 1994. Maxine has gotten her Christmas lights out and is preparing to decorate for the holidays. **Artist:** Linda Sickman
☐ Purchased 19___ Pd $_______ MIB NB DB BNT
☐ Want Orig. Ret. $20.00 **MIB** Sec. Mkt. **$30-$35**

QX 591-3 MERRY FISHMAS
Comments: Handcrafted, 2-1/8" tall, Dated 1994
This little fellow is feeding the line from his bobber through the eye of the brass hook. **Artist:** Don Palmiter
☐ Purchased 19___ Pd $_______ MIB NB DB BNT
☐ Want Orig. Ret. $8.95 **MIB** Sec. Mkt. **$14-$16**

QX 525-6 MERRY OLDE SANTA
Comments: **Fifth in Series,** Handcrafted, 4-3/16" tall
Dated 1994. Santa with a lantern, wreath and tree.
Artist: Robert Chad
☐ Purchased 19___ Pd $_______ MIB NB DB BNT
☐ Want Orig. Ret. $14.95 **NB** $15 **MIB** Sec. Mkt. **$28-$35**

QX 599-6 MISTLETOE SURPRISE
Comments: Handcrafted, 1-15/16" tall, 1-9/16" tall, Dated 1994
Set of two hang-together ornaments. A little mouse hangs overhead with mistletoe, setting the stage for a surprise kiss below.
Artist: Ed Seale
☐ Purchased 19___ Pd $_______ MIB NB DB BNT
☐ Want Orig. Ret. $12.95 **MIB** Sec. Mkt. **$22-$28**

QX 546-6 MOM
Comments: Handcrafted, 2-5/16" tall, Dated 1994
The "Most Outstanding Mom" now has a trophy to prove it!
Artist: Anita Marra Rogers
☐ Purchased 19___ Pd $_______ MIB NB DB BNT
☐ Want Orig. Ret. $7.95 **MIB** Sec. Mkt. **$10-$14**

QX 566-6 MOM AND DAD
Comments: Handcrafted, 2-15/16" tall, Dated 1994
I see mommy kissing daddy, all dressed up like Santa Claus.
Artist: Bob Siedler
☐ Purchased 19___ Pd $_______ MIB NB DB BNT
☐ Want Orig. Ret. $9.95 **NB** $9 **MIB** Sec. Mkt. **$14-$18**

QX 550-6 MOM-TO-BE
Comments: Handcrafted, 2-1/2" tall, Dated 1994
Midnight cravings never seem to be satisfied, as the soon to be mama lion is finding herself a late-night snack. **Artist:** Sharon Pike
☐ Purchased 19___ Pd $_______ MIB NB DB BNT
☐ Want Orig. Ret. $7.95 **NB** $8 **MIB** Sec. Mkt. **$14-$18**

QX 521-3 MOTHER GOOSE: HEY DIDDLE, DIDDLE
Comments: **Second in Series,** Handcrafted, 2-1/2" tall
Dated 1994. This hasn't been a widely popular series so far. Caption: "Hey diddle, diddle, the cat and the fiddle, the cow jumped over the moon." **Artist:** Ed Seale
☐ Purchased 19___ Pd $_______ MIB NB DB BNT
☐ Want Orig. Ret. $13.95 **NB** $15 **MIB** Sec. Mkt. **$35-$40**

QX 528-3 MR. AND MRS. CLAUS: A HANDWARMING PRESENT
Comments: **Ninth in Series,** Handcrafted, 3-1/4" tall
Dated 1994. "To Santa." Santa receives a pair of mittens from a loving Mrs. Claus. **Artist:** Duane Unruh
☐ Purchased 19___ Pd $_______ MIB NB DB BNT
☐ Want Orig. Ret. $14.95 **NB** $14 **MIB** Sec. Mkt. **$24-$28**

QX 554-6 NEPHEW
Comments: Handcrafted, 1-13/16" tall, Dated 1994
Santa comes to wish nephew a very merry Christmas.
Artist: John Francis (Collin)
☐ Purchased 19___ Pd $_______ MIB NB DB BNT
☐ Want Orig. Ret. $7.95 **NB** $8 **MIB** Sec. Mkt. **$12-$14**

QX 566-3 NEW HOME
Comments: Handcrafted, 2-5/16" tall, Dated 1994
The residents of this acorn home are ready for the holidays as seen by the window box of poinsettias and the wreath on the door. A plaque on the home says, "New Home 1994."
Artist: Patricia Andrews
☐ Purchased 19___ Pd $_______ MIB NB DB BNT
☐ Want Orig. Ret. $8.95 **NB** $7 **MIB** Sec. Mkt. **$15-$18**

QX 554-3 NIECE
Comments: Handcrafted, 1-1/2" tall, Dated 1994
Mrs. Santa is bringing a special doll to her niece in a cart pulled by a happy reindeer. **Artist:** John Francis (Collin)
☐ Purchased 19___ Pd $_______ MIB NB DB BNT
☐ Want Orig. Ret. $7.95 **NB** $6 **MIB** Sec. Mkt. **$14-$18**

QX 241-3 NORMAN ROCKWELL ART
Comments: White Glass Ball, 2-7/8" dia., Dated 1994
Captions: "Post Cover December 29, 1956" and "Christmas 1994. Norman Rockwell "Bottom Drawer." A famous cover from The Saturday Evening Post." **Artist:** Joyce Lyle
☐ Purchased 19___ Pd $_______ MIB NB DB BNT
☐ Want Orig. Ret. $5.00 **NB** $3 **MIB** Sec. Mkt. **$10-$12**

QX 528-6 NOSTALGIC HOUSES AND SHOPS: NEIGHBORHOOD DRUGSTORE
Comments: **Eleventh in Series,** Handcrafted, 4-1/16" tall
Dated 1994. A pharmacy and soda fountain are part of this drugstore. **Artist:** Donna Lee
☐ Purchased 19___ Pd $_______ MIB NB DB BNT
☐ Want Orig. Ret. $14.95 **NB** $12 **MIB** Sec. Mkt. **$25-$28**

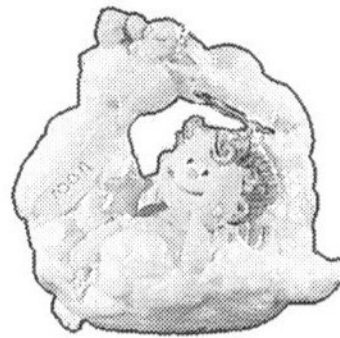

QXC 485-3 ON CLOUD NINE: KEEPSAKE CLUB
Comments: Handcrafted, 2-1/16" tall, Dated 1994
A little angel relaxes on a cloud. Available to Club Members only.
Artist: Donna Lee
☐ Purchased 19___ Pd $_______ MIB NB DB BNT
☐ Want Orig. Ret. $12.00 **NB** $10 **MIB** Sec. Mkt. **$18-$20**

QX 569-6 OPEN-AND-SHUT HOLIDAY
Comments: Handcrafted, 3-5/16" tall, Dated 1994
What better gift for a business associate. The file drawer opens to find a Christmas surprise inside. **Artist:** Bob Siedler
☐ Purchased 19___ Pd $_______ MIB NB DB BNT
☐ Want Orig. Ret. $9.95 **NB** $9 **MIB** Sec. Mkt. **$18-$22**

QX 481-6 OUR CHRISTMAS TOGETHER
Comments: Handcrafted, 2-3/8" tall, Dated 1994
A pair of flocked redbirds cuddle together. Their nest of holly leaves clips to the tree. **Artist:** Anita Marra Rogers
☐ Purchased 19___ Pd $_______ MIB NB DB BNT
☐ Want Orig. Ret. $9.95 **NB** $8 **MIB** Sec. Mkt. **$18-$20**

QX 557-6 OUR FAMILY: PHOTOHOLDER
Comments: Handcrafted, 3-5/8" dia., Dated 1994
White poinsettias, gold bells and a red bow on a bright green wreath form a frame for a favorite family photograph. Caption: "The wonderful meaning of Christmas is found in the circle of family love."
Artist: Patricia Andrews
☐ Purchased 19___ Pd $_______ MIB NB DB BNT
☐ Want Orig. Ret. $7.95 **NB** $5 **MIB** Sec. Mkt. **$12-$14**

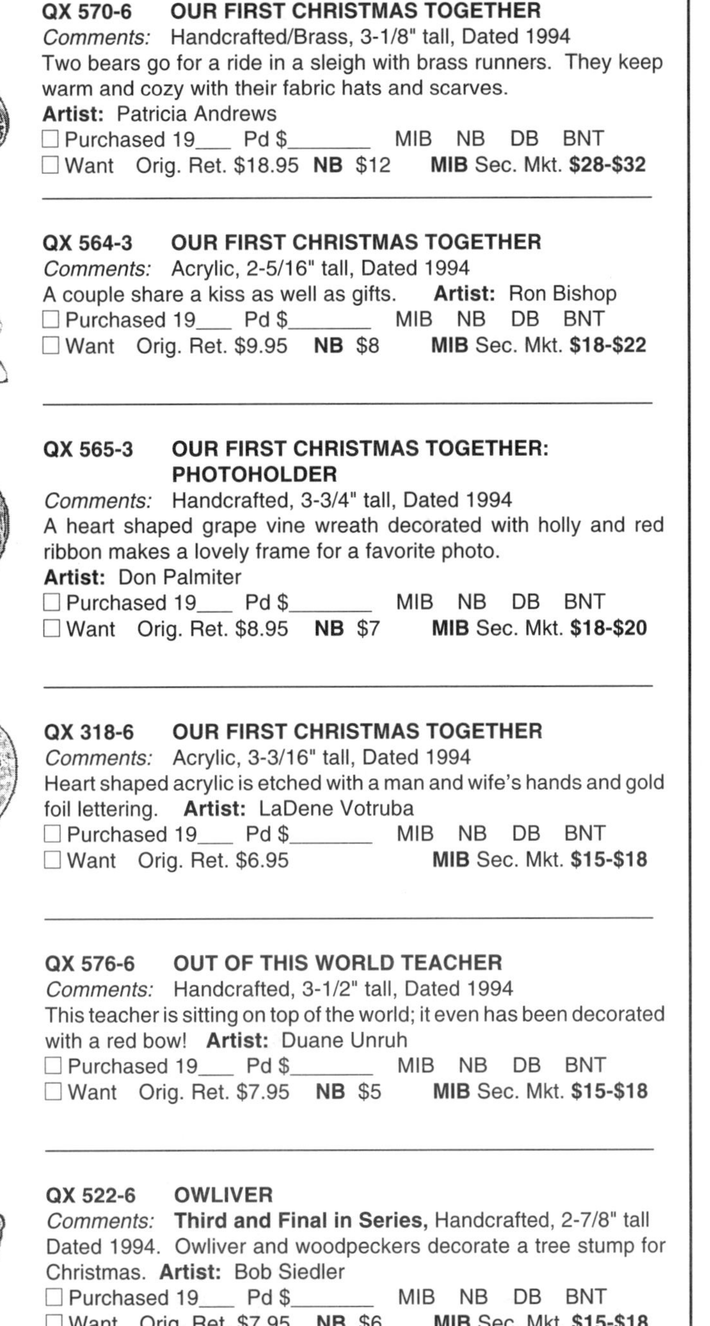

QX 570-6 OUR FIRST CHRISTMAS TOGETHER
Comments: Handcrafted/Brass, 3-1/8" tall, Dated 1994
Two bears go for a ride in a sleigh with brass runners. They keep warm and cozy with their fabric hats and scarves.
Artist: Patricia Andrews
☐ Purchased 19___ Pd $_______ MIB NB DB BNT
☐ Want Orig. Ret. $18.95 **NB** $12 **MIB** Sec. Mkt. **$28-$32**

QX 564-3 OUR FIRST CHRISTMAS TOGETHER
Comments: Acrylic, 2-5/16" tall, Dated 1994
A couple share a kiss as well as gifts. **Artist:** Ron Bishop
☐ Purchased 19___ Pd $_______ MIB NB DB BNT
☐ Want Orig. Ret. $9.95 **NB** $8 **MIB** Sec. Mkt. **$18-$22**

QX 565-3 OUR FIRST CHRISTMAS TOGETHER: PHOTOHOLDER
Comments: Handcrafted, 3-3/4" tall, Dated 1994
A heart shaped grape vine wreath decorated with holly and red ribbon makes a lovely frame for a favorite photo.
Artist: Don Palmiter
☐ Purchased 19___ Pd $_______ MIB NB DB BNT
☐ Want Orig. Ret. $8.95 **NB** $7 **MIB** Sec. Mkt. **$18-$20**

QX 318-6 OUR FIRST CHRISTMAS TOGETHER
Comments: Acrylic, 3-3/16" tall, Dated 1994
Heart shaped acrylic is etched with a man and wife's hands and gold foil lettering. **Artist:** LaDene Votruba
☐ Purchased 19___ Pd $_______ MIB NB DB BNT
☐ Want Orig. Ret. $6.95 **MIB** Sec. Mkt. **$15-$18**

QX 576-6 OUT OF THIS WORLD TEACHER
Comments: Handcrafted, 3-1/2" tall, Dated 1994
This teacher is sitting on top of the world; it even has been decorated with a red bow! **Artist:** Duane Unruh
☐ Purchased 19___ Pd $_______ MIB NB DB BNT
☐ Want Orig. Ret. $7.95 **NB** $5 **MIB** Sec. Mkt. **$15-$18**

QX 522-6 OWLIVER
Comments: **Third and Final in Series,** Handcrafted, 2-7/8" tall Dated 1994. Owliver and woodpeckers decorate a tree stump for Christmas. **Artist:** Bob Siedler
☐ Purchased 19___ Pd $_______ MIB NB DB BNT
☐ Want Orig. Ret. $7.95 **NB** $6 **MIB** Sec. Mkt. **$15-$18**

QLX 740-6 PEANUTS®
Comments: **Fourth in Series,** Flickering Light, Handcrafted 4-1/8" tall, Dated 1994. Snoopy and Woodstock ring their bells under a flickering street lamp. **Artist:** Dill Rhodus
☐ Purchased 19___ Pd $_______ MIB NB DB BNT
☐ Want Orig. Ret. $20.00 **NB** $14 **MIB** Sec. Mkt. **$38-$42**

QX 520-3 PEANUTS GANG®: LUCY
Comments: **Second in Series,** Handcrafted, 2-7/16" tall Dated 1994. Lucy has a special gift for good old Charlie Brown.
Artist: Ron Bishop
☐ Purchased 19___ Pd $_______ MIB NB DB BNT
☐ Want Orig. Ret. $9.95 **NB** $9 **MIB** Sec. Mkt. **$18-$22**

QLX 742-3 PEEKABOO PUP
Comments: Motion, Handcrafted, 3-7/8" tall, Dated 1994
The lid on the basket is opening... who is it? It's a cute little pup playing his favorite game! **Artist:** Anita Marra Rogers
☐ Purchased 19___ Pd $_______ MIB NB DB BNT
☐ Want Orig. Ret. $20.00 **NB** $15 **MIB** Sec. Mkt. **$28-$30**

QX 586-3 PRACTICE MAKES PERFECT
Comments: Handcrafted, 2-5/16" tall, Dated 1994
It takes a lot of practice to perfect a tennis game but this little pup is willing to work at it. **Artist:** Don Palmiter
☐ Purchased 19___ Pd $_______ MIB NB DB BNT
☐ Want Orig. Ret. $8.95 **NB** $6 **MIB** Sec. Mkt. **$14-$16**

QX 525-3 PUPPY LOVE
Comments: **Fourth in Series,** Handcrafted with Brass Tag 2-5/16" tall, Dated 1994. A white puppy is entangled in garland.
Artist: Anita Marra Rogers
☐ Purchased 19___ Pd $_______ MIB NB DB BNT
☐ Want Orig. Ret. $7.95 **NB** $8 **MIB** Sec. Mkt. **$12-$15**

QX 584-3 RED HOT HOLIDAY
Comments: Handcrafted, 2-5/8" tall, Dated 1994
This would be a great gift for the fireman in your life. He comes prepared in his red fire chief's cap and fire extinguisher.
Artist: Anita Marra Rogers
☐ Purchased 19___ Pd $_______ MIB NB DB BNT
☐ Want Orig. Ret. $7.95 **NB** $7 **MIB** Sec. Mkt. **$15-$18**

QX 592-6 REINDEER PRO
Comments: Handcrafted, 3-3/16" tall, Dated 1994
This reindeer golfer is set to play, rain or shine. **Artist:** Dill Rhodus
☐ Purchased 19___ Pd $_______ MIB NB DB BNT
☐ Want Orig. Ret. $7.95 **NB** $7 **MIB** Sec. Mkt. **$14-$16**

QX 535-6 RELAXING MOMENT
Comments: Handcrafted, 2-9/16" tall, Dated 1994
Santa's taking a break with his favorite beverage – Coca-Cola – as a little fawn sleeps at the base of his chair. **Artist:** John Francis
☐ Purchased 19___ Pd $_______ MIB NB DB BNT
☐ Want Orig. Ret. $14.95 **NB** $14 **MIB** Sec. Mkt. **$24-$28**

QLX 740-3 ROCK CANDY MINER
Comments: Flickering Light, Handcrafted, 2-5/8" tall, Dated 94
This little gopher is pleased with his progress. He's mined a cart full of sweet candy from the Rock Candy Mine. **Artist:** Bob Siedler
☐ Purchased 19___ Pd $_______ MIB NB DB BNT
☐ Want Orig. Ret. $20.00 **NB** $15 **MIB** Sec. Mkt. **$38-$42**

QX 501-6 ROCKING HORSE
Comments: **Fourteenth in Series,** Handcrafted, 3" tall
Dated 1994. Dark brown with white stockings and brown tail.
Artist: Linda Sickman
☐ Purchased 19___ Pd $_______ MIB NB DB BNT
☐ Want Orig. Ret. $10.95 **NB** $10 **MIB** Sec. Mkt. **$20-$24**

QX 545-3 SANTA'S LEGO® SLEIGH
Comments: Handcrafted, 1-13/16" tall, Dated 1994
Santa is making his Christmas deliveries this year in a sleigh built from LEGO® blocks! Another Lego® ornament debut in '95!
Artist: Ken Crow
☐ Purchased 19___ Pd $_______ MIB NB DB BNT
☐ Want Orig. Ret. $10.95 **NB** $8 **MIB** Sec. Mkt. **$22-$25**

QLX 747-3 SANTA'S SING-ALONG
Comments: Light and Music, Handcrafted, 3-15/16" tall
Dated 1994. Caption: "Sing Along with Santa." Santa is announcing his arrival with his calliope. Plays *Santa Claus Is Coming To Town.*
Artist: Ken Crow
☐ Purchased 19___ Pd $_______ MIB NB DB BNT
☐ Want Orig. Ret. $24.00 **NB** $22 **MIB** Sec. Mkt. **$50-$55**

XPR 945-0 SARAH, PLAIN AND TALL COLLECTION, THE: COUNTRY CHURCH, THE
Comments: Handcrafted, 5" tall, Dated 1994
This white-framed, shake-shingled church was where Sarah and Jacob danced for the first time and later married.
☐ Purchased 19___ Pd $_______ MIB NB DB BNT
☐ Want Orig. Ret. $7.95 with any Hallmark Purchase.
MIB Sec. Mkt. **$18-$20**

XPR 945-2 SARAH, PLAIN AND TALL COLLECTION, THE: HAYS TRAIN STATION, THE
Comments: Handcrafted, 5" tall, Dated 1994
Sarah arrived from Maine by train; here at the old train station she met Jacob Witting.
☐ Purchased 19___ Pd $_______ MIB NB DB BNT
☐ Want Orig. Ret. $7.95 with any Hallmark Purchase.
MIB Sec. Mkt. **$16-$18**

XPR 945-1 SARAH, PLAIN AND TALL COLLECTION, THE: MRS. PARKLEY'S GENERAL STORE
Comments: Handcrafted, 5" tall, Dated 1994
People met here at the General Store and heard the latest news as they purchased food, dry goods and other provisions.
☐ Purchased 19___ Pd $_______ MIB NB DB BNT
☐ Want Orig. Ret. $7.95 with any Hallmark Purchase.
MIB Sec. Mkt. **$15-$18**

XPR 945-4 SARAH, PLAIN AND TALL COLLECTION, THE: SARAH'S MAINE HOME
Comments: Handcrafted, 5" tall, Dated 1994
Sarah lived here off the coast of Maine with her maiden aunts - Mattie, Harriet, and Lou.
☐ Purchased 19___ Pd $_______ MIB NB DB BNT
☐ Want Orig. Ret. $7.95 with any Hallmark Purchase.
MIB Sec. Mkt. **$20-$25**

XPR 945-3 SARAH, PLAIN AND TALL COLLECTION, THE: SARAH'S PRAIRIE HOME
Comments: Handcrafted, 5" tall, Dated 1994
Sarah, a mail order bride, came to Kansas to live here with Jacob and his children, Anna and Caleb.
☐ Purchased 19___ Pd $_______ MIB NB DB BNT
☐ Want Orig. Ret. $7.95 with any Hallmark Purchase.
MIB Sec. Mkt. **$18-$22**

QX 573-6 SECRET SANTA
Comments: Handcrafted, 2-5/8" tall, Dated 1994
Who is that masked puppy with reindeer antlers? Why, it's your pal, Secret Santa! We've had several reports of ornaments being found with the caption, "From Your Secret Pal." **Artist:** Duane Unruh
☐ Purchased 19___ Pd $_______ MIB NB DB BNT
☐ Want Orig. Ret. $7.95 **NB** $6 **MIB** Sec. Mkt. **$10-$12**

QX 551-3 SISTER
Comments: Handcrafted, 2-1/8" tall, Dated 1994
A "Simply Incredible Sister" is really cool in her hot pink convertible. **Artist:** Sharon Pike
☐ Purchased 19___ Pd $_______ MIB NB DB BNT
☐ Want Orig. Ret. $6.95 **NB** $6 **MIB** Sec. Mkt. **$10-$12**

QX 553-3 SISTER TO SISTER
Comments: Handcrafted, 3-1/4" tall, Dated 1994
Two sisters spend Christmas together inside an acorn. Caption: "Sisters Fill Christmas With Joy." **Artist:** Dill Rhodus
☐ Purchased 19___ Pd $_______ MIB NB DB BNT
☐ Want Orig. Ret. $9.95 **NB** $8 **MIB** Sec. Mkt. **$18-$22**

QX 562-6 SON
Comments: Handcrafted, 3-3/16" tall, Dated 1994
What better fun could there be than to skateboard through the holidays? **Artist:** Patricia Andrews
☐ Purchased 19___ Pd $_______ MIB NB DB BNT
☐ Want Orig. Ret. $6.95 **NB** $5 **MIB** Sec. Mkt. **$12-$14**

QX 560-6 SPECIAL CAT: PHOTOHOLDER
Comments: Acrylic, 3-1/4" tall, Dated 1994
Kitty gets a place of honor at last... inside the fish bowl!
Artist: Dill Rhodus
☐ Purchased 19___ Pd $_______ MIB NB DB BNT
☐ Want Orig. Ret. $7.95 **NB** $6 **MIB** Sec. Mkt. **$10-$12**

QX 560-3 SPECIAL DOG: PHOTOHOLDER
Comments: Handcrafted, 1-13/16" tall, Dated 1994
The "Canine Edition" newspaper features your pet as the Dog of the Year. **Artist:** Dill Rhodus
☐ Purchased 19___ Pd $_______ MIB NB DB BNT
☐ Want Orig. Ret. $7.95 **NB** $8 **MIB** Sec. Mkt. **$14-$16**

QX 570-3 STAMP OF APPROVAL
Comments: Handcrafted, 1-15/16" tall, Dated 1994
Little elves help to convey their special message ASAP, "A Santa-Approved Person." **Artist:** Linda Sickman
☐ Purchased 19___ Pd $_______ MIB NB DB BNT
☐ Want Orig. Ret. $7.95 **NB** $6 **MIB** Sec. Mkt. **$14-$16**

QLX 138-6 STAR TREK®: THE NEXT GENERATION KLINGON BIRD OF PREY™
Comments: Flickering and Glowing Lights, Handcrafted 2-1/8" tall, Stardated 1994. The Klingon battle cruiser joins the line-up of space craft from The Next Generation. **Artist:** Lynn Norton
☐ Purchased 19___ Pd $_______ MIB NB DB BNT
☐ Want Orig. Ret. $24.00 **NB** $35 **MIB** Sec. Mkt. **$45-$50**

QX 580-3 SWEET GREETING
Comments: Handcrafted, 1-1/2" tall, 1-3/4" tall, Dated 1994
Set of two hang-together ornaments. Busy kittens decorate a sugar cookie greeting for the tree. **Artist:** Don Palmiter
☐ Purchased 19___ Pd $_______ MIB NB DB BNT
☐ Want Orig. Ret. $10.95 **MIB** Sec. Mkt. **$18-$20**

QX 244-3 TALE OF PETER RABBIT, THE: BEATRIX POTTER
Comments: White Glass Ball, 2-7/8" dia. Dated 1994
Caption: "Once upon a time there were four little rabbits and their names were Flopsy, Mopsy, Cotton-tail and Peter."
☐ Purchased 19___ Pd $_______ MIB NB DB BNT
☐ Want Orig. Ret. $5.00 **NB** $ 4.50 **MIB** Sec. Mkt. **$12-$14**

QX 569-3 THICK 'N' THIN
Comments: Handcrafted, 2" tall, Clip-on orn. Dated 1994
Two bears share a pizza. Caption: "Friends Stand by You Through Thick and Thin!" **Artist:** Anita Marra Rogers
☐ Purchased 19___ Pd $_______ MIB NB DB BNT
☐ Want Orig. Ret. $10.95 **NB** $10 **MIB** Sec. Mkt. **$15-$18**

QX 586-6 THRILL A MINUTE
Comments: Handcrafted, 3-11/16" tall, Dated 1994
This skier is in for a thrill, no matter which direction he travels! His destinations include "Look Out," "Earth's Edge" and "No Way."
Artist: Bob Siedler
☐ Purchased 19___ Pd $_______ MIB NB DB BNT
☐ Want Orig. Ret. $8.95 **NB** $8 **MIB** Sec. Mkt. **$14-$16**

QX 581-3 TIME OF PEACE
Comments: Handcrafted, 2-9/16" tall, Dated 1994
A lion and lamb stand together in an engraved oval which proclaims "Peace." This ornament resembles hand-carved wood.
Artist: Patricia Andrews
☐ Purchased 19___ Pd $_______ MIB NB DB BNT
☐ Want Orig. Ret. $7.95 **NB** $7 **MIB** Sec. Mkt. **$14-$18**

QX 522-3 TOBIN FRALEY CAROUSEL
Comments: **Third in Series,** Porcelain and Brass, 5-1/4" tall
Dated 1994. Collectors questioned the fact that all the horses in this series are white.
Artist: Tobin Fraley
☐ Purchased 19___ Pd $_______ MIB NB DB BNT
☐ Want Orig. Ret. $28 **NB** $28 **MIB** Sec. Mkt. **$45-$50**

QLX 749-6 TOBIN FRALEY HOLIDAY CAROUSEL
Comments: ***FIRST IN SERIES,*** Light and Music, Handcrafted 4-15/16" tall, Dated 1994. A nostalgic carousel is decorated with Santa faces. Plays *Skater's Waltz.* **Artist:** Duane Unruh
☐ Purchased 19___ Pd $_______ MIB NB DB BNT
☐ Want Orig. Ret. $32.00 **NB** $35 **MIB** Sec. Mkt. **$60-$65**

QX 564-6 TOU CAN LOVE
Comments: Handcrafted, 3" tall, Dated 1994
A pair of gaily colored toucans stand together on a gift.
Caption: "TOU-CAN make Christmas more fun!"
Artist: Anita Marra Rogers
☐ Purchased 19___ Pd $_______ MIB NB DB BNT
☐ Want Orig. Ret. $8.95 **NB** $8 **MIB** Sec. Mkt. **$15-$20**

QX 318-3 TWELVE DAYS OF CHRISTMAS: ELEVEN PIPERS PIPING
Comments: **Eleventh in Series,** Acrylic, 3-3/8" tall
Dated 1994. A Scotsman in his kilt plays his bagpipe, adding to the Christmas merriment.
☐ Purchased 19___ Pd $_______ MIB NB DB BNT
☐ Want Orig. Ret. $6.95 **NB** $5 **MIB** Sec. Mkt. **$10-$12**

QX 520-6 U.S. CHRISTMAS STAMPS
Comments: **Second in Series,** Enamel on Copper, 2-5/16" tall
Dated 1994. Caption: "Christmas 1994 Children Trimming Tree. Designer: Dollie Tingle Date of Issuance: Oct. 28, 1982; Place of Issuance: Snow, OK." This series ended with the '95 ornament.
☐ Purchased 19___ Pd $_______ MIB NB DB BNT
☐ Want Orig. Ret. $10.95 **NB** $12 **MIB** Sec. Mkt. **$25-$28**

QLX 744-3 VERY MERRY MINUTES
Comments: Light and Motion, Handcrafted, 4-5/16" tall
Dated 1994. One little mouse sleeps atop the clock as another swings playfully on the pendulum. **Artist:** LaDene Votruba
☐ Purchased 19___ Pd $_______ MIB NB DB BNT
☐ Want Orig. Ret. $24.00 **NB** $30 **MIB** Sec. Mkt. **$45-$50**

QLX 746-3 WHITE CHRISTMAS
Comments: Flickering Light/Music, Handcrafted, 3-3/16" tall
Dated 1994. The world may be covered in white but all is warm and cozy inside. Plays *White Christmas.* **Artist:** Donna Lee
☐ Purchased 19___ Pd $_______ MIB NB DB BNT
☐ Want Orig. Ret. $28.00 **NB** $40 **MIB** Sec. Mkt. **$55-$60**

QX 574-6 WINNIE THE POOH AND TIGGER
Comments: Handcrafted, 2-1/2" tall
A very excitable, bouncy Tigger has just jumped on Winnie the Pooh, putting him on his back. **Artist:** Bob Siedler
☐ Purchased 19___ Pd $_______ MIB NB DB BNT
☐ Want Orig. Ret. $12.95 **NB** $15 **MIB** Sec. Mkt. **$30-$35**

QLX 749-3 WINNIE THE POOH PARADE
Comments: Motion and Music, Handcrafted, 4-1/8" tall
Dated 1994. Pooh twirls as the gang parades around him; Tigger spins on his tail. Plays *Winnie the Pooh* theme. **Artist:** Ken Crow
☐ Purchased 19___ Pd $_______ MIB NB DB BNT
☐ Want Orig. Ret. $32.00 **NB** $40 **MIB** Sec. Mkt. **$55-$60**

QX 544-6 WIZARD OF OZ COLLECTION, THE: COWARDLY LION, THE
Comments: Handcrafted, 3-9/16" tall
The Cowardly Lion searches for courage with his tail in his hands.
Artist: Patricia Andrews
☐ Purchased 19___ Pd $_______ MIB NB DB BNT
☐ Want Orig. Ret. $9.95 **NB** $12 **MIB** Sec. Mkt. **$25-$28**

QX 543-3 WIZARD OF OZ COLLECTION, THE: DOROTHY AND TOTO
Comments: Handcrafted, 3-9/16" tall
Dorothy carries Toto in her arm as she skips down the yellow brick road. **Artist:** Joyce Lyle
☐ Purchased 19___ Pd $_______ MIB NB DB BNT
☐ Want Orig. Ret. $10.95 **NB** $20 **MIB** Sec. Mkt. **45-$48**

QX 543-6 WIZARD OF OZ COLLECTION, THE: SCARECROW
Comments: Handcrafted, 3-7/8" tall
Scarecrow looks as if he has been plucked from the fence post. **Artist:** Duane Unruh
☐ Purchased 19___ Pd $_______ MIB NB DB BNT
☐ Want Orig. Ret. $9.95 **NB** $15 **MIB** Sec. Mkt. **$28-$30**

QX 544-3 WIZARD OF OZ COLLECTION, THE: TIN MAN
Comments: Handcrafted, 3-13/16" tall
The tin man is reproduced in great detail; he even has his trusty axe. **Artist:** Duane Unruh
☐ Purchased 19___ Pd $_______ MIB NB DB BNT
☐ Want Orig. Ret. $9.95 **NB** $14 **MIB** Sec. Mkt. **$28-$32**

QX 531-6 YULETIDE CENTRAL: LOCOMOTIVE
Comments: ***FIRST IN SERIES,*** Pressed Tin, 2-9/16" tall, Dated 1994. This series will feature different train components and not just locomotives, as in the Tin Locomotive series of the past. **Artist:** Linda Sickman
☐ Purchased 19___ Pd $_______ MIB NB DB BNT
☐ Want Orig. Ret. $18.95 **NB** $40 **MIB** Sec. Mkt. **$45-$52**

Hallmark Keepsake Personalized Ornaments

No sales found in '94 or '95 on these ornaments. Any ornament with personal message is unlikely to bring a significant secondary market price. An ornament with a more general message may obtain a secondary market value faster. In my opinion, Reindeer Rooters with a message of "Hey, Santa we want to ride too" or "Hey, Hey it takes eight to pull a sleigh," would complement the Cheery Cyclists ornament.

1994

QP 603-5 BABY BLOCK
Comments: Handcrafted Photoholder, 2-13/16" tall
Reissued from 1993. **Artist:** John Francis (Collin)
☐ Purchased 19___ Pd $_______ MIB NB DB BNT
☐ Want Orig. Ret. $14.95 No Personalization
MIB Sec. Mkt. **$15-$18**

QP 604-6 COMPUTER CAT 'N MOUSE
Comments: Handcrafted, 2-3/4" tall
A kitten eyes the "mouse" gleefully from atop a computer screen which displays your Christmas message. **Artist:** Ed Seale
☐ Purchased 19___ Pd $_______ MIB NB DB BNT
☐ Want Orig. Ret. $12.95 **NB** $8 **MIB** Sec. Mkt. **$10-$12**

QP 607-3 COOKIE TIME
Comments: Handcrafted, 3-1/8" tall
This iced sugar cookie will be a hit on any Christmas tree. Your message appears as red icing. Yum, yum! **Artist:** LaDene Votruba
☐ Purchased 19___ Pd $_______ MIB NB DB BNT
☐ Want Orig. Ret. $12.95 **NB** $8 **MIB** Sec. Mkt. **$10-$12**

QP 600-6 ETCH-A-SKETCH®
Comments: Handcrafted, 2-1/4" tall
A little bear plays happily with his Etch-A-Sketch® and shows off his greeting. **Artist:** Ken Crow
☐ Purchased 19___ Pd $_______ MIB NB DB BNT
☐ Want Orig. Ret. $12.95 **NB** $8 **MIB** Sec. Mkt. **NE**

QP 602-5 FESTIVE ALBUM PHOTOHOLDER
Comments: Handcrafted Photoholder, 7-7/16" tall
Reissued from 1993. Similiar to the '95 (Premiered in July.) **Artist:** LaDene Votruba
☐ Purchased 19___ Pd $_______ MIB NB DB BNT
☐ Want Orig. Ret. $12.95 **MIB** Sec. Mkt. **$12-$14**

QP 603-6 FROM THE HEART
Comments: Handcrafted, 1-15/16" tall
A little raccoon has written his greeting in a heart carved in a snow covered tree stump. **Artist:** Dill Rhodus
☐ Purchased 19___ Pd $_______ MIB NB DB BNT
☐ Want Orig. Ret. $24.95 **MIB** Sec. Mkt. **NE**

QP 602-3 GOIN' FISHIN'
Comments: Handcrafted, 3" tall
A fisherman's tackle basket is a great spot for a little chipmunk to wish happy holidays. **Artist:** Don Palmiter
☐ Purchased 19___ Pd $_______ MIB NB DB BNT
☐ Want Orig. Ret. $14.95 **MIB** Sec. Mkt. **NE**

QP 601-2 GOING GOLFIN'
Comments: Handcrafted, 2-13/16" tall
Reissued from 1993. **Artist:** Don Palmiter
☐ Purchased 19___ Pd $__9____ MIB NB DB BNT
☐ Want Orig. Ret. $12.75 **MIB** Sec. Mkt. **$10-$12**

My wife told me not to come back until I got the latest issue of *The Ornament Collector,* but I can't even find the car!

QXR 611-6 HOLIDAY HELLO
Comments: Handcrafted, Recordable, 4-1/2" tall
Just press the button to record your own holiday message on this battery operated telephone. **Artist:** Bob Siedler
☐ Purchased 19___ Pd $_______ MIB NB DB BNT
☐ Want Orig. Ret. $24.95 **MIB** Sec. Mkt. **NE**

QP 601-5 MAILBOX DELIVERY
Comments: Handcrafted, 1-7/8" tall
Introduced in 1993, reissued in '94 and '95. **Artist:** Ken Crow
☐ Purchased 19___ Pd $_______ MIB NB DB BNT
☐ Want Orig. Ret. $14.95 **MIB** Sec. Mkt. **$10-$12**

QP 606-6 NOVEL IDEA
Comments: Handcrafted, 2-7/16" tall
A little mouse points out a special message written in the pages of a red book. **Artist:** LaDene Votruba
☐ Purchased 19___ Pd $_______ MIB NB DB BNT
☐ Want Orig. Ret. $12.95 **MIB** Sec. Mkt. **NE**

QP 602-2 ON THE BILLBOARD
Comments: Handcrafted, 2-1/8" tall
Introduced in 1993, reissued in '94 and '95. **Artist:** Ken Crow
☐ Purchased 19___ Pd $_______ MIB NB DB BNT
☐ Want Orig. Ret. $12.95 **MIB** Sec. Mkt. **$10-$12**

QP 603-2 PLAYING BALL
Comments: Handcrafted, 3-11/16" tall
Introduced in 1993, reissued in '94 and '95.
Artist: John Francis (Collin)
☐ Purchased 19___ Pd $_______ MIB NB DB BNT
☐ Want Orig. Ret. $12.95 **MIB** Sec. Mkt. **$10-$12**

QP 605-6 REINDEER ROOTERS
Comments: Handcrafted, 2-15/16" tall
Four happy reindeer, with a megaphone and waving banner, will help to send your Christmas greeting. In our opinion, this ornament with a cute saying that complements the '94 Cherry Cyclists ornament found on page 192 may obtain a secondary value faster. Reissued in '95. **Artist:** Ken Crow
☐ Purchased 19___ Pd $_______ MIB NB DB BNT
☐ Want Orig. Ret. $12.95 **MIB** Sec. Mkt. **NE**

QP 600-5 SANTA SAYS
Comments: Handcrafted, 2-15/16" tall
Introduced in 1993, reissued in '94. **Artist:** Ed Seale
☐ Purchased 19___ Pd $_______ MIB NB DB BNT
☐ Want Orig. Ret. $14.95 **MIB** Sec. Mkt. **$12-$15**

Hallmark Keepsake Showcase Ornaments

Christmas Lights - 1994

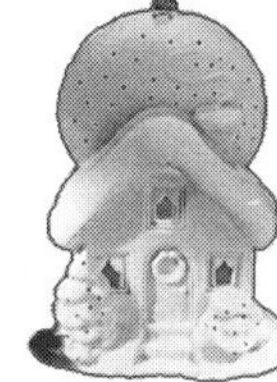

QK 112-3 HOME FOR THE HOLIDAYS
Comments: Porcelain Bisque, Lighted, 4-1/16" tall, Dated 1994
Smoke rises from a snow covered cottage and light glows through the windows. **Artist:** Don Palmiter
☐ Purchased 19___ Pd $_______ MIB NB DB BNT
☐ Want Orig. Ret. $15.75 **NB** $15 **MIB** Sec. Mkt. **$22-$28**

QK 111-6 MOONBEAMS
Comments: Porcelain Bisque, Lighted, 4-5/16" tall, Dated 1994
A star with a moon cut-out dangles from the top of a quarter moon. Light streams from the pin-hole design of this sleepy moon.
Artist: Patricia Andrews
☐ Purchased 19___ Pd $_______ MIB NB DB BNT
☐ Want Orig. Ret. $15.75 **NB** $15 **MIB** Sec. Mkt. **$22-$28**

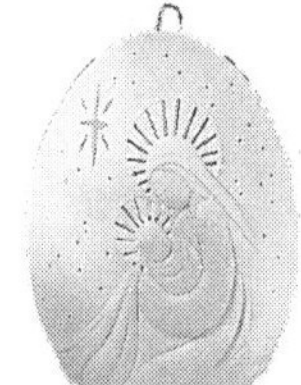

QK 112-6 MOTHER AND CHILD
Comments: Porcelain Bisque, Lighted, 3-1/2" tall, Dated 1994
A bright shining star stands above the Madonna, attending to her Holy Child. **Artist:** Anita Marra Rogers
☐ Purchased 19___ Pd $_______ MIB NB DB BNT
☐ Want Orig. Ret. $15.75 **NB** $20 **MIB** Sec. Mkt. **$28-$35**

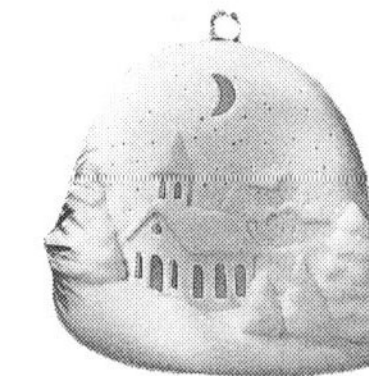
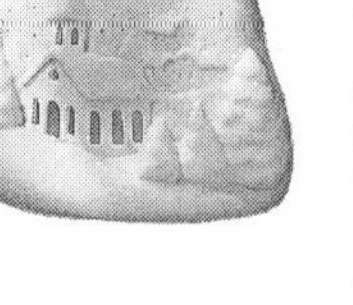

QK 110-6 PEACEFUL VILLAGE
Comments: Porcelain Bisque, Lighted, 2-13/16" tall, Dated 1994
Soft light illuminates the church in this snow covered village. Includes gold ribbon. **Artist:** Robert Chad
☐ Purchased 19___ Pd $_______ MIB NB DB BNT
☐ Want Orig. Ret. $15.75 **NB** $18 **MIB** Sec. Mkt. **$22-$28**

Folk Art Americana - 1994

QK 118-3 CATCHING 40 WINKS
Comments: Wood Look, 1-7/8" tall, Dated 1994
An elf settles down for a quick snooze among the brightly wrapped packages. **Artist:** Linda Sickman
☐ Purchased 19___ Pd $_______ MIB NB DB BNT
☐ Want Orig. Ret. $16.75 **NB** $12 **MIB** Sec. Mkt. **$24-$28**

QK 116-6 GOING TO TOWN
Comments: Wood Look, 2-7/16" tall, Dated 1994
Pouches filled with grain, an elf heads to market with his best "pack pig." **Artist:** Linda Sickman
☐ Purchased 19___ Pd $_______ MIB NB DB BNT
☐ Want Orig. Ret. $15.75 **NB** $14 **MIB** Sec. Mkt. **$24-$28**

QK 117-3 RACING THROUGH THE SNOW
Comments: Wood Look, 3-1/16" tall, Dated 1994
An elf races through the winter landscape astride a rooster on snowshoes. **Artist:** Linda Sickman
☐ Purchased 19___ Pd $_______ MIB NB DB BNT
☐ Want Orig. Ret. $15.75 **NB** $15 **MIB** Sec. Mkt. **$28-$30**

QK 119-3 RARIN' TO GO
Comments: Wood Look, 2-11/16" tall, Dated 1994
Hang on tight! This elf is in store for a quick hop through the forest atop a long-eared rabbit. **Artist:** Linda Sickman
☐ Purchased 19___ Pd $_______ MIB NB DB BNT
☐ Want Orig. Ret. $15.75 **NB** $15 **MIB** Sec. Mkt. **$35-$40**

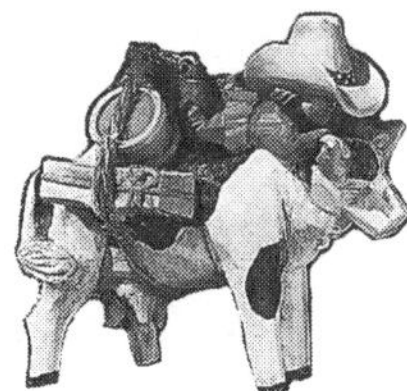

QK 117-6 ROUNDUP TIME
Comments: Wood Look, 2-11/16" tall, Dated 1994
Wrapped gifts have been tied to this fellow's unique transportation... a cow. Let's get "mooo...ving"; Christmas is just around the corner. **Artist:** Linda Sickman
☐ Purchased 19___ Pd $_______ MIB NB DB BNT
☐ Want Orig. Ret. $16.75 **NB** $14 **MIB** Sec. Mkt. **$20-$25**

Holiday Favorites - 1994

QK 105-3 DAPPER SNOWMAN
Comments: Crackled Porcelain, 3-5/8" tall, Dated 1994
This dapper fellow is highlighted with blue accents and a striped candy cane. Includes blue ribbon. **Artist:** LaDene Votruba
☐ Purchased 19___ Pd $_______ MIB NB DB BNT
☐ Want Orig. Ret. $13.75 **NB** $12 **MIB** Sec. Mkt. **$18-$20**

QK 103-3 GRACEFUL FAWN
Comments: Crackled Porcelain, 2-11/16" tall, Dated 1994
Delicately painted blue leaves circle the fawn's neck. Includes blue ribbon. **Artist:** LaDene Votruba
☐ Purchased 19___ Pd $_______ MIB NB DB BNT
☐ Want Orig. Ret. $11.75 **NB** $10 **MIB** Sec. Mkt. **$16-$18**

QK 104-6 JOLLY SANTA
Comments: Crackled Porcelain, 3-11/16" tall, Dated 1994
Santa is chuckling a happy "ho, ho, ho!" He's wearing red striped mittens and is holding a miniature tree. Includes red ribbon. **Artist:** LaDene Votruba
☐ Purchased 19___ Pd $_______ MIB NB DB BNT
☐ Want Orig. Ret. $13.75 **NB** $12 **MIB** Sec. Mkt. **$22-$26**

QK 103-6 JOYFUL LAMB
Comments: Crackled Porcelain, 2-5/16" tall, Dated 1994
A green garland graces the neck of a serene lamb. Includes green ribbon. **Artist:** LaDene Votruba
☐ Purchased 19___ Pd $_______ MIB NB DB BNT
☐ Want Orig. Ret. $11.75 **NB** $12 **MIB** Sec. Mkt. **$18-$20**

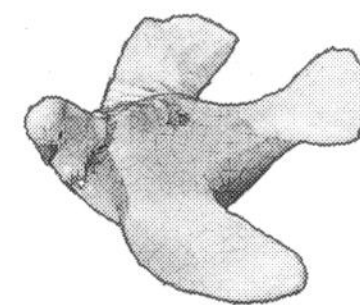

QK 104-3 PEACEFUL DOVE
Comments: Crackled Porcelain, 3-5/8" tall, Dated 1994
Trimmed in blue, this graceful dove will add a touch of grace to any tree. Includes blue ribbon. **Artist:** LaDene Votruba
☐ Purchased 19___ Pd $_______ MIB NB DB BNT
☐ Want Orig. Ret. $11.75**NB** $12 **MIB** Sec. Mkt. **$16-$22**

Old-World Silver - 1994

QK 102-6 SILVER BELLS
Comments: Silver-Plated, 3-3/16" tall, Dated 1994
Silver bells ring out the joy of Christmas, depicted in a filigree design. **Artist:** Duane Unruh
☐ Purchased 19___ Pd $_______ MIB NB DB BNT
☐ Want Orig. Ret. $24.75 **NB** $22 **MIB** Sec. Mkt. **$28-$30**

QK 102-3 SILVER BOWS
Comments: Silver-Plated, 3-5/16" tall, Dated 1994
Delicate bows add a touch of beauty to this intricate old-world ornament. **Artist:** Don Palmiter
☐ Purchased 19___ Pd $_______ MIB NB DB BNT
☐ Want Orig. Ret. $24.75 **NB** $22 **MIB** Sec. Mkt. **$30-$35**

QK 100-6 SILVER POINSETTIA
Comments: Silver-Plated, 3-1/8" tall, Dated 1994
A finely detailed poinsetta provides the focal point for this diamond shaped ornament. **Artist:** Duane Unruh
☐ Purchased 19___ Pd $_______ MIB NB DB BNT
☐ Want Orig. Ret. $24.75 **NB** $22 **MIB** Sec. Mkt. **$34-$38**

QK 101-6 SILVER SNOWFLAKES
Comments: Silver-Plated, 3-1/16" tall, Dated 1994
Intricate snowflake designs circle the ornament.
Artist: Duane Unruh
☐ Purchased 19___ Pd $_______ MIB NB DB BNT
☐ Want Orig. Ret. $24.75 **NB** $22 **MIB** Sec. Mkt. **$30-$35**

"My Christmas Angel Ornament just arrived. I'm glad they sent it airmail."

Meet Hallmark's Keepsake Creative Staff!

1. Anne Breece
2. Jim Durgin
3. Julie Parmer George
4. Dill Rhodus
5. Diana McGehee
6. Linda Sickman
7. Peggy Sixta
8. Jack Perry
9. Anita Marra Rogers
10. Ken Crow
11. Sharon Pike
12. Patricia Andrews
13. Jack Benson
14. Joyce Lyle
15. LaDene Votruba
16. Lynn Norton
17. Patti Streeper
18. Bob Siedler
19. Karla Schiller
20. Ed Seale
21. Duane Unruh
22. John "Collin" Francis
23. Don Palmiter
24. Robert Chad

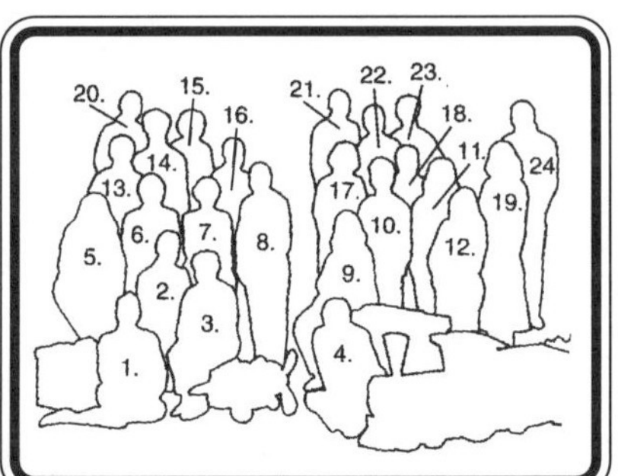

1995 Collection

Insure at these prices in 1996

QXC 416-7 1958 FORD EDSEL CITATION CONVERTIBLE: KEEPSAKE CLUB

Comments: Handcrafted, 2-3/8" tall, Dated 1995
Complements the Classic American Car Series. Price could go to $100 easily if not "stockpiled" by Club Members. Will indeed be a good money maker for the wise investor. **Artist:** Don Palmiter
☐ Purchased 19___ Pd $_______ MIB NB DB BNT
☐ Want Orig. Ret. $12.95 **MIB** Sec. Mkt. **$50-$75 up**

QX 592-9 ACORN 500

Comments: Handcrafted, 1-7/8" tall, Dated '95
A speedy chipmunk pulls into the winner's circle in his bright red race car waving the victory flag. Caption: " '95 Good Cheer."
Artist: Bob Siedler
☐ Purchased 19___ Pd $_______ MIB NB DB BNT
☐ Want Orig. Ret. $10.95 **MIB** Sec. Mkt. **$10-$12**

QX 584-7 ACROSS THE MILES

Comments: Handcrafted, 2-1/8", Dated 1995
"How many miles will I travel tonight?" wonders Santa chipmunk. The arrow on this clip-on ornament moves in the compass. Caption: "Across the Miles."
Artist: John Francis
☐ Purchased 19___ Pd $_______ MIB NB DB BNT
☐ Want Orig. Ret. $8.95 **MIB** Sec. Mkt. **$10-$12**

QX 597-7 AIR EXPRESS

Comments: Handcrafted, 1-5/16" tall, Dated '95
Flying through the skies, this chipmunk makes sure Santa's letters get to him on time. Caption: "Air Express."
Artist: Ed Seale
☐ Purchased 19___ Pd $_______ MIB NB DB BNT
☐ Want Orig. Ret. $7.95 **MIB** Sec. Mkt. **$8-$12**

QX 552-7 ALL-AMERICAN TRUCKS: 1956 FORD TRUCK

Comments: ***FIRST IN SERIES.*** Handcrafted, 1-3/4" tall Dated 1995. Celebrate Christmas with a tree and a shiny new Ford truck. Wheels turn. Will the truck series be as popular as the Classic American Car Series? Not sure-time will tell. **Artist:** Don Palmiter
☐ Purchased 19___ Pd $_______ MIB NB DB BNT
☐ Want Orig. Ret. $13.95 **MIB** Sec. Mkt. **$35-$40**

QX 581-9 ANNIVERSARY YEAR: PHOTOHOLDER

Comments: Handcrafted, Dated 1995
Place a picture of you and your loved one in this beautiful heart shaped anniversary year photo holder, which may be personalized 10 ways. **Artist:** Duane Unruh
☐ Purchased 19___ Pd $_______ MIB NB DB BNT
☐ Want Orig. Ret. $8.95 **MIB** Sec. Mkt. **$10-$12**

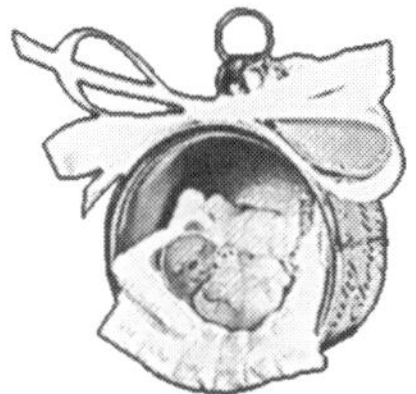

QX 554-7 BABY'S FIRST CHRISTMAS

Comments: Handcrafted and silver plate, 2-5/8" tall, Dated 1995
Baby bear dreams about sugar plums as she awaits her first Christmas. This piece is dated and has a silver tag that may be engraved. Caption: "Baby's First Christmas." **Artist:** Patricia Andrews
☐ Purchased 19___ Pd $_______ MIB NB DB BNT
☐ Want Orig. Ret. $18.95 **MIB** Sec. Mkt. **$22-$28**

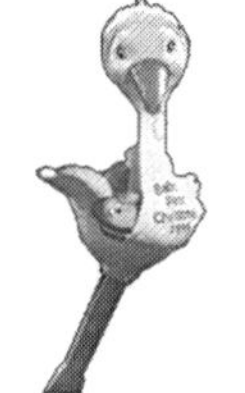

QX 555-7 BABY'S FIRST CHRISTMAS

Comments: Handcrafted, 3-11/16" tall, Dated 1995
Mr. Stork has flown a long way to surprise the new parents with this bundle of joy. Caption: "Baby's First Christmas"
Artist: Patricia Andrews
☐ Purchased 19___ Pd $_______ MIB NB DB BNT
☐ Want Orig. Ret. $9.95 **MIB** Sec. Mkt. **$12-$15**

QLX 731-7 BABY'S FIRST CHRISTMAS

Comments: Handcrafted Light, Music and Motion, 4-7/16" tall, Dated 1995 This lighted ornament is shaped like a baby's bottle. The rocking chair rocks as music plays "Rock-a-Bye, Baby."
Artist: Ken Crow
☐ Purchased 19___ Pd $_______ MIB NB DB BNT
☐ Want Orig. Ret. $22.00 **MIB** Sec. Mkt. **$22-$28**

QX 555-9 BABY'S FIRST CHRISTMAS: TEDDY BEAR YEARS COLLECTION

Comments: Handcrafted, 2-3/16" tall, Dated '95
Baby celebrates its first Christmas with a stocking and star-shaped Christmas cookie. Design is repeated from 1994. Caption: "Baby's 1st Christmas." **Artist:** Ken Crow
☐ Purchased 19___ Pd $_______ MIB NB DB BNT
☐ Want Orig. Ret. $7.95 **MIB** Sec. Mkt. **$16-$20**

QX 231-9 BABY'S FIRST CHRISTMAS - BABY BOY

Comments: White Glass Ball, 2-7/8" dia., Dated 1995
These cheerful bouncing baby boys dance around enjoying the spirit of Christmas. Caption: "Baby's First Christmas: A Baby Boy brightens your world with wonder and joy."
☐ Purchased 19___ Pd $_______ MIB NB DB BNT
☐ Want Orig. Ret. $5.00 **MIB** Sec. Mkt. **$5-$6**

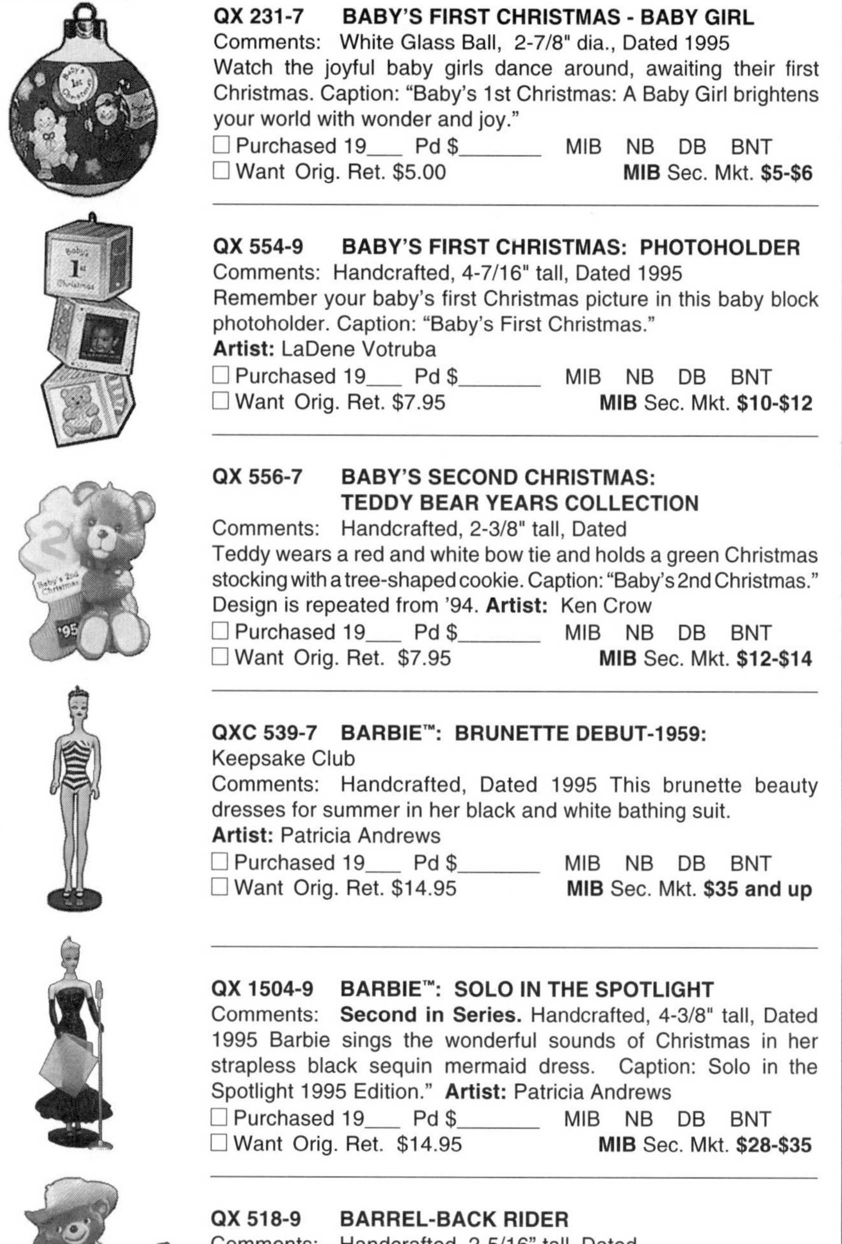

QX 231-7 BABY'S FIRST CHRISTMAS - BABY GIRL
Comments: White Glass Ball, 2-7/8" dia., Dated 1995
Watch the joyful baby girls dance around, awaiting their first Christmas. Caption: "Baby's 1st Christmas: A Baby Girl brightens your world with wonder and joy."
☐ Purchased 19___ Pd $_______ MIB NB DB BNT
☐ Want Orig. Ret. $5.00 **MIB** Sec. Mkt. **$5-$6**

QX 554-9 BABY'S FIRST CHRISTMAS: PHOTOHOLDER
Comments: Handcrafted, 4-7/16" tall, Dated 1995
Remember your baby's first Christmas picture in this baby block photoholder. Caption: "Baby's First Christmas."
Artist: LaDene Votruba
☐ Purchased 19___ Pd $_______ MIB NB DB BNT
☐ Want Orig. Ret. $7.95 **MIB** Sec. Mkt. **$10-$12**

QX 556-7 BABY'S SECOND CHRISTMAS: TEDDY BEAR YEARS COLLECTION
Comments: Handcrafted, 2-3/8" tall, Dated
Teddy wears a red and white bow tie and holds a green Christmas stocking with a tree-shaped cookie. Caption: "Baby's 2nd Christmas." Design is repeated from '94. **Artist:** Ken Crow
☐ Purchased 19___ Pd $_______ MIB NB DB BNT
☐ Want Orig. Ret. $7.95 **MIB** Sec. Mkt. **$12-$14**

QXC 539-7 BARBIE™: BRUNETTE DEBUT-1959:
Keepsake Club
Comments: Handcrafted, Dated 1995 This brunette beauty dresses for summer in her black and white bathing suit.
Artist: Patricia Andrews
☐ Purchased 19___ Pd $_______ MIB NB DB BNT
☐ Want Orig. Ret. $14.95 **MIB** Sec. Mkt. **$35 and up**

QX 1504-9 BARBIE™: SOLO IN THE SPOTLIGHT
Comments: **Second in Series.** Handcrafted, 4-3/8" tall, Dated 1995 Barbie sings the wonderful sounds of Christmas in her strapless black sequin mermaid dress. Caption: Solo in the Spotlight 1995 Edition." **Artist:** Patricia Andrews
☐ Purchased 19___ Pd $_______ MIB NB DB BNT
☐ Want Orig. Ret. $14.95 **MIB** Sec. Mkt. **$28-$35**

QX 518-9 BARREL-BACK RIDER
Comments: Handcrafted, 2-5/16" tall, Dated
Cowboy bear is ready for the rodeo! **Artist:** John Francis
☐ Purchased 19___ Pd $_______ MIB NB DB BNT
☐ Want Orig. Ret. $9.95 **MIB** Sec. Mkt. **$10-$12**

QX 502-9 BASEBALL HEROES: LOU GEHRIG
Comments: **Second in Series,** Handcrafted, 3-3/8" diameter, Dated Caption: "Lou Gehrig '95, 2,130 Consecutive Games American League MVP 1927, Batting Triple Crown 1934, .340 Lifetime Batting Average, Elected to Hall of Fame 1939."
Artist: Dill Rhodus
☐ Purchased 19___ Pd $_______ MIB NB DB BNT
☐ Want Orig. Ret. $12.95 **MIB** Sec. Mkt. **$18-$20**

QX 573-9 BATMOBILE
Comments: Handcrafted, 1-1/16" tall, Dated
Batman and Robin rush off in their Batmobile to rescue Gotham City.
Artist: Don Palmiter
☐ Purchased 19___ Pd $_______ MIB NB DB BNT
☐ Want Orig. Ret. $14.95 **MIB** Sec. Mkt. **$16-$20**

QX 541-7 BETTY AND WILMA: THE FLINTSTONES®
Comments: Handcrafted and Dated. Betty and Wilma are headed home from their Christmas shopping spree. **Artist:** Dill Rhodus
☐ Purchased 19___ Pd $_______ MIB NB DB BNT
☐ Want Orig. Ret. $14.95 **MIB** Sec. Mkt. **$16-$18**

QX 525-9 BEVERLY AND TEDDY: SPECIAL EDITION
Comments: Handcrafted, 2-7/8" tall, Dated 1995
Beverly and Teddy enjoy the true Christmas spirit. Caption: "Carols."
Artist: Duane Unruh
☐ Purchased 19___ Pd $_______ MIB NB DB BNT
☐ Want Orig. Ret. $21.75 **MIB** Sec. Mkt. **$22-$26**

QX 591-9 BINGO BEAR
Comments: Handcrafted, 2-3/4" tall, Dated '95
Bingo! Mr. Bear wins with the diagonal 1995. Caption: "Bingo."
Artist: LaDene Votruba
☐ Purchased 19___ Pd $_______ MIB NB DB BNT
☐ Want Orig. Ret. $7.95 **MIB** Sec. Mkt. **$14-$18**

QX 587-9 BOBBIN' ALONG
Comments: Handcrafted, 2-1/4" tall, Dated '95
Bucky beaver takes a nap on a mallard decoy, while hoping to catch his dinner at the same time. **Artist:** Ken Crow
☐ Purchased 19___ Pd $_______ MIB NB DB BNT
☐ Want Orig. Ret. $8.95 **MIB** Sec. Mkt. **$14-$18**

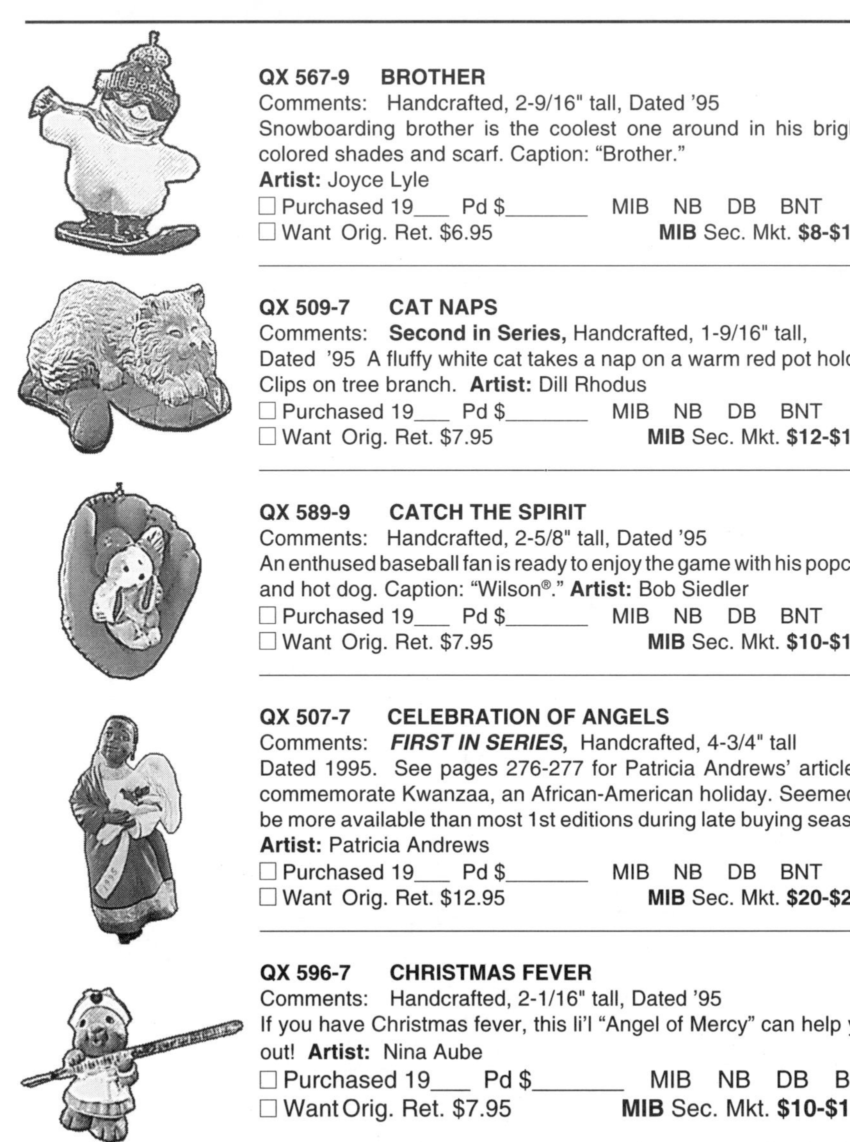

QX 567-9 BROTHER
Comments: Handcrafted, 2-9/16" tall, Dated '95
Snowboarding brother is the coolest one around in his brightly colored shades and scarf. Caption: "Brother."
Artist: Joyce Lyle
☐ Purchased 19___ Pd $_______ MIB NB DB BNT
☐ Want Orig. Ret. $6.95 **MIB** Sec. Mkt. **$8-$12**

QX 509-7 CAT NAPS
Comments: **Second in Series,** Handcrafted, 1-9/16" tall, Dated '95 A fluffy white cat takes a nap on a warm red pot holder. Clips on tree branch. **Artist:** Dill Rhodus
☐ Purchased 19___ Pd $_______ MIB NB DB BNT
☐ Want Orig. Ret. $7.95 **MIB** Sec. Mkt. **$12-$14**

QX 589-9 CATCH THE SPIRIT
Comments: Handcrafted, 2-5/8" tall, Dated '95
An enthused baseball fan is ready to enjoy the game with his popcorn and hot dog. Caption: "Wilson®." **Artist:** Bob Siedler
☐ Purchased 19___ Pd $_______ MIB NB DB BNT
☐ Want Orig. Ret. $7.95 **MIB** Sec. Mkt. **$10-$14**

QX 507-7 CELEBRATION OF ANGELS
Comments: ***FIRST IN SERIES,*** Handcrafted, 4-3/4" tall Dated 1995. See pages 276-277 for Patricia Andrews' article to commemorate Kwanzaa, an African-American holiday. Seemed to be more available than most 1st editions during late buying season.
Artist: Patricia Andrews
☐ Purchased 19___ Pd $_______ MIB NB DB BNT
☐ Want Orig. Ret. $12.95 **MIB** Sec. Mkt. **$20-$25**

QX 596-7 CHRISTMAS FEVER
Comments: Handcrafted, 2-1/16" tall, Dated '95
If you have Christmas fever, this li'l "Angel of Mercy" can help you out! **Artist:** Nina Aube
☐ Purchased 19___ Pd $_______ MIB NB DB BNT
☐ Want Orig. Ret. $7.95 **MIB** Sec. Mkt. **$10-$14**

QX 563-7 CHILD'S FIFTH CHRISTMAS: TEDDY BEAR YEARS COLLECTION
Comments: Handcrafted, 2-3/8" tall, Dated '95
Any five year old will love this special ornament. Design is repeated from '89. **Artist:** Dill Rhodus
☐ Purchased 19___ Pd $_______ MIB NB DB BNT
☐ Want Orig. Ret.$6.95 **MIB** Sec. Mkt. **$8-$10**

QX 562-9 CHILD'S FOURTH CHRISTMAS: TEDDY BEAR YEARS COLLECTION
Comments: Handcrafted, 3" tall, Dated '95
Toddler black and white teddy smiles cheerfully as he holds a red, green and white numeral 4. Caption: "My 4th Christmas." Design is repeated from '89. **Artist:** John Francis
☐ Purchased 19___ Pd $_______ MIB NB DB BNT
☐ Want Orig. Ret. $6.95 **MIB** Sec. Mkt. **$8-$10**

QX 562-7 CHILD'S THIRD CHRISTMAS: TEDDY BEAR YEARS COLLECTION
Comments: Handcrafted, 2-9/16" tall, Dated '95
Teddy holds onto his stocking filled with a frosted bell shaped cookie with the numeral 3 written on it. Caption: "My 3rd Christmas."
Artist: Ken Crow
☐ Purchased 19___ Pd $_______ MIB NB DB BNT
☐ Want Orig. Ret. $7.95 **MIB** Sec. Mkt. **$8-$12**

QLX 730-7 CHRIS MOUSE TREE
Comments: **Eleventh in Series,** Lighted, Handcrafted, 3-5/8" tall, Dated 1995 Chris Mouse climbs to the top of his cheese tree to put his gold star on top. The tree glows. **Artist:** Anita Marra Rogers
☐ Purchased 19___ Pd $_______ MIB NB DB BNT
☐ Want Orig. Ret. $12.50 **MIB** Sec. Mkt. **$14-$18**

QX 599-7 CHRISTMAS MORNING
Comments: Handcrafted, 3-5/16" tall, Dated 1995
Christmas morning just before the rush! Caption: "How Bright Joys of Christmas, How Warm the Memories." **Artist:** John Francis
☐ Purchased 19___ Pd $_______ MIB NB DB BNT
☐ Want Orig. Ret. $10.95 **MIB** Sec. Mkt. **$12-$14**

QX 595-9 CHRISTMAS PATROL
Comments: Handcrafted, 2-1/8" tall, Dated 1995
Do you have the Christmas blues? This little car won't let you, he'll pull you over and ticket you for being a scrooge.
Artist: Patricia Andrews
☐ Purchased 19___ Pd $_______ MIB NB DB BNT
☐ Want Orig. Ret. $7.95 **MIB** Sec. Mkt. **$8-$12**

QX 508-7 CHRISTMAS VISITORS: ST. NICHOLAS
Comments: ***FIRST IN SERIES,*** Handcrafted, 4-9/16" tall, Dated 1995 St. Nicolas was well known and loved in the 4th century for his kindness and love for children. His staff is brass with satin brushed finish. **Artist:** Anita Marra Rogers
☐ Purchased 19___ Pd $_______ MIB NB DB BNT
☐ Want Orig. Ret. $14.95 **MIB** Sec. Mkt. **$30-$35**

QX 523-9 CLASSIC AMERICAN CARS: 1969 CHEVROLET CAMARO
Comments: Handcrafted, 1-5/16" tall, Dated 1995
This Classic American car races down the street to get home before anyone wakes up on Christmas morning. The wheels really turn!
Artist: Don Palmiter
☐ Purchased 19___ Pd $_______ MIB NB DB BNT
☐ Want Orig. Ret. $12.95 **MIB** Sec. Mkt. **$18-$20**

QX 551-9 COLORFUL WORLD: CRAYOLA
Comments: Handcrafted, 3-3/16" tall, Dated 1995
Multi-Cultural mouse draws his friends with all the colors of the world. Caption: "Crayola® Multi-Cultural 16 Crayons (front of box), 16 Crayola® Crayons (side of box), 1995 (back of box)."
Artist: Ken Crow
☐ Purchased 19___ Pd $_______ MIB NB DB BNT
☐ Want Orig. Ret. $10.95 **MIB** Sec. Mkt. **$16-$20**

QXC 411-7 COLLECTING MEMORIES: KEEPSAKE CLUB
Comments: Handcrafted, Dated 1995
Mr. Beaver enjoys displaying his favorite Keepsake Ornaments in a wooden displayer. **Artist:** Bob Siedler
☐ Purchased 19___ Pd $_______ MIB NB DB BNT
☐ Want Membership Fee $20 **MIB** Sec. Mkt. **$18-$20**

QLX 736-9 COMING TO SEE SANTA
Comments: Handcrafted, Light, Motion and Voice 3-11/16" tall, Dated 1995 Santa says "Ho! Ho! Ho!" when the children come to see him. **Artist:** Don Palmiter
☐ Purchased 19___ Pd $_______ MIB NB DB BNT
☐ Want Orig. Ret. $32.00 **MIB** Sec. Mkt. **$35-$39**

QX 599-9 COWS OF BALI
Comments: Handcrafted, 3" tall, Dated '95
Santa's helper cow is ready for summer in his grass skirt and Christmas tree bikini top. Designed from Shoebox Greetings.
Artist: Patricia Andrews
☐ Purchased 19___ Pd $_______ MIB NB DB BNT
☐ Want Orig. Ret. $8.95 **MIB** Sec. Mkt. **$10-$12**

QX 524-7 CRAYOLA® CRAYON: BRIGHT 'N SUNNY TEPEE
Comments: **Seventh in Series,** Handcrafted, 2-11/16" tall, Dated 1995 A little Indian bear peeks out the door of his tepee to give everyone a colorful Christmas hello. Caption: "1995 Crayola® Crayons."
Artist: Patricia Andrews
☐ Purchased 19___ Pd $_______ MIB NB DB BNT
☐ Want Orig. Ret. $10.95 **MIB** Sec. Mkt. **$12-$14**

QX 564-9 DAD
Comments: Handcrafted, Dated '95
Dad is ready for Christmas as he pulls the family Christmas tree behind him. **Artist:** Bob Siedler
☐ Purchased 19___ Pd $_______ MIB NB DB BNT
☐ Want Orig. Ret. $7.95 **MIB** Sec. Mkt. **$10-$12**

QX 566-7 DAD-TO-BE
Comments: Handcrafted, 1-15/16" tall, Dated '95
The dad-to-be reads up on the latest parenting tips.
Caption: "LePaws Dad To Be."
Artist: Dill Rhodus
☐ Purchased 19___ Pd $_______ MIB NB DB BNT
☐ Want Orig. Ret. $7.95 **MIB** Sec. Mkt. **$8-$10**

QX 567-7 DAUGHTER
Comments: Handcrafted, 2-3/4" tall, Dated '95
This very sharp panda is a great student, but even she can't wait for the Christmas holiday. Caption: "Extra Sharp Daughter."
Artist: Don Palmiter
☐ Purchased 19___ Pd $_______ MIB NB DB BNT
☐ Want Orig. Ret. $6.95 **MIB** Sec. Mkt. **$7-$9**

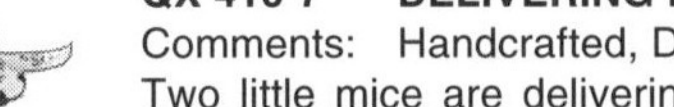

QX 410-7 DELIVERING KISSES
Comments: Handcrafted, Dated '95
Two little mice are delivering Hershey's™ Kisses to Santa to fill stockings on Christmas eve. **Artist:** Linda Sickman
☐ Purchased 19___ Pd $_______ MIB NB DB BNT
☐ Want Orig. Ret. $10.95 **MIB** Sec. Mkt. **$14-$18**

QX 600-7 DREAM ON
Comments: Handcrafted, 3-3/4" tall, Dated 1995
The want list is a little too long for Santa. Caption: "I Want."
Artist: John Francis
☐ Purchased 19___ Pd $_______ MIB NB DB BNT
☐ Want Orig. Ret. $10.95 **MIB** Sec. Mkt. **$12-$16**

QX 620-9 DUDLEY THE DRAGON
Comments: Handcrafted, 3-3/4" tall, Dated
Dudley dresses as Santa and passes out gifts to all the good little boys and girls. **Artist:** Sharon Pike
☐ Purchased 19___ Pd $_______ MIB NB DB BNT
☐ Want Orig. Ret. $10.95 **MIB** Sec. Mkt. **$12-$14**

QX 514-7 FABULOUS DECADE
Comments : **Sixth in Series**, Handcrafted, 2-5/16" tall, Dated 1995
An otter relaxes for the winter on the brass date 1995.
Artist: Ed Seale
☐ Purchased 19___ Pd $_______ MIB NB DB BNT
☐ Want Orig. Ret. $7.95 **MIB** Sec. Mkt. **$10-$14**

QX 589-7 FAITHFUL FAN
Comments: Handcrafted, 2-9/16" tall, Dated '95
This spirited beaver is cheering for his favorite team, The Snowflakes. Caption: "Go Team." **Artist:** Bob Siedler
☐ Purchased 19___ Pd $_______ MIB NB DB BNT
☐ Want Orig. Ret. $8.95 **MIB** Sec. Mkt. **$9-$12**

QX 586-9 FELIZ NAVIDAD
Comments: Handcrafted, 3-1/16" tall, Dated 1995
A mouse sends warm holiday wishes from inside his bunch of hot peppers. Caption: "Feliz Navidad." **Artist:** Dill Rhodus
☐ Purchased 19___ Pd $_______ MIB NB DB BNT
☐ Want Orig. Ret. $7.95 **MIB** Sec. Mkt. **$8-$12**

QXC 520-7 FISHING FOR FUN: KEEPSAKE CLUB
Comments: Handcrafted, Dated 1995
Santa enjoys fishing with one of his reindeer when he is not busy delivering presents. The Collectors' Club has "Arctic" misspelled on many of the ornaments as "Artic." **Artist:** Ed Seale
☐ Purchased 19___ Pd $_______ MIB NB DB BNT
☐ Want Club Fee $20 **MIB** Sec. Mkt. **$12-$16**

Photo not available at press time.

QXI 620-7 FOOTBALL LEGENDS: JOE MONTANA
Comments: Handcrafted, 4-7/16" tall
The 1995 Joe Montana ornament in the **KANSAS CITY** red, white and yellow uniform was added to the Keepsake line in direct response to consumer demand. (He played for two teams.) Secondary market price will depend on sports enthusiasts' demands for this piece. This piece was more limited than Montana in San Francisco uniform. Caption: "MONTANA 19" (back of shirt) "19" (front of shirt and on sleeve.) **Artist:** Dill Rhodus
☐ Purchased 19___ Pd $_______ MIB NB DB BNT
☐ Want Orig. Ret. $14.95 **MIB** Sec. Mkt.**$50-$75 Up**

QX 1575-9 FOOTBALL LEGENDS: JOE MONTANA
Comments: ***FIRST IN SERIES,*** Handcrafted, 4-7/16" tall Dated 1995
Joe Montana in the **SAN FRANCISCO 49ers** red and gold uniform. There are only 45 seconds in the last quarter and Joe Montana pulls back his arm and fires the winning touchdown. San Francisco's box is white. Caption: "MONTANA 16" (back of shirt) "16" (front of shirt and on sleeve.)
Artist: Dill Rhodus
☐ Purchased 19___ Pd $_______ MIB NB DB BNT
☐ Want Orig. Ret. $14.95 **MIB** Sec. Mkt. **$25-$30**

QX 572-9 FOR MY GRANDMA: PHOTOHOLDER
Comments: Handcrafted, 4-1/6" tall, Dated 1995
Keep that special picture of you and your grandma in this frosted gingerbread house picture frame. Caption: "For my grandma, I love you! From ______."
Artist: Don Palmiter
☐ Purchased 19___ Pd $_______ MIB NB DB BNT
☐ Want Orig. Ret. $6.95 **MIB** Sec. Mkt. **$8-$10**

QLX 729-9 FOREST FROLICS
Comments: **Seventh and Final in series**, Handcrafted, Motion, 4-1/8" tall. Dated 1995 The forest animals enjoy swinging back and forth on their wooden swing. Caption: "1995 Merry Christmas."
Artist: Sharon Pike
☐ Purchased 19___ Pd $_______ MIB NB DB BNT
☐ Want Orig. Ret.$28.00 **MIB** Sec. Mkt. **$35-$38**

QX 525-8 FOREVER FRIENDS BEAR
Comments: Handcrafted, 2-3/8" tall, Dated
Give your special friend a bear they will always remember you by. This bear has holly berries to share with his friends.
Artist: Andrew Brownsword
☐ Purchased 19___ Pd $_______ MIB NB DB BNT
☐ Want Orig. Ret.$8.95 **MIB** Sec. Mkt. **$14-$18**

QLX 728-9 FRED AND DINO: THE FLINTSTONES®
Comments: Light, Motion and Sound. Handcrafted, 4-11/16" tall, Dated 1995 Dino chases Fred while he calls out a holiday message: "Yabba-Dabba-Doo! Down, Dino, Down! Have a Happy Holiday."
Artist: Dill Rhodus
☐ Purchased 19___ Pd $_______ MIB NB DB BNT
☐ Want Orig. Ret. $28.00 **MIB** Sec. Mkt. **$32-$38**

An optimist is someone who tells you to cheer up when things are going their way.

QLX 734-9 FRIENDS SHARE FUN
Comments: Handcrafted, Flickering Light, 2-1/16" tall, Dated 1995
This clip-on ornament shows two little chipmunks roasting nuts over a fire. Caption: "Friends are always cooking up holiday fun."
Artist: Anita Marra Rogers
☐ Purchased 19___ Pd $_______ MIB NB DB BNT
☐ Want Orig. Ret. $16.50 **MIB** Sec. Mkt. **$22-$28**

QX 582-7 FRIENDLY BOOST
Comments: Handcrafted and Acrylic, 3-3/16" tall, Dated 1995
A little penguin gets help from his buddy putting the star atop the Christmas ice tree.
Artist: Don Palmiter
☐ Purchased 19___ Pd $_______ MIB NB DB BNT
☐ Want Orig. Ret. $8.95 **MIB** Sec. Mkt. **$10-$12**

QX 516-9 FROSTY FRIENDS
Comments: **Sixteenth is Series,** Handcrafted, 2-9/16" tall Dated 1995. A friendly eskimo takes some presents across the ice on his snowmobile with a little friend. Caption: "To Santa."
Artist: Ed Seale
☐ Purchased 19___ Pd $_______ MIB NB DB BNT
☐ Want Orig. Ret. $10.95 **MIB** Sec. Mkt. **$12-$16**

QX 500-7 GARFIELD
Comments: Handcrafted, 2-3/16" tall, Dated 1995
Garfield tries to be a sweet little angel for a minute as he toots his horn.
☐ Purchased 19___ Pd $_______ MIB NB DB BNT
☐ Want Orig. Ret.$10.95 **MIB** Sec. Mkt. **$12-$15**

QX 570-7 GODCHILD
Comments: Handcrafted, 2-3/16" tall, Dated 1995
A little bear angel with brass halo plays Christmas music for his godparents. Caption: "Godchild."
Artist: Don Palmiter
☐ Purchased 19___ Pd $_______ MIB NB DB BNT
☐ Want Orig. Ret. $7.95 **MIB** Sec. Mkt. **$8-$12**

QX 241-7 GODPARENT
Comments: White Glass Ball, 2-7/8" dia, Dated 1995
Little bear angels watch over their godparent. Caption: "A Godparent is someone special at Christmas time and always."
Artist: LaDene Votruba
☐ Purchased 19___ Pd $_______ MIB NB DB BNT
☐ Want Orig. Ret. $5.00 **MIB** Sec. Mkt. **$5-$8**

QLX 736-7 GOODY GUMBALLS!
Comments: Handcrafted, Lighted, 2-7/8" tall, Dated 1995
Two little mice raid the red gumball machine. The globe of the gumball machine glows. **Artist:** Bob Siedler
☐ Purchased 19___ Pd $_______ MIB NB DB BNT
☐ Want Orig. Ret. $12.50 **MIB** Sec. Mkt. **$18-$25**

QX 588-7 GOPHER FUN
Comments: Handcrafted, 3-1/8" tall, Dated 1995
The little gopher caddy tags along with the golfer to give him his point of view. Caption: "Score Card '95 Wilson®." **Artist:** Bob Siedler
☐ Purchased 19___ Pd $_______ MIB NB DB BNT
☐ Want Orig. Ret. $9.95 **MIB** Sec. Mkt. **$12-$15**

QX 577-7 GRANDCHILD'S FIRST CHRISTMAS

Comments: Handcrafted, 1-7/16" tall, Dated '95
This grandchild fell fast asleep waiting for Santa to come. Caption: "Grandchild's 1st Christmas." **Artist:** John Francis
☐ Purchased 19___ Pd $_______ MIB NB DB BNT
☐ Want Orig. Ret. $7.95 **MIB** Sec. Mkt. **$10-$12**

QX 577-9 GRANDDAUGHTER
Comments: Handcrafted, 2-5/16" tall, Dated 1995
Little bunny dressed up for the holidays receives a special lollipop from her grandparents. Caption: "Granddaughter-You're So Sweet."
Artist: Anita Marra Rogers
☐ Purchased 19___ Pd $_______ MIB NB DB BNT
☐ Want Orig. Ret. $6.95 **MIB** Sec. Mkt. **$10-$12**

QX 576-7 GRANDMOTHER
Comments: Handcrafted, 1-15/16" tall, Dated '95
A bluebird on the end of her watering can keeps grandma company while watering her flowers. Caption: "For Grandmother with love."
Artist: Patricia Andrews
☐ Purchased 19___ Pd $_______ MIB NB DB BNT
☐ Want Orig. Ret. $7.95 **MIB** Sec. Mkt. **$10-$12**

QX576-9 GRANDPA
Comments: Handcrafted, 3-1/16" tall, Dated
Grandpa bear pulls up a tree stump and shares a story with his grandson over warm cookies and a glass of milk.
Caption: "I ❤ Grandpa." **Artist:** Ken Crow
☐ Purchased 19___ Pd $_______ MIB NB DB BNT
☐ Want Orig. Ret. $8.95 **MIB** Sec. Mkt. **$12-$16**

QX 241-9 GRANDPARENTS
Comments: White Glass Ball, 2-7/8" Dia., Dated 1995
The picture perfect scene at grandma and grandpa's house Christmas day is shown on this dated ball. Caption: "Merry Christmas Grandparents our hearts and our lives with their love."
Artist: Joyce Lyle
☐ Purchased 19___ Pd $_______ MIB NB DB BNT
☐ Want Orig. Ret. $5.00 **MIB** Sec. Mkt. **$5-$8**

QX 578-7 GRANDSON
Comments: Handcrafted, 2-7/16" tall, Dated 1995
This happy bunny holds a most treasured "Treat" given by his grandparents. Caption: "Grandson-You're a Treat!"
Artist: Anita Marra Rogers
☐ Purchased 19___ Pd $_______ MIB NB DB BNT
☐ Want Orig. Ret. $6.95 **MIB** Sec. Mkt. **$8-$10**

QX 630-7 HAPPY HOLIDAYS: PHOTOHOLDER
Comments: Handcrafted, 3-7/16" tall
Included with this photo album is a photo of Hallmark's Keepsake artists or put your favorite photo inside. A little mouse swings from a ribbon. Was available at ornament premieres in July.
Artist: LaDene Votruba
☐ Purchased 19___ Pd $_______ MIB NB DB BNT
☐ Want Orig. Ret. $2.95 with any purchase**MIB** Sec. Mkt. **$8-$10**

QX 603-7 HAPPY WRAPPERS
Comments: Handcrafted, 2-1/8" tall, Dated 1995
Two little elves each wrap a Christmas gift for Santa.
Artist: Ken Crow
☐ Purchased 19___ Pd $_______ MIB NB DB BNT
☐ Want Orig. Ret. $10.95 **MIB** Sec. Mkt. **$14-$16**

QLX 732-7 HEADIN' HOME
Comments: Blinking Lights, Handcrafted, 1-13/16" tall, Dated 1995
Santa flies his reindeer home for the holidays in this red and white airplane. Lights glow on the inside and blink on the wings. Caption: "Polar Air." **Artist:** Julia Lee
☐ Purchased 19___ Pd $_______ MIB NB DB BNT
☐ Want Orig. Ret. $22.00 **MIB** Sec. Mkt. **$26-$30**

QX 605-7 HEAVEN'S GIFT
Comments: Handcrafted, Joseph 4-9/16" tall, Mary & Baby 2-15/16" tall, Dated 1995 The set of two ornaments rejoice in Heaven's gift of life to the world. A shepherd figurine is to debut possibly in '96. **Artist:** Patricia Andrews
☐ Purchased 19___ Pd $_______ MIB NB DB BNT
☐ Want Orig. Ret. $20.00 **MIB** Sec. Mkt. **$25-$28**

QX 517-9 HERE COMES SANTA: SANTA'S ROADSTER
Comments: **Seventeenth in Series,** Handcrafted, 2-13/16" tall, Dated 1995 Santa zooms down the road in his roadster with a Christmas tree for the Elves and Mrs. Claus to decorate. Caption: "KRUZ-N." **Artist:** Linda Sickman
☐ Purchased 19___ Pd $_______ MIB NB DB BNT
☐ Want Orig. Ret. $14.95 **MIB** Sec. Mkt. **$18-$22**

QX 591-7 HOCKEY PUP
Comments: Handcrafted, 3-5/16" tall, Dated 1995 Tucked into an oversized ice skate this Christmas dressed puppy shoots for the winning goal. Caption: "Hockey Pup 1995." **Artist:** Ken Crow
☐ Purchased 19___ Pd $_______ MIB NB DB BNT
☐ Want Orig. Ret. $9.95 **MIB** Sec. Mkt. **$10-$12**

QX 1505-7 HOLIDAY BARBIE™
Comments: **Third in Series,** Handcrafted, Dated 1995
Barbie is ready for the holiday parties in her green and white Christmas dress. She accents her gown with little silver and white bulb earrings. Caption: "Holiday Barbie™." **Artist:** Patricia Andrews
☐ Purchased 19___ Pd $_______ MIB NB DB BNT
☐ Want Orig. Ret.$14.95 **MIB** Sec. Mkt. **$22-$28**

QLX 731-9 HOLIDAY SWIM
Comments: Lighted, Handcrafted and Acrylic, 3-9/16" tall
Dated '95 Delightful aquarium glows while a festive little fish swims among seaweed decorated with red Christmas lights.
Artist: Anita Marra Rogers
☐ Purchased 19___ Pd $_______ MIB NB DB BNT
☐ Want Orig. Ret. $18.50 **MIB** Sec. Mkt. **$20-$22**

QXC105-9 HOME FROM THE WOODS: KEEPSAKE CLUB
Comments: Handcrafted, 2-1/4" tall, Dated 1995
A little man is on his way home from cutting down his Christmas tree. Complements the Folk Art Americana Collection.
Artist: Linda Sickman
☐ Purchased 19___ Pd $_______ MIB NB DB BNT
☐ Want Club Fee $15.95 **MIB** Sec. Mkt. **$22-$24**

You know you're getting older when you have to slow the aerobics tape to half-speed to keep up with the excercises.

QX 1551-7 HOOP STARS: SHAQUILLE O'NEAL
Comments: ***FIRST IN SERIES,*** Handcrafted, 5-1/2" tall, Dated It's the last possible shot as Shaq slam dunks the ball for an Orlando Magic win. Caption: "32."
☐ Purchased 19___ Pd $_______ MIB NB DB BNT
☐ Want Orig. Ret. $14.95 **MIB** Sec. Mkt. **$28-$35 up**

QX 594-7 IMPORTANT MEMO
Comments: Handcrafted, 2-3/16" tall, Dated 1995
A little mouse is exhausted from the holiday season and takes a nap under an important memo. Caption: "MEMO, Closed for the Holidays 1995." **Artist:** Linda Sickman
☐ Purchased 19___ Pd $_______ MIB NB DB BNT
☐ Want Orig. Ret. $8.95 **MIB** Sec. Mkt. **$10-$12**

QX 581-7 IN A HEARTBEAT
Comments: Handcrafted, Dated 1995
With every heartbeat these two li'l mice grow closer together. **Artist:** Patricia Andrews
☐ Purchased 19___ Pd $_______ MIB NB DB BNT
☐ Want Orig. Ret. $8.95 **MIB** Sec. Mkt. **$10-$12**

QX 604-9 IN TIME WITH CHRISTMAS
Comments: Handcrafted, 3-3/4" tall, Dated 1995
It's easy for this little violinist to keep time with the windup movement pendulum. Caption: "Music Makes Christmas Merrier." **Artist:** Ken Crow
☐ Purchased 19___ Pd $_______ MIB NB DB BNT
☐ Want Orig. Ret. $12.95 **MIB** Sec. Mkt. **$14-$18**

QX 586-7 JOY TO THE WORLD
Comments: Handcrafted, 3-15/16" tall, Dated 1995
An African-America choir boy sings the joyful sounds of Christmas carols. **Artist:** Patricia Andrews
☐ Purchased 19___ Pd $_______ MIB NB DB BNT
☐ Want Orig. Ret. $8.95 **MIB** Sec. Mkt. **$10-$14**

QLX 734-7 JUMPING FOR JOY
Comments: Handcrafted, Light and Motion, Dated 1995
Two little mice jump the barrels. The tree and lamp post light up. **Artist:** John Francis
☐ Purchased 19___ Pd $_______ MIB NB DB BNT
☐ Want Orig. Ret. $28.00 **MIB** Sec. Mkt. **$32-$38**

QX 502-7 KIDDIE CAR CLASSICS: MURRAY FIRE TRUCK
Comments: **Second in Series,** Handcrafted, 1-15/16" tall Dated 1995 This bright red fire truck is ready for any emergency. Caption: "1995 (back bumper), MURRAY 0. CLEVE. O. (on back of seat), JET FLOW DRIVE FIRE DEPT. (on sides)." This series is Hot! **Artist:** Don Palmiter
☐ Purchased 19___ Pd $_______ MIB NB DB BNT
☐ Want Orig. Ret. $13.95 **MIB** Sec. Mkt. **$28-$35**

QX 476-9 LEGO® FIREPLACE WITH SANTA
Comments: Handcrafted, 2-5/16" tall, Dated 1995
Santa comes down this Lego fireplace to find a glass of milk and cookies waiting for him. Caption: "Lego® 1995." **Artist:** Ken Crow
☐ Purchased 19___ Pd $_______ MIB NB DB BNT
☐ Want Orig. Ret. $10.95 **MIB** Sec. Mkt. **$12-$16**

QX 501-9 LOONEY TUNES: BUGS BUNNY
Comments: Handcrafted, 4-1/8" tall, Dated 1995
Our favorite mischevious Bugs Bunny is at it again! **Artist:** Robert Chad
☐ Purchased 19___ Pd $_______ MIB NB DB BNT
☐ Want Orig. Ret. $8.95 **MIB** Sec. Mkt. **$12-$16**

QX 501-7 LOONEY TUNES: SYLVESTER AND TWEETY
Comments: Handcrafted, Sylvester 4-9/16" tall Tweety 1-5/8" tall, Dated 95. Sylvester still has his eye on a Tweety for dinner. Set of 2 hang-together ornaments. **Artist:** Robert Chad
☐ Purchased 19___ Pd $_______ MIB NB DB BNT
☐ Want Orig. Ret. $13.95 **MIB** Sec. Mkt. **$18-$20**

QX 406-9 LOU RANKIN BEAR
Comments: Handcrafted, 2-5/16" tall, Dated 1995
This cute and cuddly bear is an ornament that would make anyone smile. Caption: "Rankin." **Artist:** Bob Siedler
☐ Purchased 19___ Pd $_______ MIB NB DB BNT
☐ Want Orig. Ret. $9.95 **MIB** Sec. Mkt. **$12-$15**

QX584-9 MAGIC SCHOOL BUS™, THE
Comments: Here they go again on another trip this time to the North Pole in the holiday decorated Magic School Bus.
☐ Purchased 19___ Pd $_______ MIB NB DB BNT
☐ Want Orig. Ret. $10.95 **MIB** Sec. Mkt. **$12-$14**

QX 240-9 MARY ENGELBREIT
Comments: White Glass Ball, Dated 1995
This brightly colored ball pictures a jolly Santa ready for the holiday season.
☐ Purchased 19___ Pd $_______ MIB NB DB BNT
☐ Want Orig. Ret. $5.00 **MIB** Sec. Mkt. **$6-$8**

QX 514-9 MARY'S ANGELS: CAMELLIA
Comments: **Eighth in Series,** Handcrafted/Acrylic, 2-5/8" tall
Oh, to sing like an angel... Camellia sings a duet with a feathered friend perched on her finger. Caption: "Mary." **Artist:** Robert Chad
☐ Purchased 19___ Pd $_______ MIB NB DB BNT
☐ Want Orig. Ret. $6.95 **MIB** Sec. Mkt. **$10-$14**

QX 513-9 MERRY OLDE SANTA
Comments: **Sixth in Series**, Handcrafted, 4-5/16" tall
Dated 1995 Brass bells on a gold cord enhance Santa as he carries all his goodies to children's homes. **Artist:** Patricia Andrews
☐ Purchased 19___ Pd $_______ MIB NB DB BNT
☐ Want Orig. Ret. $14.95 **MIB** Sec. Mkt. **$18-$22**

QX 602-7 MERRY RV
Comments: Handcrafted, 2-1/2" tall, Dated '95
Santa and Mrs. Claus begin their trip around the country in their holiday dressed RV on December 27th. (Santa slept all day on the 26th.) Caption: "The Claus's Merry-We-Go." **Artist:** Don Palmiter
☐ Purchased 19___ Pd $_______ MIB NB DB BNT
☐ Want Orig. Ret. $12.95 **MIB** Sec. Mkt. **$18-$20**

QX 564-7 MOM
Comments: Handcrafted, Dated '95. Mom is getting ready to decorate her Christmas tree with the popcorn she is stringing.
Artist: Bob Siedler
☐ Purchased 19___ Pd $_______ MIB NB DB BNT
☐ Want Orig. Ret. $7.95 **MIB** Sec. Mkt. **$10-$12**

QX 565-7 MOM AND DAD
Comments: Handcrafted, Dated 1995
Mom and Dad snowmen snuggle to keep warm.
Artist: Anita Marra Rogers
☐ Purchased 19___ Pd $_______ MIB NB DB BNT
☐ Want Orig. Ret. $9.95 **MIB** Sec. Mkt. **$12-$14**

QX 565-9 MOM-TO-BE
Comments: Handcrafted, Dated '95
Mom-to-be reads up on the latest bear facts about child bearing. **Artist:** Dill Rhodus
☐ Purchased 19___ Pd $_______ MIB NB DB BNT
☐ Want Orig. Ret. $7.95 **MIB** Sec. Mkt. **$10-$12**

QX 509-9 MOTHER GOOSE: JACK AND JILL
Comments: **Third in Series,** Handcrafted, 2-1/2" tall, Dated
The Mother Goose book opens to display the verse and a 3-D depiction. Caption: "Christmas 1995," "Mother Goose," "Nursery Rhymes," "Jill went up the hill ..."
Artist: Ed Seale/LaDene Votruba
☐ Purchased 19___ Pd $_______ MIB NB DB BNT
☐ Want Orig. Ret. $13.95 **MIB** Sec. Mkt. **$18-$22**

QX 515-7 MR. AND MRS. CLAUS: CHRISTMAS EVE KISS
Comments: **Tenth and Final in Series**, Handcrafted, 3-3/16" tall
Dated 1995 Mrs. Claus gives her sweetie a kiss before he heads off on his annual trip around the world. **Artist:** Duane Unruh
☐ Purchased 19___ Pd $_______ MIB NB DB BNT
☐ Want Orig. Ret. $14.95 **MIB** Sec. Mkt. **$18-$20**

QX 600-9 MULETIDE GREETINGS
Comments: Handcrafted, 3-1/16" tall, Dated 1995
Mr. Mule takes a rest from delivering gifts this holiday season. Designed from Shoebox Greetings. Caption: "Muletide Greetings."
Artist: Robert Chad
☐ Purchased 19___ Pd $_______ MIB NB DB BNT
☐ Want Orig. Ret. $7.95 **MIB** Sec. Mkt. **$10-$12**

QLX 727-9 MY FIRST HOT WHEELS™
Comments: Handcrafted 4-1/8" tall, Dated 1995
Light and motion. Children watching their Hot Wheels go 'round and 'round. Tree lights up and the car goes around the track.
Artist: Ken Crow
☐ Purchased 19___ Pd $_______ MIB NB DB BNT
☐ Want Orig. Ret. $28.00 **MIB** Sec. Mkt. **$35-$38**

A little boy looked unhappily at his dad and said, "Here's my report card... and I'm tired of watching TV anyway."

QX 583-9 NEW HOME
Comments: Handcrafted, 2-9/16" tall, Dated 1995
This cute little house dusts off the welcome mat for anyone who might come visit the new home. Caption: "Welcome New Home 1995." **Artist:** Patricia Andrews
☐ Purchased 19___ Pd $_______ MIB NB DB BNT
☐ Want Orig. Ret. $8.95 **MIB** Sec. Mkt. **$12-$14**

QX 595-7 NORTH POLE 911
Comments: Handcrafted, 3-7/8" tall, Dated '95
Fireman chipmunk is ready for any emergency. "In Case of Emergency" he can break the glass to get a candy cane. Candy cane inside box dangles. Caption: "In Case of Emergency Break Glass." **Artist:** Ed Seale
☐ Purchased 19___ Pd $_______ MIB NB DB BNT
☐ Want Orig. Ret. $10.95 **MIB** Sec. Mkt. **$12-$14**

QX 508-9 NOSTALGIC HOUSES AND SHOPS: ACCESSORIES FOR COLLECTOR'S SERIES
Comments: Handcrafted, Street Lamp: 1-9/16" tall, Evergreen 15/16" tall, Roadster: 13/16" tall, Dated
These cute accessories will add conversation to any collection of Nostaligic Houses and Shops. **Artist:** Julia Lee
☐ Purchased 19___ Pd $_______ MIB NB DB BNT
☐ Want Orig. Ret. $8.95 **MIB** Sec. Mkt. **$10-$12**

QX 515-9 NOSTALGIC HOUSES AND SHOPS: TOWN CHURCH
Comments: **Twelfth in Series,** Handcrafted, 4-11/16" tall, Dated 1995 An exececllent choice for this favorite series.
Artist: Don Palmiter
☐ Purchased 19___ Pd $_______ MIB NB DB BNT
☐ Want Orig. Ret. $14.95 **MIB** Sec. Mkt. **$20-$25**

QX 594-9 NUMBER ONE TEACHER
Comments: Handcrafted, 1-11/16" tall, Dated 1995
This little mouse slides down the bookmark to say, "You're number one in my book." More outstanding teacher ornament than others.
☐ Purchased 19___ Pd $_______ MIB NB DB BNT
☐ Want Orig. Ret. $7.95 **MIB** Sec. Mkt. **$10-$14**

QX316-9 OLYMPIC SPIRIT, THE CENTENNIAL GAMES ATLANTA 1996
Comments: Acrylic, Dated 1996
The '96 Olympic Games logo graces this oval acrylic ornament.
☐ Purchased 19___ Pd $_______ MIB NB DB BNT
☐ Want Orig. Ret. $7.95 **MIB** Sec. Mkt. **$15-$18 up**

QX 604-7 ON THE ICE
Comments: Handcrafted, 2-3/16" tall, Dated '95
On a cold winter day this Christmas mouse straps blocks of ice to his feet and enjoys himself. **Artist:** Ken Crow
☐ Purchased 19___ Pd $_______ MIB NB DB BNT
☐ Want Orig. Ret. $7.95 **MIB** Sec. Mkt. **$10-$14**

QX 580-9 OUR CHRISTMAS TOGETHER
Comments: Handcrafted, 3-9/16" tall, Dated 1995
Mr. and Mrs. Bunny decorate their new home for the holidays and their first Christmas together. Caption: "Our Christmas Together."
Artist: Joyce Lyle
☐ Purchased 19___ Pd $_______ MIB NB DB BNT
☐ Want Orig. Ret. $9.95 **MIB** Sec. Mkt. **$12-$14**

QX 570-9 OUR FAMILY
Comments: Handcrafted, 3-5/16" tall, Dated 1995
A treasure trunk full of family mementos and on the outside of the treasure chest you can picture your family. Caption: "Our Family" and "Christmas is meant to be shared." **Artist:** Robert Chad
☐ Purchased 19___ Pd $_______ MIB NB DB BNT
☐ Want Orig. Ret. $7.95 **MIB** Sec. Mkt. **$10-$12**

QX 317-7 OUR FIRST CHRISTMAS TOGETHER
Comments: Acrylic, 3-1/4" tall, Dated 1995
Heart shaped acrylic ornament is dated to remind you of the first Christmas you spent together. Caption: "Our First Christmas Together." **Artist:** Joyce Lyle
☐ Purchased 19___ Pd $_______ MIB NB DB BNT
☐ Want Orig. Ret. $6.95 **MIB** Sec. Mkt. **$8-$10**

QX 579-7 OUR FIRST CHRISTMAS TOGETHER
Comments: Handcrafted, 2-3/8" tall, Dated 1995
These two lovable bears spend their first Christmas together watching the snow fall outside their window. Caption: "Our First Christmas Together." "Christmas dreams come true when they're dreamed by two." **Artist:** Joyce Lyle
☐ Purchased 19___ Pd $_______ MIB NB DB BNT
☐ Want Orig. Ret. $16.95 **MIB** Sec. Mkt. **$18-$22**

QX 579-9 OUR FIRST CHRISTMAS TOGETHER
Comments: Handcrafted Water Globe, 2-15/16" tall, Dated 1995
Two mice have the key to each others' hearts as they spend their first Christmas together. Caption: "Our First Christmas Together."
Artist: Bob Siedler
☐ Purchased 19___ Pd $_______ MIB NB DB BNT
☐ Want Orig. Ret. $8.95 **MIB** Sec. Mkt. **$10-$12**

QX 580-7 OUR FIRST CHRISTMAS TOGETHER: PHOTOHOLDER

Comments: Handcrafted, 3-11/16" tall, Dated 1995
Put your favorite picture of you and yours in this "Love Bug" photoholder. Caption: "Our First Christmas Together"
Artist: Ed Seale
☐ Purchased 19___ Pd $_______ MIB NB DB BNT
☐ Want Orig. Ret. $8.95 **MIB** Sec. Mkt. **$10-$12**

QX 520-9 OUR LITTLE BLESSINGS

Comments: Handcrafted, 3-9/16" tall, Dated 1995
Two children sit side by side discussing what they want Santa to bring them for Christmas. **Artist:** Ken Crow
☐ Purchased 19___ Pd $_______ MIB NB DB BNT
☐ Want Orig. Ret. $12.95 **MIB** Sec. Mkt. **$15-$18**

QX 563-9 PACKED WITH MEMORIES: PHOTOHOLDER

Comments: Handcrafted, 3-5/8" tall, Dated 1995
New commemorative ornament. Keep your child's first school photo is this cute little pouch with a bear peeking out.
Artist: Ed Seale
☐ Purchased 19___ Pd $_______ MIB NB DB BNT
☐ Want Orig. Ret. $7.95 **MIB** Sec. Mkt. **$10-$12**

QLX 727-7 PEANUTS®

Comments: **Fifth and Final in Series,** Light and Motion, Handcrafted, 4-1/8" tall, Dated 1995 Snoopy spins gracefully on the ice. His message, "Merry Christmas." **Artist:** Dill Rhodus
☐ Purchased 19___ Pd $_______ MIB NB DB BNT
☐ Want Orig. Ret. $24.50 **MIB** Sec. Mkt. **$28-$32**

QX 505-9 PEANUTS® GANG

Comments: **Third in Series,** Handcrafted, 2-7/8" tall, Dated
Charlie Brown holds onto his sled as he flies down the largest hill in cartoon land. **Artist:** Bob Siedler
☐ Purchased 19___ Pd $_______ MIB NB DB BNT
☐ Want Orig. Ret. $9.95 **MIB** Sec. Mkt. **$12-$14**

QX 592-7 PERFECT BALANCE

Comments: Handcrafted, 3-11/16" tall, Dated '95
A seal from team St. Nicholas shows off his talents spinning a soccer ball on his nose. Caption: "St. Nicks." **Artist:** Bob Siedler
☐ Purchased 19___ Pd $_______ MIB NB DB BNT
☐ Want Orig. Ret. $7.95 **MIB** Sec. Mkt. **$8-$10**

QX 616-7 PEWTER ROCKING HORSE: ANNIVERSARY EDITION

Comments: Handcrafted, 3" tall, Dated 1995
This anniversary edition pewter rocking horse celebrates 15 years of the rocking horse ornament collection. Caption: "1995 15th Year 1981-1995" (each side of rocker). **Artist:** Linda Sickman
☐ Purchased 19___ Pd $_______ MIB NB DB BNT
☐ Want Orig. Ret. $20.00 **MIB** Sec. Mkt. **$28-$30**

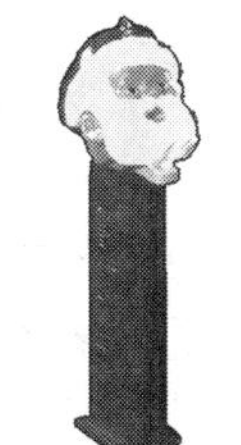

QX 526-7 PEZ® SANTA

Comments: Handcrafted 3-13/16" tall, Dated
Your favorite candy treat is now an ornament. Hang PEZ Santa on your tree to make the holiday season even sweeter. Caption: "PEZ®." **Artist:** John Francis
☐ Purchased 19___ Pd $_______ MIB NB DB BNT
Want Orig. Ret. $7.95 **MIB** Sec. Mkt. **$10-$14**

QX1616-9 POCAHONTAS: CAPTAIN JOHN SMITH AND MEEKO

Comments: Handcrafted, 4-1/2" tall, Dated
Meeko steals a biscuit while Captain John Smith watches out for savages. **Artist:** Ken Crow
☐ Purchased 19___ Pd $_______ MIB NB DB BNT
☐ Want Orig. Ret. $12.95 **MIB** Sec. Mkt. **$14-$18**

QX 1617-9 POCAHONTAS: PERCY, FLIT AND MEEKO

Comments: Handcrafted, 1-13/16" tall, Dated
These three friends love to play, but Percy never likes to have any fun. **Artist:** Ken Crow
☐ Purchased 19___ Pd $_______ MIB NB DB BNT
☐ Want Orig. Ret. $9.95 **MIB** Sec. Mkt. **$18-$22**

QX 1617-7 POCAHONTAS

Comments: Handcrafted, 2-15/16" tall, Dated 1995
Pocahontas rows "just around the river bend" with her little hummingbird friend, Flit. **Artist:** Ken Crow
☐ Purchased 19___ Pd $_______ MIB NB DB BNT
☐ Want Orig. Ret. $12.95 **MIB** Sec. Mkt. **$18-$22**

QX 1619-7 POCAHONTAS: POCAHONTAS AND CAPTAIN JOHN SMITH

Comments: Handcrafted, 2-9/16" tall, Dated 1995
You will fall in love at first sight just like these two did, when you see this ornament. **Artist:** Ken Crow
☐ Purchased 19___ Pd $_______ MIB NB DB BNT
☐ Want Orig. Ret. $14.95 **MIB** Sec. Mkt. **$16-$20**

QX 611-7 POLAR COASTER
Comments: Handcrafted, 2-1/2" tall, Dated '95
It's winter fun at its best when this li'l penguin is sliding off his polar bear friend's back. **Artist:** Ken Crow
☐ Purchased 19___ Pd $_______ MIB NB DB BNT
☐ Want Orig. Ret. $8.95 **MIB** Sec. Mkt. **$10-$12**

QX 525-7 POPEYE
Comments: Handcrafted, 3-11/16" tall, Dated
No turkey or ham for him. Even on Christmas day spinach is the only thing Popeye eats. Caption: "SPINACH." **Artist:** Robert Chad
☐ Purchased 19___ Pd $_______ MIB NB DB BNT
☐ Want Orig. Ret. $10.95 **MIB** Sec. Mkt. **$16-$18**

QX 513-7 PUPPY LOVE
Comments: **Fifth in Series,** Handcrafted, 2-1/16" tall, Dated '95
A brown and black puppy tries his best to help with wrapping presents, but all he really wants to do is play.
Artist: Anita Marra Rogers
☐ Purchased 19___ Pd $_______ MIB NB DB BNT
☐ Want Orig. Ret. $7.95 **MIB** Sec. Mkt. **$10-$14**

QX 406-7 REFRESHING GIFT
Comments: Handcrafted, Dated
Santa stocks up on cold Coca-Cola® for all his little helpers.
Artist: Duane Unruh
☐ Purchased 19___ Pd $_______ MIB NB DB BNT
☐ Want Orig. Ret. $14.95 **MIB** Sec. Mkt. **$18-$20**

QX 598-7 REJOICE!
Comments: Handcrafted, 3-15/16" tall, Dated 1995
Everyone rejoices with the birth of baby Jesus. Caption: "A Child is Born." "The world rejoices!" **Artist:** Joyce Lyle
☐ Purchased 19___ Pd $_______ MIB NB DB BNT
☐ Want Orig. Ret. $10.95 **MIB** Sec. Mkt. **$12-$16**

Remember:
You can't judge a book by its movie.

QX 516-7 ROCKING HORSE
Comments: **Fifteenth in Series**, Handcrafted, 3" tall, Dated 1995
A painted pony with red saddle and green rockers joins this popular series. See page VI. **Artist:** Linda Sickman
☐ Purchased 19___ Pd $_______ MIB NB DB BNT
☐ Want Orig. Ret. $10.95 **MIB** Sec. Mkt. **$14-$16**

QX 593-7 ROLLER WHIZ
Comments: Handcrafted, 2-1/2" tall, Dated '95
Santa turtle roller blades his way home to open the gifts he received.
Artist: Ed Seale
☐ Purchased 19___ Pd $_______ MIB NB DB BNT
☐ Want Orig. Ret. $7.95 **MIB** Sec. Mkt. **$10-$12**

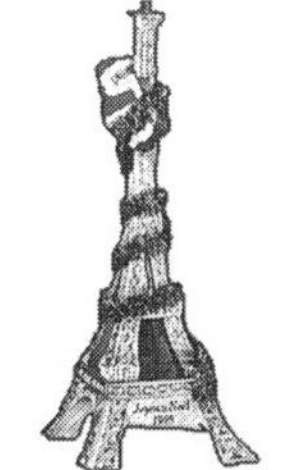

QX 587-7 SANTA IN PARIS
Comments: Handcrafted, 3-9/16" tall, Dated 1995
Santa climbs the Eiffel Tower to decorate it with real garland for Christmas. Caption: "Joyeux Noel 1995."
Artist: Linda Sickman
☐ Purchased 19___ Pd $_______ MIB NB DB BNT
☐ Want Orig. Ret. $8.95 **MIB** Sec. Mkt. **$10-$12**

QLX 733-7 SANTA'S DINER
Comments: Handcrafted, Lighted, 2" tall, Dated 1995
Santa stands at the door and greets customers into his diner. Sign glows. Caption Santa's Diner."
Artist: LaDene Votruba
☐ Purchased 19___ Pd $_______ MIB NB DB BNT
☐ Want Orig. Ret. $24.50 **MIB** Sec. Mkt. **$28-$30**

QX 601-7 SANTA'S SERENADE
Comments: Handcrafted, 3" tall, Dated '95
Cowboy Santa sings Christmas carols with the help of Mr. Owl on his hat who is playing the harmonica. **Artist:** Ken Crow
☐ Purchased 19___ Pd $_______ MIB NB DB BNT
☐ Want Orig. Ret. $8.95 **MIB** Sec. Mkt. **$12-$14**

QX 240-7 SANTA'S VISITORS: NORMAN ROCKWELL
Comments: White Glass Ball, Dated 1995
Santa makes sure he checks his list for these two little ones as they tell him what they want for Christmas.
Artist: Norman Rockwell
☐ Purchased 19___ Pd $_______ MIB NB DB BNT
☐ Want Orig. Ret. $5.00 **MIB** Sec. Mkt. **$10-$12**

QX 615-9 SIMBA, PUMBAA, AND TIMON: THE LION KING
Comments: Handcrafted, 3-1/16" tall, Dated
Simba, Pumbaa and Timon walk across a log singing their favorite song "Hakuna Matata." Caption: "Hakuna Matata."
Artist: Ken Crow
☐ Purchased 19___ Pd $_______ MIB NB DB BNT
☐ Want Orig. Ret. $12.95 **MIB** Sec. Mkt. **$16-$18**

QX 568-7 SISTER
Comments: Handcrafted, 2-5/8" tall, Dated '95
Skier sister is heading for the slopes. Caption: "Sister."
Artist: Joyce Lyle
☐ Purchased 19___ Pd $_______ MIB NB DB BNT
☐ Want Orig. Ret. $6.95 **MIB** Sec. Mkt. **$8-$10**

QX 568-9 SISTER TO SISTER
Comments: Handcrafted, 2-3/4/" tall, Dated 1995
These two sisters share everything from secrets to spices with each other. Caption: "SPICES" and "Sisters Add Spice to the Holidays."
Artist: LaDene Votruba
☐ Purchased 19___ Pd $_______ MIB NB DB BNT
☐ Want Orig. Ret. $8.00 **MIB** Sec. Mkt. **$10-$14**

QX 566-9 SON
Comments: Handcrafted, 2-13/16" tall, Dated '95
This sharp son panda will study hard so there will be no homework during Christmas break. Caption: "Super Sharp Son."
Artist: Don Palmiter
☐ Purchased 19___ Pd $_______ MIB NB DB BNT
☐ Want Orig. Ret. $6.95 **MIB** Sec. Mkt. **$8-$10**

QX 590-9 SKI HOUND
Comments: Handcrafted, 1-15/16" tall, Dated 1995
One ski, one dachshund-off he goes.
Artist: Dill Rhodus
☐ Purchased 19___ Pd $_______ MIB NB DB BNT
☐ Want Orig. Ret. $8.95 **MIB** Sec. Mkt. **$10-$12**

QLX 739-6 SPACE SHUTTLE
Comments: Lighted, Handcrafted, 2-1/8" tall, Dated 1995
Stringer ornament. Commemorates the first Earth-orbiting flight of the U.S. Space Shuttle Columbia and the 30th Anniversary of the first U.S. spacewalk. Cargo door opens to allow an astronaut to space walk. **Artist:** Ken Crow
☐ Purchased 19___ Pd $_______ MIB NB DB BNT
☐ Want Orig. Ret. $24.50 **MIB** Sec. Mkt. **$28-$35**

QX 571-7 SPECIAL CAT
Comments: Handcrafted, 2-1/4" tall, Dated 1995
That special cat will love you even more when you hang his picture on your tree. Caption: "Good Kitties." **Artist:** Robert Chad
☐ Purchased 19___ Pd $_______ MIB NB DB BNT
☐ Want Orig. Ret. $7.95 **MIB** Sec. Mkt. **$8-$10**

QX 571-9 SPECIAL DOG
Comments: Handcrafted, 2-1/4" tall, Dated 1995
Every dog should have its photo in this special dog frame. Caption: "Good Doggies."
Artist: Robert Chad
☐ Purchased 19___ Pd $_______ MIB NB DB BNT
☐ Want Orig. Ret. $7.95 **MIB** Sec. Mkt. **$8-$10**

QX 1553-9 STAR TREK®: CAPTAIN JAMES T. KIRK
Comments: Handcrafted, Dated
Boldly headed where no ornament has gone before, the captain of the first Starship Enterprise, along with captain Picard, are the first Star Trek characters produced in this collection.
Artist: Anita Marra Rogers
☐ Purchased 19___ Pd $_______ MIB NB DB BNT
☐ Want Orig. Ret. $13.95 **MIB** Sec. Mkt. **$28-$35**

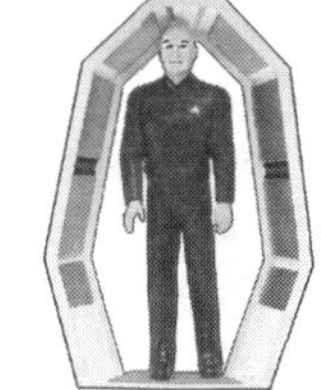

QX 1573-7 STAR TREK®: CAPTAIN JEAN-LUC PICARD
Comments: Handcrafted, Dated
The captain prepares to call all senior officers to the bridge for further instructions. **Artist:** Anita Marra Rogers
☐ Purchased 19___ Pd $_______ MIB NB DB BNT
☐ Want Orig. Ret. $13.95 **MIB** Sec. Mkt. **$25-$30**

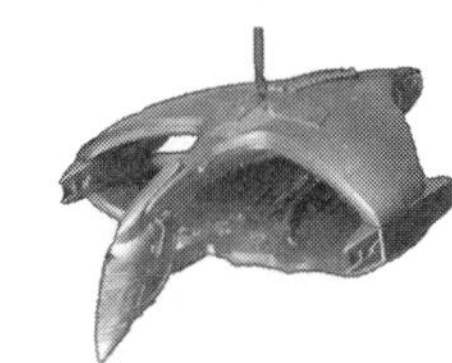

QX 1726-7 STAR TREK: ROMULAN WARBIRD™
Comments: Handcrafted, 1-7/8" tall, Dated
Caption: "Romulans have been the bad guys of the Star Trek universe since the beginning." It looks like this ship forgot its cloaking device. **Artist:** Lynn Norton
☐ Purchased 19___ Pd $_______ MIB NB DB BNT
☐ Want Orig. Ret. $24.00 **MIB** Sec. Mkt. **$28-$32**

QLX 730-9 SUPERMAN™
Comments: Handcrafted, Light and Motion, 5-1/8" tall, Dated 1995
The sign on top of the telephone booth glows as Clark Kent turns into Superman. (Rotates) **Artist:** Robert Chad
☐ Purchased 19___ Pd $_______ MIB NB DB BNT
☐ Want Orig. Ret. $28.00 **MIB** Sec. Mkt. **$28-$35**

QX 601-9 SURFIN' SANTA
Comments: Handcrafted, 2-5/8" tall, Dated '95
Santa rips a few tides on his break from delivering presents. Caption: "Yuletide." **Artist:** Ken Crow
☐ Purchased 19___ Pd $_______ MIB NB DB BNT
☐ Want Orig. Ret. $9.95 **MIB** Sec. Mkt. **$10-$12**

QX 602-9 TAKIN' A HIKE
Comments: Handcrafted. 2-1/16" tall, Dated '95
This mouse tags along anywhere you may go on your Christmas journies. **Artist:** John Francis
☐ Purchased 19___ Pd $_______ MIB NB DB BNT
☐ Want Orig. Ret. $7.95 **MIB** Sec. Mkt. **$12-$14**

QX 590-7 TENNIS, ANYONE?
Comments: Handcrafted, 3-7/8" tall, Dated '95
Play tennis with this little mouse; she is sure to help with your game. **Artist:** Nina Aube
☐ Purchased 19___ Pd $_______ MIB NB DB BNT
☐ Want Orig. Ret. $7.95 **MIB** Sec. Mkt. **$8-$10**

QX 585-7 THOMAS THE TANK ENGINE- NO. 1
Comments: Handcrafted, 1-11/16" tall, Dated 1995
Thomas the Tank Engine makes it up another hill to teach the young children all about Christmas. **Artist:** Dill Rhodus
☐ Purchased 19___ Pd $_______ MIB NB DB BNT
☐ Want Orig. Ret. $9.95 **MIB** Sec. Mkt. **$10-$14**

QX 597-9 THREE WISHES
Comments: Handcrafted, 2-5/16" tall, Dated '95
The little girl dreams of her three wishes: love, joy and peace. Caption: "Love Joy Peace." **Artist:** Patricia Andrews
☐ Purchased 19___ Pd $_______ MIB NB DB BNT
☐ Want Orig. Ret. $7.95 **MIB** Sec. Mkt. **$8-$12**

QX 506-9 TOBIN FRALEY CAROUSEL
Comments: **Fourth and Final in Series**, Handpainted Fine Porcelain, 5-7/8" tall, Dated 1995 This porcelain hand painted carousel is decorated for the Christmas season with its gold star and red and green trimmings. **Artist:** Tobin Fraley
☐ Purchased 19___ Pd $_______ MIB NB DB BNT
☐ Want Orig. Ret. $28.00 **MIB** Sec. Mkt. **$28-$30**

QLX 726-9 TOBIN FRALEY HOLIDAY CAROUSEL
Comments: **Second in Series,** Handcrafted, Light and Music, 5-9/16" tall. Dated 1995 A horse prances inside a lighted carousel. Plays "Over The Waves." **Artist:** Tobin Fraley
☐ Purchased 19___ Pd $_______ MIB NB DB BNT
☐ Want Orig. Ret. $32.00 **MIB** Sec. Mkt. **$35-$38**

QX 300-9 TWELVE DAYS OF CHRISTMAS: TWELVE DRUMMERS DRUMMING
Comments: **Twelfth and Final in Series,** Handcrafted, 3-7/8" tall, Dated 1995 As soon as you see this piece you will start singing the Twelve Days of Christmas. Caption: "The Twelve Days of Christmas 1995" "...twelve drummers drumming..."
☐ Purchased 19___ Pd $_______ MIB NB DB BNT
☐ Want Orig. Ret. $6.95 **MIB** Sec. Mkt. **$8-$10**

QX 582-9 TWO FOR TEA
Comments: Handcrafted, 1-11/16" tall, Dated 1995
Two mice join together in a cup of tea. Caption: "Friendship is a Special Gift" **Artist:** Julia Lee
☐ Purchased 19___ Pd $_______ MIB NB DB BNT
☐ Want Orig. Ret. $9.95 **MIB** Sec. Mkt. **$10-$12**

QX 506-7 U.S. CHRISTMAS STAMPS
Comments: **Third and Final in Series,** Handcrafted, 3-3/8" tall, Send your love to anyone with this Christmas greetings postage stamp. Caption: "25 USA Greetings," "1995 Christmas" and "Christmas Tree."
☐ Purchased 19___ Pd $_______ MIB NB DB BNT
☐ Want Orig. Ret. $10.95 **MIB** Sec. Mkt. **$11-$14**

QX 553-7 VERA THE MOUSE
Comments: Fine Porcelain, 3-7/32" Diameter, Dated 1995
This fine porcelain Marjolein Bastin collector's plate includes stand or can be hung on your tree. **Artist:** Marjolein Bastin
☐ Purchased 19___ Pd $_______ MIB NB DB BNT
☐ Want Orig. Ret. $8.95 **MIB** Sec. Mkt. **$9-$12**

QLX 735-7 VICTORIAN TOY BOX: SPECIAL EDITION
Comments: Handcrafted, Light, Motion and Music 4-5/16" tall
The Christmas tree glows, jack-in-the-box goes up and down, top spins and Santa wobbles. Plays "Toyland." **Artist:** Joyce Lyle
☐ Purchased 19___ Pd $_______ MIB NB DB BNT
☐ Want Orig. Ret. $42.00 **MIB** Sec. Mkt. **$45-$50**

QX 610-6 WAITING UP FOR SANTA
Comments: Handcrafted, 2-9/16" tall, Dated '95
This tired little bear drags his toy bear along while waiting up for Santa. **Artist:** Don Palmiter
☐ Purchased 19___ Pd $_______ MIB NB DB BNT
☐ Want Orig. Ret. $8.95 **MIB** Sec. Mkt. **$10-$14**

QX 603-9 WATER SPORTS
Comments: Handcrafted, Boat 1-5/8" tall, Ms. Claus 1-15/16" tall, Dated '95 A set of two clip-on ornaments. Santa takes time off from his busy schedule to enjoy the summer sport of water skiing with Mrs. Claus. **Artist:** Bob Siedler
☐ Purchased 19___ Pd $_______ MIB NB DB BNT
☐ Want Orig. Ret. $14.95 **MIB** Sec. Mkt. **$18-$20**

QLX 732-9 WEE LITTLE CHRISTMAS
Comments: Lighted, Handcrafted, 3" tall, Dated '95
The Christmas tree glows when Santa comes to deliver his gifts. There is a surprise Christmas scene behind the wall.
Artist: Ken Crow
☐ Purchased 19___ Pd $_______ MIB NB DB BNT
☐ Want Orig. Ret. $22.00 **MIB** Sec. Mkt. **$22-$26**

QX 618-7 WHEEL OF FORTUNE®: ANNIVERSARY EDITION
Comments: Handcrafted, Dated 1995
Check your luck to see if the letters spell out what you want for Christmas. Caption: "Wheel of Fortune You're A Winner 1995" and "Wheel of Fortune 20 Years 1975-1995." Popular ornament.
Artist: Linda Sickman
☐ Purchased 19___ Pd $_______ MIB NB DB BNT
☐ Want Orig. Ret. $12.95 **MIB** Sec. Mkt. **$22-$28**

QX 588-9 WINNING PLAY, THE
Comments: Handcrafted, 1-7/8" tall, Dated '95
The athletic mouse takes the court. He dribbles left then right, shoots and scores. The Christmas mice win the game. **Artist:** Bob Siedler
☐ Purchased 19___ Pd $_______ MIB NB DB BNT
☐ Want Orig. Ret. $7.95 **MIB** Sec. Mkt. **$12-$14**

QX 500-9 WINNIE THE POOH AND TIGGER
Comments: Handcrafted, Dated '95
Tigger gives Pooh a boost to put the star atop the tree.
Artist: Bob Siedler
☐ Purchased 19___ Pd $_______ MIB NB DB BNT
☐ Want Orig. Ret. $12.95 **MIB** Sec. Mkt. **$18-$22**

QLX 729-7 WINNIE THE POOH - TOO MUCH HUNNY
Comments: Handcrafted, Motion, 4-1/8" tall, Dated 1995
Tigger is pulling the hunny loving Pooh through the narrow hole at "Rabbit's House." **Artist:** Bob Siedler
☐ Purchased 19___ Pd $_______ MIB NB DB BNT
☐ Want Orig. Ret. $24.50 **MIB** Sec. Mkt. **$45-$50**

QX 585-9 WISH LIST: ORNAMENT PREMIERE
Comments: Handcrafted, 2-3/8" tall, Dated '95
A small Tender Touches mouse writes a letter "to Santa."
Artist: Ed Seale
☐ Purchased 19___ Pd $_______ MIB NB DB BNT
☐ Want Orig. Ret. $15.00 **MIB** Sec. Mkt. **$16-$20**

QX 574-9 WIZARD OF OZ™: GLINDA, WITCH OF THE NORTH
Comments: Handcrafted, 4-3/8" tall
Last year's Wizard of Oz characters were happy to have Glinda join them in 1995. **Artist:** Joyce Lyle
☐ Purchased 19___ Pd $_______ MIB NB DB BNT
☐ Want Orig. Ret. $13.95 **MIB** Sec. Mkt. **$22-$25**

QX 507-9 YULETIDE CENTRAL
Comments: **Second is Series,** Pressed Tin, 2" tall, Dated 1995
A li'l train car carries all of the goodies for children on Christmas day.
Artist: Linda Sickman
☐ Purchased 19___ Pd $_______ MIB NB DB BNT
☐ Want Orig. Ret. $18.95 **MIB** Sec. Mkt. **$22-$24**

QP 615-7 BABY BEAR
Comments: Handcrafted, 2-5/8 tall, new design
Personalize this baby bear's bib to commemorate the birth of your little bundle of joy. **Artist:** Patricia Andrews
☐ Purchased 19___ Pd $_______ MIB NB DB BNT
☐ Want Orig. Ret. $12.95 **MIB** Sec. Mkt. **$13-$15**

QP 612-7 CHAMP, THE
Comments: Handcrafted, 2-9/16" tall
Baby chipmunk holds on to a winners cup.
Artist: LaDene Votruba
☐ Purchased 19___ Pd $_______ MIB NB DB BNT
☐ Want Orig. Ret.$12.95 **MIB** Sec. Mkt. **$13-$15**

QP 604-6 COMPUTER CAT 'N MOUSE
Comments: Handcrafted, 2-3/4" tall
A little white kitten watches over your mouse from the top of your computer. Caption: "Happy Holidata." **Artist:** Ed Seale
☐ Purchased 19___ Pd $_______ MIB NB DB BNT
☐ Want Orig. Ret. $12.95 **MIB** Sec. Mkt. **$13-$15**

QP 607-3 COOKIE TIME
Comments: Handcrafted, 2-3/4" tall
An iced Christmas cookie will make your tree even sweeter.
Artist: LaDene Vortruba
☐ Purchased 19___ Pd $_______ MIB NB DB BNT
☐ Want Orig. Ret. $12.95 **MIB** Sec. Mkt. **$13-$15**

QP 601-5 ETCH-A-SKETCH®
Comments: Handcrafted, 2-1/4" tall
A little brown bear sketches a warm Christmas wish you. Caption: "Etch-A-Sketch®." **Artist:** Ken Crow
☐ Purchased 19___ Pd $_______ MIB NB DB BNT
☐ Want Orig. Ret. $12.95 **MIB** Sec. Mkt. **$13-$16**

QP 603-6 FROM THE HEART
Comments: Handcrafted, 1-15/16" tall
This little raccoon is willing to brave the cold snow to show his sweetheart how much he loves her.
Artist: Dill Rhodus
☐ Purchased 19___ Pd $_______ MIB NB DB BNT
☐ Want Orig. Ret. $14.95 **MIB** Sec. Mkt. **$15-$16**

QP 614-9 KEY NOTE
Comments: Handcrafted, 2-5/8" tall
A li'l mouse holds the golden key to your new home. The tag he sits on can be personalized. Artist: Ed Seale
☐ Purchased 19___ Pd $_______ MIB NB DB BNT
☐ Want Orig. Ret. $12.95 **MIB** Sec. Mkt. **$13-$18**

QP 601-5 MAILBOX DELIVERY
Comments: Handcrafted, 1-7/8" tall
What a surprise when Mr. Raccoon delivers the mail in person. Mail box opens. **Artist:** Ken Crow
☐ Purchased 19___ Pd $_______ MIB NB DB BNT
☐ Want Orig. Ret. $14.95 **MIB** Sec. Mkt. **$15-$16**

QP 606-6 NOVEL IDEA
Comments: Handcrafted, 2-7/16" tall
Mr. Mouse will help deliver your message on this "novel" ornament.
Artist: LaDene Votruba
☐ Purchased 19___ Pd $_______ MIB NB DB BNT
☐ Want Orig. Ret. $12.95 **MIB** Sec. Mkt. **$13-$16**

QP 602-2 ON THE BILLBOARD
Comments: Handcrafted, 2-1/8" tall
Have Santa's helper paint a Christmas message on a billboard for you. Caption: "Santa Sign Co." **Artist:** Ken Crow
☐ Purchased 19___ Pd $_______ MIB NB DB BNT
☐ Want Orig. Ret. $12.95 **MIB** Sec. Mkt. **$13-$15**

603-2 PLAYING BALL
Comments: Handcrafted, 3-11/16" tall
This little bear is ready to play ball. He carries a bat that can be personalized for your "little winner." **Artist:** John Francis
☐ Purchased 19___ Pd $_______ MIB NB DB BNT
☐ Want Orig. Ret. $12.95 **MIB** Sec. Mkt. **$13-$15**

QP 605-6 REINDEER ROOTERS
Comments: Handcrafted, 2-15/16" tall
Reissued from 1994. This peppy squad of reindeer will help anyone send that special Christmas message.
Artist: Ken Crow
☐ Purchased 19___ Pd $_______ MIB NB DB BNT
☐ Want Orig. Ret. $12.95 **MIB** Sec. Mkt. **$13-$15**

Hallmark Keepsake Showcase Ornaments

Offered by Gold Crown Stores only

Turn of the Century Parade - 1995

QK 102-7 THE FIREMAN
Comments: ***FIRST IN SERIES,*** Die-cast metal, 3-1/8" tall Dated 1995 No fire truck would be complete without a brass bell and red ribbon; the wheels turn and bell rings. **Artist:** Ken Crow
☐ Purchased 19___ Pd $_______ MIB NB DB BNT
☐ Want Orig. Ret. $16.95 **MIB** Sec. Mkt. **$25-$28**

Holiday Enchantment - 1995

QK 109-7 AWAY IN A MANGER
Comments: Fine Porcelain, 4-5/16" tall, Dated 1995
Caption: "...The little Lord Jesus, asleep on the hay" "Away in a Manger." **Artist:** LaDene Votruba
☐ Purchased 19___ Pd $_______ MIB NB DB BNT
☐ Want Orig. Ret. $13.95 **MIB** Sec. Mkt. **$15-$18**

QK 109-9 FOLLOWING THE STAR
Comments: Fine Porcelain, 3-7/16" diameter, Dated 1995
Caption: "...we have seen his star in the east, and are come to worship him. Matthew 2:2." **Artist:** LaDene Votruba
☐ Purchased 19___ Pd $_______ MIB NB DB BNT
☐ Want Orig. Ret. $13.95 **MIB** Sec. Mkt. **$15-$18**

Nature's Sketchbook - 1995

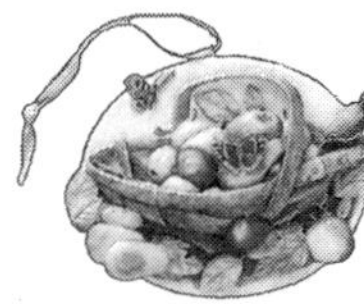

QK 106-9 BACKYARD ORCHARD
Comments: Handcrafted, 3-3/16" tall, Dated 1995
This basket full of fruit feeds everyone from the birds to the butterflies.
Artists: Marjolein Bastin and John Francis
☐ Purchased 19___ Pd $_______ MIB NB DB BNT
☐ Want Orig. Ret. $18.95 **MIB** Sec. Mkt. **$20-$25**

QK 107-7 CHRISTMAS CARDINAL
Comments: Handcrafted, 3-5/8" tall, Dated 1995
This handcrafted ornament pictures mama bird feeding her baby bird. Gorgeous! **Artists:** Marjolein Bastin and Joyce Lyle
☐ Purchased 19___ Pd $_______ MIB NB DB BNT
☐ Want Orig. Ret. $18.95 **MIB** Sec. Mkt. **$20-$25**

QK 106-7 RAISING A FAMILY
Comments: Handcrafted, 3-5/8" diameter, Dated 1995
Artists: Marjolein Bastin and Joyce Lyle
☐ Purchased 19___ Pd $_______ MIB NB DB BNT
☐ Want Orig. Ret. $18.95 **MIB** Sec. Mkt. **$20-$25**

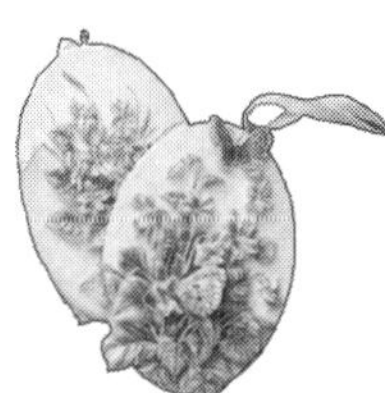

QK 107-9 VIOLETS AND BUTTERFLIES
Comments: Handcrafted, 4-1/8" tall, Dated 1995
This two-sided, hand crafted ornament pictures the butterflies enjoying the flowers of spring. Nice!
Artists: Marjolein Bastin and Joyce Lyle
☐ Purchased 19___ Pd $_______ MIB NB DB BNT
☐ Want Orig. Ret. $16.95 **MIB** Sec. Mkt. **$20-$25**

Symbols of Christmas - 1995

QX 108-7 JOLLY SANTA
Comments; Handcrafted, 2-1/4" tall, Dated '95
Jolly Santa brings home a Christmas tree for the family to enjoy.
☐ Purchased 19___ Pd $_______ MIB NB DB BNT
☐ Want Orig. Ret. $15.95 **MIB** Sec. Mkt. **$18-$22**

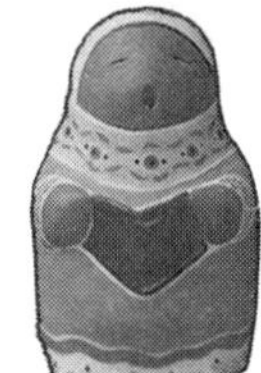

QX 108-9 SWEET SONG
Comments: Handcrafted, 2-5/16" tall, Dated '95
This hand painted caroler sings her favorite Christmas carols.
☐ Purchased 19___ Pd $_______ MIB NB DB BNT
☐ Want Orig. Ret. $15.95 **MIB** Sec. Mkt. **$18-$22**

Invitation To Tea - 1995

The handle, spout and removable lid of each ornament are concealed in the design of the teapot.

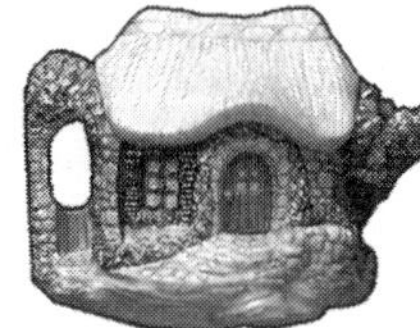

QK 112-7 COZY COTTAGE TEAPOT
Comments: Handcrafted, 2-7/16" tall, Dated 1995
A quaint cottage with an ivy covered arch make a lovely teapot design. **Artist:** Patricia Andrews
☐ Purchased 19___ Pd $_______ MIB NB DB BNT
☐ Want Orig. Ret. $15.95 **MIB** Sec. Mkt. **$18-$20**

A financial genius is someone who earns money faster than it's spent.

QK 112-9 EUROPEAN CASTLE
Comments: Handcrafted, 3-5/16" tall, Dated 1995
Turrets and Balconies add to the charm of this ivory castle.
Artist: Patricia Andrews
☐ Purchased 19___ Pd $_______ MIB NB DB BNT
☐ Want Orig. Ret. $15.95 **MIB** Sec. Mkt. **$18-$20**

QX 111-9 VICTORIAN HOME TEAPOT
Comments: Handcrafted, 2 7/16" tall, Dated 1995
All the elegance and style of a Victorian home are captured in this unique teapot. **Artist:** Patricia Andrews
☐ Purchased 19___ Pd $_______ MIB NB DB BNT
☐ Want Orig. Ret. $15.95 **MIB** Sec. Mkt. **$18-$20**

All Is Bright - 1995

QK 115-9 ANGEL OF LIGHT
Comments: Handcrafted, 4-9/16" tall, Dated 1995
Beautiful angel has a holiday golden glow; she dreams of the joy of Christmas. "GOLD LEAF" look **Artist:** Patricia Andrews
☐ Purchased 19___ Pd $_______ MIB NB DB BNT
☐ Want Orig. Ret. $11.95 **MIB** Sec. Mkt. **$12-$16**

QK 115-7 GENTLE LULLABY
Comments: Handcrafted, 4-5/16" tall, Dated 1995
A beautiful golden angel rocks her precious baby to sleep. "GOLD LEAF" look. **Artist:** Patricia Andrews
☐ Purchased 19___ Pd $_______ MIB NB DB BNT
☐ Want Orig. Ret. $11.95 **MIB** Sec. Mkt. **$12-$16**

Angel Bells - 1995

QX 114-7 CAROLE
Comments: Fine Porcelain, 3-9/16" tall, Dated 1995
Carole is a devout African-American angel. Her feet are the clapper for the bell.
☐ Purchased 19___ Pd $_______ MIB NB DB BNT
☐ Want Orig. Ret. $12.95 **MIB** Sec. Mkt. **$18-$20**

QK 113-7 JOY
Comments: Fine Porcelain, 3-1/2" tall, Dated 1995
The Joy bell ornament seemed to be the hardest one to find. All three were not abundently produced.
Artist: LaDene Votruba
☐ Purchased 19___ Pd $_______ MIB NB DB BNT
☐ Want Orig. Ret. $12.95 **MIB** Sec. Mkt. **$25-$30**

QK 113-9 NOELLE
Comments: Fine Porcelain, 3-5/8" tall, Dated 1995
A lovely Asian angel, her feet are the clapper for the bell.
Artist: LaDene Votruba
☐ Purchased 19___ Pd $_______ MIB NB DB BNT
☐ Want Orig. Ret. $12.95 **MIB** Sec. Mkt. **$18-$20**

Folk Art Americana - 1995

QK 103-7 GUIDING SANTA
Comments: Handcrafted, 3-3/8" tall, Dated '95
A little angel guides Santa as he takes an unusual ride.
☐ Purchased 19___ Pd $_______ MIB NB DB BNT
☐ Want Orig. Ret. $18.95 **MIB** Sec. Mkt. **$24-$30**

QK105-7 FETCHING THE FIREWOOD
Comments: Handcrafted, Dated '95
A li'l man hugs his dog after a long day on the trail.
☐ Purchased 19___ Pd $_______ MIB NB DB BNT
☐ Want Orig. Ret. $16.95 **MIB** Sec. Mkt. **$22-$28**

QK 103-9 FISHING PARTY
Comments: Handcrafted, 1-7/8" tall, Dated '95
Everyone should have a pet walrus.
☐ Purchased 19___ Pd $_______ MIB NB DB BNT
☐ Want Orig. Ret. $15.95 **MIB** Sec. Mkt. **$22-$28**

QK 104-7 LEARNING TO SKATE
Comments: Handcrafted, 2-1/4" tall, Dated '95
Learning to ice skate requires a pillow or two.
☐ Purchased 19___ Pd $_______ MIB NB DB BNT
☐ Want Orig. Ret. $14.95 **MIB** Sec. Mkt. **$22-$28**

Specialty Ornaments

QX 524-9 FLAG OF LIBERTY
Comments: Handcrafted, 3-5/16" tall, Dated 1991
A pearlized yellow banner carries the caption: "God Bless America 1991" on this commemorative ornament of Desert Shield/Desert Storm. For each ornament sold, Hallmark donated $1.00 to the American Red Cross. The first shipment in June was very limited but Hallmark began shipping the ornaments again in August.
Artist: Donna Lee
☐ Purchased 19___ Pd $_______ MIB NB DB BNT
☐ Want Orig. Retail $6.75 **NB** $4 **MIB** Sec. Mkt. **$8-$10**

Hall Ornaments

The Hall ornaments were given by the Hall family to employees and friends. The ornaments were attached to their Christmas cards. The value of these ornaments is very sentimental to those who receive them, thus not many are on the secondary market. They are coveted by avid collectors. No price has been established to date. If one has these special ornaments and plans to sell them, *The Ornament Collector* would recommend advertising them for sale at "Best Offer," and of course *The Ornament Collector* is a great magazine for such advertisements. Call now and subscribe. You'll be glad you did! 1-800-445-8745 ☺

CRAYOLA CRAYON ORNAMENT
Comments: Handcrafted
Came as free gift in tin box of Crayola Crayons.
☐ Purchased 19___ Pd $_______ MIB NB DB BNT
☐ Want
Orig. Ret. $5.99-$9.99 (depending on location of purchase)
without tin box **$5-$10** **MIB** Sec. Mkt. **$10-$12**

COLLECTOR'S SURVIVAL KIT PREMIERE '94
Comments: Handcrafted
Given as a free gift during premiere week of 1994.
☐ Purchased 19___ Pd $_______ MIB NB DB BNT
☐ Want **MIB** Sec. Mkt. **$10-$12**

What do you call a dog with ticks?
A watch dog.

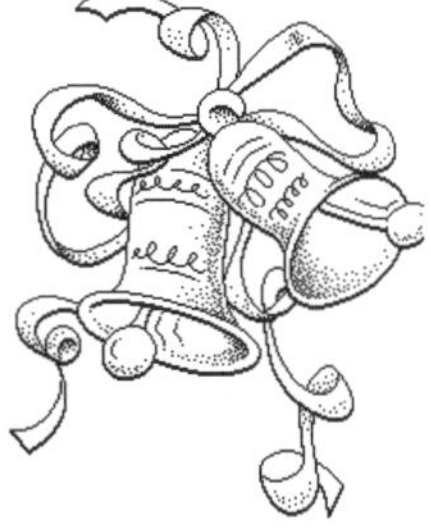

Convention Ornaments

KANSAS CITY SANTA: SPECIAL EDITION
Comments: Silver-Plated, Dated "K.C. 1991"
This special edition Santa was given as a parting gift to all who attended the 1991 Keepsake Ornament Convention in June. Santa holds a plate with the Club logo. Has anyone sold one?
☐ Purchased 19___ Pd $_______ MIB NB DB BNT
☐ Want **MIB** Sec. Mkt.-**NE**

KANSAS CITY ANGEL: SPECIAL EDITION
Comments: Silver-Plated, Dated "K.C. 1993"
This special edition Angel was given as a parting gift to all who attended the 1993 Keepsake Ornament Conventions in June and September.
☐ Purchased 19___ Pd $_______ MIB NB DB BNT
☐ Want **MIB** Sec. Mkt.-**NE**

Keepsake Signature Collection

SANTA'S FAVORITE STOP

Comments: Handcrafted, 1993 with removable Santa ornament. Sculpted by 14 artists, this tabletop was available only at Hallmark stores hosting special 1993 Artist's Appearances; only 200 per event were available. **Artists:** Removable Santa, Ken Crow; Stocking Holder Snowman, Trish Andrews; Elf on Mantel, Robert Chad; Hearth/Puppy, John Francis (Collin); Cat, Julia Lee; Victorian Doll, Joyce A. Lyle; Santa's Bag, Don Palmiter; Fireplace, Dill Rhodus; Cookies and Milk for Santa/Garland, Anita Marra Rogers; Stocking Holder Teddy Bear, Ed Seale; Toy Train/Kindling Box, Linda Sickman; Stocking Holder Mouse, Bob Siedler; Clock on the Mantel, Duane Unruh; and Teddy Bear, LaDene Votruba.
☐ Purchased 19___ Pd $_______ MIB NB DB BNT
☐ Want Orig. Ret. $55 with $25 purchase of Keepsake Ornaments
MIB Sec. Mkt. **$250-$275** if signed by all

As Sarah was feeding her pet hare, her brother David asked, "Do you really think carrots are good for the eyesight?" "Sure," said Sarah. "After all, I've never seen a rabbit with glasses."

Hallmark Expo Ornaments

Expo 1994

The '93 Old-World Silver Ornments from the Showcase line were finished in a gold color and sold to Expo '94 attendees for $10 each. These were very popular and by the time of San Francisco Expo, they were sold out. The '94 Bows and Poinsetta Old-World Silver Ornaments were then also dipped in a gold colored finished and sold to lucky Expo attendees.

GOLD BOWS
Comments: '94 Old-World Silver ornament dipped in a gold colored finish with attached ribbon that said Expo '94.
☐ Purchased 19___ Pd $_______ MIB NB DB BNT
☐ Want Orig. Ret. $10.00 **MIB** Sec. Mkt. **$ NE**

GOLD DOVE OF PEACE
Comments: '93 Old-World Silver ornament dipped in a gold colored finish with attached ribbon that said Expo '94.
☐ Purchased 19___ Pd $_______ MIB NB DB BNT
☐ Want Orig. Ret. $10.00 **MIB** Sec. Mkt. **$ NE**

GOLD POINSETTIA
Comments: '94 Old-World Silver ornament dipped in a gold colored finish with attached ribbon that said Expo '94.
☐ Purchased 19___ Pd $_______ MIB NB DB BNT
☐ Want Orig. Ret. $10.00 **MIB** Sec. Mkt. **$ NE**

GOLD SANTA
Comments: '93 Old-World Silver ornament dipped in a gold colored finish with attached ribbon that said Expo '94.
☐ Purchased 19___ Pd $_______ MIB NB DB BNT
☐ Want Orig. Ret. $10.00 **MIB** Sec. Mkt. **$ NE**

GOLD SLEIGH
Comments: '93 Old-World Silver ornament dipped in a gold colored finish with attached ribbon that said Expo '94.
☐ Purchased 19___ Pd $_______ MIB NB DB BNT
☐ Want Orig. Ret. $10.00 **MIB**Sec. Mkt. **$ NE**

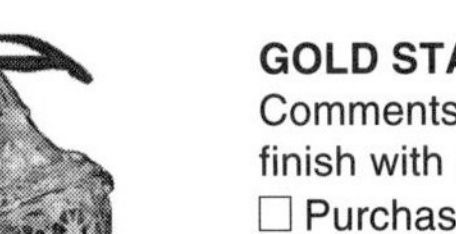

GOLD STAR AND HOLLY
Comments: '93 Old-World Silver ornament dipped in a gold colored finish with attached ribbon that said Expo '94.
☐ Purchased 19___ Pd $_______ MIB NB DB BNT
☐ Want Orig. Ret. $10.00 **MIB** Sec. Mkt. **$ NE**

QXC 484-3 MRS. CLAUS' CUPBOARD
Comments: Handcrafted, 1994. Only available at eight 1994 Hallmark Expos held across the USA. Mrs. Claus' Cupboard is filled with delightful surprises... miniature copies of favorite Keepsake ornaments such as Cheerful Santa, Noah's Ark, the 1993 Folk Art Polar Bear Adventure, a Nativity and more!
☐ Purchased 19___ Pd $_______ MIB NB DB BNT
☐ Want Orig. Ret. $55 with $25 purchase of Keepsake Ornaments
MIB Sec. Mkt. **$200-$250**

Expo '94 Prizes

Available at the '94 Expo were several gifts given to fortunate attendees by entering different drawings. Gifts given included, a signed Star Trek ornament, a '94 Looney Tunes set, complete set of all mini ornaments from '94, a signed Mary Engelbreit ball and an original signed artist sketch. Also available by special drawings, the '93 Circle of Friendship (a member's only ornament in '93), Red '94 First Edition Murray Champion (5 given away per each Expo) and the Red '94 Chevy which could have been signed by Don Palmiter at the two Expos he attended.

Expo 1995

1956 FORD TRUCK ORNAMENT, SPECIAL EDITION
Comments: Handcrafted
Available only to Expo '95 attendees by special drawing.
☐ Purchased 19___ Pd $_______ MIB NB DB BNT
☐ Want Orig. Ret. $ Free **MIB** Sec. Mkt. $

ARTISTS' CARICATURE BALL ORNAMENT
Comments: Signed.
☐ Purchased 19___ Pd $_______ MIB NB DB BNT
☐ Want Orig. Ret. $7.95 **MIB** Sec. Mkt. $

CHRISTMAS EVE BAKE-OFF
Comments: Handcrafted, Dated 1995
Rts work of 14 studio artists. Mrs. Claus is an ornament.
Artist: All 14 Studio Artists
☐ Purchased 19___ Pd $_______ MIB NB DB BNT
☐ Want Orig. Ret. $60 **MIB** Sec. Mkt. $

COOKIE TIME – SPECIAL EDITION
Comments: Handcrafted, Dated 1995
Caption: "EXPO 95 Cooking Up Fun!"
☐ Purchased 19___ Pd $_______ MIB NB DB BNT
☐ Want Orig. Ret. $12.95 **MIB** Sec. Mkt. $

KIDDIE CAR CLASSICS SPECIAL EDITION COLLECTIBLE
Comments: Kiddie Car
Available only to Expo '95 attendees by special drawing.
☐ Purchased 19___ Pd $_______ MIB NB DB BNT
☐ Want Orig. Ret. $Free **MIB** Sec. Mkt. $

Keep Up To Date
on ornament collecting by reading
The Ornament Collector™
magazine.
One year, only $23.95
Call Now!!

MURRAY FIRE TRUCK, – SPECIAL EDITION
Comments: Cast Metal
Available only to Expo '95 attendees by special drawing.
White with red trim. Photo not available.
☐ Purchased 19___ Pd $_______ MIB NB DB BNT
☐ Want Orig. Ret. $Free **MIB** Sec. Mkt. **$ NE**

MURRAY CHAMPION ORNAMENT – SPECIAL EDITION
Comments: Cast Metal Miniature Ornament
Available only to Expo '95 attendees by special drawing.
☐ Purchased 19___ Pd $_______ MIB NB DB BNT
☐ Want Orig. Ret. $Free **MIB** Sec. Mkt. $

ROCKING HORSE ORNAMENT – SPECIAL EDITION
Comments: Pewter Miniature Ornament
Hot! Collectors were seeking unwanted redemption forms for this ornament during the Expos!
☐ Purchased 19___ Pd $_______ MIB NB DB BNT
☐ Want Orig. Ret. $7.95 **MIB** Sec. Mkt. **$25-$30**

Expo '95 Prizes

1995 Keepsake Signature Collection Piece, Signed.
Expo-Exclusive Ball Ornament, Signed.
Kiddie Car Classics Collectible, Expo Special Edition.
Murray® Fire Truck Ornament, Expo Special Edition.
1956 Ford Truck Ornament, Expo Special Edition.
Miniature Murray® Champion Ornament, Expo Special Edition
Holiday Memories™ Barbie® Doll
Regional NFL Ornament Collection
Expo Artists' Caricatures Original Sketch, Signed
When You Care Enough, Book Signed by Don Hall, Sr. and Don Hall, Jr.

NFL Ornaments

Pictured are Chicago Bears.
Ten NFL Teams were offered in 1995:

Eagles	Panthers
Patriots	Redskins
Kansas City Chiefs	Dallas Cowboys
Chicago Bears	Vikings
Raiders	San Francisco 49ers

Not all Hallmark stores carried these. Some only offered "their" area team's logo.

FOOTBALL HELMET ORNAMENTS
Comments: Handcrafted, Dated 1996
☐ Purchased 19___ Pd $_______ MIB NB DB BNT
☐ Want Orig. Ret. $9.95 **MIB** Sec. Mkt. **$NE**

NFL BALL ORNAMENTS
Comments: White Glass Ball, Dated 1996. Quite attractive.
☐ Purchased 19___ Pd $_______ MIB NB DB BNT
☐ Want Orig. Ret. $5.95 **MIB** Sec. Mkt. **$ NE**

Agnes - Did you advertise for ornaments that are out of this world?

1996 Olympic Ornaments

(Not produced at press time)

QXE 551 1 INVITATION TO THE GAMES
Comments: 3-1/2" x 2-1/2", Dated 1996
These two ceramic plaque ornaments feature posters from the 1896 and 1996 Olympics. Each comes with display stand and commemorative copy. **Artist:** Diana McGehee
☐ Purchased 19___ Pd $_______ MIB NB DB BNT
☐ Want Orig. Ret. $14.95

QXE 744 4 LIGHTING THE FLAME
Comments: 4-15/16" x 2-5/8", battery operated, Dated 1996
Plays *Bugler's Dream* from the Opening Ceremony. Features commemorative copy and a flickering light. **Artist:** Duane Unruh
☐ Purchased 19___ Pd $_______ MIB NB DB BNT
☐ Want Orig. Ret. $28

QXE 573 1 OLYMPIC TRIUMPH KEEPSAKE ORNAMENT
Comments: 4-1/16" x 2-13/16", Dated 1996
This sculpted discus thrower includes commemorative copy.
Artist: Ed Seale
☐ Purchased 19___ Pd $_______ MIB NB DB BNT
☐ Want Orig. Ret. $10.95

QXE 404 1 CLOISONNE MEDALLION
Comments: 1" in diameter, Dated 1996
This miniature ornament features the artwork for the Atlanta Olympic Games for 1996. **Artist:** Diana McGehee
☐ Purchased 19___ Pd $_______ MIB NB DB BNT
☐ Want Orig. Ret. $9.75

QXE 574 1 PARADE OF NATIONS
Comments: 3-3/16" diameter, porcelain, Dated 1996
Includes display stand and features flags from various nations.
☐ Purchased 19___ Pd $_______ MIB NB DB BNT
☐ Want Orig. Ret. $10.95

QXE 572 4 IZZY – The Mascot
Comments: 3-11/16" x 2-11/16", Dated 1996
Here's *Izzy*, the official 1996 Olympic mascot.
☐ Purchased 19___ Pd $_______ MIB NB DB BNT
☐ Want Orig. Ret. $9.95

Anniversary Ornaments

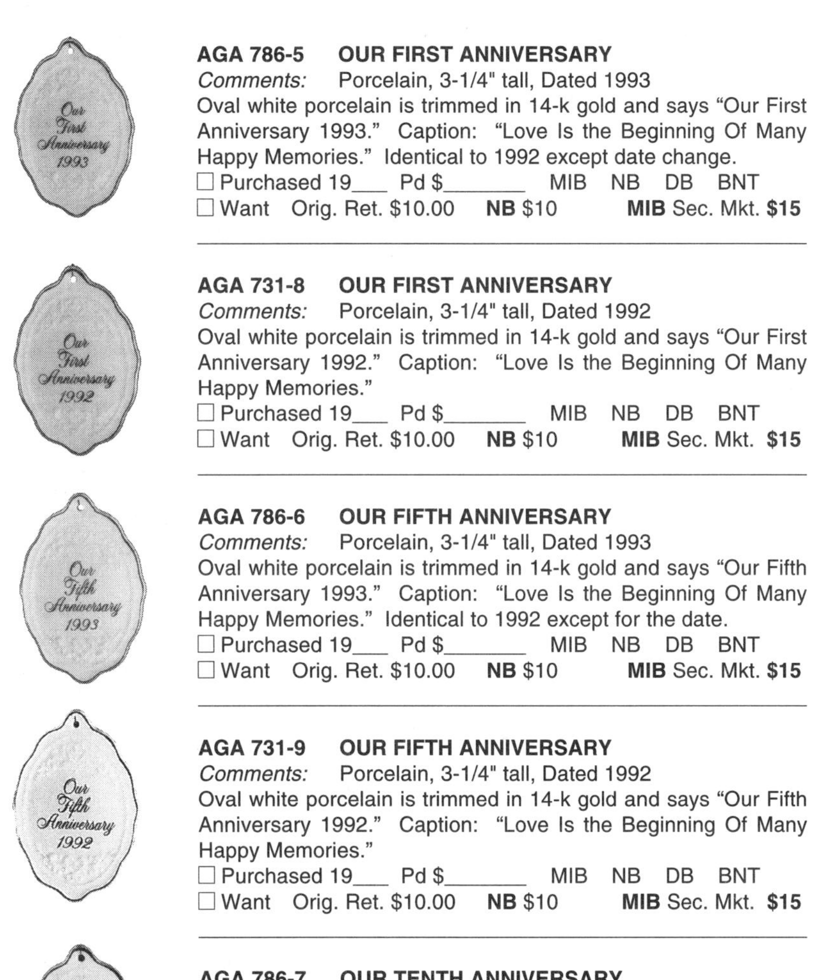

AGA 786-5 OUR FIRST ANNIVERSARY
Comments: Porcelain, 3-1/4" tall, Dated 1993
Oval white porcelain is trimmed in 14-k gold and says "Our First Anniversary 1993." Caption: "Love Is the Beginning Of Many Happy Memories." Identical to 1992 except date change.
☐ Purchased 19___ Pd $_______ MIB NB DB BNT
☐ Want Orig. Ret. $10.00 **NB** $10 **MIB** Sec. Mkt. **$15**

AGA 731-8 OUR FIRST ANNIVERSARY
Comments: Porcelain, 3-1/4" tall, Dated 1992
Oval white porcelain is trimmed in 14-k gold and says "Our First Anniversary 1992." Caption: "Love Is the Beginning Of Many Happy Memories."
☐ Purchased 19___ Pd $_______ MIB NB DB BNT
☐ Want Orig. Ret. $10.00 **NB** $10 **MIB** Sec. Mkt. **$15**

AGA 786-6 OUR FIFTH ANNIVERSARY
Comments: Porcelain, 3-1/4" tall, Dated 1993
Oval white porcelain is trimmed in 14-k gold and says "Our Fifth Anniversary 1993." Caption: "Love Is the Beginning Of Many Happy Memories." Identical to 1992 except for the date.
☐ Purchased 19___ Pd $_______ MIB NB DB BNT
☐ Want Orig. Ret. $10.00 **NB** $10 **MIB** Sec. Mkt. **$15**

AGA 731-9 OUR FIFTH ANNIVERSARY
Comments: Porcelain, 3-1/4" tall, Dated 1992
Oval white porcelain is trimmed in 14-k gold and says "Our Fifth Anniversary 1992." Caption: "Love Is the Beginning Of Many Happy Memories."
☐ Purchased 19___ Pd $_______ MIB NB DB BNT
☐ Want Orig. Ret. $10.00 **NB** $10 **MIB** Sec. Mkt. **$15**

AGA 786-7 OUR TENTH ANNIVERSARY
Comments: Porcelain, 3-1/4" tall, Dated 1993
Oval white porcelain is trimmed in 14-k gold and says "Our Tenth Anniversary 1993." Caption: "Love Is the Beginning Of Many Happy Memories." Identical to 1992 except for the date.
☐ Purchased 19___ Pd $_______ MIB NB DB BNT
☐ Want Orig. Ret. $10.00 **NB** $10 **MIB** Sec. Mkt. **$15**

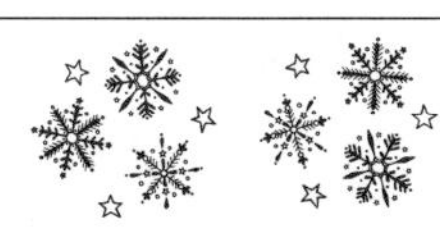

AGA 731-7 OUR TENTH ANNIVERSARY
Comments: Porcelain, 3-1/4" tall, Dated 1992
Oval white porcelain is trimmed in 14-k gold and says "Our Tenth Anniversary 1992." Caption: "Love Is the Beginning Of Many Happy Memories."
☐ Purchased 19___ Pd $_______ MIB NB DB BNT
☐ Want Orig. Ret. $10.00 **NB** $10 **MIB** Sec. Mkt. **$15**

AGA 768-6 25 YEARS TOGETHER
Comments: Porcelain, 3-1/4" tall, Dated 1993
Oval white porcelain is trimmed in silver and says "25 Years Together 1993." Caption: "Silver Christmas Memories Are Keepsakes Of The Heart." Identical to 1992 except for the date.
☐ Purchased 19___ Pd $_______ MIB NB DB BNT
☐ Want Orig. Ret. $10.00 **NB** $10 **MIB** Sec. Mkt. **$15**

AGA 711-3 25 YEARS TOGETHER
Comments: Porcelain, 3-1/4" tall, Dated 1992
Oval white porcelain is trimmed in silver and says "25 Years Together 1992." Caption: "Silver Christmas Memories Are Keepsakes Of The Heart."
☐ Purchased 19___ Pd $_______ MIB NB DB BNT
☐ Want Orig. Ret. $10.00 **NB** $10 **MIB** Sec. Mkt. **$15**

AGA 786-8 40 YEARS TOGETHER
Comments: Porcelain, 3-1/4" tall, Dated 1993
Oval white porcelain is trimmed in 14 k gold and says "40 Years Together 1993." Caption: "Love Is The Beginning Of Many Happy Memories." Identical to 1992 except for the date.
☐ Purchased 19___ Pd $_______ MIB NB DB BNT
☐ Want Orig. Ret. $10.00 **NB** $10 **MIB** Sec. Mkt. **$15**

AGA 731-6 40 YEARS TOGETHER
Comments: Porcelain, 3-1/4" tall, Dated 1992
Oval white porcelain is trimmed in 14 k gold and says "40 Years Together 1992." Caption: "Love Is The Beginning Of Many Happy Memories."
☐ Purchased 19___ Pd $_______ MIB NB DB BNT
☐ Want Orig. Ret. $10.00 **NB** $10 **MIB** Sec. Mkt. **$15**

AGA 778-7 50 YEARS TOGETHER
Comments: Porcelain, 3-1/4" tall, Dated 1993
Oval white porcelain is trimmed in 14 k gold and says "50 Years Together 1993." Caption: "Golden Christmas Memories Are Keepsakes Of The Heart." Identical to 1992 except for the date.
☐ Purchased 19___ Pd $_______ MIB NB DB BNT
☐ Want Orig. Ret. $10.00 **NB** $10 **MIB** Sec. Mkt. **$15**

AGA 721-4 50 YEARS TOGETHER
Comments: Porcelain, 3-1/4" tall, Dated 1992
Oval white porcelain is trimmed in 14 k gold and says "50 Years Together 1992." Caption: "Golden Christmas Memories Are Keepsakes Of The Heart."
☐ Purchased 19___ Pd $_______ MIB NB DB BNT
☐ Want Orig. Ret. $10.00 **NB** $10 **MIB** Sec. Mkt. **$15**

AGA 768-7 25 YEARS TOGETHER ANNIVERSARY BELL
Comments: Porcelain, 3" tall, Dated 1993
White porcelain bell is trimmed in silver and says "25 Years Together 1993." Caption: "Silver Christmas Memories Are Keepsakes Of The Heart." Identical to 1992 except for the date.
☐ Purchased 19___ Pd $_______ MIB NB DB BNT
☐ Want Orig. Ret. $10.00 **NB** $10 **MIB** Sec. Mkt. **$15**

AGA 713-4 25 YEARS TOGETHER ANNIVERSARY BELL
Comments: Porcelain, 3" tall, Dated 1992
White porcelain bell is trimmed in silver and says "25 Years Together 1992." Caption: "Silver Christmas Memories Are Keepsakes Of The Heart."
☐ Purchased 19___ Pd $_______ MIB NB DB BNT
☐ Want Orig. Ret. $10.00 **NB** $10 **MIB** Sec. Mkt. **$15**

AGA 778-8 50 YEARS TOGETHER ANNIVERSARY BELL
Comments: Porcelain, 3" tall, Dated 1993
White porcelain bell is trimmed in 14 k gold and says "50 Years Together 1993." Caption: "Golden Christmas Memories Are Keepsakes Of The Heart." Identical to 1992 except for the date.
☐ Purchased 19___ Pd $_______ MIB NB DB BNT
☐ Want Orig. Ret. $10.00 **NB** $10 **MIB** Sec. Mkt. **$15**

AGA 723-5 50 YEARS TOGETHER ANNIVERSARY BELL
Comments: Porcelain, 3" tall, Dated 1992
White porcelain bell is trimmed in 14 k gold and says "50 Years Together 1992." Caption: "Golden Christmas Memories Are Keepsakes Of The Heart."
☐ Purchased 19___ Pd $_______ MIB NB DB BNT
☐ Want Orig. Ret. $10.00 **NB** $10 **MIB** Sec. Mkt. **$15**

"HAVE YOU CALLED OUR 900 LINE FOR HOT COLLECTING TIPS ON HALLMARK ORNAMENTS OR TO BUY OR SELL HALLMARK ORNAMENTS?"
1-900-740-7575 – Press #2
CHANGES EVERY THURSDAY...
$2.00 per minute or portion thereof.
Must be 18 yrs. old.
Touch tone phone required.

Baby Celebrations

A B C D E

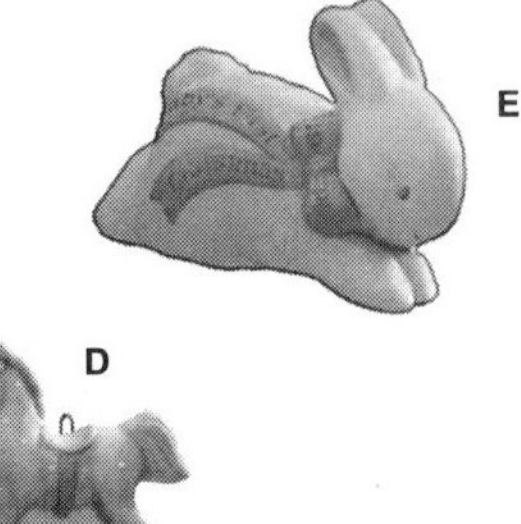

1989

A **BBY 132-5** **1989 BABY'S CHRISTENING KEEPSAKE**
Acrylic, 3-3/4" tall, Dated 1989
☐ Purchased 19___ Pd $_______ MIB NB DB BNT
☐ Want Original Retail $7.00
NB $25 **MIB** Sec. Mkt. **$32-$35**

B **BBY 172-9** **1989 BABY'S FIRST BIRTHDAY**
Acrylic, 4-1/2" tall, Dated 1989
☐ Purchased 19___ Pd $_______ MIB NB DB BNT
☐ Want Original Retail $5.50
NB $25 **MIB** Sec. Mkt. **$32-$38**

BBY 145-3 **1989 BABY'S FIRST CHRISTMAS - BABY BOY**
Blue Satin Ball, 2-7/8" dia. See page 118, QX 272-5
☐ Purchased 19___ Pd $_______ MIB NB DB BNT
☐ Want Original Retail $4.75
NB $10 **MIB** Sec. Mkt. **$12-$16**

BBY 155-3 **1989 BABY'S FIRST CHRISTMAS - BABY GIRL**
Pink Satin Ball, 2-7/8" dia. See page 118, QX 272-2
☐ Purchased 19___ Pd $_______ MIB NB DB BNT
☐ Want Original Retail $4.75
NB $8 **MIB** Sec. Mkt. **$10-$14**

1990

C **BBY 132-6** **BABY'S CHRISTENING**
Hand-Painted Porcelain, 2-1/4" tall, Dated 1990
☐ Purchased 19___ Pd $_______ MIB NB DB BNT
☐ Want Original Retail $10.00
NB $15 **MIB** Sec. Mkt. **$25-$30**

D **BBY 155-4** **BABY'S FIRST CHRISTMAS**
Hand-Painted Porcelain, 2-1/8" tall, Dated 1990
☐ Purchased 19___ Pd $_______ MIB NB DB BNT
☐ Want Original Retail $10.00
NB $15 **MIB** Sec. Mkt. **$25-$30**

E **BBY 145-4** **BABY'S FIRST CHRISTMAS**
Hand-Painted Porcelain, 2-5/8" tall, Dated 1990
☐ Purchased 19___ Pd $_______ MIB NB DB BNT
☐ Want Original Retail $10.00
NB $15 **MIB** Sec. Mkt. **$25-$30**

1991

BBY 131-7 **BABY'S CHRISTENING**
Hand-Painted Porcelain, 2-1/4" tall, Dated 1991, Identical to 1990.
☐ Purchased 19___ Pd $_______ MIB NB DB BNT
☐ Want Original Retail $10.00
NB $10 **MIB** Sec. Mkt. **$14-$18**

BBY 151-4 **BABY'S FIRST CHRISTMAS**
Hand-Painted Porcelain, 2-1/8" tall, Dated 1991, Identical to 1990.
☐ Purchased 19___ Pd $_______ MIB NB DB BNT
☐ Want Original Retail $10.00
NB $10 **MIB** Sec. Mkt. **$14-$18**

BBY 141-6 **BABY'S FIRST CHRISTMAS**
Hand-Painted Porcelain, 2-5/8" tall, Dated 1991, Identical to 1990.
☐ Purchased 19___ Pd $_______ MIB NB DB BNT
☐ Want Original Retail $10.00
NB $10 **MIB** Sec. Mkt. **$14-$18**

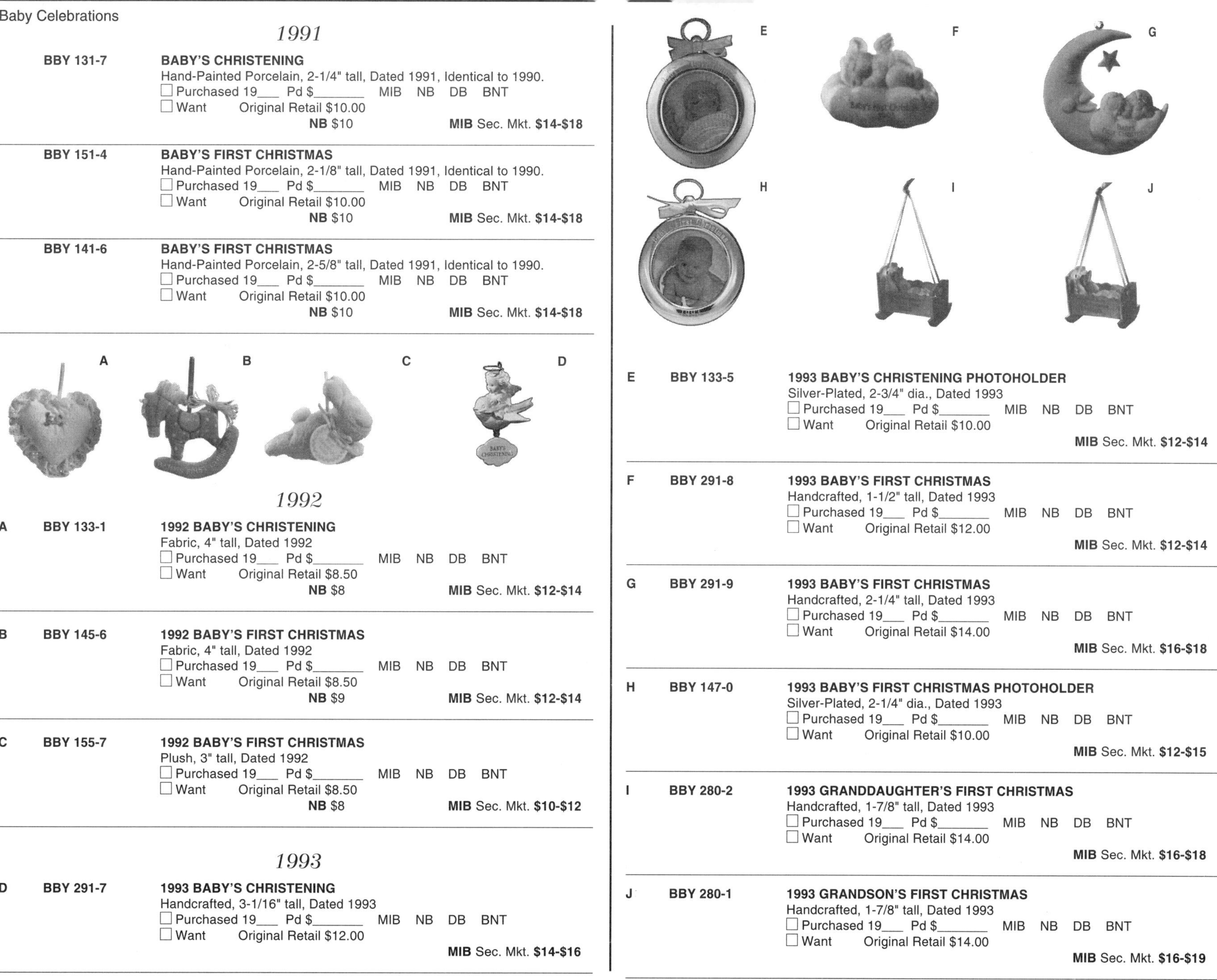

1992

A **BBY 133-1** **1992 BABY'S CHRISTENING**
Fabric, 4" tall, Dated 1992
☐ Purchased 19___ Pd $_______ MIB NB DB BNT
☐ Want Original Retail $8.50
NB $8 **MIB** Sec. Mkt. **$12-$14**

B **BBY 145-6** **1992 BABY'S FIRST CHRISTMAS**
Fabric, 4" tall, Dated 1992
☐ Purchased 19___ Pd $_______ MIB NB DB BNT
☐ Want Original Retail $8.50
NB $9 **MIB** Sec. Mkt. **$12-$14**

C **BBY 155-7** **1992 BABY'S FIRST CHRISTMAS**
Plush, 3" tall, Dated 1992
☐ Purchased 19___ Pd $_______ MIB NB DB BNT
☐ Want Original Retail $8.50
NB $8 **MIB** Sec. Mkt. **$10-$12**

1993

D **BBY 291-7** **1993 BABY'S CHRISTENING**
Handcrafted, 3-1/16" tall, Dated 1993
☐ Purchased 19___ Pd $_______ MIB NB DB BNT
☐ Want Original Retail $12.00
MIB Sec. Mkt. **$14-$16**

E **BBY 133-5** **1993 BABY'S CHRISTENING PHOTOHOLDER**
Silver-Plated, 2-3/4" dia., Dated 1993
☐ Purchased 19___ Pd $_______ MIB NB DB BNT
☐ Want Original Retail $10.00
MIB Sec. Mkt. **$12-$14**

F **BBY 291-8** **1993 BABY'S FIRST CHRISTMAS**
Handcrafted, 1-1/2" tall, Dated 1993
☐ Purchased 19___ Pd $_______ MIB NB DB BNT
☐ Want Original Retail $12.00
MIB Sec. Mkt. **$12-$14**

G **BBY 291-9** **1993 BABY'S FIRST CHRISTMAS**
Handcrafted, 2-1/4" tall, Dated 1993
☐ Purchased 19___ Pd $_______ MIB NB DB BNT
☐ Want Original Retail $14.00
MIB Sec. Mkt. **$16-$18**

H **BBY 147-0** **1993 BABY'S FIRST CHRISTMAS PHOTOHOLDER**
Silver-Plated, 2-1/4" dia., Dated 1993
☐ Purchased 19___ Pd $_______ MIB NB DB BNT
☐ Want Original Retail $10.00
MIB Sec. Mkt. **$12-$15**

I **BBY 280-2** **1993 GRANDDAUGHTER'S FIRST CHRISTMAS**
Handcrafted, 1-7/8" tall, Dated 1993
☐ Purchased 19___ Pd $_______ MIB NB DB BNT
☐ Want Original Retail $14.00
MIB Sec. Mkt. **$16-$18**

J **BBY 280-1** **1993 GRANDSON'S FIRST CHRISTMAS**
Handcrafted, 1-7/8" tall, Dated 1993
☐ Purchased 19___ Pd $_______ MIB NB DB BNT
☐ Want Original Retail $14.00
MIB Sec. Mkt. **$16-$19**

1991 Easter Ornament Collection

A QEO 518-9 **BABY'S FIRST EASTER**
Hand-Painted/Handcrafted, 1-1/2" tall, Dated 1991
☐ Purchased 19___ Pd $_______ MIB NB DB BNT
☐ Want Original Retail $8.75
NB $14 **MIB** Sec. Mkt. **$24-$28**

B QEO 517-9 **DAUGHTER**
Hand-Painted/Handcrafted, 1-1/2" tall
☐ Purchased 19___ Pd $_______ MIB NB DB BNT
☐ Want Original Retail $5.75
NB $8 **MIB** Sec. Mkt. **$22-$25**

C QEO 513-7 **EASTER MEMORIES PHOTOHOLDER**
Fabric, 2-1/2" tall, Dated 1991
☐ Purchased 19___ Pd $_______ MIB NB DB BNT
☐ Want Original Retail $7.75
NB $12 **MIB** Sec. Mkt. **$14-$16**

D QEO 514-9 **FULL OF LOVE**
Hand-Painted/Handcrafted, 2" tall, Dated 1991
☐ Purchased 19___ Pd $_______ MIB NB DB BNT
☐ Want Original Retail $7.75
NB $15 **MIB** Sec. Mkt. **$38-$40**

E QEO 515-9 **GENTLE LAMB**
Hand-Painted/Handcrafted, 2" tall, Dated '91
☐ Purchased 19___ Pd $_______ MIB NB DB BNT
☐ Want Original Retail $6.75
NB $8 **MIB** Sec. Mkt. **$14-$16**

F QEO 517-7 **GRANDCHILD**
Hand-Painted/Handcrafted, 2-1/2" tall, Dated 1991
☐ Purchased 19___ Pd $_______ MIB NB DB BNT
☐ Want Original Retail $6.75
NB $10 **MIB** Sec. Mkt. **$16-$18**

G QEO 514-7 **LI'L DIPPER**
Hand-Painted/Handcrafted, 2-1/2" tall
☐ Purchased 19___ Pd $_______ MIB NB DB BNT
☐ Want Original Retail $6.75
NB $10 **MIB** Sec. Mkt. **$20-$22**

H QEO 513-9 **LILY EGG**
Hand-Painted Fine Porcelain, 2" tall, Dated 1991
☐ Purchased 19___ Pd $_______ MIB NB DB BNT
☐ Want Original Retail $9.75
NB $10 **MIB** Sec. Mkt. **$16-$20**

I QEO 518-7 **SON**
Hand-Painted/Handcrafted, 1-1/2" tall
☐ Purchased 19___ Pd $_______ MIB NB DB BNT
☐ Want Original Retail $5.75
NB $12 **MIB** Sec. Mkt. **$18-$20**

J QEO 516-9 **SPIRIT OF EASTER**
Hand-Painted/Handcrafted, 2" tall, Dated 1991
☐ Purchased 19___ Pd $_______ MIB NB DB BNT
☐ Want Original Retail $7.75
NB $18 **MIB** Sec. Mkt. **$25-$30**

K QEO 5167 **SPRINGTIME STROLL**
Hand-Painted/Handcrafted, 2-1/2" tall, Dated 1991
☐ Purchased 19___ Pd $_______ MIB NB DB BNT
☐ Want Original Retail $6.75
NB $14 **MIB** Sec. Mkt. **$20-$22**

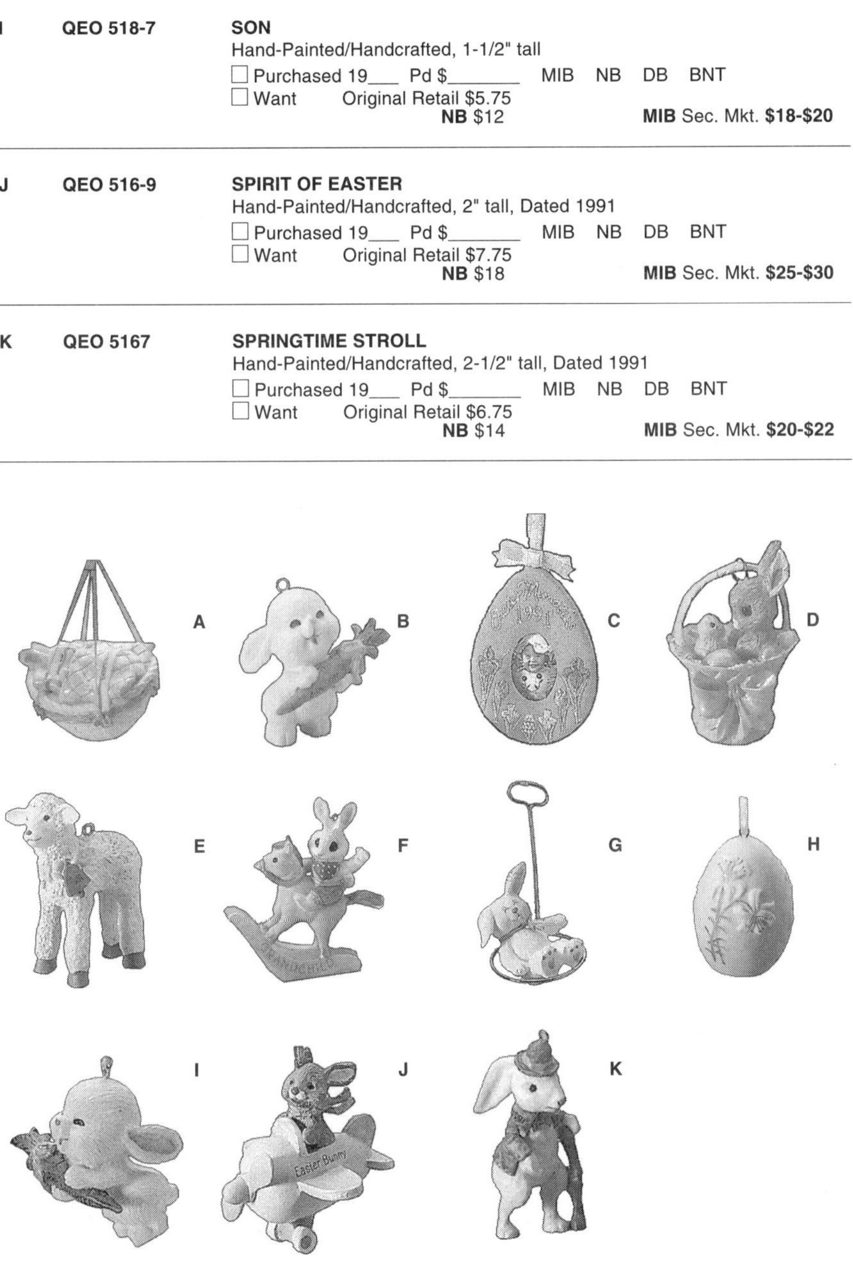

1992 Easter Ornament Collection

A QEO 927-1 **BABY'S FIRST EASTER**
Handcrafted, 3" tall, Dated 1992. **Artist:** John Francis (Collin)
☐ Purchased 19___ Pd $_______ MIB NB DB BNT
☐ Want Original Retail $6.75
NB $10 **MIB** Sec. Mkt. **$18-$20**

B QEO 935-4 **BELLE BUNNY**
Porcelain, 3" tall, Dated '92. **Artist:** LaDene Votruba
☐ Purchased 19___ Pd $_______ MIB NB DB BNT
☐ Want Original Retail $9.75
NB $12 **MIB** Sec. Mkt. **$18-$20**

C QEO 929-1 **BLESS YOU**
Handcrafted, 3" tall. **Artist:** John Francis (Collin)
☐ Purchased 19___ Pd $_______ MIB NB DB BNT
☐ Want Original Retail $6.75
NB $9 **MIB** Sec. Mkt. **$18-$22**

D QEO 936-4 **COSMIC RABBIT**
Handcrafted, 3" tall, Dated '92. **Artist:** Bob Siedler
☐ Purchased 19___ Pd $_______ MIB NB DB BNT
☐ Want Original Retail $7.75
NB $9 **MIB** Sec. Mkt. **$14-$18**

E QEO 930-4 **CRAYOLA® BUNNY**
Handcrafted, 3" tall, Dated '92. **Artist:** Anita Marra Rogers
☐ Purchased 19___ Pd $_______ MIB NB DB BNT
☐ Want Original Retail $7.75
NB $18 **MIB** Sec. Mkt. **$28-$30**

F QEO 935-1 **CULTIVATED GARDENER**
Handcrafted, 3" tall, Caption: "Carrots 92". **Artist:** Bob Siedler
☐ Purchased 19___ Pd $_______ MIB NB DB BNT
☐ Want Original Retail $5.75
NB $6 **MIB** Sec. Mkt. **$15-$18**

G QEO 928-4 **DAUGHTER**
Handcrafted, 3" tall, Dated 1992. **Artist:** Anita Marra Rogers
☐ Purchased 19___ Pd $_______ MIB NB DB BNT
☐ Want Original Retail $5.75
NB $10 **MIB** Sec. Mkt. **$15-$18**

H QEO 930-1 **EASTER PARADE**
FIRST IN SERIES, 3" tall, Handcrafted, Dated '92. **Artist:** Ken Crow
☐ Purchased 19___ Pd $_______ MIB NB DB BNT
☐ Want Original Retail $6.75
NB $15 **MIB** Sec. Mkt. **$25-$30**

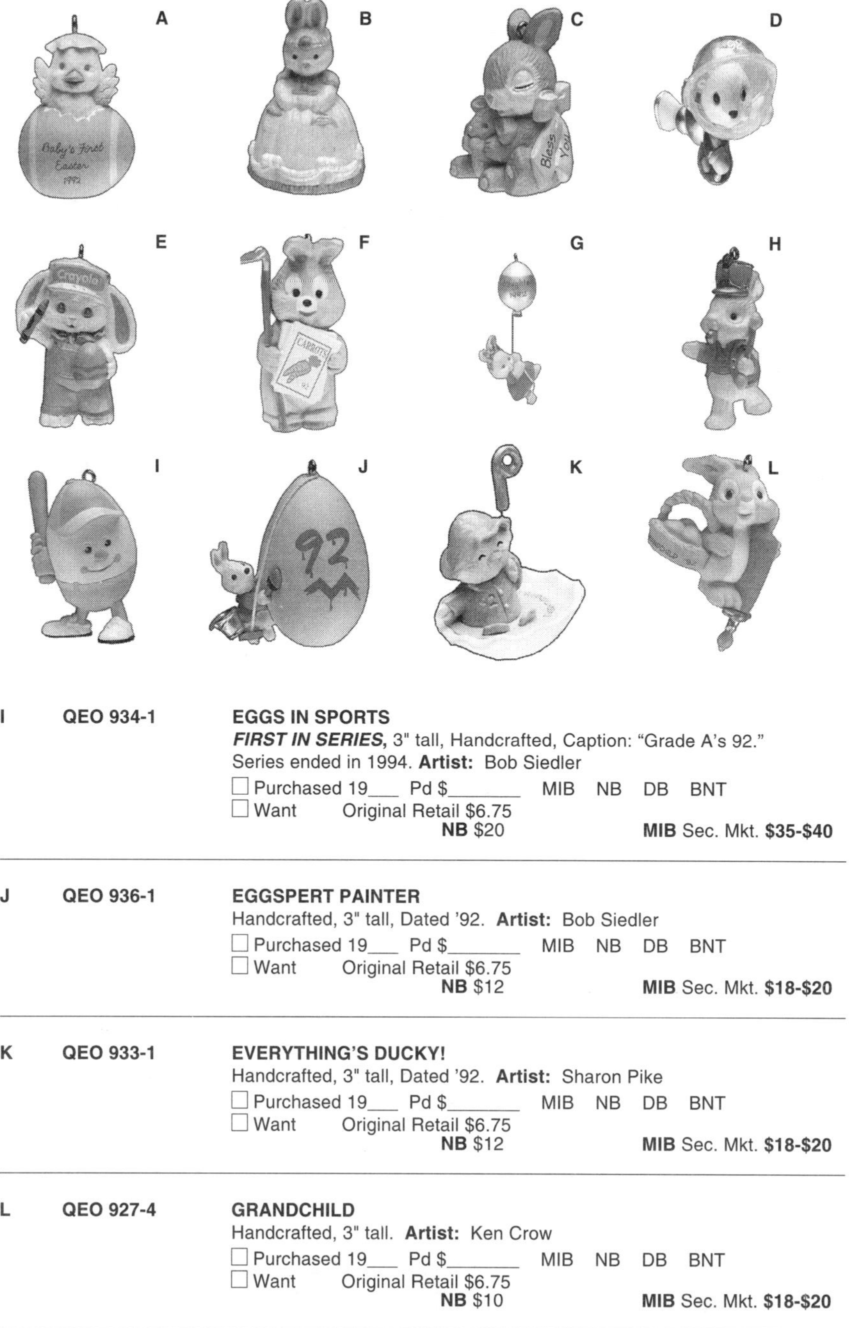

I QEO 934-1 **EGGS IN SPORTS**
FIRST IN SERIES, 3" tall, Handcrafted, Caption: "Grade A's 92." Series ended in 1994. **Artist:** Bob Siedler
☐ Purchased 19___ Pd $_______ MIB NB DB BNT
☐ Want Original Retail $6.75
NB $20 **MIB** Sec. Mkt. **$35-$40**

J QEO 936-1 **EGGSPERT PAINTER**
Handcrafted, 3" tall, Dated '92. **Artist:** Bob Siedler
☐ Purchased 19___ Pd $_______ MIB NB DB BNT
☐ Want Original Retail $6.75
NB $12 **MIB** Sec. Mkt. **$18-$20**

K QEO 933-1 **EVERYTHING'S DUCKY!**
Handcrafted, 3" tall, Dated '92. **Artist:** Sharon Pike
☐ Purchased 19___ Pd $_______ MIB NB DB BNT
☐ Want Original Retail $6.75
NB $12 **MIB** Sec. Mkt. **$18-$20**

L QEO 927-4 **GRANDCHILD**
Handcrafted, 3" tall. **Artist:** Ken Crow
☐ Purchased 19___ Pd $_______ MIB NB DB BNT
☐ Want Original Retail $6.75
NB $10 **MIB** Sec. Mkt. **$18-$20**

A QEO 933-4 **JOY BEARER**
Handcrafted, Dated '92. **Artist:** Don Palmiter
☐ Purchased 19___ Pd $_______ MIB NB DB BNT
☐ Want Original Retail $8.75
NB $14 **MIB** Sec. Mkt. **$28-$30**

B QEO 931-4 **PROMISE OF EASTER**
Porcelain, 3" tall, Dated 1992. **Artist:** Joyce A. Lyle
Caption: "God's love shines everywhere."
☐ Purchased 19___ Pd $_______ MIB NB DB BNT
☐ Want Original Retail $8.75
NB $14 **MIB** Sec. Mkt. **$18-$20**

C QEO 932-4 **ROCKING BUNNY**
Handcrafted and Nickel-Plated, 3" tall. **Artist:** LaDene Votruba
Caption: "Happy Easter 1992"
☐ Purchased 19___ Pd $_______ MIB NB DB BNT
☐ Want Original Retail $9.75
NB $14 **MIB** Sec. Mkt. **$20-$22**

D QEO 929-4 **SOMEBUNNY LOVES YOU**
Handcrafted, 3" tall. **Artist:** John Francis (Collin)
☐ Purchased 19___ Pd $_______ MIB NB DB BNT
☐ Want Original Retail $6.75
NB $12 **MIB** Sec. Mkt. **$24-$28**

E QEO 928-1 **SON**
Handcrafted, 3" tall, Dated 1992. **Artist:** Anita Marra Rogers
☐ Purchased 19___ Pd $_______ MIB NB DB BNT
☐ Want Original Retail $5.75
NB $8 **MIB** Sec. Mkt. **$15-$18**

F QEO 932-1 **SPRINGTIME EGG**
Handcrafted, 3" tall, Dated 1992. **Artist:** Julia Lee
☐ Purchased 19___ Pd $_______ MIB NB DB BNT
☐ Want Original Retail $8.75
NB $10 **MIB** Sec. Mkt. **$15-$18**

G QEO 934-4 **SUNNY WISHER**
Handcrafted, 3" tall. **Artist:** Sharon Pike
Caption: "Sunny Easter Wishes"
☐ Purchased 19___ Pd $_______ MIB NB DB BNT
☐ Want Original Retail $5.75
NB $10 **MIB** Sec. Mkt. **$14-$18**

H QEO 931-1 **WARM MEMORIES**
Embroidered Fabric Photoholder, 4: tall, Dated 1992
Artist: LaDene Votruba. Caption: "Easter brings warm memories."
☐ Purchased 19___ Pd $_______ MIB NB DB BNT
☐ Want Original Retail $7.75
NB $12 **MIB** Sec. Mkt. **$14-$16**

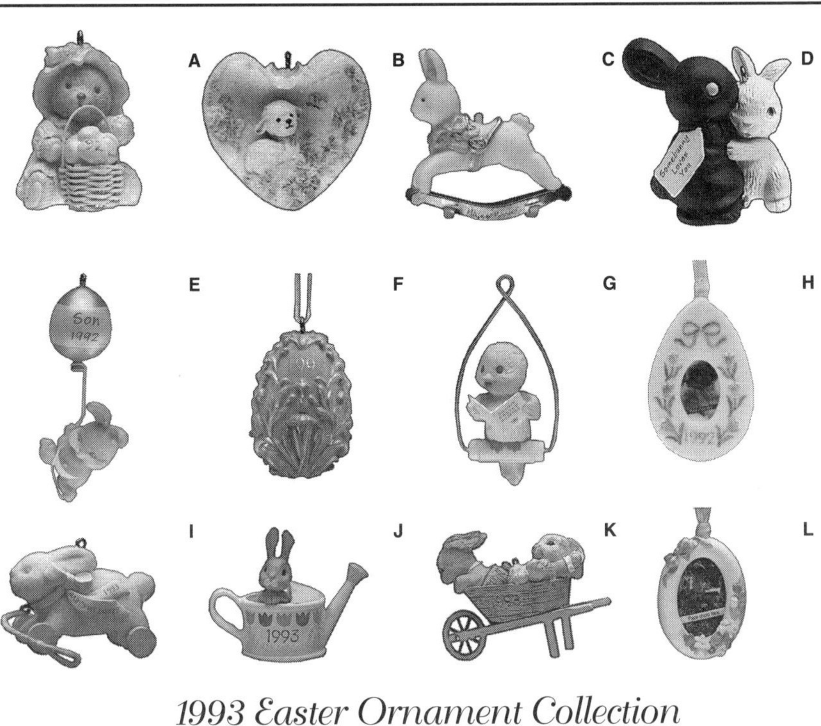

1993 Easter Ornament Collection

I QEO 834-5 **BABY'S FIRST EASTER**
Handcrafted, 1-1/4" tall, Dated 1993. **Artist:** Don Palmiter
☐ Purchased 19___ Pd $_______ MIB NB DB BNT
☐ Want Original Retail $6.75
NB $8 **MIB** Sec. Mkt. **$10-$14**

J QEO 840-5 **BACKYARD BUNNY**
Handcrafted, 2" tall, Dated 1993. **Artist:** Linda Sickman
☐ Purchased 19___ Pd $_______ MIB NB DB BNT
☐ Want Original Retail $6.75
NB $8 **MIB** Sec. Mkt. **$14-$16**

K QEO 840-2 **BARROW OF GIGGLES**
Handcrafted, 1-7/8" tall, Dated 1993. **Artist:** Patricia Andrews
☐ Purchased 19___ Pd $_______ MIB NB DB BNT
☐ Want Original Retail $8.75
NB $12 **MIB** Sec. Mkt. **$18-$20**

L QEO 836-2 **BEAUTIFUL MEMORIES**
Handcrafted Photoholder, 2-1/2" tall. **Artist:** Duane Unruh
Caption: "1993 Beautiful Easter Memories"
☐ Purchased 19___ Pd $_______ MIB NB DB BNT
☐ Want Original Retail $6.75
NB $8 **MIB** Sec. Mkt. **$12-$16**

A QEO 839-2 **BEST-DRESSED TURTLE**
Handcrafted, 1-7/8" tall. **Artist:** Julia Lee
☐ Purchased 19___ Pd $_______ MIB NB DB BNT
☐ Want Original Retail $5.75
NB $8 **MIB** Sec. Mkt. **$14-$16**

B QEO 837-5 **CHICKS-ON-A-TWIRL**
Handcrafted Twirl-About, 3" tall, Dated 1993
Artist: Joyce A. Lyle
☐ Purchased 19___ Pd $_______ MIB NB DB BNT
☐ Want Original Retail $7.75
NB $9 **MIB** Sec. Mkt. **$15-$16**

C QEO 834-2 **DAUGHTER**
Handcrafted, 2-1/2" tall, Dated '93. **Artist:** Patricia Andrews
☐ Purchased 19___ Pd $_______ MIB NB DB BNT
☐ Want Original Retail $5.75
NB $9 **MIB** Sec. Mkt. **$16-$18**

D QEO 832-5 **EASTER PARADE**
Second in Series, Handcrafted, 2-7/8" tall, Dated '93
Artist: Julia Lee
☐ Purchased 19___ Pd $_______ MIB NB DB BNT
☐ Want Original Retail $6.75
NB $10 **MIB** Sec. Mkt. **$18-$20**

E QEO 833-2 **EGGS IN SPORTS**
Second in Series, Handcrafted, 2" tall. **Artist:** Bob Siedler
Caption: "Tennis 93 Ace"
☐ Purchased 19___ Pd $_______ MIB NB DB BNT
☐ Want Original Retail $6.75
NB $10 **MIB** Sec. Mkt. **$18-$20**

F QEO 835-2 **GRANDCHILD**
Handcrafted, 1-7/8" tall, Dated 1993. **Artist:** Bob Siedler
☐ Purchased 19___ Pd $_______ MIB NB DB BNT
☐ Want Original Retail $6.75
NB $10 **MIB** Sec. Mkt. **$15-$18**

G QEO 831-2 **LI'L PEEPER**
Handcrafted, 1-7/8" tall. **Artist:** Julia Lee
☐ Purchased 19___ Pd $_______ MIB NB DB BNT
☐ Want Original Retail $7.75
NB $10 **MIB** Sec. Mkt. **$15-$18**

H QEO 831-5 **LOP-EARED BUNNY**
Handcrafted, 7/8" tall. **Artist:** Linda Sickman
☐ Purchased 19___ Pd $_______ MIB NB DB BNT
☐ Want Original Retail $5.75
NB $6 **MIB** Sec. Mkt. **$15-$16**

I QEO 837-2 **LOVELY LAMB**
Porcelain, 3" tall, Dated '93. **Artist:** LaDene Votruba
☐ Purchased 19___ Pd $_______ MIB NB DB BNT
☐ Want Original Retail $9.75
NB $9.50 **MIB** Sec. Mkt. **$18-$20**

J QEO 839-5 **MAYPOLE STROLL**
Handcrafted. **Artists:** John Francis (Collin) and Robert Chad
Dollie Duck, Ricky Rabbit and Chester Chipmunk, 2" - 2-1/2" tall in Basket, 4-1/4" tall
☐ Purchased 19___ Pd $_______ MIB NB DB BNT
☐ Want Original Retail $28.00
NB $22 **MIB** Sec. Mkt. **$38-$40**

K QEO 838-2 **NUTTY EGGS**
Handcrafted, 1-7/8" tall. **Artist:** Julia Lee
☐ Purchased 19___ Pd $_______ MIB NB DB BNT
☐ Want Original Retail $6.75
NB $10 **MIB** Sec. Mkt. **$18-$20**

L QEO 836-5 **RADIANT WINDOW**
Handcrafted, 3-1/4" tall. **Artist:** Duane Unruh
☐ Purchased 19___ Pd $_______ MIB NB DB BNT
☐ Want Original Retail $7.75
NB $10 **MIB** Sec. Mkt. **$14-$16**

A | QEO 832-2 | **SPRINGTIME BONNETS**
First in Series, Handcrafted, 2-1/4" tall, Dated '93
Artist: Donna Lee
☐ Purchased 19___ Pd $_______ MIB NB DB BNT
☐ Want Original Retail $7.75
NB $15 **MIB** Sec. Mkt. **$25-$30**

B | QEO 833-5 | **SON**
Handcrafted, 2-1/2" tall, Dated '93, **Artist:** Patricia Andrews
☐ Purchased 19___ Pd $_______ MIB NB DB BNT
☐ Want Original Retail $5.75
NB $8 **MIB** Sec. Mkt. **$14-$16**

C | QEO 838-5 | **TIME FOR EASTER**
Handcrafted, 3-1/2" tall, **Artist:** Robert Chad
Caption: "1993 Time for Easter Fun!"
☐ Purchased 19___ Pd $_______ MIB NB DB BNT
☐ Want Original Retail $8.75
NB $12 **MIB** Sec. Mkt. **$18-$22**

1994 Easter Ornament Collection

D | QEO 815-3 | **BABY'S FIRST EASTER**
Handcrafted, 2" tall, Dated 1994
Sleeping bunny in basket. **Artist:** John Francis
☐ Purchased 19___ Pd $_______ MIB NB DB BNT
☐ Want Original Retail $6.75
MIB Sec. Mkt.**$16-$18**

E | QEO 823-3 | **COLLECTOR'S PLATE**
FIRST IN SERIES, Porcelain, 3" dia. **Artist:** LaDene Votruba
Caption: "Gathering Sunny Memories 1994"
☐ Purchased 19___ Pd $_______ MIB NB DB BNT
☐ Want Original Retail $7.75
NB $15 **MIB** Sec. Mkt.**$25-$30**

F | QEO 816-6 | **COLORFUL SPRING**
Handcrafted, 3" tall, Caption: "Crayola® Crayon 1994"
Was very popular. **Artist:** Ken Crow
☐ Purchased 19___ Pd $_______ MIB NB DB BNT
☐ Want Original Retail $7.75
NB $15 **MIB** Sec. Mkt. **$26-$30**

G | QEO 815-6 | **DAUGHTER**
Handcrafted, 2" tall, Dated 1994 **Artist:** Patricia Andrews
Girl bunny in yellow dress.
☐ Purchased 19___ Pd $_______ MIB NB DB BNT
☐ Want Original Retail $5.75
NB $8 **MIB** Sec. Mkt.**$12-$15**

H | QEO 818-3 | **DIVINE DUET**
Handcrafted, 2" tall, Caption: "Easter Hymns" **Artist:** LaDene Votruba
☐ Purchased 19___ Pd $_______ MIB NB DB BNT
☐ Want Original Retail $6.75
NB $8 **MIB** Sec. Mkt.**$12-$15**

I | QEO 819-3 | **EASTER ART SHOW**
Handcrafted, 2-1/4" tall, Dated 1994
Stringer Ornament, hangs from two branches. **Artist:** LaDene Votruba
☐ Purchased 19___ Pd $_______ MIB NB DB BNT
☐ Want Original Retail $7.75
NB $6 **MIB** Sec. Mkt.**$12-$15**

J | QEO 813-6 | **EASTER PARADE**
Third and Final in Series, Handcrafted, 1-1/4" tall, Dated '94
Artist: Dill Rhodus
☐ Purchased 19___ Pd $_______ MIB NB DB BNT
☐ Want Original Retail $6.75
NB $8 **MIB** Sec. Mkt. **$16-$20**

K | QEO 813-3 | **EGGS IN SPORTS**
Third and Final in Series, Handcrafted, 2" tall
Caption: "Golf Club 94." **Artist:** Bob Siedler
☐ Purchased 19___ Pd $_______ MIB NB DB BNT
☐ Want Original Retail $6.75
NB $8 **MIB** Sec. Mkt.**$16-$20**

A QEO 809-3 **HERE COMES EASTER**
FIRST IN SERIES, Handcrafted, 1-3/4" tall
Caption: "Hop-N-Go 1994." **Artist:** Ken Crow
☐ Purchased 19___ Pd $_______ MIB NB DB BNT
☐ Want Original Retail $7.75
NB $15 **MIB** Sec. Mkt. **$30-$32**

B QEO 820-6 **JOYFUL LAMB**
Handcrafted, 1-3/4" tall **Artist:** Duane Unruh
☐ Purchased 19___ Pd $_______ MIB NB DB BNT
☐ Want Original Retail $5.75
NB $7 **MIB** Sec. Mkt. **$10-$12**

C QEO 817-6 **PEANUTS®**
Handcrafted, 2-1/4" tall, Caption: "Easter Beagle 1994"
Was the hottest Easter ornament for 1994.
Artist: Duane Unruh
☐ Purchased 19___ Pd $_______ MIB NB DB BNT
☐ Want Original Retail $7.75
NB $18 **MIB** Sec. Mkt. **$28-$34**

D QEO 820-3 **PEEPING OUT**
Handcrafted, 1-1/4" tall **Artist:** Duane Unruh
☐ Purchased 19___ Pd $_______ MIB NB DB BNT
☐ Want Original Retail $6.75
NB $10 **MIB** Sec. Mkt. **$14-$16**

E QEO 821-3 **RIDING A BREEZE**
Handcrafted, 2-1/2" tall, Caption: "Happy Spring 94"
Artist: Don Palmiter
☐ Purchased 19___ Pd $_______ MIB NB DB BNT
☐ Want Original Retail $5.75
NB $8 **MIB** Sec. Mkt. **$14-$16**

F QEO 816-3 **SON**
Handcrafted, 2" tall, Dated 1994. **Artist:** Patricia Andrews
☐ Purchased 19___ Pd $_______ MIB NB DB BNT
☐ Want Original Retail $5.75
NB $8 **MIB** Sec. Mkt. **$12-$15**

G QEO 809-6 **SPRINGTIME BONNETS**
Second in Series, Handcrafted, 2-1/4" tall, Dated '94
☐ Purchased 19___ Pd $_______ MIB NB DB BNT
☐ Want Original Retail $7.75
NB $10 **MIB** Sec. Mkt. **$20-$24**

H QEO 813-6 **SUNNY BUNNY GARDEN**
Handcrafted, 1-1/4" tall, Set of Three
Caption: "Teeny Tiny Daisies 1994" **Artist:** Ed Seale
☐ Purchased 19___ Pd $_______ MIB NB DB BNT
☐ Want Original Retail $15.00
NB $15 **MIB** Sec. Mkt. **$20-$22**

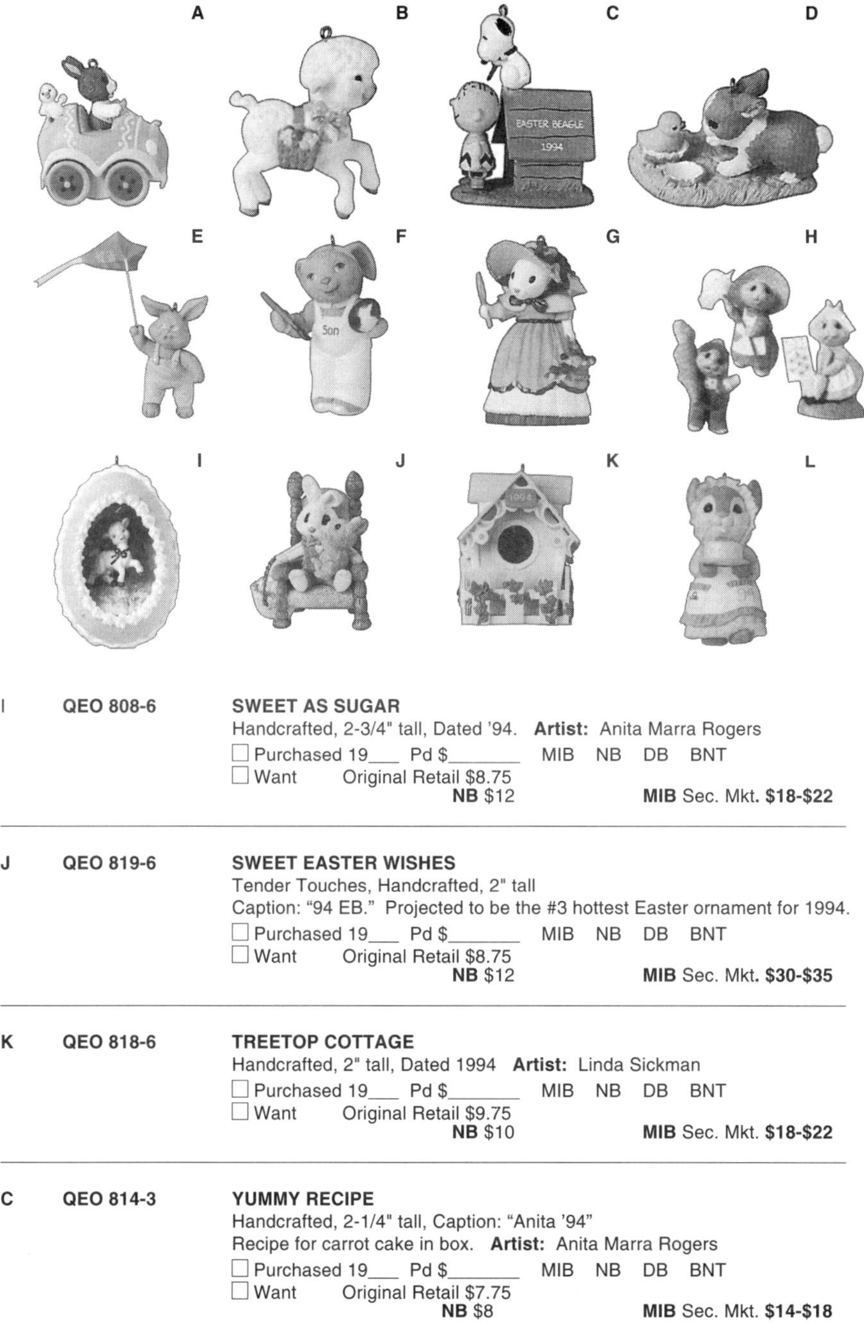

I QEO 808-6 **SWEET AS SUGAR**
Handcrafted, 2-3/4" tall, Dated '94. **Artist:** Anita Marra Rogers
☐ Purchased 19___ Pd $_______ MIB NB DB BNT
☐ Want Original Retail $8.75
NB $12 **MIB** Sec. Mkt. **$18-$22**

J QEO 819-6 **SWEET EASTER WISHES**
Tender Touches, Handcrafted, 2" tall
Caption: "94 EB." Projected to be the #3 hottest Easter ornament for 1994.
☐ Purchased 19___ Pd $_______ MIB NB DB BNT
☐ Want Original Retail $8.75
NB $12 **MIB** Sec. Mkt. **$30-$35**

K QEO 818-6 **TREETOP COTTAGE**
Handcrafted, 2" tall, Dated 1994 **Artist:** Linda Sickman
☐ Purchased 19___ Pd $_______ MIB NB DB BNT
☐ Want Original Retail $9.75
NB $10 **MIB** Sec. Mkt. **$18-$22**

C QEO 814-3 **YUMMY RECIPE**
Handcrafted, 2-1/4" tall, Caption: "Anita '94"
Recipe for carrot cake in box. **Artist:** Anita Marra Rogers
☐ Purchased 19___ Pd $_______ MIB NB DB BNT
☐ Want Original Retail $7.75
NB $8 **MIB** Sec. Mkt. **$14-$18**

1995 Easter Ornament Collection

A QEO 825-3 **APRIL SHOWERS**
Handcrafted, Dated 1995
☐ Purchased 19___ Pd $_______ MIB NB DB BNT
☐ Want Original Retail $6.95
MIB Sec. Mkt. **$10-$14**

B QEO 823-7 **BABY'S FIRST EASTER**
Handcrafted, Dated 1995
☐ Purchased 19___ Pd $_______ MIB NB DB BNT
☐ Want Original Retail $7.95
MIB Sec. Mkt. **$12-$14**

C QEO 821-9 **COLLECTOR'S PLATE**
Second in Series, Porcelain, Dated 1995
☐ Purchased 19___ Pd $_______ MIB NB DB BNT
☐ Want Original Retail $7.95
MIB Sec. Mkt. **$14-$16**

D QEO 824-9 **CRAYOLA: BUNNY WITH CRAYONS**
Handcrafted, Dated '95
☐ Purchased 19___ Pd $_______ MIB NB DB BNT
☐ Want Original Retail $7.95
NB $10 **MIB** Sec. Mkt. **$15-$18**

E QEO 823-9 **DAUGHTER**
Handcrafted, Dated 1995
☐ Purchased 19___ Pd $_______ MIB NB DB BNT
☐ Want Original Retail $5.95
MIB Sec. Mkt. **$12-$14**

F QEO 820-7 **EASTER EGG COTTAGES**
FIRST IN SERIES, Handcrafted, Dated 1995
☐ Purchased 19___ Pd $_______ MIB NB DB BNT
☐ Want Original Retail $8.95
NB $10 **MIB** Sec. Mkt. **$18-$20**

G QEO 820-9 **GARDEN CLUB**
FIRST IN SERIES, Handcrafted
☐ Purchased 19___ Pd $_______ MIB NB DB BNT
☐ Want Original Retail $7.95
NB $10 **MIB** Sec. Mkt. **$16-$20**

H QEO 827-7 **HAM 'N EGGS**
Handcrafted
☐ Purchased 19___ Pd $_______ MIB NB DB BNT
☐ Want Original Retail $7.95
NB $8 **MIB** Sec. Mkt. **$12-$14**

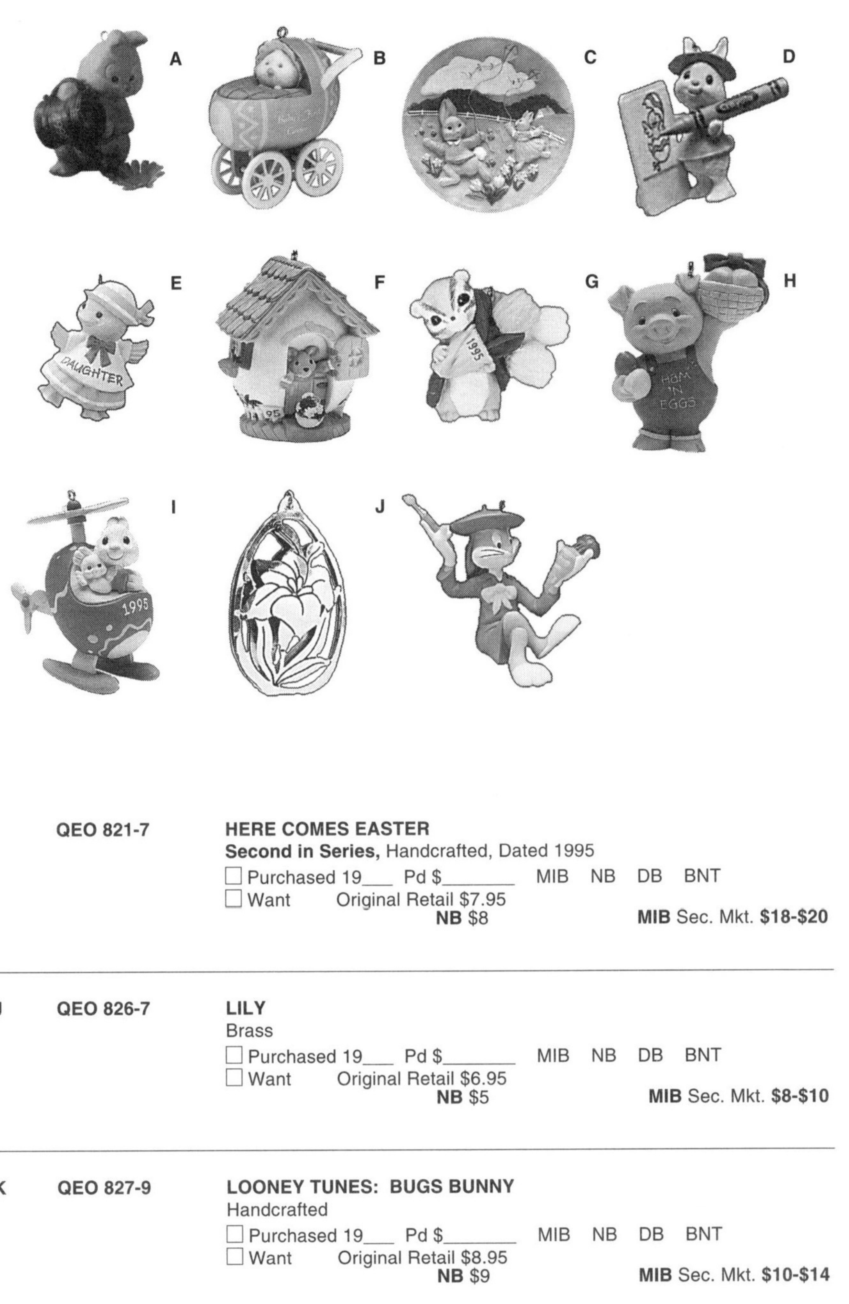

I QEO 821-7 **HERE COMES EASTER**
Second in Series, Handcrafted, Dated 1995
☐ Purchased 19___ Pd $_______ MIB NB DB BNT
☐ Want Original Retail $7.95
NB $8 **MIB** Sec. Mkt. **$18-$20**

J QEO 826-7 **LILY**
Brass
☐ Purchased 19___ Pd $_______ MIB NB DB BNT
☐ Want Original Retail $6.95
NB $5 **MIB** Sec. Mkt. **$8-$10**

K QEO 827-9 **LOONEY TUNES: BUGS BUNNY**
Handcrafted
☐ Purchased 19___ Pd $_______ MIB NB DB BNT
☐ Want Original Retail $8.95
NB $9 **MIB** Sec. Mkt. **$10-$14**

A QEO 826-9 **MINIATURE TRAIN**
Handcrafted, Dated '95
☐ Purchased 19___ Pd $_______ MIB NB DB BNT
☐ Want Original Retail $4.95
MIB Sec. Mkt. **$8-$12**

B QEO 825-7 **PEANUTS: EASTER BEAGLE**
Handcrafted, Dated 1995
☐ Purchased 19___ Pd $_______ MIB NB DB BNT
☐ Want Original Retail $7.95
NB $10
MIB Sec. Mkt. **$20-$24**

C QEO 824-7 **SON**
Handcrafted, Dated 1995
☐ Purchased 19___ Pd $_______ MIB NB DB BNT
☐ Want Original Retail $5.95
MIB Sec. Mkt. **$10-$14**

D QEO 806-9 **SPRINGTIME BARBIE**
FIRST IN SERIES, Handcrafted
☐ Purchased 19___ Pd $_______ MIB NB DB BNT
☐ Want Original Retail $12.95
NB $20
MIB Sec. Mkt. **$40-$45**

E QEO 822-7 **SPRINGTIME BONNETS**
Third in Series, Handcrafted, Dated '95
☐ Purchased 19___ Pd $_______ MIB NB DB BNT
☐ Want Original Retail $7.95
NB $10
MIB Sec. Mkt. **$14-$16**

F QEO 825-9 **TENDER TOUCHES: BUNNY WITH SEED PACKETS**
Handcrafted, Dated 1995
☐ Purchased 19___ Pd $_______ MIB NB DB BNT
☐ Want Original Retail $8.95
NB $10
MIB Sec. Mkt. **$14-$18**

G QEO 822-9 **THREE FLOWERPOT FRIENDS**
Handcrafted, Dated 1995
☐ Purchased 19___ Pd $_______ MIB NB DB BNT
☐ Want Original Retail $14.95
NB $15
MIB Sec. Mkt. **$20-$25**

"My sister got in a lot of trouble yesterday,"
Ernie said to Ruth.
"What did she do?"
"She was feeding the tropical fish."
"What's wrong with that?" Ruth asked.
Ernie said, "She was feeding them to our cat."

"We started living up here after Doris's Hallmark Ornaments took over."

1996 Easter Ornament Collection

A	QEO 808-4	**APPLE BLOSSOM LANE** **Second in Series**, Handcrafted, 2-1/2" tall, Dated 1996 **Artist:** John Francis ☐ Purchased 19___ Pd $_______ MIB NB DB BNT ☐ Want Original Retail $8.95
B	QEO 815-4	**DAFFY DUCK** Looney Tunes™, Handcrafted 2 -1/2" tall, Will be popular. **Artist:** Anita Rogers ☐ Purchased 19___ Pd $_______ MIB NB DB BNT ☐ Want Original Retail $8.95
C	QEO 816-4	**EASTER MORNING** Handcrafted, 2-1/4" tall, Dated 1996 **Artist:** Duane Unruh ☐ Purchased 19___ Pd $_______ MIB NB DB BNT ☐ Want Original Retail $7.95
D	QEO 816-1	**EGGSTRA SPECIAL SURPRISE** Tender Touches, Handcrafted 2 -1/4" tall, Dated 1996, Will be top seller. **Artist:** Ed Seale ☐ Purchased 19___ Pd $_______ MIB NB DB BNT ☐ Want Original Retail $8.95
E	QEO 809-1	**GARDEN CLUB** Handcrafted, 1-1/4" tall, Dated 1996 **Artist:** Don Palmiter ☐ Purchased 19___ Pd $_______ MIB NB DB BNT ☐ Want Original Retail $7.95
F	QEO 809-4	**HERE COMES EASTER** **Third in Series**, Handcrafted, 2" tall, Dated 1996 **Artist:** Ken Crow ☐ Purchased 19___ Pd $_______ MIB NB DB BNT ☐ Want Original Retail $7.95
G	QEO 814-4	**HIPPITY HOP DELIVERY** Crayola® Crayon, Handcrafted, 2" tall, Dated 1996 **Artist:** Ken Crow ☐ Purchased 19___ Pd $_______ MIB NB DB BNT ☐ Want Original Retail $7.95
H	QEO 818-4	**JOYFUL ANGELS** ***FIRST IN SERIES,*** Handcrafted, 3" tall, Dated 1996, Be sure to get this one. **Artist:** Joyce Lyle ☐ Purchased 19___ Pd $_______ MIB NB DB BNT ☐ Want Original Retail $9.95
I	QEO 822-1	**KEEPING A SECRET** Porcelain Collector's Plate, 3" tall, Dated 1996 **Artist:** LaDene Votruba ☐ Purchased 19___ Pd $_______ MIB NB DB BNT ☐ Want Original Retail $7.95

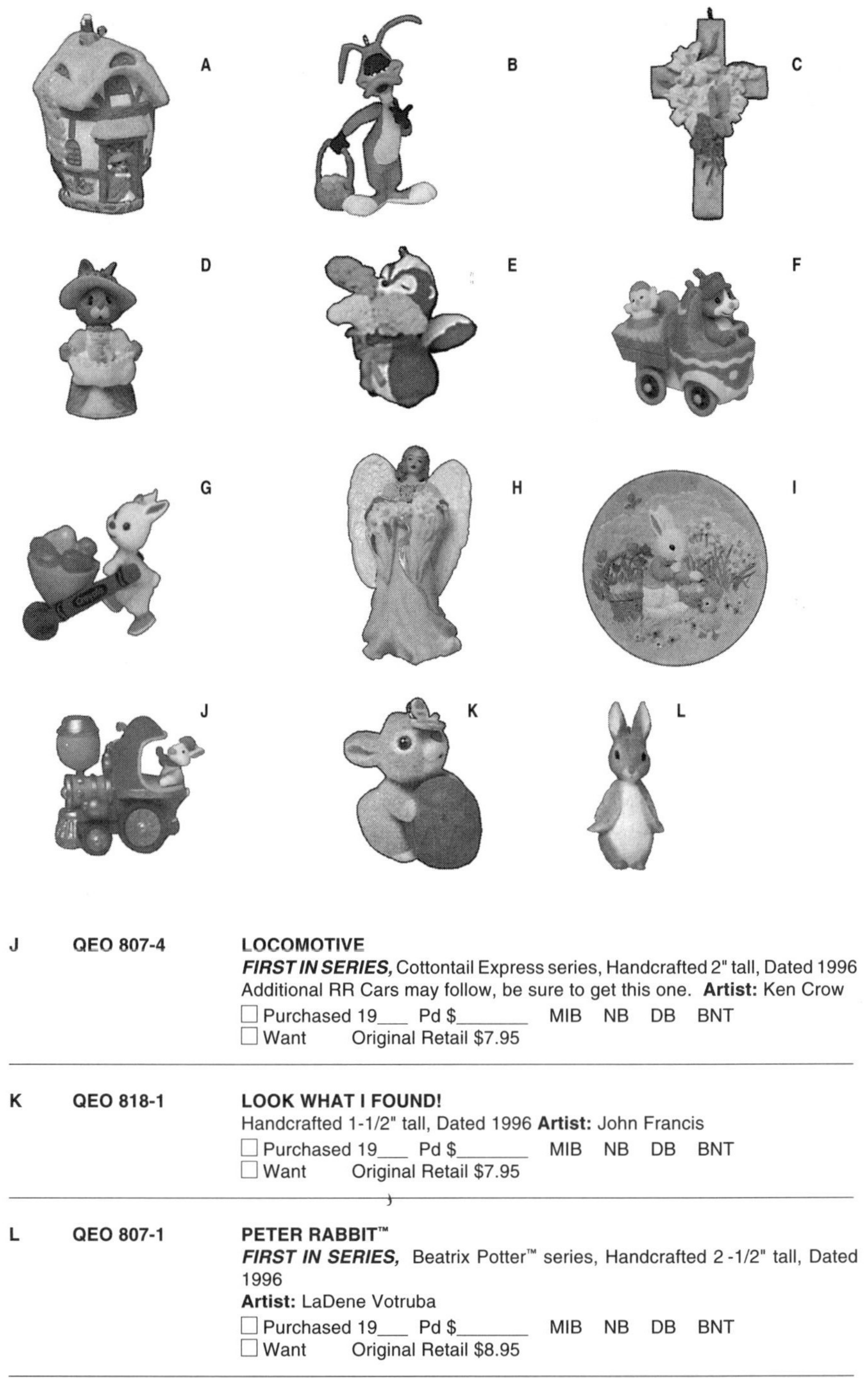

J	QEO 807-4	**LOCOMOTIVE** ***FIRST IN SERIES,*** Cottontail Express series, Handcrafted 2" tall, Dated 1996 Additional RR Cars may follow, be sure to get this one. **Artist:** Ken Crow ☐ Purchased 19___ Pd $_______ MIB NB DB BNT ☐ Want Original Retail $7.95
K	QEO 818-1	**LOOK WHAT I FOUND!** Handcrafted 1-1/2" tall, Dated 1996 **Artist:** John Francis ☐ Purchased 19___ Pd $_______ MIB NB DB BNT ☐ Want Original Retail $7.95
L	QEO 807-1	**PETER RABBIT™** ***FIRST IN SERIES,*** Beatrix Potter™ series, Handcrafted 2 -1/2" tall, Dated 1996 **Artist:** LaDene Votruba ☐ Purchased 19___ Pd $_______ MIB NB DB BNT ☐ Want Original Retail $8.95

1996 Easter Ornaments

A

B

C

D

A	QEO 815-1	**PARADE PALS** Peanuts ®, Handcrafted, 2-1/4" tall, Dated 1996 **Artist:** Dill Rhodus ☐ Purchased 19___ Pd $_______ MIB NB DB BNT ☐ Want Original Retail $7.95
B	QEO 817-4	**PORK 'N BEANS** Handcrafted, 2" tall, Dated 1996 **Artist:** Robert Chad ☐ Purchased 19___ Pd $_______ MIB NB DB BNT ☐ Want Original Retail $7.95
C	QEO 817-1	**STRAWBERRY PATCH** Handcrafted, 3" tall, Dated 1996 **Artist:** Ed Seale ☐ Purchased 19___ Pd $_______ MIB NB DB BNT ☐ Want Original Retail $6.95
D	QEO 814-1	**STRIKE UP THE BAND!** Set of three, Handcrafted, Bugle Bunny: 2 - 1/4" tall, Tweedle-Dee Duck: 1-1/2" tall, Nutty Squirrel: 1-1/2" tall, Dated 1996 **Artist:** Duane Unruh ☐ Purchased 19___ Pd $_______ MIB NB DB BNT ☐ Want Original Retail $14.95

Hallmark Keepsake Ornament Collectors' Club Ornaments

Year	Item #	Description	Comments	Price
1987	QXC 580-9	Wreath of Memories, Dated	Membership	$55-$60
1987	QXC 581-7	Carousel Reindeer	Members Only	$65-$70
1988	QXC 580-4	Our Clubhouse, Dated	Membership	$45-$48
1988	QXC 570-4	Hold On Tight, Mini	Early Renewal Gift	$65-$70
1988	QXC 580-1	Sleighful of Dreams	Members Only	$62-$65
1988	QX 406-4	Holiday Heirloom, II	Club - LE 34,600	$28-$32
1988	QX 408-4	Angelic Minstrel	Club - LE 49,900	$32-$35
1988	QX 407-1	Christmas Is Sharing	Club - LE 49,900	$38-$40
1989	QXC 580-2	Visit From Santa, Dated	Membership	$35-$40
1989	QXC 428-5	Collect A Dream	Members Only	$35-$40
1989	QXC 581-2	Sitting Purrty, Mini	Special Gift	$10-$15
1989	QXC 451-2	Christmas Is Peaceful	Club - LE 49,900	$35-$40
1989	QXC 448-3	Noelle	Club - LE 49,900	$35-$38
1989	QXC 460-5	Holiday Heirloom, III	Club- LE 34,600	$33-$35
1990	QXC 445-6	Club Hollow, Dated	Membership	$30-$35
1990	QXC 445-3	Armful of Joy	Members Only	$35-$40
1990	QXC 560-3	Crown Prince, Mini	Special Gift	$25-$30
1990	QXC 447-6	Dove of Peace	Club - LE 25,400	$60-$65
1990	QXC 476-6	Christmas Limited	Club - LE 38,700	$95-$100
1990	QXC 447-3	Sugar Plum Fairy	Club - LE 25,400	$52-$55
1991	QXC 476-9	Hidden Treasure/Li'l Keeper	Membership	$35-$45
1991	QXC 315-9	Five Years Together	Charter Member Gift	$50-$55
1991	QXC 725-9	Beary Artistic (Lighted)	Members Only	$38-$42
1991	QXC 479-7	Secrets for Santa	Club - LE 28,700	$50-$55
1991	QXC 477-9	Galloping Into Christmas	Club - LE 28,400	$70-$75
1992	QXC 508-1	Rodney Takes Flight	Membership	$22-$25
1992	QXC 729-1	Santa's Club List	Members Only	$35-$38
1992	QXC 519-4	Chipmunk Parcel Service, Mini	Special Gift	$18-$24
1992	QXC 546-4	Christmas Treasures	Club - LE 15,500	$150-$165
1992	QXC 406-7	Victorian Skater	Club - LE 14,700	$50-$55
1993	QXC 527-2	It's in the Mail	Membership	$22-$25
1993	QXC 543-2	Trimmed With Memories	Members Only	$24-$26
1993	QXC 543-5	Sharing Christmas	Club - LE 16,500	$32-$35
1993	QXC 544-2	Gentle Tidings	Club - LE 17,500	$38-$40
1993	QXC 529-4	Forty Winks, Mini	Membership	$18-$22
1994	QXC	First Hello	Membership Promotion	
1994	QXC	Happy Collecting MM	Renewal Bonus	
1994	QXC 482-3	Holiday Pursuit	Membership	$18-$20
1994	QXC 483-3	Jolly Holly Santa	Club - LE	$35-$40
1994	QXC 483-6	Majestic Deer	Club - LE	$28-$30
1994	QXC 485-3	On Cloud Nine	Members Only	$25-$28
1994	QXC 480-6	Sweet Bouquet - Mini	Membership	$20-$22
1995	QXC 416-7	1958 Ford Edsel Citation Conv.	Members Only	$50-$75
1995	QXC 539-7	Barbie™: Brunette Debut - 1959	Members Only	$22-$28
1995	QXC 105-9	Home From The Woods	Members Only	$22-$24
1995	QXC 412-9	A Gift From Rodney - Mini	Membership Promotion	$10-$12
1995	QXC 411-7	Collecting Memories	Membership Promotion	$18-$20
1995	QXM 445-7	Cool Santa - Mini	Membership Promotion	$10-$14
1995	QXC 520-7	Fishing for Fun	Membership Promotion	$12-$16

1988 Miniature Ornament Collection

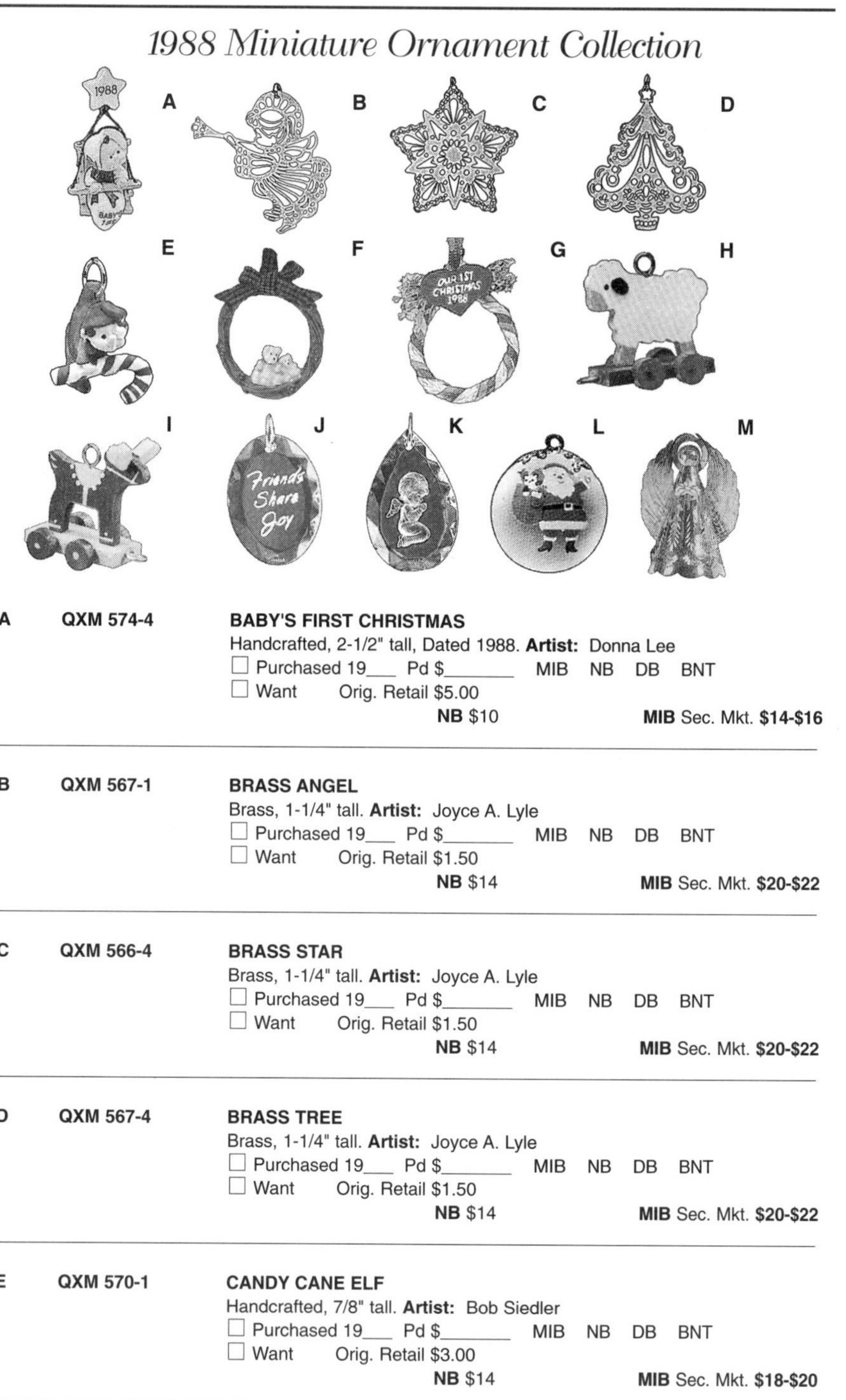

A **QXM 574-4** **BABY'S FIRST CHRISTMAS**
Handcrafted, 2-1/2" tall, Dated 1988. **Artist:** Donna Lee
☐ Purchased 19___ Pd $_______ MIB NB DB BNT
☐ Want Orig. Retail $5.00
NB $10 **MIB** Sec. Mkt. **$14-$16**

B **QXM 567-1** **BRASS ANGEL**
Brass, 1-1/4" tall. **Artist:** Joyce A. Lyle
☐ Purchased 19___ Pd $_______ MIB NB DB BNT
☐ Want Orig. Retail $1.50
NB $14 **MIB** Sec. Mkt. **$20-$22**

C **QXM 566-4** **BRASS STAR**
Brass, 1-1/4" tall. **Artist:** Joyce A. Lyle
☐ Purchased 19___ Pd $_______ MIB NB DB BNT
☐ Want Orig. Retail $1.50
NB $14 **MIB** Sec. Mkt. **$20-$22**

D **QXM 567-4** **BRASS TREE**
Brass, 1-1/4" tall. **Artist:** Joyce A. Lyle
☐ Purchased 19___ Pd $_______ MIB NB DB BNT
☐ Want Orig. Retail $1.50
NB $14 **MIB** Sec. Mkt. **$20-$22**

E **QXM 570-1** **CANDY CANE ELF**
Handcrafted, 7/8" tall. **Artist:** Bob Siedler
☐ Purchased 19___ Pd $_______ MIB NB DB BNT
☐ Want Orig. Retail $3.00
NB $14 **MIB** Sec. Mkt. **$18-$20**

F **QXM 573-1** **COUNTRY WREATH**
Handcrafted, 1-1/2" tall. Reissued in 1989 **Artist:** Anita Marra Rogers
☐ Purchased 19___ Pd $_______ MIB NB DB BNT
☐ Want Orig. Retail $4.00
NB $6 **MIB** Sec. Mkt. **$12-$14**

G **QXM 574-1** **FIRST CHRISTMAS TOGETHER**
Wood/Straw Wreath, 1-3/4" tall, Dated 1988 **Artist:** Diana McGehee
☐ Purchased 19___ Pd $_______ MIB NB DB BNT
☐ Want Orig. Retail $4.00
NB $6 **MIB** Sec. Mkt. **$12-$14**

H **QXM 568-1** **FOLK ART LAMB**
Wood, 1" tall. **Artist:** Joyce Pattee
☐ Purchased 19___ Pd $_______ MIB NB DB BNT
☐ Want Orig. Retail $2.75
NB $12 **MIB** Sec. Mkt. **$22-$24**

I **QXM 568-4** **FOLK ART REINDEER**
Wood, 1-1/8" tall. **Artist:** Joyce Pattee
☐ Purchased 19___ Pd $_______ MIB NB DB BNT
☐ Want Orig. Retail $3.00
NB $12 **MIB** Sec. Mkt. **$18-$20**

J **QXM 576-4** **FRIENDS SHARE JOY**
Faceted Acrylic, 1-1/4" tall. **Artist:** Joyce Pattee
☐ Purchased 19___ Pd $_______ MIB NB DB BNT
☐ Want Orig. Retail $2.00
NB $9 **MIB** Sec. Mkt. **$15-$18**

K **QXM 577-1** **GENTLE ANGEL**
Acrylic, 1 1/2" tall. **Artist:** LaDene Votruba
☐ Purchased 19___ Pd $_______ MIB NB DB BNT
☐ Want Orig. Retail $2.00
NB $10 **MIB** Sec. Mkt. **$15-$18**

L **QXM 561-4** **HAPPY SANTA**
Frosted Glass Ball, 3/4" dia. **Artist:** Joyce Pattee
☐ Purchased 19___ Pd $_______ MIB NB DB BNT
☐ Want Orig. Retail $4.50
NB $10 **MIB** Sec. Mkt. **$18-$20**

M **QXM 566-1** **HEAVENLY GLOW TREE TOPPER**
Brass. Reissued in 1989.
☐ Purchased 19___ Pd $_______ MIB NB DB BNT
☐ Want Orig. Retail $9.75
NB $8 **MIB** Sec. Mkt. **$20-$22**

A QXC 570-4 **HOLD ON TIGHT: KEEPSAKE CLUB**
Handcrafted, 15/16" tall. **Artist:** Bob Siedler
☐ Purchased 19___ Pd $_______ MIB NB DB BNT
☐ Want Orig. Retail - Free to Renewing Members
NB $40 **MIB** Sec. Mkt. **$65-$70**

B QXM 561-1 **HOLY FAMILY**
Handcrafted, 1-3/4" tall, Reissued in 1989.
Artist: Duane Unruh
☐ Purchased 19___ Pd $_______ MIB NB DB BNT
☐ Want Orig. Retail $8.50
NB $9 **MIB** Sec. Mkt. **$14-$16**

C QXM 572-1 **JOLLY ST. NICK**
Handcrafted Santa, 1-3/8" tall.
Artist: Duane Unruh
☐ Purchased 19___ Pd $_______ MIB NB DB BNT
☐ Want Orig. Retail $8.00
NB $25 **MIB** Sec. Mkt. **$35-$38**

D QXM 569-1 **JOYOUS HEART**
Wood, 1-1/8" tall. **Artist:** Diana McGehee
☐ Purchased 19___ Pd $_______ MIB NB DB BNT
☐ Want Orig. Retail $3.50
NB $15 **MIB** Sec. Mkt. **$28-$30**

E QXM 562-1 **KITTENS IN TOYLAND; TRAIN**
FIRST IN SERIES, Handcrafted, 3/4" tall. **Artist:** Ken Crow
☐ Purchased 19___ Pd $_______ MIB NB DB BNT
☐ Want Orig. Retail $5.00
NB $12 **MIB** Sec. Mkt. **$28-$32**

F QXM 578-4 **LITTLE DRUMMER BOY**
Handcrafted, 1-1/4" tall. **Artist:** Bob Siedler
☐ Purchased 19___ Pd $_______ MIB NB DB BNT
☐ Want Orig. Retail $4.50
NB $12 **MIB** Sec. Mkt. **$24-$26**

G QXM 577-4 **LOVE IS FOREVER**
Acrylic, 1" tall. **Artist:** Joyce Pattee
☐ Purchased 19___ Pd $_______ MIB NB DB BNT
☐ Want Orig. Retail $2.00
NB $8 **MIB** Sec. Mkt. **$15-$18**

H QXM 572-4 **MOTHER**
Handcrafted Heart, 1-1/4" tall, Dated 1988. **Artist:** Sharon Pike
☐ Purchased 19___ Pd $_______ MIB NB DB BNT
☐ Want Orig. Retail $3.00
NB $6 **MIB** Sec. Mkt. **$12-$14**

I QXM 563-4 **OLD ENGLISH VILLAGE: FAMILY HOME**
FIRST IN SERIES, Handcrafted, 1-1/4" tall Dated 1988.
Artist: Donna Lee
☐ Purchased 19___ Pd $_______ MIB NB DB BNT
☐ Want Orig. Retail $8.50
NB $25 **MIB** Sec. Mkt. **$45-$50**

J QXM 563-1 **PENGUIN PAL: GIFT**
FIRST IN SERIES, Handcrafted, 1" tall. **Artist:** Bob Siedler
☐ Purchased 19___ Pd $_______ MIB NB DB BNT
☐ Want Orig. Retail $3.75
NB $14 **MIB** Sec. Mkt. **$25-$28**

K QXM 562-4 **ROCKING HORSE: DAPPLED**
FIRST IN SERIES, Handcrafted, 1-1/8" tall, Dated 1988
Artist: Linda Sickman
☐ Purchased 19___ Pd $_______ MIB NB DB BNT
☐ Want Orig. Retail $4.50
NB $20 **MIB** Sec. Mkt. **$42-$45**

L QXM 560-1 **SKATER'S WALTZ**
Handcrafted, 1-3/8" tall. **Artist:** Duane Unruh
☐ Purchased 19___ Pd $_______ MIB NB DB BNT
☐ Want Orig. Retail $7.00
NB $10 **MIB** Sec. Mkt. **$18-$22**

A B  C  D

E  F  G  H

I  J  K  L

A B  C  D  E  F  G  H 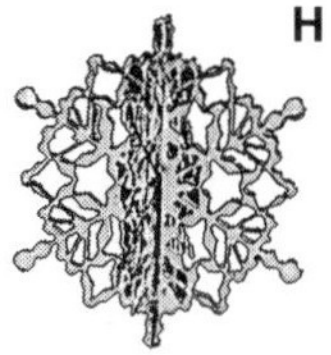 I

A QXM 571-1 **SNEAKER MOUSE**
Handcrafted, 1/2" tall
☐ Purchased 19___ Pd $_______ MIB NB DB BNT
☐ Want Orig. Retail $4.00
NB $9 **MIB** Sec. Mkt. **$18-$20**

B QXM 571-4 **SNUGGLY SKATER**
Handcrafted, 1-1/8" tall. **Artist:** Bob Siedler
☐ Purchased 19___ Pd $_______ MIB NB DB BNT
☐ Want Orig. Retail $4.50
NB $10 **MIB** Sec. Mkt. **$26-$30**

C QXM 560-4 **SWEET DREAMS**
Handcrafted, 1-1/2" tall
☐ Purchased 19___ Pd $_______ MIB NB DB BNT
☐ Want Orig. Retail $7.00
NB $8 **MIB** Sec. Mkt. **$18-$22**

D QXM 569-4 **THREE LITTLE KITTIES**
Handcrafted/Willow, 15/16" tall, Reissued in 1989
Artist: Sharon Pike
☐ Purchased 19___ Pd $_______ MIB NB DB BNT
☐ Want Orig. Retail $6.00
NB $8 **MIB** Sec. Mkt. **$18-$20**

1989 Miniature Ornament Collection

E QXM 568-2 **ACORN SQUIRREL**
Handcrafted, 1-3/8" tall, Reissued in 1990. **Artist:** Sharon Pike
☐ Purchased 19___ Pd $_______ MIB NB DB BNT
☐ Want Orig. Retail $4.50
NB $6 **MIB** Sec. Mkt. **$8-$10**

F QXM 573-2 **BABY'S FIRST CHRISTMAS**
Handcrafted/Acrylic, 1-3/8" tall, Dated '89. **Artist:** Sharon Pike
☐ Purchased 19___ Pd $_______ MIB NB DB BNT
☐ Want Orig. Retail $6.00
NB $6 **MIB** Sec. Mkt. **$12-$14**

G QXM 572-5 **BRASS PARTRIDGE**
Etched Brass, 1-1/4" dia. **Artist:** Joyce A. Lyle
☐ Purchased 19___ Pd $_______ MIB NB DB BNT
☐ Want Orig. Retail $3.00
NB $6 **MIB** Sec. Mkt. **$12-$14**

H QXM 570-2 **BRASS SNOWFLAKE**
Dimensional Brass, 1-3/8" tall. **Artist:** Joyce A. Lyle
☐ Purchased 19___ Pd $_______ MIB NB DB BNT
☐ Want Orig. Retail $4.50
NB $6 **MIB** Sec. Mkt. **$12-$14**

I QXM 577-5 **BUNNY HUG**
Etched, Faceted Acrylic, 1-1/4" tall. **Artist:** LaDene Votruba
☐ Purchased 19___ Pd $_______ MIB NB DB BNT
☐ Want Orig. Retail $3.00
NB $5 **MIB** Sec. Mkt. **$10-$12**

Here's a close-up of the Shearers' Tree filled with Hallmark ornaments!

QXM 573-1 **COUNTRY WREATH**
Handcrafted, 1-1/2" tall
Artist: Anita Marra Rogers
See page 228. Reissued from 1988.
☐ Purchased 19___ Pd $_______ MIB NB DB BNT
☐ Want Orig. Retail $4.50
NB $6 **MIB** Sec. Mkt. **$12-$14**

A QXM 573-5 **COZY SKATER**
Handcrafted, 1-3/8" tall, Reissued in 1990. **Artist:** Joyce A. Lyle
☐ Purchased 19___ Pd $_______ MIB NB DB BNT
☐ Want Orig. Retail $4.50
NB $8 **MIB** Sec. Mkt. **$10-$14**

B QXM 564-2 **FIRST CHRISTMAS TOGETHER**
Ceramic, 1-3/8" tall, Dated 1989. **Artist:** LaDene Votruba
☐ Purchased 19___ Pd $_______ MIB NB DB BNT
☐ Want Orig. Retail $8.50
NB $8 **MIB** Sec. Mkt. **$10-$12**

C QXM 569-2 **FOLK ART BUNNY**
Handcrafted, 1" tall. **Artist:** Joyce Pattee
☐ Purchased 19___ Pd $_______ MIB NB DB BNT
☐ Want Orig. Retail $4.50
NB $7 **MIB** Sec. Mkt. **$8-$10**

D QXM 566-2 **HAPPY BLUEBIRD**
Handcrafted, 7/8" tall, Reissued in 1990. **Artist:** Anita Marra Rogers
☐ Purchased 19___ Pd $_______ MIB NB DB BNT
☐ Want Orig. Retail $4.50
NB $8 **MIB** Sec. Mkt. **$10-$14**

QXM 566-1 **HEAVENLY GLOW TREE TOPPER**
See page 228. Reissued from 1988.
☐ Purchased 19___ Pd $_______ MIB NB DB BNT
☐ Want Orig. Retail $9.75
NB $8 **MIB** Sec. Mkt. **$20-$22**

E QXM 577-2 **HOLIDAY DEER**
Faceted Acrylic Teardrop, 1-1/2" tall. **Artist:** LaDene Votruba
☐ Purchased 19___ Pd $_______ MIB NB DB BNT
☐ Want Orig. Retail $3.00
NB $5 **MIB** Sec. Mkt. **$10-$12**

QXM 561-1 **HOLY FAMILY**
Handcrafted, 1-3/4" tall, **Artist:** Duane Unruh
See page 229. Reissued from 1988.
☐ Purchased 19___ Pd $_______ MIB NB DB BNT
☐ Want Orig. Retail $8.50
NB $9 **MIB** Sec. Mkt. **$14-$16**

F QXM 561-2 **KITTENS IN TOYLAND: SCOOTER**
Second in Series, Handcrafted, 1" tall. **Artist:** Ken Crow
☐ Purchased 19___ Pd $_______ MIB NB DB BNT
☐ Want Orig. Retail $4.50
NB $12 **MIB** Sec. Mkt. **$18-$20**

G QXM 572-2 **KITTY CART**
Wood, 1-1/8" tall. **Artist:** Joyce Pattee
☐ Purchased 19___ Pd $_______ MIB NB DB BNT
☐ Want Orig. Retail $3.00
NB $3 **MIB** Sec. Mkt. **$8-$10**

H QXM 562-5 **KRINGLES, THE: GIFT**
FIRST IN SERIES, Handcrafted, 1-1/8" tall. **Artist:** Anita Marra Rogers
☐ Purchased 19___ Pd $_______ MIB NB DB BNT
☐ Want Orig. Retail $6.00
NB $25 **MIB** Sec. Mkt. **$32-$36**

I QXM 567-5 **LITTLE SOLDIER**
Handcrafted, 1-3/8" tall, Reissued in 1990. **Artist:** Linda Sickman
☐ Purchased 19___ Pd $_______ MIB NB DB BNT
☐ Want Orig. Retail $4.50
NB $5 **MIB** Sec. Mkt. **$10-$12**

J QXM 562-2 **LITTLE STAR BRINGER**
Handcrafted Blue Angel, 1-1/4" tall, Dated 1989
Artist: Joyce A. Lyle
☐ Purchased 19___ Pd $_______ MIB NB DB BNT
☐ Want Orig. Retail $6.00
NB $8 **MIB** Sec. Mkt. **$16-20**

A  B  C  D

E  F  G  H

I  J

(Photos shown on this page.)

A **QXM 574-5** **LOAD OF CHEER**
Handcrafted, 7/8" tall, Dated 1989. **Artist:** Dill Rhodus
☐ Purchased 19___ Pd $_______ MIB NB DB BNT
☐ Want Orig. Retail $6.00
NB $8 **MIB** Sec. Mkt. **$15-$18**

B **QXM 563-5** **LOVEBIRDS**
Handcrafted/Brass, 1-1/8" tall. **Artist:** Sharon Pike
☐ Purchased 19___ Pd $_______ MIB NB DB BNT
☐ Want Orig. Retail $6.00
NB $8 **MIB** Sec. Mkt. **$13-$15**

C **QXM 575-5** **MERRY SEAL**
Hand Painted Porcelain, 7/8" tall. **Artist:** John Francis (Collin)
☐ Purchased 19___ Pd $_______ MIB NB DB BNT
☐ Want Orig. Retail $6.00
NB $8 **MIB** Sec. Mkt. **$12-$15**

D **QXM 564-5** **MOTHER**
Blue Cameo, Chrome Bezel, 1-1/4" dia., Dated 1989
☐ Purchased 19___ Pd $_______ MIB NB DB BNT
☐ Want Orig. Retail $6.00
NB $6 **MIB** Sec. Mkt. **$14-$16**

E **QXM 576-2** **NOEL R.R.: LOCOMOTIVE**
FIRST IN SERIES, Handcrafted, 1" tall, Dated 1989
Artist: Linda Sickman
☐ Purchased 19___ Pd $_______ MIB NB DB BNT
☐ Want Orig. Retail $8.50
NB $25 **MIB** Sec. Mkt. **$45-$50**

F **QXM 561-5** **OLD ENGLISH VILLAGE: SWEET SHOP**
Second in Series, Handcrafted, 1-1/4" tall, Dated 1989. **Artist:** Julia Lee
☐ Purchased 19___ Pd $_______ MIB NB DB BNT
☐ Want Orig. Retail $8.50
NB $22 **MIB** Sec. Mkt. **$32-$38**

G **QXM 569-5** **OLD WORLD SANTA**
Handcrafted, 1-3/8" tall. Reissued in 1990. **Artist:** Bob Siedler
☐ Purchased 19___ Pd $_______ MIB NB DB BNT
☐ Want Orig. Retail $3.00
NB $3 **MIB** Sec. Mkt. **$8-$10**

H **QXM 560-2** **PENGUIN PAL: CANDY CANE**
Second in Series, Handcrafted/Acrylic, 1-3/8" tall
☐ Purchased 19___ Pd $_______ MIB NB DB BNT
☐ Want Orig. Retail $4.50
NB $12 **MIB** Sec. Mkt. **$18-$22**

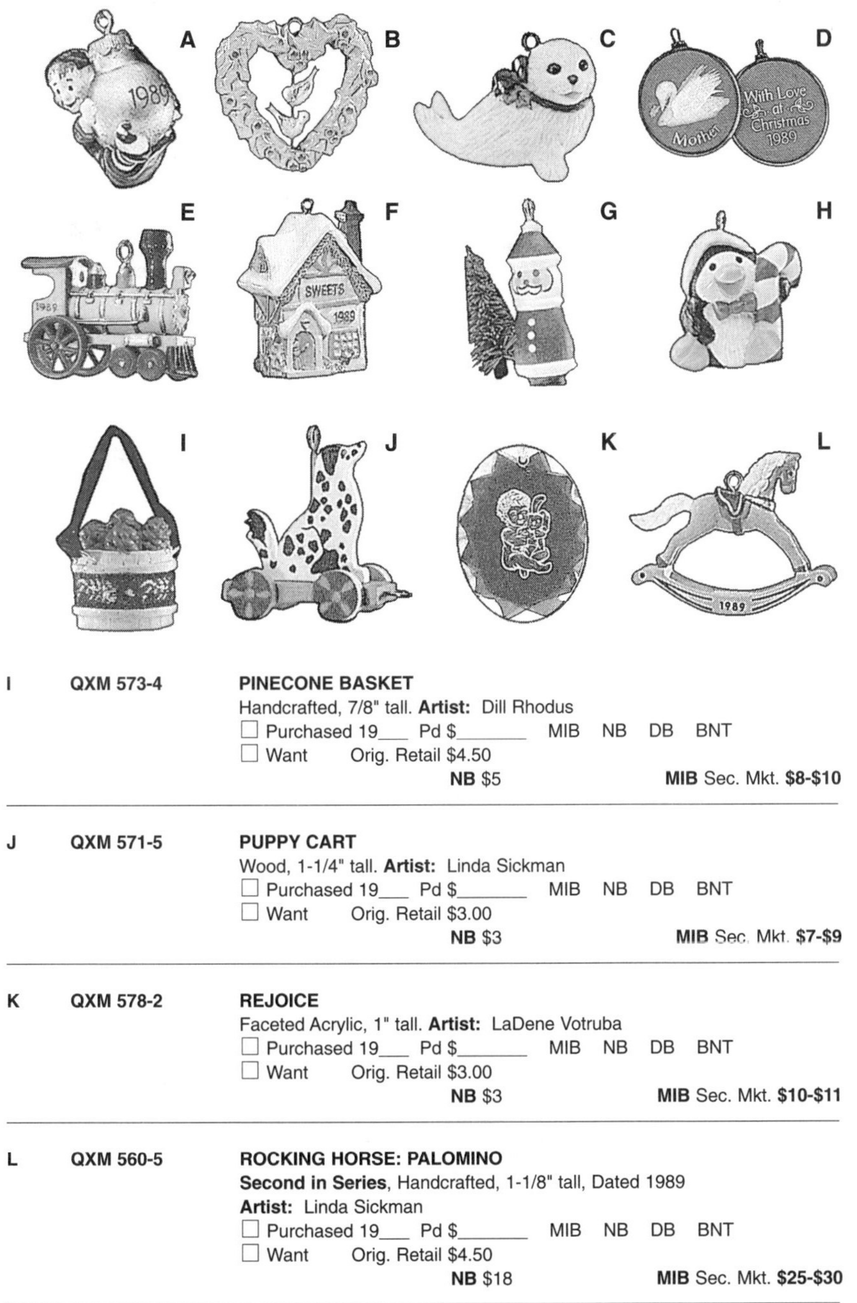

I **QXM 573-4** **PINECONE BASKET**
Handcrafted, 7/8" tall. **Artist:** Dill Rhodus
☐ Purchased 19___ Pd $_______ MIB NB DB BNT
☐ Want Orig. Retail $4.50
NB $5 **MIB** Sec. Mkt. **$8-$10**

J **QXM 571-5** **PUPPY CART**
Wood, 1-1/4" tall. **Artist:** Linda Sickman
☐ Purchased 19___ Pd $_______ MIB NB DB BNT
☐ Want Orig. Retail $3.00
NB $3 **MIB** Sec. Mkt. **$7-$9**

K **QXM 578-2** **REJOICE**
Faceted Acrylic, 1" tall. **Artist:** LaDene Votruba
☐ Purchased 19___ Pd $_______ MIB NB DB BNT
☐ Want Orig. Retail $3.00
NB $3 **MIB** Sec. Mkt. **$10-$11**

L **QXM 560-5** **ROCKING HORSE: PALOMINO**
Second in Series, Handcrafted, 1-1/8" tall, Dated 1989
Artist: Linda Sickman
☐ Purchased 19___ Pd $_______ MIB NB DB BNT
☐ Want Orig. Retail $4.50
NB $18 **MIB** Sec. Mkt. **$25-$30**

A QXM 571-2 **ROLY-POLY PIG**
Handcrafted, 7/8" tall, Reissued in 1990. **Artist:** Sharon Pike
☐ Purchased 19___ Pd $_______ MIB NB DB BNT
☐ Want Orig. Retail $3.00
NB $6 **MIB** Sec. Mkt. **$12-$14**

B QXM 570-5 **ROLY-POLY RAM**
Handcrafted, Handcrafted, 7/8" tall
☐ Purchased 19___ Pd $_______ MIB NB DB BNT
☐ Want Orig. Retail $3.00
NB $5 **MIB** Sec. Mkt. **$10-$14**

C QXM 563-2 **SANTA'S MAGIC RIDE**
Special Edition**,** Handcrafted, 1-3/16" tall.
Artist: Anita Marra Rogers
☐ Purchased 19___ Pd $_______ MIB NB DB BNT
☐ Want Orig. Retail $8.50
NB $8 **MIB** Sec. Mkt. **$14-$18**

D QXM 566-5 **SANTA'S ROADSTER**
Handcrafted, 15/16" tall, Dated 1989. **Artist:** Ken Crow
☐ Purchased 19___ Pd $_______ MIB NB DB BNT
☐ Want Orig. Retail $6.00
NB $10 **MIB** Sec. Mkt. **$18-$22**

E QXM 568-5 **SCRIMSHAW REINDEER**
Handcrafted, 15/16" tall. **Artist:** LaDene Votruba
☐ Purchased 19___ Pd $_______ MIB NB DB BNT
☐ Want Orig. Retail $4.50
NB $5 **MIB** Sec. Mkt. **$8-$10**

F QXM 576-5 **SHARING A RIDE**
Handcrafted, 1-1/4" tall. **Artist:** Peter Dutkin
☐ Purchased 19___ Pd $_______ MIB NB DB BNT
☐ Want Orig. Retail $8.50
NB $10 **MIB** Sec. Mkt. **$12-$16**

G QXC 581-2 **SITTING PURRTY: KEEPSAKE CLUB**
Handcrafted, 1-1/4" tall, Dated 1989
Artist: Peter Dutkin
☐ Purchased 19___ Pd $_______ MIB NB DB BNT
☐ Want Orig. Retail -- Free to Club Members
NB $7 **MIB** Sec. Mkt. **$10-$15**

H QXM 575-2 **SLOW MOTION**
Handcrafted, 1" tall. **Artist:** Bob Siedler
☐ Purchased 19___ Pd $_______ MIB NB DB BNT
☐ Want Orig. Retail $6.00
NB $6 **MIB** Sec. Mkt. **$12-$16**

I QXM 565-2 **SPECIAL FRIEND**
Handcrafted/Willow, 1-3/8" tall, Dated 1989
☐ Purchased 19___ Pd $_______ MIB NB DB BNT
☐ Want Orig. Retail $4.50
NB $6 **MIB** Sec. Mkt. **$12-$14**

J QXM 565-5 **STARLIT MOUSE**
Handcrafted, 1-3/16" tall, Dated 1989. **Artist:** Dill Rhodus
☐ Purchased 19___ Pd $_______ MIB NB DB BNT
☐ Want Orig. Retail $4.50
NB $8 **MIB** Sec. Mkt. **$14-$16**

K QXM 567-2 **STOCKING PAL**
Handcrafted, 1" tall, Reissued in 1990. **Artist:** Julia Lee
☐ Purchased 19___ Pd $_______ MIB NB DB BNT
☐ Want Orig. Retail $4.50
NB $5 **MIB** Sec. Mkt. **$8-$10**

L QXM 574-2 **STROLLIN' SNOWMAN**
Hand Painted Fine Porcelain, 1-1/4" tall. **Artist:** Bob Siedler
☐ Purchased 19___ Pd $_______ MIB NB DB BNT
☐ Want Orig. Retail $4.50
NB $6 **MIB** Sec. Mkt. **$10-$14**

QXM 569-4 **THREE LITTLE KITTIES**
Handcrafted, 15/16" tall **Artist:** Sharon Pike
See page 230. Reissued from 1988.
☐ Purchased 19___ Pd $_______ MIB NB DB BNT
☐ Want Orig. Retail $6.00
NB $8 **MIB** Sec. Mkt. **$16-$18**

A B C D
E F G H
I J K L

1990 Miniature Ornament Collection

	QXM 568-2	**ACORN SQUIRREL** Handcrafted, 1-3/8" tall. **Artist:** Sharon Pike See page 230. Reissued from 1989. ☐ Purchased 19___ Pd $_______ MIB NB DB BNT ☐ Want Orig. Retail $4.50 **NB** $6 **MIB** Sec. Mkt. **$8-$10**
A	QXM 568-6	**ACORN WREATH** Handcrafted, 1-1/4" tall. **Artist:** Ken Crow ☐ Purchased 19___ Pd $_______ MIB NB DB BNT ☐ Want Orig. Retail $6.00 **NB** $8 **MIB** Sec. Mkt. **$12-$14**
B	QXM 565-6	**AIR SANTA** Handcrafted, 1/2" tall, Dated 1990 ☐ Purchased 19___ Pd $_______ MIB NB DB BNT ☐ Want Orig. Retail $4.50 **NB** $6 **MIB** Sec. Mkt. **$12-$13**
C	QXM 570-3	**BABY'S FIRST CHRISTMAS** Handcrafted Cradle, 1-1/8" tall, Dated 1990 **Artist:** John Francis (Collin) ☐ Purchased 19___ Pd $_______ MIB NB DB BNT ☐ Want Orig. Retail $8.50 **NB** $10 **MIB** Sec. Mkt. **$16-$18**
D	QXM 569-6	**BASKET BUDDY** Handcrafted, 1-3/16" tall. **Artist:** Anita Marra Rogers ☐ Purchased 19___ Pd $_______ MIB NB DB BNT ☐ Want Orig. Retail $6.00 **NB** $8 **MIB** Sec. Mkt. **$10-$12**
E	QXM 563-3	**BEAR HUG** Handcrafted, 15/16" tall. **Artist:** Don Palmiter ☐ Purchased 19___ Pd $_______ MIB NB DB BNT ☐ Want Orig. Retail $6.00 **NB** $7 **MIB** Sec. Mkt. **$12-$14**
F	QXM 577-6	**BRASS BOUQUET** Antiqued Brass Medallion, 1-1/4" tall. **Artist:** Joyce A. Lyle ☐ Purchased 19___ Pd $_______ MIB NB DB BNT ☐ Want Orig. Retail $6.00 **NB** $5 **MIB** Sec. Mkt. **$7-$8**
G	QXM 579-3	**BRASS HORN** Etched, Pierced Brass, 3/4" tall, Dated 1990 ☐ Purchased 19___ Pd $_______ MIB NB DB BNT ☐ Want Orig. Retail $3.00 **NB** $3 **MIB** Sec. Mkt. **$6-$8**

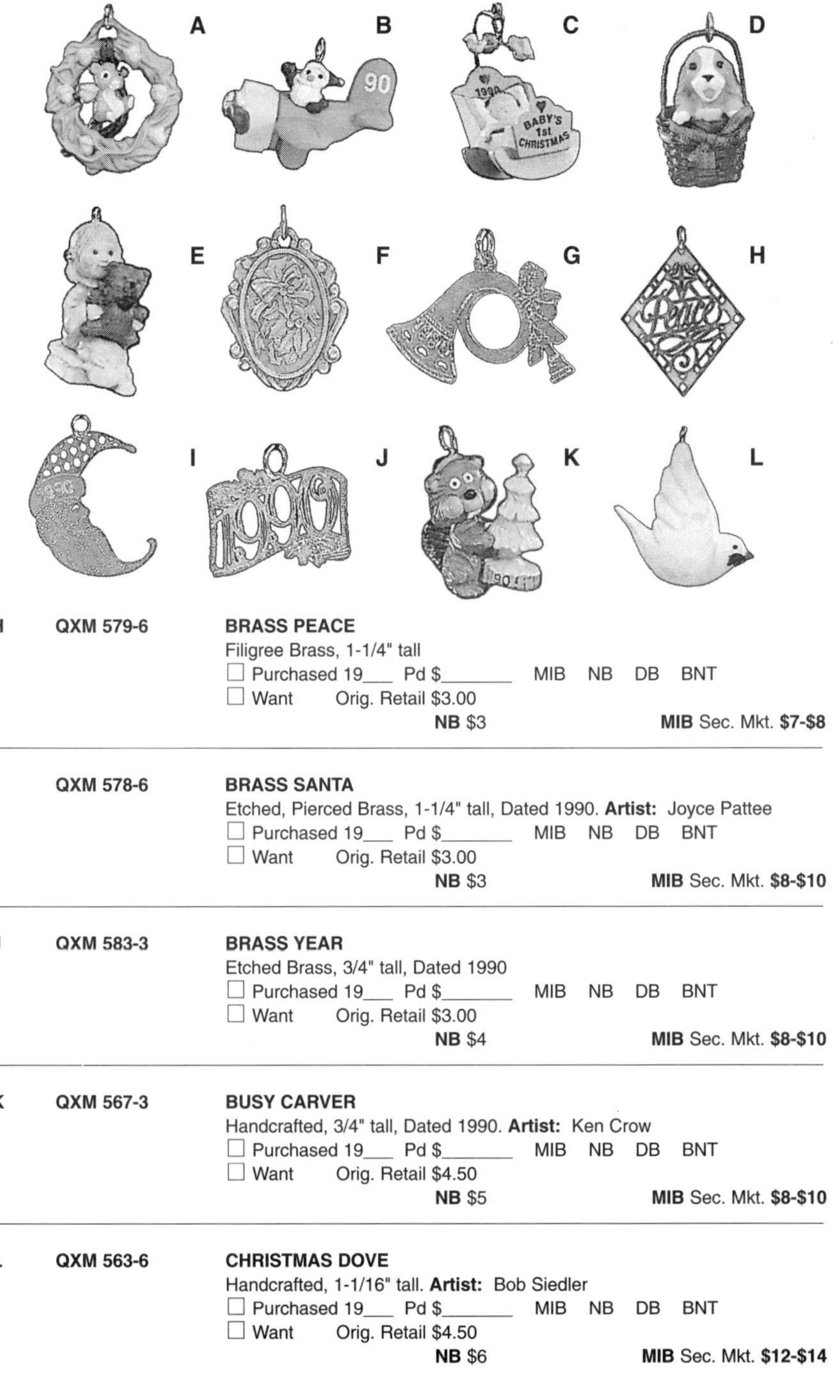

H	QXM 579-6	**BRASS PEACE** Filigree Brass, 1-1/4" tall ☐ Purchased 19___ Pd $_______ MIB NB DB BNT ☐ Want Orig. Retail $3.00 **NB** $3 **MIB** Sec. Mkt. **$7-$8**
I	QXM 578-6	**BRASS SANTA** Etched, Pierced Brass, 1-1/4" tall, Dated 1990. **Artist:** Joyce Pattee ☐ Purchased 19___ Pd $_______ MIB NB DB BNT ☐ Want Orig. Retail $3.00 **NB** $3 **MIB** Sec. Mkt. **$8-$10**
J	QXM 583-3	**BRASS YEAR** Etched Brass, 3/4" tall, Dated 1990 ☐ Purchased 19___ Pd $_______ MIB NB DB BNT ☐ Want Orig. Retail $3.00 **NB** $4 **MIB** Sec. Mkt. **$8-$10**
K	QXM 567-3	**BUSY CARVER** Handcrafted, 3/4" tall, Dated 1990. **Artist:** Ken Crow ☐ Purchased 19___ Pd $_______ MIB NB DB BNT ☐ Want Orig. Retail $4.50 **NB** $5 **MIB** Sec. Mkt. **$8-$10**
L	QXM 563-6	**CHRISTMAS DOVE** Handcrafted, 1-1/16" tall. **Artist:** Bob Siedler ☐ Purchased 19___ Pd $_______ MIB NB DB BNT ☐ Want Orig. Retail $4.50 **NB** $6 **MIB** Sec. Mkt. **$12-$14**

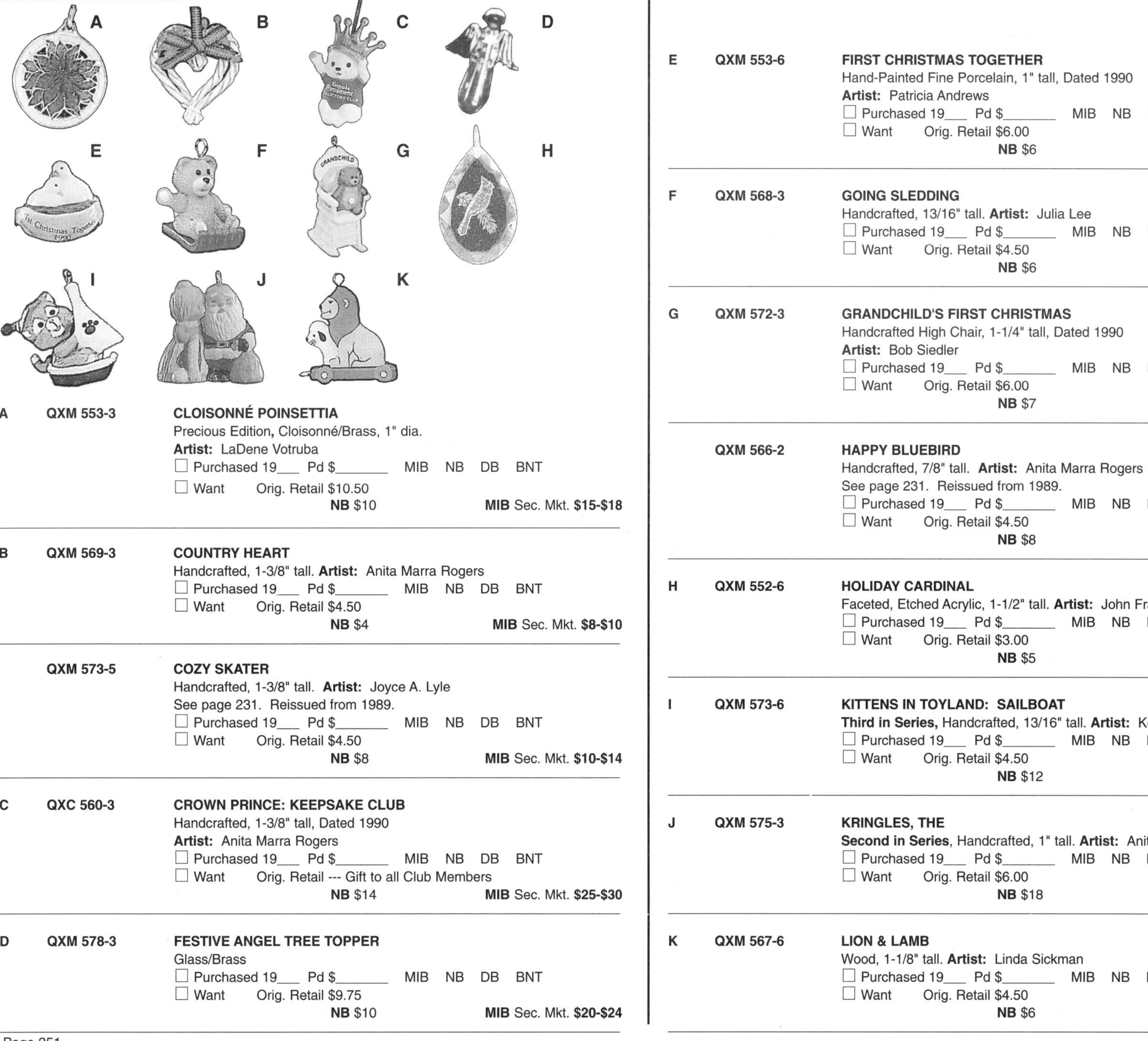

A **QXM 553-3** **CLOISONNÉ POINSETTIA**
Precious Edition, Cloisonné/Brass, 1" dia.
Artist: LaDene Votruba
☐ Purchased 19___ Pd $_______ MIB NB DB BNT
☐ Want Orig. Retail $10.50
NB $10 **MIB** Sec. Mkt. **$15-$18**

B **QXM 569-3** **COUNTRY HEART**
Handcrafted, 1-3/8" tall. **Artist:** Anita Marra Rogers
☐ Purchased 19___ Pd $_______ MIB NB DB BNT
☐ Want Orig. Retail $4.50
NB $4 **MIB** Sec. Mkt. **$8-$10**

QXM 573-5 **COZY SKATER**
Handcrafted, 1-3/8" tall. **Artist:** Joyce A. Lyle
See page 231. Reissued from 1989.
☐ Purchased 19___ Pd $_______ MIB NB DB BNT
☐ Want Orig. Retail $4.50
NB $8 **MIB** Sec. Mkt. **$10-$14**

C **QXC 560-3** **CROWN PRINCE: KEEPSAKE CLUB**
Handcrafted, 1-3/8" tall, Dated 1990
Artist: Anita Marra Rogers
☐ Purchased 19___ Pd $_______ MIB NB DB BNT
☐ Want Orig. Retail --- Gift to all Club Members
NB $14 **MIB** Sec. Mkt. **$25-$30**

D **QXM 578-3** **FESTIVE ANGEL TREE TOPPER**
Glass/Brass
☐ Purchased 19___ Pd $_______ MIB NB DB BNT
☐ Want Orig. Retail $9.75
NB $10 **MIB** Sec. Mkt. **$20-$24**

E **QXM 553-6** **FIRST CHRISTMAS TOGETHER**
Hand-Painted Fine Porcelain, 1" tall, Dated 1990
Artist: Patricia Andrews
☐ Purchased 19___ Pd $_______ MIB NB DB BNT
☐ Want Orig. Retail $6.00
NB $6 **MIB** Sec. Mkt. **$14-$16**

F **QXM 568-3** **GOING SLEDDING**
Handcrafted, 13/16" tall. **Artist:** Julia Lee
☐ Purchased 19___ Pd $_______ MIB NB DB BNT
☐ Want Orig. Retail $4.50
NB $6 **MIB** Sec. Mkt. **$10-$15**

G **QXM 572-3** **GRANDCHILD'S FIRST CHRISTMAS**
Handcrafted High Chair, 1-1/4" tall, Dated 1990
Artist: Bob Siedler
☐ Purchased 19___ Pd $_______ MIB NB DB BNT
☐ Want Orig. Retail $6.00
NB $7 **MIB** Sec. Mkt. **$12-$14**

QXM 566-2 **HAPPY BLUEBIRD**
Handcrafted, 7/8" tall. **Artist:** Anita Marra Rogers
See page 231. Reissued from 1989.
☐ Purchased 19___ Pd $_______ MIB NB DB BNT
☐ Want Orig. Retail $4.50
NB $8 **MIB** Sec. Mkt. **$10-$14**

H **QXM 552-6** **HOLIDAY CARDINAL**
Faceted, Etched Acrylic, 1-1/2" tall. **Artist:** John Francis (Collin)
☐ Purchased 19___ Pd $_______ MIB NB DB BNT
☐ Want Orig. Retail $3.00
NB $5 **MIB** Sec. Mkt. **$10-$12**

I **QXM 573-6** **KITTENS IN TOYLAND: SAILBOAT**
Third in Series, Handcrafted, 13/16" tall. **Artist:** Ken Crow
☐ Purchased 19___ Pd $_______ MIB NB DB BNT
☐ Want Orig. Retail $4.50
NB $12 **MIB** Sec. Mkt. **$18-$21**

J **QXM 575-3** **KRINGLES, THE**
Second in Series, Handcrafted, 1" tall. **Artist:** Anita Marra Rogers
☐ Purchased 19___ Pd $_______ MIB NB DB BNT
☐ Want Orig. Retail $6.00
NB $18 **MIB** Sec. Mkt. **$22-$26**

K **QXM 567-6** **LION & LAMB**
Wood, 1-1/8" tall. **Artist:** Linda Sickman
☐ Purchased 19___ Pd $_______ MIB NB DB BNT
☐ Want Orig. Retail $4.50
NB $6 **MIB** Sec. Mkt. **$10-$12**

A XPR 972-3 **LITTLE FROSTY FRIENDS: LITTLE BEAR**
Handcrafted, 1" tall, Dated 1990
Artist: Bob Siedler
☐ Purchased 19___ Pd $_______ MIB NB DB BNT
☐ Want Orig. Retail $2.95 w/$5 purchase.
NB $4 **MIB** Sec. Mkt. **$6-$8**

B XPR 972-0 **LITTLE FROSTY FRIENDS: LITTLE FROSTY**
Handcrafted, 1-7/16" tall, Dated 1990 **Artist:** Bob Siedler
☐ Purchased 19___ Pd $_______ MIB NB DB BNT
☐ Want Orig. Retail $2.95 w/$5 purchase.
NB $4 **MIB** Sec. Mkt. **$8-$10**

C XPR 972-2 **LITTLE FROSTY FRIENDS: LITTLE HUSKY**
Handcrafted, 1-1/8" tall, Dated 1990 **Artist:** Ed Seale
☐ Purchased 19___ Pd $_______ MIB NB DB BNT
☐ Want Orig. Retail $2.95 w/$5 purchase.
NB $4 **MIB** Sec. Mkt. **$9-$12**

D XPR 972-1 **LITTLE FROSTY FRIENDS: LITTLE SEAL**
Handcrafted, 1-1/8" tall, Dated 1990 **Artist:** Julia Lee
☐ Purchased 19___ Pd $_______ MIB NB DB BNT
☐ Want Orig. Retail $2.95 w/$5 purchase.
NB $4 **MIB** Sec. Mkt. **$8-$10**

E XPR 972-4 **LITTLE FROSTY FRIENDS: MEMORY WREATH**
Handcrafted, 5" dia., Dated 1990. **Artist:** Donna Lee
☐ Purchased 19___ Pd $_______ MIB NB DB BNT
☐ Want Orig. Retail $2.95 w/any purchase.
NB $3 **MIB** Sec. Mkt. **$8-$10**

QXM 567-5 **LITTLE SOLDIER**
Handcrafted, 1-3/8" tall. **Artist:** Linda Sickman
See page 231. Reissued from 1989.
☐ Purchased 19___ Pd $_______ MIB NB DB BNT
☐ Want Orig. Retail $4.50
NB $5 **MIB** Sec. Mkt. **$10-$12**

F QXM 552-3 **LOVING HEARTS**
Faceted Acrylic, 1-1/4" tall
☐ Purchased 19___ Pd $_______ MIB NB DB BNT
☐ Want Orig. Retail $3.00
NB $4 **MIB** Sec. Mkt. **$8-$12**

G QXM 564-3 **MADONNA AND CHILD**
Handcrafted, 1-1/4" tall. **Artist:** Anita Marra Rogers
☐ Purchased 19___ Pd $_______ MIB NB DB BNT
☐ Want Orig. Retail $6.00
NB $8 **MIB** Sec. Mkt. **$12-$14**

H QXM 571-6 **MOTHER**
Rose Cameo, 1-1/8", Dated 1990. **Artist:** Joyce A. Lyle
☐ Purchased 19___ Pd $_______ MIB NB DB BNT
☐ Want Orig. Retail $4.50
NB $4 **MIB** Sec. Mkt. **$15-$18**

I QXM 570-6 **NATIVITY**
Handcrafted, 1-3/8" tall, Dated 1990. **Artist:** Duane Unruh
☐ Purchased 19___ Pd $_______ MIB NB DB BNT
☐ Want Orig. Retail $4.50
NB $8 **MIB** Sec. Mkt. **$12-$14**

J QXM 573-3 **NATURE'S ANGELS: BUNNY**
FIRST IN SERIES, Handcrafted, 1-1/4" tall. **Artist:** Ed Seale
☐ Purchased 19___ Pd $_______ MIB NB DB BNT
☐ Want Orig. Retail $4.50
NB $14 **MIB** Sec. Mkt. **$25-$28**

K QXM 575-6 **NOEL R.R.: COAL CAR**
Second in Series, Handcrafted, 3/4" tall, Dated 1990
Artist: Linda Sickman
☐ Purchased 19___ Pd $_______ MIB NB DB BNT
☐ Want Orig. Retail $8.50
NB $15 **MIB** Sec. Mkt. **$28-$32**

A B C D

E F G H

I J K

A QXM 576-3 **OLD ENGLISH VILLAGE: SCHOOL**
Third in Series, Handcrafted, 1-1/8" tall, Dated 1990. **Artist:** Julia Lee
☐ Purchased 19___ Pd $_______ MIB NB DB BNT
☐ Want Orig. Retail $8.50
NB $15 **MIB** Sec. Mkt. **$22-$26**

QXM 569-5 **OLD WORLD SANTA**
Handcrafted, 1-3/8" tall. **Artist:** Bob Siedler
See page 232. Reissued from 1989.
☐ Purchased 19___ Pd $_______ MIB NB DB BNT
☐ Want Orig. Retail $3.00
NB $3 **MIB** Sec. Mkt. **$8-$10**

B QXM 561-6 **PANDA'S SURPRISE**
Handcrafted, 7/8" tall, Dated '90. **Artist:** John Francis (Collin)
☐ Purchased 19___ Pd $_______ MIB NB DB BNT
☐ Want Orig. Retail $4.50
NB $5 **MIB** Sec. Mkt. **$12-$14**

C QXM 574-6 **PENGUIN PAL**
Third in Series, Handcrafted, 7/8" tall
☐ Purchased 19___ Pd $_______ MIB NB DB BNT
☐ Want Orig. Retail $4.50
NB $12 **MIB** Sec. Mkt. **$18-$20**

D QXM 551-6 **PERFECT FIT**
Handcrafted, 15/16" tall, Dated 1990. **Artist:** Robert Chad
☐ Purchased 19___ Pd $_______ MIB NB DB BNT
☐ Want Orig. Retail $4.50
NB $8 **MIB** Sec. Mkt. **$12-$14**

E QXM 566-6 **PUPPY LOVE**
Handcrafted, 1" tall. **Artist:** Don Palmiter
☐ Purchased 19___ Pd $_______ MIB NB DB BNT
☐ Want Orig. Retail $6.00
NB $6 **MIB** Sec. Mkt. **$12-$14**

F QXM 574-3 **ROCKING HORSE: PINTO**
Third in Series, Handcrafted, 1-1/8" tall, Dated 1990
Artist: Linda Sickman
☐ Purchased 19___ Pd $_______ MIB NB DB BNT
☐ Want Orig. Retail $4.50
NB $15 **MIB** Sec. Mkt. **$22-$26**

QXM 571-2 **ROLY-POLY PIG**
Handcrafted, 7/8" tall. **Artist:** Sharon Pike
See page 233. Reissued from 1989.
☐ Purchased 19___ Pd $_______ MIB NB DB BNT
☐ Want Orig. Retail $3.00
NB $6 **MIB** Sec. Mkt. **$12-$14**

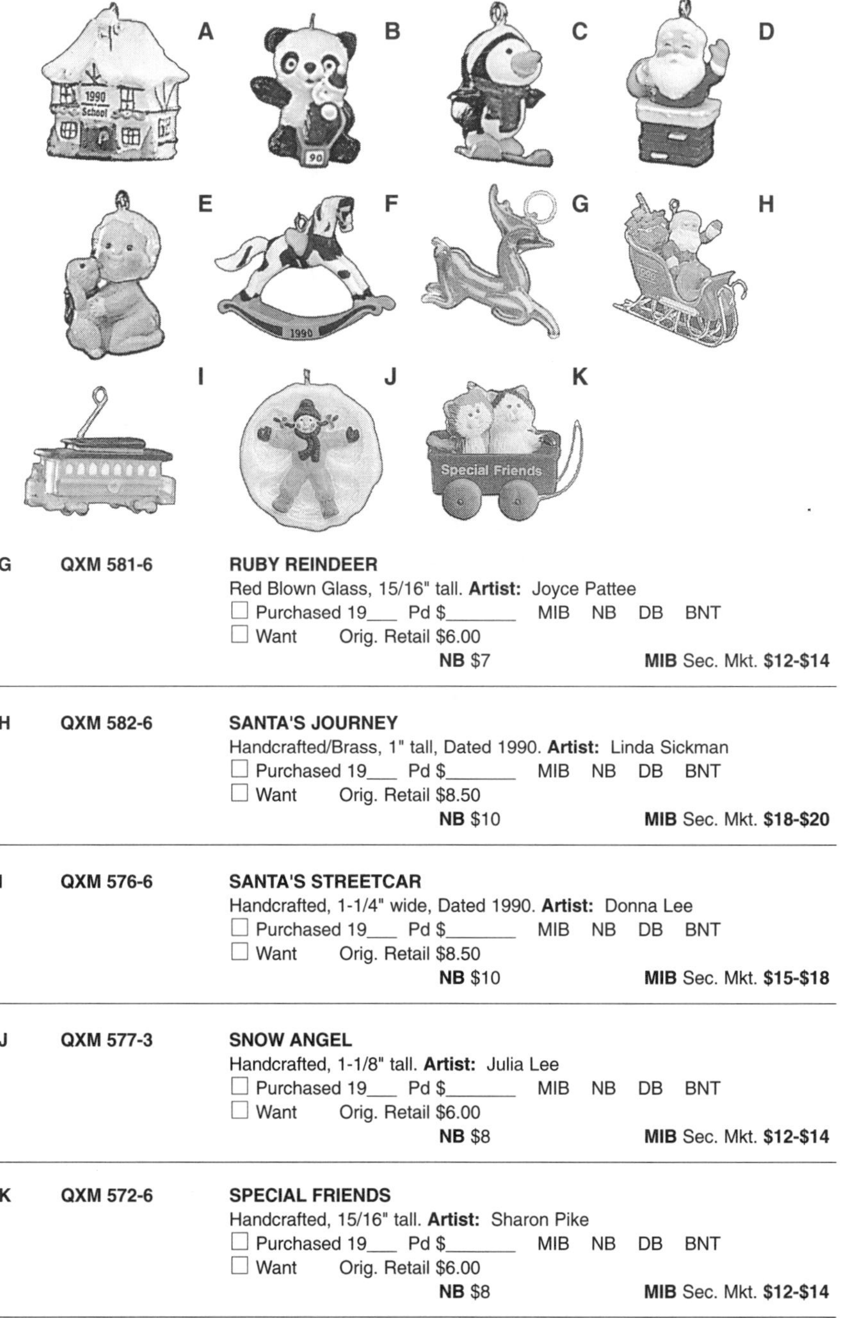

G QXM 581-6 **RUBY REINDEER**
Red Blown Glass, 15/16" tall. **Artist:** Joyce Pattee
☐ Purchased 19___ Pd $_______ MIB NB DB BNT
☐ Want Orig. Retail $6.00
NB $7 **MIB** Sec. Mkt. **$12-$14**

H QXM 582-6 **SANTA'S JOURNEY**
Handcrafted/Brass, 1" tall, Dated 1990. **Artist:** Linda Sickman
☐ Purchased 19___ Pd $_______ MIB NB DB BNT
☐ Want Orig. Retail $8.50
NB $10 **MIB** Sec. Mkt. **$18-$20**

I QXM 576-6 **SANTA'S STREETCAR**
Handcrafted, 1-1/4" wide, Dated 1990. **Artist:** Donna Lee
☐ Purchased 19___ Pd $_______ MIB NB DB BNT
☐ Want Orig. Retail $8.50
NB $10 **MIB** Sec. Mkt. **$15-$18**

J QXM 577-3 **SNOW ANGEL**
Handcrafted, 1-1/8" tall. **Artist:** Julia Lee
☐ Purchased 19___ Pd $_______ MIB NB DB BNT
☐ Want Orig. Retail $6.00
NB $8 **MIB** Sec. Mkt. **$12-$14**

K QXM 572-6 **SPECIAL FRIENDS**
Handcrafted, 15/16" tall. **Artist:** Sharon Pike
☐ Purchased 19___ Pd $_______ MIB NB DB BNT
☐ Want Orig. Retail $6.00
NB $8 **MIB** Sec. Mkt. **$12-$14**

A QXM 562-3 **STAMP COLLECTOR**
Handcrafted, 7/8" tall. Dated Christmas 1990. **Artist:** Ken Crow
☐ Purchased 19___ Pd $_______ MIB NB DB BNT
☐ Want Orig. Retail $4.50
NB $7 **MIB** Sec. Mkt. **$10-$12**

QXM 567-2 **STOCKING PAL**
Handcrafted, 1" tall. **Artist:** Julia Lee
See page 233. Reissued from 1989.
☐ Purchased 19___ Pd $_______ MIB NB DB BNT
☐ Want Orig. Retail $4.50
NB $5 **MIB** Sec. Mkt. **$8-$10**

B QXM 560-6 **STRINGING ALONG**
Handcrafted, 1-1/8" tall. **Artist:** Ed Seale
☐ Purchased 19___ Pd $_______ MIB NB DB BNT
☐ Want Orig. Retail $8.50
NB $10 **MIB** Sec. Mkt. **$16-$18**

C QXM 566-3 **SWEET SLUMBER**
Handcrafted, 9/16" tall. **Artist:** Bob Siedler
☐ Purchased 19___ Pd $_______ MIB NB DB BNT
☐ Want Orig. Retail $4.50
NB $6 **MIB** Sec. Mkt. **$9-$12**

D QXM 565-3 **TEACHER**
Handcrafted owl/pencil, 7/8" tall, Dated 1990. **Artist:** Sharon Pike
☐ Purchased 19___ Pd $_______ MIB NB DB BNT
☐ Want Orig. Retail $4.50
NB $4 **MIB** Sec. Mkt. **$8-$10**

E QXM 554-3 **THIMBLE BELLS**
FIRST IN SERIES, Fine Porcelain, 1-1/8" tall, Dated 1990
Artist: Michele Pyda-Sevcik
☐ Purchased 19___ Pd $_______ MIB NB DB BNT
☐ Want Orig. Retail $6.00
NB $14 **MIB** Sec. Mkt. **$28-$30**

F QXM 564-6 **TYPE OF JOY**
Handcrafted, 11/16" tall. **Artist:** Robert Chad
☐ Purchased 19___ Pd $_______ MIB NB DB BNT
☐ Want Orig. Retail $4.50
NB $5 **MIB** Sec. Mkt. **$9-$10**

G QXM 571-3 **WARM MEMORIES**
Handcrafted, 1-1/8" tall, Dated 1990. **Artist:** Ed Seale
☐ Purchased 19___ Pd $_______ MIB NB DB BNT
☐ Want Orig. Retail $4.50
NB $8 **MIB** Sec. Mkt. **$10-$14**

H QXM 584-3 **WEE NUTCRACKER**
Handcrafted, 1-1/4" tall, Dated 1990. **Artist:** Bob Siedler
☐ Purchased 19___ Pd $_______ MIB NB DB BNT
☐ Want Orig. Retail $8.50
NB $10 **MIB** Sec. Mkt. **$15-$18**

1991 Miniature Ornament Collection

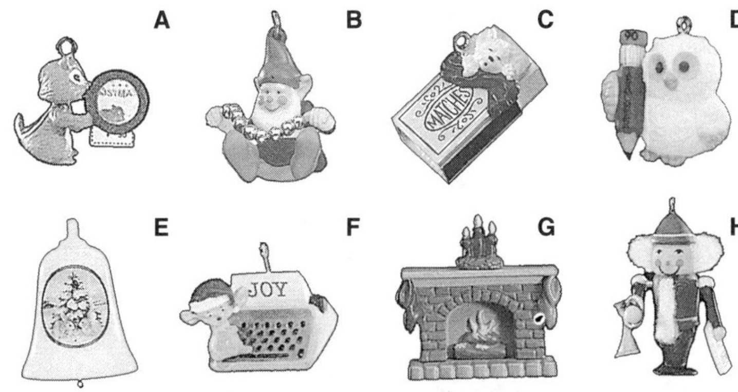

Lois Winter displays her Hallmark ornaments cleverly with lights and an older doll house!

A QXM 586-9 **ALL ABOARD**
Handcrafted, 1" tall, Dated 1991. **Artist:** Robert Chad
☐ Purchased 19___ Pd $_______ MIB NB DB BNT
☐ Want Orig. Retail $4.50
NB $8 **MIB** Sec. Mkt. **$16-$18**

B QXM 579-9 **BABY'S FIRST CHRISTMAS**
Handcrafted Carriage, 1" tall, Dated 1991
Artist: John Francis (Collin)
☐ Purchased 19___ Pd $_______ MIB NB DB BNT
☐ Want Orig. Retail $6.00
NB $10 **MIB** Sec. Mkt. **$18-$22**

C QXM 597-7 **BRASS BELLS**
Etched, Pierced Brass, 1-1/4" tall, Dated 1991. **Artist:** Patricia Andrews
☐ Purchased 19___ Pd $_______ MIB NB DB BNT
☐ Want Orig. Retail $3.00
NB $4 **MIB** Sec. Mkt. **$8-$10**

D QXM 597-9 **BRASS CHURCH**
Etched Brass, 1-1/4" tall, Dated 1991
☐ Purchased 19___ Pd $_______ MIB NB DB BNT
☐ Want Orig. Retail $3.00
NB $4 **MIB** Sec. Mkt. **$8-$10**

A B C D E F G H I J K L

E QXM 598-7 **BRASS SOLDIER**
Etched Brass, 1-1/4" tall, Dated 1991
☐ Purchased 19___ Pd $_______ MIB NB DB BNT
☐ Want Orig. Retail $3.00
NB $4 **MIB** Sec. Mkt. **$8-$10**

F QXM 587-7 **BRIGHT BOXERS**
Handcrafted, 1" tall, Dated 1991. **Artist:** Dill Rhodus
☐ Purchased 19___ Pd $_______ MIB NB DB BNT
☐ Want Orig. Retail $4.50
NB $8 **MIB** Sec. Mkt. **$16-$18**

G QXM 593-9 **BUSY BEAR**
Wood, 1-7/16" tall. **Artist:** Dill Rhodus
☐ Purchased 19___ Pd $_______ MIB NB DB BNT
☐ Want Orig. Retail $4.50
NB $6 **MIB** Sec. Mkt. **$12-$14**

H QXM 595-7 **CARDINAL CAMEO**
Handcrafted, 1-7/16" tall, Dated "Season's Greetings 1991."
Artist: Joyce A. Lyle
☐ Purchased 19___ Pd $_______ MIB NB DB BNT
☐ Want Orig. Retail $6.00
NB $8 **MIB** Sec. Mkt. **$14-$18**

I QXM 594-9 **CARING SHEPHERD**
Hand-Painted Porcelain, 1-1/16" tall. **Artist:** John Francis (Collin)
☐ Purchased 19___ Pd $_______ MIB NB DB BNT
☐ Want Orig. Retail $6.00
NB $9 **MIB** Sec. Mkt. **$16-$20**

J QXM 586-7 **COOL 'N' SWEET**
Hand-Painted Fine Porcelain, 1-3/16" tall, Dated 1991
Artist: Sharon Pike
☐ Purchased 19___ Pd $_______ MIB NB DB BNT
☐ Want Orig. Retail $4.50
NB $10 **MIB** Sec. Mkt. **$18-$20**

K QXM 599-9 **COUNTRY SLEIGH**
Enamel, 1" tall, Dated 1991. **Artist:** LaDene Votruba
☐ Purchased 19___ Pd $_______ MIB NB DB BNT
☐ Want Orig. Retail $4.50
NB $5 **MIB** Sec. Mkt. **$13-$15**

L QXM 585-7 **COURIER TURTLE**
Handcrafted, 1-1/8" tall. **Artist:** Sharon Pike
☐ Purchased 19___ Pd $_______ MIB NB DB BNT
☐ Want Orig. Retail $4.50
NB $7 **MIB** Sec. Mkt. **$12-$15**

A QXM 591-7 **FANCY WREATH**
Handcrafted, 1-1/16" tall. **Artist:** Joyce A. Lyle
☐ Purchased 19___ Pd $_______ MIB NB DB BNT
☐ Want Orig. Retail $4.50
NB $7 **MIB** Sec. Mkt. **$14-$15**

B QXM 588-7 **FELIZ NAVIDAD**
Handcrafted/Straw, 1" tall, Dated 1991. **Artist:** Anita Marra Rogers
☐ Purchased 19___ Pd $_______ MIB NB DB BNT
☐ Want Orig. Retail $6.00
NB $8 **MIB** Sec. Mkt. **$12-$16**

C QXM 581-9 **FIRST CHRISTMAS TOGETHER**
Handcrafted/Brass, 1-1/8" tall, Dated 1991
Artist: Duane Unruh
☐ Purchased 19___ Pd $_______ MIB NB DB BNT
☐ Want Orig. Retail $6.00
NB $10 **MIB** Sec. Mkt. **$16-$18**

D QXM 585-9 **FLY BY**
Handcrafted, 7/8" tall, Dated 1991. **Artist:** Ken Crow
☐ Purchased 19___ Pd $_______ MIB NB DB BNT
☐ Want Orig. Retail $4.50
NB $6 **MIB** Sec. Mkt. **$15-$18**

E QXM 594-7 **FRIENDLY FAWN**
Handcrafted, 1-1/8" tall, Dated 1991. **Artist:** Julia Lee
☐ Purchased 19___ Pd $_______ MIB NB DB BNT
☐ Want Orig. Retail $6.00
NB $8 **MIB** Sec. Mkt. **$14-$16**

F QXM 569-7 **GRANDCHILD'S FIRST CHRISTMAS**
Hand-Painted Fine Porcelain, 1-1/16", Dated 1991
Artist: Anita Marra Rogers
☐ Purchased 19___ Pd $_______ MIB NB DB BNT
☐ Want Orig. Retail $4.50
NB $7 **MIB** Sec. Mkt. **$14-$15**

G QXM 568-7 **HEAVENLY MINSTREL**
Handcrafted, 1-3/16" tall. **Artist:** Donna Lee
☐ Purchased 19___ Pd $_______ MIB NB DB BNT
☐ Want Orig. Retail $9.75
NB $12 **MIB** Sec. Mkt. **$25-$28**

H QXM 599-7 **HOLIDAY SNOWFLAKE**
Etched, Faceted Acrylic, 1-15/32" tall, 1991. **Artist:** Dill Rhodus
☐ Purchased 19___ Pd $_______ MIB NB DB BNT
☐ Want Orig. Retail $3.00
NB $5 **MIB** Sec. Mkt. **$10-$12**

I QXM 568-9 **KEY TO LOVE**
Handcrafted, 1" tall, Dated "Love 1991." **Artist:** Ken Crow
☐ Purchased 19___ Pd $_______ MIB NB DB BNT
☐ Want Orig. Retail $4.50
NB $9 **MIB** Sec. Mkt. **$15-$18**

J QXM 563-9 **KITTENS IN TOYLAND: AIRPLANE**
Fourth in Series, Handcrafted, 7/8" tall. **Artist:** Ken Crow
☐ Purchased 19___ Pd $_______ MIB NB DB BNT
☐ Want Orig. Retail $4.50
NB $9 **MIB** Sec. Mkt. **$18-$22**

K QXM 587-9 **KITTY IN A MITTY**
Handcrafted, 1" tall, Dated 1991. **Artist:** Patricia Andrews
☐ Purchased 19___ Pd $_______ MIB NB DB BNT
☐ Want Orig. Retail $4.50
NB $5 **MIB** Sec. Mkt. **$12-$14**

L QXM 564-7 **KRINGLES, THE: CAROLING**
Third in Series, Handcrafted, 1" tall. **Artist:** Anita Marra Rogers
☐ Purchased 19___ Pd $_______ MIB NB DB BNT
☐ Want Orig. Retail $6.00
NB $12w **MIB** Sec. Mkt. **$20-$24**

M QXM 589-7 **LI'L POPPER**
Handcrafted, 1-3/4" tall. **Artist:** Linda Sickman
☐ Purchased 19___ Pd $_______ MIB NB DB BNT
☐ Want Orig. Retail $4.50
NB $10 **MIB** Sec. Mkt. **$16-$18**

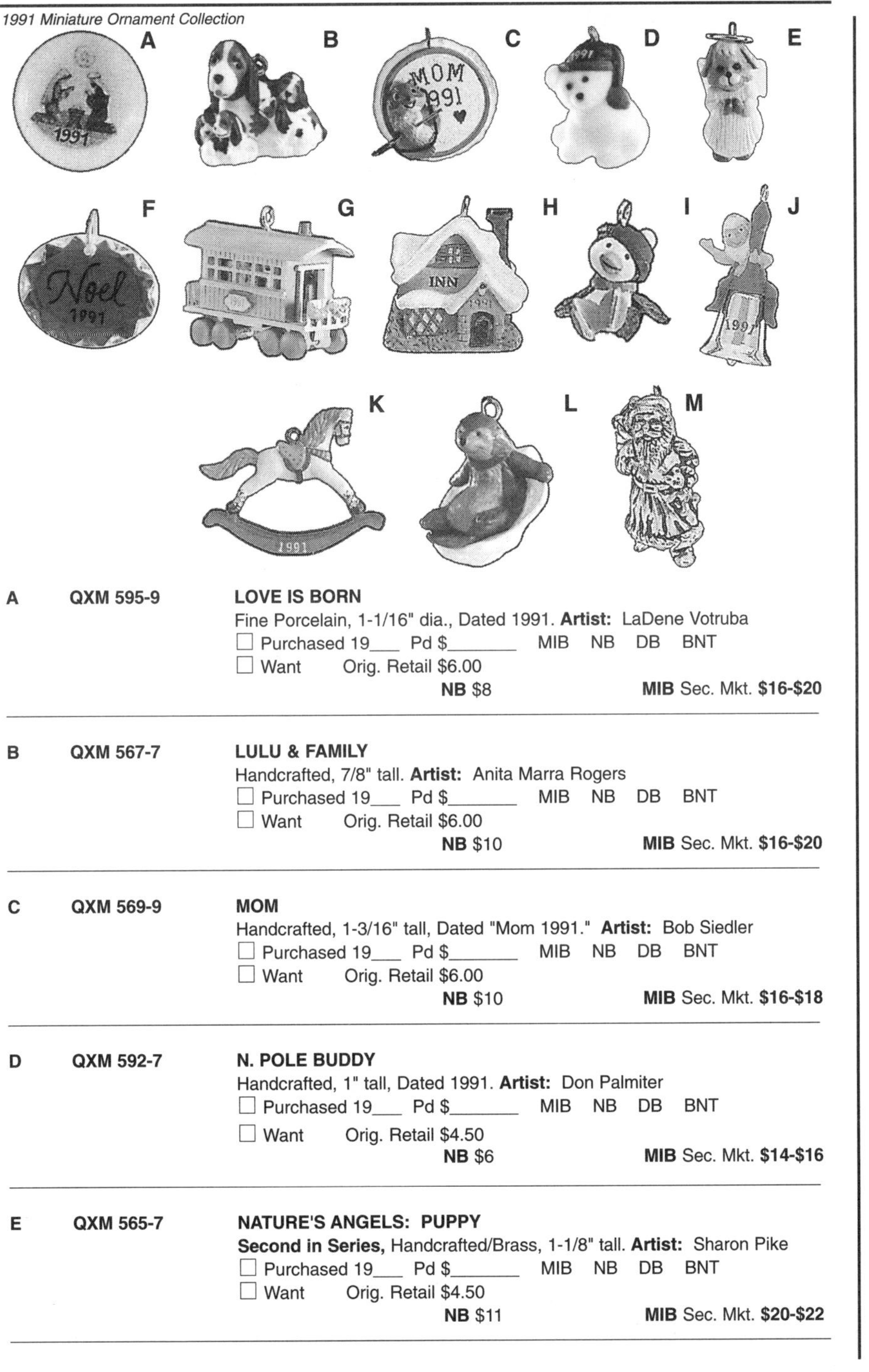

A QXM 595-9 **LOVE IS BORN**
Fine Porcelain, 1-1/16" dia., Dated 1991. **Artist:** LaDene Votruba
☐ Purchased 19___ Pd $_______ MIB NB DB BNT
☐ Want Orig. Retail $6.00
NB $8 **MIB** Sec. Mkt. **$16-$20**

B QXM 567-7 **LULU & FAMILY**
Handcrafted, 7/8" tall. **Artist:** Anita Marra Rogers
☐ Purchased 19___ Pd $_______ MIB NB DB BNT
☐ Want Orig. Retail $6.00
NB $10 **MIB** Sec. Mkt. **$16-$20**

C QXM 569-9 **MOM**
Handcrafted, 1-3/16" tall, Dated "Mom 1991." **Artist:** Bob Siedler
☐ Purchased 19___ Pd $_______ MIB NB DB BNT
☐ Want Orig. Retail $6.00
NB $10 **MIB** Sec. Mkt. **$16-$18**

D QXM 592-7 **N. POLE BUDDY**
Handcrafted, 1" tall, Dated 1991. **Artist:** Don Palmiter
☐ Purchased 19___ Pd $_______ MIB NB DB BNT
☐ Want Orig. Retail $4.50
NB $6 **MIB** Sec. Mkt. **$14-$16**

E QXM 565-7 **NATURE'S ANGELS: PUPPY**
Second in Series, Handcrafted/Brass, 1-1/8" tall. **Artist:** Sharon Pike
☐ Purchased 19___ Pd $_______ MIB NB DB BNT
☐ Want Orig. Retail $4.50
NB $11 **MIB** Sec. Mkt. **$20-$22**

F QXM 598-9 **NOEL**
Faceted Acrylic, 31/32" tall, Dated 1991. **Artist:** Linda Sickman
☐ Purchased 19___ Pd $_______ MIB NB DB BNT
☐ Want Orig. Retail $3.00
NB $6 **MIB** Sec. Mkt. **$10-$12**

G QXM 564-9 **NOEL R.R.: PASSENGER CAR**
Third in Series, Handcrafted, 13/16" tall, Dated 1991
Artist: Linda Sickman
☐ Purchased 19___ Pd $_______ MIB NB DB BNT
☐ Want Orig. Retail $8.50
NB $12 **MIB** Sec. Mkt. **$24-$28**

H QXM 562-7 **OLD ENGLISH VILLAGE: COUNTRY INN**
Fourth in Series, Handcrafted, 1-1/8" tall, Dated 1991
Artist: Julia Lee.
☐ Purchased 19___ Pd $_______ MIB NB DB BNT
☐ Want Orig. Retail $8.50
NB $14 **MIB** Sec. Mkt. **$25-$30**

I QXM 562-9 **PENGUIN PAL**
Fourth & Final in Series, Handcrafted, 3/4" tall. **Artist:** Bob Siedler
☐ Purchased 19___ Pd $_______ MIB NB DB BNT
☐ Want Orig. Retail $4.50
NB $7 **MIB** Sec. Mkt. **$12-$16**

J QXM 566-9 **RING-A-DING ELF**
Handcrafted/Brass, 1-1/4' tall, Dated 1991. **Artist:** Robert Chad
☐ Purchased 19___ Pd $_______ MIB NB DB BNT
☐ Want Orig. Retail $8.50
NB $12 **MIB** Sec. Mkt. **$16-$20**

K QXM 563-7 **ROCKING HORSE: GREY ARABIAN**
Fourth in Series, Handcrafted, 1-1/8" tall, Dated 1991
Artist: Linda Sickman
☐ Purchased 19___ Pd $_______ MIB NB DB BNT
☐ Want Orig. Retail $4.50
NB $14 **MIB** Sec. Mkt. **$20-$22**

L QXM 590-9 **SEASIDE OTTER**
Handcrafted, 7/8" tall. **Artist:** Bob Siedler
☐ Purchased 19___ Pd $_______ MIB NB DB BNT
☐ Want Orig. Retail $4.50
NB $6 **MIB** Sec. Mkt. **$10-$14**

M QXM 567-9 **SILVERY SANTA**
Precious Edition, Silver-Plated, 1-1/8" tall, Dated 1991
Artist: Julia Lee
☐ Purchased 19___ Pd $_______ MIB NB DB BNT
☐ Want Orig. Retail $9.75
NB $15 **MIB** Sec. Mkt. **$20-$23**

A QXM 579-7

SPECIAL FRIENDS
Handcrafted/Wicker, 13/16" tall, Dated 1991. **Artist:** Julia Lee
☐ Purchased 19___ Pd $_______ MIB NB DB BNT
☐ Want Orig. Retail $8.50
NB $12 **MIB** Sec. Mkt. **$18-$20**

B QXM 565-9

THIMBLE BELLS
Second in Series, Handcrafted, 1-1/8" tall, Dated 1991
Artist: Michele Pyda-Sevcik
☐ Purchased 19___ Pd $_______ MIB NB DB BNT
☐ Want Orig. Retail $6.00
NB $12 **MIB** Sec. Mkt. **$20-$24**

C QXM 582-7

TINY TEA PARTY SET
Fine **Porcelain**/Handcrafted, Dated 1991. Other mini sets not porcelain. These porcelain ornaments were "first of their kind." They were not bought up on the secondary market due to the inital retail. Following sets were artplas, not porcelain. The second issue was over-ordered and plentiful.
Artist: Ed Seale
Cookie Plate, 11/16" tall — Teacup Lounger, 5/8" tall
Teacup Taster, 13/16" tall — Teapot, 1" tall
Creamer, 1-3/16" tall — Sugar Bowl, 15/16" tall
☐ Purchased 19___ Pd $_______ MIB NB DB BNT
☐ Want Orig. Retail $29.00
NB $100 **MIB** Sec. Mkt. **$150-$160**

D QXM 588-9

TOP HATTER
Handcrafted, 1" tall, Dated 1991. **Artist:** Ed Seale
☐ Purchased 19___ Pd $_______ MIB NB DB BNT
☐ Want Orig. Retail $6.00
NB $10 **MIB** Sec. Mkt. **$16-$18**

E QXM 589-9

TREELAND TRIO
Handcrafted, 7/8" tall, Dated 1991. **Artist:** Robert Chad
☐ Purchased 19___ Pd $_______ MIB NB DB BNT
☐ Want Orig. Retail $8.50
NB $12 **MIB** Sec. Mkt. **$16-$18**

F QXM 590-7

UPBEAT BEAR
Handcrafted/Metal, 1-1/16" tall, Dated 1991
Artist: John Francis (Collin)
☐ Purchased 19___ Pd $_______ MIB NB DB BNT
☐ Want Orig. Retail $6.00
NB $10 **MIB** Sec. Mkt. **$16-$18**

G QXM 593-7

VISION OF SANTA
Handcrafted, 1-1/16" tall, Dated 1991. **Artist:** Robert Chad
☐ Purchased 19___ Pd $_______ MIB NB DB BNT
☐ Want Orig. Retail $4.50
NB $10 **MIB** Sec. Mkt. **$14-$16**

H QXM 596-7

WEE TOYMAKER
Handcrafted, 1" tall, Dated 1991. **Artist:** Ron Bishop
☐ Purchased 19___ Pd $_______ MIB NB DB BNT
☐ Want Orig. Retail $8.50
NB $10 **MIB** Sec. Mkt. **$16-$18**

I QXM 566-7

WOODLAND BABIES
FIRST IN SERIES, Handcrafted, 1" tall. **Artist:** Ken Crow
☐ Purchased 19___ Pd $_______ MIB NB DB BNT
☐ Want Orig. Retail $6.00
NB $12 **MIB** Sec. Mkt. **$22-$25**

A  B  C  D  E  F G H  I

1992 Miniature Ornament Collection

A QXM 551-1 **A+ TEACHER**
Handcrafted, 1-1/8" tall, Dated 1992. **Artist:** Duane Unruh
☐ Purchased 19___ Pd $_______ MIB NB DB BNT
☐ Want Orig. Retail $3.75
NB $4 **MIB** Sec. Mkt. **$6-$8**

B QXM 552-4 **ANGELIC HARPIST**
Handcrafted, 1-1/4" tall. **Artist:** Joyce A. Lyle
☐ Purchased 19___ Pd $_______ MIB NB DB BNT
☐ Want Orig. Retail $4.50
NB $8 **MIB** Sec. Mkt. **$13-$15**

C QXM 549-4 **BABY'S FIRST CHRISTMAS**
Handcrafted, 1-1/4" tall, Dated 1992
Artist: Joyce A. Lyle
☐ Purchased 19___ Pd $_______ MIB NB DB BNT
☐ Want Orig. Retail $4.50
NB $8 **MIB** Sec. Mkt. **$17-$20**

D QXM 554-4 **BEARYMORES, THE**
FIRST IN SERIES, Handcrafted, 1-1/8" tall, Dated 1992
Artist: Anita Marra Rogers
☐ Purchased 19___ Pd $_______ MIB NB DB BNT
☐ Want Orig. Retail $5.75
NB $14 **MIB** Sec. Mkt. **$20-$22**

E QXM 548-4 **BLACK-CAPPED CHICKADEE**
Handcrafted, 1-3/8" tall, Dated 1992
Artist: John Francis (Collin)
☐ Purchased 19___ Pd $_______ MIB NB DB BNT
☐ Want Orig. Retail $3.00
NB $8 **MIB** Sec. Mkt. **$12-$16**

F QXM 584-1 **BRIGHT STRINGERS**
Handcrafted, 1-1/8" tall. **Artist:** Ed Seale
☐ Purchased 19___ Pd $_______ MIB NB DB BNT
☐ Want Orig. Retail $3.75
NB $8 **MIB** Sec. Mkt. **$12-$14**

G QXM 581-4 **BUCK-A-ROO**
Handcrafted, 1-1/8" tall, Dated 1993. **Artist:** Ken Crow
☐ Purchased 19___ Pd $_______ MIB NB DB BNT
☐ Want Orig. Retail $4.50
NB $8 **MIB** Sec. Mkt. **$12-$15**

H QXC 519-4 **CHIPMUNK PARCEL SERVICE: KEEPSAKE CLUB**
Handcrafted, Dated 1992. **Artist:** Ed Seale
☐ Purchased 19___ Pd $_______ MIB NB DB BNT
☐ Want Early Renewal Gift to Keepsake Orn. Club Members
NB $14 **MIB** Sec. Mkt. **$18-$22**

I QXM 581-1 **CHRISTMAS BONUS**
Handcrafted, 1-3/16" tall, Dated 1992. **Artist:** Don Palmiter
☐ Purchased 19___ Pd $_______ MIB NB DB BNT
☐ Want Orig. Retail $3.00
NB $6 **MIB** Sec. Mkt. **$8-$10**

J QXM 584-4 **CHRISTMAS COPTER**
Handcrafted, 7/8" tall, Dated 1992. **Artist:** John Francis (Collin)
☐ Purchased 19___ Pd $_______ MIB NB DB BNT
☐ Want Orig. Retail $5.75
NB $8 **MIB** Sec. Mkt. **$14-$16**

K QXM 588-4 **COCA-COLA SANTA**
Handcrafted, 1-3/16" tall. **Artist:** Duane Unruh
☐ Purchased 19___ Pd $_______ MIB NB DB BNT
☐ Want Orig. Retail $5.75
NB $9 **MIB** Sec. Mkt. **$17-$19**

L QXM 556-1 **COOL UNCLE SAM**
Handcrafted, 1" tall, Dated '92. **Artist:** Julia Lee
Election Year Commemorative
☐ Purchased 19___ Pd $_______ MIB NB DB BNT
☐ Want Orig. Retail $3.00
NB $8 **MIB** Sec. Mkt. **$15-$17**

A  B  C 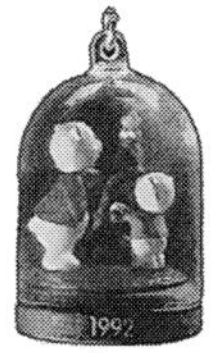 D
E  F  G  H 
I  J  K  L

A **QXM 555-1** **COZY KAYAK**
Handcrafted, 3/4" tall, Dated 1992. **Artist:** Julia Lee
☐ Purchased 19___ Pd $_______ MIB NB DB BNT
☐ Want Orig. Retail $3.75
NB $8 **MIB** Sec. Mkt. **$10-$14**

B **QXM 589-1** **DANCING ANGELS TREE TOPPER**
Dimensional Brass, 2-7/8" tall. Reissued in 1993.
☐ Purchased 19___ Pd $_______ MIB NB DB BNT
☐ Want Orig. Retail $9.75
NB $10 **MIB** Sec. Mkt. **$12-$14**

C **QXM 530-1** **FAST FINISH**
Handcrafted, 7/8" tall, Dated '92. **Artist:** Dill Rhodus
☐ Purchased 19___ Pd $_______ MIB NB DB BNT
☐ Want Orig. Retail $3.75
NB $6 **MIB** Sec. Mkt. **$12-$14**

D **QXM 548-1** **FEEDING TIME**
Handcrafted, 1" tall, Dated '92. **Artist:** Ken Crow
☐ Purchased 19___ Pd $_______ MIB NB DB BNT
☐ Want Orig. Retail $5.75
NB $9 **MIB** Sec. Mkt. **$14-$16**

E **QXM 587-4** **FRIENDLY TIN SOLDIER**
Pressed Tin, 1-1/16" tall. **Artist:** Linda Sickman
☐ Purchased 19___ Pd $_______ MIB NB DB BNT
☐ Want Orig. Retail $4.50
NB $6 **MIB** Sec. Mkt. **$14-$16**

F **QXM 552-1** **FRIENDS ARE TOPS**
Handcrafted, 1-1/8" tall, Dated '92. **Artist:** Ken Crow
☐ Purchased 19___ Pd $_______ MIB NB DB BNT
☐ Want Orig. Retail $4.50
NB $6 **MIB** Sec. Mkt. **$10-$12**

G **QXM 592-4** **GERBIL, INC.**
Handcrafted, 7/8" tall, Dated '92. **Artist:** Bob Siedler
☐ Purchased 19___ Pd $_______ MIB NB DB BNT
☐ Want Orig. Retail $3.75
NB $5 **MIB** Sec. Mkt. **$10-$12**

H **QXM 587-1** **GOING PLACES**
Handcrafted, 1" tall, Dated 1992. **Artist:** Patricia Andrews
☐ Purchased 19___ Pd $_______ MIB NB DB BNT
☐ Want Orig. Retail $3.75
NB $6 **MIB** Sec. Mkt. **$10-$12**

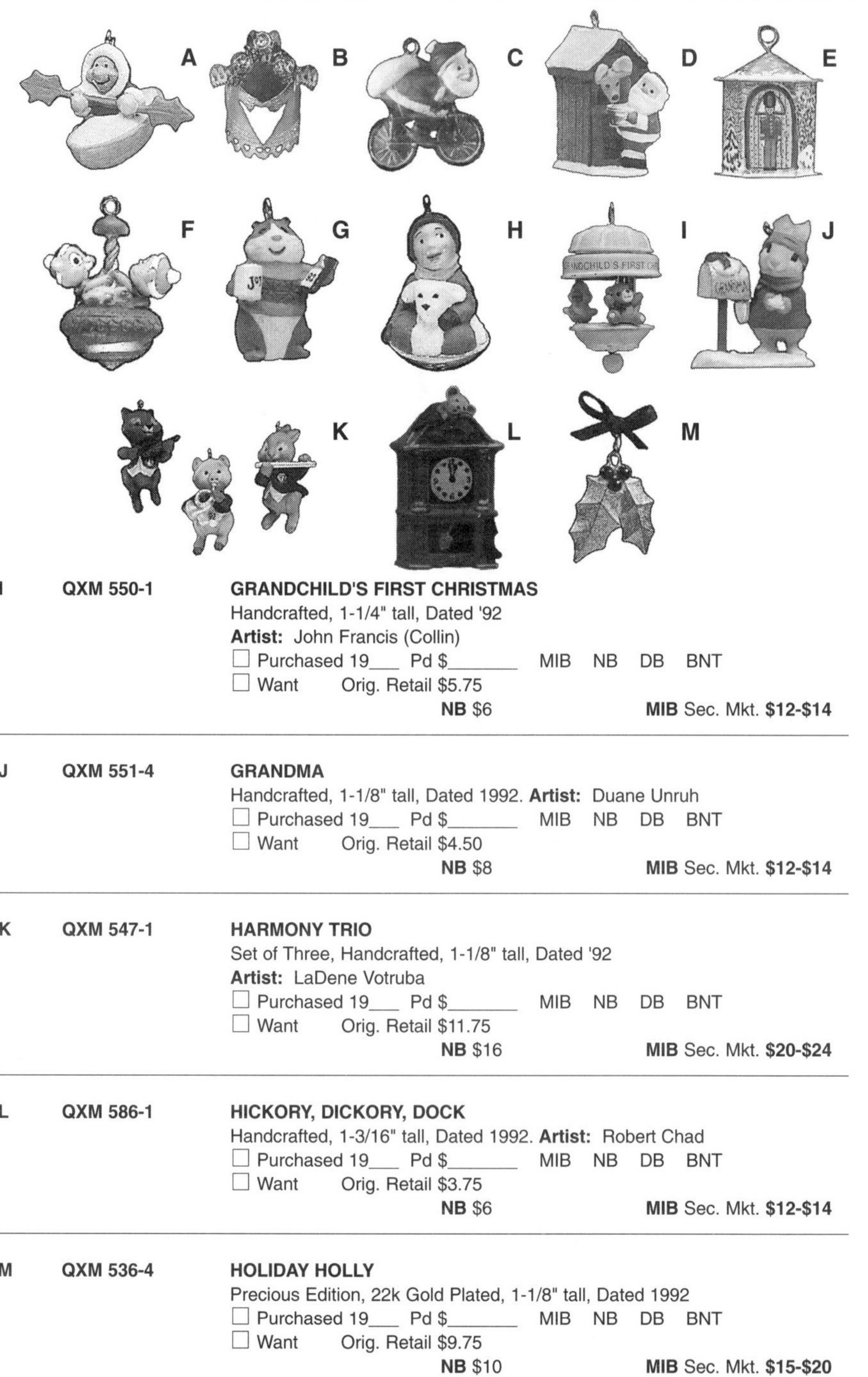

I **QXM 550-1** **GRANDCHILD'S FIRST CHRISTMAS**
Handcrafted, 1-1/4" tall, Dated '92
Artist: John Francis (Collin)
☐ Purchased 19___ Pd $_______ MIB NB DB BNT
☐ Want Orig. Retail $5.75
NB $6 **MIB** Sec. Mkt. **$12-$14**

J **QXM 551-4** **GRANDMA**
Handcrafted, 1-1/8" tall, Dated 1992. **Artist:** Duane Unruh
☐ Purchased 19___ Pd $_______ MIB NB DB BNT
☐ Want Orig. Retail $4.50
NB $8 **MIB** Sec. Mkt. **$12-$14**

K **QXM 547-1** **HARMONY TRIO**
Set of Three, Handcrafted, 1-1/8" tall, Dated '92
Artist: LaDene Votruba
☐ Purchased 19___ Pd $_______ MIB NB DB BNT
☐ Want Orig. Retail $11.75
NB $16 **MIB** Sec. Mkt. **$20-$24**

L **QXM 586-1** **HICKORY, DICKORY, DOCK**
Handcrafted, 1-3/16" tall, Dated 1992. **Artist:** Robert Chad
☐ Purchased 19___ Pd $_______ MIB NB DB BNT
☐ Want Orig. Retail $3.75
NB $6 **MIB** Sec. Mkt. **$12-$14**

M **QXM 536-4** **HOLIDAY HOLLY**
Precious Edition, 22k Gold Plated, 1-1/8" tall, Dated 1992
☐ Purchased 19___ Pd $_______ MIB NB DB BNT
☐ Want Orig. Retail $9.75
NB $10 **MIB** Sec. Mkt. **$15-$20**

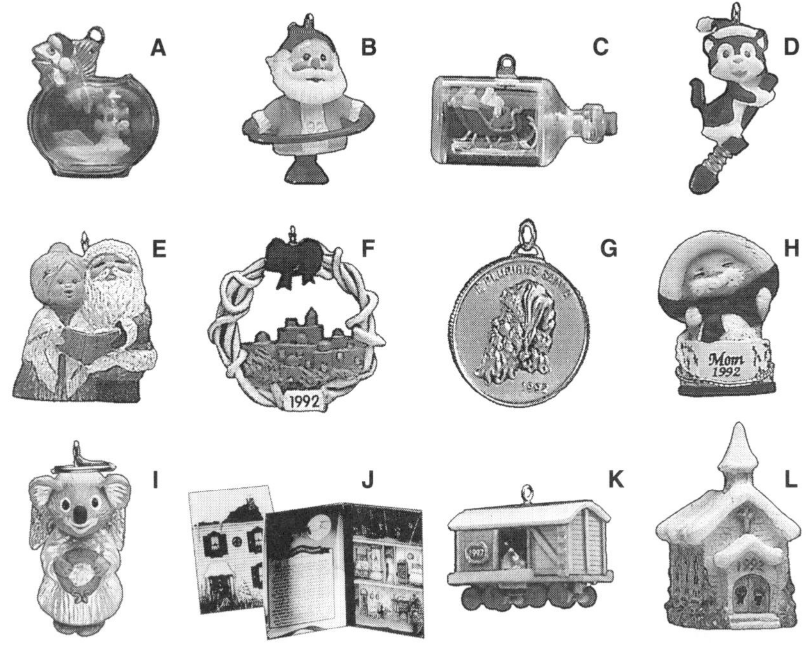

A QXM 583-4 **HOLIDAY SPLASH**
Handcrafted, 1" tall, Dated 1992. **Artist:** John Francis (Collin)
☐ Purchased 19___ Pd $_______ MIB NB DB BNT
☐ Want Orig. Retail $5.75
NB $6 **MIB** Sec. Mkt. **$12-$14**

B QXM 583-1 **HOOP IT UP**
Handcrafted, 1" tall, Dated '92, **Artist:** Ken Crow
☐ Purchased 19___ Pd $_______ MIB NB DB BNT
☐ Want Orig. Retail $4.50
NB $6 **MIB** Sec. Mkt. **$12-$14**

C QXM 588-1 **INSIDE STORY**
Handcrafted, 3/4" tall, Dated 1992. **Artist:** Ed Seale
☐ Purchased 19___ Pd $_______ MIB NB DB BNT
☐ Want Orig. Retail $7.25
NB $9 **MIB** Sec. Mkt. **$16-$18**

D QXM 539-1 **KITTENS IN TOYLAND: POGO STICK**
Fifth and Final in Series, Handcrafted, 1-3/16" tall
Artist: Ken Crow
☐ Purchased 19___ Pd $_______ MIB NB DB BNT
☐ Want Orig. Retail $4.50
NB $8 **MIB** Sec. Mkt. **$15-$18**

E QXM 538-1 **KRINGLES, THE**
Fourth in Series, Handcrafted, 1" tall. **Artist:** Anita Marra Rogers
☐ Purchased 19___ Pd $_______ MIB NB DB BNT
☐ Want Orig. Retail $6.00
NB $12 **MIB** Sec. Mkt. **$16-$20**

F QXM 586-4 **LITTLE TOWN OF BETHLEHEM**
Handcrafted, 1" dia., Dated 1992. **Artist:** Linda Sickman
☐ Purchased 19___ Pd $_______ MIB NB DB BNT
☐ Want Orig. Retail $3.00
NB $10 **MIB** Sec. Mkt. **$18-$20**

G QXM 585-4 **MINTED FOR SANTA**
Copper, 1" dia., Dated 1992. **Artist:** Duane Unruh
☐ Purchased 19___ Pd $_______ MIB NB DB BNT
☐ Want Orig. Retail $3.75
NB $6 **MIB** Sec. Mkt. **$12-$16**

H QXM 550-4 **MOM**
Handcrafted, 1-3/16" tall, Dated 1992. **Artist:** Patricia Andrews
☐ Purchased 19___ Pd $_______ MIB NB DB BNT
☐ Want Orig. Retail $4.50
NB $9 **MIB** Sec. Mkt. **$12-$16**

I QXM 545-1 **NATURE'S ANGELS**
Third in Series, Handcrafted, 1" tall. **Artist:** Sharon Pike
☐ Purchased 19___ Pd $_______ MIB NB DB BNT
☐ Want Orig. Retail $4.50
NB $10 **MIB** Sec. Mkt. **$16-$20**

J QXM 554-1 **NIGHT BEFORE CHRISTMAS, THE: HOUSE**
FIRST IN SERIES, Tin/Handcrafted
Tin Display House, 8" tall x 5-1/2" wide; Rocker w/Mouse, 1-1/8" tall
Due to the house being produced only in '92 this series will not be as popular, as there are too many "new" buyers each year who will not have the house for the remaining pieces in the series.
Artists: LaDene Votruba and Duane Unruh
☐ Purchased 19___ Pd $_______ MIB NB DB BNT
☐ Want Orig. Retail $13.75
NB $22 **MIB** Sec. Mkt. **$30-$35**

K QXM 544-1 **NOEL R.R.: BOX CAR**
Fourth in Series, Handcrafted, 13/16" tall, Dated 1992
Artist: Linda Sickman
☐ Purchased 19___ Pd $_______ MIB NB DB BNT
☐ Want Orig. Retail $7.00
NB $12 **MIB** Sec. Mkt. **$18-$22**

L QXM 538-4 **OLD ENGLISH VILLAGE: CHURCH**
Fifth in Series, Handcrafted, 1-5/16" tall, Dated 1992
Artist: Julia Lee
☐ Purchased 19___ Pd $_______ MIB NB DB BNT
☐ Want Orig. Retail $7.00
NB $15 **MIB** Sec. Mkt. **$25-$30**

A QXM 557-1 **PERFECT BALANCE**
Handcrafted, 1-1/4" tall, Dated '92. **Artist:** Anita Marra Rogers
☐ Purchased 19___ Pd $_______ MIB NB DB BNT
☐ Want Orig. Retail $3.00
NB $5 **MIB** Sec. Mkt. **$12-$14**

B QXM 553-4 **POLAR POLKA**
Handcrafted, 1-13/16" tall, Dated 1992. **Artist:** Ed Seale
☐ Purchased 19___ Pd $_______ MIB NB DB BNT
☐ Want Orig. Retail $4.50
NB $8 **MIB** Sec. Mkt. **$14-$16**

C QXM 557-4 **PUPPET SHOW**
Handcrafted, 1" tall, Dated '92. **Artist:** Bob Siedler
☐ Purchased 19___ Pd $_______ MIB NB DB BNT
☐ Want Orig. Retail $3.00
NB $6 **MIB** Sec. Mkt. **$12-$14**

D QXM 545-4 **ROCKING HORSE: BROWN HORSE**
Fifth in Series, Handcrafted, 1-1/8" tall, Dated 1992
Artist: Linda Sickman
☐ Purchased 19___ Pd $_______ MIB NB DB BNT
☐ Want Orig. Retail $4.50
NB $10 **MIB** Sec. Mkt. **$18-$22**

E 2QXM 579-4 **SEW, SEW TINY**
Handcrafted, Dated 1992. Not Porcelain **Artist:** Ed Seale
A. Basket Break, 1-1/8" tall D. Cutting Edge, 7/8" tall
B. Threaded Thru, 1-1/4" tall E. Buttoned Up, 3/4" tall
C. Pinned On, 1-1/8" tall F. Thimble Full, 13/16" tall
☐ Purchased 19___ Pd $_______ MIB NB DB BNT
☐ Want Orig. Retail $29.00
NB-$30 **MIB** Sec. Mkt. **$50-$55**

F QXM 582-1 **SKI FOR TWO**
Handcrafted, 15/16" tall, Dated '92. **Artist:** Patricia Andrews
☐ Purchased 19___ Pd $_______ MIB NB DB BNT
☐ Want Orig. Retail $4.50
NB $6 **MIB** Sec. Mkt. **$13-$15**

G QXM 556-4 **SNOWSHOE BUNNY**
Handcrafted, 1-1/16" tall. **Artist:** LaDene Votruba
☐ Purchased 19___ Pd $_______ MIB NB DB BNT
☐ Want Orig. Retail $3.75
NB $6 **MIB** Sec. Mkt. **$10-$12**

H QXM 555-4 **SNUG KITTY**
Handcrafted, 1" tall, Dated '92. **Artist:** Sharon Pike
☐ Purchased 19___ Pd $_______ MIB NB DB BNT
☐ Want Orig. Retail $3.75
NB $5 **MIB** Sec. Mkt. **$10-$12**

I QXM 592-1 **SPUNKY MONKEY**
Handcrafted, 1-3/8" tall, Dated '92. **Artist:** Robert Chad
☐ Purchased 19___ Pd $_______ MIB NB DB BNT
☐ Want Orig. Retail $3.00
NB $8 **MIB** Sec. Mkt. **$14-$16**

J QXM 546-1 **THIMBLE BELLS**
Third in Series, Porcelain, 1-1/8" tall, Dated 1992
Artist: Joyce A. Lyle
☐ Purchased 19___ Pd $_______ MIB NB DB BNT
☐ Want Orig. Retail $6.00
NB $10 **MIB** Sec. Mkt. **$20-$22**

K QXM 585-1 **VISIONS OF ACORNS**
Handcrafted, 1-3/16" tall, Dated '92. **Artist:** Patricia Andrews
☐ Purchased 19___ Pd $_______ MIB NB DB BNT
☐ Want Orig. Retail $4.50
NB $8 **MIB** Sec. Mkt. **$12-$14**

L QXM 553-1 **WEE THREE KINGS**
Handcrafted, 1-3/16" tall, Dated 1991. **Artist:** Don Palmiter
☐ Purchased 19___ Pd $_______ MIB NB DB BNT
☐ Want Orig. Retail $5.75
NB $8 **MIB** Sec. Mkt. **$16-$18**

M QXM 544-4 **WOODLAND BABIES**
Second in Series, Handcrafted, 1" tall, Dated 1992
Artist: Don Palmiter
☐ Purchased 19___ Pd $_______ MIB NB DB BNT
☐ Want Orig. Retail $6.00
NB $10 **MIB** Sec. Mkt. **$16-$18**

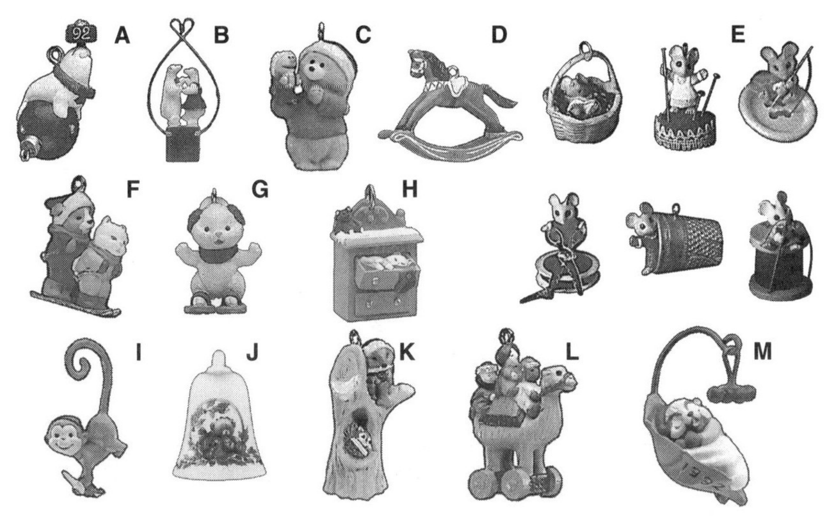

1993 Miniature Ornament Collection

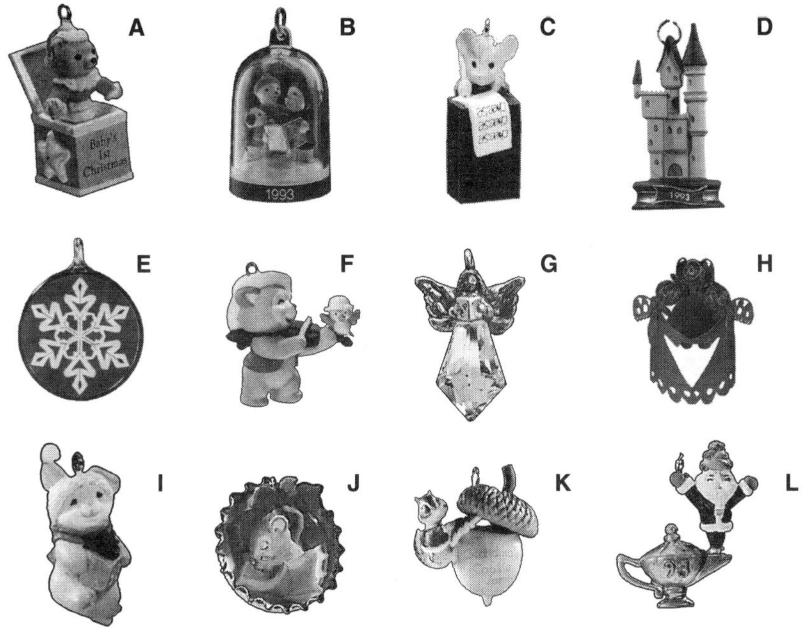

A QXM 514-5 **BABY'S FIRST CHRISTMAS**
Handcrafted, 1-1/16" tall, Dated 1993. **Artist:** LaDene Votruba
☐ Purchased 19___ Pd $_______ MIB NB DB BNT
☐ Want Orig. Retail $5.75
NB $8 **MIB** Sec. Mkt. **$12-$14**

B QXM 512-5 **BEARYMORES, THE**
Second in Series, Handcrafted, 1-1/8" tall, Dated 1993
Artist: Anita Marra Rogers
☐ Purchased 19___ Pd $_______ MIB NB DB BNT
☐ Want Orig. Retail $5.75
NB $9 **MIB** Sec. Mkt. **$14-$18**

C QXM 407-2 **CHEESE PLEASE**
Handcrafted, 1 1/4" tall, Dated 1993. **Artist:** Bob Siedler
☐ Purchased 19___ Pd $_______ MIB NB DB BNT
☐ Want Orig. Retail $3.75
NB $5 **MIB** Sec. Mkt. **$9-$10**

D QXM 408-5 **CHRISTMAS CASTLE**
Handcrafted, 1 1/8" tall, Dated 1993. **Artist:** Ed Seale
☐ Purchased 19___ Pd $_______ MIB NB DB BNT
☐ Want Orig. Retail $5.75
NB $6 **MIB** Sec. Mkt. **$10-$12**

E QXM 401-2 **CLOISONNÉ SNOWFLAKE**
Precious Edition. Cloisonné/Brass, 1" dia. Being used as earrings and necklaces. **Artist:** LaDene Votruba
☐ Purchased 19___ Pd $_______ MIB NB DB BNT
☐ Want Orig. Retail $9.75
NB $12 **MIB** Sec. Mkt. **$18-$20**

F QXM 406-2 **COUNTRY FIDDLING**
Handcrafted, 1" tall, Dated '93. **Artist:** John Francis (Collin)
☐ Purchased 19___ Pd $_______ MIB NB DB BNT
☐ Want Orig. Retail $3.75
NB $5 **MIB** Sec. Mkt. **$8-$10**

G QXM 401-5 **CRYSTAL ANGEL**
Full lead crystal and gold-plated, 1" tall, Dated '93. Being used as a necklace! A sleeper in '94. **Artist:** Don Palmiter
☐ Purchased 19___ Pd $_______ MIB NB DB BNT
☐ Want Orig. Retail $9.75
NB $45 **MIB** Sec. Mkt. **$60-$65**

H QXM 589-1 **DANCING ANGELS TREE-TOPPER**
Dimensional brass 2 7/8" tall, Reissued from 1992
☐ Purchased 19___ Pd $_______ MIB NB DB BNT
☐ Want Orig. Retail $9.75
NB $10 **MIB** Sec. Mkt. **$12-$14**

I QXM 407-5 **EARS TO PALS**
Handcrafted, 1 3/16" tall, Dated '93. **Artist:** Patricia Andrews
☐ Purchased 19___ Pd $_______ MIB NB DB BNT
☐ Want Orig. Retail $3.75
NB $5 **MIB** Sec. Mkt. **$8-$10**

J QXC 529-4 **FORTY WINKS: KEEPSAKE CLUB**
Handcrafted, 1 3/16" tall. **Artist:** John Francis (Collin)
☐ Purchased 19___ Pd $_______ MIB NB DB BNT
☐ Want Orig. Retail---Free with Membership
NB $15 **MIB** Sec. Mkt. **$18-$22**

K QXM 516-2 **GRANDMA**
Handcrafted, 1" tall, Dated 1993. **Artist:** Ed Seale
☐ Purchased 19___ Pd $_______ MIB NB DB BNT
☐ Want Orig. Retail $4.50
NB $6 **MIB** Sec. Mkt. **$12-$14**

L QXM 405-5 **I DREAM OF SANTA**
Handcrafted, 1 1/8" tall, Dated 1993. **Artist:** Linda Sickman
☐ Purchased 19___ Pd $_______ MIB NB DB BNT
☐ Want Orig. Retail $3.75
NB $8 **MIB** Sec. Mkt. **$12-$14**

A QXM 404-5 **INTO THE WOODS**
Handcrafted, 1" tall, Dated '93. **Artist:** Ed Seale
☐ Purchased 19___ Pd $_______ MIB NB DB BNT
☐ Want Orig. Retail $3.75
NB $6 **MIB** Sec. Mkt. **$8-$10**

B QXM 513-5 **KRINGLES, THE: WREATH**
Fifth and Final in Series, Handcrafted, 1" tall. **Artist:** Anita Marra Rogers
☐ Purchased 19___ Pd $_______ MIB NB DB BNT
☐ Want Orig. Retail $5.75
NB $8 **MIB** Sec. Mkt. **$15-$18**

C QXM 412-2 **LEARNING TO SKATE**
Handcrafted, 1 1/8" tall. **Artist:** Robert Chad
☐ Purchased 19___ Pd $_______ MIB NB DB BNT
☐ Want Orig. Retail $3.00
NB $5 **MIB** Sec. Mkt. **$8-$10**

D QXM411-5 **LIGHTING A PATH**
Handcrafted, 1 1/16" tall. **Artist:** Robert Chad
☐ Purchased 19___ Pd $_______ MIB NB DB BNT
☐ Want Orig. Retail $3.00
NB $5 **MIB** Sec. Mkt. **$9-$10**

E QXM 400-5 **MARCH OF THE TEDDY BEARS**
FIRST IN SERIES, Handcrafted, 1-7/16" tall, Dated 1993
Artist: Duane Unruh
☐ Purchased 19___ Pd $_______ MIB NB DB BNT
☐ Want Orig. Retail $4.50
NB $8 **MIB** Sec. Mkt. **$15-$18**

F QXM 404-2 **MERRY MASCOT**
Handcrafted, 1 3/8" tall, Dated '93. **Artist:** Bob Siedler
☐ Purchased 19___ Pd $_______ MIB NB DB BNT
☐ Want Orig. Retail $3.75
NB $6 **MIB** Sec. Mkt. **$10-$12**

G QXM 515-5 **MOM**
Handcrafted, 1-1/8" tall, Dated 1993. **Artist:** Patricia Andrews
☐ Purchased 19___ Pd $_______ MIB NB DB BNT
☐ Want Orig. Retail $4.50
NB $7 **MIB** Sec. Mkt. **$10-$12**

H QXM 409-2 **MONKEY MELODY**
Stringer ornament, Handcrafted, 15/16" tall, Dated 1993
Artist: Linda Sickman
☐ Purchased 19___ Pd $_______ MIB NB DB BNT
☐ Want Orig. Retail $5.75
NB $10 **MIB** Sec. Mkt. **$14-$16**

I QXM 512-2 **NATURE'S ANGELS**
Fourth in Series, Handcrafted, 1-1/8" tall, Dated 1993
Artist: Patricia Andrews
☐ Purchased 19___ Pd $_______ MIB NB DB BNT
☐ Want Orig. Retail $4.50
NB $8 **MIB** Sec. Mkt. **$12-$15**

J QXM 511-5 **NIGHT BEFORE CHRISTMAS, THE: BED**
Second in Series, Handcrafted, 1-1/8" tall, Dated '93
Artist: LaDene Votruba
☐ Purchased 19___ Pd $_______ MIB NB DB BNT
☐ Want Orig. Retail $4.50
NB $12 **MIB** Sec. Mkt. **$18-$20**

K QXM 510-5 **NOEL R.R.: FLATBED CAR**
Fifth in Series, Handcrafted, 1-1/8" tall, Dated 1993
Artist: Linda Sickman
☐ Purchased 19___ Pd $_______ MIB NB DB BNT
☐ Want Orig. Retail $7.00
NB $12 **MIB** Sec. Mkt. **$18-$21**

A

B

C

D

E

F

G

H

I

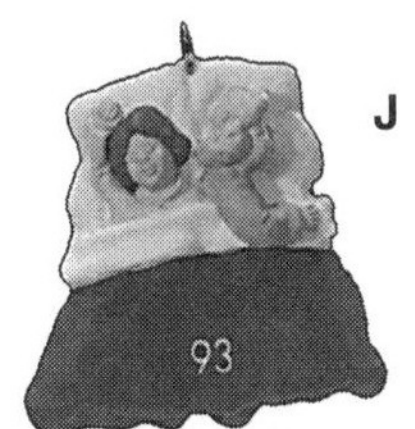

J

K

A QXM 410-5 **NORTH POLE FIRE TRUCK**
Handcrafted, 5/8" tall, Dated '93. **Artist:** Don Palmiter
☐ Purchased 19___ Pd $_______ MIB NB DB BNT
☐ Want Orig. Retail $4.75
NB $8 **MIB** Sec. Mkt. **$12-$14**

B QXM 513-2 **OLD ENGLISH VILLAGE: TOY SHOP**
Sixth in Series, Handcrafted, 1-3/16" tall, Dated 1993
Artist: Julia Lee
☐ Purchased 19___ Pd $_______ MIB NB DB BNT
☐ Want Orig. Retail $7.00
NB $10 **MIB** Sec. Mkt. **$17-$20**

C QXM 400-2 **ON THE ROAD**
FIRST IN SERIES, Pressed Tin, 7/16" tall, Dated 1993
Artist: Linda Sickman
☐ Purchased 19___ Pd $_______ MIB NB DB BNT
☐ Want Orig. Retail $5.75
NB $10 **MIB** Sec. Mkt. **$14-$16**

D QXM 405-2 **PEAR-SHAPED TONES**
Handcrafted, 1" tall, Dated 1993. **Artist:** Joyce A. Lyle
☐ Purchased 19___ Pd $_______ MIB NB DB BNT
☐ Want Orig. Retail $3.75
NB $4 **MIB** Sec. Mkt. **$6-$8**

E QXM 409-5 **PULL OUT A PLUM**
Handcrafted, 5/8" tall, Dated '93. **Artist:** John Francis (Collin)
☐ Purchased 19___ Pd $_______ MIB NB DB BNT
☐ Want Orig. Retail $5.75
NB $6 **MIB** Sec. Mkt. **$12-$14**

F QXM 411-2 **REFRESHING FLIGHT**
Handcrafted, 7/8" tall. **Artist:** Robert Chad
☐ Purchased 19___ Pd $_______ MIB NB DB BNT
☐ Want Orig. Retail $5.75
NB $10 **MIB** Sec. Mkt. **$14-$16**

G QXM 545-2 **REVOLVING TREE BASE: HOLIDAY EXPRESS**
Train circles on track, Free miniature tree w/purchase.
Reissued in '94 and '95.
☐ Purchased 19___ Pd $_______ MIB NB DB BNT
☐ Want Orig. Retail $50.00
NB NE **MIB** Sec. Mkt. **NE**

H QXM 511-2 **ROCKING HORSE: APPALOOSA**
Sixth in Series, Handcrafted, 1-1/8" tall, Dated 1993
Artist: Linda Sickman
☐ Purchased 19___ Pd $_______ MIB NB DB BNT
☐ Want Orig. Retail $4.50
NB $9 **MIB** Sec. Mkt. **$13-$15**

I QXM 402-5 **'ROUND THE MOUNTAIN**
Handcrafted, 1-11/16" tall, Dated 1993. **Artist:** Ken Crow
☐ Purchased 19___ Pd $_______ MIB NB DB BNT
☐ Want Orig. Retail $7.25
NB $12 **MIB** Sec. Mkt. **$18-$20**

J QXM 512-7 **SECRET PAL**
New Commemorative, Handcrafted, 1" tall, Dated 1993
Artist: Anita Marra Rogers
☐ Purchased 19___ Pd $_______ MIB NB DB BNT
☐ Want Orig. Retail $3.75
NB $5 **MIB** Sec. Mkt. **$8-$10**

K QXM 518-2 **SNUGGLE BIRDS**
Handcrafted, 1-9/16" tall, Dated '93. **Artist:** Patricia Andrews
☐ Purchased 19___ Pd $_______ MIB NB DB BNT
☐ Want Orig. Retail $5.75
NB $7 **MIB** Sec. Mkt. **$12-$15**

L QXM 516-5 **SPECIAL FRIENDS**
Handcrafted, 1" tall, Dated 1993. **Artist:** John Francis (Collin)
☐ Purchased 19___ Pd $_______ MIB NB DB BNT
☐ Want Orig. Retail $4.50
NB $5 **MIB** Sec. Mkt. **$8-$10**

A B C D

E F G H

I J K L

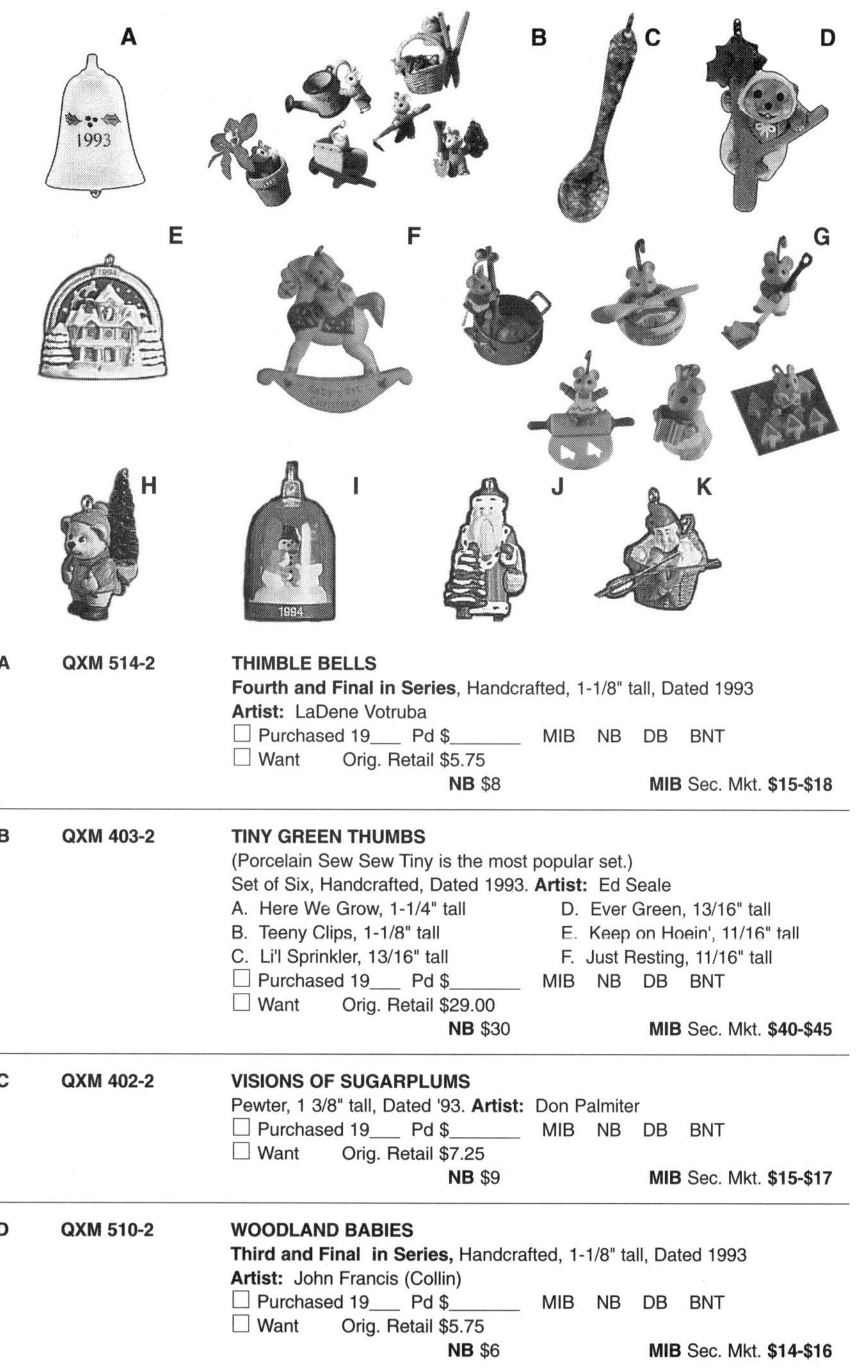

A QXM 514-2 **THIMBLE BELLS**
Fourth and Final in Series, Handcrafted, 1-1/8" tall, Dated 1993
Artist: LaDene Votruba
☐ Purchased 19___ Pd $_______ MIB NB DB BNT
☐ Want Orig. Retail $5.75
NB $8 **MIB** Sec. Mkt. **$15-$18**

B QXM 403-2 **TINY GREEN THUMBS**
(Porcelain Sew Sew Tiny is the most popular set.)
Set of Six, Handcrafted, Dated 1993. **Artist:** Ed Seale
A. Here We Grow, 1-1/4" tall
B. Teeny Clips, 1-1/8" tall
C. Li'l Sprinkler, 13/16" tall
D. Ever Green, 13/16" tall
E. Keep on Hoein', 11/16" tall
F. Just Resting, 11/16" tall
☐ Purchased 19___ Pd $_______ MIB NB DB BNT
☐ Want Orig. Retail $29.00
NB $30 **MIB** Sec. Mkt. **$40-$45**

C QXM 402-2 **VISIONS OF SUGARPLUMS**
Pewter, 1 3/8" tall, Dated '93. **Artist:** Don Palmiter
☐ Purchased 19___ Pd $_______ MIB NB DB BNT
☐ Want Orig. Retail $7.25
NB $9 **MIB** Sec. Mkt. **$15-$17**

D QXM 510-2 **WOODLAND BABIES**
Third and Final in Series, Handcrafted, 1-1/8" tall, Dated 1993
Artist: John Francis (Collin)
☐ Purchased 19___ Pd $_______ MIB NB DB BNT
☐ Want Orig. Retail $5.75
NB $6 **MIB** Sec. Mkt. **$14-$16**

1994 Miniature Ornament Collection

E QXM 407-3 **A MERRY FLIGHT**
Handcrafted, 1" tall, Dated 1994. Caption:"Santa's flight is the merriest sight!" Turn dial with thumb and Santa circles the village. **Artist:** Ken Crow
☐ Purchased 19___ Pd $_______ MIB NB DB BNT
☐ Want Orig. Retail $5.75
MIB Sec. Mkt. **$8-$10**

F QXM 400-3 **BABY'S FIRST CHRISTMAS**
Handcrafted, 1-1/4" tall, Dated 1994. **Artist:** Joyce Lyle
☐ Purchased 19___ Pd $_______ MIB NB DB BNT
☐ Want Orig. Retail $5.75
NB $6 **MIB** Sec. Mkt. **$10-$12**

G QXM 403-3 **BAKING TINY TREATS**
Handcrafted, Set of Six, Dated 1994. **Artist:** Ed Seale
A. Merry Mixer, 1-1/8" tall
B. Standin' By, 3/4" tall
C. Just Dozin', 1/2" tall
D. Rollin' Along, 13/16" tall
E. Scoop, 11/16" tall
F. Official Taster, 9/16" tall
☐ Purchased 19___ Pd $_______ MIB NB DB BNT
☐ Want Orig. Retail $29.00
NB $35 **MIB** Sec. Mkt. **$50-$55**

H QXM 407-6 **BEARY PERFECT TREE**
Handcrafted, 1-3/16" tall, Dated 1994. **Artist:** Ron Bishop
☐ Purchased 19___ Pd $_______ MIB NB DB BNT
☐ Want Orig. Retail $4.75
MIB Sec. Mkt. **$8-$10**

I QXM 513-3 **BEARYMORES, THE**
Third and Final in Series, Handcrafted, 1-1/8" tall, Dated 1994.
Artist: Anita Marra Rogers
☐ Purchased 19___ Pd $_______ MIB NB DB BNT
☐ Want Orig. Retail $5.75
NB $6 **MIB** Sec. Mkt. **$12-$15**

J QXM 515-3 **CENTURIES OF SANTA**
FIRST IN SERIES, Handcrafted, 1-1/4" tall, Dated 1994.
Artist: Linda Sickman
☐ Purchased 19___ Pd $_______ MIB NB DB BNT
☐ Want Orig. Retail $6.00
NB $14 **MIB** Sec. Mkt. **$25-$28**

K QXM 406-3 **CORNY ELF**
Handcrafted, 1" tall, **Artist:** Dill Rhodus
☐ Purchased 19___ Pd $_______ MIB NB DB BNT
☐ Want Orig. Retail $4.50
MIB Sec. Mkt. **$8-$10**

A QXM 410-3 **CUTE AS A BUTTON**
Handcrafted, 13/16" tall, Dated 1994. **Artist:** Ken Crow
☐ Purchased 19___ Pd $_______ MIB NB DB BNT
☐ Want Orig. Retail $3.75
MIB Sec. Mkt. **$8-$10**

B QXM 589-1 **DANCING ANGELS TREE-TOPPER**
Dimensional Brass, 2 7/8" tall, Reissued from 1992
☐ Purchased 19___ Pd $_______ MIB NB DB BNT
☐ Want Orig. Retail $9.75
NB$10 **MIB** Sec. Mkt. **$12-$14**

C QXM 402-6 **DAZZLING REINDEER**
Precious Edition, Pewter, 1-3/8" tall
Artist: LaDene Votruba
☐ Purchased 19___ Pd $_______ MIB NB DB BNT
☐ Want Orig. Retail $9.75
NB$12 **MIB** Sec. Mkt. **$18-$22**

D QXM 401-6 **FRIENDS NEED HUGS**
Handcrafted, 13/16" tall, Dated 1994. **Artist:** Joyce Lyle
☐ Purchased 19___ Pd $_______ MIB NB DB BNT
☐ Want Orig. Retail $4.50
MIB Sec. Mkt. **$8-$12**

E QXM 405-6 **GRACEFUL CAROUSEL HORSE**
Pewter, 1-1/4" tall, Dated 1994. **Artist:**
☐ Purchased 19___ Pd $_______ MIB NB DB BNT
☐ Want Orig. Retail $7.75
MIB Sec. Mkt. **$12-$14**

F QXM 516-6 **HAVE A COOKIE**
Handcrafted, 7/8" tall, Dated 1994, Artist's Favortie
Artist: Donna Lee
☐ Purchased 19___ Pd $_______ MIB NB DB BNT
☐ Want Orig. Retail $5.75
MIB Sec. Mkt. **$12-$14**

G QXM 400-6 **HEARTS A-SAIL**
Handcrafted, 15/16" tall, Dated 1994. **Artist:** Ron Bishop
☐ Purchased 19___ Pd $_______ MIB NB DB BNT
☐ Want Orig. Retail $5.75
MIB Sec. Mkt. **$10-$12**

H QXM 545-2 **HOLIDAY EXPRESS: REVOLVING TREE BASE**
Handcrafted, 4-1/4" tall Reissued from 1993.
Train circles track, Miniature tree sold separately.
☐ Purchased 19___ Pd $_______ MIB NB DB BNT
☐ Want Orig. Retail $50.00
NB-NE **NE**

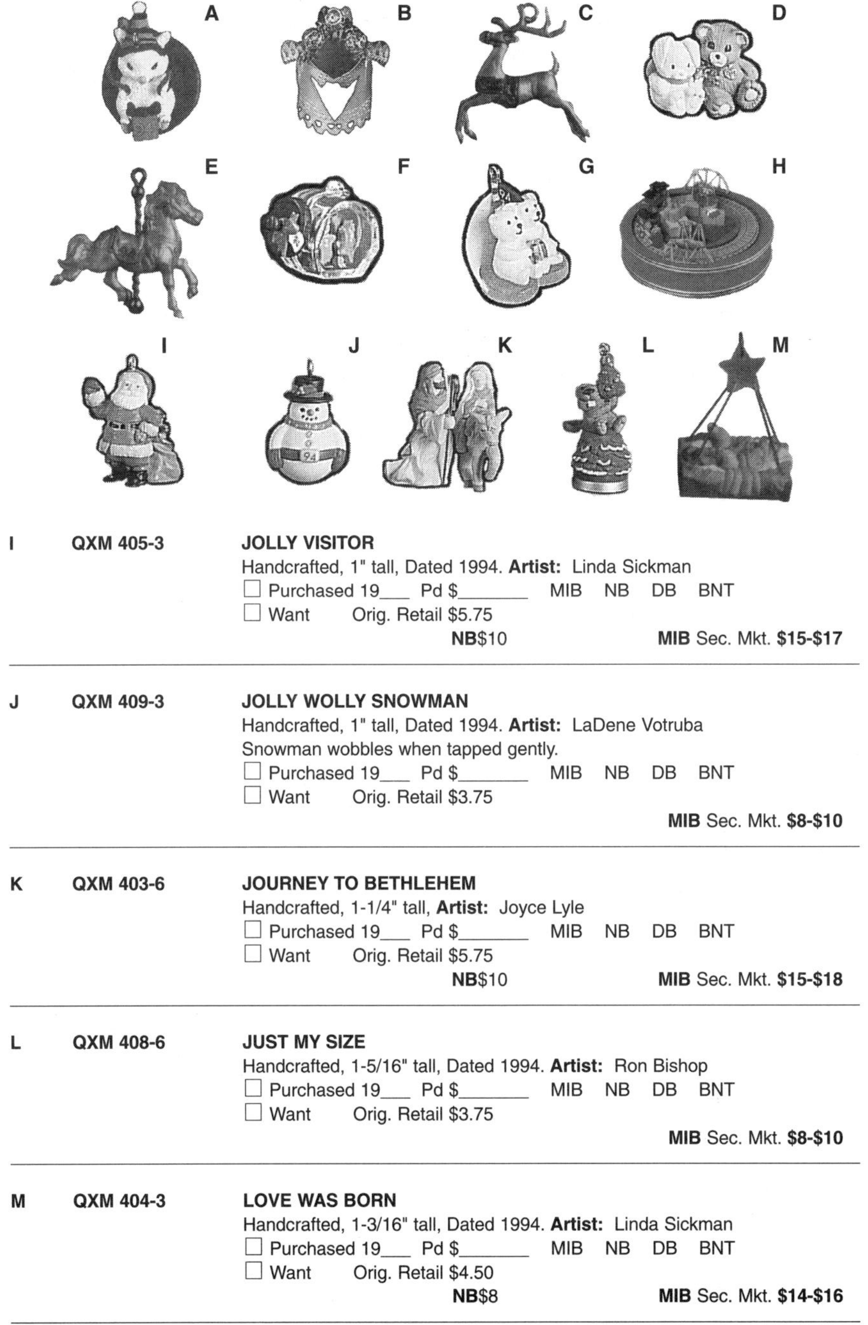

I QXM 405-3 **JOLLY VISITOR**
Handcrafted, 1" tall, Dated 1994. **Artist:** Linda Sickman
☐ Purchased 19___ Pd $_______ MIB NB DB BNT
☐ Want Orig. Retail $5.75
NB$10 **MIB** Sec. Mkt. **$15-$17**

J QXM 409-3 **JOLLY WOLLY SNOWMAN**
Handcrafted, 1" tall, Dated 1994. **Artist:** LaDene Votruba
Snowman wobbles when tapped gently.
☐ Purchased 19___ Pd $_______ MIB NB DB BNT
☐ Want Orig. Retail $3.75
MIB Sec. Mkt. **$8-$10**

K QXM 403-6 **JOURNEY TO BETHLEHEM**
Handcrafted, 1-1/4" tall, **Artist:** Joyce Lyle
☐ Purchased 19___ Pd $_______ MIB NB DB BNT
☐ Want Orig. Retail $5.75
NB$10 **MIB** Sec. Mkt. **$15-$18**

L QXM 408-6 **JUST MY SIZE**
Handcrafted, 1-5/16" tall, Dated 1994. **Artist:** Ron Bishop
☐ Purchased 19___ Pd $_______ MIB NB DB BNT
☐ Want Orig. Retail $3.75
MIB Sec. Mkt. **$8-$10**

M QXM 404-3 **LOVE WAS BORN**
Handcrafted, 1-3/16" tall, Dated 1994. **Artist:** Linda Sickman
☐ Purchased 19___ Pd $_______ MIB NB DB BNT
☐ Want Orig. Retail $4.50
NB$8 **MIB** Sec. Mkt. **$14-$16**

A QXM 510-6

MARCH OF THE TEDDY BEARS
Second in Series, Handcrafted, 1-3/16" tall, Dated 1994
Artist: Duane Unruh
☐ Purchased 19___ Pd $_______ MIB NB DB BNT
☐ Want Orig. Retail $4.50
NB$10 **MIB** Sec. Mkt. **$14-$16**

B QXM 406-6

MELODIC CHERUB
Handcrafted, 1-5/16" tall, Dated 1994. **Artist:** Anita Marra Rogers
☐ Purchased 19___ Pd $_______ MIB NB DB BNT
☐ Want Orig. Retail $3.75
MIB Sec. Mkt. **$8-$10**

C QXM 401-3

MOM
Handcrafted, 1" tall, Dated 1994. **Artist:** Anita Marra Rogers
☐ Purchased 19___ Pd $_______ MIB NB DB BNT
☐ Want Orig. Retail $4.50
MIB Sec. Mkt. **$8-$10**

D QXM 512-6

NATURE'S ANGELS
Fifth in Series, Handcrafted, 1-3/16" tall. **Artist:** LaDene Votruba
☐ Purchased 19___ Pd $_______ MIB NB DB BNT
☐ Want Orig. Retail $4.50
NB$6 **MIB** Sec. Mkt. **$12-$14**

E QXM 512-3

NIGHT BEFORE CHRISTMAS, THE: FATHER
Third in Series, Handcrafted, 1-3/16" tall, Dated 1994.
Artist: Duane Unruh
☐ Purchased 19___ Pd $_______ MIB NB DB BNT
☐ Want Orig. Retail $4.50
NB$10 **MIB S**ec. Mkt. **$14-$16**

F QXM 410-6

NOAH'S ARK
Special Edition**,** Handcrafted, Three piece set.
Ark, 3-1/8" tall; bears, 5/8" tall; seals, 5/8" tall;
deck lifts off and ladder lowers. Merry Walruses and
Playful Penguins were added in '95.
Artist: Linda Sickman
☐ Purchased 19___ Pd $_______ MIB NB DB BNT
☐ Want Orig. Retail $24.50
NB$30 **MIB** Sec. Mkt. **$50-$55**

G QXM 511-3

NOEL R.R.: STOCK CAR
Sixth in Series, Handcrafted, 13/16" tall, Dated 1994.
Doors slide open and closed **Artist:** Linda Sickman
☐ Purchased 19___ Pd $_______ MIB NB DB BNT
☐ Want Orig. Retail $7.00
NB$10 **MIB** Sec. Mkt. **$16-$20**

H QXM 514-6

NUTCRACKER GUILD
FIRST IN SERIES, Handcrafted, 1-3/16" tall, Dated 1994
Opens and closes like real nutcrackers. **Artist:** Linda Sickman
☐ Purchased 19___ Pd $_______ MIB NB DB BNT
☐ Want Orig. Retail $5.75
NB $10 **MIB** Sec. Mkt. **$18-$22**

I QXM 514-3

OLD ENGLISH VILLAGE: HAT SHOP
Seventh in Series, Handcrafted, 7/8" tall, Dated 1994
Artist: Patricia Andrews
☐ Purchased 19___ Pd $_______ MIB NB DB BNT
☐ Want Orig. Retail $7.00
NB $10 **MIB** Sec. Mkt. **$16-$20**

J QXM 510-3

ON THE ROAD
Second in Series Pressed Tin, 7/16" tall, Dated 1994
Wheels turn. Pressed tin ornaments do well on Secondary Market.
Artist: Linda Sickman
☐ Purchased 19___ Pd $_______ MIB NB DB BNT
☐ Want Orig. Retail $5.75
NB $9 **MIB** Sec. Mkt. **$13-$16**

A  B 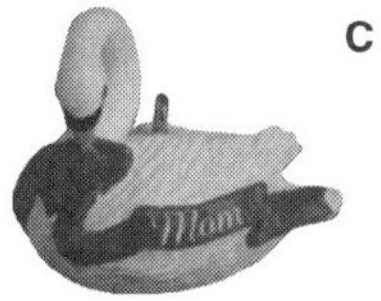 C  D

E  F

G  H  I  J

A **QXM 515-6** **POUR SOME MORE**
Handcrafted, 1-9/16" tall
Caption: "Enjoy Coca-Cola®" **Artist:** Robert Chad
☐ Purchased 19___ Pd $_______ MIB NB DB BNT
☐ Want Orig. Retail $5.75
NB $10 **MIB** Sec. Mkt. **$12-$18**

B **QXM 511-6** **ROCKING HORSE: WHITE**
Seventh in Series, Handcrafted, 1-1/8" tall, Dated 1994
Artist: Linda Sickman
☐ Purchased 19___ Pd $_______ MIB NB DB BNT
☐ Want Orig. Retail $4.50
NB $6 **MIB** Sec. Mkt. **$12-$15**

C **QXM 517-3** **SCOOTING ALONG**
Handcrafted, 1-3/16" tall, Dated 1994, Artist's Favorite
Artist: John Francis
☐ Purchased 19___ Pd $_______ MIB NB DB BNT
☐ Want Orig. Retail $6.75
NB $8 **MIB** Sec. Mkt. **$14-$16**

D **QXC 480-6** **SWEET BOUQUET: KEEPSAKE COLLECTOR'S CLUB**
Handcrafted, 1-3/16" dia. Caption: " Santa's Club Soda."
☐ Purchased 19___ Pd $_______ MIB NB DB BNT
☐ Want Orig. Retail - Included with Membership Kit
MIB Sec. Mkt. **$20-$22**

E **QXM 409-6** **SWEET DREAMS**
Handcrafted, 11/16" tall. **Artist:** Ken Crow
☐ Purchased 19___ Pd $_______ MIB NB DB BNT
☐ Want Orig. Retail $3.00
NB $5 **MIB** Sec. Mkt. **$10-$12**

F **QXM 404-6** **TEA WITH TEDDY**
Handcrafted, 15/16" tall. Dated 1994. **Artist:** Anita Marra Rogers
☐ Purchased 19___ Pd $_______ MIB NB DB BNT
☐ Want Orig. Retail $7.25
MIB Sec. Mkt. **$12-$14**

G **QXM 411-6** **TINY TOON ADVENTURES: BABS BUNNY**
Handcrafted, 1-5/16" tall. **Artist:** Don Palmiter
☐ Purchased 19___ Pd $_______ MIB NB DB BNT
☐ Want Orig. Retail $5.75
MIB Sec. Mkt. **$12-$15**

H **QXM 516-3** **TINY TOON ADVENTURES: BUSTER BUNNY**
Handcrafted, 1-5/16" tall. **Artist:** Don Palmiter
☐ Purchased 19___ Pd $_______ MIB NB DB BNT
☐ Want Orig. Retail $5.75
MIB Sec. Mkt. **$12-$15**

I **QXM 413-3** **TINY TOON ADVENTURES: DIZZY DEVIL**
Handcrafted, 15/16" tall. **Artist:** Don Palmiter
☐ Purchased 19___ Pd $_______ MIB NB DB BNT
☐ Want Orig. Retail $5.75
NB $10 **MIB** Sec. Mkt. **$15-$20**

J **QXM 412-6** **TINY TOON ADVENTURES: HAMTON**
Handcrafted, 1-1/16" tall. **Artist:** Don Palmiter
☐ Purchased 19___ Pd $_______ MIB NB DB BNT
☐ Want Orig. Retail $5.75
MIB Sec. Mkt. **$12-$15**

K **QXM 412-3** **TINY TOON ADVENTURES: PLUCKY DUCK**
Handcrafted, 1-1/8" tall. **Artist:** Don Palmiter
☐ Purchased 19___ Pd $_______ MIB NB DB BNT
☐ Want Orig. Retail $5.75
MIB Sec. Mkt. **$12-$15**

A  B  C  D

E  F  G  H

I  J  K

1995 Miniature Ornament Collection

A QXC 412-9 **A GIFT FROM RODNEY: KEEPSAKE CLUB**
Handcrafted, Dated 1995
Artist: Linda Sickman
☐ Purchased 19___ Pd $_______ MIB NB DB BNT
☐ Want Free with '95 Club Membership
MIB Sec. Mkt. **$10-$12**

B QXM 483-9 **A MOUSTERSHIRE CHRISTMAS: SPECIAL EDITION**
Handcrafted,13/16" tall, House 2-5/8" tall, Dated 1995
A. Moustershire Cottage C. Violet
B. Robin D. Dunne
Artist: Dill Rhodus
☐ Purchased 19___ Pd $_______ MIB NB DB BNT
☐ Want Orig. Retail $24.50
MIB Sec. Mkt. **$28-$30**

C QXM 477-7 **ALICE IN WONDERLAND**
FIRST IN SERIES, Handcrafted, 1-7/16" tall, Dated 1995
Artist: Patricia Andrews
☐ Purchased 19___ Pd $_______ MIB NB DB BNT
☐ Want Orig. Retail $6.75
MIB Sec. Mkt. **$10-$12**

D QXM 402-7 **BABY'S FIRST CHRISTMAS**
Handcrafted, 1-1/16" tall, Dated 95
Artist: Ed Seale
☐ Purchased 19___ Pd $_______ MIB NB DB BNT
☐ Want Orig. Retail $4.75
MIB Sec. Mkt. **$8-$10**

E QXM 478-9 **CENTURIES OF SANTA**
Second in Series, Handcrafted, 1-1/4" tall, Dated 95
Artist: Linda Sickman
☐ Purchased 19___ Pd $_______ MIB NB DB BNT
☐ Want Orig. Retail $5.75
MIB Sec. Mkt. **$8-$10**

F QXM 400-7 **CHRISTMAS BELLS**
FIRST IN SERIES, Handcrafted and Metal, 1-1/4" tall, Dated 1995
Artist: Ed Seale
☐ Purchased 19___ Pd $_______ MIB NB DB BNT
☐ Want Orig. Retail $4.75
MIB Sec. Mkt. **$10-$12**

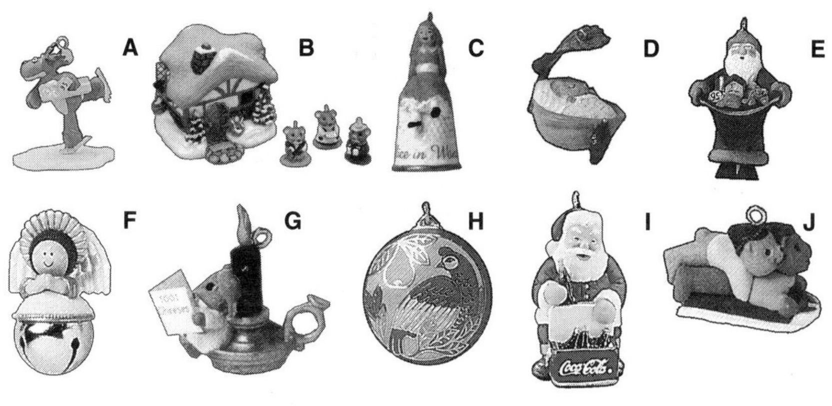

G QXM 408-7 **CHRISTMAS WISHES**
FIRST IN SERIES, Handcrafted, 1-1/16" tall, Dated 1995
Artist: Ed Seale
☐ Purchased 19___ Pd $_______ MIB NB DB BNT
☐ Want Orig. Retail $3.75
MIB Sec. Mkt. **$10-$12**

H QXM 401-7 **CLOISONNÉ PARTRIDGE: PRECIOUS EDITION**
Cloisonné, 1" dia. If this would have been a "First in Series" the Secondary Market would be more effected. We'll know by March if more are coming.
Artist: Ed Seale
☐ Purchased 19___ Pd $_______ MIB NB DB BNT
☐ Want Orig. Retail $9.75
MIB Sec. Mkt. **$10-$12**

I QXM 445-7 **COOL SANTA: KEEPSAKE CLUB**
"Coca-Cola®"
Artist: John Francis
☐ Purchased 19___ Pd $_______ MIB NB DB BNT
☐ Want Free with '95 Club Membership
MIB Sec. Mkt. **$10-$14**

J QXM 483-7 **DOWNHILL DOUBLE**
Handcrafted, 5/8" tall, Dated 1995
Artist: Don Palmiter
☐ Purchased 19___ Pd $_______ MIB NB DB BNT
☐ Want Orig. Retail $4.75
MIB Sec. Mkt. **$6-$8**

A QXM 401-9 **FRIENDSHIP DUET**
Handcrafted, 1-1/4" tall, Dated 95
Artist: Duane Unruh
☐ Purchased 19___ Pd $_______ MIB NB DB BNT
☐ Want Orig. Retail $4.75
MIB Sec. Mkt. **$6-$8**

B QXM 482-9 **GRANDPA'S GIFT**
Handcrafted, 1" tall, Dated 1995
Artist: Anita Marra Rogers
☐ Purchased 19___ Pd $_______ MIB NB DB BNT
☐ Want Orig. Retail $5.75
MIB Sec. Mkt. **$8-$9.50**

C QXM 403-7 **HEAVENLY PRAISES**
Handcrafted, 1-5/16" tall, Dated 1995
Artist: Patricia Andrews
☐ Purchased 19___ Pd $_______ MIB NB DB BNT
☐ Want Orig. Retail $5.75
MIB Sec. Mkt. **$7-$8**

D QXM 545-2 **HOLIDAY EXPRESS**
Miniature Tree Base, able to hold any standard miniature tree.
Train moves on track. 4-1/4" tall
Artist: Linda Sickman
☐ Purchased 19___ Pd $_______ MIB NB DB BNT
☐ Want Orig. Retail $50.00
MIB Sec. Mkt. **NE**

E QXM 408-9 **JOYFUL SANTA**
Handcrafted, 1-1/8" tall, Dated 1995
Artist: Duane Unruh
☐ Purchased 19___ Pd $_______ MIB NB DB BNT
☐ Want Orig. Retail $4.75
MIB Sec. Mkt. **$6-$8**

F QXM 479-9 **MARCH OF THE TEDDY BEARS**
Third in Series, Handcrafted, 1-5/16" tall, Dated 1995
Artist: Duane Unruh
☐ Purchased 19___ Pd $_______ MIB NB DB BNT
☐ Want Orig. Retail $4.75
MIB Sec. Mkt. **$6-$8**

G QXM 409-7 **MINIATURE CLOTHESPIN SOLDIER**
FIRST IN SERIES, Handcrafted, 1-1/8" tall
Artist: Linda Sickman
☐ Purchased 19___ Pd $_______ MIB NB DB BNT
☐ Want Orig. Retail $3.75
MIB Sec. Mkt. **$8-$12**

H QXM 407-9 **MINIATURE KIDDIE CAR CLASSICS: MURRAY® BLUE "CHAMPION"**
FIRST IN SERIES, Cast Metal, 9/16" tall, Dated 1995
Hot! Disappeared from shelves early in buying season!
Artist: Don Palmiter
☐ Purchased 19___ Pd $_______ MIB NB DB BNT
☐ Want Orig. Retail $5.75
MIB Sec. Mkt. **$20-25**

I QXM 480-9 **NATURE'S ANGELS**
Sixth in Series, Handcrafted, Brass Halo, 1-1/8" tall
Artist: Patricia Andrews
☐ Purchased 19___ Pd $_______ MIB NB DB BNT
☐ Want Orig. Retail $4.75
MIB Sec. Mkt. **$6-$8**

J QXM 480-7 **NIGHT BEFORE CHRISTMAS, THE**
Fourth in Series, Handcrafted, 1-1/4" tall, Dated 95
Artist: Duane Unruh
☐ Purchased 19___ Pd $_______ MIB NB DB BNT
☐ Want Orig. Retail $4.75
MIB Sec. Mkt. **$6-$8**

K QXM 405-7 **NOAH'S ARK: MERRY WALRUSES**
Handcrafted, 9/16" tall. Addition to Noah's Ark Special Edition (1994).
Artist: Linda Sickman
☐ Purchased 19___ Pd $_______ MIB NB DB BNT
☐ Want Orig. Retail $5.75
MIB Sec. Mkt. **$7-$8**

A B  C  D  E

F  G  H  I  J

K

A QXM 405-9

NOAH'S ARK: PLAYFUL PENGUINS
Handcrafted, 11/16" tall. Addition to Noah's Ark Special Edition (1994).
Artist: Linda Sickman
☐ Purchased 19___ Pd $_______ MIB NB DB BNT
☐ Want Orig. Retail $5.75
MIB Sec. Mkt. **$7-$8**

B QXM 481-7

NOEL R.R.: MILK TANK CAR
Seventh in Series, Handcrafted, 13/16" tall, Dated 1995
Artist: Linda Sickman
☐ Purchased 19___ Pd $_______ MIB NB DB BNT
☐ Want Orig. Retail $6.75
MIB Sec. Mkt. **$10-$12**

C QXM 478-7

NUTCRACKER GUILD
Second in Series, Handcrafted, 1-1/8" tall, Dated 1995
Artist: Linda Sickman
☐ Purchased 19___ Pd $_______ MIB NB DB BNT
☐ Want Orig. Retail $5.75
MIB Sec. Mkt. **$8-$10**

D QXM 481-9

OLD ENGLISH VILLAGE: TUDOR HOUSE
Eighth in Series, Handcrafted, 1" tall, Dated 1995
Artist: Julia Lee
☐ Purchased 19___ Pd $_______ MIB NB DB BNT
☐ Want Orig. Retail $6.75
MIB Sec. Mkt. **$8-$10**

E QXM 479-7

ON THE ROAD
Third in Series, Pressed Tin, 7/16" tall, Dated 1995
Artist: Linda Sickman
☐ Purchased 19___ Pd $_______ MIB NB DB BNT
☐ Want Orig. Retail $5.75
MIB Sec. Mkt. **$8-$10**

F QXM 475-7

PEBBLES AND BAMM-BAMM: THE FLINTSTONES®
Handcrafted, 1-1/8" tall
Artist: Dill Rhodus
☐ Purchased 19___ Pd $_______ MIB NB DB BNT
☐ Want Orig. Retail $9.75
MIB Sec. Mkt. **$12-$14**

G QXM 407-7

PRECIOUS CREATIONS
Handcrafted, 1-1/4" tall, Dated 1995
Artist: Linda Sickman
☐ Purchased 19___ Pd $_______ MIB NB DB BNT
☐ Want Orig. Retail $9.75
MIB Sec. Mkt. **$12-$15**

A B C D E F G H I J K

H QXM 482-7

ROCKING HORSE
Eighth in Series, Handcrafted, 1-1/8" tall, Dated 1995
Artist: Linda Sickman
☐ Purchased 19___ Pd $_______ MIB NB DB BNT
☐ Want Orig. Retail $4.75
MIB Sec. Mkt. **$8-$10**

I QXM 477-9

SANTA'S LITTLE BIG TOP
FIRST IN SERIES, Handcrafted, 1-5/8" tall, Dated 1995
Artist: Ken Crow
☐ Purchased 19___ Pd $_______ MIB NB DB BNT
☐ Want Orig. Retail $6.75
MIB Sec. Mkt. **$10-$12**

J QXM 404-7

SANTA'S VISIT
Lighted, Batteries included, Handcrafted, 1-7/16" tall, Dated 1995
Artist: Ken Crow
☐ Purchased 19___ Pd $_______ MIB NB DB BNT
☐ Want Orig. Retail $7.75
MIB Sec. Mkt. **$12-$14**

K QXM 414-1

SHINING STAR TREE-TOPPER
Dimensional Brass
☐ Purchased 19___ Pd $_______ MIB NB DB BNT
☐ Want Orig. Retail $9.95
MIB Sec. Mkt. **$10-$12**

A QXM 403-9 **STARLIT NATIVITY**
Lighted, Batteries included, Handcrafted, 1-7/16" tall, Dated 1995
Artist: Duane Unruh
☐ Purchased 19___ Pd $_______ MIB NB DB BNT
☐ Want Orig. Retail $7.75
MIB Sec. Mkt. **$12-$14**

B QXM 409-9 **SUGARPLUM DREAMS**
Third in Series, Handcrafted, 15/16" tall, Dated 1995
Artist: Ken Crow
☐ Purchased 19___ Pd $_______ MIB NB DB BNT
☐ Want Orig. Retail $4.75
MIB Sec. Mkt. **$6-$8**

C QXM 446-7 **TINY TOON ADVENTURES: CALAMITY COYOTE**
Handcrafted, 1-7/16" tall
Artist: Anita Marra Rogers
☐ Purchased 19___ Pd $_______ MIB NB DB BNT
☐ Want Orig. Retail $6.75
MIB Sec. Mkt. **$8-$10**

D QXM 445-9 **TINY TOON ADVENTURES: FURRBALL**
Handcrafted, 7/8" tall
Artist: Anita Marra Rogers
☐ Purchased 19___ Pd $_______ MIB NB DB BNT
☐ Want Orig. Retail $5.75
MIB Sec. Mkt. **$8-$10**

E QXM 446-9 **TINY TOON ADVENTURES: LITTLE BEEPER**
Handcrafted, 3/4" tall
Artist: Anita Marra Rogers
☐ Purchased 19___ Pd $_______ MIB NB DB BNT
☐ Want Orig. Retail $5.75
MIB Sec. Mkt. **$8-$10**

F QXM 400-9 **TINY TREASURES**
Set of Six Ornaments, Handcrafted, 5/8" tall to 1-3/8" tall, Dated 1995
A. Precious Gem D. Smelling Sweet
B. Glamour Girl E. All Tied Up
C. Powder Puff Pal F. Just Reflecting
Artist: Ed Seale
☐ Purchased 19___ Pd $_______ MIB NB DB BNT
☐ Want Orig. Retail $29.00
MIB Sec. Mkt. **$35-$38**

G QXM 402-9 **TUNNEL OF LOVE**
Handcrafted, 13/16" tall, Dated 1995 **Artist:** Ken Crow
☐ Purchased 19___ Pd $_______ MIB NB DB BNT
☐ Want Orig. Retail $4.75
MIB Sec. Mkt. **$6-$8**

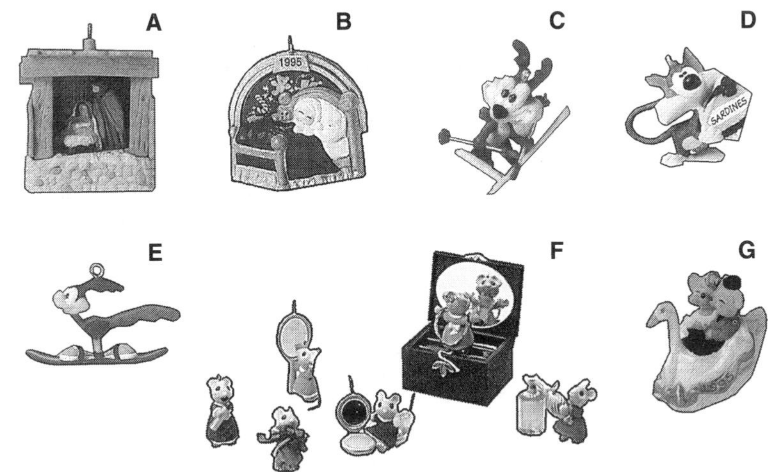

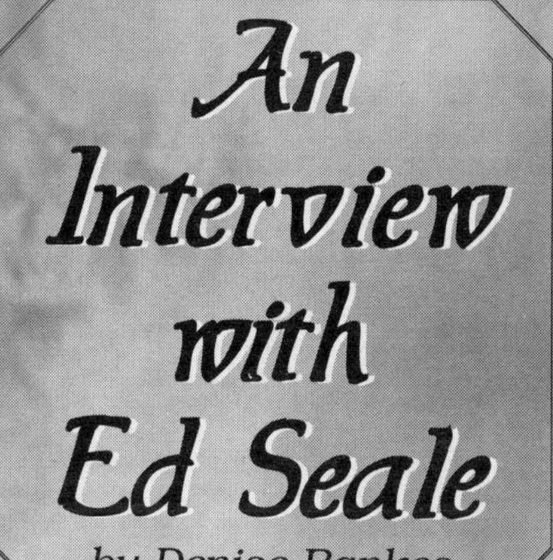

An Interview with Ed Seale

by Denise Bankes

We spoke recently with Ed Seale, long-time Hallmark artist. The following are excerpts from the conversation.

Ed, when and how did you realize you enjoyed art? Was this as a young child?

I think I was pretty much like a lot of kids. I used to draw. I guess my earliest memories are because I grew up during World War II. I used to love to draw pictures of airplanes, Spitfires, bombers and that sort of thing. I went to rural schools for a lot of my elementary education and we didn't really have art programs. So as far as what form it took, I think my strongest inclination as a kid was making things with my hands. I was always building things with scrap lumber, nailing things together and trying to build my own toys. That was an early sign, unnoticed by me at the time, that I was gravitating toward three-dimensional forms of expression. Even though I liked drawing, I didn't have the passion for it that I had for making things in three dimension.

Did you ever whittle things when you were young?

Yes, I did. I liked to carve things. I tried making puppets and all kinds of things. I would take a try at just about anything. In fact, when I was just old enough to get my driver's license, I set about building my own car from the ground up. I decided I wanted a sports car and I couldn't afford one, so I bought an old Ford, stripped the body totally off and rebuilt a new low-slung body of my own on it. It took about a year and a half to do.

You've had many different kind of jobs, including carpentry and building boats before you attended art school. How did you come to attend the Ringling School of Art in Sarasota, Florida.

After several years of working nomadically in Canada and Florida, roaming around doing different jobs and basically enjoying myself, I realized the jobs weren't going to lead anywhere particularly. I did choose jobs that I liked, building things, but other people told me what they wanted built. Somebody else was designing and I was building. I wanted to design as well as build – I wanted more involvement. I was observing that every time I thought about something that appealed to me, it came back to making things. I was renting an apartment in Florida from a lady who was a high school art teacher and one day I asked her where the best art school was in the area. She said that Ringling was the best school in the southeast. I looked into it and decided she was right. I enrolled there in 1965 in a three year program. Drawing, painting and advertising design were heavily emphasized. If I would have foll[illegible] ing in an agency somewhere. But as it turned out, Hallmark sent recruiters around the country to different art schools. Ringling was one of those schools they recruited from. They came around before I graduated and interviewed a bunch of us and they asked some of us to send our portfolios in, which we did. We waited in great suspense – two weeks later they said they were going to fly me in for an interview.

What did you feel, as a younger person, getting that kind of opportunity? Were you nervous?

I was nervous before I found out because they kind of keep you waiting for a decision. But I was just elated when they sent me the final letter saying they felt I would work well there. This was all before I was graduating from Ringling so I was really happy because I already had a job. I went back to Canada that summer, then joined Hallmark in the fall. It was great, all the way around! I think I was lucky that I didn't go off into advertising because I don't think I would have been happy. I probably would have had some fun in the creative side of advertising but it's very stressful and crazy with deadlines and 60-70 hour work weeks. Hallmark is a much more people-friendly place to work.

You're originally from Canada. Do you visit there frequently?

I do go up there to visit. I have several cousins there.

Are Hallmark ornaments as widespread in Canada as they are in the United States?

No, they're not, but they are getting that way. The Hallmark Collectors' Club was just started in Canada. I was the first artist to go to Canada for a signing event in Toronto. I think they let me do that because I was from Canada.

It probably meant a lot to the Canadian collec-[illegible]

town boy. We went to two stores and they were just thrilled with the whole thing. The events were smaller than in the United States, but since they were just starting up there, everyone was very happy with the results. Canadians haven't gotten the collecting bug as the Americans have, but the Hallmark people in Canada think this is just the beginning.

Do you sketch your work first before you sculpt it? Duane Unruh (another Hallmark artist) told me that sometimes he just starts to sculpt.

We work on a project basis to generate ideas, so we'll have a week or two to come up with ideas. Then we can either sketch or make prototypes. Most people do sketches, but for several years I have made prototypes that are not finished but are three dimensional. I like it better because the person looking at them can see them in the round and see how they work dimensionally. Sketches sometimes don't give enough information.

What type of material do you use?

When I first started we worked in clay, a kind of brown modeling clay used in Detroit for automobile mock-ups. That was really pretty bad stuff, and we got out of that in a year or so and started experimenting with waxes. Hallmark developed a wax that has some great properties for sculpting; Duane Unruh was very instrumental in getting that formula. In the last three to five years we've had Super Sculpy,™ which is a material made for sculpting. Each artist has a favorite material. We all have different combinations. I use maybe a half dozen materials on the same ornament if I have to. Sometimes a piece of wood, metal or plastic will create one part of the ornament better than anything else, depending on the effect you want…

When you started working for Hallmark in 1968, did you start in paper products?

When I first interviewed with the company, I asked, "Do you do any three dimensional products?" since I was increasingly going in that direction. They didn't have a lot at the time – they had party units, with folding centerpieces and things like that. But they had just started a little fledgling group called New Product Design about a year before I arrived. There were about four or five people in this group and their job was to explore new products for Hallmark. During the summer, I was in Canada and somebody from Hallmark sent me a form which gave away the fact that they had me slated to go to work in New Product Design, although I was not supposed to know where I was going to work until later on. I was really happy; it was just what I was looking for. I spent about five years in that department until it was phased into another department. I've always been outside of the greeting card area.

Did you start with the beginning of the Keepsake line?

I started with the beginning of Keepsakes as a separate business entity in 1980 when the first business unit was formed at Hallmark. As far as the actual beginning, 1973 was the year we started to make the ornaments. Before 1980, the ornaments were done in the Specialty Design department, along with other products. But then as the business grew, they said, "We've got too much work here. We need to concentrate on this because it's growing. We need to break off a group of people who just work on ornaments."

When did you and others at Hallmark realize the impact of the ornaments… was this in the '80s? Were you surprised that the ornaments took off the way they did?

Well, yes and no – when I joined in 1980, the ornaments had been done since 1973 and had been growing every year. So when we got them as a business unit, a full-time operation, they were rising each year. We could see that it was going to keep on growing. I think we underestimated how much it was going to grow. I don't think the amount of business we do now was predicted by anybody. I think we surprised management more than anybody because we were this little side business for years. We were a greeting card company, after all!

Do you remember your first ornament?

There are a couple of ornaments I think I worked on almost at the same time. One that was very close to the first was the Baby's First Christmas rat-

years ago and I'm a little foggy on which one was the very first ornament.

Have you kept track of how many ornaments you've designed?

I can't give you an exact figure, but it's in the hundreds. I've done well over 100 Tender Touches designs, too. We've all become more productive over the years. In the first year or two, most of us wouldn't have done more than ten or twelve ornaments a year. I do double and triple that amount now. After 15 years, we've learned a lot.

Do you have any favorite ornaments?

I have so many. I could sit down and go through the book and talk to you about why I like this one or that one. There are so many I like for different reasons. There is no way I could ever pick a favorite ornament.

I suppose you go through stages, too. You like the ornaments you are working on at the time.

Well, yes. First I like the idea for the ornament. I don't want to turn in any ideas I don't think are strong. Then when I do an ornament, sometimes I don't think I've done as well as I thought I would and I don't think I've done justice to the idea behind it. Then other times an ornament turns out even a little bit better than I thought it would. It's a mysterious process.

Tender Touches.

I did a retail test way back there with a miniature version of Tender Touches called Mini Memories in about 16 stores around the country. By the time people found they were out there, they were pulled in off the test. Meanwhile, it was decided that these pieces would be better up-sized to a larger scale, so we set about redesigning some of the miniatures to about twice as big. Hallmark had a couple of guys come in and help me sculpt these originals that went out to card shops under the label Tender Touches because there was a period there when we were trying to increase the number of designs and I was really busy. Different people would sculpt the pieces in different ways and they would come out looking funny so I went back to sculpting all of them. The Tender Touches evolved a lot over several years.

Will we see the Tender Touches come back?

After the Galleries line was discontinued, we immediately started getting calls and letters asking why we wouldn't be doing Tender Touches. Consumer Affairs at Hallmark was getting letters and they are still getting some many months later. Ever since then, the word I've been getting is, "We are studying the situation and trying to decide what to do and how we would handle it if we

some new artists recently to get more work done. Collectibles had taken a back seat to ornaments, but now here are these people saying, "We like Tender Touches and we collect them." The pieces have started showing up on the secondary market with some pretty decent prices.

Ed Seale has created collectibles for Hallmark since 1980 and has been a Hallmark artist since 1968. He has worked in several new-product development areas at Hallmark and thinks being a Hallmark Keepsake Ornament studio artist is "the best of all!" Born in Toronto, Ed grew up in the rolling wooded countryside of southern Ontario. At Hallmark, he is noted for drawing on past experiences, future trends and his own intuition to create some of the most memorable Hallmark Keepsake Ornaments, including the highly prized *Frosty Friends* series.

I think people were surprised to see the line discontinued.

When Galleries was discontinued, the Tender Touches line was the second best selling line in Galleries next to the Kiddie Cars, and Kiddie Cars have been really outstanding in the way they have sold. There was a considerable gap between Tender Touches and Kiddie Cars in sales, but Tender Touches was in the number two spot out of all the other Galleries collections. But the Galleries line was only in a few hundred stores, which handicapped everything. We had trouble getting stores that were confident in retailing collectibles. People were always asking me, "Where can I get Tender Touches? I can't find a store with them." The year before they pulled the plug on the Galleries line, I was getting more questions about them, like "When are you going to start a club? We want one…" and just general talk about the secondary market value.

The Tender Touches have a childlike and nostalgic quality to them. What did you draw on for ideas for this line?

I drew on life experiences and memories and they started showing up in my work, whether consciously or unconsciously. I grew up in a simpler age in Canada with its countryside. There was a feeling of the simplicity of life in basic things and doing things for yourself. When you bring those experiences to bear in doing something now, it's a pretty nostalgic feeling to a lot of people. Tender Touches were always kind of nostalgic to me.

I like Tender Touches because they have a friendly, homey feel and I can relate to them. For example, the two bunnies sleeping in the same bed – anyone who has ever had to share a bed with a sister or brother or maybe had a cousin who stayed all night can

ing cookies.

I think those are such universal experiences that they reach a lot of people. They are not some sort of exotic or rarefied experience that people can't relate to. I began to realize that the things I was intuitively putting into Tender Touches were things that a broad mass of people have experienced and therefore when they see the pieces, they react to them immediately.

Your animals have such friendly faces.

The expressions are very important. Without it, Tender Touches could be just anything. A lot of artists will mimic a cute animal style that another artist has done, but I don't believe in that. I go back to real animals, study them and then interpret them my own way. They are not totally realistic by any means, but they're not cute copies of somebody else's animals. They are my interpretation of the personalities and so forth of those animals.

I remember seeing a picture of you and your truck, which had been decorated for Christmas, in a past issue of The Courier.

About three or four years ago I started putting garland and things on my truck just for fun. One year some people at Hallmark said, "Hey, we would like to take a picture of your truck," so I drove it into the studio. I had a couple of light strings on it and they put even more on it. I came back and this truck was really looking neat!

Do you still decorate your truck?

I still do. As a matter of fact I have a better way of laying it out so that I can plug more lights into my electrical system.

What will we see in the future from Ed Seale?

All kinds of things – I can't say too much. I'd love to tell you everything, but it's a surprise! We're all doing a lot of neat things.

We'll look forward to seeing your new ornaments in 1996. Thanks so much, Ed, for sharing with us. We enjoy your work and the work of all the artists at Hallmark!

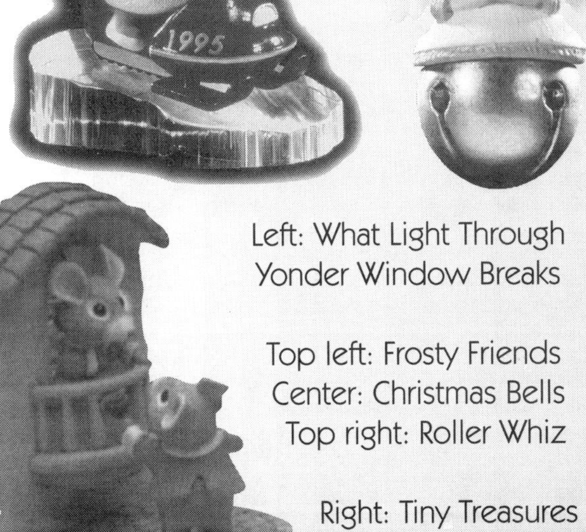

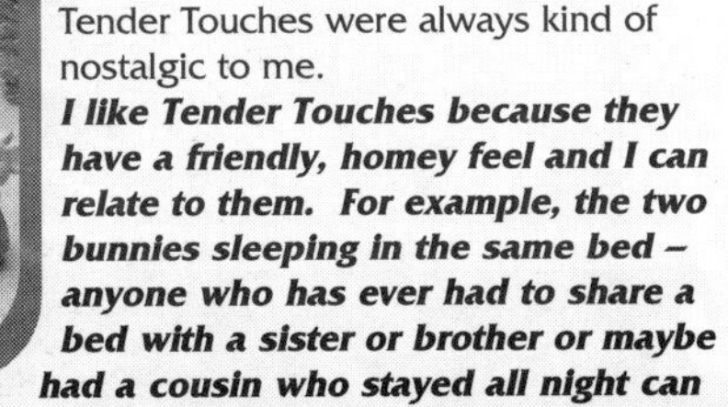

Left: What Light Through Yonder Window Breaks

Top left: Frosty Friends
Center: Christmas Bells
Top right: Roller Whiz

Right: Tiny Treasures
(Photo by Hallmark)

Reprinted from The Ornament Collector™ Magazine, Fall 1995.

An Interview with Patricia Andrews

by Kathie Huddleston

Rosie Wells Enterprises Staff

I had the pleasure of chatting with Hallmark's Patricia (Trish) Andrews. Here are some excerpts from our conversation.

What is your background in art?
I grew up drawing every day. It was always part of my life. I went to college and received a Bachelor of Fine Arts degree from Auburn University in Alabama. I majored in drawing and graphic design. As soon as I graduated from college, I went to work for Hallmark.

You've worked at Hallmark for 19 years. Has your whole career been at Hallmark?
Yes... I was born here.

Have you always sculpted ornaments?
No. I started out as an engraver at Hallmark. I worked in that position for a little over ten years. Then I was able to transfer to this department and I put together a portfolio of sculptures. I just sat at home and experimented with it. I knew I could draw, but I wasn't sure about the sculpting part. The engraving that I did was very applicable to the sculpting.

What type of media do you work in?
I use a pro mat. It's similar to a plastic clay. When you heat it, it hardens into a plastic. We sculpt actual size. When we do a miniature ornament we have to use very small tools. Then when we do the larger ornaments, larger tools are used.

Third in Series

The miniature ornaments must be a tremendous challenge.
It's hard on the eyesight.

I reviewed the 1995 Dream Book and discovered you had designed approximately 25 of this year's ornaments for Hallmark. Do you work on more than one at a time?
They're spread out through the whole year. Usually, I do one at a time. Sometimes there's an overlap. We do our own original painting on them, too, so we have some overlap time with that.

Is that to give a guide to the people who do the hand-painting later on?
Right. We have to pick out our original colors and actually paint it. It really doesn't come to life until you put color on it.

What is your favorite ornament you designed this year?
The black angel, *Celebration of Angels*.

It is so real looking.
I used photographs of faces to bring that out.

Joy to the World ***also looks very real.***
I wanted to create an ornament that had a lot of feeling and was relevant to the African-American culture. I didn't want it to look like a white ornament that had been painted brown. I wanted it to be part of their culture. It meant a lot to me to do those.

What has the response been?
Excellent, so far. I've had lots of good responses. I've even had people call me on the telephone and thank me. People at Hallmark usually don't get calls from their colleagues, but I've been getting phone calls saying they really like them and thanking me for doing them. So... I thanked them for calling.

I think you've done most of the African-American ornaments.
Yes, I have. I did a miniature this year also.

What draws you to that culture?
It's very different. Not only different facial features, but you're dealing with different colors and patterns. The pieces are very different from what we normally work with. In order to make them more authentic I had to do a lot of research on the clothing styles, patterns and colors. I incorporated the black angel into the holiday of Kwanzaa.

What is Kwanzaa?
It is a holiday developed by a chairman of black studies at California State University back in 1966. It is celebrated the week after Christmas. It almost reminds you of Hanukkah. It lasts seven days; they burn a different candle every day. Each day represents a different principle. It's to help the African-Americans have a relationship with their roots and ethnic heritage

celebrate their history. I've incorporated the symbols from Kwanzaa into the *Celebration Angel*. Every year there will be a different symbol.

The Cowardly Lion

What is your favorite ornament that you have designed, and why?
Probably the *Cowardly Lion*. It was just so much fun. I love the *Wizard of Oz*. I grew up watching it every year at Thanksgiving. The Cowardly Lion is just so cute. And what a great personality he has. I just really enjoyed that one.

You've designed all the Barbie ornaments for Hallmark. Did you play with Barbie dolls as a child?
Oh, yes. I still have mine.

Did you ever think you were going to be a Barbie artist?
No. That was a surprise. I still have my dolls. They're a little old and ratty looking, but I still have them. Now my daughter likes to play with them. I have to tell her to be really careful because they're pretty old. I think Ken's foot was half eaten by my dog and I think Barbie's eyelashes are worn off.

What is your favorite subject to design? You seem to do a little bit of everything.
I like to stay pretty versatile. If you stay on one thing for any length of time it starts to get a little bit overbearing. I like a lot of different things. I guess I prefer doing people more than anything.

It must be a challenge to make them realistic.
Yes. I enjoy doing portrait-type faces. It can be a challenge. Even people with an untrained eye can tell if something is wrong. But if you do a cute, fuzzy animal you can do whatever you want. That is a lot easier. It sure is nice to break up the day to do some loose things and then come really tight things

I thought the gold angels, Always Bright, were very pretty.

Patricia Andrews has worked for Hallmark since 1976. She is married to fellow Hallmark artist, Dill Rhodus, and they have two children.

Angel of Light

Thank you. That was the first time I had ever played with gold leaf. It wasn't as hard as I thought it would be.

What is the biggest challenge when you start a project?

Finding accurate research. Especially if we're doing a licensed design where we are paying a royalty to use their design. The *Holiday Barbie* was difficult because of the time restraints on it. Then, too, I'm just working from photographs.

You mean they don't send an actual doll to work from?

They're working with a prototype doll. They don't have anything to send. So they send us photographs and we hope that the design is not impossible to do.

When you get an idea for a new series or an unusual ornament, do you present it to Hallmark? What is the process?

We do that on a regular basis. We call that project time and the whole art staff is involved. They will specify certain parts of our line to do, because we can't do it all at once. We'll come up with many ideas that would work for say, *Sister to Sister* or new designs for series. We

reviews the ideas and tries to create a nice balance of the ideas. Then they're handed back to us to sculpt. So we're always presenting ideas. Not all of them are chosen. If you really like your idea and it wasn't chosen, you save it and turn it in the next time.

Jolly Santa

Heavenly Praises

Merry Olde Santa

Solo in the Spotlight

New Home

What is the most enjoyable aspect of your position with Hallmark?

It's a very fun atmosphere. The art staff stays; it never goes away. We've had one person retire. We've had a couple of people move, but for the most part the staff stays the same. It becomes a family atmosphere. Then you're doing something people really enjoy. It's very rewarding to have so many people tell you how much they like your work. You really feel appreciated. Not many people get that with their job. It's a real plus. We are allowed to do our own designs and make a lot of our own decisions. They're very good to us here.

Probably feelings more than anything else, really strong feelings of joy. Or with the ethnic ornaments, trying to get something across that's relevant to them. A lot of childhood memories are tapped into. I like to review a lot of children's story books. I think that takes one back to being a "kid" and makes one more creative. You can get your childhood mind back.

What factor leads you to creating an ornament?

The *New Home* ornament (house sweeping its own welcome mat) strongly relates to memories of story books and the cartoons I used to watch. I got to be a kid again, imagining the house come to life. It has a little face, little arms, little hands and a big fluffy bow. It's definitely a kid memory.

You must love going to work every morning.

It's not something I complain about. We get paid, too. There's not much stress here at all.

Even when you're on a deadline?

Well, we have deadlines, but we all understand what they're about and why they have to be there. We're all really dedicated to it and we want it to work. So we try our very best to get things out as quickly as we can and still have the right look and quality to it.

Earlier, you mentioned your daughter. She must be fascinated with your occupation.

My little girl just loves it. She's six. She comes in and plays with my Barbies. She says, "Oh, Mommy, I think you do such beautiful things. I wish I could make Barbies too." I have a display set up of Barbies that I had to use for research and some of our Classic Barbie greeting cards that can stand up. When she comes, she gets to play with all of these characters. She has a great time.

What will we see in the future from Patricia Andrews?

Probably more of the same. Probably more Barbies. I can't give away too many secrets. I do have a shepherd coming along with the black nativity for next year. It's not a series, it's just an addition.

Thank you, Patricia for this interview. I know the collectors will thoroughly enjoy reading about you.

A Celebration of Angels (left), *Heaven's Gift* (center and right).

KWANZAA

Kwanzaa means "first fruits" in the East African language of Swahili. This seven-day African-American family observance reflect is traditional African harvest festivals. The celebration begins Dec. 26 and continues through Jan. 1.

Kwanzaa was created in 1966 by Maulana Ron Karenga, chairman of black studies at California State University.

Reprinted from The Ornament Collector™ Magazine, Spring 1996.

Many collectors have admired and collected Hallmark products for much of their lives. We are especially partial to the Hallmark Keepsake Ornaments. Some of us, however, actually know very little about this highly respected and diversified company called Hallmark. This article will hopefully give a little insight into the heart of Hallmark as a business that strives to be "the very best."

To Be the Very Best

by Shirley Trexler

Hallmark was founded in 1910 by Mr. Joyce C. Hall. The company was called Hall Brothers, Inc., until 1954 when the name was changed to Hallmark Cards, Inc. Mr. Hall died in 1982. At present, the Chairman of the Board of Directors at Hallmark is Donald J. Hall, Sr. The current President and Chief Executive Officer is Irvine O. Hockaday, Jr. Hallmark employs about 21,000 full time employees and 15,000 part time employees. These include about 5,700 in the Kansas City Headquarters as well as about 12,700 throughout the United States. Hallmark also includes in these figures many subsidiaries and international operations. A profit sharing and ownership plan makes it possible for the employees to own about one third of the company. Annual sales for Hallmark are approximately $3.8 billion. This makes Hallmark rank thirty-first on the FORBES list of the largest privately owned companies in the United States.

The world's largest creative staff is employed by Hallmark. Seven hundred artists, stylists, designers, writers, editors and photographers offer about 21,000 greeting card designs and messages each year. About 9,000 related items are also produced annually. Hallmark produces greeting cards and other products under the brand names of Hallmark, Ambassador, Crayola, Hallmark Connections, Heartline, Keepsake Ornaments, Liquitex, Magic Marker, Party Express, Revell-Monogram, Shoebox Greetings, Springbok and Verkerke. These products include all of the following: Albums, art supplies, calendars, candles, Christmas ornaments, collectibles, crayons, creativity software, frames, gifts, gift wrap, greeting cards,

(WOW! Quite an extensive and impressive list of products.)

Hallmark has, for some time, produced the acclaimed dramatic television series called Hallmark Hall of Fame. In addition, Hallmark proclaims its corporate mission is to enrich peoples' lives and enhance their relationships. Hallmark Corporate Foundation produces a traveling creative workshop for children which is based in Kansas City, MO. The program is called *Kaleidoscope*. This foundation has also created a video series called *Talking with T.J.* which helps kids with social skills. This series helps to benefit many organizations in the communities where Hallmark operates.

Hallmark's distribution of their products is widespread. There are 21,783 retail outlets in the United States. Specialty shops account for about 8,360 of the retail outlets. The rest of the outlets are department stores, drug stores, college bookstores, military bases and a variety of other retailers. Hallmark still owns approximately two hundred stores. There are 5,190 certified Gold Crown stores. The Ambassador brand serves to distribute their products to a mass market. This distribution includes many supermarkets. Ambassador brand adds over 19,000 retailers in the United States.

Hallmark has four major production centers. These are located in Kansas City, MO; Lawrence, KS; Leavenworth, KS and Topeka, KS. Hallmark has two distribution centers for their products located in Liberty, MO and Enfield, CT. Regional offices for Hallmark are located in White Plains, NY; Atlanta, GA; Oak Brook, IL and Newport Beach, CA. Hallmark has eight major subsidiaries and divisions. These are Binney and Smith in Easton, PA; Crown Center in Kansas City, MO; Graphics International in Kansas City, MO; Hallmark Entertainment, Inc., in New York, NY; Hallmark International in Kansas City, MO; Hall Merchandising in Kansas City, MO and Litho-Krome Company in Columbus, GA. These divisions and subsidiaries make for a very diverse and varied product line.

Hallmark has, from the onset of the company, strived to maintain only the highest level of integrity for its business and to produce superior products. We the collector/consumer recognize and love the quality and creativity given us by Hallmark. I hope this glimpse of what Hallmark is all about will give you an even greater sense of why we collect "the very best."

Alphabetical Listing of Hallmark Keepsake Easter Ornaments

Miniature Ornaments Alphabetical Listing

Oh, Christmas Tree
Oh, Christmas Tree
How lovely are
thy branches.

Miniature Ornaments Subject Listing

At left is Audrey Advey's Merry Miniature display.

Pictured right is a scene done by Helen Settles.

Right is Carolyn Brown's wreath display. Below is the Sew, Sew Tiny Mice displayed on a pincushion by Ruth Moody.

The display in this shadow box belongs to Betty Willing.

The tree pictured at right displays Helen Settles' miniature collection.

Kids enjoy collecting, too!

Pictured above is Jacob Buescher from IL. He stands in front of his Grandma's collection of Hallmark ornaments.
Pictured left are Brandon and Brittany Hubschman of FL. They enjoy mom's collection as much as they enjoy each other's company.

Alphabetical Listing of Hallmark Keepsake Ornaments

C

H

M

Q

R

S

Subject Listing of Hallmark Keepsake Ornaments

Deck the halls with Keepsake Treasures!

Fa La La La
La, La La
La La

Other Collector Publications

by Rosie Wells Ent.

The Ornament Collector™

Since 1986

Magazine For
HALLMARK ORNAMENT
Collectors & Others!
4 Issues a Year $23.95

Precious Collectibles™

Since 1983

Collector Magazine For Precious Moments® Collectors!
4 Issues a Year $23.95
Less than the cost of one figurine for news all year through.

To buy or sell Precious Moments collectibles
call: **1-900-740-7575**

Press #1 for Hot Tips on Precious Moments. Press #3 to buy or sell.
$2 per minute, avg. call 2 min.
Touch-tone phone required. Must be 18 years of age.

Weekly Collectors' Gazette™

Exciting news every week on Hallmark Ornaments!

What's New, Retirement Announcements,
Secondary Market Updates, More!
By subscription only. This weekly publication
is only $2 a week. 12 weeks $24, 26 weeks $48
1 year $84 (saves $20)

Call 1-800-445-8745

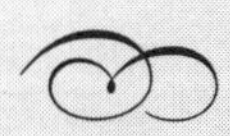

Collector's Bulletin™

Featuring articles and up-to-date news on HALLMARK
Ornaments, Precious Moments®, Cherished Teddies™, Barbie™,
David Winter, Boyds Bears and many more collectibles!
"Hundreds of Collectors' Ads" Specializing in
Precious Moments collector ads.
6 Issues a Year $23.95

Rosie Wells Enterprises, Inc.
22341 E. Wells Road, Dept. G
Canton, IL 61520

Rosie's NEW Secondary Market Price Guides

for Enesco's Precious Moments® Collection & The Cherished Teddies™ Collection

1996

©1996 Precious Moments, Inc. Licensee, Rosie Wells Enterprises, Inc. All Rights Reserved

Cherished Teddies ©1991-1996 Priscilla Hillman.
Cherished Teddies® is a registered trademark of Enesco Corporation.

Available Early Spring 1996!

• Easy-to-read • Line cuts for each piece • Alphabetical and Descriptive Index© • Informative articles and more! • Use as a guide for insuring. • Spiral binding at top of guide (per collector request)!

$21.95 plus $1.50 shipping

IL Residents Add $1.37 Sales Tax

A "Must Have" for Precious Moments® and Cherished Teddies Collectors! Check with your favorite dealer or call us:

1-800-445-8745

Premiere Edition!

Easy to use format • Alphabetical Index • Vivid color photos of each piece! • Informative articles • Use as a guide for insuring and to know what has been produced to date.

$13.25 includes shipping

IL Residents Add $.75 Sales Tax

Rosie Wells Enterprises, Inc.

22341 E. Wells Rd., Dept. G, Canton, IL 61520
Ph: 1-800-445-8745 Fax 1-800-337-6743

Notes

This Guide Belongs To:

Name ______________________________

Address ______________________________

Phone ______________________________

Please Return to **Desperate** Collector